CONCEPT AND CONTROVERSY

W. W. Rostow   1916–2003

CONCEPT AND CONTROVERSY
SIXTY YEARS OF
TAKING IDEAS TO MARKET

by W. W. Rostow

University of Texas Press
Austin

Publication of this book was supported by a grant from the
Sid Richardson Foundation.

Requests for permission to reproduce material from this work should
be sent to Permissions, University of Texas Press, P.O. Box 7819,
Austin, TX 78713-7819.

♾ The paper used in this book meets the minimum requirements of
ANSI/NISO Z39.48-1992 (R1997) (Permanence of Paper).

LIBRARY OF CONGRESS CATALOGING-IN-PUBLICATION DATA

Rostow, W. W. (Walt Whitman), 1916–
Concept and controversy : sixty years of taking ideas to market /
by W. W. Rostow.
          p.   cm.
Includes index.
ISBN 0-292-77124-x (hardcover : alk. paper)
1. Cold War.   2. United States—Foreign relations—1945-
3. Statesmen—United States—Biography.   4. World politics—
20th century.   I. Title.
D843.R656   2003
327.73'009'045—dc21
2002015038

TO

all those who took part in these adventures
And, in particular, Eugene Rostow,
Richard Bissell, Edward Mason, Charles Kindleberger,
Frederick Anderson, Richard D'Oyly Hughes, Constance
Babington-Smith, Max Millikan, C. D. Jackson, Jean Monnet,
Gunnar Myrdal, Albert Kervyn, Phillipe de Selliers, Dwight
Eisenhower, Nelson Rockefeller, Andrew Goodpaster, John
Kennedy, B. K. Nehru, Lyndon Johnson, Dean Rusk, Henry
Owen, William Westmoreland, Bruce Todd, Robert
Rutishauser, Reverend Sterling Lands, Betty Jo Hudspeth,
Martha Garcia, Frank Bean, Jose del Valle

And, above all, to Elspeth Davies Rostow, supporter and critic,
who shared in almost all of them

CONTENTS

FIGURES

TABLES

PREFACE

This book is about one man's efforts to relate ideas to action in the last sixty years of the twentieth century. Although it is an eclectic memoir rather than an autobiography, it begins with a section on my early years, when my ideas and convictions took shape through the usual mysterious blend of inheritance, environment, and accident. America's interwar landscape within which I grew up provided the context for my professional life and shaped the manner in which I addressed the dilemmas of the post–World War II world. Let me explain.

I was born six months before America entered World War I and grew up during the brief period of U.S. prosperity in the 1920s. My teenage years, however, were spent in the shadow of the depression. In my twenties, I was involved in the Second World War. Subsequently I embarked upon a career split three ways amongst academia, government service, and a preoccupation with the process of economic growth, as a matter of both thought and action. With a desire to apply theory to concrete circumstances, my career as a development economist took me first to postwar Europe, then to the developing world, and finally, to the disadvantaged sections of my last hometown, Austin, Texas. In all, my triangular activities carried me through forty years of Cold War and into a new century. Behind my three-part life has been a persistent and conscious effort to translate abstract ideas into operational policy by weaving together short-run and long-term forces. This is the central theme of Chapter 13. This is also the link between my academic life and the years I have spent as a public servant.

I should note here a distinctive part of my academic life reflected in Chapter 12. I had for long followed the course of population growth in my work in economic history. As a teacher of economic history I sought to link the rate of increase of population to the stages of growth. I also accepted from the beginning that "trees did not grow to the sky"; and therefore I speculated about the limits to growth, only in the last few years coming to a conviction on how the limits to growth might come about.

In *The Stages of Economic Growth,* originally delivered as a series of lectures to undergraduates at Cambridge University in 1958, I allowed myself a few pages (90–92) to talk about "Beyond High Mass Consumption." I concluded, in the midst of the Cold War:

> For the moment — for this generation and probably the next — there is a quite substantial pair of lions in the path. First, the existence of modern weapons of mass destruction which, if not tamed and controlled, could solve this and all other problems of the human race, once and for all. Second, the fact that the whole southern half of the globe plus China is caught up actively in the stage of preconditions for take-off or in the take-off itself. They have a reasonably long way to go; but their foreseeable maturity raises this question: shall we see, in a little while, a new sequence of political leaders enticed to aggression by their new-found technical maturity; or shall we see a global reconciliation of the human race.

In *The World Economy* (twenty years later), I spent more time examining whether diminishing returns would set in and limit growth as foodstuffs and raw materials, water and air became more expensive (Part Six, "The Future of the World Economy," pp. 571–658). Along the way I gave some thought also to whether we were approaching the time growth might be limited by the diminishing marginal utility of money itself — by abundance (especially, pp. 154, 796–798). I concluded that the human race was still a long way from the time it would have trouble spending money. In *Theorists of Economic Growth from David Hume to the Present* in 1990 I spent considerable time on the fact that population growth rates had flattened out markedly in the industrialized countries but were still high in the developing countries. A substantial change of proportions between the two populations was foreshadowed. I concluded:

> For the moment it is sufficient to note that the world community is likely to confront simultaneously in the several generations ahead anxieties centered, in different parts of the world, on excessive increase and excessive decrease in population; that the richness of contemporary statistical data is not yet matched by firm knowledge of the determinants of fertility; and it is likely — perhaps certain — that the old unresolved issue of how to define an optimum population level will arise again, if it is not already upon us. (p. 457)

In general, I felt there were ample acute problems of growth immediately ahead, and I again put to one side the limits to growth for a later time.

In the 1990s, however, another two decades had passed. It was not only the rapid fall of fertility in the large developed countries after 1965 but the quite unexpected fall in fertility among many developing countries that caught my attention. And the more I studied the demographic statistics in the 1990s, the more I became convinced that we were entering a time of a clear and present danger. I therefore wrote *The Great Population Spike* (1998) and continued with the work on population policy reflected in Chapter 12, which presents one of a series of recent policy papers focusing on the immediate and forthcoming problems of the twenty-first century.

I am past eighty and still involved in academic life and community affairs. It seems appropriate for me to take a look back. After all, my idealistic young parents chose to name me after Walt Whitman: I borrow his "Backward Glance o'er Travel'd Roads" as my point of departure.

Six of the eleven episodes chosen for this book fall, in part, within the period when I was either a consultant to the Eisenhower administration (1953–1960) or a public servant (1961–1969) in Washington. The perspective herein is somewhat different than in my previous writing. The reader interested in a more detailed narrative of this period can find it in *The United States in the World Arena* (1960) and *The Diffusion of Power* (1972). That latter book also contains a long section on Vietnam and my views as of the end of the 1960s. The short chapter on Vietnam and Southeast Asia (Chapter 10), while consistent with my earlier view, addresses a different question: how most usefully to frame the continuing debate about Vietnam.

In five chapters (2–5, and 7) I have used materials from a series of books that I wrote around the theme of ideas and action, and that were published in the 1980s by the University of Texas Press. These were short works containing primary source material or documents hard to come by. In all cases these chapters now conclude with reflections from the perspective of 2002.

Looking back over these years I found there was something of a difference between working, for example, as an assistant to a president (or elsewhere in a big bureaucracy) and writing a book. In the former case what one learns is the difference between advice and responsibility. As Dean Rusk used to say, if you give advice to a president and it turns out badly, you can resign and disappear from public life. He must live with his decisions before the public and in history. In the reflections that follow at the end of all chapters except the first, I accept the responsibility and freedom of an author.

Most of the book is concerned with foreign and military policy, with a few touching on domestic policy. I have put the chapters in roughly the chronological sequence in which they occurred for this reason: domestic issues (e.g., the balance of payments and domestic inflation) have an important foreign policy effect to be taken into account. From the president's point of view foreign and domestic policy are closely interwoven, and a president is never allowed the luxury of dealing with them separately.

As the dedication of this book—and its text—make clear, I have not been alone in these adventures. But the study of history did teach me that Keynes was wrong when he counseled: "In the long run we'll all be dead." I would hold: "The long run is with us every day of our lives."

A final word about the dedication. I list a good many people. As I wrote about the issues of policy on which I happen to have been engaged it was driven home that on each step of the way I had many comrades. Indeed, the list could have been much longer. It reaches from the presidents of the United States to the two principals of elementary schools with whom we shared hard problems in East Austin. When they went to bed at night they all asked what can I do tomorrow to make things a little better in my domain. They took responsibility for themselves and for others.

I don't think we were unique. In fact, no teacher in an American university—now highly international—can be pessimistic about those coming along. As I recalled in my conversation with Kim Chai Ik (Chapter 7), the American and British young people gave a quite good account of themselves in the Second World War and the Cold War after a not very heroic passage in the interwar years. They had, it is true, great challenges before them. But so will those who will try to make sense of the twenty-first century in Korea, as Chapters 7 and 12 suggest.

In preparing this book, I have been aided by many technical experts, companions in arms, and indeed, opponents of views I have held. Their names are too numerous to report here; but I take this opportunity to thank them collectively.

I have been aided, in particular, by my wife, Elspeth Davies Rostow, and by my friend Herbert Addison of the Oxford University Press. In both cases this book intruded on their urgent professional tasks; and I am greatly in their debt. With great competence and good cheer, Patricia Schaub produced many drafts of each chapter.

W. W. ROSTOW, MARCH 2002

CONCEPT AND CONTROVERSY

One

A BACKWARD GLANCE

1916–1938

My parents, Victor and Lillian, born respectively in 1886 and 1894, belonged to the generation before the First World War. They communicated their values and concerns to their three sons without pressure or preaching, mainly by how they lived. My elder brother, Eugene, was born in 1913; I came along in 1916; and my younger brother Ralph in 1920. Each of our parents had been the eldest child of a fairly large family: five children on my father's side, six on my mother's. They met their responsibilities, conventional at the time, as the first children of their respective families.

A word about Ralph, who appears infrequently in this largely academic and policy-oriented book. He early showed an aptitude for business — unlike his older brothers but following a path pursued by a number of our uncles. During World War II, Ralph volunteered to serve as a spotter for artillery, slogging across France from Cherbourg to the edge of the Siegfried Line where the Seventy-ninth Division bogged down for the winter of 1944–1945. There his unit of three men was hit by German artillery. His two colleagues were killed; Ralph was seriously wounded. Evacuated via Italy, he recovered slowly, but was able in time to start a business career. He ended up owning his own small department store and retiring relatively early to Florida, where winters are not as hard on the residual shrapnel he carries in his body. He and his wife, Millie, have two talented children: Victoria, a Washington lawyer and public servant, and Ron, a health-care administrator. A fine man, Ralph, and a good brother.

Both Victor and Lillian Rostow were interested in ideas; their house was filled with books. An academic strand runs through our family. For example, my cousin Robert Rosenbaum, once my roommate at Yale, went on to become a Henry Fellow at Cambridge, England, a distinguished mathematician and a respected university administrator. Now emeritus, he teaches math to promising students from the underdeveloped part of Middletown, Connecticut. But not all our relatives appeared to share a passion for learning. Perhaps the best way to put it is that academic pursuits were regarded as respectable.

Our parents represented a fusion of different waves of emigration from eastern Europe. Victor, born in Russia, came to America at the age of eighteen in 1904, already independent and mature. As a boy, he had worked in my grandfather's soap factory where he picked up the rudiments of chemistry, a field he was to pursue in the United States. He also worked on the family farm—without developing any notable attachment to the soil.

Life for a young Jew was not always peaceful. One story Victor told on himself may have been typical. When he was about sixteen, some households in his village were attacked one Saturday night by drunken Cossacks from a nearby town. Outraged, young Victor next morning rode the family horse into the Cossack domain, where he upbraided any male he could spot for attacking defenseless people. Instead of getting the angry response he was inviting, he was met with sullen silence; the Saturday-night marauders were nursing world-class hangovers. The deflated hero turned around and went home.

Soon, however, Victor was caught up in a larger struggle, the fight against both absolutist czarist rule and the local communists. Associated with a group of democratic socialists, he argued against the communists over Lenin's pamphlet *What Is to Be Done?* The crux of the matter was whether, as Lenin insisted, the Communist Party, a minority of dedicated revolutionaries, on its own should define the "correct" historical line without regard to the opinions of the majority.[1] Victor, then and always, believed in majority rule and tried to make his case. He didn't win. It was from this early exposure to Leninists that Victor derived his lifelong aversion to communism. I remember asking Father what he thought of a young Soviet citizen whom someone had brought to our house in Irvington, New Jersey, in the 1920s. His reply was categorical: "In politics, the objectives you seek are not determined solely by your formal pronouncements but by the methods you use. The Bolsheviks are worse than the czars. Czars sent to Siberia only the dissidents; Communists send whole families. No good will ever come of them."

Despite this retrospectively dispassionate view of "the Tsars," it was their police who triggered Victor's hasty departure from Russia. Word from the underground indicated that demo-socialists were to be rounded up. A family decision determined that Victor and two of his cousins, Misha and Grisha, should leave for America at once.

Embarking from a Black Sea port via Scotland, the trio arrived at Ellis Island. (1904 was a good year to travel: some foreign steamship lines had just cut steerage rates for immigrants to the United States to $10.) Victor and (I believe) both his cousins found work as waiters—an occupation for which Father later said he had absolutely no aptitude. Was he fired? Possibly. At any rate, his career turned up when he was admitted to Pratt Institute in Brooklyn, where he studied metallurgical chemistry. At the same time, a benign Columbia University professor allowed the young immigrant to use his laboratory. There Victor concentrated on white metals: lead, tin, and antimony. He must have done well, both academically and financially, for he was soon able to help bring his whole family to America. They settled on a substantial farm in Bloomfield, Connecticut, near Hartford.

My grandfather, former soap-factory owner and Russian farmer, somehow mutated into a New Englander. I have a small boy's memory of going with him to a swimming hole on his land, picking tomatoes, plums, or carrots to eat along the way. Later I accompanied him behind a blind, well-loved horse to market in Hartford to sell whatever was in season.

Misha and Grisha found life less satisfactory in the Northeast and soon moved away. Misha got as far as Terre Haute, Indiana, where he set up a general store. Grisha, even more adventurous, put down roots in Melbourne, Australia, where his watchmaking shop formed the fulcrum of a dynasty that produced a spate of academicians, lawyers, public servants, and businessmen. I met with some twenty-five of them in Melbourne in 1983.

To an American child, Victor's Russian past was exotic, even romantic. Perhaps for that reason I recall more about it than I do about Lillian's more familiar upbringing. Her parents were also immigrant Russian Jews, but their six children were all born in this country. Lillian, the firstborn, apparently took seriously her responsibilities to help rear the younger ones. An ambitious student, with a passion for reading that lasted until her death, she hoped to go to college, and in fact won a scholarship. Her high school record was good; she was articulate, a competent athlete, and possessed a nice sense of humor. But her parents decided that she had to contribute to the support of the five siblings who trailed behind her. As a secretary and a bookkeeper she did just that. When my wife once asked her if there was anything in her life she would have liked to change, she replied with uncharacteristic bitterness: "Yes. I should have gone to college!" Lillian's devoted support of her sons' academic careers may have been, in part, wish fulfillment. It was she who put into my head, for example, the thought of applying for a Rhodes scholarship. But her sacrificial career as a secretary paid off too. In what I now regard as an excess of maternal zeal, she typed my first academic papers at Yale.

As for Victor and Lillian's courtship I know little. I believe they met at the farm run by Victor's aunt and uncle—Rose and Mendel Schaenen. This may account for the deep tie to the Schaenen family. Their sons, who were to go to Cornell, became older role models for us. My great uncle and his elder son were, among other things, the first exurbanites I ever knew: they commuted for many years between their work in New York City and their 160-acre farm in Basking Ridge (near Morristown), New Jersey. The family lore, as I remember it, was that Victor stole Lillian from a young man who was courting her, a fact the latter never forgot. The courtship of my parents evidently went forward briskly. The only comment Lillian ever made was that she regarded it—smiling—as somewhat arrogant that Victor, in advancing his case, said: "Think of what wonderful children we will have." What they read and talked about is indicated by the names given to their sons: Eugene Victor, named for Debs as well as his father; Walt Whitman, and Ralph Emerson. Lillian was not only a devoted mother but she corresponded with and knew a great deal about both sides of our large family.

The most important thing to convey about Victor and Lillian as parents doesn't lend itself to anecdote. They were much in love. This was a fact—an atmosphere that permeated all our lives. We would hear them laughing behind their bedroom door. It was a bit lonely for children to realize that we were not wholly the center of our parents' lives; but it also was a reminder of what maturity might bring—if one was lucky.

Second, perhaps because Victor and Lillian had a life of their own, perhaps because they were simply wise, they never pressed their ideas upon us. Although they encouraged us to make our way, we were supported in every way by them. There was not a sense of being pushed out of the nest too soon. But I can still hear my father's voice: "Make up your own mind. I shall have my opinion, and I will tell you what it is. But make up your own mind." As a result, I don't remember a period of revolt against received family views.

IRVINGTON, NEW JERSEY

I was born in Brooklyn in 1916; but we moved to Irvington, New Jersey, when I was one year old. Our active young mother (she was eighteen when she married) kept notes on all three of her boys. She ended her meticulous account of our weight and other aspects of our first year with bold and quite accurate predictions on what kind of men we would be. Although she later showed us these memoirs and her conclusions, the texts were somehow lost, at least mine. Later, one of my colleagues at MIT, Elting Morison, propounded a theory (for which he had thin statistical evidence); that middle sons like ourselves had an easier time. Subsequent research has tended to bear this out. In any case, I was from all accounts a cheerful baby—blond, chubby, and spared the burdens and responsibilities of being the firstborn.

We stayed in Irvington until I was nine years old. It was—at least in retrospect—a pleasantly rural period. We had a car, I recall, a Buick touring car with celluloid curtains we put up if it rained. We went almost every weekend to the Schaenen home in Basking Ridge. It was there I learned something of the round of life on a farm; for the Rostow boys were put to work no doubt to give the grown-ups some quiet time to talk. The tasks varied with the seasons and our ages. (I remember weeding the family garden in the late spring.)

At school Gene and I spent only half a year each in the first three grades. This was mainly due to our early instruction at home, which included reading and arithmetic from our parents. From the fourth grade on we stayed with our respective classes. This resulted in my elder brother and I graduating from Yale at 19. (I wouldn't recommend this procedure to anyone else; but it did us no harm because we were both tolerably good athletes and were quite comfortable with children a bit older than we were.)

Irvington, New Jersey, was then a small town on the outskirts of Newark. Our parents had the Old and New Testaments among our books but had no formal religious ties—as befitted democratic socialists. My only marginally religious memories of those days are two.

After school one day, the brother of my brother Gene's best friend called him a "dirty Jew." A fight followed. My brother clearly won, but he emerged with a cut in his eyebrow that required some attention. We went home together. I played Sancho Panza to the great warrior. Our mother patched Gene up without fuss. When my father came home from work, we told him about the fight and showed off the wound. He surprised us by laughing gently and explaining: "Look, if anyone calls you a 'dirty Jew' that's his problem not yours. I'm glad you can look after yourself. But you would be wiser to ignore that kind of talk."

The only other Jewish memory I can recall was a Sunday trip to a synagogue in Newark. The occasion, however, was a lecture by a Norwegian explorer on summer in Alaska. All I remember was that, with the sun out a good part of the long day, the flowers and vegetables were big—as well as the mosquitoes.

Gene was memorably chivalrous. Three years older than I, he taught me to play tennis. (There were grass courts in Irvington's park.) He took me on the handlebars of his bike to play baseball and football with his friends. He would let me play a bit while keeping a shrewd eye on me. This rather sophisticated mixture of support and encouragement continued through my freshman year at Yale when he was a distinguished senior.

In the Irvington years Father rose to be head of the laboratory at Federated Metals, a firm specializing in white metals, where he designed an application to white metals of the method created by Frederick Gardener Cottrell for iron and steel. This method extracted by electric current metal particles from the smoke going up in chimneys. One of my most vivid memories of these years was Father taking me up a ladder outside a chimney at his plant to show me his adaptation in operation. I climbed the ladder, straddled by my Father, until the machine was reached, perhaps halfway up, emplaced inside the chimney. After coming down I was rewarded with a Hershey bar.

In 1926, the whole family was shaken when Federated Metals was bought out by another firm. It had its own chemist to take over what had been my father's laboratory. Father, aged forty, was fired. However, he soon received an offer from a Detroit firm at an equivalent salary. After consideration with Mother, he announced his decision to his two older sons. He would not accept the offer from Detroit; he would set up an independent firm in New Haven, where he had learned that there were eight full tuition scholarships from Hillhouse High to Yale. Mother and he thought we both would qualify. Father added that he might be the last member of the family who would have his own firm; but that is what he wanted.

I would record one more memory of Irvington. Mother and Father subscribed to the Theater Guild in New York. Among the plays was a visit of the Moscow Art Theater, which performed in Russian. I remember one night my brother Gene and I stole down to the landing on the staircase to hear Father speaking in Russian. He was translating Chekhov's *Cherry Orchard* from Russian to English, preparing Mother to see the show. The only other memory of Father using Russian was a nightly ritual when we were small. Often arriving home when we were already in bed, he would recite a round: "A priest had a dog. The dog ate a piece of meat that was poisoned. The dog died. The priest put on his tombstone: 'A priest had a dog etc., etc. . . .'" I sometimes astonished Russians who asked me at diplomatic gatherings if I spoke Russian. I replied, "No, but I know a round." A surprising number knew this round and recited it correctly in Russian.

NEW HAVEN

WORTHINGTON HOOKER AND HILLHOUSE

In New Haven I entered Worthington Hooker Grammar School in the seventh grade just before my tenth birthday and graduated from Hillhouse High School at fifteen.

During these years I became conscious — even fascinated — with events in the wider world. Like other boys in the 1920s I was much interested in airplanes and read everything I could find on flying. I knew precisely when the two major airplane magazines arrived at the New Haven Library. Therefore, I followed with excitement the flight of Lindbergh across the Atlantic to

Paris in May 1927. Lindbergh was in competition with Admiral Byrd (who flew with a substantial crew in a multiengine Fokker) as well as with Chamberlain and Levine (in a Bellanca); Lindbergh flew alone in a Ryan. When I met Lindbergh in the White House many years later, despite all that had happened that lowered the Colonel in my eyes, I could still feel echoes of a young boy's hero-worship.

I also remember the family's deep concern with the trial of Sacco and Vanzetti and its denouement in August 1927. They didn't follow the details of the evidence, but as social democrats they sympathized instinctively with the prisoners.

The third memory of a large outside-the-family event sparked breakfast debates between Father and Gene. The subject was the 1928 race for the presidency between Herbert Hoover and Al Smith. Gene was an ardent and hopeful supporter of Al Smith. Father, while he sympathized with Gene's advocacy, explained that the New York governor's chances were slim: (a) because he was a Catholic, and (b) because the country was prosperous. As I worked in support of John Kennedy in 1960, I remembered this family discussion; for Kennedy wanted to prove that a Catholic could not only win but be a great president.

From ten to fifteen I was a voracious reader of novels. (I kept notes at the time but they are now lost.) As best I remember the list included the works of Thomas Hardy, Somerset Maugham, the Russian classics, Thomas Mann,[2] the early works of James Joyce, Mark Twain — in short, a fairly conventional list. They taught me something of the human condition; and what it was like to live in another society, in another time, in another skin.

It was in this period that my father made a decision affecting my education. It came when in my last year of grammar school, I was awarded a full-tuition scholarship to the Hopkins Grammar School. I was quite excited. Father explained to me that the students at this private school were a fine group, and the school had a good reputation. But they reflected a rich minority of the American population. I would do better to go to New Haven's Hillhouse High School. There I would encounter a cross section of my contemporaries. At the time I felt a bit of disappointment, but I soon learned that Hillhouse, indeed, contained an excellent cross section of my contemporaries, and I never looked back. I think that the experience of Hillhouse led to an abiding view of the American people as "we," not "they."

At Worthington Hooker there occurred an incident long remembered in the family. I played the clarinet in a small band of which the father of one of my friends was the pianist. I brought the clarinet to the third floor homeroom of the high-ceilinged school building before playing basketball in the schoolyard. Leaving my homeroom I peered over the banister and fell three stories. I missed by a small margin a bust of Julius Caesar, hit the last step a glancing blow on my back, and ended up on the carpet at the bottom of the stairs out of breath. Pop Sullivan, the school janitor, saw the last stage of my descent. He found me alive and recovering my wind; and after telling me to lie still he summoned Miss Betts the principal, an authority figure of consequence. They walked me gingerly to her car and drove me to the New Haven hospital.

My mother was there paying the bill for my younger brother's appendectomy. He was about to be released. A member of the hospital staff came up to her and said, "Your son Walt is arriving at the hospital. You will wish to see him." My mother said, "You mean my son Ralph. I am about to take him home." When this confusion was straightened out, my mother rushed to see me. I tried to reassure her that I was not injured. They X-rayed me, found me fit, and sent me home.

Meanwhile, at an afternoon assembly, there was a speaker on the importance of following safety-first rules. By this time mother was convinced that I was not only all right but also getting in the way. Her first job, she felt, was to look after my recovering younger brother. So she suggested that I go back to school, shaking her head and muttering, "I guess God is saving you for some purpose." When I arrived, the assembly was still going on. I sat in the last row. The speaker, to drive home his message, said, "Only this morning one of your classmates fell three stories over the banister. We don't know yet if he is seriously injured. We hope not. But that is the sort of thing that proper care will avoid." After some laughter and joking about the return of the exemplar of carelessness, my moment as center of attention was over.

My days at grammar school were also marked by a memorable encounter with two brothers who were the self-appointed schoolyard bullies. One was thirteen years old, the other fifteen, older than their contemporaries. The younger one was appointed by his elder brother to beat me up. As we were playing basketball in the schoolyard, he picked a fight. I fought back, got him against the fence, and broke his nose. I think it was the first time I ever swore. I said, "Goddamn it, you started it." The next day his elder brother attacked me, knocking me down. I somersaulted backward, came to my feet, and piled into him fiercely with little effect. At this point, Pop Sullivan appeared carrying a shovel, and speaking fiercely to my opponent: "If you pick on any of the younger kids in this schoolyard again I'll take this shovel to you." That was the end of schoolyard bullying—at least for a while. However, the episode was not without cost for me. For a special English class, my mother had let me take to school one of her favorite books, the poems of Edna St. Vincent Millay. The book was knocked about in the schoolyard dirt. I felt angry—and guilty.

The second intervention of my father came in the first year at Yale. An overeager fifteen-year-old, I began playing quarterback on the freshman team; going out for the *Yale Daily News* (which was natural for a former editor of his high school newspaper); and earning a bit of money ushering at the New Haven Arena. I was working hard and losing weight. Father said I was trying to do too much. I would do better, he said, to drop football and the college paper, and concentrate on my freshman studies. Next year, he argued, I would be able to think about playing competitive sports and writing for the *News*. He was right; and, with some regret, I recognized this. It led to my having the time and energy to do a long paper on a French Revolutionary journalist.

In high school I went out for its newspaper (*The Sentinel*) and made the staff. In time I became the editor-in-chief, a post Gene had held a few years earlier. The associate editor was Mary Goode, who became a special friend as well as colleague. She and I were, respectively, salutatorian and valedictorian of our class.

A close friend of mine, Jirayr Zorthian, was also on the *Sentinel* staff. He is a remarkable artist who was to get his degree at the Yale Art School, and subsequently to launch a distinguished and colorful career. Jirayr did some cartoons, and together we conducted interviews with visitors to town ranging from the boxer Max Schmeling to Professor Harold Laski, who taught for a time at the Yale Law School. Laski was both a professor at the London School of Economics and something of a guru for the Labour Party as well as for left-wing students. I disappointed Schmeling when I didn't jump in surprise when we shook hands. He wore a buzzer as a ring—a familiar trick for an American high school kid.

While still a high school editor, I joined the group of reviewers organized by Charles Ives, editor of one of the two newspapers in New Haven, the *Journal Courier*. Opposite the editorial page Ives ran a page of book reviews. Most of the reviewers were students at Yale. As a fifteen-year-old, I was low man on the totem pole and assigned at first either cheap novels (given some 250 words per review) or academic books too unexciting to attract the more senior reviewers (for example, Perry Miller's *Orthodoxy in Massachusetts*).

Ives' instruction was clear. "Ninety percent of your review," he said, "should consist of what the reader wishes to know; that is, a sympathetic statement of what the author was trying to say. Ten percent at the most should consist of your own view." Although I have at times stretched the 90-10 percent rule in reviewing academic books, on the whole I have lived by the Ives rule and found it salutary.

During these high school years—and subsequently at Yale—I spent summers at camp: as a camper, a junior counselor, and then as a senior counselor. I went first to the New Haven Boys Club Camp (Clearview, near Wallingford). As I recall, middle-class campers paid a small sum, while others came free. The counselors, who were drawn from prep schools, included John Hersey, whom I knew later as a classmate at Yale. The camp was exceedingly well run. The two major figures were Mr. Pastore, a gifted raconteur and humorist who on rainy days could hold the campers' attention for long periods, and Mr. Bender, who handled sports and discipline. As a boy of ten I received two honors of which I was inordinately proud. The first was the award of a blue ribbon (first prize) for "Chivalry." I suspect this stemmed from a long hike in which one of the campers was wearing inappropriate shoes, found his knapsack onerous, and I offered to carry it. After I received this award I remember before I went to sleep looking out at the clear sky, the distant stars, and thinking what a strange thing it was: here was a large universe that evidently didn't give a damn about a ten-year-old boy, yet for him this award meant so much.

The second high honor was permission to play second base with the counselors' baseball team against Wallingford, the nearest town. Our pitcher was Spade Petrovsky, who had a hop on his fastball and once tried out for the Newark team, a minor league outfit of fairly good repute. Unfortunately Spade's fastball broke the finger of the starting catcher. I was put in for the last few innings. Although mighty scared, I survived.

Brother Gene's high school activities were particularly important to the family. For example, he did exceedingly well in the 1929 College Board examinations, which largely guaranteed his entrance to Yale. In fact, he received a perfect score in each of the four exams that then constituted the College Board's requirement. The rotogravure section of the *New York Times* announced him as "Yale's perfect freshman." The picture, taken on our porch, showed a tieless, gangly youth of fifteen sitting in a rocker. Although the picture portrayed a rather odd version of perfection, it was to us a big event.

Even more important were the friends Gene brought home on Sundays for dinner. I remember, above all, Dick Bissell (who later played major roles in the Second World War, the Marshall Plan, and the Cold War); Fritz Liebert (later director of the Beinecke Rare Book Library at Yale); and Alistair Cooke (later a major transatlantic figure in radio and TV). Bill Harpham, one of Gene's roommates, and also a history major, was a frequent visitor. It was then Yale's custom to hand out the examination for majors (at least in history) on Friday to be turned in by 9:00 A.M. on Monday. Bill and Gene ended that custom, I believe, by working sleeplessly through the nights on the key weekend and turning in on Monday morning an awesome pile of blue books. Bill, who introduced us via records to western cowboy music, died of appendicitis shortly after graduation from Yale, a tragedy for all the family in addition to Gene.

After Yale, Gene went to King's College, Cambridge, on a Henry Scholarship. It is hard to recall in the year 2002 what it meant in the 1930s to have a member of the family in a British college. Europe was far away; Gene was the first in the family to go abroad since Father came to America in 1904. In the midst of a busy life at King's, Gene wrote regularly and in detail. The arrival of each letter was a family event, read aloud at the dinner table and discussed with not a little wonder.

YALE

As already indicated, I lived a two-track life during my high-school years; a vigorous Hillhouse existence combined with exposure to a more sophisticated Yale world. When I finally became a freshman, I was in one sense a vicarious junior. I lived at home my first year at Yale. Gene continued to have me meet his friends. This included a memorable cocktail party just before the Volstead Act was repealed. No "bathtub gin" was present; rather the gin was in a basin in a shower.

The most important intervention of Gene on my behalf was in the Yale Library's Research Room. The problem stemmed directly from my father's advice to drop as a freshman both football and going out for the *Yale News*.

I had quite a lot of surplus energy available. One day I ran my finger down a page in the index of Schevill's *History of Europe,* the textbook in my history course. It stopped at "Hébertistes." The central figure in Schevill's account was Jacques René Hébert, a left-wing journalist.[3] I decided to write a paper about him. It was, perhaps, the only account of Hébert in English at that time. Hébert was a minor figure who did not yet attract Anglo-American historians.

Using a back door reserved for those who worked in the library, I stole into the stacks. There I found not only a long row of histories of the French Revolution, but also the newspaper *Le Moniteur Universel* (the *New York Times* of Paris), plus interminable pamphlets and journals including a complete file of Hébert's journal, *Le Père Duchêne.* It is difficult to describe the impression made upon me by the scale and richness of all this—that lay behind the terse recording of Hébert's name in Schevill's index.

This was my first extended piece of research. I found the histories of the French Revolution to be little more than party pamphlets themselves. The footnotes were all in order; but each was an essay from a strongly held and clearly definable point of view that was never stated.

My difficulties, however, flowed not from such problems of philosophy and method but from the fact that I was in violation of the rules governing the use of the Research Room. First, it was against the rules for undergraduates to enter the stacks; and second, the maximum number of books permitted a graduate student in the Research Room was fifty at a time, and I was grossly in violation of that rule too.

The head of the Research Room called in Gene and said: "What should we do about Walt?" In what may have been my brother's first negotiation on behalf of a client (he later attended Yale Law School and became for ten years its dean), he achieved permission for me to enter the stacks, but I had to accept the fifty-book limit.

My research on Hébert continued. From it I derived certain abiding impressions: the complexity of the forces let loose by the Revolution; the romantic violence in Paris of the early revolutionary leaders who successively cut off each other's heads; the conflict between the countryside and Paris; the synthesis achieved for a time by Napoleon at the cost of a trail of military conquests that ultimately failed, yielding however a more modern France and Europe; a triumphant and confident Britain. I also learned a good many swear words in French.

In this freshman year I also won an English prize in books comparing the treatments of the Arthurian legend by Malory and Edwin Arlington Robinson. Unfortunately I remember little about these efforts. I would like to think that these exercises in history and literature led me to regard economic theory as interesting and respectable but grossly inadequate for dealing with the human condition, or with historical events, or with the setting of contemporary economic policy. But I may be elaborating.

Between completing my first college year at home and moving to Pierson College at Yale, I again spent a summer as a camp counselor in southern Maryland. The camp was some distance southeast of Washington, D.C., where I was to meet camp representatives. This turned out to be quite adventurous.

I arrived at Union Station early in the morning after all night on a daycoach. I decided that it was too early to call on anyone so I went to sleep on one of the lions in front of Union Station. Later that day I met the major characters who would run the camp — the chief administrator, a trained dietitian, and a doctor. It was 1933, and I recall the newspapers were full of General "Iron Pants" Johnson, his horse, and the NRA (National Recovery Administration) that he ran.

The camp started out peacefully enough. It was sited some sixteen feet above the Potomac at Maryland Point — a newly built, fine installation, run by the Catholic diocese of Washington. Once a week a priest came out to camp, preached a sermon (which we all attended), and the Catholics among us took communion. Things proceeded normally except that we had to make up games that children and young people from six to sixteen could play together, there not being enough campers to permit conventional games by age groups.

Toward the end of the summer there were, however, four events that were not in the camp's prospectus. First, I discovered that the doctor—who was extremely competent when sober—became dangerously erratic when he took drugs or drank. (He did both.) I discovered this problem one day when I took my campers to the end of our dock, which was several hundred yards long—a length determined because the water was not deep enough to swim in comfortably until one was that far out. The swimming area was marked off by empty oil drums between which ropes were strung. The summer was extremely hot, and one could catch a breeze only at the end of the dock.

I was telling my campers a story that I made up as I went along. At a certain point I heard several shots. I turned to find the doctor in full military uniform shooting from the bank. I later discovered he was once in the army and put on the uniform and took out his rifle when drunk. His target, I guessed, was not the group of campers and myself but the nearby oil drums. I made a quick calculus that it would not be helpful to send the children in panic down the length of the dock. I thus continued the story I was telling as if the shooting was perfectly normal. When the oil drums were all sunk, the doctor moved on. I reported the incident to the head of the camp, who did nothing.

Second, I saw the doctor shortly thereafter, quite sober, in a different role. One of my campers was Roger Mudd, later the well-known TV news anchor and commentator. He was then a charming eight-year-old. At swimming periods he would hold his breath and swim with me underwater, his hands on my shoulders. He came down suddenly with pneumonia. There were no antibiotics in the thirties. Roger's temperature rose. The doctor said there was nothing to do but keep cold compresses on him regularly, make sure he had enough liquids, and count on his constitution to see him through. We stayed up with him several nights of great anxiety with this primitive routine. At last his temperature broke, and he recovered.

Third, we were informed by one of the older girls that the mother of a farm family nearby was having labor pains and was about to give birth prematurely. The doctor asked me to assist him. While he was making a quick examination, he asked me to find the father because the cows had not been milked and were roaming around. I finally found the father when he fell out of the hayloft above the cow stalls. He was dead drunk and asleep. After making him comfortable and bringing the cows in, I reported to the doctor. I literally boiled some water and was otherwise as helpful as I could be.

The baby was premature in the extreme. The mother asked the doctor to try to keep it alive long enough for it to be buried in the family graveyard. He did. The last we saw of this family was the husband, now sober, driving off to bury the dead child, wrapped in white cloth, on a board across the mother's knees.

Fourth, a heavy storm struck the camp on August 23.[4] The administrator of the camp was away in Washington, and did not return until after the storm had passed two days later. Responsibility fell on Sammy Agnew, a Catholic seminarian, aged eighteen, and myself, aged sixteen. The Potomac gradually rose some fourteen feet carrying away the camp's dock. The water swirled around the camp—yellow, ominous, filled with dead animals and debris from the nearby woods. The camp, on a slight elevation, was totally surrounded by water. During dinner the night before, a tree had crashed on one of the bunkhouses. Fortunately the children were not there, and they could easily be accommodated in the remaining bunkhouses. Agnew and I decided that we should, if possible, build a raft out of the badly damaged bunkhouse. We spent the night at this task while the rain poured down. But by morning the rain relented before the camp was engulfed. The raft was never used. The Potomac gradually subsided. And with the resilience of young people we resumed the routine of camp for the relatively few days left of summer. Agnew and I became good friends that night, but we lost touch. I'm not sure, but I may have learned something about crises that summer.

My sophomore year worked out much as my father envisaged a year earlier: I played football, basketball, baseball, and tennis for my college (Pierson) during the first year of the College Plan at Yale. I earned a bursary stipend for room and board, delivering intracollege mail.

After my foray as a freshman into revolutionary Paris, I did a research paper on the British revolution of the seventeenth century—specifically, on an egalitarian group called the Levellers and Diggers. Again I found the Yale Library full of pamphlets as well as a rich secondary literature. I remember, in particular, the Marxist essay of Christopher Hill (later master of Balliol College, Oxford) that told a complex tale in fairly simplistic terms.

More important was the unofficial seminar organized by Dick Bissell that met on Thursday nights—a formative part of my education during my sophomore year and beyond. At each session Bissell gave a talk, after which there was extended discussion, culminating with hamburgers at a tiny shop on Chapel Street called Louie's. An early lecture was given on the scientific method in the social sciences by a graduate student philosopher,

Julian Ripley. The four regular members were Max Millikan, who defected in the end from physics to economics; Lyman Spitzer, who remained loyal to physics and later played a key role in the design of the Hubbell telescope; Bill Hull, a lawyer; and myself, somewhat junior to the others. Bissell, fresh out of the London School of Economics, was writing his dissertation: a mathematical version of the theory of capital. His talks were a synthesis of micro- and macroeconomics expounded in essentially mathematical terms. I had taken freshman calculus, as well as an elementary economics course taught by a freshman football coach, but this was on another level of discourse.

I emerged from this exciting experience not intent on becoming a mathematical economist, but with two other objectives: (a) to apply economic theory to economic history, then a rather descriptive, institutional field; and (b) to try my hand at relating the economic sectors of society to the cultural, social, and political sectors assuming, contrary to Marxism, that the various sectors interacted. This was, of course, a by-product of my essays on the French and British revolutions. My agenda deviated sharply from Bissell's. On the other hand, this warm and highly collegial gathering was clearly the most important intellectual experience of my life.

Our differences, however, were not purely academic. We had quite different views about American policy toward Hitler. Some of my friends were isolationists, believing that involvement in the war would irreparably damage American society. Conversely, I believed we had to fight Hitler sooner or later. If we and our allies did not prevail, American society would never again be the same, and the ideals of the Enlightenment would leave us. We carried on this debate at one level or another until Pearl Harbor. The experience taught me how to debate civilly on deeply felt issues with good friends. Bissell, Millikan, and I remained in touch until their deaths.

Max Millikan and I were also held together by the continuity of the *Harkness Hoot*, a magazine founded in 1930–1931 by William Harlan Hale, who felt the staid *Yale Literary Magazine* was outdated.[5] By 1934 only graduate students were mainly concerned to carry on the tradition. Besides, an issue recommending at length serious changes in the Yale curriculum was sent by the university administration to members of the Yale Corporation. We were becoming too respectable. It was decided, therefore, to close down the *Harkness Hoot*. Millikan and I in 1934–1935 wrote a weekly column for the *Yale News* under, respectively, the pseudonyms Gog and Magog.

Academically, my last undergraduate years were productive. In 1934, I tried to fashion a satisfactory framework for explaining the inflation and deflation in Britain during and after the Revolutionary and Napoleonic wars. In 1935, I wrote an analysis of the famous crisis of 1873. In the senior year,

I produced a systematic account of the British economy during the price upswing, 1896-1914. The last exercise pretty much followed the format I was to use in my doctoral thesis (covering 1868-1896), the Gayer study, volume 1 (covering 1790-1850); and it was used also in my first published book, *The Growth and Fluctuations of the British Economy, 1790-1914* (Oxford: Clarendon Press, 1948).

It was the sense that I was clearly laying the groundwork for later research that led my senior tutor, David Owen, to say: "You will undoubtedly be doing this sort of thing all your life. Why not write a different term paper now?" We talked of what it might be, deciding on (of all things) the initial reception in the press of the Gilbert and Sullivan operas. It was about time for me to lighten up. I enjoyed it immensely.

James Harvey Rogers, a distinguished economist, lived in our college. As a bachelor, he often ate with our group of incipient economists. In fact, he made a practice of inviting small groups of undergraduates to dinners in his suite to meet some of his exalted friends from New York and Washington. In the early days of the first Roosevelt administration Rogers was in the Brain Trust and often in the newspapers. After a period in Washington, he returned to the Pierson dining room. He was asked by an overeager undergraduate: "What did you talk about with the president?" Rogers replied with an enigmatic smile: "Various economic facts in general." I often recalled Rogers' gentle rebuff in the 1960s when I worked for two presidents.

I was gradually moving forward as an economist-historian in my junior and senior years, following the conclusions from Bissell's seminar. I was also having a fine time. In these years my college assignment was to organize sports. This gave me a chance to play football, basketball, baseball, and tennis.

Bill House, an accomplished mountain climber, also led a group of us in climbing on Yale's rooftops. This dangerous but exciting activity continued until the night when we were spotted by campus cops on the roof of Harkness quadrangle. Quickly descending to a dormer window and climbing in, we awoke the resident, a classics scholar named (I believe) Godwin, who sat up in bed half asleep to witness our group, trailing ropes, our faces smudged, clambering into his bedroom. He said, almost in disbelief: "Don't you fellows have anything better to do than this?"

After we evaded the cops by hurrying to the basement and making our way out to a safe place, I gave some thought to Godwin's question. I decided he was right and never climbed again at Yale, although I was later to scale Monte Rosa in the Alps with my Geneva colleague Albert Kervyn, several of his sons, and an excellent guide.

I spent my last three undergraduate summers at Camp Scatico, about one hundred miles north of New York City. A camp for both boys and girls, it was run by Nat and Jack Holman, half brothers related to my mother. Nat was a well-known basketball player and coach of the same generation (but not as famous) as Bobby Jones, Babe Ruth, and Gene Tunney.

At Scatico, I was assistant to the man running dramatics. We were near enough to the city that families came up to see the plays on Saturday night, a major feature of the camp's routine. I wrote some plays for the children; and put together a musical comedy based on the songs of Irving Berlin. A high point came when I directed fellow counselor Cornel Wilde (later an actor on Broadway and in Hollywood) in *Trial by Jury* and *The Emperor Jones*.

The major event of my senior year at Yale was the competition for a Rhodes scholarship. The first round was a state competition meeting at Hartford designed to send two men to the regional finals in Boston. I was asked what proved to be a single question: "Rostow, define liberalism." I paused perhaps fifteen seconds before speaking to this unexpected question. Having collected my wits more or less, I gave a reasonably coherent answer. I was promptly dismissed, thinking I had bombed.

However, both Dwight Robinson (the other Yale candidate) and I were sent on to the regionals. In Boston, the twelve nervous aspirants gathered in a hotel room. I had brought along a book to read: George Santayana's *Character and Opinion in America*. My turn came early. One of my examiners—John Fulton (I believe), a historian of medicine at the Yale Medical School—said genially: "Rostow, at the Connecticut finals you were asked to define liberalism. Tell us, how would you define fascism?" Again I paused, not as long as I had earlier. And I gave a moderately shapely reply. Again I was dismissed.

It was a long day. A number of the candidates were called back and re-interviewed. Not me. Robinson and I had concluded that the inquisitors might pick one from Yale, but not two. One candidate from Harvard seemed (to us) to assume that they would obviously pick him: he looked over the rest of the field as if to guess which of these peasants would go on to Oxford in his company. Robinson and I decided no matter how it turned out we would celebrate together at the house of a friend of his and go to see *Three Men on a Horse*, which was playing in Boston. At about six o'clock in the evening the twelve of us were lined up and the names of the four winners were read: both Robinson and Rostow made it; the Harvard man did not.

Next morning when the Federal Express dropped us off in the New Haven railroad yard, we found our pictures on the front page of the *Journal-Courier*.

The last days before I caught the small Cunarder *Laconia* for England were made memorable and, in time, poignant because my father asked that I budget time for us to talk alone after I came home from saying good-bye to friends. We talked about everything: our family; Oxford in prospect; even briefly and tersely, about sex. I remember, in particular, what he said about politics: the goals that Mother and he dreamed of as young democratic socialists, he felt had mainly come to pass. He was content to be a Democrat, a New Dealer, and above all, an American.

It was possible that he knew he was seriously ill, and that we might not have a chance to talk again. Later I was to wish we had had more time.

It was while I was in high school that the Great Depression struck. It hit Father's firm with particular force, for its products (for example, heavy bars of lead, light bars of solder) were largely sold to firms building houses or commercial and industrial buildings. And this form of construction fell off dramatically. The price of tin, for example, fell from 50 cents per pound in 1929 to 22 cents in 1932; and it was only back to 42 cents in 1938.[6]

Father maintained the loyalty of his customers by the integrity and quality of his work. The tasks in his plant were below the sophistication of the laboratory he had left. And yet he somehow managed to make enough to keep our family going through the depression years. He and my mother, who kept the books, must have had some bad moments. But they never let on.

OXFORD

When I joined thirty-one other Rhodes scholars of our year to make our way across the Atlantic on the *Laconia,* it turned out that only one had ever been to Europe before. My great discovery on the ten-day trip was Gordon Craig, a Princetonian who was a talented lyric writer in search of a tune writer. I was an aspiring tune writer who lacked someone to write lyrics. Our collaboration in time included such classics as "She's Only a Sherry Party Girl" and "P-A-R-I-S Paree, What a Fool You Made of Me" — in all some thirty songs now to be found in the Balliol College Library, the Smithsonian, and the LBJ Library. Craig also was assigned to Balliol. He was a serious historian, writing at Oxford what turned out to be his Ph.D. thesis on the building of the Belgian railways and their economic and strategic significance. We thus made common cause over a wide front. Gordy later taught at Princeton and Stanford, becoming an outstanding historian of modern Germany, recognized in Europe as well as the United States. We have remained in touch to the present; but on the *Laconia* we mainly devoted our time to getting to work as long-sought musical collaborators.

Our first view of a foreign country was at Southampton. It all was new: the double-decker buses, the cars driving on the left side of the street, the distinctive trains — and still more distinctive vowel sounds.

We went to Oxford and fanned out to our several colleges. Term had not yet begun. Three of us were at Balliol. In addition to Craig and me, there was Philip Kaiser who roomed next door to me and became a friend to both of us as well to many others. However, Craig reported his first conversation with an Englishman: Craig: "I'm Gordon Craig (offering his hand). I live on this staircase." Englishman, deadpanned: "Yes, I know," and walked on. But, by and large, we found our British, Australian, New Zealander, and Canadian colleagues most congenial.

I was assigned to a personal adviser, Humphrey Sumner. Sumner was a scholar of Russian history, a shy bachelor, who rocked precariously on the fender of his fireplace during tutorials. I often feared that he would fall in. He was also a central character in Somerset Maugham's stories of Switzerland during the First World War, where Sumner was a spy. He was later warden of All Souls.

It was easy to become fond of Sumner. A wise, sensitive judge of his colleagues, he had evidently given my academic career some thought (if truth be told, more thought than I had given it). I laid out my plan which was to plunge forthwith into writing my Ph.D. thesis on the British economy in the period 1868–1896, which included post-1873, the so-called "Great Depression." [7] He countered with a plan of his own. Echoing David Owens' advice at Yale, he said: "You'll be doing this sort of thing for the rest of your life, why don't you devote two terms to reading in economic theory and history? Then in the third term you can turn to your thesis. You'll never have another chance just to read and write papers for tutorials. I would suggest Maurice Allen in Balliol for economics and economic theory, and A. B. Rodger in economic history. Rodger is great on bibliography and will supervise your thesis in time. I have spoken to them, and they are quite agreeable to taking you on." I accepted Sumner's carefully prepared and thought-out plan, and I found he was quite right. I enjoyed and benefited greatly from reading articles in professional journals and writing for tutorials, and I was quite ready for my thesis in the last term. Rodger accorded me special attention not only because economic historians were quite rare but because I played rugger (rugby) and made Balliol's first team.

I had planned to play rugby and bought W. W. Wakefield's classic book on the sport—but had not gotten around to reading it. Soon after term started, on the bulletin board of the college there was a notice of an initial practice. I went out and was told practice would consist of a game. I was assigned to the left wing of the second team and told two things: don't get ahead of the ball, and only pass backward. Aside from these two injunctions, I was told to keep my eyes open and see how the game was played.

The upshot was that I made the second team, where I might have stayed

but for a communication failure. It happened during a game with Hereford. At left wing, I was sometimes near the sidelines, where I thought I heard the scraggly crowd call, "Up Harvard"; for that was the way they pronounced Hereford. I took this as a personal slight, and I lifted my game in honor of Yale, scoring three tries (goals) and earning a place on the first team.

The Balliol first rugby team turned out to be a lot of fun. We played with spirit and cohesion, and much laughter. In the first term, the varsity (blues) did not play with the college team. Balliol had only one blue, but the rest of us were quite good. We beat the Greyhounds (junior varsity), the Metropolitan Police, and St. Guys Hospital, which had a tolerably good team of medical students. We won most of the games against the other college teams.

In the second term the blues came back to their respective colleges, and there was an elimination tournament.[8] Balliol got to the finals against University College. University had eight blues and internationals, who had represented their countries in international competition. Somehow the regular game ended in a tie. In the second overtime period we committed a foul and they scored a penalty goal and thus won the game. The *Times* agreed that Balliol had lost honorably. I still have the picture of that rugger team on our wall. About a third of them were killed in World War II.

In the first term, word got around Oxford that two Americans could perform their own songs. (Craig had a good voice and sang the songs well; I played the piano.) And so we were invited to a good many sherry parties. A certain number of our friends were acquired this way. After the first term we cut down on going to these outside parties and mainly wrote songs for our circle of friends at Balliol, which now contained a number of Englishmen as well as a Canadian and a New Zealander.

Due to an invitation passed along by the warden of Rhodes House, Christmas was spent at a country house in Monmouthshire that contained, so I was told, the only private pack of foxhounds in England. It was a nice break and a glimpse of an older England. The house was presided over by a woman who had been crippled in a hunting accident in her youth. A portrait of her as a proud and handsome girl moved me considerably. We dressed for dinner, and had port later.

I then went to London where I became engulfed in the Abdication crisis that began (in England) on December 3, 1936.[9] The head of the NBC office in London was on a boat bound for New York. The No. 2 was Alistair Cooke, whom I knew from days when he enjoyed Sunday dinners with our family in New Haven. Alistair had to broadcast four times a day to America, using BBC facilities. He was hard-pressed for staff to meet this schedule largely because there was no news for days on end. Ruth Cooke and I were enlisted to drum up some material for these broadcasts. Late at night the BBC had

an engineering staff at work, but no announcers. For the better part of a week I served as the BBC announcer.

In our search for copy, Ruth Cooke and I visited the party headquarters (there were five of them); reported the editorials in the press, visited the endless large crowds outside Buckingham Palace and small crowds outside 10 Downing Street. I remember a Sunday essay by Harold Laski in the *News of the World* in which he argued that the heart of the issue was whether in all circumstances the sovereign should follow the policy of the prime minister. In terms of that principle King Edward VIII should either resign or refrain from marrying Mrs. Simpson.

As it happened, the king did resign a few days later. The dramatic announcement came on December 10 while I was seeing a movie with a friend who brought along the actress June Knight. At a certain point the movie was interrupted. King Edward's voice came over the loudspeaker system as he read his famous "Woman I Love" resignation.

I went shortly thereafter to the Liberal Party ball, invited by the parents of one of Gene's English friends: David Layton. David's father, Sir Walter Layton, was then editor of the *Economist.* The actor Robert Donat and his wife were at the party. Not much of a dancer, I was impressed by the style and gusto with which the elderly Lord and Lady Samuels waltzed.

Shortly after these events, I packed and set out for Paris and the Côte d'Azur. It was my first trip to Paris—I was twenty. My main preparation for France had been *A Tale of Two Cities* and *Le Père Duchêne.* Was there culture shock? Perhaps—but my most vivid memory of Paris is the smell of Gallois cigarettes in the Metro. I also saw signs of the bitterly contentious French election that had brought to power in June 1936 a Popular Front government. It sought to display its orthodoxy with large posters featuring a gold franc. The election posters were now frayed. The Popular Front government lasted only a year.

A group of friends from Oxford had taken rooms in a pension on the outskirts of Nice since none of us could afford the splendid hotels at the center of town. The weather was surprisingly cold. I have a picture of me reading Keynes' *General Theory* huddled on a rocky beach in an overcoat.

A feature of our stay was a group trip to Monte Carlo, where we had to show our passports to enter the Casino. Mine showed that I was some nine months short of my twenty-first birthday. My friends, all older, were permitted to enter and play baccarat, roulette, and so on while I was consigned to the outside terrace slot machines. The only recompense for this humiliation was that I made a small profit while the rest of our group uniformly lost money.

Back in Oxford for the third term, I started on my B.Litt.-Ph.D. thesis, and dull hours were spent reducing to comparable index numbers the data for Great Britain, 1868–1896, in the Oxford Statistical Institute. But that did not keep me from enjoying college tennis on the grass or from playing village cricket with The Erratics. We played on Saturday afternoons. Time was determined by when the pubs opened, which differed from village to village.

Term was followed by a tour acting with the Balliol Players,[10] a college theatrical group that performed Greek comedies in English. In 1937 we put on Aristophanes' *The Frogs*. We performed in villages west of Oxford; then in The Pump Room at Bath; then along the south coast of England, including a performance in the ruins of Corfe Castle; then the gardens of the palace of the bishop of Chichester. After a call on Reverend William Temple, who was uncle of one of the Balliol Players and later archbishop of Canterbury, we ended in the Grammar School at Croydon.

On this fairly rugged tour we slept outdoors in sleeping bags. Our set, a Greek theater, was carried in a truck: we erected it for every performance. Craig and I, as part of the 1937 chorus, were encouraged to preserve — even to flatten — our American accents. Aristophanes would have approved.

In July I went directly from the Balliol Players to Paris to meet my colleagues from all over Europe, the United States, and Canada bound for a Geneva seminar on international affairs, run by the Students' International Union (SIU) based in New York. It was by no means inevitable that I should be at this seminar. First, I considered joining a British tour and visiting the USSR. I was brought up short by a letter from my father. He said: "Don't do it. There's no one there you would wish to visit." Agreeing, I contemplated going home and having my vacation in the States. At about this time I received word from my friend Max Millikan that I would probably receive the offer of a scholarship to a Geneva seminar to which he had been the previous year. I wrote back that I was thinking of an alternative plan for the summer. But Max had, I assume, stuck out his neck to get me an offer of the scholarship, so he persisted. He wrote again enclosing a girl's picture from the *New York Times* of May 10, 1937. Below it he wrote: "Enclosed please find sample seminar student. She may not be a dodo, most of them are." The picture was a profile shot of Elspeth Davies, a junior at Barnard College who had won two awards including a scholarship to the SIU seminar. I stared at the picture, put it in my wallet, and wrote to Max that I would accept a scholarship if offered. As I wrote in the fiftieth anniversary album of my class at Yale: "The seminar members gathered in Paris en route to Geneva. I met Elspeth at 12:30 P.M., July 13, 1937 at the Cercle Interallié, Rue St. Honoré. From that day, the round of life has been suffused with magic."[11]

The year being 1937, sessions in Geneva focused on war or peace in

Europe. The seminar was run by Sir Norman Angell. The seminar's co-leader and chaperone was José Castillejo, a scholar of Roman law from Spain. It was rumored that both sides had put a price on Professor Castillejo's head. An anarchist at heart, he was an ideal chaperone because he did not believe he should interfere in the decisions of other human beings — even those of students.

Obviously, the seminar did not produce peace in Europe and the world. But it provided six pleasant weeks in which I got to know Elspeth. We never lost touch, but did not marry until 1947. After I saw Elspeth off to New York from Southampton, I buried myself in the files of the *Economist,* which was a major source for my B.Litt.-Ph.D. thesis.

Work on that thesis dominated 1937–1938. I continued playing sports, but our rugger team was not up to the previous year's standard. Craig and I continued to write songs. But he, too, had settled down to focus on his thesis.

Sometime in 1938 — I have no record of when — the Rhodes scholars of my generation received something of a shock. Ambassador Joseph Kennedy was invited to speak at Rhodes House. We all turned up. I recall that he came, as was proper, in a rather grand car, which the chauffeur kept running at his parking place outside Rhodes House.

Ambassador Kennedy gave an impassioned speech urging that we not fight the Germans. The world war that would then result would, he said, destroy capitalism. It was evidently a deeply felt point of view, but seemed a bit odd for an American ambassador to elaborate it to an audience of young students.

In the question period one member of the audience replied politely to the ambassador's thesis and made a reference in passing to Keynes' latest book, *The General Theory,* which was then much in vogue. Something in what was said by this young man inflamed the ambassador, who denounced him wholeheartedly as a Communist, and Keynes too. As the senior economist in the audience, I replied to Ambassador Kennedy, again politely, mainly trying to make clear that Keynes was not a Communist but was simply trying to produce a policy that would cut unemployment in Britain and save capitalism. Then, without a word, the ambassador walked out, got in his car, and returned to London.

A group of us walked over to the Mitre Hotel and had a cup of coffee. I recall that we were rather stunned, and we collectively discussed whether we had done anything rude or disrespectful to bring on the ambassador's wrath.

Years later when I told John Kennedy this story, he replied, "Sounds like the old man."

I had agreed to do two things in the break between the second and third terms of 1938. One was to go out with another student to the Welsh mining fields and help build a Quaker-financed (Pilgrim Trust) communal house on a hill above Bargoed in the Rymney Valley. The town, Cefn Hangoed, had experienced 50 percent unemployment for more than ten years. The unemployed lived on the dole that supplied an exceedingly low income and was strictly administered. We were billeted in the home of an employed miner—the Morrises'—because if the family of an unemployed man earned even bed and breakfast money from itinerant students he would lose the dole.

My colleague had never before dealt with working men. He asked how we should talk with them. I said: "We're here to help build a house for this community. Concentrate on that task. If they decide we're serious about that, they'll initiate conversation." After a few days of work, the leader of the unemployed miners abruptly asked: "What do you think of the civil war in Spain?" From that time on, we conversed over a wide range of topics and became friends. I was unexpectedly recruited to play hymns in the very small Episcopal Church in a largely Baptist town. The congregation was made up mainly of elderly women—mainly miners' widows. Their church organist had died and a replacement was needed for a few weeks until a successor could be arranged. I went around to the church to see whether I could handle the organ and play their hymns. I decided I could.

I came to admire this community. With their miserable rations the women would organize teas for one another mainly consisting of margarine and rather thin jam. They kept their children in school; went to church on Sunday with the children all wearing immaculate white shirts, ties, and black suits; maintained a soccer league, and—of course (it being Wales)—had a fine choir.

I visited the village with Elspeth in the spring of 1950, when we were at Cambridge. I was glad to see that the unemployment had virtually disappeared; manufactures had diversified; and the atmosphere of quiet desperation had dissipated. However, our visit was sad: Morris had died, not long after losing his only son, who had become a coal chemist. A tearful Mrs. Morris, who shared her husband's desire to keep the young man out of the mines, told us he had been killed when his trench coat caught in the elevator machinery and he was pulled to his death.

I bicycled back to Oxford from Cefn Hangoed after helping build the communal house and found a pile of mail waiting. One was a long letter from Gene. It opened with words I still remember: "I have terrible news to tell you." Father had died suddenly, late in March. Gene also explained that the family would be stretched for funds, and that I should come home with some money in my pocket if possible. In the summer before the Yale graduate term opened the family hoped I would help Ralph run the factory.

It was not clear that this would be Ralph's choice for the long run; but some help would be needed to keep the factory going until final decisions were made. I should therefore come home as soon as I could, given my academic responsibilities.

After writing home, I set to work changing my schedule. Sumner was away, but I saw Roy Ridley, another senior fellow of the college. He was extremely helpful and as an act of sympathy offered an unprecedented glass of sherry early in the morning. Ridley first established the earliest date I could leave for home given the B.Litt. requirements to stay two full years. It turned out I could leave a bit earlier than the end of term, but not much. Then he thought of some Balliol ties to the BBC and before long I had an agreement to do a series of articles for the *Listener* (a BBC publication). They were about a Tank's experience in England and broadcast in the BBC's Third Programme. The articles earned some money, which was helpful.

Leaving Ridley, I ran into an Indian friend. When I told him my news, he took me as therapy to an Indian restaurant with the hottest food in town.

Life had to go on. I proceeded to the other job I had planned for vacation. I spent some weeks in London at the merchant banking firm of Guinness, Mahan. I spent a week in each of four departments where I learned some odd things; for example, there was only a few pence of ale in the price of a Guinness bottle, the rest being advertisement, bottling, and so on. Although the news of my father's death hovered over this period, the experience of the City from the inside was a useful distraction.

At Balliol Sumner called me in early in the third term. The conversation went about as follows:

SUMNER: I assume you know we'll be at war with the Germans before too long.
WWR: Yes, sir.
SUMNER: I assume you also know that sooner or later the United States will be drawn into that war. You're young enough to fight in the war, and you may be killed.
WWR: Yes, sir.
SUMNER: On the other hand, you may survive.
WWR: That's possible, sir.
SUMNER: In that case it's important that you publish something before the war so that you have some sort of academic reputation at the end of the war.
WWR: That makes sense.
SUMNER: I have been reading a draft of your [B.Litt.] thesis; and I do believe you can quickly make one or two articles out of it.
WWR: I had not thought of doing that but it seems possible.

SUMNER: I've taken the liberty of sending off your thesis to Munia
   Postan at Cambridge. He's editor, as you know, of the *Economic
   History Review*. He wrote back that you better get an article to him in
   three weeks.
WWR: I believe that is possible.

I fulfilled Sumner's advice. In fact, this led to two articles in the *Review*
and one in *Economic History*, a supplement to the *Economic Journal*. As
Sumner predicted, they also led to a postwar job (1946–1947) as the Harmsworth Professor of American History at Oxford—a job I undertook despite
having never taught American political history before.

My friends sought to make my departure from Balliol memorable. After
I completed my examination on the B.Litt. thesis, I was invited to dine at
High Table on my last night in college. A number of friends helped me pack.
One of them was Bill Sitwell, who was known to take off the odd term and
go to sea as a merchant seaman, for which he carried a license. Bill took a
proprietary interest in the Atlantic Ocean. He insisted on going with me to
Southampton, looked over the *Queen Mary,* and pronouncing it in reason-
ably good shape, said good-bye.

Two

THE USE OF AIR POWER IN EUROPE, 1942-1945

SHOULD THE ALLIES HAVE WON THE WAR IN EUROPE IN 1944?

BACKGROUND: THE TRANSITION FROM ACADEMIC LIFE TO WAR

Between coming home in 1938 to complete my thesis at Yale and going to Washington in the late summer of 1941, I was involved wholly in academic work. There was first of all a dissertation to complete and oral Ph.D. examinations to get through. I was a graduate proctor at Yale earning pocket money by tutoring and serving as a teaching assistant. It was the only conventional graduate student year I was to know. I remember it best as a period of hard work with clear-cut immediate objectives. There was a touch of magic — of holiday — about the two years at Oxford. In coming home to New Haven, there was no sense of letdown, but of return to reality.

Early in 1939 I was enlisted to work for the next academic year on A. D. Gayer's massive study of Great Britain from 1790 to 1850. It was a period on which Gayer had written in his doctoral thesis at Oxford. Gayer taught economics at Barnard College, but his work at Oxford covered the early days of the Industrial Revolution as well as the Revolutionary and Napoleonic Wars and their aftermath. But now he was handsomely supported by a foundation and by a team that collected much additional material. I was granted a Social Science Research Council Fellowship to help this team and to pull the data together. Gayer had heard in New York of the structure I had designed over the years to tell the story of a whole economy in motion. My thesis, for example, covered the years 1868-1896 in the British economy. It was natural that I convert the material the Gayer team had collected, plus material I already knew rather well from previous studies, into a coherent narrative.

I therefore moved to New York. The year 1939-1940 was taken up with writing the history that forms a considerable part of volume 1 of the Gayer study. Then in the next year, I taught at Columbia and worked on volume 2, which provided both a theoretical explanation of the main movements set out in the first volume plus an application to this historical data of the National Bureau of Economic Research method of cyclical analysis. Anna Jacobson Schwartz did the laborious statistical calculations for this exercise. She supplied the statistical patterns, I supplied the historical and theoretical explanation for them on which at the time we agreed. (In the preface to the second edition we amiably disagreed about the analysis of prices. Mrs. Schwartz had become a distinguished disciple of the monetarists.)

Elspeth was starting the first course of American Studies in the country and was just down the hall in a large and rather grand room. It was not a wholly professional time.

Throughout this period my generation was painfully aware of the looming possibility of active engagement in the war as the Nazis gathered relative strength by invading western Europe and the Japanese moved more deeply into China. We were also aware of the shifts in U.S. public opinion. In the early part of 1940 70 percent of Americans were for aiding the Allies short of war. By the end of that year 70 percent of Americans were for aiding the Allies at the risk of war. This shift was, above all, brought about by the miraculous salvage of some 200,000 British and 140,000 French troops from Dunkirk; the RAF's defensive success in the Battle of Britain; and the gutsy response of the British public — reported vividly from London by Edward R. Murrow and his radio colleagues.

In common with many young academics, I received offers to go to Washington. I chose the Coordinator of Information, soon to be the Office of Strategic Services (OSS). I spent a year as assistant to Edward S. Mason, a Harvard economist who headed the research department of OSS working on economic-military problems. I found him an admirable man: an excellent economist, spare of talk, with a rare gift of practical judgment. In a committee of high military officers and senior civilians, he was soon addressed as "Sir." But he had great compassion for refugees, many of whom he placed in confidence in universities. In fact, he did a great deal of good in stealth. We were lifelong friends.

In September 1942 I flew to England in an elegant but underpowered and uncertain Sikorsky "flying boat." (The Atlantic was treacherous — for planes as well as shipping. Mason later was nearly drowned when his plane broke apart on takeoff.)

The focus of this chapter is the decision regarding which targets to attack that would bring war to an end in the shortest possible period of time. The story is told from the perspective of a small group of up to twelve professionals: ten were members of the Office of Strategic Services (OSS), and two were members of the Board of Economic Warfare (BEW). On arrival, we were assigned to the staff of Colonel Richard D'Oyly Hughes. Technically, this was labeled the Enemy Objectives Unit (EOU) of the Economic

Warfare Division of the U.S. Embassy. A high-security operation, EOU was housed in 40 Berkeley Square; only Ambassador John G. Winant, Colonel Hughes, and a few associates of Hughes were permitted to enter EOU's suite of offices.

By and large, the EOU group was recruited by the OSS in the latter half of 1941 or early 1942, mainly from the economic division of its Research and Analysis Branch. The earlier work done in Washington by the OSS economists included three exercises that proved a useful background for EOU's later target work. The first exercise comprised studies of the logistical problems involved in a possible German invasion of French territory in northwestern Africa, an analysis that later formed part of the foundation for planning the 1942 Allied landing in that region. The second task was to analyze an unanticipated German thrust in the spring of 1942 through southern Russia to Stalingrad, a study in which the OSS analysts concluded correctly that the German situation would become progressively more precarious unless they captured the city of Voronezh and its double-track railroad to Stalingrad. If captured that line could have supplied the German forces, and they might have taken Stalingrad. The Soviets evidently agreed with us. Voronezh, heavily protected, was never captured, and the Germans lacked the logistical strength to take Stalingrad. The third assignment focused on the supply possibilities and limitations of the Japanese offensive in the southwestern Pacific, with special attention to the Japanese capacity to secure a landing in Australia. All three of these studies required detailed analysis of the scale and character of supply requirements, under combat conditions of varying intensity, as well as close attention to the carrying capacity of roads, railway lines, and ships.

The professional bias of the airmen in both Britain and the United States in the Second World War was to strike industrial targets systematically, that is, all the plants in the same economic sector. But in the early stages of the war the RAF did not have sufficient force and especially long-range fighter aircraft to protect bombers while striking systematically industrial targets in central and eastern Europe. The frustrated British turned to bombing German cities at night and built the bombers to do this job. They were protected from German night fighters by crews that included some machine gunners.

The U.S. Army Air Corps had built its bombers and trained its airmen solely for precision bombing in daylight. Its bombing aircraft were more heavily armored than the British and their bomb load was lighter. Targeting staff work was devoted wholly to the comparison and choice among various industrial target systems in Germany.

When the United States entered the war and, after some months, dispatched the Eighth Air Force to Britain in the summer of 1942, it was discovered that training in the American Southwest was quite inadequate preparation for European weather as well as for the opposition of German fighter planes and antiaircraft weapons. Until the Americans proved quite dramatically in February 1944, after much painful adjustment and the arrival in quantity of long-range fighters, that they could indeed carry out systematic daylight precision bombing of important target systems, most British, with tact but insistence, argued that we should join the RAF in the assault against German cities. A minority simply wished us well in our romantic quest of efficient daylight precision bombing.

IDEAS

THE ORIGINS OF EOU

The London we encountered in September 1942 had changed considerably from the city that I left four years earlier. Uniforms were everywhere — on women as well as men. The blackout was enforced strictly, as was rationing, which supplied dull but healthy fare. At the same time, London was bustling with purpose and energy. There were no unemployed. The theaters opened early, so that one could get home before the (then) rare nighttime attacks by the German Air Force. And the theaters were full. Together wartime Britons put on a historic performance that was unforgettable.

Colonel Hughes was the father of the Enemy Objectives Unit. He was actually born in America, but came back to England, where his father was a physician, at the age of three. A Sandhurst graduate, and an officer in the British army, he had followed an American girl, Frances Chase, whom he met in India, to the United States. After their marriage, Hughes took out U.S. citizenship. When war came, he promptly joined the Army Air Forces and became the chief planner on General Carl Spaatz' staff. When Spaatz moved with the Eighth Air Force to England in 1942, Hughes found himself in London, wholly dependent on British sources of intelligence, without an independent staff capable of evaluating the flow of material on which planning had to be based.

Hughes was a memorable character in London. He at first startled his British colleagues because he wore a British combat insignia as well as Northwest Frontier ribbons. His uniforms looked as if he had slept in them at night. His pockets bulged with classified papers. He had an acute stutter. Before long he was universally respected, trusted, and loved.

With General Eisenhower's assent, Hughes induced Ambassador Winant to request that appropriately trained staff be sent to London to work, in fact, for Hughes, but formally within the embassy. After some bureaucratic infighting, the Office of Strategic Services and the Board of Economic

Warfare combined to supply the staff that was needed. The first contingent, consisting of Chandler Morse, the unit's first chief; Roselene Honerkamp, its secretary; and me, arrived in London on September 13, 1942. Charles P. Kindleberger took over from Morse as chief in March 1943.

The previous experience of those who served EOU and its outposts over the subsequent thirty-two months converged in a quite particular way with Hughes' intellectual biases. As a professional soldier, he had been trained in the principles of concentration of effort at the enemy's most vulnerable point and of maximum follow-through when a breakthrough was achieved. And, for a curious reason, he had thought, long before the rest of us, about the appropriate principles that should govern bombing policy. He had carried with him, as a British army officer in India, a book by Ernest Swinton, *The Green Curve*. Swinton, a British staff officer in the First World War, is remembered in history as the inventor of the tank. His creative enthusiasm for his invention was initially frustrated by the War Office, only to be salvaged, after a tragic delay, by Winston Churchill at the Admiralty—a fact for which the War Office never forgave Swinton. His *Green Curve* consists of a series of vividly evoked abstract military situations, each illustrating a basic military principle. One chapter, initially published in January 1907, four years after the Wright brothers' first successful flight, envisaged bombing aircraft. It articulates the pure theory of interdiction: "Railways are the arteries of modern armies. Vitality decreases when they are blocked, and terminates when they are permanently severed" (*Imperial Strategy*). Like Dick Hughes before me, I read and reread *The Green Curve*.

Hughes, in addition to fathering EOU, formed a critical link to Fred Anderson and, later, Carl Spaatz, both of whom some EOU members came to know well. This tie proved valuable since Anderson and Spaatz became, respectively, the deputy commander and commander of the Eighth and Fifteenth American Air Forces.

EOU was initially put to work by Hughes not on high-flown theories of target selection, but on a task as narrowly focused and painstaking as the logistical studies done in Washington: aiming-point reports. In effect, Hughes found out by this exercise what kind of a team Washington had sent him. These reports were analyses of particular German industrial plants or installations. They contained stylized maps based on photos taken by Allied reconnaissance aircraft. The reports were designed to establish the most vulnerable point of attack and were accompanied by a text that would state:

a. The effect on the plant if the vulnerable point is destroyed;
b. How long it is likely to take to effect repairs;
c. The effect on the German war potential if the plant is out of action to the extent given in (a) for the period given in (b).

Some 285 aiming-point reports were produced by EOU. They were an invaluable education, requiring, among other things, visits to the nearest equivalent plants in Britain, as well as detailed exploitation of virtually all the intelligence London could provide. (The qualifier is necessary because EOU as an institution never had access to ULTRA, based on British intercepts of German military communications. However, I at the Air Ministry from mid-1943, Charles P. Kindleberger later at Twenty-first and then Twelfth Army Group, and perhaps others who later dispersed from 40 Berkeley Square to join fighting units after D-Day may have been introduced to ULTRA's erratic but remarkable mysteries.)

THE THEORY OF EOU

By December 1942, having passed, as it were, Hughes' examination, EOU was drawn into the formulation of its own concepts of target-system selection.

Did we consider the question of civilian casualties? On one hand, the Air Corps (and EOU) were committed to daylight precision bombing, which of its nature minimized civilian casualties for the simple reason that factories were rarely in built-up areas where civilians mostly lived. On the other, European weather was such that our aircraft often were forced to bomb through clouds with radar. The bomb patterns thus at times lapped over into civilian areas; indeed, the bombers occasionally missed their targets in the heat of the battle in the air. But we took a certain pride that we sought to make strategic bombing, an inherently clumsy operation, into an instrument of war, not of random slaughter of civilians.

We sought target systems where the destruction of the minimum number of targets would have the greatest effect. One had to ask, in assessing the potential results of an attack, how large would its effect be within its own sector of the economy or military system; how quickly would the impact be felt in front-line German strength; how long would the effect last; and what its direct military (as opposed to economic) consequences would be. The application of these criteria was a serious and rather rigorous intellectual business. It required, among other things, taking fully into account the extent to which the military effect of an attack could be cushioned by the Germans, notably, by diverting civilian output or services to military purposes or buying time for repair by drawing down stocks of finished products. The EOU view was, in short, a doctrine of warfare, not of economics or politics. In elaborating this doctrine in particular contexts, EOU's contribution had a distinguishing characteristic: it was the product of an intelligence organization at the working level. It was a continuing rule of the unit that its personnel remain close to the basic raw information; and its papers, even at their most theoretical, stood against a background of research: the steady reading of the flow of ground reports, the building-by-building analysis of the targets themselves, the measurement of the bridges, the cleaning and recording of serial numbers from a pile of German ball bearings that revealed roughly their rate of production. These grubby exercises were never far from the surface of thought. The unit was sufficiently large to handle the full flow of intelligence and sufficiently small and flexible so that the major items in each field were shared. Long-term specialization was not encouraged. At one time or another most members of the unit were reigning experts on aircraft, ball bearings, and oil.

There were in London two other distinct doctrines plus the memory of a doctrine, much like EOU's, that had failed in the early months of the war. The doctrine that had failed, associated with Bomber Operations (an Air Ministry unit under British Air Chief Marshal Charles Portal), was precision attack on whole target systems — for example, oil plants, aircraft factories, electric-power stations, ball bearing plants, and so on. The theory, like that of EOU, was that concentration of effort on a system was the optimum use of strategic air power, if the system could be hit in its entirety and if bombing could be sustained long enough. As already indicated, the relative strength of the RAF Bomber Command and the British long-range fighters in the early days of the war was not such as to give this theory a fair test. Precision attacks had to be carried out in daylight, and British bombers and fighters were simply not numerous enough to implement this strategy until well into 1944. But memory of this brief early experience was not wholly forgotten.

The British moved over to another theory and built Bomber Command around that theory. It was a theory of nighttime attacks against the heart of cities. The hope was that such attacks would produce in time a breakdown in German morale and an end to the war. The wartime RAF was thus built around three bombers — the Lancaster, the Halifax, and the Stirling — that could find their way to German cities at night. They carried heavier loads than American planes (3–4 versus 5 tons) and needed smaller crews (6–7 men versus 10), less defensive firepower, and above all, many fewer or no fighter escorts. The accuracy of the RAF bombers gradually improved during the war, and they did a distinguished job in the oil offensive, this time accompanied in daylight by an adequate number of fighters. But the major theoretical argument with respect to strategic bombing was between precision bombing — a military concept — and area bombing — a political or social concept.

A third theory existed and had a brief dramatic life. It might be called a GNP (gross national product) theory. It proposed precision attacks against the biggest plants in a whole series of target systems. Such attacks might lower GNP, but would mainly affect the civilian economy rather than the German war effort; and it was scrapped before application.

The essence of the situation confronted in 1943–1944, however, was that time was short before the invasion of France would take place. Eisenhower and his British deputy Arthur Tedder only arrived in London in January 1944, five months or less before the planned landings. American air supremacy over Germany was only attained by February 25, 1944. The criteria for both strategic and tactical bombing thus had to be considered together. We did not have the luxury of endless debate. And this led to a controversy so major that both Eisenhower and Spaatz contemplated resignation from their respective commands before it was more or less resolved.

THE TEDDER-ZUCKERMAN DOCTRINE

From the perspective of ideas there was symmetry between the precision versus city-busting strategy and the even more heated tactical controversy over oil and bridges versus railroad marshaling yards.

Briefly, the controversy was between those who felt that all air forces should join in the few weeks before and after D-Day in the attack on French and Belgian marshaling yards and those (including members of the EOU) who believed the optimum program in support of the invasion was to attack oil installations, bridges, and military dumps. The issues in support of the marshaling yard attacks were that they would, by their cumulative effect, "paralyze" the movement of German troops and weaponry to the Normandy beachheads. In that sense, it was a case parallel to the area bombing argument. Marshaling yards consisted of many tracks for sorting out civilian traffic for many destinations. They were big targets, easy to locate. They had, however, a fatal weakness: it was easy to repair an attack promptly, run the military trains to their destinations, and transfer the burden of the attack to the civilian economy. The case for oil, bridges, and military dumps was that their destruction would have greater, more immediate direct military effect on the capabilities of the German ground and air forces both within and outside the invasion area.

The background to Tedder's initial support for the bombing of marshaling yards came from ideas developed by Solly Zuckerman, laid out most fully in his autobiography, *From Apes to Warlords* (1978). Trained as a doctor, he had, in fact, not practiced medicine, but rather had studied the sexual and social life of apes and monkeys, publishing two books on this theme. In 1934 he became a research fellow and university lecturer in the Anatomy Department at Oxford. Against this background, it was natural for Zuckerman to use monkeys—and, later, other laboratory animals—to establish, in controlled experiments, the physical effects of blast and high-velocity fragments. That was the initial link between Zuckerman's academic work and the bombing business, where he worked to establish whether there was any risk that people in underground home shelters might suffer from concussion as the result of shock waves that passed through the earth when a bomb exploded nearby.

This experimental work widened, in 1940–1942, into broader analyses of German raids on Britain, including, especially, an analysis of the physical and morale impact of the German attacks on Birmingham and Hull. These studies involved analyses of the effects of bombs of different sizes and fusing and the relative efficacy of high explosives versus incendiaries in attacks on housing and factories.

After a brief tour in Louis Mountbatten's Combined Operations, Zuckerman was sent to Cairo. On the spot, Zuckerman recommended altered fusing and improvements in the destructive power of British bombs, and greater use of smaller rather than larger bombs. But most important of all, Zuckerman met Tedder and evidently impressed him favorably: He became Tedder's scientific adviser.

Zuckerman soon found himself in Algiers, where he was designated a planner for the assault on the island of Pantelleria. The Italian commander did, indeed, surrender just before the planned assault from landing craft. The special circumstances of the island and the early withdrawal of six hundred Germans virtually dictated the outcome. However, Tedder feared and Zuckerman acknowledged that excessively broad lessons might be drawn from the special advantageous circumstances of the Pantelleria exercise.

It was logical, then, that Zuckerman should be asked to contribute his advice on air operations in support of the forthcoming assault on Sicily. Here is how he describes his position, introducing the anti-interdiction theme that is found throughout:

> When Tedder had first asked me to give him my ideas about what bombing operations should precede the invasion of Sicily, I had suggested a plan to destroy the rail and road communications on which the enemy depended. . . . [It] focused on the destruction of the nodal points [e.g., marshalling yards] which controlled the railway system of Sicily and Southern Italy.[1]

It is perhaps permissible to deduce, from Zuckerman's experience, that his attraction to marshaling yards related to his study of the physical effects of bombing. As late as June 1979 Zuckerman states what may have been, for him, the controlling insight: "Only a direct hit counted on a bridge, whereas any bomb on a railway centre caused damage."[2] From the earliest British and American planning, such transport targets had been seriously considered among the options examined. But long before the issue became inflamed, some, on balance, came to the conclusion that, despite their evident attractions, marshaling yards were an inherently civilian target, and too easy to repair for military purposes.

Zuckerman's summary of the Sicily Report, in subsequent months and in Zuckerman's autobiography, is cited as the primary empirical basis for the proposition he subsequently applied to northwestern Europe. Its general conclusions include these passages:

> The strategical effect of destroying the enemy's means of rail communications is best achieved by attacks on large railway centres which contain important repair facilities and large concentrations of locomotives and rolling-stock. . .
>
> The efficiency of a railway system appears to fall very rapidly when bombing simultaneously leads to an increase in the calls upon, and a decrease in the capacity of the repair facilities. . . .
>
> A far more costly air effort would be needed to achieve a tactical success, in the sense of a sudden blocking of communications at any given series of points, than has proved necessary to produce the strategical effect of reducing traffic potential by the destruction of rolling-stock and repair facilities.[3]

The "Special Conclusions" of the Sicily Report included this terse sentence, which, like a theme in a symphony, was to be greatly elaborated: "Railway and road bridges are uneconomical and difficult targets, and in general do not appear to be worth attacking except where special considerations demand it in the tactical area."

Zuckerman's autobiography states that he had never "heard anyone criticizing the factual analysis which I had made of the breakdown of railway communications in Southern Italy and Sicily."[4] The contemporary text, as opposed to Zuckerman's later summary, did indeed belie this conclusion.

Zuckerman found that a tactical air support plan had been drawn up in 1943 by those engaged in preliminary planning for OVERLORD. In concept it was similar to the initial plan drawn up for the invasion of Sicily, which Zuckerman had opposed. It called for sustained attacks before D-Day, designed to isolate the battlefield in the limited sense of forcing German support forces to detrain a considerable distance from the coast. Zuckerman reports his reaction in terms that are almost identical to his reaction to the preliminary plan for the support of the invasion of Sicily:

> Kingston [author of the preliminary plan for OVERLORD] accepted my immediate comment that it would be hazardous in the extreme to rely on good flying weather in the two to three weeks before the proposed

date of the assault, and on the very precise bombing operations which the plan demanded. I also expressed doubts about the ability of our fighter-bombers to cut railway lines and destroy tunnels and bridges in order to force the enemy to detrain some hundred miles from the assault area. Kingston was also ready to believe, what Italian experience had revealed, that the desired disruption of communications could be more securely achieved by a "strategic" attack on the railway network than by any attempt to cut it at specific points. We therefore agreed that the moment I got back to London I would prepare an alternative plan which he would then submit to Leigh-Mallory.[5]

This doctrine of strategic, attritional attack on rail facilities for tactical purposes was incorporated in an AEAF (Allied Expeditionary Air Force) planning paper of January 22, 1944, titled "Delay and Disorganization of Enemy Movement by Rail," of which Zuckerman was the principal author.[6] The paper called for attack on the seventy-six most important servicing and repair facilities in northwestern Europe; promised to "paralyze movement in the whole region they serve and render almost impossible the subsequent movement by rail of major reserves into France"; and foreshadowed Zuckerman's post-D-Day advocacy of the assault on German railroads as a strategic target system, a successful attack on which would reduce German war production.

The paper estimated that the pre-D-Day bombing of rail centers would require less than half the capabilities of RAF Bomber Command and well over half the U.S. strategic bombing force.

In the historic meeting of March 25, 1944, chaired by Eisenhower, the marshaling yard attacks clearly won. Oil and bridges clearly lost. But before D-Day, the stubborn proponents of the latter (including me) had launched their counterattack to good effect. That is the story which I shall tell in time. But before turning to that saga, I shall deal briefly with the unlikely movement of the American strategic air forces from trivial capabilities in early 1943 to air supremacy over Germany by the end of February 1944.[7]

ACTION

By early 1943, then, our common grasp on what EOU regarded as the correct principles of target selection for precision bombing outranged the capabilities of the Eighth Air Force. As it slowly built up its strength, it confronted the realities of European weather, Germany's powerful antiaircraft batteries, and the German daylight single-engine fighter force, well equipped and expertly manned.

On June 10, 1943, Portal, working closely with the Eighth Air Force, narrowed the spacious set of target systems in POINTBLANK to German submarine construction yards, the aircraft industry, and plants producing ball bearings. The German transport system and oil production were dropped from the Casablanca directive as beyond the existing capacity of the Eighth Air Force.

But execution of this reduced list was by no means easy. Just when RAF Bomber Command was demonstrating a capacity to do considerable damage to German cities, the Eighth Air Force was finding it exceedingly difficult to penetrate deeply into Germany to strike significant targets. The targets most relevant to the invasion of Europe in 1944 were the factories producing German fighter aircraft. In 1943 a massive expansion in production and first-line strength was under way and well described in our intelligence. The acceptance of single-engine fighter aircraft into the German Air Force almost tripled between January and July 1943. Strength in units rose proportionately. The figures were expected to double again by the end of the year. Production remained concentrated at well-known plants whose expanding contours were measured and watched with anxious fascination in aerial photographs. Because of their location, the Germans believed these factories were not subject to massive precision attack.

British pressure on the Eighth Air Force to join the RAF in nighttime area bombing was resisted at high and low levels while the American air forces struggled to create the conditions that would make their commitment to daylight precision bombing effective. The development of the long-range fighter was accelerated; the bomber's defensive capabilities were strengthened by chin turrets, tighter formations, and other devices; area bombing in daylight with radar was introduced to permit bad weather days over target areas to be used even with reduced accuracy; and methods for dealing with poor weather conditions on takeoff were devised. But only time could bring the buildup of the long-range fighters that were needed if Germany was to be effectively attacked by daylight, and the superiority of American long-range fighters over German short-range fighters could by no means be guaranteed in advance. Out of the experience of the Battle of Britain, in fact, many in London, both American and British, believed short-range fighters would always command a substantial inherent advantage over pilots and planes that had to come to the scene of battle over long distances.

The Army Air Forces thus faced in mid-1943 a most painful choice: either to postpone by perhaps by six months (until long-range fighters were available on a large scale) the precision attack on objectives in Germany, while the German fighter defense forces doubled; or to attack German targets immediately without long-range fighter support, with high losses.

The American command decided that, despite the evident limitations of its air forces and the promise of more bombers and long-range fighters by early 1944, it would proceed immediately with precision bombing attacks deep into Germany. More than any other man, Fred Anderson, then chief of Bomber Command, Eighth Air Force, was responsible for that painful decision—although many, both in the United States and in Europe, shared in shaping and executing it.

The modern U.S. Army Air Forces (USAAF) as a fighting establishment rather than a small body of dedicated pilots, production plans, and untested convictions emerged directly from the crisis imposed by the need to make this choice, a crisis that can be dated from July to December 1943. A generation of leaders, a firm operational doctrine, a set of mature staff concepts, and a fighting style crystallized over these decisive months. The character of the modern U.S. Air Force cannot be understood outside the context of that experience.

Between July and December 1943 some sixteen attacks were delivered against the German aircraft and antifriction bearing industries. These were mainly mounted from Britain, but a few were carried out by the Fifteenth Air Force, which was primarily engaged in support of ground-force operations in the Mediterranean theater.

Forty-six hundred tons of bombs were dropped on aircraft factories in these crucial six months: a mere 4 percent of the total American effort during this period, about one-third of 1 percent of the total bombing effort of the American air forces in the Second World War in Europe. These few attacks were, however, of immense importance. Germany's monthly single-engine fighter production, which had risen from less than 400 in January 1943 to 1,050 in July, was down to less than 600 by December, a decline caused by direct bomb damage combined with the effects of dispersal induced by the fear of further damage. In the absence of bombing attacks, the figure by December might well have been on the order of 2,000 per month. Table 2.1 lists the monthly figures for 1943.

The unexpected success of these few gallant, costly missions led the Germans to disperse their production at a crucial stage of the war. This dispersal was conducted with energy and success, but its timing was disastrous to German interests. Just when German fighter production was beginning to recover from the 1943 attacks, the USAAF made its bid for daylight air supremacy over Germany, backed at last by an effective long-range fighter, the British-designed P-51, which was finally available in quantity. A limited break in the winter weather occurred on January 11, 1944, and several attacks on aircraft plants were carried out. The major result was the demonstration that the long-range fighters could deal successfully with the German defensive fighter force. Then came the Big Week.

Exploiting a remarkable sequence of clear days in the European winter,

TABLE 2.1 GERMAN SINGLE-ENGINE FIGHTER AIRCRAFT
ACCEPTANCES, 1943

January	381		July	1,050
February	725		August	914
March	819		September	853
April	790		October	955
May	847		November	775
June	957		December	560

Source: U.S. Strategic Bombing Survey, Overall Economic Effects Division, "The Effects of Strategic Bombing on the German War Economy," October 31, 1945, p. 156.

the American air forces executed Portal's directive of June 10, 1943. They attacked the aircraft and bearing industries of Germany in great force on February 20-25, 1944, following a plan that had been developed and held in readiness for many months. The attack had been ordered on the night of February 19 on the assumption that it might cost one hundred or more American bombers and their crews. Spaatz made this extremely difficult command decision knowing that either the Americans had to act on their air force concepts, and take their losses, or admit they had been wrong. And he was fully aware of the repercussions suffered by the Army Air Forces for the loss of sixty bombers in a single raid in October 1943. It had shaken confidence that precision bombing could succeed. The losses on February 20, 1944, were only twenty-two planes. Following fundamental military principle, the breakthrough was driven home day after day, despite the strain on the crews (and the understandable resistance of their commanders), until normal winter weather again closed in on the 26th.

Substantial damage was done to German aircraft, and the Germans were forced into accelerated dispersal. But this was a military victory for the American air forces, not merely a victory over German production capabilities. The attack of February 1944 was important because the German fighter force was tactically defeated in the air in close and bitter battle, and it never again recovered major capabilities for sustained defensive operations in daylight. This tactical defeat took the form of the progressive loss of experienced pilots at a greater rate than in the American fighter force; and, partly due to later attacks on oil installations and their effects on pilot training, this loss could never again be made good by the Germans.

Adolf Galland, wartime commander of the German fighter force, captures vividly the operational sequence in which this critical process occurred:

The German destroyer [fighter aircraft], which so far had achieved good results in the fight against the multiengined bombers, now suffered unbearable losses because of the American fighter escort. The fighters that accompanied the [German] destroyers were soon involved in dogfights with the numerically superior enemy, so that they were fully occupied themselves and the destroyers had to fend for themselves. . . .

. . . Therefore we used the tactic of combat formations. . . .

. . . These combat formations were an emergency measure forced on us by the enemy and it was anything but ideal. . . . According to orders the combat formations were not to attack the American fighter escort, thus losing the initiative and making it easier for the enemy to take the decisive step from the defensive. . . . The results were devastating, because only the fighter that attacks has the advantage. Our losses rose irresistibly. Forced onto the defensive our units forgot how to conduct a dogfight. . . .

. . . Only in this way can it be explained that the great struggle for air supremacy over Germany between the opposing fighters never took place.

In April, 1944, I said in one of my reports: "The ratio in which we fight today is about 1 to 7. The standard of the Americans is extraordinarily high. The day fighters have lost more than 1000 aircraft during the last four months, among them our best officers. These gaps cannot be filled. During each enemy raid we lose about 50 fighters. Things have gone so far that the danger of a collapse of our arm exists."[8]

Thus the strategic attacks on fighter production in 1943 may well have succeeded in containing the German fighter force at a size that permitted the close tactical victory of February 1944. Precision bombing was the instrument and the occasion by which the equivalent of the Battle of Britain was won by the Allied air forces over Germany. American bomber forces continued to suffer losses, sometimes heavy losses; but never again was their ability to sustain significant operations throughout Europe in question. The indispensable foundation for OVERLORD was at last established.

We come, then, to the second and third of the great action issues: what target should be hit (a) to achieve a safe landing in Normandy and (b) to support subsequently a successful campaign on the Continent.

THE ARENA OF DECISION, MARCH 25, 1944: POWER, VESTED INTEREST, AND PERSONALITY

From the perspective of EOU the issue before General Eisenhower and his senior colleagues was oil, bridges, and military dumps versus marshaling yards. General Spaatz chose not to present at that time the case for bridges and dumps versus marshaling yards for two reasons. First, he was in command of a strategic, not a tactical, air force. He was prepared to argue that the bombing of oil would have tactical effects, that the attacks on oil would keep the German fighter force in Germany and impose on it the heavy attrition needed to reduce its tactical capabilities for D-Day and beyond. The marshaling-yards plan would risk permitting a revival of German fighter strength. But, following military etiquette, he was not prepared to argue — at least not in the formal showdown of March 25 — for a tactical plan involving the use of the tactical bombers not under his direct command.

This rather strict military correctness was reinforced by a second consideration. The American air commanders (like a great many of the British military) were by no means sure that the landings in Normandy would succeed. Spaatz, in particular, had grave doubts about the viability of the operation. If it failed, he believed the USAAF would be called upon, along with the RAF, to try to win the war by the maximum application of air power. But, should the landings fail, Spaatz was determined the record would show that he had done everything Eisenhower had asked him to do. As Hughes' family memoir says: "At this tense juncture, the intellectual niceties of planning were far from his [Spaatz'] mind. If Eisenhower had asked him, in writing, to drop his bombs in the Arctic Ocean on D-Day he would have complied."

There was undoubtedly more to it than that. Like everyone else, Spaatz passionately wanted the landing to succeed. Moreover, he had been with Eisenhower and Tedder through the difficult Mediterranean campaign. He understood the importance of harnessing ground, naval, and air power into a team; and, by instinct and temperament, he was a team man as well as a dedicated USAAF officer. His ties to Eisenhower went back to West Point, where they were contemporaries, Spaatz being one class ahead. Although Spaatz regarded the proposed transport plan as a second-rate method for supporting the invasion force in the critical early days, he would not have felt comfortable — in human as well as hierarchical terms — in challenging Tedder directly with a tactical plan of his own in the field of responsibility that Tedder had been assigned, gravely embarrassing Eisenhower in the bargain.

Tedder, too, had several problems that transcended optimum targeting. He arrived in January 1944, as Eisenhower's deputy, with special responsibilities for the use of air power in support of the invasion. But he found Arthur Harris, chief of British Bomber Command, and, from Tedder's perspective, Spaatz, as well, determined to pursue their respective attacks on Germany. He needed a plan that would bring the strategic as well as tactical bombers to bear on his and Eisenhower's problem and under their command. Specifically, Tedder was confronted with a proposal to put bombing policy under several committees, an idea to which he reacted strongly to Portal on February 22: "I do not think that a unified plan can be evolved by a number of independent committees, and I am quite certain that successful operations cannot result from control by committees."[9] In conferences with Spaatz and Harris, Tedder found agreement that in the weeks immediately before and after D-Day they were prepared to concentrate their forces on tactical targets. Tedder argued "that paralysis of the French railway system could not be achieved in a week or two. Unless we did the job properly, there would be little advantage in trying to do it at all; and if we did decide on the Transportation Plan, it must be carried out with our full resources. Even though the alternative was heavy damage to the German synthetic oil plants, that could not vitally affect the enemy's efforts in time for 'Overlord'"[10] Evidently, in his mind the question of timing and targets related also to the question of who would exercise control over the strategic bombers and for how long.

Quite aside from Tedder's honest assessment of what the optimum targeting plan should be, it is clear that the marshaling-yard approach appealed to him as a way of solving the problem of command. Here was a program requiring the concentration of all bomber forces, for a protracted period, under centralized command. And, certainly, there was an understandable element of personal pride in all this: "The new plan, based on my Mediterranean experience, was to paralyse the railways by systematic attack on railway centres, and came to be known as the Transportation plan. This plan was to run like a thread through all the operations up to the end of the war; true, sometimes a very tangled thread—tangled sometimes by deliberate intrigue and sometimes by ignorance and misunderstanding."[11]

As Tedder's evocation of "intrigue . . . ignorance and misunderstanding" suggests, he found it difficult or impossible to believe that the lessons of his Mediterranean experience were open to legitimate debate or that, quite aside from the Mediterranean experience, knowledgeable men could believe that his transport plan was not sufficient to prevent the Germans from bringing military forces and supplies forward to the Channel by rail. It is unclear whether he was aware of a fully developed bridge-and-dump alternative. Almost certainly he was, for the papers advocating this course were widely distributed. But he was clearly not in a mood to lay it before Eisenhower on March 25. Marshaling yards versus oil presented much more comfortable terms for debate. Tedder significantly referred to all alternative tactical plans as requiring coordinated attacks for a short period straddling D-Day. This was not the case, for the bridge-and-dump plan (excepting the Loire bridges) could have been conducted over a protracted period without compromising the area chosen for the invasion landing. As we shall see, the bridge plan was, in fact, launched a month before D-Day and could well have been initiated earlier, to good effect.

Eisenhower's central problem in all this, as he saw it, was still more remote from the question of optimum targeting. He was determined — understandably so — that in assuming responsibility for the success of the invasion he should have at his disposal all the resources available in his theater, including the strategic bombers. The importance of this to Eisenhower is worth underlining. In a memorandum for the record of March 22, 1944, reviewing his first three months of command, Eisenhower identified the issue as one of his major problems:

> The air problem has been one requiring a great deal of patience and negotiation. . . .
>
> The actual air preparatory plan is to be the subject of a formal meeting on this coming Saturday, March 25, between Portal, Spaatz, Harris, Leigh-Mallory, Tedder and myself.
>
> If a satisfactory answer is not reached I am going to take drastic action and inform the Combined Chiefs of Staff that unless the matter is settled at once I will request relief from this Command.[12]

In asserting his authority successfully, however, Eisenhower was clearly sensitive to the complex of differing interests in play. Tedder's status as the highest-ranking British figure in OVERLORD ensured that his views on targeting would be given great weight. Although General Hap Arnold and the other American members of the Joint Chiefs of Staff strongly supported Eisenhower in demanding control of the strategic bombers, Spaatz was also a man whose views had to be taken into account. Moreover, he, like Eisenhower, carried the weapon suggested in the last sentence of the memorandum quoted above — the threat to quit. A request by Spaatz for relief from his command would not, of course, have been as explosive as one from Eisenhower; but he was the senior U.S. airman in the field, the most experienced, the most respected in both Washington and London. Harris, similarly, had to be brought along diplomatically. He had established a quasi-independent status, which neither Portal nor Churchill was in a position to override bluntly. On air matters, Portal was close by, representing the Combined Chiefs of Staff, but inclined to back Eisenhower and Tedder even against the views of his own staff.

Churchill, however, was another matter. It was Churchill who held up the formal settlement of the target and command question in the wake of the March 25 meeting. He did not like Tedder's plan. He appears to have preferred the attack on oil.[13] Although Eisenhower formally acquired control over the British and American bombers on April 14, the wrangle with

Churchill over civilian casualties continued into May when Churchill referred the matter to Roosevelt. The latter backed Eisenhower in a message of May 11.

Thus, Eisenhower and Tedder had their way but, so far as the latter is concerned, only after a fashion.

The many considerations that entered the decision in Washington as well as London did not, then, conform to the conventional view of how military decisions were made. One could not help feeling, as an impassioned observer of the scene, that this was one hell of a way to run a railroad. But, after all, Eisenhower was appointed because he had, from the beginning of his career, displayed great political skills. And he was surely called upon to exercise them before D-Day as well as afterward.

THE OIL AND BRIDGES GOT IN

I kept a cryptic personal diary during my war years in London. The notation for March 26, 1944, when Hughes informed us of the outcome of the high-level meeting of the previous day, reads in part: "A sad and even historic day. We're licked. Marshaling yards. Bet 2 d. they [oil targets] will be attacked—even too late." Oil was flatly turned down as a target system on March 25, and it does not appear in the April 14 directive. Nevertheless, the Fifteenth Air Force began its attacks on the oil refineries at Ploesti, Romania, on April 5; on May 12 Spaatz attacked a substantial group of oil targets in central Germany, including Leuna, the largest synthetic oil plant. Intelligence, including ULTRA, immediately indicated acute German alarm over these attacks including the sending of antiaircraft units from single-engine fighter factories to synthetic oil plants. At the time, Tedder, responding to the intelligence, was reported to have said: "I guess we'll have to give the customer what he wants." And the oil target system was, at last, fully legitimized.[14]

One reason this happened is that the attacks had a much more rapid effect on German military dispositions than any of us except Spaatz had calculated. The collective judgment of the oil experts in London was that German stocks amounted to a three-month supply; but there was considerable uncertainty about when the attacks would affect German military dispositions. Spaatz' assessment—that the Germans would anticipate shortages and reduce military allocations from the time serious attacks began—proved most nearly correct. As early as May 27 the British Joint Intelligence Subcommittee reported to the War Cabinet that there was evidence of interference, due to oil shortages, of training of combat divisions; a substantial cut in the allocation of oil to the German navy; the outfitting of certain types of motor transport with wood fuel generators; and, most impressive of all at the time, the reallocation of antiaircraft units protecting three of the principal German aircraft factories, hitherto enjoying highest priority, to protect hydrogenation plants not yet attacked. Aircraft fuel production, which reached a peak of 180,000 tons in March 1944, was cut to 54,000 tons in June and was down to 10,000 tons in September. Overall the attacks cut total German oil production and imports from a peak in March 1944 of 968,000 tons to a trough of 281,000 tons in September — a decline of 71 percent.

This prompt appearance of acute military consequences occurred, in part, because, by the time of the mid-May attack on major synthetic plants, Ploesti had already been attacked by the Fifteenth Air Force on April 5, 15, and 24. These Romanian attacks came about in a rather curious way, described as follows by Craven and Cate:

> There was, however, a chance to open the oil campaign by dispatching the Fifteenth Air Force to attack the crude-oil refineries around Ploesti, already attacked in the famous mission of August 1943. On 17 March 1944, Arnold notified Spaatz that the Combined Chiefs had no objection to his ordering attacks on Ploesti at the first opportunity, but even so it was thought wise to begin the undertaking surreptitiously under the general directive which called for bombing transportation targets supporting German forces that faced the Russians, who were then breaking into Rumania. . . . By 4 May, MAAF [Mediterranean Allied Air Forces] headquarters fortified the authority for the Fifteenth Air Force's oil missions by granting permission for them to continue if tactical considerations allowed.[15]

One basis for quiet acquiescence in the attacks on Ploesti lay in a memorandum of March 31, 1944, from Spaatz to Eisenhower. Spaatz not only repeated his general agreement for the superiority of oil over marshaling yards but argued for the first time that the successful attacks on Ploesti would heighten the priority for oil elsewhere. Accepting the verdict of March 25 with respect to attack on the French railroads, Spaatz argued, in general, that the attack on oil in Germany would prove more beneficial for OVERLORD than attack on the several German marshaling yards included in Tedder's plan: "The effect from the oil attack, while offering a less definite impact in time, is certain to be more far-reaching. It will lead directly to sure disaster for Germany. The rail attack can lead to harassment only." After then pointing out that bombing capabilities existed beyond the needs of currently assigned targets, Spaatz proposed that the transportation lines in the Romanian area be interdicted; if this were done, it would "lend weight to the advantages of early attack upon the Synthetics in order to obtain the earliest possible impact. That impact might well be far earlier than currently estimated."

This memorandum can only be understood (a) as the effort of a recently defeated but unbowed group to return to the attack after a week of painful regrouping and (b) in the light of knowledge from aerial photographs of the transport facilities serving the Romanian refineries. Tedder's plan restricted the strategic target system assigned to the Fifteenth Air Force to aircraft and transportation. He rightly feared that if the Ploesti refineries were attacked, the case for attacking the oil targets in Germany would be heightened. The marshaling yards at Ploesti were, however, listed by Tedder as a legitimate target. What Tedder did not perceive was that each Ploesti refinery had associated with it a small marshaling yard for parking tanker cars, making up trains, and similar activities. These were, literally, the aiming points chosen in the April 5 attack on Ploesti. The spacing of the bombs was arranged to enlarge the bombing patterns and overlap onto the nearby refineries

There was a similar backdoor quality to Spaatz' acquiring permission for two pre-D-Day raids on oil plants in central Germany:

> While the Fifteenth Air Force was inaugurating the oil campaign, the way was partly cleared for the Eighth Air Force participation. . . .
>
> . . . Eisenhower's directive to the strategic air forces on 17 April 1944 gave the German Air Force first priority in USSTAF [U.S. Strategic Air Forces] target listings. The Luftwaffe used oil products and, as Allied Air Force Headquarters pointed out, attacks on oil installations could come under the general heading of POINTBLANK without disturbing the Combined Chiefs or the British with efforts to change the existing system of priorities; moreover, the destruction of German fighters which rose to defend the oil plants was undoubtedly a major purpose of the Eighth Air Force. General Eisenhower . . . granted verbal permission on 19 April for the bombing of German oil targets on the next two days of good visual conditions.[16]

Tedder tried to divert those attacks to CROSSBOW (flying bomb launchers), but Spaatz preserved his two days granted by Eisenhower. The fact was that Spaatz had proved correct in his predictions that the German fighters would not rise in large numbers to defend the marshaling yards of northwestern Europe and that Eisenhower's caveat on March 25 about the primacy of air supremacy as an objective for D-Day could come into play.[17] But it was also the case that in a quiet, osmotic way the notion was spreading in the higher echelons of command, in London and Washington, that it had been a mistake on March 25 to postpone the attack on oil.

The attack on the Seine and Meuse bridges before D-Day (and the Loire bridges thereafter) also came about in an unorthodox, faintly comic way.

As late as May 1, 1944, Zuckerman's view, derived from his Mediterranean experience, that the bombing of bridges was excessively costly, still prevailed in AEAF.[18] But this view had long since been overtaken by later experience in the Mediterranean. The contention that targeting rail and road bridges was "uneconomical and difficult" met "sharp disagreement" from various "target experts." As the official war history details:

> . . . They pointed to a brief period of bridge-busting in late October and early November 1943 which had so successfully cut the main rail lines in central Italy that, according to General D'Aurelio, former chief of the Italian liaison staff with Kesselring, the Germans were "mentally preparing themselves" for a withdrawal to above Rome—and might well have done so had not the Allies abandoned the program before the end of November because of other commitments and bad weather. The exponents of attacks on bridges received a strong boost early in March when an OSS report concluded that an air assault on marshaling yards and repair shops by any force likely to be available in the theater would not produce significant military results, and asserted that "nothing in the record to date shows that a simultaneous interdiction of all north-south rail lines by bombing bridges is beyond the capabilities of MAAF, given a scale of effort comparable to that currently being expended against other transport targets. . . ." On 19 March, MATAF [Mediterranean Allied Tactical Air Forces] issued a definitive directive for the interdiction program, which in code soon was appropriately designated Operation STRANGLE.[19]

As word of these developments was transmitted to London directly, and through visits of a high-ranking officer to Italy, advocates of bridge attacks renewed the old debate with fresh support that deserves full quotation:

> [D]uring the spring of 1944 General Spaatz began to urge that experimental attacks be carried out on bridges, for it was apparent that success in this matter would greatly contribute to the transportation campaign. General Brereton likewise pressed for efforts to remove bridges leading toward or into the invasion area. Substantiation for the views of these air generals came out of Italy, where operation STRANGLE showed not only that bridge-breaking was feasible but that it was the most effective way to block the enemy's movements. . . . Pressure for a bridge campaign grew when it was realized that an experimental attack carried out by RAF Typhoons on 21 April 1944 on several French and Belgian bridges had rendered the crossings unusable even if it had failed to destroy them. Soon afterward, on 3 May, Montgomery's headquarters officially requested the air forces to take out several bridges over which the enemy might move reinforcements into Normandy, and his representative subsequently expressed to Leigh-Mallory the view that bridge destruc-

tion would be more decisive than "pin-pricking on rail communications." Still there was hesitation. The British railway expert, E. D. Brant, estimated that 1,200 tons [Zuckerman's figure] would have to be expended on each of the Seine bridges, a costly undertaking which could hardly be afforded in view of other preinvasion commitments. . . .

On 7 May all serious doubts were swept away by a notable Ninth Air Force operation. Eight P-47's dropped two 1,000-pound bombs apiece on a 650-foot steel railway crossing over the Seine near Vernon and demolished it. . . . SHAEF [Supreme Headquarters Allied Expeditionary Force], alarmed by a report of its G-2 that the rail center bombings were causing only "some slight delay" in enemy rail movements, soon prepared an extensive interdiction program for the air forces which called for cutting all bridges up the Seine to Mantes and up the Loire to Blois and at critical points in the so-called Paris-Orléans gap stretching between the two rivers. . . .

Last-minute attacks on the Seine bridges produced the maximum results: the impassability of all crossings below Paris. Marauders, Thunderbolts, Lightnings, and Typhoons attacked every day and night, bombing and rebombing until every bridge was unusable. The Germans, of course, made desperate attempts to repair their shattered bridges, but strafing made it difficult and demoralizing work, and even when reconstruction was successful, the Allies would promptly bomb again. Strafing also interfered with the enemy's efforts to unload freight from trains at the broken crossings for ferrying across the Seine to trains on the other side, and the Allies could strand the trains by cutting lines or destroying locomotives. The line of interdiction along the Seine was a fact by D-Day.[20]

In the pre-D-Day attacks, tonnage requirements per bridge knocked out proved to be less than one-fifth of Leigh-Mallory's (Zuckerman's) estimate of May 1—that is, 220 versus 1,200.[21]

The bridge target system was, evidently, legitimized by the May 7 experimental attack on the Seine bridge at Vernon. The equivalent of the ULTRA and other intelligence in the wake of the May 12 attack on Leuna, was a remarkable post-attack aerial photograph with the Vernon bridge roadway lying quietly on the bottom of the Seine. On May 8 it was on the desk of every major (and minor) figure concerned with the bombing business. The debate in London on whether bridges could be attacked with reasonable economy was settled.

Statistically, however, the result was a sport. The Vernon bridge was dropped in an attack by twelve P-47 (Thunderbolt) fighter-bombers, each carrying two 1,000-lb. bombs. The bridge was, in fact, destroyed by only eight sorties in which the bombs, with delayed fuses, were released at pointblank range, in low-level attacks, into the north and center supports of the bridge. Surplus sorties were directed to a nearby ammunition factory, which blew up throwing debris three thousand feet into the air, severely damaging two of the attacking aircraft. The group chosen for the venture against Vernon and the other bridges targeted for May 7 had been specially trained for this kind of low-level, delayed-fuse attack; but in no sense was this a reasonable statistical test of the likely number of sorties required to damage a bridge severely. And even the greatest enthusiasts for bridge-busting would not have predicted the result, in which three other bridges were also significantly damaged by the attacking fighter-bomber group.

I shall leave the full story of the shenanigans that introduced the bridges to more compulsive historians who might establish why Fred Anderson of the USSTAF and, perhaps, Winston Churchill or his personal staff got into the act.[22] Two facts are significant. First, by early May the weight of Spaatz' command was thrown behind the bridge attacks even though it was tactical rather than strategic aircraft that would be involved. Spaatz' reserved stance of March 25 had ended. The technical success of Operation STRANGLE in Italy was clearly the cause of this shift. Second, as with the oil campaign, Tedder was prepared to shift his position as the evidence came in. His commentary on the bridges in his memoir is terse but candid: "The rail and road bridges began to receive attention. Though expert opinion, with which I had concurred, had earlier held these targets to be relatively unprofitable for attack, our bomber crews now surpassed even their own standards."[23]

And so, by D-Day bridges and oil installations as well as railroad centers were legitimate target systems. In an odd, uphill battle the apparent decision of March 25 had been radically altered; and the mixture of target systems that evolved between March 25 and D-Day persisted over the next three months, with a distinguished contribution to the oil offensive from RAF Bomber Command.

CONCLUSIONS

There were a number of circumstances in this group of decisions that make them understandable.

1. There was, in part, a clash between two branches of the military, each of which was flushed with victory. Eisenhower and his team in January 1944 came to London to take over the management of the invasion of Europe, after defeating the Germans in North Africa and pursuing them up the Italian peninsula. And, to the surprise of many Americans as well as some British, Spaatz and his team had achieved in the week of February 20–25, 1944, unequivocal supremacy over the German Air Force, vindicating the American choice of precision versus area bombing. And the Americans

knew how they wanted to exploit that supremacy. There were other important players. British Air Chief Marshal Charles Portal; Arthur Tedder, Eisenhower's deputy; Arthur Harris, chief of the Royal Air Force Bomber Command. Each had distinct interests to consolidate or protect. There was also Winston Churchill, who had, as always, his own view of military affairs and played his hand from the wings. But it turned out in the end to be a struggle between Eisenhower and Spaatz, in which chance played a considerable part, but primarily because Spaatz' assessment of March 25 was validated by subsequent events.

2. Timing required that strategic and tactical considerations be merged, with tactical considerations having distinct priority. D-Day was scheduled for early June 1944, and the crucial decision was made at the meeting on March 25.

3. On March 25 Spaatz decided that his role as chief of the U.S. strategic bombers precluded him from advocating tactical targets. He made his case for oil, however, on both tactical and strategic grounds: strategically, the attack on oil would devastate the enemy's air forces and reduce the mobility drastically of their ground forces; tactically, the enemy would both anticipate the shortages imposed on him from the first attack on the oil system and "would defend oil installations to the last fighter aircraft." This would guarantee Allied air supremacy at D-Day. The transport plan would not. Spaatz alone made this tactical argument.

Eisenhower, however, decided on March 25 that the transport action plan alone would guarantee reduced enemy strength in the beachhead area; but he ruled that half the U.S. strategic bombers' strength would be devoted to continuing attack on the German Air Force. Oil would be left to the period after D-Day.

4. Spaatz did not give up. He exploited an overzealous Tedder mistake in putting the Ploesti marshaling yards on the target list. The marshaling yards close by each Ploesti refinery were successfully attacked on April 5, 15, and 24, constituting in fact the opening of the oil offensive.

5. The German reaction to the three Ploesti attacks in turn was so strong that Eisenhower granted permission to Spaatz on April 19 to execute two attacks on synthetic oil plants by the Eighth Air Force before D-Day. This agreement may have been influenced by Spaatz pointing to evidence that German fighters were not rising to contest the bombing of marshaling yards. If he could not attack oil, he could not guarantee Allied air supremacy on D-Day, which was his assignment from the Combined Chiefs of Staff.

6. As a result of this agreement of Spaatz and Eisenhower, Leuna was attacked by the Eighth Air Force on May 12.

7. Just as Spaatz was vindicated by the failure of the German Air Force to

fight in defense of the marshaling yards, the bombing team that succeeded Tedder in the Mediterranean found that Zuckerman had grossly overestimated the average number of tons needed to take out a bridge: say, 1,200 as opposed to 250–375 in fact. Word of the changed attitude toward bridge attacks in the Mediterranean spread in London; and Spaatz, who had been reserved about advocating bridge attacks, became an advocate. Through a complicated series of events, maneuvers, and shenanigans, a test was carried out on May 7, 1944, against the bridge at Vernon by eight P-47 fighter-bombers. By no reasonable calculation was this a fair statistical test. The fighter-bombers, nevertheless, dropped the bridge into the Seine.

8. The war did not end until another year had almost passed. I once called the time when the heavy bombers were returned to their own staffs (September 1, 1944) to the end of the war (May 1945) "the neo-classical period."[24] There were three phases in this period: September–October 1944, in which the RAF as well as the U.S. strategic bombers concentrated on oil, a military supplies working committee provided a set of military targets directly relevant to the battlefield, and the transport targets in France and Belgium were overrun. A second period followed from the end of October to Field Marshal Karl von Runstedt's counteroffensive of December in the Ardennes, in which the military supplies targets were sacrificed to the resumed Tedder-inspired attack on German transport targets. The third phase led to a limited rise in transport targets, due to their role in defeating Runstedt's counter-offensive. Hughes — then at the Twelfth Air Force — gave Vandenburg a set of road cuts, which had an important part in blunting the German attack on Bastogne. In particular, the later scheme for interdicting the Ruhr resulted from this effort against the failed German thrust into the Ardennes, which was followed by a resumed Allied offensive. The argument continued until the end of the war between the advocates of the interdiction versus marshaling yards. But, in EOU's view, there were by the spring no targets worth strategic attack from the air. It was up to the ground forces to mop up.[25]

CODA: COUNTERFACTUAL REFLECTIONS ON THE OUTCOME

So much for how ideas related to action in this episode. One can take two views in retrospect. One is a benign view; the other would raise the question of whether there were serious negative consequences to this sequence of decisions.

On the side of tolerance, there is the view of Charles Kindleberger, one of the ardent contestants for oil and bridges: "A more serious irony of history is that Nature does not conduct controlled experiments. Frequently when protagonists have long debated alternative courses of action, decision is taken to do both, so that it is impossible to tell in retrospect which course was right."[26] One is tempted, especially since things turned out reasonably well, to conclude that there was some higher wisdom in letting, in the end, all the protagonists do what they, for whatever reasons, so passionately wanted to do.

On the side of tolerance there is also the problem of Eisenhower dealing with Tedder, Spaatz, Leigh-Mallory, and Churchill, and Portal dealing with Tedder, Spaatz, and Harris, while representing the Combined British and American Chiefs of Staff. One feels for Eisenhower and Portal a certain compassion. Effective power was so diffused among these quasi-autonomous figures in the extraordinary circumstances of Europe in 1944 that both Eisenhower and Portal were forced to operate on what might be called the Charlie Curtis Principle (Charles Curtis was a distinguished Boston lawyer and a member of the Harvard Corporation in the 1950s): "It may be that truth is best sought in the market of free speech, but the best decisions are neither bought nor sold. They are the result of disagreement, where the last word is not 'I admit you're right,' but 'I've got to live with the son of a bitch, haven't I.'"[27] This conciliatory precept may be fundamental to the successful workings of political democracy in times short of crisis; but it is not necessarily the optimum process for making military decisions.

A highly centralized, effective command structure and process might, of course, have yielded a worse result: bridges might have been totally excluded and oil postponed still further. As Andrew Goodpaster observed in a letter to me of April 8, 1980: "[T]he somewhat messy process by which the attack on bridges and on oil finally came into being is testimony to the value of a degree of flexibility, pragmatism and open-mindedness — rather than rigidity or preconceptions based on deficient analysis. I would suggest that the art of command is knowing where flexibility descends into mere muddling and indecision. Since the events finally turned out 'right,' although late and at greater cost, I would assume it was 'flexibility' that we were seeing, along with some understandable limitations reflecting less than perfect knowledge."

Then there is the Smuts criterion, again on the side of tolerance. (The reference is to General Jan Smuts, former premier of South Africa): "My boy, it is the greatest mistake to imagine that it is the great victories that decide wars; on the contrary, it is the great blunders. We ought, for instance, to erect a statue to Hitler in Trafalgar Square for having been such a fool as to attack Russia."[28] In terms of the war against Germany, Eisenhower did not make any "great blunders." He fulfilled the directive given him and received the German surrender.

On the other hand, consider at length the final views of Webster and Frankland, British historians of the air war:

Could this result [the virtual elimination of oil production] have been obtained two or three months earlier if a greater effort had been made in the autumn to complete the destruction of the remaining Bergius hydrogenation and Fischer-Tropsch plants? There can be no certain answer to this question because no one can say exactly how successful the attempt would have been or how far it would have reduced the German resistance. But as has been seen . . . there seems to have been at least a fair chance that the attacks would have been almost as successful in October and November as they undoubtedly were in December and January.

In December also the attention of the strategic forces was diverted to the protection of the armies during the Ardennes offensive. Had that offensive not taken place undoubtedly more attacks would have been made on the oil targets. How many could have been made in the three months October–December if Sir Arthur Harris had had the same view of the situation as Sir Charles Portal it is impossible to say. In any case some production would have been possible in the smaller plants and the distilleries. But if the supply of aviation spirit could have been prevented from rising above the September level, the Luftwaffe might have been in almost the same position by the end of January as it in fact was three months later.

It is by no means certain that this would have stopped altogether the Ardennes offensive for the final stocks might have been used for that purpose. Nor would it have induced the Russians to resume their offensive on the main Eastern front for their inaction was due to other causes. In any case the Germans would have prolonged this resistance by the stubborn fighting of their infantry as they did in the final stages of the war. All that can be said is that, if it had been possible to press home the attack earlier, there can be little doubt that the collapse of Germany would have come sooner.

It is thus hardly possible not to agree with the judgment which Sir Charles Portal had at the time that neglect of the opportunities provided by the oil offensive might prolong the war for several months. . . . [T]his view was shared neither by Sir Arthur Harris nor by some others in a position to influence the objectives of the attack. Fortunately when Sir Charles Portal made the observation the turning point had already come. But had it come earlier the unreasoning pessimism of the Western Alliance in January might have been avoided and the more optimistic view of October might have continued to persist. In this case less thought would have been given to using the strategic air forces to assist the Russian offensive and more to winning a rapid victory in the West. If this could have been achieved not only would many German and Allied lives been saved, but there would also have been political consequences of great importance to the future of Europe. So great were the stakes of the oil offensive.[29]

If one adds to Webster and Frankland's "several months" lost in the autumn of 1944 the two and a half months lost between, say, March 1 and mid-May, the cost of delay and diversion may indeed have been high. In terms of Table 2.2, the counterfactual question is: How would the war have gone if German oil availabilities at the September 1944 low point had been achieved by June—say, 200,000 tons overall, 10,000 tons of aircraft fuel?[30] The costs of failing to produce this result may have been high not only in human life foregone but also in terms of postwar diplomacy; for, in the end, the location of the Soviet and Western armies on V-E Day certainly played a role—the extent of which can be debated—in leading Stalin to conceive as realistic the creation of a Soviet empire in Eastern Europe, yielding a split and an intensely armed continent, rather than a united but disarmed Germany with democracy free to flourish in the East as well as the West. That, presumably, is the grand issue raised in the last two sentences of Webster and Frankland's summation.

Harris' gracious acknowledgment that the Americans were correct, if lucky, to advocate the attack on oil has, in this view, its sinister side:

> In the spring of 1944 the Americans began a series of attacks against German synthetic oil plants, and a week after D-Day Bomber Command was directed to take part in the same campaign by attacking the ten synthetic oil plants situated in the Ruhr. At the time, I was altogether opposed to this further diversion, which, as I saw it, would only prolong the respite which the German industrial cities had gained from the use of the bombers in a tactical role. I did not think that we had any right to give up a method of attack which was indisputably doing the enemy enormous harm for the sake of prosecuting a new scheme the success of which was far from assured. In the event, of course, the offensive against oil was a complete success, and it could not have been so without the co-operation of Bomber Command, but I still do not think it was reasonable, at that time, to expect that the campaign would succeed; what the Allied strategists did was to bet on an outsider, and it happened to win the race.[31]

But, in fact, Harris gave Portal a hard time over oil. Despite his retrospective acquiescence, it proved impossible at the time to harness the combined bomber forces in a sustained way to the oil offensive. The nominal priority for oil that emerged after D-Day was systematically eroded by Tedder's hankering for transportation and Harris' for city-busting. Total concentration

TABLE 2.2 GERMAN PRODUCTION AND IMPORTS OF TOTAL FINISHED OIL PRODUCTS AND AIRCRAFT FUEL,
JANUARY 1944–MARCH 1945 (in thousand metric tons)

Year and Month	Synthetic Production		Domestic Refining of Crude Oil	Production in Occupied Territories	Imports	Total	Aircraft Fuel
	Hydrogenation and Fischer-Tropsch Process	Other Synthetic Production					
1944							
January	336	162	175	48	179	900	160
February	306	172	160	48	200	886	164
March	341	201	191	49	186	968	180
April	348	153	157	48	104	810	175
May	285	151	170	47	81	734	156
June	145	153	129	44	40	511	54
July	86	143	115	38	56	438	35
August	47	137	134	16	11[a]	345	17
September	26	126	113	5	11	281	10
October	38	117	124	3	34	316	21
November	78	107	105	10	37	337	39
December	56	108	108	9	22	303	25
1945							
January	37	—	—	—	—	—	—
February	13	—	—	—	—	—	—
March	12	—	—	—	—	—	—

Source: Data drawn from tables in Webster and Frankland, *Strategic Air Offensive against Germany* 4:516–517.

[a] The Soviet army occupied Ploesti on August 22, 1944.

on oil targets would have been impossible to sustain for reasons of weather and irreducible tactical diversions in support of the ground battle. But there were, in effect, three setbacks to the oil offensive: (1) the delay between, say, early March and mid-May 1944, as the debate preceding the March 25 decision ate up the clock; (2) the negative March 25 decision on oil, which was only laboriously undone; and (3) the dilution of oil priority, notably in the autumn of 1944.

Webster and Frankland's counterfactual question cannot be answered dogmatically. But it is a legitimate question—and, given the stakes, a haunting one.

Now a final observation that should have imposed—and should impose—an important degree of modesty on those who argued and may argue in the future about the use of air power in Europe during the Second World War. Air power helped mightily to win the war. Indeed, the war was almost certainly not winnable without virtually total Allied air supremacy over the battlefield on D-Day and in the critical period of consolidating the Normandy bridgehead on the Continent. The pre-D-Day attacks on the bridges and dumps and the direct attack on enemy forces after D-Day certainly helped ease—and ease substantially—the task of the men fighting on the ground. The attacks on oil and military production targets in Germany certainly helped. The attacks on transport centers in Germany, although less productive, in my view, than a more persistent and concentrated attack on oil, certainly had an impact on military as well as civilian production and other diffuse but not trivial military effects. Something of the same could be said for the area bombing of German cities. But the ultimate fact is that the war had to be won on the ground by the armies.

F. M. Sallagar makes the point temperately and well in a 1972 study of Operation STRANGLE.[32] In specifying the precise effects of the technically successful interdiction of railway lines in Italy, Sallagar notes that in one way or another essential military supplies did get through even if mainly by road. What the air attacks did was to reduce radically the mobility of the German forces and to impair significantly their effectiveness in many other rather impressive ways; but they did not achieve the air-power strategist's dream of rendering unnecessary the bloody struggle on the ground.

This certainly proved to be the case with respect to OVERLORD and its aftermath. The buildup of the German forces against the beachhead was slower than it would have been without prior bombing attacks and consistent harassment; German units often arrived piecemeal at the front after incredible difficulties and significant depletion; but they arrived nonetheless and fought, postponing for eight weeks the breakout from Normandy. And after the disheveled German retreat across France in midsummer and early autumn, they fought hard again, postponing final defeat until eleven months after D-Day.

There is something ironic as well as understandable in the various schemes and enterprises to use air power "decisively" in the final weeks of the war. Despite as massive an array of non-nuclear air power as is ever likely to be assembled, the bombers remained to the end a supporting force to the infantry, although all three target systems had their chance: marshaling yards, area bombing, and oil. In retrospect, I am glad EOU understood and accepted with some perspective and maturity — but without loss of ardor — the limits as well as the possibilities of the enterprise in which its members were privileged to play a part.

So far as the narrow theme of this book is concerned, the saga is a remarkable demonstration of the power of abstract intellectual concepts over the emotions of men and the behavior of institutions. It is not a unique phenomenon, but it is not often that deeply felt debate over rival concepts persists among men fifty-five years after the days when their clash had operational meaning and consequence.

Three

THE UNITED STATES AND THE
SOVIET UNION, 1945-1989

THE HINGE WAS POLAND

BACKGROUND

It was suggested after V-E Day that I might go out to the Pacific and help bring our experiences in Europe to the war against Japan, but things seemed to be well in hand. After a brief stint in the OSS on British postwar problems, I accepted the post of assistant chief of the German-Austrian Economic Division (GA) in the State Department. As I will explain below, a number of us from EOU, London, were recruited. The chief of the GA division was Charles Kindleberger.

I was soon out of uniform and plunged into the problems of postwar Europe. However, I regarded this work as temporary and wished to return as soon as possible to academic life. I therefore accepted Harvard's invitation to become an associate professor and to begin teaching again in September 1946. This orderly transition was symbolized by a correspondence with George Homans, a Harvard professor, about a course that we would jointly teach and by an appointment to a fellowship at Eliot House. Things were falling in place, and I looked forward to a conventional academic career.

Then a strange thing happened. My brother Gene received from Ambassador Averell Harriman, then in London, what appeared to be an invitation to take a year off from the Yale Law School to be Harmsworth Visiting Professor in American History at Oxford. He was given permission to accept by the president of Yale, Whitney Griswold. At the last moment, Gene had a thought and wired Harriman: "Which Rostow do you want?" It turned out that, as Sumner had predicted in 1938, they wanted Walt, probably because three articles on the British economy of the nineteenth century deriving from my thesis at Oxford had been published. Harvard was informed and graciously suggested that a year at Oxford would knock off the rust and get me back into academic life. (Incidentally, Gene was later Eastman Professor at Oxford and Pitt Professor of American History at Cambridge.) But a year in a British university became a hiatus abroad of three years and then a career at MIT, down the road from Harvard.

I had a full and satisfying academic year at Oxford. Elspeth came over in the spring of 1947. She had been independently appointed to a summer seminar in Geneva. We were married at the old Registry Office in St. Giles.

My inaugural lecture centered around the subject of this chapter: the importance of Europe moving toward unity as it reconstructed. In late June 1947, while we were honeymooning in Paris, Gunnar Myrdal, executive secretary of the Economic Commission for Europe (ECE), tracked me down and asked me to join him in helping set up the commission in Geneva. Such a commission was a feature of the draft Plan for a European Settlement I had written more than a year before (outlined in Appendix A). He said that he understood I had a hand in the parentage of the institution, and that it was coming to life at a difficult time. He challenged me to back my play. My wife and I, after a visit to Geneva, decided to cast our lot for a few years with the all-European enterprise as a small personal contribution to the long future of Europe. By the time we made our decision, Molotov had left Paris and it was clear the Marshall Plan would proceed on a Western basis. I resigned from Harvard without ever turning up and worked in Geneva as special assistant to Myrdal from 1947 to 1949 and as a consultant in the summer of 1950. Albert Kervyn, of Belgium, was also a special assistant and became a lifelong friend.

Thus, while my bureaucratic crusading on behalf of an all-European settlement in the State Department in 1946 had only an extremely limited immediate impact on the course of history, it had a considerable effect on my professional life.[1]

U.S.-SOVIET RELATIONS: ALLY OR ENEMY?

A good deal was stirring in the vastly more important field of U.S.-Soviet relations. In May 1945 Soviet and U.S. troops met in central Germany as conquering Allies. There was a widespread awareness in the United States that the Soviet Union had suffered great casualties in the war, had experienced a terrible invasion, and had fought its way back to capture Berlin. American and British Lend-Lease assistance to the Soviet effort was not begrudged. At the same time, there was a suspicion of the Soviet government that had deep roots. The Bolshevik counterrevolution against the Kerensky government was not only opposed, but U.S. forces had taken up positions on Russian soil. Diplomatic relations were not reestablished until November 1933. Then the Ribbentrop-Molotov Pact of August 1939 confirmed the view that the Soviet Union was still not our friend. There were also moments of doubt about Soviet policy during the war, and some questioned Soviet postwar ambitions.

But there was also some hope in 1945, and to a diminishing degree thereafter, that the Soviet Union would change course now that it was a victorious major power in the world. There was great sympathy for the Soviet peoples, but there was also a gathering underlying suspicion. It was accompanied by a profound unwillingness to accept that, after a great war to defeat German and Japanese enemies, the United States faced, in succession to them, a new, formidable if not sanguinary enemy. From the end of the war in May 1945 it took until, perhaps, the departure from Paris of Molotov and the Soviet delegation, in the wake of Secretary of State George Marshall's Harvard speech of June 5, 1947, for that double-minded perspective to be resolved.

The first portion of this chapter is concerned with that transition in American policy—and public outlook. It does not deal in detail with the gradual movement of American public opinion. It is sufficient to note that 62 percent of Americans felt "harshly or coolly" toward the Soviet Union in September 1946 than a year earlier; but in early October existing disagreements did not justify going to war.[2] The first part of this chapter is mainly concerned with the clash of two views—two ideas—as to how U.S.-Soviet relations should unfold. That clash ended with Truman's enunciation of the Truman Doctrine on March 12, 1947, Marshall's speech of June 5, 1947, Molotov's rejection of the American proposal at Paris, and the national policy that followed. In a curious way that policy was a synthesis of both views, arrived at through the workings of democracy in response to a variety of changing forces in the outside world and at home.

The second portion of this chapter reflects on the whole course of the Cold War which ended with the collapse of the Soviet Union. And it concludes with an examination of the reasons why the emerging Russian nation reluctantly accepted a united East-West Europe, which had been offered by the Western powers some forty-five years before as the road to peace.

SETTING

1946, A "DISASTROUS YEAR"

In a chapter heading of his book on Harry Truman, Robert J. Donovan calls 1946 a "Disastrous Year." The description is apt. Released from the disciplines of war, the American people turned inward, in a manner evocative of 1919-1920, to pursue private and material goals. Under intense (but not universal) popular pressure, including demonstrations by men in the services, the armed forces were hastily dismantled, dropping from 11.4 million in 1945 to 3.4 million in 1946 to 1.6 million in 1947.[3] National defense expenditures on goods and services fell from $87 billion in 1945 to $19 billion in 1946, from 41 percent of the GNP to 9 percent. More important, the reductions in forces and expenditures left many military units essentially non-operational, lacking key technical personnel. By March 1946 the army was down to 400,000 men, mainly new recruits. Price controls were substantially but not wholly abandoned, yielding a 16 percent inflation rate. Spending on durable consumer goods, constrained during the war years, almost doubled (in constant prices). But the surge of inflation had a sharp impact on real wages, which declined about 10 percent in 1946. This led to a series of acrimonious strikes for higher wages, which generated in turn a popular wave of hostility toward labor unions.

Starting with the interim report from Ottawa of a royal commission, which revealed a massive Soviet espionage effort in Canada, the issue was raised of Soviet recruitment of American public servants, a matter that was to haunt American politics for a decade. Within the Democratic Party Truman's support eroded in both conservative southern and liberal northern camps. In late June Congress passed a bill weakening price controls in general and providing that price controls on meat could be reimposed only after August 20. When controls were, in fact, reimposed, cattle producers held their herds on the farm in a de facto strike, forcing a beef shortage. On October 14, Truman was forced to lift all price controls on agricultural products, but politically it was too late.

Thus, domestic political life turned very lively indeed in 1946. The Gallup poll registering presidential approval fell from 87 percent in July 1945 to 32 percent in October 1946. On November 6, 1946, the Republicans won their first congressional majority in both houses in fifteen years in what is often called the Beefsteak Election.[4] In the wake of this defeat, Truman was almost universally judged to be a lame-duck president, to be superseded by a Republican in January 1949.

All this disarray, plain for all to see, within a nation that had emerged by V-J Day in a position of greater primacy even than Great Britain's after the Napoleonic Wars, had its impact throughout the world community and on the minds of those who bore responsibility for U.S. foreign policy. In his famous "X" article, published in the July 1947 issue of *Foreign Affairs,* George Kennan, a senior foreign service officer, evokes, in terms relevant to other periods since 1945 as well, its impact on the Communist world:

> [E]xhibitions of indecision, disunity and internal disintegration within this country have an exhilarating effect on the whole Communist movement. At each evidence of these tendencies, a thrill of hope and excitement goes through the Communist world; a new jauntiness can be noted in the Moscow tread; new groups of foreign supporters climb on to what they can only view as the band wagon of international politics; and Russian pressure increases all along the line in international affairs.[5]

Kennan wrote the article while at the National War College. In 1946-1947, however, he was the reigning American expert on Russia in the Foreign Service and the deputy chief of mission to the American ambassador in Moscow, Averell Harriman. He took advantage of Harriman's pre-Potsdam trip to Washington to respond at great length to a routine circular cable asking each mission to outline the likely position of its country to the forthcoming peace treaty conference of the foreign ministers' meeting in Paris. On the way home from Moscow, at the Berlin airport, he bracketed the Soviet government with Hitler's and was declared non grata by the Soviets. Thus his temporary transfer to the War College.

THE INITIAL SOVIET IDEAS AND ACTION

Kennan's proposition was clearly at work during 1946 in every dimension of Soviet policy toward Europe, although, simultaneously, American public opinion was rapidly hardening in its view of Soviet politics and intentions in Eastern Europe, however, Soviet policy faced a dilemma. On the one hand, the disposition of its armies in 1945 provided unlimited de facto power to do politically whatever the Soviet government wished to do. On the other hand, under the exigencies of war and wartime diplomacy, Stalin had made serious commitments to free secret elections in Eastern Europe in general, Poland in particular. After all, Britain had gone to war in defense of Poland, and, as Roosevelt had made clear, Americans had a strong interest in Poland's political future. Poland was an obsessive subject of discussion and negotiation at Yalta. Churchill reports: "Poland was discussed at no fewer than seven of the eight plenary meetings of the Yalta Conference, and the British record contains an interchange on this topic of nearly eighteen thousand words between Stalin, Roosevelt, and myself."[6] Stalin was evidently resistant, seeking to maximize the power of the Polish Communists initially installed, but he gave ground under pressure from Washington and London.

Since this is a book about ideas and action, it is worth asking—rather than taking for granted that we know—what Stalin had in mind. It so happens that a quarter century earlier, in a letter to Lenin, he had addressed himself in abstract terms to the question of how Communist states in Eastern Europe, assuming they emerged, should relate to the Soviet Union:

> For the nations constituting the old Russia, our [Soviet] type of federation can be regarded as of the greatest assistance on the road toward international unity. The reasons are obvious: these national groups either had no state organization in the past or had long ago lost it, so that the Soviet (centralized) type of federation could be grafted on without any special friction.

The same cannot be said of those national groups not included in the old Russia as independent formations but having developed a specific state organization of their own, and which, if they become Soviet, will perforce have to enter into some State relation with Soviet Russia. Take for instance a future Soviet Germany, Poland, Hungary or Finland. It is doubtful whether these nations, who have their own State, their own army, their own finances, would, after becoming Soviet, at once agree to enter into a federal relationship with Soviet Russia of the Bashkir or Ukrainian type.... [T]hey would regard federation of the Soviet type as a form of reducing their national independence and as an attempt against it.

I do not doubt that the most acceptable form of rapprochement to these nationalities would be confederation.... I am leaving out the backward nationalities, e.g. Persia, Turkey, in relation to whom or for whom the Soviet type of federation and federation in general would be still more unacceptable.

Bearing all this in mind, I think that it is indispensable to include at some point in your minutes on the transition forms of rapprochement between the workers of the various nations the mention of confederation (alongside federation). Such an amendment would lend your proposals more elasticity, enrich them with one more transition form of rapprochement as described, and would render State rapprochement with the Soviet easier to the national groups which did not previously form part of old Russia.[7]

It would be quite unwarranted to assume that Stalin simply decided, as a matter of fixed plan, to implement after 1945 the "confederation" concept he commended to Lenin in 1920. A more general notion probably governed Soviet thought in the immediate postwar period. Built into the memory and doctrines of the Soviet leaders was an acute awareness that societies emerging from the political and social as well as physical disruptions of major war represented targets of great opportunity. After all, it was by exploiting such possibilities that the Bolsheviks had come to power in Russia in 1917; and it had been a close thing elsewhere in Central and Eastern Europe. From their perspective they no doubt felt a sense of historic duty to make the most of immediate postwar circumstances and extend communism to the outer limits of the possible, short of direct military conflict with the United States. Their ambition was not limited to the areas controlled by the Soviet armies. The potentialities in France and Italy, western Germany, Greece, Turkey, and Iran evidently interested them. Stalin, whose style included elements of candor as well as guile, may have revealed his perspective quite succinctly in responding to then Ambassador Averell Harriman at Potsdam: "The first time I saw [Stalin] at the conference I went up to him and said that it must be very gratifying for him to be in Berlin, after all the struggle and tragedy. He hesitated a moment and then replied, 'Czar Alexander got to Paris.' It didn't need much of a clairvoyant to guess what was in his mind."[8] Stalin simply did not know how far Moscow would be able to extend its power in the postwar world; but his ambitions were ample, supported by a sense of how much Russia had suffered and achieved in the Second World War, a determination to guarantee Soviet security from another German assault, converging with a Communist's sense of duty to exploit an interval of palpable opportunity.

As far as Eastern Europe was concerned, something like Stalin's earlier confederation scheme, with ultimate power firmly centered in Moscow, was what emerged as the primary intent of the Soviet government. How far and how fast this could proceed, however, depended on the strength and determination of Americans in requiring that the Yalta commitments be carried out, notably with respect to Poland. In 1945 and subsequently, Stalin was not about to risk a confrontation that carried with it the risk of war with the United States. Nevertheless, Poland was critical from Moscow's point of view for fundamental reasons. If Poland was taken over by more or less pliant Communists and became part of the confederation, a continuous area of military as well as political power could be built from Moscow as far west as the Elbe. If it were politically democratic, Poland might well be rendered harmless to the Soviet Union in narrow military terms, as Finland and Austria were to be; but it could not be relied on as a working member of a Moscow-dominated confederation. Eastern Germany, blocked off from the USSR by a democratic Poland, would then be useful only as a diplomatic bargaining counter, in dealings with the West, to assure reparations or aid in the short run, the disarmament of a united democratic Germany in the long run. But Stalin's ambitions were higher. It was not accidental that Stalin's vision of empire in Eastern Europe was brought together under the rubric of the Warsaw Pact.

Churchill and Roosevelt had a contrary vision of postwar Europe. Their overriding concern was to establish whether they could agree with Stalin. Then all three countries could preside together over a united Germany limited in arms—in a Europe at last reunited. If Stalin disagreed the British (and French) thought there would be a split Europe backed, they hoped, by the United States. Churchill and Roosevelt, on the one hand, and Stalin, on the other, were thus quite right to make Poland the central issue at Yalta. The final exchanges between the two Western leaders on the eve of Roosevelt's death reflect their anxiety about Stalin's evident procrastination in carrying out the Yalta agreement to broaden the government in Warsaw and to proceed with free elections; and this was the first major foreign policy issue addressed by Truman in his contentious meeting with Vyacheslav Molotov on April 23, 1945, followed by his dispatch of the ailing Harry Hopkins to Moscow a month later.

Hopkins got Stalin to agree that a Polish government of national unity be formed, including Stanislaw Mikolajczyk (a member of the wartime Polish government in London) as vice premier. Three additional ministries were granted to non-Lublin Poles acceptable to Great Britain and the United States. With this and several lesser concessions, the ground was cleared for the Big Three meeting at Potsdam.

At Potsdam the recognition of the reorganized Polish Provisional Government was confirmed, and agreement was made to hold free and unfettered elections on the basis of universal suffrage and secret ballot, with guarantees of access by the world press to report events before and during the elections. In a sense, then, Truman's diplomacy on Poland in the first four months of his administration appeared to have moved the Polish question forward in terms of the Yalta agreement.

Mikolajczyk arrived in Warsaw as vice premier to find the Communists quite solidly entrenched. The Ministry of the Interior was divided in two at the start, with public administration (routine bureaucratic matters) under Wladyslaw Kiernik, a follower of Mikolajczyk, and security (secret political police, internal security corps, and militia) under a Communist, Stanislaw Radkiewicz. What was left of the army was also controlled, at least at the top, by Communists and included many who had served in the Red Army. The third crucial position occupied by the Communists was the Ministry of Regained Territories (the Oder-Neisse region), a separate administration under Wladyslaw Gomulka. Since the territory was comparatively rich in industrial and agricultural opportunities, and since a complete resettlement of Poles from the East was called for after the Germans were expelled, ample possibilities for patronage and control were available to Gomulka, who was also at that time secretary of the Polish Communist Party.

But, from a Communist point of view, the real enemy was Mikolajczyk. His original Peasant Party was taken over by bringing in Communists from the outside to take key posts. Mikolajczk then established a new Polish Peasant Party. Two leaders of the new party were promptly murdered. Mikolajczyk's protests and demands for investigation were taken to exhibit a "lack of confidence in the Ministry of Security." A subsequent trial brought a suitable confession from an underground Communist agent.

Nevertheless, Mikolajczyk was able to hold a party congress in January 1946 and, despite harassment, maintained a distinctive political position. In the plebiscite of June 1946 — conducted with many irregularities but more or less by Western election standards — the government announced, after a delay of ten days and with much embarrassment, an antigovernment, pro-Mikolajczyk majority of 68 percent on the one disputed question (the abolition of the Senate); but according to Mikolajczyk the result would have been 83 percent in his favor had there not been arrests and falsification. It was Mikolajczyk who had urged the Polish people to vote "no" on this issue, which was universally taken to be a test of his strength.

From this time on, the Polish government, frightened by Mikolajczyk's evident grass-roots support, moved quickly under Moscow's guidance. To prepare for the parliamentary elections of January 1947, the western territories, safe under Gomulka's control, were given disproportionate electoral representation. Mikolajczyk and his followers were incriminated by the confessions of certain political prisoners who asserted they were foreign agents. Two bogus parties were set up to drain off the peasant vote toward Communist-controlled groups. Thousands of members of the new pro-Mikolajczyk Polish Peasant Party were at least temporarily arrested, and "preliminary open voting" took place in many districts. The resulting parliament, overwhelmingly backing the government bloc, passed a new provisional constitution in February 1947. Britain and the United States protested that the Yalta provisions on Poland were being violated, but by this time it was clear to both the Soviet leadership and the Polish Communists that such paper protests could be safely ignored.

This, in effect, was the end of the road for Yalta and Mikolajczyk; but he did not give up the uneven struggle and leave Poland until the fall of 1947, when he was informed of his imminent arrest. The fact is that, after Potsdam, the question of the fate of democracy in Poland virtually disappeared from Truman's and Secretary of State Byrnes' agenda.[9] The confrontation between Soviet and Western conceptions of postwar Europe shifted to Germany and the Control Council in Berlin. General Marshall succeeded Byrnes as secretary of state on January 7, 1947.

THE AMERICAN STANCE ON GERMANY

The story of U.S. postwar policy toward Germany begins formally with the Potsdam meeting and its decisions, although a good deal was foreshadowed in the earlier European Advisory Commission agreement in London on the location of occupation zones and the creation of a quadripartite Control Council in Berlin. As it related to Germany, the Potsdam communiqué issued on August 2, 1945, contained several elements. In part, it proclaimed general principles that were to govern the occupation of each zone in Germany. The principles were to be interpreted and administered by the several occupying powers; but the four-power Control Council in Berlin was to handle all-German issues, and a Council of Foreign Ministers was created to deal, among other matters, with German issues not resolved in Berlin and ultimately with a German treaty. The principles covered the elimination of existing military equipment and uniquely military production facilities as well as the democratization of German institutions: the schools, the judiciary, local government, and the trade unions. The principles of freedom of speech and assembly and of free elections were proclaimed.

The second set of agreements on Germany related to economic policy and, most specifically, to reparations; and it laid down a number of operating procedures. Germany was to be treated as an economic unit, and central German agencies were to be created in economic fields, to operate under the general stipulation of earning for itself a standard of subsistence accommodated to an average European level and with a specific limit of paying for current imports out of current exports. Soviet and Polish reparations were to come from the Soviet Zone; but, in view of heavy Russian war losses, 15 percent of Western Zone capital equipment removed would be traded against current exports from the Soviet Zone, and an additional 10 percent would be available as pure reparations to the Soviet Union. A general reparations plan was to be negotiated in the Control Council within six months. Advance reparation deliveries on a limited basis were to be made, pending a general accord, in order to accelerate European recovery.

Diplomatic explorations and technical studies of the reparations problem had been going forward since the Yalta conference, the negotiations being conducted on the American side mainly under a special group headed by Edwin Pauley, a western oil executive who had distinguished himself as a Democratic fund-raiser. That group was ill-coordinated with other arms of American foreign policy, and there was still no clear American position on reparations at the time of the Potsdam conference.

At Potsdam, however, the American delegation underwent a vivid experience that clarified its collective mind. Americans saw in Berlin (including the Western zones of Berlin) that, without inter-Allied agreement, the Russians were moving equipment out of factories as fast as their technicians could dismantle it—faster even than the equipment could be properly crated and transported. It was evident that this process of Soviet seizure was proceeding throughout much of Eastern Europe as well as in Manchuria. American reparations policy quickly focused around the problem of preventing the kind of denuding of West Germany that the Russians were effecting in East Germany.

Mindful of the Russian war losses, Americans found it hard in July 1945 to put their hearts into protesting what was being done in the Soviet Zone, even though the hasty unilateral removal of machinery was viewed as inefficient as well as illegal. American efforts, therefore, were devoted primarily to limiting the extent of Soviet claims on West German capital equipment and to laying down rules under which it would be impossible for the United States to pour emergency aid into Germany from the West (or finance a German foreign exchange deficit) while current German production was being drained off to the East as reparations. Thus, while Potsdam's general political and economic principles looked to a united four-power policy in Germany, the unilateral principle was strengthened once unilateral action on reparations was accepted as legitimate in the Soviet Zone; and reparations went to the heart of short-run economic and political policy. To a significant degree, then, the postwar negotiations on German unity began on the basis of a split Germany.

From the Potsdam meetings to April 1946, the question of reparations remained the central issue of four-power diplomacy in Germany, although the larger issues emerged and were gradually clarified. On December 12, 1945, the Department of State issued a long statement on German economic policy. Its formal purpose was to clarify the principle on which the reparations clauses of Potsdam should be negotiated. Its broader aim, however, was to define the stages whereby the German economy would move from a role of subservience to the needs of other states for recovery to one of resumed economic development when once again German standards of living would be a matter determined by German efforts and efficiency in utilizing German resources. This document symbolized the rapid transition in the post-Potsdam period from a negative to a constructive approach to Germany, a transition that was inevitable given Western values but that was certainly accelerated by a Soviet policy that evidently sought to profit from poverty and frustration in Central and Western Europe.

Although the economists and industrial technicians concentrated in Berlin made valiant efforts to construct an economic plan to meet the complex Potsdam conditions, the essence of U.S. policy in this period was political. The American purpose was to force at an early stage a clear-cut test of whether or not the Soviet Union was prepared to move promptly toward a united Germany. The architect of this policy, as well as its chief practitioner, was General Lucius Clay. He had succeeded Eisenhower as the senior officer in the American Zone and was a clear and forceful member of the Control Council.

The reparations plan was essentially a definition of the initial complement of industrial equipment necessary to make postwar Germany economically viable if it were effectively unified. The reparations pool would be defined by subtracting this minimum level of industry from the capacity actually in Germany. Clay's policy was to work hard and cooperatively with the Soviets in getting an agreed level-of-industry plan for Germany as a whole and then to make actual reparation deliveries hinge on Soviet agreement to treat the German economy as an economic unit. Because of the intimate interconnections between economic and other institutions, it was clear that political and economic unity would come together if they came at all. What appeared a highly remote and often fantastic technicians' game was, in fact, a negotiation to test whether the split of Germany would persist.

The outcome was clean-cut, although its full implications took some time to absorb. A level-of-industry plan was agreed to on March 26, 1946, with the American negotiators making every possible concession to meet Soviet demands. Within a month, however, Clay had openly disengaged from the reparations plan on the grounds that the Soviets were clearly unprepared to join in a common program for foreign trade and for the German economy as a whole. Clay's statement in the Coordinating Committee of the Control Council on April 26, 1946, reveals his mind:

> I submit that reparations were only one of the bricks that built the house. If you pull out any of the bricks the house collapses, and it seems to me we have pulled out so many already we are on the verge of collapse. I don't believe we can ever reach a solution on any one of them without reaching a solution on all of them. Certainly the question of the ability to meet the export-import program is tied up definitely with the question of reparations.[10]

On May 3 Clay stopped advance reparation deliveries to the Soviet Union from the American Zone—a major benchmark in the evolution of postwar diplomacy.

Hopes for an all-German settlement were not immediately and definitively abandoned; but, from this time forward, the American position moved toward the unification of the Western zones and the gradual acceptance of a split Germany. This trend was broken only by George Marshall's last-ditch effort to negotiate German unity in Moscow in March and April 1947 and, in a sense, by his offer in June 5, 1947, to treat the whole of Europe ("to the Urals") as an economic unit under the Marshall Plan proposal.

It is difficult to recapture the mood of the post-Potsdam negotiations in the Berlin Control Council as American hopes came up against the positions of the Soviet Union, Britain, and France, each of which, for different reasons, were not anxious to move toward German unity. Eisenhower and Clay—the former remaining in Germany only until November 1945—felt that the Control Council and its negotiations represented a historic occasion to seek a fundamental understanding with the Soviets.

From the beginning, Eisenhower was encouraged by the responsiveness of Georgy K. Zhukov; and between Clay and Vasily Sokolovsky, their deputies and successors, there developed a relationship of mutual respect and, to a degree, of friendship.[11] This reaching out between Americans and Russians, within the narrowing limits the course of events permitted, extended far down into the maze of technical committees into which the Control Council was organized. Although reparations were at the center of high diplomacy in Berlin, there was an interminable array of housekeeping questions that required one form or another of expertise. Neither the Americans nor the Russians involved in this business were professional diplomats. They were, for the most part, technicians, emerging from searching experiences of war, full of national pride, and touched with a human desire to make the peace work. The Berlin Control Council was the most extensive Western contact with the rising second generation of well-trained technicians in Soviet society; and many who shared the experience emerged with a sense that Soviet society had the capability of producing in time a policy easier to live with than Stalin's.

The Control Council quickly established a common law of decorous, dignified debate, a tradition that survived long after the council had clearly failed in its central mission. On at least one occasion Sokolovsky, furnished by the increasingly powerful Soviet political adviser with a conventional diplomatic script full of the recriminations against the West, did his duty but in a manner that clearly disassociated himself from the text. In part, the Control Council style was a carryover of mutually understood military etiquette as among the military chiefs; in part, it reflected a sense of a larger mission that, in differing degree, touched men from all of the four nations represented in Berlin.

The human relations that developed initially between the Americans and Russians in Berlin were watched with mixed feelings by the British and French. The French had tried but failed to achieve the agreement of the United States, Great Britain, and the Soviet Union to the detachment of the Ruhr from Germany. As at Versailles, they felt about equally that Germany would revive and the United States would leave Europe. The rapprochement raised the possibility of a Soviet-American bilateral agreement that would, in effect, settle Europe's affairs and reduce all other powers to secondary status, and then the Americans would go home. More important, as far as the American hopes in the Control Council were concerned, neither the French nor the British believed then that German unity was a practical or a particularly desirable goal—a view that persisted in Paris and London until the Berlin Wall fell in 1989.

The French, having failed to get agreement on the detachment of the Ruhr, sought to delay the revival of German economic and political strength at every stage, sensing that a revived Germany would ultimately overshadow postwar France on the European scene. British policy, on narrower economic grounds, aimed to ensure a more rapid recovery of the British than the German economy, notably in export markets; but, since the costs of British occupation in Germany were high, there was a countervailing interest in making the British Zone, which contained the bulk of German industry, a going concern. Neither France nor Britain shared the American anxiety to force a showdown on the issue of German unity, both nations being reasonably content with the split of Europe on the Elbe. It represented a tolerable, if not happy, distribution of power between East and West in the short run and, perhaps, in the long run as well. Given their recent experiences of Germany and their intense domestic preoccupations in the immediate postwar period, their attitudes were wholly understandable; but they were not in harmony with the more ambitious hopes and more ardent mood of Americans caught up in the German problem.

Some British and French undoubtedly shared the sense of promise implicit in the human understanding that briefly flowered in the Control Council. On the whole, however, Clay, in actively seeking an accord with the Soviet Union on the level of industry and then provoking a sharp crisis on the issue of German economic unity, was doubly out of step with his Western colleagues.

Early in 1946 it became evident that Stalin was disturbed at the developing friendly relationship in Berlin, which indeed had within it the seeds of German unity on democratic terms. There were changes in Soviet personnel, and the role of Soviet political adviser was increased. Marshal Georgy Zhukov was recalled as early as November 1945 and soon isolated in Odessa. Sokolovsky operated with progressively diminished flexibility and freedom for independent action.

After the failure of the reparations negotiation in April, the notion of linking the British and American zones began seriously to be considered. On July 20, 1946, a formal offer was made in the Control Council to link the American Zone with any other (or all three), and this was accepted by the British on July 30. Aside from aiding German recovery and strengthening the Western bargaining hand vis-à-vis Moscow, the agreement lifted to a degree the pressing financial burden of occupation on London and gave Clay a strong voice in the administration of West German resources, including the critical supply of coking coal from the Ruhr. It had rankled among the Americans in Berlin that their authority extended directly only over the wooded hills and farms that mainly characterized the American Zone in the south.

The American position taken in the Control Council shared one general limitation of U.S. policy. It sought to test Soviet intentions at a key point, but it incorporated no clear, positive concept of Europe or of the American interest in its structure. German unity was sought in a vacuum, as a goal in itself or as a generalized test of Soviet intentions. Above all, the American view failed to recognize adequately the forces shaping Soviet policy and the extent to which Soviet policy hinged on what Stalin thought the United States would or would not do to enforce agreements he intended to break if violation proved safe.

The American assumption in the Control Council was that Moscow's position was determined by forces essentially independent of the American performance outside Berlin, and that the maximum course open to the United States, having honestly reassured the Soviets that the nation's intentions were peaceful, was to accept the split on the Elbe.[12] The reaction in Berlin to the concept of an American initiative looking to an all-European settlement was that the question of unity or schism in Europe would be settled in Germany and in Berlin. If the Soviets were willing to see a free unified Europe, that fact would emerge in the German negotiations; if not, then a split on the Elbe would be inevitable. There was little awareness that the fate of Germany might hinge on Mikolajczyk's fate in Poland and on what the United States did or failed to do in backing the Yalta and Potsdam commitments in Eastern Europe. And, in other respects as well, American policy in postwar Germany was clear, strong, but narrow.

Clay's performance in the eight post-Potsdam months had one important consequence for those charged with making American policy. His effort to seek German unity by negotiation with the Soviet Union had been so wholehearted and was conducted with such evident sincerity, and the Soviet unwillingness to proceed seriously toward unity was so patent, that no one who knew the circumstances could feel that a postwar opportunity for accord had been lost for lack of trying in Berlin. That could not be said about Poland or, indeed, Europe as a whole.

BYRNES AND THE SATELLITE TREATIES

As Stalin progressively consolidated his position in Eastern Europe and the Control Council in Berlin moved into stalemate, the de facto acceptance of the split of Germany was accented. Byrnes and his staff worked their way laboriously through the peace treaties. It was clear at the time to those working from day to day in the State Department and it is clear from Byrnes' account in *Speaking Frankly* that, at a crucial juncture in world history, the American secretary of state was overwhelmingly preoccupied with what were geographically and, in substance, peripheral issues. The relevant chapter headings of Byrnes' book suggest rather well the story of his treaty-making peregrinations over the critical sixteen months from September 1945 through December 1946: "Setback at London," "Moscow Ends an Impasse," "London Again, and Paris Twice," "The Paris Peace Conference and Its New York Finale." Of his 562 days as secretary of state, Byrnes spent 245 outside the United States, 350 away from Washington.

In all conscience, the negotiation of the treaties was hard and frustrating work, marked at every step by the skillful, patient, stubborn roadblocks and obfuscations for which Molotov was justly famous. The Council of Foreign Ministers was a very difficult committee. At the end, one can understand Byrnes' pride and relief that the job was done. And it was a job that had to be done. It brought Finland and Italy, as well as the other states, formally back into the family of nations. Byrnes took great pains to carry with him the leaders of both parties in the Senate. And on June 5, 1947, the politically most difficult of the treaties—the Italian—cleared the Senate. But, as they emerged, the treaties merely tidied up one dimension of the division of Europe, for they left Eastern Europe and eastern Germany in Soviet hands.

In Acheson and Clayton, Byrnes had exceedingly able deputies operating steadily in Washington. But the position of the secretary of state is— or should be—rather different from, say, that of Molotov. Molotov was an instrument of the policy agreed upon in Stalin's Politburo. The secretary of state is—or should be—the principal and most intimate collaborator of the president in the making of foreign policy.

Byrnes' preoccupation with the treaties in 1946, was combined with his rather peculiar arm's-length relationship to Truman. Byrnes never appeared to have forgiven Truman for accepting Roosevelt's offer of the nomination as vice president—a post he felt should have gone to him. That would have made him president rather than Truman. In any case, he permitted the process of division to go forward—in Eastern Europe, Berlin, and the treaty negotiations themselves—without any coherent, determined effort to reverse it. For this would have required that he work closely with Truman.

THE DREADFUL WINTER OF 1946–1947

These rather depressing developments in the world of politics and diplomacy took place against a background of uneven and financially precarious economic revival in Europe. The main features of the situation were these:

Industrial production, except in Germany, revived moderately well but declined or decelerated in the extremely severe European winter of 1946–1947. This was felt in Western Europe particularly in the first quarter of 1947. Overall industrial production remained well below the 1938 level.

Agricultural production, recovering more slowly, was far below the 1938 level.

Sustained by ad hoc pre–Marshall Plan credits, European imports from non-European countries were reasonably high (91.9 percent of 1938 in 1946), exports low (51 percent of 1938 in 1946), and intra-European trade disastrously low (45.3 percent of 1938 in 1946). These 1946 foreign trade figures were in substantial part due to the extremely low level of economic activity in Germany.

The European balance of payments deficits were much greater than in 1938 due not only to the trade deficit but also to lesser earnings from investments and invisibles. The balance of payments deficits reflected the urgent European need for enormous imports from the United States in foodstuffs, coal, and manufactured goods that could not be paid for by exports to the United States; for the undamaged American economy easily met the country's basic needs.

This situation, heightened by the hard winter of 1946–1947, translated itself into mass impoverishment in Germany, straitened circumstances to a varying degree elsewhere, and a generally disheartening setting for social and political life. The sense gradually spread that something had to be done about the European dollar deficit and the revival of German economic life in 1947, or Western Europe was headed for disaster.

All this was brought home with particular force to Will Clayton, who spent considerable time in Geneva on trade negotiations, as well as in London, which was greatly depressed by Britain's running out of its coal stockpile in the midst of the coldest winter of the century. Clayton's most influential memorandum, which no doubt helped focus Washington's collective mind sharply, was based on notes made on a flight from Geneva to Washington on May 19, 1947, completed and given to Marshall on May 27. It included this passage: "Europe is steadily deteriorating. . . . Millions of people in the cities are slowly starving. . . . Without further and substantial aid from the United States economic, social, and political disintegration will overwhelm Europe."[13]

These, then, were the corrosive forces operating, on the whole quietly, without dramatic crises, during the year 1946: in Eastern Europe, in the Control Council in Berlin, among the economies of Western Europe, and at home.

THE TRUMAN DOCTRINE

The Truman Doctrine was laid before Congress on March 12, 1947. Vandenberg, whom many regarded as Truman's logical Republican successor in 1949, had impressed on the president that he had to lay out the case publicly, in the full and stark terms Marshall and Acheson had used to the bipartisan congressional leadership. Truman was not only asking for aid for Greece, bedeviled by a guerrilla civil war waged by Communists supplied from Yugoslavia; not merely asking for aid for Turkey in the face of Soviet pressure for an expanded role in the Dardanelles; not merely dramatizing the financial weakness of Britain as the United States took over its responsibilities in the Eastern Mediterranean and the Middle East; he was declaring that, in general, it is the "policy of the United States to support free peoples who are resisting attempted subjugation by armed minorities or by outside pressures." This was not a declaration of war; but it crossed a line the American public had been reluctant to cross: from a receding hope that the Soviet Union would cooperate with the West in building the postwar world into open confrontation.

The Truman Doctrine stirred much discussion and some controversy in the United States and Western Europe. There were fears that its rhetoric would lead the nation into expenditures beyond its means; that the Soviet Union would be antagonized; that the doctrine did not deal with the economic instability of Europe as a whole; and that, in general, it was an excessively negative approach to a complex situation in which the corrosive Communist role was only one part.

The Marshall Plan speech restored an important degree of balance. It was, however, a reaction to Marshall's negotiations in Moscow of March and April 1947. Marshall concluded—as had many others over the previous year and a half—that Stalin did not intend to move toward a unified democratic Germany; but he did not stop there. Unlike Byrnes, Marshall also concluded that the economic, social, and political disarray of Western Europe, with all the opportunities it appeared to open for Soviet penetration, was a major reason for Stalin's complacency in the face of delay over the German problem. As Joseph Jones, one of the best chroniclers of this period, reports, one lesson of Moscow was that "to deal with the problem of Germany it was necessary to deal with the problem of Europe."[14] Marshall clearly understood that the policy of the United States, as perceived by Moscow, was one determinant of Soviet policy. And he decided the United States would have to act. George Kennan paraphrases Marshall's pithy view as of April 29, 1947: "Europe was in a mess. Something would have to be done. If he [Marshall] did not take the initiative, others would."[15]

The Marshall Plan consisted of some $13 billion (say, $90 billion in current prices) of unrequited aid to seventeen Western and Southern European countries. From the low point in the winter of 1946-1947, the aid produced in Europe a rise in gross national product of 15 to 25 percent in four years. It had an enormous psychological as well as material reaction among the peoples of Western Europe.

The Marshall Plan—and all that immediately followed down to, say, 1951—also ended the contention within the Department of State and, more important, laid the basis for European policy and American policy toward Europe for a half century and more.

THE IDEAS

THE FOREIGN SERVICE OUTLOOK
ON THE PROSPECTS FOR EUROPE

We turn now to the ideas in contention in this transition between 1945 and 1947. The setting in which these ideas were applied had all the dimensions indicated in the section above. But it was an argument, in the end, about the split or unity of Europe. As nearly as the records show, the issue of a purposeful U.S. effort to avoid, or accept, the split of Europe or its acceptance never came before Truman. It was laid before Byrnes by Acheson and Clayton with their support on April 20, 1946, but not firmly decided by Byrnes. At the working level the major partisans were the members of the Foreign Service concerned with European affairs and the economists of the Office of German Austrian Economic Affairs (GA), in particular Charles Kindleberger, its chief, and myself.

The issue — a purposeful effort to avoid the split of Europe or its acceptance — was not new. As early as February 3, 1945, Kennan had written to Charles Bohlen, a friend and fellow Foreign Service officer. According to the latter's recollection in *Witness to History,* Kennan explained:

> "I am aware of the realities of this war, and of the fact that we were too weak to win it without Russian cooperation. I recognize that Russia's war effort has been masterful and effective and must, to a certain extent, find its reward at the expense of other peoples in eastern and central Europe.
>
> "But with all of this, I fail to see why we must associate ourselves with this political program, so hostile to the interests of the Atlantic community as a whole, so dangerous to everything we need to see preserved in Europe. Why could we not make a decent and definitive compromise with it — divide Europe frankly into spheres of influence — keep ourselves out of the Russian sphere and keep the Russians out of ours?"

Kennan also proposed that "[t]he United States 'accept as an accomplished fact the complete partition of Germany' and begin consultations with the British and French about the formation of a Western European federation, which would include West German states." Bohlen's reply and his reflections on the exchange capture well the balance of considerations that governed American policy at Yalta:

> . . . As hopeless as the outlook seemed the United States must try to get along with the Soviets. The American people, who had fought a long,

hard war, deserved at least an attempt to work out a better world. If the attempt failed, the United States could not be blamed for not trying.

In short, foreign policy in a democracy must take into account the emotions, beliefs and goals of the people. The most carefully thought-out plans of the experts, even though 100 percent correct in theory, will fail without broad public support. The good leader in foreign affairs formulates his policy on expert advice and creates a climate of public opinion to support it.

Between February 1945 and February 22, 1946, when George Kennan's famous five-part "long cable" from Moscow began to arrive in the State Department, the notion had spread within the Foreign Service that the task of the West was to contain the outward thrust of Communist power rather than seek an agreed-upon settlement embracing all of Europe. Kennan's eloquent and influential essay helped crystallize that judgment in Washington. Its effect was perhaps heightened because its somewhat fevered prose was read on the pink cable forms that usually transmitted terse, professional messages. Kennan did not take the occasion to restate his earlier call for Eastern and Western spheres of influence, although two weeks later he reaffirmed it.[16] In fact, his famous cable had remarkably little to say in specific terms about U.S. policy. But his portrait of implacable, hostile Soviet purposes and the need for "cohesion, firmness, and vigor" in the Western world, geared to "a constructive picture of the sort of world we would like to see," fitted well the views of those who envisaged a split of Europe and the formation of a Western bloc.

Although the process of exploration envisaged by Bohlen, in his response to Kennan at Yalta, proceeded in 1946, an increasing proportion of the relevant Foreign Service officers came to Kennan's conclusion about a split Europe.

The anxiety in 1946 that pursuit of German unity would lead to a Soviet-dominated Germany was not confined to the U.S. Foreign Service. It was, as noted above, a recurrent theme in French diplomatic exchanges with the United States, often linked to the notion of a future American withdrawal of its effective weight from Europe.[17] For example, Robert Murphy, another distinguished Foreign Service officer, reported on February 24 that "members of the French delegation here [in Berlin] have admitted privately that present French policy is based not simply on fear of future German aggression but equally, if not more, on fear that the United States will lose interest, eventually withdraw from Germany, and that some fine morning they will wake up and find themselves face to face with the Russians on the Rhine."[18]

The British Foreign Office had, perhaps even earlier, come to the view that a permanently divided Germany was the best that could be wrested from the military and diplomatic situation that was emerging after the Second World War. Robert Murphy, in his memoir, reports that "the British decided very soon after Potsdam that Germany probably was permanently divided between East and West."[19]

Although its accent and emphasis were different, a similar schismatic view of the appropriate outcome in Europe was forming in what, for want of a better term, is called the liberal wing of the Democratic Party. It was reflected, for example, in Henry Wallace's speech on foreign policy of September 12, 1946, which led to his being removed by Truman from his post as secretary of commerce at Byrnes' insistence. After providing a rationale out of Russian history for Moscow's concern with its security in Eastern Europe and eastern Germany and blaming the British as well as the Russians for conducting postwar power politics, Wallace called for a formal recognition of the split of Germany and Europe and an understanding between the United States and the Soviet Union about subsequent behavior.

In a curious way the Wallace position and that of the Foreign Service were identical, with one not trivial exception: Wallace assumed that a treaty assuring Soviet good behavior on the noncommunist side of the line was negotiable; the Foreign Service, regarding this stance as naive, assumed that we would have to "keep the Russians out" of our sphere.

As the issue of policy toward the Soviet Union emerged in the first half of 1946, Truman took an independent initiative, as his earlier confidence waned that he and Stalin could work things out. In June he ordered his special counsel, Clark Clifford, to survey expert opinion in the government and report on the state of Soviet motivations, policies, and apparent intentions. Clifford's top secret report to the president, "American Relations with the Soviet Union," is dated September 24, 1946.[20] Clifford first evoked Soviet motivation and ambitions, along the lines of Kennan's February 1946 cable, the record of broken agreements, Soviet activities against U.S. interests beyond Eastern Europe, and the buildup of Soviet military strength. Clifford's final recommendations included the following:

> The Soviet Government will never be easy to "get along with." The American people must accustom themselves to this thought, not as a cause for despair, but as a fact to be faced objectively and courageously. If we find it impossible to enlist Soviet cooperation in the solution of world problems, we should be prepared to join with the British and other Western countries in an attempt to build up a world of our own which will pursue its own objectives and will recognize the Soviet orbit as a distinct entity with which conflict is not predestined but with which we cannot pursue common aims. . . .
> It must be made apparent to the Soviet Government that our strength

will be sufficient to repel any attack and sufficient to defeat the USSR decisively if a war should start. The prospect of defeat is the only sure means of deterring the Soviet Union. . . .

In addition to maintaining our own strength, the United States should support and assist all democratic countries which are in any way menaced or endangered by the USSR. . . .

Even though the Soviet leaders profess to believe that the conflict between Capitalism and Communism is irreconcilable and must eventually be resolved by the triumph of the latter, it is our hope that they will change their minds and work out with us a fair and equitable settlement when they realize that we are too strong to be beaten and too determined to be frightened.

This paper, as opposed to Kennan's "long cable," is explicit about the military aspect of containment. It was no doubt carefully read by Truman. It foreshadows the Truman Doctrine, elements in the Marshall Plan, and a good deal more in future U.S. foreign policy. From the perspective of this chapter, it also reflects a fatalistic acceptance of the split of Europe.

This, then, was the emerging climate of opinion in which the Acheson-Clayton proposal to Byrnes was formulated.

HOW THE ACHESON-CLAYTON PLAN CAME TO BE FORMULATED

One of the liveliest, most relaxed documents ever to be published among the solemn papers in *Foreign Relations of the United States* is a memorandum for the files on the origins of the Marshall Plan.[21] It was written by Charles Kindleberger, who had been much involved in the evolution of the plan. It is dated July 22, 1948, when the European Recovery Program, approved by Congress in April, was a going concern. Kindleberger evidently wrote from memory, without going back to the files. At one point he says: "In early 1946, Walt Rostow had a revelation that the unity of Germany could not be achieved without the unity of Europe, and that the unity of Europe could best be approached crabwise through technical cooperation in economic matters, rather than bluntly in diplomatic negotiations."

I would not quite rate my memorandum that went forward to Clayton on February 25, 1946, "a revelation," and I would describe the strategy it incorporated in somewhat different terms, since it transcended "technical cooperation in economic matters." But it did represent the crystallization in my mind of a line of approach quite different from the one we had been taking in the German-Austrian division of the Department of State; its scope far exceeded our bureaucratic mandate; and it no doubt startled Kindleberger, whose deputy I then was, and my other colleagues. But we soon made common cause.

Several of us from the Office of Strategic Services who had worked, for target purposes, on aspects of the German economy during the war were drawn into the State Department on the grounds that our expertise was transferable to problems of occupation and reconstruction. Five former members of the Enemy Objectives Unit (EOU) of the U.S. Embassy in London were among those recruited: Charles Kindleberger, John De Wilde (of the Board of Economic Warfare), Harold Barnett, William Salant, and myself. We took the wry view that there was a certain rude justice in all this; having helped through our work on bombing target selection to knock the place down, it was fair enough to ask us to help rebuild it. About half the members of the GA were drawn from outside EOU, including two hired fresh from the navy. At a higher bureaucratic level, Emile Despres and (later) Edward Mason of OSS also served under Clayton, the latter becoming his deputy and, later, Marshall's chief economic adviser at the Moscow conference of 1947. John Kenneth Galbraith, the Harvard economist, served for a time in 1946 as office director, presiding over the divisions concerned with Japanese as well as German-Austrian economic policy. I came out of the military to work in the State Department the day the Potsdam communiqué was published. On receiving the document and then talking with colleagues returned from the Potsdam meetings, we quickly appreciated that the result was of two minds. Depending on what subsequently transpired, it might lead either to German unity or to a split. By and large, we aligned ourselves with Clay and those backstopping his operation in Washington who sought to maximize the chance for German unity.

Our work, however, did not concern directly issues of high strategy. I, for example, concentrated on problems of German coal production and export. From 1945 to 1946 and for several years thereafter the availability of coal, especially coking coal for steel, determined the rate of recovery of a number of the economies of Western Europe and Yugoslavia. I also played an ancillary role on the level-of-industry reparations issue and had in my domain one of the most complex and frustrating issues encountered in postwar years: the settlement of Allied (including Russian) claims on German assets in Austria.

Our work moved forward, day by day, reaching interim crystallization in the policy document released by the State Department on December 12, 1945. This reflected an accord among the three major working groups in Washington dealing with German occupation problems: the political group working on Europe (EUR), the GA, and the initially military (later State Department) unit (headed by General John Hildring) that supported, day by day, the occupation authorities in Germany, Austria, and Japan.

It was in the wake of that communal effort that a series of dissatisfactions converged in my mind. They took the form of an array of questions that current U.S. policy failed to answer. I am reasonably sure of what they were; but, as every historian knows, it is an extremely uncertain business to reconstruct the past without valid documents; and the intellectual origins of a memorandum, even one's own, are inherently difficult to recapture.

Two fundamental questions were raised by my participation in the Franco-American conversations held in Washington November 13-20, 1946.[22] The first was, simply, what was the appropriate long-run relationship of Germany to the rest of Europe. The French team, headed by Couve de Murville, a major French diplomat, made the case, as it did also in London and Moscow, for the detachment of the Ruhr-Rhineland area from the rest of Germany. He argued that it should be placed under a special international authority independent of the Control Council in Berlin. At this time the French government was withholding its support from the Potsdam provisions for the setting up of central German administrative units until the Ruhr-Rhineland issue was settled. As the reigning Washington working-level expert on German coal production, I was invited along to some of the sessions despite my quite junior status in the State Department.

The French presented the case with their usual logic, precision, and elegance. But I found the piece of surgery they proposed unsatisfactory and unrealistic. By removing Germany's major industrial base, it not only would have radically reduced Germany's economic potential, already attenuated by the transfer of Silesia to Poland, but also would have provided a long-run focus for revived German resentment; and, besides, the proposal was unlikely to commend itself to Britain, the Soviet Union, or the United States. On the other hand, the underlying question had to be answered: how should the countries of Europe, dependent on German coal exports in particular, and its industrial capacity in general, be assured for the long pull that Germany's inevitable economic bargaining power would not be translated into inappropriate military strength or bilateral political bargaining power? My thoughts turned to a long-run institutionalization of the already existing European Coal Organization (ECO), which was operating to allocate coal from European sources, including Poland, and from the United States. The further thought developed that if institutions of economic unity on a wider front could emerge—embracing the European Central Inland Transport Organization (ECITO), in which the Soviet Union also participated, and the Emergency Economic Committee for Europe (EECE)—a revived and united Germany might be safely fitted into Europe. It was already evident that those three ad hoc organizations, which had emerged in the wake of the armies advancing from the west, provided a forum in which the smaller countries, by combining their interests, could insist on evenhanded standards of equity in a way that simple bilateralism might not permit.

The second question, posed informally by the French, was how the security of France was to be guaranteed vis-à-vis a united Germany, perhaps Soviet-dominated, if an effective U.S. role in Europe was withdrawn. The question of Americans' staying power in Europe was endemic in diplomatic conversations of late 1945 and early 1946, but here it was sharply focused in the off-the-record exchanges on the French Ruhr-Rhineland proposals.[23] This might seem strange from the perspective of the year 2002, a half century after U.S. loyalty to NATO proved exemplary. But in 1946 the Europeans were thinking of Wilson and Versailles and its aftermath.

The role of European unity was raised with me in December 1945 from a quite different direction. In discussing the State Department's policy document of December 9, which had just been published, my brother Eugene, who was teaching at the Yale Law School, said, in effect: "This is all very well, but it won't work unless Germany is part of a united Europe."[24] The economic situation in Europe, quite apart from the dreadful living conditions in Germany, cried out for rapid German revival. But only a united Europe was likely to have the inner confidence and strength to receive and balance a revived Germany. Thus, my brother's criticism of our policy document converged with my reflections on the Franco-American conversations of the previous month.

As the position of the British and Continental economies became increasingly clear, it was palpable that a vastly larger flow of American aid to Europe would be required and for a much longer period than anyone had yet envisaged if Europe was, in fact, fully and promptly, to recover. If this were to happen, however, a new basis for U.S. congressional support would be required. This lesson was driven home to all of us by the intense effort required to achieve the rather grudging passage by Congress of the special loan to Britain. The appeal in terms of British requirements and its wartime service to the Allied cause in standing alone from 1939 to the end of 1941, only barely succeeded. It was clear that if additional U.S. aid to Europe was going to be organized, it would have to be in terms of a large enterprise that looked forward rather than backward.

Finally, there was gathering evidence that Stalin viewed the postwar world as an arena of opportunity with the limits of that opportunity not yet set and, evidently, dependent in good part on his assessment of what the United States was prepared to do. I concluded that it was essential to establish the extent to which this forbidding stance was based on the assumption of progressive U.S. withdrawal from Europe; and, if it were not, and if it represented fixed purposes irrespective of U.S. policy, a much more vigorous and purposeful U.S. policy was, in any case, required.

Just what brought these elements all together and induced me to set down the proposal for a unified Europe, I simply do not recall. In sending the memorandum forward to Kindleberger, I simultaneously gave a copy to James Riddleberger of EUR at the very heart of the opposition. I did not think EUR's opposition would be softened by advance warning; but what I was proposing far exceeded our mandate. It simply seemed to be the correct thing to do. That occasion I remember well. I delivered and explained the memo's background at Riddleberger's home in Chevy Chase on a Sunday. His Dutch wife was present and responded more positively than her husband to my vision of how a drive for a united Europe might help solve some of the problems for which none of us yet had satisfactory answers.

After a generally favorable response within Clayton's domain, the second version of the plan, geared to the forthcoming foreign ministers' meeting, was formulated. It was at this stage that Jean Monnet was brought into the act. Monnet, director of the French modernization plan, was in Washington with Léon Blum, a former prime minister during a part of the 1930s. They were negotiating assistance for the French plan. This occupied eleven weeks, starting on March 19, 1946.[25] Monnet was thus in town in the period after our advocacy of European unity had been formulated and during the time when it moved up to Byrnes. I met Monnet not in connection with the French loan talks but because of his friendship with my brother, Eugene, stemming from their days together in North Africa in 1943. We talked in general terms about the theme of my memorandum. Knowing in April that the latest and most operational form of our proposal was moving up to higher levels, I informed my brother and asked his advice. He came down to Washington and talked to Monnet in, as he recalls, the garden of the French embassy. Monnet supported the plan and so informed Acheson.

So much by way of anecdote.

The substantive question arises: why did the leaders of the European Division of the State Department—James Dunn, H. Freeman Matthews, James Riddleberger, and other serious, knowledgeable officials—oppose the plan? In part, I am sure, they realized Soviet intentions were expansionist and thus had already written off Eastern Europe, including eastern Germany. The best outcome they could envisage was a split Europe with a Western bloc emerging. They had long since concluded that negotiations with the Soviet Union were fruitless and might open up the West to extensions of Soviet power. And, to a degree, they mistrusted the soundness and steadiness of the vision of Soviet intentions held by Truman and Byrnes, whom they tended to lump together. They feared that elements of naïveté persisted concerning the possibility of general negotiated settlements. In short, they tended to identify the split of Europe with a tough policy toward the Soviet Union, efforts to avoid the split as, in some sense, soft.

Put another way, I believe the senior members of the Foreign Service believed that their primary mission in 1946 was to educate American leaders in the nature of Soviet intentions.

Those initiating the Acheson-Clayton proposal of April 1946 took a somewhat different view. We took it for granted that Stalin was intent on pressing Soviet power as far as he safely could; we were acutely aware that the position of the United States, in its widest sense, tended to encourage him to aim high; we were conscious that the assets and inherent strength of the United States had not been effectively mobilized to indicate the options that the Soviet Union would eventually face. We were, moreover, sensitive to the likely costs of a split Europe: the loss of human freedoms for those in Eastern Europe, where the struggle, as of February to April 1946, had by no means been wholly lost; a perpetual confrontation and arms race on either side of the line; a United Nations bedeviled and weakened by that confrontation for which once consolidated, we could see no end. We thought all this would be a pretty poor outcome for those in the Soviet Union as well as the West who had fought and died in the recent struggle. We understood the EUR argument that all-German institutions and an all-European settlement would offer the Soviet Union room for maneuver in the West as well as Western influence in the East, but we rejected the notion that the United States — and the West as a whole — was incapable of coping with such Soviet efforts. As far as Germany was concerned, this was the view of Clay and the Americans on the Control Council staff. In short, we believed that acceptance of the split was a weak, not a strong, policy. We did not know whether our proposals could succeed, but we believed that, in the American interest and the general human interest, they were worth a college try so long as we kept our powder dry.

Behind the difference in perspective between EUR and GA lay differences in training and experience. The stance of EUR was wholly consonant with the tradition of diplomacy in general, American diplomacy in particular. A diplomat reports the situations he sees about him in foreign areas and the professional conversations in which he engages. He negotiates on the basis of instructions dispatched to him from the capital. He is trained to report accurately and with perception and, above all, to communicate both ways with as near absolute lucidity as possible.

With the Roosevelt administration forces came into play that radically altered the role of the Department of State and the American diplomatic tradition. Unlike his three immediate predecessors, Roosevelt was actively interested in the details of diplomacy as well as in broad foreign policy positions. He was unwilling to delegate day-to-day operations to the same degree as Harding, Coolidge, and Hoover; and, like Wilson, he was not prepared to regard the secretary of state as his sole agent in foreign affairs. But the truly revolutionary factor that progressively affected the role of the Department of State was that the United States began consciously to throw into the world power balance its military, economic, and political and psychological weight.

The coordination of the sprawling foreign affairs empire lay uniquely in the president's hands. Although the Department of State itself expanded greatly in the course of the war years, and its personnel shared many of the adventures and enterprises of the time, its monopoly position under the president was broken, never to be fully regained in the postwar decades.

This deeply rooted image of the American diplomat's task and its limitations substantially explains, I now believe, why the senior European experts of the Foreign Service undertook as their central mission in 1946 to educate the president, the secretary of state, and the foreign policy establishment generally on the realities of Soviet thought and policy. As they observed the ambiguities and uncertainties of American policy, they regarded that mission as serious and fundamental; but it was not for them to define the military, political, and economic consequences and requirements for bringing that mission to completion.

The young men in the GA did not instinctively accept the limitations Kennan described. It was this sense that the framework within which we operated was subject to change, including the domestic political base, that distinguished us from our Foreign Service colleagues. We were comfortable with operations that transcended the narrow terrain of diplomacy. Our experience in public policy had been relatively brief and narrow; but it had involved making an assessment of the situation, defining goals, and helping design courses of action to achieve them. As economists, we understood one of the major instruments that had to be brought to bear, and we knew something as well about military power. I remember my reaction to reading Kennan's long cable of February 22 as it came across my desk in delayed installments: "OK, but what are we going to do about it?" And, by the time I read that cable, I had already defined and recently sent forward my notion of what ought to be done. When I turned to write the first draft of my memorandum, I echoed my military draft of two years before: "The Deployment of Heavy Diplomacy, Spring 1946," as opposed to "The Deployment of Heavy Bombers, Spring 1944."

But our effort of February to April 1946 clearly failed. The year 1946 was taken up not with the launching of our proposed enterprise to attempt to forestall the split of Europe but with a series of tests of Soviet intentions. In Eastern Europe, did the Soviet Union intend to live up to the Yalta commitments? In Berlin, did the Soviet Union intend to permit the creation of central economic agencies and a democratic Germany embracing the Soviet Zone? In the peripheral treaties, was the Soviet Union prepared for a sharing of power — East and West? In Germany, was the Soviet Union interested in a long-term disarmament treaty for a unified Germany? For EUR the negative responses to these questions were a satisfactory justification of the educational process it took as its central task. For GA these negative responses foreshadowed an unsatisfactory, second-order outcome. We believed Soviet intentions depended to a significant degree on the Soviet view of what the United States intended to do; and we thought a satisfactory test of Soviet policy required a stance quite different from the defensive, uncertain, questioning American posture of 1946. That is also what I had in mind in the concluding passages of my inaugural lecture at Oxford on November 12, 1946.[26] After evoking the potentially creative role of the United States in helping build federal structures in Europe and elsewhere, transcending old-fashioned nationalism, I went on:

> . . . Although the recent revolution of American diplomacy is likely to hold the United States actively in world affairs, fluctuations in the degree and efficacy of American intervention are to be expected.
>
> American history has been marked by only occasional periods when the full strength of the nation has been unified and made effective — usually in the face of crisis and under great leadership — but the intervening periods have not been without purpose.

It was not in 1946 but in the late winter and spring of 1947 that the full strength of the United States was unified and made effective, in the face of crisis and under great leadership; but by that time the forces making for the split of Europe were much stronger than they were a year earlier. And the building of a Western bloc proved the maximum attainable goal in the short run.

ACTION

THE UNITY OF ALL OF EUROPE REMAINS ON THE AGENDA

So far as the Acheson-Clayton proposal is concerned, the Marshall Plan initiative conforms to the sixth of the "just and obvious queries" to be made of that proposal:

> f) *U.S. initiative in pressing for such a European solution may fail.* The nature of the alternative to a European Organization . . . makes it desirable in the U.S. interest to press for the superior solution, however

small the chances of success may initially appear to be. Only after exhaustion of the line of approach it represents does acceptance of a bloc
alternative appear justified.[27]

Kindleberger, Harlan Cleveland, and their fellow economists, who had
for a year been building toward such a plan, threw themselves fully into the
task of filling the empty boxes left in the wake of Marshall's speech.

The fact that Marshall defined his offer of aid as including "Europe to
the Urals" — thus inviting the Soviet Union as a full partner in what became
the Marshall Plan — was in the long run as well as the short run extremely
important. But by the time Molotov left Paris with his delegation, and the
expressed hopes of Poland and Czechoslovakia were frustrated (and an intense debate had occurred within the Soviet government), the "exhaustion"
of this line of approach had, for the time being, happened.

The United States, however, has remained faithful to the stance of Secretary of State Marshall in June 1947; and since the end of the Cold War,
it has been caught up in the economic and political transition of Eastern
Europe and Russia itself from communism to democracy and private enterprise. For some forty years the United States has steadily held out the vision
of a Europe united and democratic.

Why, in the end, did Europeans, pulled by historic ties of nationalism, regionalism, culture, and religion, support the movement toward continental
unity? The answer as of 1947 was that these sources of national action, while
still strong, on balance, had run their course. Europe had twice in the twentieth century engaged in desperate fraternal struggles. In the Second World
War it had to be rescued in terrible battles by two extra-European powers —
plus Britain. One of those powers — the United States — not only helped revive Western Europe but also threw its weight behind European unity. It
had remained loyal to Truman's basic decision that the United States would
not play a divide-and-rule game with Europe but would gamble that a united
Europe would be a partner, not an adversary. And at a critical moment in
1951, it invested four divisions in NATO that would have met French fears
of Germany expressed at the Versailles Conference in 1919 and after 1945.

From a European point of view, however, there was an anti-American
as well as an anti-Soviet strand in the movement toward European unity.
Europe wanted to stand on its own feet and deal with dignity, not subservience, with the United States and the Soviet Union. And, to its eternal credit,
the United States encouraged this sentiment.

The original coalition for European unity was led by four men who were
old enough to know the world before 1914: Konrad Adenauer of Germany,
Alcide De Gasperi of Italy, Jean Monnet and Robert Schuman of France.

They made common cause not with the interwar generation of leaders, who had failed and largely disappeared from the scene, but with the younger men who survived combat, the resistance, and the prison camps. These two generations—the grandparents and the grandsons—shared a determination that some five centuries of internecine struggles by European states would come to an end.

All this, however, would prove to be empty rhetoric if France and Germany did not make common cause. From the West German currency reform of 1948 the German economy moved rapidly forward. The focal point of French anxiety was the Ruhr and Germany's capacity to produce far more coking coal and steel than France. This fact was greatly heightened by the Soviet demonstration in 1949 that it could produce nuclear weapons. NATO, after careful studies, concluded that its conventional forces would have to be substantially increased. It was in the common interest that Western Europe be defended if possible without initiating nuclear war. It was natural to turn to Germany for an important part of this increase. Thus Monnet spoke to Adenauer in their important meeting of May 23, 1950:

> "We want to put Franco-German relations on an entirely new footing," I said. "We want to turn what divided France from Germany—that is, the industries of war—into a common asset, which will also be European. In this way, Europe will rediscover the leading role which she used to play in the world and which she lost because she was divided. Europe's unity will not put an end to her diversity—quite the reverse. That rich diversity will benefit civilization and influence the evolution of powers like America itself.
>
> "The aim of the French proposal, therefore, is essentially political. It even has an aspect which might be called moral. Fundamentally, it has one simple objective, which our Government will try to attain without worrying, in this first phase, about any technical difficulties that may arise."
>
> I stressed this point because it now seemed to me essential to turn from the problems to the method, and to agree on a certain conception of our common task. My visit to London had convinced me that the French proposal, so clear and simple in its form and spirit, might be totally distorted by an approach that was too scrupulously or too insidiously technical. I saw a similar risk, though for different reasons, in dealing with the Germans, and especially with their industrialists and diplomats.

On January 11, 1952, the West German Bundestag ratified the Schuman Plan. The French at last had their international control of the Ruhr but it was not imposed on Germany; rather, it was the product of European cooperation.

I have included this long passage from the Adenauer-Monnet dialogue of 1950 because it was, I believe, the foundation of European unity. As Monnet envisaged, this was a first step. A series of European institutions followed, culminating in the 1957 Treaty of Rome, the resulting European Economic Community (now the European Union), and the great experiment with the euro. Nationalism in Europe was still alive and well, as indicated by the failure of a "European Army" in the French parliament in 1953 and the pre-eminence of General Charles de Gaulle in the decade after 1958. But the European idea, rescued by Monnet, Adenauer, and Schuman, was firmly established and translated into a living institution.

CONCLUSIONS

There are two issues that stand out in this story of ideas in action. The first is the question of whether a general peace could have been negotiated in the period 1945-1947 if the United States had been as clear about its abiding interests as it was in the later years. There is no doubt that American dispositions, military and political, in 1945-1946 encouraged Stalin to set up his empire in Eastern Europe. In particular, it is striking that after the pressure exerted at Yalta for free elections in Poland, the strong position taken by Truman in his dialogue with Molotov on April 23, 1945, and the subsequent dispatch of Hopkins to Moscow, the Americans, in effect, gave up in the short run on Eastern Europe. The treaties with the smaller countries of Europe confirmed Stalin's free hand in the East. Byrnes fought hard only on the Italian treaty. Finally, in Berlin the alternative to an agreed-upon economic policy was the unification of the British and American zones. In the course of 1946 Stalin was given every reason to think that if he implemented an imperial policy in the East he would not be seriously challenged by the Americans.

But we do not know if he would have done the same if he knew that the Americans would be emplaced in Western Europe for a half century and more, or that the disheveled state of Western Europe in 1947 would give way to its extraordinary revival of the 1950s, 1960s, and beyond. What we do know is that the American stance in 1945-1947 encouraged him to follow an imperial—or "confederation"—policy in Eastern Europe and to push west in Greece, Turkey, Italy, France, and Germany as opportunity offered.

He was confronted in 1947 with the Truman Doctrine and the Marshall Plan. But his dispositions were by then made. His de facto priorities were clearly indicated by his brutal consolidation of Czechoslovakia, which proved to have some predictable cost in the Italian election of 1948.

Yet one cannot dogmatically take this as the story of a missed opportunity parallel to the missed opportunity to attack German oil installations from

March 1, 1944. For one thing, the United States was willing to fight for the balance of power in Europe, as indicated in 1917 and 1941. And it gave every evidence that it would fight to hold the line at the Elbe and in West Berlin. But Stalin remembered more vividly that the United States did little to support the dispositions of Versailles in eastern Europe during the 1920s. And its isolationist behavior down to 1941 did nothing to dispel this limited view of the American interest before the atomic weapons and modern means of delivery came on the scene. But when Stalin made his dispositions in 1945-1946 American behavior after Versailles was more resonant than after the later Truman Doctrine and the Marshall Plan speeches. Besides, Soviet leaders never forgot what Roosevelt had said at the first meeting at Yalta, which Churchill characterized as a "momentous" — but false — prediction; namely, that although the United States would take all reasonable steps to preserve peace, it would not keep a large army in Europe, and its occupation of Germany could be envisaged for only two years.[28]

Moreover, the French and the British felt more comfortable with a split Europe and a split Germany; and they thought that a split had a better chance of holding the United States in Europe than an all-European settlement.

Finally, there is the question of Stalin's bias. His inclination was in general to hold total power over a smaller area than dilute power over a larger area. His brutal and dictatorial style made him suspicious of the latter.

Consequently, his decisions on Finland and Austria permitted, in time, each to go their own way politically.

What should one conclude?

My tentative view in retrospect is that if there was any chance of achieving an all-European settlement in the wake of the Second World War, it lay in American insistence on free elections and political freedom in Poland promptly in the wake of Yalta and thereafter. A bloc or "confederation" solution was impossible to achieve without a puppet regime in Warsaw — a fact confirmed by the swift breakup of the Soviet empire circa 1989, which began with the decision in Moscow that Soviet troops would not contest the thrust of the Polish people for freedom.

The second question posed by this tale of a half century is this: Why did it end not with a bang but with a whimper? The confrontation of the Soviet Union and the West was a grave affair marked by large conventional and nuclear forces on both sides; by many serious crises, some of which raised the possibility of unintended nuclear war; and by significant conventional wars, notably in Korea and Southeast Asia. Surely, it is a rare, perhaps a unique event in history for a confrontation of this magnitude — a convergent confrontation of both power and ideology — to end without a full test

TABLE 3.1 RATES OF GROWTH IN SOVIET INDUSTRY (%), ANNUAL
AVERAGE RATE OF INCREASE

Annual average rate of increase	Rates of growth in Soviet industry (%)					
	Coal	Oil	Pig-iron	Steel	Electric power	Cement
1955-1960	8.6	13.6	10.0	8.5	13.5	19.5
1957-1972	2.8	9.4	5.3	5.3	9.7	8.6

Source: W. W. Rostow, *The Stages of Economic Growth* (Cambridge: Cambridge University Press, 1960, 1971, 1990), p. 102.

Note: These projections were first published from Soviet sources in the *E.C.E. (Economic Commission for Europe) Survey of Europe in 1957,* published in 1958. I note in *Stages* (p. 102, 1971 and 1990 eds.) that these projections are not markedly inconsistent with the 1965 goals presented by Khrushchev to the Twenty-first Congress of the Soviet Communist Party in January 1959.

of arms. Here we will undoubtedly be wiser with the passage of time; but it may be useful to set out, without dogmatism, a tentative explanation.

First, there was a dramatic economic deceleration in the Soviet economy. This deceleration can be dated from the late 1950s and was noted as early as the first edition of *The Stages of Economic Growth.*[29] It is necessary to beware of linear projections. A variety of forces at work in Russia, already evident in her projected figures for expansion, were making for deceleration. The ECE (Economic Commission for Europe) Survey of Europe in 1957 (published in 1958) presented, for example, the official projected rates of growth in key sectors of Soviet (and Russian) industry shown in Tables 3.1 and 3.2.

As predicted by Soviet planners the classic heavy industries decelerated and the sectors of high mass consumption (notably automobiles) never took hold sufficiently to counter their drag. Overall industrial production declined dramatically. And it continued to decline as computers took over from automobiles as a leading sector in the civilian economies of Japan, Western Europe, and the United States.

Meanwhile, even deeper forces helped bring the Soviet Union to the Brezhnev stagnation of the early 1980s: the need to allocate increased investment resources to a perverse, inherently low-productivity agricultural system; the need to rely increasingly on distant and expensive sources of raw materials and energy; and the continued allocation of the society's best scientific, engineering, and entrepreneurial talent to military production, including space.[30] These depressing forces were compounded by extraordinary neglect of the physical environment and demographic trends. The latter yielded an absolute decline in the able-bodied population of European Russia (including Belarus and Ukraine), where most of Soviet industry was located. This circumstance rendered further Soviet growth increasingly dependent on accelerated improvement in productivity rather than on population increase or the transfer of the working force from rural to urban life. In fact, the rate of productivity increase declined.

This grinding to a virtual halt of a massive economy—investing more than 30 percent of GNP to achieve an increase in output that barely matched its decelerating rate of population increase—was climaxed by the palpable inability of the Soviet Union, endowed with ample cadres of well-trained scientists and engineers, to absorb and diffuse efficiently to the civil society the array of new technologies that moved from invention to innovation during the mid-1970s: microelectronics, genetic engineering, lasers, and a batch of new industrial materials. The Soviet system, with its bureaucratic compulsion to meet quantitative targets irrespective of quality, set up powerful perverse incentives that discouraged innovation except in the one field where Russia inescapably confronted international competition—the military and space. I have the impression that the Soviet Union was falling rapidly behind the United States, Japan, and Western Europe in the new technologies; and this fact may have helped significantly to crystallize an elite consensus that a radical restructuring of Soviet society was imperative.

This sense of a failing system was heightened by the heavy casualties and ultimate defeat suffered in Afghanistan. Soviet troops entered Afghanistan on December 24, 1979. The last Soviet soldier left Afghanistan on February 15, 1989. By this time Mikhail Gorbachev had been negotiating a Soviet withdrawal for some time.

Arms were supplied to the insurgents in Afghanistan by the United

TABLE 3.2 USSR: AVERAGE ANNUAL GROWTH RATE OF INDUSTRIAL OUTPUT, 1961-1986

	%		%
1961-1965	6.5	1976-1980	2.7
1966-1970	6.4	1981-1985	1.9
1971-1975	5.5		

Source: Laurie Kurtzweg, "Trends in Soviet Gross National Product," in Gorbachev's Economic Plans, Studies submitted to the Joint Economic Committee, U.S. Congress, November 23, 1987 (Washington, D.C.: GPO, 1987), 1:140.

Note: While the U.S. official figures for Soviet industrial production over this interval may have been too high, they correctly tracked this trend.

States, Britain, China, and the Muslim states. The Pakistani border was virtually an open frontier. And the Soviets faced seven major guerrilla groups who came to make common cause against the invader, some of whom are still vying for power more than a decade after Soviet withdrawal.

There was a third factor at work on the Soviet Union in the 1980s, namely, the remarkable surge forward of the Chinese economy under the reforms of Deng Xiaoping. At the core, these reforms stemmed from the Family Responsibility policy installed in 1979 in the countryside. This policy left to the Chinese peasants rather than the party cadres the choice of what to produce for the market and set a ceiling on what the government would take in taxes. This yielded not only an abundance of food in the cities but a shift of industry inland from the coast to meet the enlarged purchasing power of the Chinese farmer. At just the moment when the Soviet Union was feeling the results of a deceleration in its economy and reeling from a failed military campaign in Afghanistan, the Chinese appeared to be moving rapidly forward in industry, agriculture, and foreign trade.

The Russians have never forgotten that the Mongol Golden Horde occupied the south of their country for two centuries, and Russian nationalism, centered on Moscow, arose from this invasion, Moscow being too far north for the reach of the Golden Horde.

The memory of this historical circumstance among Russians and the endemic fear of China was brought home to a group of Americans at Glassboro, New Jersey, where President Johnson met with Premier Aleksey Kosygin in 1967. As the president, Kosygin, and their two translators talked alone in one room, Soviets and Americans sat around outside and made conversation. The American group included Secretary Rusk, Secretary McNamara, and their Soviet counterparts. McNamara at a certain point spoke to the group about a Chinese film we had acquired from Hong Kong of the firing of their first atomic bomb. Chinese ground forces could be seen moving in quite closely following the explosion of the bomb. And there was a general celebration, fireworks and all. McNamara said that the film worried him. The Chinese did not seem to understand the power of the bomb or the radioactive danger it posed.

One of the Soviet delegation took the lead in reply, saying: "Suppose there were a billion people in Canada. The Canadian government every day declared that the U.S.-Canadian border was an arbitrary product of imperialism and was not legitimate. And supposing the Canadians had atomic weapons. Would you worry?"

In short, the fear of China, still alive in Russia, was heightened by the Chinese surge forward at a time of Soviet stagnation.

But these concurrent factors—the stagnation of the economy, Afghanistan, the rise of the Chinese economy—do not in themselves explain the drastic decisions taken by the ruling elite to dismantle the Soviet empire and abandon an official ideology.

The missing element in the saga is the "Buddenbrooks' dynamics"—the dynamics that leads a third generation from a revolution to decide the game is not worth the candle. In speaking to an undergraduate audience in 1958 in Cambridge, England, I said this, ending with a quotation from my father:

> The Buddenbrooks' dynamics moves on, generation by generation; those who seized power and used it to build an industrial machine of great resource may be succeeded by men who, if that machine cannot produce a decisive international result, decide that there are other and better objectives to be sought, both at home and abroad.
>
> In short, while Lenin and Stalin—and now Mao—have succeeded in overcoming the weaknesses in Marx's analysis of the historical process, it does not follow that their techniques will prove to have long run viability. Both Marxism and modern Communism are conceptions which set transcendent goals, independent of the techniques used to achieve them; but the long lesson of history is that the ends actually achieved are largely a function of the means used to pursue them.[31]

Lenin was born in 1870, Khrushchev in 1894, Gorbachev in 1931.

In short, Communist Russia—or the Soviet leadership—declared bankruptcy in the second half of the 1980s in roughly the third generation after the revolution as the system was weakened by economic stagnation, a fruitless war, and the incipient rise of its old enemy, China. All this produced at the top a loss of will to save a system that had failed.

To this result, American policy contributed not only by helping save Western Europe with the Marshall Plan and U.S. participation in NATO, not only by compounding Soviet difficulties in Afghanistan, but by steadily holding out to one and all the inevitability of Eastern Europe rejoining Western Europe with which it had religious and cultural ties that would not die.

Four

THE DEATH OF STALIN, 1953

THE TIMING MAY HAVE BEEN OFF

INTRODUCTION

As indicated in Chapter 3, I devoted the two years 1947–1949 to work on European reconstruction as special assistant to Gunnar Myrdal, executive director of the United Nations Economic Commission for Europe in Geneva. I joined Myrdal after Molotov left Paris and was under no illusion that Geneva would be at the center of affairs. The Cold War was under way in earnest. While the annual meetings of the commission were the occasion for much Cold War rhetoric, by common agreement the work in the committees of the ECE was strictly businesslike. The ECE in its early years thus turned out to be quite a lively place.

First, in general, despite the split of Europe, the Western Europeans did not wish to turn their backs on Eastern Europe; nor did the United States. As for the governments of Eastern Europe, they did not wish wholly to cut their ties to the West.

Second, Poland, in particular, wished to sell as much coal as possible to earn dollars in the West; and, in general, its government wished to maintain ties to the West. This conformed with the interest and the policy of the United States. In the first years of the Marshall Plan the bottleneck of industrial production in Europe was steel; and the supply of steel hinged, in turn, on the supply of coking coal. Thus, the Coal and Steel Committees in Geneva became the center for the allocation of coal, including coking coal, from (mainly) Germany, the United States, and Poland. These allocations were based on the principle that the Europeans (except Germany) would receive enough coal to revive their economies to the same relative level as 1938. The allocation system depended on the integrity of the two men in the Secretariat who headed the Coal and Steel Committees—Charles Jeffers, an American coal expert and Tony Rollman, a steel expert from Luxembourg—and the trust the governments placed in them. They earned that trust. Thus, important business was carried on in Geneva.

Third, the other committees of the ECE (Housing, Timber, Electricity, Raw Materials, Transport) found a great deal of work to do that did not involve the allocation of American dollars, such as developing a system of uniform traffic signs for Europe and documents for facilitating the crossing of frontiers, which were forerunners of later Common Market developments; studying housing requirements country by country, which served as the basis for national housing plans; and developing a study of Europe's future steel requirements, *European Steel Trends in the Setting of the World Market*,[1] which played a part in Jean Monnet's design of the European Coal and Steel Community. At Monnet's request Myrdal sent Philippe de Selliers, who had participated in the study, to Paris to help.

Finally, the Research Division established from the beginning a reputation for both analytic rigor and integrity in its annual reports on the European economy: those reports were of help to the various European governments and to the U.S. Congress.

Although the ECE was in many ways a diplomatic backwater as Europe split, it was not only a busy place in 1947–1949 but a useful part of my education. It was in traveling around Eastern Europe and in Geneva, meeting both Communist officials and people outside the Party, that I formed the conviction that Stalin's empire was historically unsound and would not last.

In 1949–1950 Elspeth and I surprised many of our friends in the United States by not returning at long last to an American university but accepting an invitation for both of us to teach for a year at Cambridge. The reason was simple enough. Elspeth had twice been to Europe but had never experienced the round of life at a British university. It was a delightful year. Elspeth was told there was no examination subject in American social history, the field in which she planned to lecture. Therefore, perhaps twenty or so students might turn up at first. In fact, her lectures soon built up to an audience of more than a hundred.

After a brief period of consulting once more in Geneva, we were both invited to teach at MIT, where Elspeth was the first woman member of the faculty. To the astonishment of our friends, who had concluded we had an incurable case of wanderlust, we spent a peaceful decade there. At MIT both Max Millikan and I were asked to take up posts in Washington as the United States faced up to war in Korea. We, however, thought the Cold War was a long-term proposition and instead proposed that we set up a center for international studies to help the nation and government with analyses of three dimensions of the Cold War: the dynamics of the Communist world, the dynamics of the developing world, and the evolution of American society. One of our first efforts was a book I did with the help of several others entitled *The Dynamics of Soviet Society* (New York: W. W. Norton, 1952). It focused in the end on the likely impact of the death of Stalin. It was turned in to the government in the late summer of 1952 and was circulated widely in the incoming Eisenhower administration. All this got us involved early in March 1953 with the new administration.

THE DECISION

The occasion examined here was, perhaps, the first potentially serious opportunity to seek reconciliation with the Soviet Union since Vyacheslav Molotov left the Marshall Plan conference in Paris in June 1947. Although the effort, marked, as we shall see, by uncertainty and ambivalence, failed in 1953, it illustrates well the complexity of the problem confronted by those who during the Cold War sought to find a better way to order international affairs than the dangerous, confrontational format that dominated the world scene for some forty years, overhung after 1949 by nuclear weapons commanded by the Soviet Union as well as the West.

Six weeks after assuming responsibility, the Eisenhower administration was galvanized, early on Wednesday morning, March 4, 1953, by the news that Stalin was gravely ill. His death was announced on March 6. The debate within the administration on an appropriate course of action reopened, after a fashion, the central issue of this chapter: should the United States initiate a proposal to undo the split of Europe and actively propose a democratic unified Germany, within a structure of appropriate political, economic, and security arrangements?

A National Security Council (NSC) directive promptly instructed the CIA to provide an evaluation of the impact of Stalin's death and the State Department and C. D. Jackson, at the White House, to recommend appropriate courses of action. Jackson was a special assistant to Eisenhower for what was then called psychological warfare. He and his successor, Nelson Rockefeller, functioned, in fact, as sources of presidential initiatives of substance in foreign policy.

The heart of Jackson's proposal was "A Message to the Soviet Government and the Russian Peoples" from President Eisenhower, which he urged be delivered the day after Stalin's funeral. After discussion with Jackson and at his request, I drafted in Cambridge the message, a rationale for its content, and an outline of possible follow-up actions, during the late afternoon and evening of March 5.

Among a good many other things, the draft "Message" flatly proposed a quadripartite negotiation and contained this passage:

> The United States shall propose measures for the general control of armaments and special security arrangements for Europe.
> The United States shall propose measures for the unification of Ger-

many by free elections as well as proposals designed to end the occupation of Austria. We believe that, within a structure of general and regional security and economic arrangements, a Germany unified by democratic means would constitute a creative force in Europe, without danger to East or West.

Briefly, we felt that it was the duty of the United States to hold up to the new Soviet leadership the option of ending the confrontation in the center of Europe and elsewhere, even though the chance of its acceptance was slight; that a pacific stance by the United States at this juncture would maximize the chance for liberalizing changes within Soviet society; that the initiative should be taken promptly for maximum effect, among other reasons, to preempt a possible Soviet peace offensive; and that the initiative could be mounted in ways that might reinforce rather than obtrude upon the European Defense Community (EDC) initiative. The bargaining position would be stronger with EDC in hand than without it. Letters from Eisenhower to the major European leaders were drafted, explaining his initiative, to be delivered before the event.

I was invited to come promptly to Washington, arriving on the afternoon of March 6. The concept of such a presidential statement and its broad contents were explored that day (before my arrival) in a meeting that included Jackson and Emmet Hughes from the White House and Charles Bohlen and Paul Nitze from the State Department. Although the discussion was indecisive, there appeared to be agreement that any meaningful statement by the president would have to include a concrete proposal for a high-level four-power meeting. On Monday, March 9, however, it was evident that there would be quite significant opposition from the State Department. This emerged when Hughes, at Jackson's direction, showed the documents we had drafted to Bohlen and Nitze.

The objections of the State Department to an early presidential speech were crystallized in a memorandum of March 11 transmitted by the undersecretary of state (Walter Bedell Smith) to Jackson and others at the undersecretary level in the foreign affairs community. It constituted the brief presented to Secretary John Foster Dulles by his aides for the NSC meeting of that day and contained four main points:

1. A presidential speech should be postponed "until an important opportunity arises."

2. No meeting of foreign ministers should be advocated until U.S. proposals had been formulated.

3. The proposal of a foreign ministers' meeting without prior consultation with major allies would be divisive.

4. "[A] meeting of Foreign Ministers would indefinitely delay progress on

EDC. No action could be expected by European Governments on EDC pending outcome and evaluation of the Ministers' meeting."

On the 9th it had been decided to postpone a formal discussion of the matter with the president until Wednesday, March 11, since Dulles would be out of Washington until late afternoon of the tenth. On his return, Dulles received the Jackson proposal, conferred with his State Department colleagues, and breakfasted with Jackson early on the morning of the eleventh. He said he found Jackson's proposed initiative "intriguing" but had certain reservations, which he did not discuss with Jackson at the time.

At my suggestion, George Kennan, recently declared persona non grata as ambassador to the Soviet Union, was brought to Washington by Jackson from his farm in Pennsylvania. They conferred on March 10. Kennan gave Jackson's proposal strong intellectual and moral support, although he was not then in a position of influence in Washington. Kennan told Jackson that the proposed initiative required great clarity concerning its implications for Germany on the part of two men: the president and the secretary of state. If this condition were fulfilled, there was no need to worry excessively about other opinions in Washington or about the short period of excitement in the foreign offices in London, Paris, and Bonn. Kennan expressed his faith that Washington would respond with vigor and unity to the initiative, as it had to the Marshall Plan proposal, and that our allies would come along without much difficulty. The initial showdown came in a two-hour NSC meeting on March 11. Jackson's report to me as he emerged from the meeting, which I summarized soon afterward, follows:

> Rostow saw Jackson again as he emerged from the NSC meeting at about 12:30 P.M. Jackson announced that he did not know whether he was a man "carrying a shield or being carried upon it." He reported that
>
> (a) he had had his full day in court;
> (b) the President, remembering his experience with previous four-power meetings, was not enthusiastic about the Council of Foreign Ministers;
> (c) Dulles took the position that our relations with France and Britain would be damaged by a unilateral initiative of this kind; that the governments of [Alcide] de Gasperi, [Konrad] Adenauer and [René] Mayer would fall in a week; and that EDC would be postponed, if not destroyed. It was, nevertheless, agreed that a Presidential statement should be made and made soon, and that the bulk of the text as drafted was suitable. . . .
>
> It was further decided that the references to Korea would be expanded and a truce in Korea would be made even more clearly a condition for

further movement toward the larger objectives of peace than the original draft had provided. Jackson was instructed to prepare a new text in the sense of the meeting.

While Jackson was at lunch on Wednesday, March 11, Rostow re-drafted the message as instructed by Jackson. The essential device was to hold up a vision of the specific long-range objectives of American diplomacy but to make the negotiations designed to achieve that vision contingent upon a prior Korean settlement.[2]

At the close of business on March 11, Eisenhower dispatched a cable to Winston Churchill, who had proposed a prompt Big Four summit meeting. It contained the three basic decisions that were to shape U.S. policy on this matter over the next year: a Big Four summit was rejected; Eisenhower indicated his desire to make a speech soon "giving to the world some promise of hope"; it held out the possibility of a Western summit meeting including the U.K. and "probably the French."

A presidential statement of the kind envisaged on March 11 was not, in fact, made until five weeks had passed, exchanges had taken place with the major European leaders, and some fourteen drafts had been formulated.[3] Three factors account for the delay:

1. The seizure of the peace initiative by Georgy M. Malenkov, starting with his statement before the Supreme Soviet, published on March 16: "At the present time there is no disputed or unresolved question that cannot be settled peacefully or unresolved question that cannot be settled peacefully by mutual agreement of the interested countries. This applies to our relations with all states, including the United States of America."[4]

2. Dulles' anxiety that nothing be done at American initiative to interfere with the passage of EDC, then before the Continental parliaments.

3. Dulles' skepticism about negotiations with the Soviet Union and anxiety about major presidential pronouncements on foreign policy—an anxiety that was to emerge on several occasions over his tenure in office.

Eisenhower, after considerable uncertainty, finally decided to proceed with the speech despite Dulles' lack of enthusiasm, although the latter's initial flat opposition gradually eroded as it became clear that the Soviet peace offensive was, in any case, holding up forward movement on EDC and generating political pressures on the Western European governments for a positive response. The president delivered his most famous speech before the American Society of Newspaper Editors on April 16, entitled "The Chance for Peace." It defined Eisenhower before the world, in his first major presidential pronouncement, as a statesman actively seeking peace. It was also published in *Pravda* and *Izvestia,* along with a temperate but quite precise critique. Most analysts of the period would agree with Sherman Adams' assessment that, however meager its direct policy consequences, "it was the most effective speech of Eisenhower's public career, and certainly one of the highlights of his presidency."[5] Two days later Dulles delivered a speech of his own, covering similar ground but considerably harsher in tone—a fact duly noted in Soviet commentaries.

The president's speech, as delivered, dealt with the German question in much the style of the draft prepared in the wake of the March 11 NSC meeting: that is, a broad vision of what American policy ultimately sought was held up, with action toward it dependent on the prior settlement of other issues, notably Korea:

> We are ready not only to press forward with the present plans for closer unity of the nations of western Europe but also, upon that foundation, to strive to foster a broader European community, conducive to the free movement of persons, of trade, and of ideas.
>
> This community would include a free and united Germany, with a government based upon free and secret ballot.
>
> This free community and the full independence of the East European nations could mean the end of the present unnatural division of Europe.

THE BACKGROUND: EUROPE, THE SOVIET UNION, AND THE UNITED STATES

First, the background in Europe that rendered the EDC such a critical issue in alliance policy in the late winter and early spring of 1953.

As early as March 1947, France and Britain signed a pact of mutual defense, the Dunkirk Treaty. The Anglo-French arrangement was joined by Belgium, the Netherlands, and Luxembourg in the Brussels Pact of March 1948. Stalin's Berlin blockade of 1948–1949 heightened anxieties about European defense, yielding the NATO treaty, which embraced seven additional countries, including Canada and the United States. The treaty was ratified by the Senate in July 1949. NATO was, at that stage, a symbol of mutual commitment with the U.S. Strategic Air Command, exercising a nuclear monopoly, judged to be a sufficient deterrent against an unleashing of ground forces by the Soviet Union.

This concept was shaken by the Soviet explosion of a nuclear weapon in September 1949 and the North Korean assault on South Korea in June 1950. These events suggested between them that Moscow, within the framework of a nuclear stalemate, might be prepared to exploit its ground force superiority in Europe. The shock of the North Korean attack was profound in Europe as well as in the United States. A consensus emerged that NATO would have to be given sufficient resources to defend Western Europe on the ground.

Thus, the difficult issue of German rearmament was first posed. Britain, France, Italy, and the United States were, in different ways, under political and economic inhibitions that precluded the development of a sufficient counterforce on the Central Front without a substantial German contribution.

For Germany the problem was difficult for a range of other reasons. Nevertheless, under Adenauer's guidance, the move was accepted in principle. Adenauer, the incarnation of much in the Germany that had been lost when Prussia came to domination in the wake of the Revolution of 1848, may, in his heart, have been somewhat ambivalent about a united Germany. But he certainly believed in the end that the only safe course for Germany was to associate itself inextricably with the West and move toward unity as part of a strong Western European base supported by the United States.

Adenauer's position on this matter and his capacity to carry his countrymen were tested by Moscow in 1952. Evidently wishing to avoid the militarization of West Germany within the NATO structure, the Soviet Union launched on March 10 a proposal for a Four-Power Peace Conference that would define the framework for a unified demilitarized Germany. In a joint response of March 25 the West agreed to insist on free all-German elections, under United Nations supervision, and the right of a future German government to choose its friends and allies. The U.N. General Assembly formed a commission to define the conditions for the holding of a free all-German election. West Germany accepted. Soviet acceptance of the presence of the commission to do its work in East Germany became the touchstone for the seriousness of Moscow's intentions. The commission was banned from East Germany. And the terms of a Soviet note of August 29, 1952, called for elections only after a peace treaty had been signed by a German government formed on a fifty-fifty East-West basis. Thus, West Germany objected, and Adenauer was able to proceed in good conscience and with majority support.

In France, of course, the reemergence of German military strength set in motion profound instinctive fears, despite the existence of NATO. Partly to diminish those fears, the United States, after searching congressional and public debate, made in 1951 the commitment to maintain four divisions in Europe, a momentous decision in terms of previous American reactions to French requests for a security guarantee, stretching back to Versailles.

To the British, NATO had several attractive features. At the time, the British commitment to the European continent was essentially in naval and air strength, and this fitted British plans and military thought. Moreover, the organization of NATO gave the British great influence through General Hastings Ismay's role in the secretary-generalship and Bernard Montgomery's command over the ground forces. Finally, London found satisfaction in the wholehearted manner in which Canada could participate in NATO arrangements. For Canadians an enterprise that attracted the support of the United States, Britain, and France was the optimum setting in which to play an active role on the world scene, given the nature of Canadian social and political life.

NATO rapidly gathered strength in 1951-1952 as Congress agreed to station the American divisions, Eisenhower built Supreme Headquarters, Allied Powers, Europe (SHAPE), and substantial U.S. aid helped build the infrastructure; that is, the airfield, logistical and communications base of the enterprise. But a critical issue remained: what form should the German ground force contribution take? The formula that appeared for a time to reconcile this requirement with fears of a national German army came from France; and it came, quite particularly, from Jean Monnet.[6] He perceived, on the Sunday of the North Korean attack, that the war in Asia, with all its repercussions, might upset the schedule for bringing to life the Schuman Plan, then at a critical stage. As the second half of 1950 unfolded, it became apparent that France could not resist indefinitely a large German contribution to European defense. Monnet proposed, therefore, that the German forces become part of a Continental European defense structure administered, like the Coal and Steel Community, by a supranational institution. He suggested the concept to René Pleven, then French prime minister, who tentatively laid it before the French parliament on October 24, 1950. After much complex negotiation and many vicissitudes, the EDC treaty was signed in Paris on May 27, 1952, but it still had to face the French parliament. In the face of opposition, the supporters of EDC in the French government delayed a parliamentary showdown for many months, but the treaty came before the National Assembly in January 1953. As Monnet notes: "For more than a year, the dispute about EDC had underlain all political attitudes in France, in the parties, in Parliament, and in the Government itself."[7] That was where the matter stood in Paris—precarious and undecided—when Stalin died on March 6.

Although the question of EDC posed some problems for Adenauer, on balance it represented a step forward for Germany in the recovery of a place of full equality in the Western community; and it conformed to the majority judgment that Germany's destiny, including the possibility of ultimate German unification, lay in intimate association with a strong and united West.

In his first major move as secretary of state, Dulles toured Western Europe. Accompanied by Harold Stassen, he visited Rome, Paris, London, Bonn, The Hague, Brussels, and Luxembourg. His primary objective was to urge the European governments to complete ratification of EDC.

Dulles arrived in Bonn on February 5 and spoke with Social Democratic leaders as well as with Adenauer and his government colleagues.[8] He urged that the treaty be passed definitively on its third reading by the Bundestag. On March 19, the Bundestag accepted the treaty by a somewhat larger majority than in its second reading, and the Federal Republic of Germany became its first signatory.

Plunged as he was into the diplomacy and politics of EDC in the several capitals, Dulles' uneasiness on March 11 about presidential statements and initiatives toward an all-German settlement is not difficult to understand. For Dulles, Stalin's death, and all the attendant fuss, was intruding on serious business.

The death of the Soviet dictator occurred at a particular moment not only in the affairs of the West but also in the rhythm of relations between the Soviet Union and the world beyond. He died when exertions to expand Soviet power in the context of postwar disarray in Eurasia had just about reached their limits. In a manner resonant of Russian history, he had pressed first in the West and, then, when frustrated, turned to apparent opportunities in the East.

In the course of 1946 the negotiations for a truce in China also broke down and all-out civil war began. In 1946 Stalin probably advised against an all-out effort by the Communists to seize power, but once Mao was well started, he was backed by Stalin from 1947 to 1949. Communist policy in Asia formally had changed in the course of 1947. Ambitious new objectives were being enunciated by Andrey A. Zhdanov at the founding meeting of the Cominform in September. Open guerrilla warfare began in Indochina as early as November 1946, in Burma in April 1948, in Malaya in June of that year, and in Indonesia and the Philippines in the autumn. The Indian and Japanese Communist parties, with less scope for guerrilla action, nevertheless sharply increased their militancy in 1948. As final victory was won in China in November 1949, Mao's political-military strategy was openly commended by the Cominform to the Communist parties in those areas where guerrilla operations were under way. Stalin and Mao met early in 1950 and confirmed the ambitious Asian strategy, planning its climax, in response to Kim Il Sung's appeal, in the form of the North Korean invasion of South Korea, which took place at the end of June 1950.

The American and United Nations response to the invasion of South Korea, the landing at Inch'on, the march to the Yalu, the Chinese Communist entrance into the war, and the successful U.N. defense against the massive Chinese assault in April and May 1951 at the thirty-eighth parallel brought this phase of military and quasi-military Communist effort throughout Asia to a gradual end. Neither Moscow nor Beijing was willing to undertake all-out war with the United States or even accept the cost of a continued Korean offensive. And elsewhere the bright Communist hopes of 1946 and 1947 had dimmed. Nowhere in Asia was Mao's success repeated. Indonesia, Burma, and the Philippines largely overcame their guerrillas. At great cost to Britain, the Malayan guerrillas were contained and driven back. Only in Indochina, where French colonialism offered a seedbed as fruitful as postwar China, was there real Communist momentum. When Stalin died the Korean negotiations had been indecisively under way for some twenty months and China, rather than the Soviet Union, was most active in support of the Vietminh.

Like his postwar offensive, Stalin himself had been winding down for some time. From the quite consistent accounts of his daughter Svetlana and Khrushchev, Stalin's health was failing progressively in 1951-1952, and with this came a heightening of his pathological distrust of all around him. Stalin's last days, his macabre death, and the Byzantine maneuvers it set in motion, climaxed by the brutal execution of Lavrenti P. Beria in July, all have the flavor of an earlier century. It had all the earmarks of an inner struggle for power, possibly to be accompanied by purges evocative of the 1930s. Among those who followed Soviet events, the period between mid-January and early March was one of considerable concern about the course that nation was likely to take in the time ahead.

As an era was ending in Moscow, a page also turned in Washington with the arrival of the first Republican president since the departure of Herbert Hoover. In an oral history interview in 1970, Charles Bohlen, looking back on the early days of the Eisenhower administration, observed: "In fact, I used to think to myself that the Republicans came into the State Department rather like a wagon train going into hostile Indian territory, and every night they'd group their wagons around the fire."[9] Knowing both some of the Republicans who had recently come to responsibility and some of the older State Department hands — and having the privilege of observing their interaction in the early days — I can attest that Bohlen's image was apt, but the suspicion was mutual.

After all, this was the first Republican administration in twenty years. Its members arrived in Washington after a political campaign in which Korea, communism, and corruption were major directions of attack on the Truman administration. The Hiss affair was still a corrosive and vivid memory. Even those Republicans who took a more sophisticated and tolerant view of the outgoing Democrats felt authentically that their predecessors were burned out, and it was time for a fresh start in new directions. Dulles, in particular, was extremely sensitive — in Eisenhower's view, occasionally oversensitive — to the possible charge that he was merely carrying forward Acheson's policies, notably in Asia, which he had been so recently denouncing with vigor. But both Eisenhower and Dulles were understandably anxious to avoid the exacerbated relations between the executive branch and the Congress on foreign policy that marked the latter Truman years.[10]

Moreover, the old hands with whom the newly arrived Republicans had to deal had lived most, if not all, of their professional lives under Democratic administrations, were probably voting Democrats, and were judged, prima facie, to be antagonistic to the new team. And there was something in that view. C. D. Jackson, for example, was initially regarded in the State Department as a somewhat superficial sloganeer without a serious grounding in the realities of diplomacy. When I talked to two of my old friends in the State Department in the immediate aftermath of Stalin's death, their reaction was that the White House should "do nothing" on the grounds that the new boys were likely to do something irresponsible. Quite soon, however, their professional instincts took over. For example, Nitze, director of the Policy Planning Staff, was soon working in reasonable harmony with the White House speech drafters. But it took a good deal longer for the State Department as a whole to get over the first meeting of Dulles with department officials: "Dulles's words were cold and raw as the weather that February day. He said that he was going to insist that every member of the department extend not just loyalty but 'positive loyalty.' He did not define the difference, but his intent was clear. It was a declaration by the secretary of state that the department was indeed suspect. The remark disgusted some Foreign Service officers, infuriated others, and displeased even those who were looking forward to the new administration."[11]

There was another complicating dimension to all this: the strong McCarthyite mood in Congress that came sharply into focus with the nomination of Bohlen to the post of ambassador to the Soviet Union.[12] Bohlen was one of the most respected senior members of the Foreign Service, as well as a man of charm, vivacity, and courage. Rather to his surprise, he was nominated on January 23, 1953, to succeed Kennan. The proceedings in the Senate gradually built up into an ugly, harrowing affair, with Joseph McCarthy challenging the 15-0 favorable vote of the Foreign Affairs Committee and demanding the withdrawal of the nomination. Dulles, extremely sensitive to the Republican right wing but also conscious that the morale of his department was at stake, was much concerned. Eisenhower, however, stood firm; Senators Taft and Sparkman were permitted to read Bohlen's security file and vouched for the harmlessness of its contents; and on April 4 Bohlen left for Moscow.[13] But the first month of the period we are considering—March 4 to April 16, 1953—was suffused by this controversy with the special intensity that only Washington, essentially an inbred company town, can generate in such matters.

Aside from these human and institutional tensions, larger considerations helped shape the setting in which Eisenhower finally decided to give his speech. The nation had gone through an exceedingly hard time during the Korean War: the initial setback, MacArthur's brilliant riposte at Inch'on, the surge of hubris that led to the movement north toward the Yalu, the unexpected entrance of the Chinese Communists into the war, the firing of MacArthur with its attendant bitter debate, the little-noted defensive victories of April and May 1951 under General Ridgway leading to the opening of truce talks; and then month after month of indecisive combat at the thirty-eighth parallel, with substantial casualties and little progress in the negotiations. All this was heightened by a regime of irksome price and wage controls. Truman's approval rating, which had fallen as low as 24 percent during the MacArthur controversy, stood at just 31 percent when he left office. As the nation was to learn again during the struggle in Southeast Asia, its style and instincts did not accommodate easily to limited, protracted war. The hope that General Eisenhower could end that war was a major, but by no means the singular reason for his victory in November 1952. In the wake of Stalin's death, Eisenhower understood viscerally and correctly that the war-weary nation yearned for peace and a more hopeful future.

This judgment converged with the basic budgetary and military strategy the new administration adopted. Those who dominated the Republican Party looked to a reduction in the role of the federal government in American life as the necessary condition for retaining the sort of society to which they were attached. For twenty years, in political impotence or active opposition, they had watched the absolute size of federal expenditures rise. Above all, it was the aspiration of a substantial group of Republicans to undo these believed evils when political power was regained and to move American society back toward an older balance between government and private capitalism, which they found more congenial. They were convinced that minimum essential American interests could be protected with diminished direct responsibility and at less cost. Further, many Republicans had convinced themselves that the nation's costly military and foreign policy, including the Korean War, was the result of incompetent meddling in the world rather than of an inescapable, if belated, effort to protect straightforward American interests. With authentic passion, they sought to cut the federal budget, to reduce the scope of federal power in the economy, and to reduce the nation's commitments on the world scene.

Two things are clear about the new administration's dispositions. First, maximum economic strength was viewed primarily as the maximum degree of freedom for the private sector of the economy, minimum tax revenues, and hopefully, a relatively stable price level. Second, the assumption was initially made that the new military technology would cheapen the costs of military defense. This was a somewhat static conception, in which a kind of once-and-for-all substitution of nuclear weapons delivery capabilities for manpower was envisaged. This view did not embrace a realistic vision of the costly succession of new weapons systems—each leaving a prompt trail of obsolescence—which was just over the horizon. Eisenhower understood this process better than some in his administration.

Once in power, certain inescapable facts of the world arena in which the nation lived and operated and certain inescapable requirements of national security were respected. But in the formative months, when policy wavered in the councils of the executive branch, there was Senator Taft to remind them of the meaning of the Republican victory:

> The full import of their words [George Humphrey, Joseph Dodge, and Roger Kyes] was nevertheless that heavy military spending would continue, that more deficits lay ahead and that the first Republican budget would be out of balance. When this hit Robert A. Taft, he went off like a bomb.
>
> The sedate discussion was rent by his hard, metallic voice. Fairly shouting and banging his fist on the Cabinet table, Taft declared that all the efforts of the Eisenhower Administration to date had merely produced the net result of continued spending on the same scale as the Truman Administration. Unless the inconceivable step of raising taxes was taken, he said, the new budget—the budget for the fiscal year 1954—would carry a large deficit. He denounced the budget total as one that exceeded 20 per cent of the national income, a limit Taft thought high enough.
>
> The President was taken aback as Taft barked out a prediction that the first Eisenhower budget would drive a wedge between the administration and the economy-minded Republicans in Congress and drag the party to defeat in the 1954 elections.
>
> "The one primary thing we promised the American people," he shouted, "was a reduction of expenditures. Now you're taking us right down the same road Truman traveled. It's a repudiation of everything we promised in the campaign."
>
> Taft said that he could see no prospect of future reductions so long as emphasis was placed upon military preparedness for which, he said, funds could be spent without limit.[14]

Thus, in 1953, as the nation was confronted by the expensive consequences of the revolutionary forces at work both in weapons technology and in the underdeveloped areas of the world, its policy was controlled by a powerful and purposeful thrust to reduce the size of the federal budget.

Eisenhower's instinct to reach out for the possibility of peace, like that of all the other post-1945 American presidents, was no doubt rooted in fundamental values and aspirations. In his case his instinct was heightened by a thoroughly professional knowledge of the nature of nuclear weapons and the irrationality of their use except to deter their use by others. But a strand of budgetary concern was also present. As Eisenhower encountered opposition, in the course of drafting his speech — to a peaceful gesture in general and, as we shall see, to limiting the preconditions in Asia for a settlement in Korea and a negotiation on Germany — the budgetary costs of continued conflict and confrontation were much on his mind.

In the interval that followed the Korean truce — roughly from June 1951 to March 1953 — a fresh assessment of Soviet society and its future was made both within and outside the government. That assessment benefited greatly from the gradual fruition of the analyses, based in part on interviews with Soviet defectors in Germany, conducted by the emerging younger generation of American experts on the Soviet Union. Their conclusions fitted, in general, both the less formal perceptions of Kennan and Bohlen and the insights of the best older scholars. They permitted, however, a more systematic and complete picture of how a modern bureaucratic society had emerged in the Soviet Union out of the dynamics of the prewar Five-Year Plans, the World War II experience, and the postwar Soviet efforts at reconstruction and expansion of external power. Specifically, they confirmed the likelihood that the Soviet Union was not operating on a fixed timetable for the achievement of world domination but was engaged in a systematic effort to maximize its external power within the limits imposed by the need to cope with its internal problems, on the one hand, and by resistance met in the external world, on the other.

In the year or so preceding Stalin's death, there were widespread efforts in the United States to achieve a new vision of where Soviet society was headed and what influence the removal of Stalin was likely to have. There was obviously a problem for both social scientists and policymakers in speculating on the relationship between a massive bureaucratic structure, with evident momentum of its own, and the extraordinary concentrated power of one ruthless man. What would his withdrawal from the system mean? Those professionally concerned with this issue disagreed significantly in their predictions, as well as in the confidence with which they were prepared to predict, but there was virtually universal agreement that the Soviet Union as of the early 1950s was a complex societal structure in which there were many built-in resistances to radical change as well as some potentially explosive frictions. On the whole, the weight of professional analysis fell to the view that Stalin's death would release certain limited changes — backed by forces that the dictator had hitherto suppressed — without radically altering the contours of Soviet society or the content of the Soviet Union's external objectives.

The effort to clarify the prospects for change in Soviet society intertwined with an effort to develop more mature conceptions of what was then called psychological warfare. As the Cold War years rolled on, it became evident that some part in the conflict was being played by the American impact on the minds and attitudes of men and women in other societies, including Communist societies. When the Soviet Union acquired nuclear weapons, and the possibilities of a standoff in major weapons became more real, the psychological element in the struggle rose in priority.

Simultaneously, a technical problem emerged when, in 1949–1950, the Soviet Union invested major resources in jamming American radio broadcasts toward Eastern Europe and beyond. This crisis led to Project TROY, an analysis conducted at MIT of the technical, psychological, and political problems of communication from the United States to the Communist world. What emerged from Project TROY and the studies that succeeded it was a somewhat paradoxical conclusion: the American problem of communicating effectively was neither technical nor psychological in any narrow professional sense. The essential task was to project a clear, consistent image of U.S. purposes and policies that would match what, in fact, the nation did from day to day and that could be related to the lives and perspectives of other peoples. From this conclusion flowed few suggestions for new psychological tricks but, rather, the recommendation that the national government find better means for coordinating the flow of policy and action among the various arms, military and civil, that, in fact, dealt with the outside world. The problem of psychological warfare came to be conceived primarily as the task of making, executing, and articulating a coordinated policy that would dramatize the areas of overlap between the purposes of the United States and those of other nations. This was the approach adopted explicitly in 1953 by the committee headed by William Jackson to review policy in this area. Although the two Jacksons were friends, they are to be distinguished from one another.

Thus, the Psychological Strategy Board, created in 1951, gave way, under the Eisenhower administration, to the Operations Coordinating Board, a useful committee at the undersecretary level that normally met over lunch on Thursdays, with a mandate, among other things, to render day-to-day operations mutually consistent and reinforcing. In addition, the role of special adviser to the president on the psychological impact of national policy was maintained during Eisenhower's first term.

The president-elect evidently had other responsibilities in the period preceding his assumption of authority than to follow the development of a more mature image of the dynamics of Soviet society and a more mature conception of the nature and limits of psychological warfare. Nevertheless, three elements in Eisenhower's experience and policy converged to make him look toward the possibilities of change in Soviet society and toward a negotiation with the Soviet Union of a peace settlement.

First, like most Americans in the Control Council in Berlin in 1945 and 1946, Eisenhower had seen something of the generation of modern soldiers and technicians who had matured during the Five-Year Plans and the Second World War. While these men were obviously the instruments of Stalin's policy, they exhibited in human and professional interchange the existence of values and manners quite different from those of the dedicated professional international revolutionary; and the impression they left among Americans, including Eisenhower, fostered a sense that Soviet society might evolve in time into something different from what it appeared to be under Stalin, difficult still but more livable in terms of American interests.

Second, this temperate optimism about the potentialities for change converged with Eisenhower's appreciation of the terrible destructiveness of the emerging new weapons. As with most professional soldiers, Eisenhower understood that the capabilities for destruction in nuclear weapons, compared with the weapons of the Second World War, made a major war not only irrational but almost unthinkable. While recognizing the need to deter the use of Soviet military force, he deeply believed that the nation would have to look to nonmilitary instruments to protect its interests; and this conclusion directly influenced his interest in psychological warfare.

Third, as noted earlier, the commitment of the new administration to seek a substantial reduction in defense outlays, combined with the drawing to a close of the Korean War, made it logical to conceive of a test of Moscow's purposes by the new administration.

Thus, it was natural that Eisenhower should not be reluctant to consider the possibility of negotiations with the Soviet Union centered about the question of the control of armaments.

IDEAS

There were, then, essentially three views at work on the Washington scene in the days following Stalin's death. First, there was Foster Dulles' view. Basically his mind was fastened on the difficult immediate diplomacy of the European Defense Community in French political life. He wanted no summit meeting. He wanted no presidential speech that would divert thought in the West away from the task of getting the EDC through the relevant parliaments. In short, Stalin's death was a diversion from the serious, difficult work of the State Department.

Second, there was Eisenhower's view. He was conscious of Stalin's death as an occasion when the American president should address the Soviet people and, indeed, the world. He wanted no summit meeting. On the other hand, he was aware that the Soviet Union's possession of nuclear weapons imposed a dangerous, expensive stalemate upon the world. He wanted the world to break out of the Cold War and, as American president, wanted to be seen as one wishing this outcome.

The third view had three partisans in Washington (Jackson, Kennan, and me) plus Winston Churchill, returned as British prime minister, across the ocean. We thought there should be a summit meeting soon to deal with central issues of arms control and a united free Germany and Europe.

This curious team and its view needs some explaining.

I was caught up in this process in a quite particular way. After a year at Cambridge and a summer consulting at the ECE, Elspeth and I returned to the States. I took up teaching at MIT in 1950 (see Chapter 5). As the Korean War appeared to signal a new, intense, and protracted phase of the Cold War, extending far beyond Europe, it was decided to set up at MIT a Center for International Studies (CENIS). Its director, Max F. Millikan, a professor of economics, had done both wartime and postwar public service in Washington. He was also one of my oldest and closest friends, a tie reaching back to 1933–1934, when we learned our first economics, with two others, in an informal seminar. CENIS was created to bring to bear academic research on issues of public policy. It was financed by grants from both the government and the private foundations.

As a social scientist without prior commitments in the field of Soviet affairs, I was asked, in 1951, to undertake an analysis of the dynamics of Soviet society while continuing my teaching of economic history. I put together a small research team, drew on all the learning and insights of academia and government, but made my own synthesis. The study (*The Dynamics of Soviet Society*) was turned in to the government in August 1952, published later in that year, with further editions in 1954 and 1967. We devoted a good deal of attention in the first edition to what effects Stalin's death might have on Soviet domestic life and its foreign policy.

Our central perception arose from a triangular view of Soviet dispositions. In exercising power within the Soviet system, we viewed the rulers as confronted with the need to allocate their energies among three often competing objectives: the overriding requirement of managing high-level politics in ways that would maintain Communist Party control over the country;

the maintenance of minimum necessary popular support, including allocations to the production of consumer goods; and the extension of Soviet power abroad, including the buildup of potential military power at home. Over the span of Communist rule, a systematic pattern emerged among these objectives. When a crisis arose affecting one of them, pressure from the government eased in the other two directions. When, for example, Lenin found himself caught up in a serious challenge to his power with the Kronstadt revolt of 1920, he concentrated on consolidating his control over the Communist Party but eased pressures on the people with his New Economic Policy and avoided external confrontations. Stalin behaved in a similar way while conducting his massive purges in the 1930s. It was a time when the constitution was promulgated, jazz, Christmas trees, and lipstick permitted, and a Popular Front policy conducted abroad. When the Germans attacked in 1941 and the security issue became overriding, Russian nationalism was evoked as the nation's binding cement, rather than Communist doctrine; and Stalin looked abroad for allies, nominally liquidating the Comintern.

On the basis of this recurrent pattern, we drew two major conclusions:

1. Since Stalin's death would constitute a major crisis in the organization of Soviet power, absorbing a great deal of attention among his possibly contentious heirs, its immediate aftermath was most unlikely to include Soviet adventures abroad.

2. If the American objective was to act in ways that maximized the chance of benign internal changes—an objective we commended—U.S. actions should not be threatening. External pressure was likely to force the Soviet leadership into a rigid unity unlikely to yield liberalization in domestic policy.

As for the possibilities of prompt major changes in Soviet foreign policy, our conclusions before the event were not highly optimistic.[15] We perceived Germany and arms control as the two central issues of the Cold War as of 1952. The argument was that a reversion of East Germany to democratic rule, as part of a unified nation under severe arms limitations, and acceptance of the mutual inspection required for serious arms control in general had implications for the stability of Communist domestic rule that rendered progress on these two central issues rather unlikely:

> It is, thus, our judgment that the ultimate obstacles to a diplomatic agreement on the decisive issues of the Cold War stem not from problems of Russian national security, but from the overriding priority of Soviet policy, namely, the maintenance of that regime's power over its Russian base. It follows, therefore, that a true liquidation of the Cold War—as opposed to a mitigation convenient, perhaps, for both sides—hinges on

the possibility of change in the nature of the Soviet regime, which would make its foreign policy a reflex of Russian national interest rather than the interests of a regime in perpetuating its own domestic power.[16]

Our bias, therefore, was for an American policy in the wake of Stalin's death that did what it could to encourage domestic changes toward a more liberal and nationalistic Soviet Union rather than one that looked with high expectations to a prompt and definitive resolution of the Cold War.

On the other hand, we felt that we had no right to be so confident in our conclusions as to rule out an effort to explore the possibility of radical change in Soviet external policy and that, if the exploration were properly conducted, it might provide a framework that would maximize the possibilities of liberalizing domestic change within the USSR.

This frame of reference, elaborated in some detail in *The Dynamics of Soviet Society,* explains the following suggestion from CENIS, passed to Washington on March 4, the day Stalin's illness was announced:

Given the acute but temporary traumatic state of emotion in the Soviet Union and in the Communist bloc, we believe the government should consider a major Presidential initiative within the week made with Congressional backing if possible, along the following lines.

1. He should state that Stalin's death marks the end of an era and opens up fresh options for the Russian peoples. In particular it offers them a unique opportunity to remake their relations with the rest of the world;

2. The President should evoke the common wartime effort and the common wartime goals of the two nations for a peaceful, orderly world;

3. He should emphasize and illustrate in concrete terms that there is no incompatibility between American interests and objectives and the legitimate interests and objectives of the Russian nation and its peoples; and

4. He should announce his intention to initiate in concert with our allies a meeting in the near future designed to reexamine the possibilities of agreement on controlled armaments, Germany, Austria, and other substantive issues in contention. There are, we believe, four reasons for such action:

(a) as a matter of historical record, the United States must not let this possibly brief period of unsettlement in the Russian outlook go by without holding up an image of our true intentions and purposes;

(b) such an initiative would solidify the Free World in its posture toward our future relations with the Soviet Union;

(c) such an initiative would help counter the fears of American aggression cultivated by Soviet propaganda and inevitably heightened by

Stalin's removal from the scene. It would thus encourage those close to power who may be prepared to consider internal and external policies different from those of Stalin; and

(d) such an initiative would immediately confront the regime with a major policy decision of the first order of magnitude and help reveal its inner constitution and conflicts.

These were propositions underpinning the draft I wrote two days later in Washington after discussion with C. D. Jackson.

The convergence of George Kennan's views with ours was, on the face of it, less likely, but he had fallen into a somewhat dissident position as containment unfolded under the leadership of Truman and Acheson.[17] The generalized phrases in his 1947 "X" article in *Foreign Affairs* might easily lend themselves to interpretation as including tight military containment of the Soviet Union. In fact, Walter Lippmann accused Kennan of holding precisely that view. But Kennan drew back from the arming of Germany and from a security pact with Japan. His instinctive judgment was that it was not necessary to confront the Soviet ground forces in Eastern Europe with a balancing counterforce, that Moscow would not attack even a thinly defended NATO area. He feared that Western force expansion, although undertaken for defensive purposes, would stir in Moscow fears of attack and generate a mood that all-out war with the West was inevitable. He also felt that, as a society, the United States was not capable of sustaining for the long pull a decisive military role in the European power balance. Here is Kennan's own description of his views and of his differences with his colleagues:

> My opponents, thinking in defensive terms, wished to see American military power held tightly at every point to the borders of the Soviet orbit—exactly the aberration of which Lippmann had accused me in 1947. I, in each case, wanted to hold the door open to permit the eventual emergence of large areas (a united, demilitarized Germany, a united Europe, a demilitarized Japan) that would be in the military sense uncommitted, as between the two worlds. In each case, I was prepared to see us withdraw our military forces if Soviet power would be equivalently withdrawn and if we could look forward to the rise, in the areas thus thrown open, of political authority independent of Soviet domination. . . .
>
> . . . [T]he second [objective] was to get us as soon as possible out of the position of abnormal political-military responsibility in Western Europe which the war had forced upon us. I had no confidence that a status quo dependent on so wide an American commitment could be an enduring one. Such bipolarity, I thought, might do for a few years; it could not endure indefinitely. . . . What was important was our plans for the future

should be laid in such a way as to permit that "something" to come into being when the time for it was ripe—not in such a way as to constitute an impediment to it.[18]

These views lay behind a paper formulated in the Policy Planning Staff during the Berlin blockade and submitted to Acheson on November 15, 1948.[19] It was a package of proposals for a general German settlement, known as Plan A. It involved the early creation of an all-German provisional government by free elections, as well as the mutual withdrawal of Western and Soviet forces from Germany except for garrison positions on the German periphery. Thus, from 1948 on Kennan was prepared to contemplate a negotiation in which German democratic unity was traded for substantial demilitarization.

Jackson and I did not share Kennan's reasoning about NATO, and we believed a negotiation on German unity with Moscow would be more likely to succeed if the EDC had been agreed to in principle—that is, prior agreement on EDC would constitute the most powerful bargaining chip available to the West in negotiating an all-German settlement with quite different security arrangements for Germany. But Jackson and I did share Kennan's view that existing dispositions in Western Europe were not an end in themselves and that we should be prepared radically to alter security arrangements in Europe if the Soviet Union were to agree to a Germany unified by free democratic elections. We also felt it was essential for the unity of the noncommunist world that the United States put forward, in good faith, credible proposals to this end, even if the odds of their immediate acceptance appeared low. We felt that the split of Europe was dangerous as well as historically unnatural; that it could not be rationally resolved by war with the Soviet Union; that the human plight of the Eastern Europeans should not be callously accepted; and therefore, that the effort should be made for peace in Europe consistent with Soviet as well as Western security interests and with expanded freedom for those who lived east of the Elbe. Kennan also took the view, at which we had arrived in *The Dynamics of Soviet Society*, that, in all probability, major changes in Soviet foreign policy were likely to emerge only as the result of slow but cumulative changes in the character of the Soviet system itself.

It is not difficult to understand, then, why Kennan, on the afternoon of March 10, responded positively to a reading of our draft of Eisenhower's proposed statement.

Kennan arrived in Washington in the wake of Stalin's death by a kind of back door. On the night of March 5, Kennan happened to be in Cambridge and came to dinner at the home of Max Millikan, who gathered a group of friends, including, I believe, McGeorge Bundy, Kingman Brewster, and

Elting Morison.[20] Millikan and I were full of the ideas CENIS had transmitted to the government the previous day. I was about to catch the night
train to Washington, and we talked at length about what ought to be done.
Kennan evoked eloquently, on his own, a case similar to that CENIS had
just made for a major presidential initiative to explore the possibility of a
more peaceful resolution of problems with the Soviet Union.

I felt it was somehow quite wrong for me, a newcomer to the field of
Soviet studies, to be going to Washington at this critical juncture while Kennan, one of the few authentic experts the nation possessed, was not being
consulted. On arrival, I raised the matter with Jackson. Without a moment's
hesitation he ran down Kennan at his Pennsylvania farm and asked him to
come to town. Kennan saw, I believe, Allen Dulles, as well as Bohlen and
other old friends, but the secretary of state did not receive him.[21]

As Jackson went into his NSC confrontation with the secretary of state
the next day, I believe he felt a bit strengthened that at least one member of
the Foreign Service was in support of his effort.

ACTION

FROM MARCH 11 TO APRIL 16, 1953

Eisenhower's April 16 speech emerged in the five weeks after the March 11
NSC meeting from the interplay of three tracks: the evolution of the Soviet
peace offensive; the exchanges of views between the United States and its
major allies; and the speech-drafting process that engaged the president and
his staff, on the one hand, and Dulles and his staff, on the other.

The Soviet peace offensive began, in a small way, with a passage in Malenkov's funeral oration of March 10, which included this sentence: "In the
sphere of foreign policy, our principal concern is not to permit a new war,
to live in peace with all countries." There was a good deal more in this vein,
including "a policy based on the Lenin-Stalin premise of the possibility of
prolonged coexistence and peaceful competition of two different systems,
capitalist and socialist." There was nothing remarkable in Malenkov's evocation of the peace theme. The language was familiar and, in the past, had
proved consistent with some exceedingly unpleasant confrontations. But,
still, Malenkov's words were noted; and there was interest, even if skeptical
interest, in what the words might come to mean, if anything.

The next move came six days later with the publication of Malenkov's
brief but more operational statement to the Supreme Soviet: "At the present
time there is no disputed or unresolved question that cannot be settled
peacefully by mutual agreement of the interested countries. This applies to
our relations with all states, including the United States of America."

The State Department immediately expressed "interest"; and, in a press

conference of March 19, Eisenhower opened with a prepared statement including the following:

> [A]s you know, there has been an expression of an intent to seek peace,
> from the Kremlin. I can only say that that is just as welcome as it is sincere.
>
> There is a very direct relationship between the satisfaction of such a
> thing and the sincerity in which it is meant. These will never be met less
> than halfway, that I assure you; because the purpose of this administra-
> tion will forever be to seek peace by every honorable and decent means,
> and we will do anything that will be promising towards that direction.

Some limited acts of substance followed Malenkov's statement published
on March 16. On March 21, the Soviet government threw its weight behind a proposal, laid before the Korean negotiators by the United Nations
commander in December 1951 and ignored for fifteen months, that ill and
disabled prisoners of war be exchanged in Korea. On April 2, after the
first positive Communist move in Korea, Eisenhower reinforced his positive
pragmatic stance: "[W]e should take at face value every offer that is made to
us, until it is proved not to be worthy of being so taken." There were, at this
time, further indications that the truce stalemate at Panmunjom might be
ending. At the other end of Eurasia, traffic tie-ups around Berlin were lifted
and an atmosphere of quadripartite bonhomie regenerated. In New York
the Soviet delegation at the United Nations agreed to Dag Hammarskjöld
as secretary-general, ending a long impasse. As Philip Mosely was to point
out later in the year in *Foreign Affairs:* "Some of the first steps in carrying
out the new line were little more than gestures. . . . Some . . . have simply
meant the scrapping of profitless obstinacy. . . . The most striking shift in
Soviet policy has been the conclusion of the Korean truce, the liquidation
of one of Stalin's most glaring mistakes."[22] On Germany, there were vague
suggestions, including one from the Soviet commander in Berlin that the
negotiation of German unity might be possible.

All this was sufficient for the *New York Times* to observe as early as April 2
in an editorial that "since the death of Stalin an unmistakably softer wind
has begun to blow out of Moscow and the various Communist moves are
beginning to fall into a pattern which, if completed and validated, holds out
the promise of at least a temporary easing of international tensions." And
Eisenhower was prepared to acknowledge in his April 16 speech that "recent statements and gestures of Soviet leaders give some evidence that they
may recognize this critical moment."

Soviet moves, gestures, and rhetoric, accompanied by some tentative re-
laxation of pressure on the Soviet peoples, were also sufficient to complicate
diplomacy. Each of the leaders of the major allies in different ways faced the

problem of responding to a public opinion that welcomed signs of an easing of tension with the Soviet Union. Their reactions are well summarized in Louis L. Gerson's account of their responses in April to a near final draft of Eisenhower's proposed speech:

> The President sent drafts of his speech to Churchill, Mayer, and Adenauer. He did not want to say anything publicly until he knew the allies were in agreement. He was anxious to have Churchill's reaction. All of the allied leaders thought the statement was excellent, but only Adenauer gave unqualified support.
>
> The French Premier [who had ended a visit to the United States on April 2] applauded American initiative on the peace front and favored pressure on the Soviets to make agreements. He felt Soviet acceptance of an Austrian treaty followed by evacuation of troops from Austria, Hungary, and Rumania would give evidence of readiness to consider other problems. Mayer opposed a summit conference, which pleased Dulles. His only comments of substance related to Germany and Indochina. The Premier feared a reunited Germany, which he assumed would be a neutral and disarmed Germany, before reaching an agreement with the Soviet Union. A reunited Germany might deal with the Soviet Union and Eastern Europe. France, he said, could not permit this unless with a simultaneous general disarmament. He supported EDC and rearmament of Germany as a means of convincing the Soviet Union of the desirability of general disarmament. The Premier requested the President to couple the demand for a Korean settlement with an end to the war in Indochina.
>
> Churchill questioned some of the proposed address's assumptions. He felt that a change in Soviet mood and perhaps in policy had become apparent with the death of Stalin, and that the time was ready for informal, private conversation among a few leaders of the major powers. The Prime Minister doubted the wisdom of too many conditions as a means of testing Soviet intentions.[23]

Eisenhower's reply to Churchill "doubted the wisdom" of a summit meeting with the Soviets but raised again the possibility of a gathering of the leaders of Britain, France, and the United States. As we shall see, Churchill was not that easily put off. As for the excessive conditions Churchill found in the draft, Eisenhower, using Churchill's language, replied on April 13: "I agree with the tenor of your comments and shall certainly strive to make my talk one that will not freeze the tender buds of sprouting decency, if indeed they are really coming out." Churchill's suggestion that the speech might be postponed until the Soviet stance was better defined was, after some uncertainty, set aside. There was even some suspicion in Eisenhower's entourage that Churchill hoped to make the first grand response of the West to the new situation in Moscow.

Adenauer had come to visit the United States after the passage of the EDC treaty by the Bundestag and was in Washington April 7 to 11. His assessment of the situation in the wake of Stalin's death and of the attitudes encountered in America are set down at length in his memoirs and captured in the following passage:

> This peace offensive had produced a very insecure political situation. It seemed as though a large part of American public opinion was only too ready to succumb to the blandishments of a détente which for the time being was nothing but a pipe dream. American families wanted their sons to come back from Korea. People were tired of war and its tensions. . . .
>
> I was very interested to learn what the attitude of the United States was regarding the Soviet peace feelers that had been put out recently. . . .
>
> There were no indications that Russia had desisted from her intentions. Rearmament was continuing unabated in the Soviet Union, especially along the Western front. . . .
>
> . . . If the Soviet Union offered something concrete, one should accept it, but for the rest one should continue on the previous course and not be diverted from it. The Federal Republic certainly did not want war, but the danger of war would increase if the West relaxed its rearmament efforts. It would decrease if the West continued to rearm. . . .
>
> On the reunification of Germany I said that this problem was not an isolated one, but a question closely and intimately linked with the question of Europe as such. A neutralized Germany was no solution. . . . [T]he influence of Soviet power and Soviet strength would be so great—it could be compared to a magnet which attracts iron—that after some time the Soviet Union would attract all the weakened European countries.[24]

It is likely that Adenauer welcomed Eisenhower's call for German unity for domestic political purposes. Later in the year, Adenauer was to press Dulles to initiate negotiations on German unity in order to assist him in the German general election of September 6.[25]

Thus, Eisenhower was in a position to deliver his speech, having consulted in exemplary fashion and with his major allies more or less in support. In different ways each welcomed, for domestic reasons, the peaceful stance of the American leader; but they had quite different concerns and priorities, as the course of events in 1953–1954 was to reveal. Barring a Soviet willingness to accept German unity on something like Western terms, those differences were bound to assert themselves; and the French did not want German unity in any form, although they would have found it difficult to oppose if, in fact, it had been offered by Moscow in a form acceptable to Adenauer, Churchill, and Eisenhower.

The real problems in formulating the speech, however, lay in Washington, not abroad; and to evoke them we must backtrack a month to the aftermath of Eisenhower's decisions at the NSC meeting of March 11.

There was the usual luncheon meeting of the Psychological Strategy Board (PSB) on Thursday, March 12, in the wake of the NSC session on the previous day. The group included Bedell Smith, Allen Dulles, and C. D. Jackson. There seemed unanimity that the government should move forward on the basis of the redrafted version of the proposed "Statement," and Smith promised to help with Foster Dulles.

But it was not all that easy. In the first place, what I had left behind with Jackson, as I returned to my teaching at MIT, was a rather austere draft of a possible presidential "Message to the Soviet Government and the Russian Peoples." It was initially designed for publication, not personal delivery. By the afternoon of March 12, it was envisaged that what the president had to say would be delivered either to the American people on television or to the U.N. General Assembly on Thursday, March 19. In addition, of course, and despite apparent agreement in principle, there were bound to be differences of view about what, in fact, the president should say. All this resulted in a weekend of hard work.

This communal enterprise yielded four drafts, three dated March 16, one March 17, presumably the synthesis of the Hughes and Jackson drafts. All were geared to delivery before the U.N. General Assembly. Along the way it was evidently decided that the speech was not ready, and the notion of delivering it before the General Assembly was dropped. By March 21, Eisenhower was thinking of delivery on April 12 at the Pan-American Union.

In substance, what might be called the weekend drafts shifted the emphasis rather heavily to Eastern Europe, reflecting, no doubt, Jackson's concerns; and a format evolved counterposing what the United States sought in the world with the question: what is the Soviet Union prepared to do? The call for immediate negotiations with the Soviet Union on Germany had, of course, been dropped after the March 11 NSC meeting. I was shown one of these drafts while briefly in Washington during the week of the sixteenth and expressed the view that it was excessively negative. It was in response to one of these drafts that Eisenhower intervened rather dramatically in "mid March," according to Emmet Hughes' account:

> On this occasion . . . he grew more excited and intense. He began talking with the air of a man whose thoughts, after a permissive spell of meandering, were fast veering toward a conclusion. . . .

"Look, . . . just *one* thing matters: what have *we* got to offer the world? What are *we* ready to do, to improve the chances of peace? . . .

"*Here* is what I would like to say.

"The jet plane that roars over your head costs three-quarters of a million dollars. That is more money than a man earning ten thousand dollars every year is going to make in his lifetime. What world can afford this sort of thing for long? . . . Where will it lead us? At worst, to atomic warfare. At best, to robbing every people and nation on earth of the fruits of their own toil. . . .

"Now, there could be another road before us—the road of disarmament. What does this mean? It means for everybody in the world: bread, butter, clothes, homes, hospitals, schools—all the good and necessary things for decent living. . . .

"What do we say about the Soviet Government? I'd like to get up and say: I am *not* going to make an indictment of them. The past speaks for itself. I am interested in the future. Both their government and ours now have new men in them. The slate is clean. Now let us begin talking to each other. *And let us say what we've got to say so that every person on earth can understand it.* Here is what *we* propose. If you—the Soviet Union—can improve on it, we want to hear it.

"This is what I want to say. And if we don't really *have* anything to *offer,* I'm not going to make a speech about it."

The excitement of the man and the moment was contagious and stirring.[26]

The discussion on the seventeenth yielded a draft of March 19, which contained "America's Four-Year Plan for Peace": arms expenditures not to exceed 10 percent of "national industrial product"; savings from arms reductions to go to a World Aid Fund; U.N.-inspected arms control; the peaceful use of atomic energy; "peace in Asia," including Indochina and Malaya as well as Korea; a "gradual lifting" of the Iron Curtain; unification of Germany and an Austrian peace treaty; withdrawal of U.S. and Soviet forces, and the forces of their allies, from "foreign soil."

In responding to the March 19 draft, Paul Nitze, head of the Policy Planning Staff, raised sharply again, in a memorandum to Dulles, some of the concerns he and his colleagues had felt from the beginning—notably, the slowing down of EDC, and being forced into a negotiation with the Soviet Union.

Thus, what had begun as a call for prompt negotiation with the Soviet Union on Germany and other outstanding issues, to be transmitted immediately in the wake of Stalin's death, became, six weeks later, an eloquent definition of the American vision of what peace required in Europe, Asia, and the control of arms, coming to rest on a question put to the new Soviet leaders: how far are you willing to go? A good deal of the bone structure of the statement proposed on March 6 survived the many subsequent drafts: the evocation of wartime alliance; the contrast between the U.S. and Soviet post-1945 concepts for achieving security; the dangers to all in existing dispositions; the opportunity the moment offered for a fresh start; the ending of hostilities in Korea as a precondition, the need for reduced armaments and the commitment of direct savings to assist developing countries; the need for an Austrian treaty; the requirement of ending the division of Germany and Europe; and the assertion that the United States and its allies would persist in their joint efforts until effective measures of collective security were agreed to with the Soviet Union and put into effect. But, in the course of the exercise, Eisenhower had put his mark on the speech in several important ways: by setting aside an explicit call for negotiation, by strengthening and greatly elaborating the passages on the need for arms control, by resisting inflammatory language on the liberation of Eastern Europe, and by resisting elaborate preconditions for a Korean settlement on the thirty-eighth parallel. As delivered, it was an authentic expression of his vision of what a peaceful world community required, and it was a vision that an overwhelming majority of the American people were prepared to support. But, in itself, it set in motion no courses of action to move the world closer to that vision.

THE AFTERMATH

Preparations by C. D. Jackson for the distribution of the speech had been thorough, and the immediate popular reaction to the speech at home and abroad was extraordinarily positive. On April 16, before the returns were in, Jackson, in a letter to Secretary of State Dulles, returned to the issue of negotiations with Moscow on which he and I (and Kennan) had fought and lost on March 11. After noting that the burden of implementing the president's speech would fall with greatest weight on diplomacy and hence the State Department, he raised the possibility again of U.S. initiation of a four-power conference; urged, in any case, advance planning for such a conference; and underlined the virtue of persuading the Western European allies that the optimum stance for a four-power meeting was with the EDC ratification complete. Dulles' response on April 21 was confined to the statement that advance planning was necessary and under way.

The government as a whole, however, was not so sharply focused on what the next steps should or should not be. When the cabinet met in Eisenhower's absence under Nixon's chairmanship on April 17, the talk was all of domestic politics and budgets; there was no reference to the president's initiative. Hughes wrote in his diary: "I suppose a lot of people thought we spent this day in the White House talking about the peace of the world."[27]

On the eighteenth Dulles addressed the American Society of Newspaper Editors. He argued that Eisenhower's words, which could have been spoken "at any time during these past ninety days, . . . gained immensely in significance because they come against a background of cohesive, positive action." He then marched through his agenda as he saw it: EDC and NATO, the role of the Seventh Fleet in protecting Formosa but not the Chinese mainland, aid to the French in Indochina, a tightening of the blockade of the Chinese mainland, the Captive Nations Resolution before Congress. He described the recent Soviet moves as "peace defensive," responding to the strength of U.S. policy. He called on Moscow to meet "the Eisenhower tests" and to "abolish and abandon, in fact as well as in name, the Cominform." It was pretty much a business-as-usual Cold War speech. And this was noted in a *Pravda* commentary on April 25, when the full text of Eisenhower's talk was published. Referring to the secretary's "belligerence," *Pravda* concluded that "if the real meaning of Eisenhower's statement is what was represented in Dulles' more detailed speech, delivered after the President's, before the same audience and in the same hall, it cannot produce positive results from the point of view of the interests of strengthening peace."

With respect to Eisenhower's text, *Pravda* provided a long, temperate but firm reply, point by point. It resisted the notion of preconditions and special requirements which the Soviet Union had to meet, suggesting that the responsibility for moving forward was joint and that Moscow was ready for a "serious, businesslike discussion of problems both by direct negotiations and, when necessary, within the framework of the U.N."

Then, on May 11 and 12, Churchill spoke out. Acting as foreign secretary, with Anthony Eden ill, as well as prime minister, he returned to the theme of his earlier exchanges with Eisenhower:

> It would, I think, be a mistake to assume that nothing can be settled with Soviet Russia unless or until everything is settled. A settlement of two or three of our difficulties would be an important gain to every peace-loving country. For instance, peace in Korea, the conclusion of an Austrian Treaty—these might lead to an easement in our relations for the next few years, which might in itself open new prospects to the security and prosperity of all nations and every continent. . . .
>
> I must make it plain that, in spite of all the uncertainties and confusion in which world affairs are plunged, I believe that a conference on the highest level should take place between the leading Powers without long

delay. It might well be that no hard-faced agreements would be reached, but there might be a general feeling among those gathered together that they might do something better than tear the human race, including themselves, into bits. . . .

I only say that this might happen, and I do not see why anyone should be frightened at having a try for it.

Eisenhower and Dulles were not pleased with Churchill's intervention, and Harold Macmillan and Eden thought the proposed summit meeting with Moscow might be premature.[28] In much the mood of Dulles and Adenauer, Eden doubted "whether the policy of sustained pressure on Russia and the building up of strength in Europe had yet gone far enough to permit of such an attempt at détente." But Churchill, brooding about the probable early emergence of Soviet as well as American fusion weapons, with all they implied for the character of a major war between the great powers, felt the moment had to be seized and direct conversations undertaken with Moscow at the highest level.

It was clearly time for the West to align its policies toward Moscow. Eisenhower's March 11 suggestion of a possible Big Three summit meeting was adopted and scheduled for Bermuda on June 17. The meeting was first delayed by a prolonged interregnum in the French government, as Mayer fell and a month passed before Joseph Lanier was found as an acceptable successor on June 26. The next day Churchill's inability to go to Bermuda was announced. He had suffered a stroke on June 23.

The aftermath of Stalin's death also generated two dramatic events in the East; the June riots in East Germany, which began on the night of June 16, after some six weeks of movement toward liberalization; and, in early July, the arrest of Beria, possibly connected with the East German uprising. Beria's arrest occurred just as the three Western foreign ministers were meeting in Washington in lieu of the Bermuda summit. It was at these sessions, which ended on July 14, that it became apparent that a conference on Germany with the Soviet Union was required: Bidault, then French foreign minister, made it clear to Dulles that the French parliament would not pass EDC unless a good-faith effort to solve the German problem by negotiation with the Soviet Union had been made and had failed. And, despite his skepticism regarding the outcome, Adenauer sent a message to Dulles asking for the announcement of a four-power meeting on Germany to assist him in the general elections of September 6. Thus, by mid-July 1953, some four months after Stalin's death, the Allies offered to negotiate about Germany with Moscow; and they did so not because the signals from Moscow were more propitious than they had been earlier but because the enterprises of the alliance could not move forward until the Soviet position on Germany had been tested.

After a "dreary interchange" of diplomatic notes in the autumn, to use Macmillan's characterization, the four foreign ministers, meeting in Berlin, finally came to grips with the German question in January 1954. By that time the Soviet Union had weathered tolerably well the East German revolt, had exploded a hydrogen bomb on August 20, had shot Beria, and had decided it was prepared to make no concessions whatsoever on Germany. The Western powers were well prepared for the Berlin sessions, strengthened by the holding, at last, of a summit meeting in Bermuda in December 1953. The meeting generated no new propositions but permitted the foreign ministers, with support from their principals, to consolidate their positions before heading for Berlin and the long-delayed confrontation with Molotov. Before they arrived, Eisenhower had launched on December 8 his "Atoms for Peace" proposal at the United Nations General Assembly and, two weeks later, Dulles had evoked his "agonizing reappraisal" threat; that is, the United States might have to consider withdrawing its troops from Europe unless the French parliament accepted the EDC.

Whether this possibility affected Soviet dispositions in Berlin we do not know. It is clear that Molotov was under instructions to give no ground on Germany or, indeed, on anything else.

Whether Molotov was trying to encourage Britain and France to accept Dulles' threat of an "agonizing reappraisal" by the United States or simply overplayed his hand is not clear. His blunt, dogmatic manner pulled the Allies closer together. But Dulles handled well this and other aspects of the conference;[29] and Molotov's position left no doubt in the minds of the Western governments that, as of early 1954, there was no realistic possibility of negotiating German unity or avoiding the absorption of the Federal Republic into the enterprises of the West as a full partner.

But this did not happen through the EDC. The French assembly rejected the EDC on August 30, 1954, by a vote of 319 to 264. At British suggestion, the Federal Republic of Germany was invited to join a Western European Union (WEU) superseding the Brussels Pact of 1948. This looser organization, with full British membership, filled the gap left by the failure of the EDC. The French retained their national army and had the British at their side. Thus, the Allied occupation of the Federal Republic ended on October 23, 1954, with the formal signing of the WEU agreement and its entrance into NATO.

The major operational result of the Berlin conference arose from the powerful pressures in French political life to negotiate some kind of Indochina settlement. It yielded agreement to hold a further foreign ministers meeting in Geneva on unresolved Asian problems in which Communist China would participate. That protracted conference (April 26 to July 21) finally produced the armistice in Indochina at the seventeenth parallel with Communist control north of the line. A few years of relative peace descended on that bedeviled region. In 1955, the negotiations on the Austrian State Treaty were completed and that country assumed fully its place in the international community. And, in general, the period from Stalin's death in 1953 to, say, the nationalization of the Suez Canal by Nasser on July 26, 1956, was the least troubled period in the protracted struggle between the Soviet Union and the West. When a period of acute tension resumed, its regional focus shifted from Europe and Korea to the Middle East, Africa, and Latin America, although the struggle in Southeast Asia revived in 1958. The new phase of confrontation was framed by the arms race in missiles, tipped with fusion weapons, which were developed on both sides during the somewhat illusory quiet of the three years that followed Stalin's death.

SOME CONCLUSIONS

In terms of ideas and action, the U.S. government's decisions from Stalin's death to Eisenhower's April 16 speech constitute the resolution of a series of clashes. Among them was Eisenhower's instinct to speak out promptly versus Dulles' reserve; between those, including Churchill, who felt that high-level diplomatic contact with the Soviets should be sought at Western initiative, versus those, including Eisenhower, who drew back from summitry, in particular, quadripartite negotiation in general; between those who judged that the democratic unification of Germany, and the ending of military confrontation in the center of Europe, justified the exploration of radically new security dispositions versus those who either felt German unity was undesirable on any terms (the French and British) or were prepared to pursue it only on the basis of the further consolidation of the Western security position along familiar lines (Adenauer). Behind their dialogue was a largely unexplored difference of view between those who felt that Soviet policy would be determined on grounds quite independent of what the United States and the West did versus those who felt that there was a margin of Western influence on Soviet dispositions and that it should be exercised. Then there were elements of personality—notably, Eisenhower, Dulles, and the relationship between them. And, as always, there was politics—notably, the shadow of the Republican right wing, including not only Senators William Knowland and Robert Taft but also Joseph McCarthy. Out of this mélange came five weeks of delay, a benign and successful speech, and a sterile negotiation at the foreign minister level nine months later forced on the United

States by the domestic political requirements of the French and German governments.

The first question to pose is, was anything lost by this outcome? Was an opportunity forgone when Eisenhower turned down Churchill's suggestion for a prompt summit meeting and backed Dulles against Jackson in the NSC meeting of March 11?

One of the most interesting judgments on this matter is the retrospective view of Charles Bohlen, incorporated in a June 1964 interview:

> [L]ooking back on it, there are a number of things that might have been done, and I think that one of them might have been to have gone along with Winston Churchill's appeal in the spring of '53 for a Summit conference. . . . And from what we know now, this would have been a very fruitful period and might easily have led to a radical solution in our favor of the German question—because subsequent to that in '54—or later on in '59   there were a number of rumors around Moscow that the Russians had been thinking of the possibility of giving up East Germany. A year or so ago, Khrushchev made the same charge against Malenkov and Beria. But I think this was a mistake. I think it would have been very useful to have had a Summit conference in '53. We might have gotten a great deal out of it. I must say, I didn't advise it then, because I didn't see the situation as it looks now.[30]

Richard Goold-Adams reports, without providing his source, a similar retrospective view of Foster Dulles:

> By the time that January, 1954, arrived Dulles felt that the chances of reaching any significant agreement with the Russians, never more than slim, had grown even slimmer. He was inclined to think that, if a conference had been possible immediately after Stalin's death, or if the famous riots in East Berlin had never taken place, the chances of a breakthrough would have been better. But, with the passage of time, the psychological elements in the situation were hardening as it was inevitable that they would in a period when the realities of nuclear power were so patently shifting.[31]

Of all the possible reasons for regret over the delay in negotiations with the Soviet Union, the most interesting—even tantalizing—centers on the course of Soviet policy in East Germany from, say, early May to the riots that began on the evening of June 16.[32] Evidently under Soviet pressure, the German Communist leaders undertook a wide-ranging set of moves that appeared, at least, to liberalize marginally life in East Germany. It was announced that consumer goods production would be increased; controls over labor were somewhat relaxed; farmers were reassured that they would not be forced into collectives; amiable gestures were made toward the German clergy and even noncommunist politicians; criticisms of the FRG were somewhat muted.

It seems reasonably clear from a variety of sources, including several East German Communist defectors, that Wilhelm Zaisser, minister of state security in East Germany, was associated with this policy, and that his sponsor in Moscow was Beria. A decade later, in March 1963, Khrushchev, in fact accused Beria of having plotted with Malenkov to liquidate East Germany as a Communist state in negotiation with the West. Those who accept something like this interpretation argue that the liberalization was designed to render East Germany a more respectable negotiating partner in an all-German settlement. Even before later evidence developed, the rather hard-minded Philip Mosely presented something approximating this assessment in his *Foreign Affairs* article of October 1953. And it may be that when Churchill spoke in the House of Commons on May 11 he had not only observed what was beginning to happen in East Germany but had in hand some intriguing intelligence. Others have remained skeptical that the limited liberalizing moves in East Germany had any such grand purpose.

In any case, the possibility—such as it may or may not have been—disappeared with the East German riots in June, the intervention of Soviet forces, and the reconsolidation of a hard-line Communist dictatorship in East Germany. The whole episode, however, with its vivid demonstration of the feelings of the East Germans, heightened the issue of German unity in the West German elections, helping lead Adenauer to advocate an early Western negotiation on the subject of the Soviet Union.

In the ten months between Stalin's death and the opening of the Berlin talks, five things had happened, then, that bear on Bohlen's and Dulles' second thoughts: (1) there had been time for the new men in Moscow to get over the shock and, after eliminating Beria, to settle into an uneasy collective leadership; (2) the East German riots erupted in June, resulting in the successful reconsolidation of Communist power after the intervention of elements from more than twenty Soviet divisions; (3) the first Soviet fusion weapon was exploded in August; (4) Moscow was able to observe the acute difficulty confronted by the French government in mobilizing parliamentary support for EDC, leading Dulles to evoke his "agonizing reappraisal"; and (5) the United States substantially reduced its military budget. With these factors taken altogether, it is not difficult to understand that the Soviet government judged, as of January 1954, that it could afford to stand pat on Germany, observe what transpired with the EDC, and see whether, in fact, the United States might reduce or withdraw its military commitment from

Western Europe. From Roosevelt's statement at Yalta that U.S. forces could not be maintained in Germany for more than two years down to the 1980s, the possibility of American detachment from Europe remained a recurrent Soviet hope—almost an obsession—explicitly evoked, for example, at the Berlin conference in February 1954, at the Geneva summit in July 1955, in the Kennedy-Khrushchev exchange in Vienna in June 1961, and in Georgi Arbatov's authoritative article published in the United States in April 1980.[33]

There is no solid evidence that Moscow would have been prepared in the spring of 1953 or in the immediate aftermath of the East German revolt in June to have contemplated a radical change in German policy; but it does seem likely that the chances for a substantial alteration in the contours of the Cold War would have been higher at a summit meeting in, say, April or May 1953 than at a foreign ministers' meeting in early 1954 (see Appendix B). There may have been an interval of fluidity, although the evidence for it is limited and inconclusive; but at the Berlin foreign ministers' conference the status quo ante was firmly reestablished.

What, then, explains Eisenhower's curious position: he clearly felt there was a historic moment to be exploited, but he drew back from a meeting with the Soviets at his initiative. He regretted that he had, in effect, been prevented by Dulles from preempting Malenkov in the launching of a post-Stalin peace offensive; but, in his April 16 speech, he left it wholly up to Moscow to propose or not to propose diplomatic courses of action. From the beginning the State Department, as well as Jackson, perceived that serious progress on Germany, Austria, arms control, and the other issues placed on the agenda by the president could occur only in the context of negotiation. Why did Eisenhower resist?

In broad terms, Eisenhower addresses himself at some length in his memoirs to the question of summitry.[34] He reviews the disappointing experiences of Wilson and Franklin Roosevelt and describes his general attitude toward such meetings in these terms: "I was still not willing to meet with Communist leaders unless there was some likelihood that the confrontation could produce results acceptable to the peoples of the West." On the post-Stalin period, he notes Dulles' opposition to a summit, Churchill's advocacy, Eden's reservations, and continued press discussion. He concludes:

> At home and abroad the subject continued a live one. The constant debate—pro and con—assured the persistent interest of the press; so I developed a stock answer to any question about a possible Summit. I would not go to a Summit merely because of friendly words and plausible promises by the men in the Kremlin; actual deeds giving some indication of a Communist readiness to negotiate constructively will have to be produced before I would agree to such a meeting.

There is no reason to doubt that Eisenhower faithfully recorded the basic reasons for his reserve.

But I suspect three other elements converged to help produce his stance on this matter. First, summit meetings with the Soviets were not in good repute in Republican circles as of early 1953. There had been a good deal of Republican talk during the campaign about the alleged failure of Yalta and Potsdam. Here the shadow of the Republican right wing may have mattered. Eisenhower did not wish, I suspect, to begin his period of responsibility with a meeting of uncertain outcome in which he would be a central figure.[35] Thus, he turned off Churchill's proposals on March 11 and again on April 13, preferring a politically safer Western summit.

Second, Eisenhower did not regard himself as a professional diplomatic negotiator. He had a clear picture of what leadership at his level demanded: setting a broad course for the nation and the world, administering the executive branch and its relations with Congress in a way that maintained reasonable consensus and courses of action that did not grossly violate the general directions in which he proposed to move. But, quite unlike Churchill, Eisenhower did not regard himself as both maker and implementer of policy. He had risen in the military as an officer of the staff rather than the line. He came to the top of his profession, through no fault of his own, without a field command. He was as successful as a man could be as an executive organizing and managing others in large enterprises. He did not shirk tough decisions in what he regarded as his proper domain. He was a natural and accomplished politician. Without question he rather than Dulles made the basic foreign policy decisions of his administration. But, both in military and political life, he drew back from imposing on his subordinates his concept of how operations should be conducted in detail. In the wake of Stalin's death, he lacked Churchill's confident eagerness, despite the latter's seventy-eight years and gathering infirmities, to come directly to grips with the new Soviet leadership and assess what could or could not be wrung from the new situation.

Third, there was John Foster Dulles. Eisenhower accepted Dulles as a skilled professional in diplomacy. He had chosen him, was pleased with his choice, and was determined to work with him.[36] But at this juncture Eisenhower could not achieve with Dulles the common vision and common conception of the course of action to be followed that Kennan correctly defined as the necessary and sufficient condition for implementing the draft "Statement" Jackson showed Kennan on March 10. Not for the last time during his tenure as president, Eisenhower acted at his level as his instincts told him to act, but he did not insist on the operational follow-through implicit in the rhetorical position he took.[37]

Thus, Eisenhower reached out and spoke on April 16 with evident sincerity about peace. In phrases he used on another occasion, he aimed "to attack the future" rather than "worry about the past."[38] As a professional soldier, he knew better than most that in a world where thermonuclear weapons would be in the hands of both the Soviet Union and the United States, a military resolution of the conflict between the two countries was irrational. Describing Eisenhower's view of political warfare in a letter to me of December 31, 1952, Jackson wrote that Eisenhower "appreciates that practically every other golf club in his bag is broken." Abstracting from the vocabulary of the day, Eisenhower was trying to use his position and his personality to nudge the world toward peace. As he said to his aide Andrew Goodpaster in 1956: "Of course we have got to have a concern and respect for fact and reiteration of official positions, but we are likewise trying to 'seek friends and influence people.'"[39] But, lacking a secretary of state who shared his view of what was required and being uncertain about the appropriate diplomatic course to be followed, he settled for a good speech.

C. D. Jackson's style in this conflict was rather deceptive. This tall, vigorous figure in his fifties had about him a boyish exuberance. In small talk his vocabulary smacked more of journalism and advertising than politics and diplomacy. He was systematically unpompous, humorous, and a companion to be enjoyed. But, when he settled down to the task at hand, he could be thoroughly professional—comfortable and firm in loyalty to his own values and insights and his large vision of what the United States should stand for on the world scene. It was easy to underestimate Jackson, as a good many men in the Washington bureaucracy did; and, in a curious way, this was an asset to the administration.[40]

Dulles is generally portrayed in this policy debate as the hard-hearted cold warrior, resisting and then diluting the decent and generous impulses of his chief. Dulles' reaction to Jackson's draft "Statement" was, simply, that its issuance would gravely endanger his major, fragile Western (EDC) enterprise in mid-passage. Even when the call for negotiation was removed, after the March 11 NSC meeting, the president's speech still, he thought, carried with it that danger which, however, he came to regard as inevitable once Malenkov launched Moscow's peace offensive. As one who differed with Dulles at the time and would differ still, in retrospect, I believe he must be accorded the kind of acknowledgment Kennan made to Acheson's 1948 opposition to the Planning Staff's Plan A for a united Germany:

> I was far then, and am far today, from being without sympathy for
> Mr. Acheson's position. The responsibility that rested on him was great.
> For him, too, the London Program, adopted and put in hand long before
> he became Secretary of State, represented a species of *fait accompli*. It

could not be lightly placed in jeopardy. He had a solemn duty to preserve Western unity, to carry forward the improvement and consolidation of political and economic conditions in Western Germany, to avoid things that could unduly excite the ready suspicions and anxieties of our Western European Allies. No immediate Russian agreement could have been expected at that time to proposals along the lines of Plan A. The imprudent advancement of them, on the other hand, could easily alarm and disorient Western opinion. To ask him to toy with such proposals was, in the circumstances, asking a great deal.[41]

Dulles' failure, in my view, lay not in his skepticism that the German issue could be solved in 1953 by negotiation with Moscow but in certain quite specific and narrow professional errors: his gross overstatement at the March 11 NSC meeting of the consequences of the president's proceeding with the proposed "Statement" (that is, the French and German governments would fall in a week, etc.); his failure to find a formula—or even seek a formula—that might have persuaded the European Allies that a negotiation on Germany had a much greater chance of success if EDC were, in principle, agreed to than if its fate were still moot when the negotiation took place; his failure to anticipate the possibility of a Soviet peace offensive and thus the reluctant, defensive posture in which he found himself from Malenkov's statement published on March 16, a posture that may have been costly because it was quite apparent to Moscow and may well have colored their dispositions at the Berlin conference of January and February 1954; his failure to sense at the time that the softening of Soviet policy in East Germany might conceivably represent an opening for serious diplomacy on a German settlement; and his apparent failure to take into account the possible effects in Moscow of his threat to Western Europe of an American "agonizing reappraisal," if EDC were not consummated.

As a professional diplomat, Dulles had reason to have looked back with some regret at this technical performance in the days immediately after Stalin's death, as Goold-Adams suggests he did.

There is an even larger issue—or question—embedded in this story. The secretary of state is an important official in the executive branch—next to the president and the vice president, the most important official. But he is appointed by the president, does not submit himself to the electorate, and serves at the president's pleasure. Like everyone else in the executive branch except the president and vice president, he is, in the best sense, a hired hand. His duty is to advise the president, understand as profoundly and sympathetically as he can the reasons for the president's decision, and then execute the letter and spirit of that decision, unless he chooses to resign.

The simple fact is that Dulles resisted the president's impulse to speak out promptly after Stalin's death, agreed only when he found unanticipated pressure in Europe for a Western peace gesture and negotiation with Moscow, and then delivered a speech, two days after the president's, that appeared to undercut the spirit if not the letter of what Eisenhower had said on April 16.

There is some reason to believe that there was, in fact, an incomplete meeting of the minds between Eisenhower and Dulles in the wake of Stalin's death. Eisenhower sensed immediately that men and women in the United States and everywhere else, skeptical as they might have been, still ached for peace and asked: "Is this a moment when things could be changed for the better?" However small the opportunities for any fundamental change in relations between Moscow and the West were reckoned to be by qualified experts, that popular feeling was a force with which professional diplomacy had to reckon. The secretary of state should have been capable of responding to his president's sensitivity to this powerful sentiment and of swiftly adjusting his approach to EDC and other matters to take it into account.

Eisenhower's assessment of Dulles is set down in an entry in his diary for May 14, 1953:

> He is not particularly persuasive in presentation and, at times, seems to have a curious lack of understanding of how his words and manner may affect another personality. Personally, I like and admire him; my only doubts concerning him lie in the general field of personality, not in his capacity of foreign affairs.[42]

Thus, elements of personality helped prevent the emergence of a fully coherent American policy in the wake of Stalin's death. Despite the almost compulsive detail of the communications between Eisenhower and Dulles, their minds did not quite meet. Their relationship evokes something of a Victorian novel in which two characters, closely aligned, cannot quite communicate the deepest thoughts in their minds.

There is no firm reason to believe that if Dulles had designed a diplomatic track responsive to the president's instinct and taken the initiative on Germany and other matters promptly after Stalin's death, the outcome would have been greatly different. Certainly, the tactical position of the United States and the West would have been stronger, but a unified Germany and an end to the military confrontation in the center of Europe might have eluded negotiations in the spring of 1953 as they did early in 1954. We shall never know.

What the story illuminates is the power over the behavior of men in public life of the often unarticulated images they carry in their heads, including their images of each other; and, as in the earlier chapters, this essay suggests the critical importance of timing: two months or so lost for the attack on German oil in 1944, a year or so lost in 1946–1947 before confronting Stalin on both Germany and the offer of large-scale American aid in European reconstruction, nine months or so lost before representatives of the West met with the representatives of Stalin's successors—and not at the summit. Of course, earlier is not always better. In these three cases I am still inclined to believe it would have been better. In the rhythms of public life there may emerge a moment for an idea when its time has come, and it is translated into effective action; but that moment may not necessarily be the moment of greatest opportunity. The unambiguous point is that, one way or the other, timing matters.

Five

OPEN SKIES, 1955

A USEFUL FAILURE

THE DECISION

At 6:00 P.M. on Wednesday, July 20, 1955, President Eisenhower assembled an impressive group of American public servants in the library at the Chateau du Creux de Genthod, an eighteenth-century villa on Lake Geneva where he stayed while attending the summit conference of July 18–23. Those present included his major national security advisers, excepting the secretary of defense and the director of Central Intelligence who had remained in Washington: John Foster Dulles, secretary of state; Robert B. Anderson, deputy secretary of defense; Livingston Merchant, assistant secretary of state for European affairs; Arthur W. Radford, chairman of the Joint Chiefs of Staff; Harold E. Stassen, special assistant to the president on disarmament; Dillon Anderson, special assistant to the president for national security affairs; Nelson A. Rockefeller, special assistant to the president; and Andrew J. Goodpaster, White House staff secretary. Alfred M. Gruenther, supreme Allied commander in Europe, was also present.

With Eisenhower and Dulles side by side in easy chairs by the fireplace and the others distributed informally around the room, the subject of discussion was what the president should say the next day at the meeting with his three colleagues: Prime Minister Anthony Eden, Edgar Faure, the French premier, and Nikolay Bulganin, nominally the head of the Soviet delegation.[1] Disarmament was the scheduled subject, and it was agreed that Eisenhower would focus on the problem of mutual inspection.

The choice before Eisenhower was, essentially, this: after discussing the critical role of inspection, should he refer the issue to Harold Stassen for negotiation elsewhere; or should he personally propose a concrete scheme for mutual aerial inspection, which had been advocated within the government by Nelson Rockefeller since June 10?

Stassen had prepared a draft statement for the president to make the next day. Stassen's draft made the case for the critical importance of inspection, recommended that the Big Four instruct their representatives in the United Nations Subcommittee on Disarmament to give priority attention to the matter, and added the following:

> The United States is ready to proceed in the study and testing of a reliable system of inspections and reporting, and when that system is proved, then to reduce armaments with all others to the extent that the system will provide assured results.
>
> The successful working out of such a system would do much to develop the mutual confidence which will open wide the avenues of progress for all our peoples.

Eisenhower's thoughts, however, were ranging well beyond Stassen's somewhat chaste bureaucratic draft and moving toward support for Rockefeller's proposal. In fact, he reported to the meeting that he had already indicated to Eden and his British colleagues at breakfast that morning that "a plan for mutual overflights in the East and the West, to include Russia and the United States, would not be unacceptable to him."

As often happens, the official minutes and memoranda for the record are not wholly clear about the course and texture of the discussion on the evening of the twentieth. They suggest, however, that Stassen initially took the position that such schemes "would tend to fix 'the iron curtain' more formally." Eisenhower said they would have the opposite effect. Stassen was also concerned that the ground inspections, envisaged to supplement mutual photographic coverage, might reveal "our own advanced technology." Robert Anderson of the Pentagon said that, while lists of military installations would be furnished, "not everything would be available for examination" on the ground. Dulles thought the United States would be under obligation to inform the British and French before the president made any such proposal. Evidently this might make its presentation the next day difficult, if not impossible.

After statements of support from the senior military men present (Radford and Gruenther), a consensus emerged. For some six weeks Dulles and Stassen had been resisting the concept of a specific presidential initiative for mutual aerial inspection; but with Radford and Gruenther aboard, as well as the deputy secretary of defense, on what was, essentially, a military proposal, they were evidently outgunned in narrow bureaucratic terms. But the decisive fact was that Eisenhower was strongly drawn to the proposal.

Stassen then stated that the initiative by the president the next day would "constitute a splendid opening step in the move toward disarmament." Dulles proceeded to reverse his earlier position: he opined that as both "drama and substance" the proposal was "very promising" and would have a "very great effect," but that there must be no advance word to anyone. Much of the impact would be lost if a leak occurred. So far as the records show, Nelson Rockefeller did not speak at this evening meeting, but he had met with Eisenhower and Stassen in midmorning and certainly discussed the plan.

The evening meeting closed with an agreement on tactics: "[I]t would be best for the President to make a broad and basic opening statement giving his overall views in the matter, and then on the "second round" put forward the proposal for overflights as a specific, more or less spontaneous, suggestion."

Eisenhower's text and tactics were refined the next morning, but the decision to go forward with the proposal had been made.

On Thursday afternoon, July 21, Eisenhower played out the script with éclat, including its planned quasi-spontaneous passage. He proceeded about two-thirds through the Stassen draft and then interjected the following.

> Gentlemen, since I have been working on this memorandum to present to this conference, I have been searching my heart and mind for something that I could say here that could convince everyone of the great sincerity of the United States in approaching this problem of disarmament.
>
> I should address myself for a moment principally to the delegates from the Soviet Union, because our two great countries admittedly possess new and terrible weapons in quantities which do give rise in other parts of the world, or reciprocally, to the fears and dangers of surprise attack.
>
> I propose, therefore, that we take a practical step, that we begin an arrangement, very quickly, as between ourselves—immediately. These steps would include:
>
> To give to each other a complete blueprint of our military establishments, from beginning to end, from one end of our countries to the other; lay out the establishments and provide the blueprints to each other.
>
> Next, to provide within our countries facilities for aerial photography to the other country—we to provide you the facilities within our country, ample facilities for aerial reconnaissance, where you can make all the pictures you choose and take them to your own country to study; you to provide exactly the same facilities for us and we to make these examinations, and by this step to convince the world that we are providing as between ourselves against the possibility of great surprise attack, thus lessening danger and relaxing tensions.
>
> Likewise we will make more easily attainable a comprehensive and effective system of inspection and disarmament, because what I propose, I assure you, would be but a beginning.

He then picked up the Stassen draft with its recommendation for instructing the U.N. Subcommittee on Disarmament.

Thus ended almost two months of internecine strife within the federal bureaucracy in which John Foster Dulles and Nelson Rockefeller were the central antagonists, but in which a substantial part of the regular bureaucracy concerned with national security affairs was arrayed against Rockefeller and his scheme.

As for the immediate aftermath of Eisenhower's initiative, his memoirs supply the best account.[2] After describing the clap of thunder and brief failure of lighting in the hall, Eisenhower notes the hearty approval of the British and French prime ministers and the apparently sympathetic response of the nominal head of the Soviet delegation, Mr. Bulganin. As they moved to the cocktail lounge, Eisenhower walked with Khrushchev who said: "I don't agree with the chairman." Eisenhower subsequently elaborated thereafter to Khrushchev the case for aerial inspection in some detail: ". . . but to no avail. He [Khrushchev] said the idea was nothing more than a bald espionage plot against the USSR, and to this line of argument he stubbornly adhered."

Despite Khrushchev's prompt, dour, but smiling rejection, the Open Skies proposal was generally accounted a great Eisenhower success. It provided, as Dulles had predicted the second time around, drama and substance for Eisenhower's five otherwise rather barren days on the world stage; and it strongly reinforced his image as a statesman trying to lead the world toward peace.

This was not the end of the story of aerial inspection or, indeed, the beginning. At the time of the Geneva summit conference the United States was at work on a program to photograph the USSR, both from balloons and from the U-2 aircraft, then being built. Less urgent work was going forward on the possibilities of satellite photography.[3] The balloon program actually ran from November 1955 to the spring of 1956; it ended presumably because the U-2 was under rapid development. The U-2 was test-flown from an American base on August 6, 1955, and made its first overflight of the Soviet Union in July 1956. Satellite photography was not attempted until February 1959 and was conducted successfully for the first time on August 18, 1960.[4] Operations were held up, in part, because appropriate rocket boosters did not become available until the end of 1957 (THOR) and late August 1958 (ATLAS).

Of those around the table at the president's villa in Geneva on July 20, 1955, Eisenhower, Dulles, Radford, and Goodpaster certainly knew of these possibilities. There is not a line I could find in the documentary records suggesting how they viewed the Open Skies proposal in relation to the U.S.

intention to initiate unilaterally aerial inspection of the Soviet Union. One can assume that Eisenhower concluded the world would be better off if such aerial inspection were done by agreement and that the U.S. position would be stronger in the future with regard to unilateral aerial photography if the Open Skies offer were made before the U.S. flights over the USSR began.

The initial upshot of the Soviet rejection of Open Skies and of the United States proceeding with its unilateral plans was trouble. In May 1960 Khrushchev used the shooting down of a U-2 as the occasion to break up the summit conference in Paris and to withdraw an invitation for a Soviet visit. Three months later the United States successfully began regular satellite photography of the USSR. The Soviet Union reciprocated with *Kosmos 1,* launched on March 16, 1962.[5] Both sides came to accept the procedure, the Soviet Union, no doubt, after considerable uncertainty and inner debate; but, in a sense, the overflight of the United States by the *Sputnik 1* in October 1957 tended to settle the matter. It would have been difficult for the USSR to object to photographic satellites, having already set the precedent that overflight in space was to be regarded by other nations as acceptable.[6]

Indeed, Khrushchev acknowledged as much in the midst of the turbulent exchanges at the Paris summit meeting of May 1960, as Eisenhower reports:

> When I finished, General de Gaulle made the interesting observation that within the last few days a Soviet satellite had been passing over France and for all that the French had been told about the nature of the orbiting vehicle, reconnaissance photographs could have been made of all French territory.
>
> Khrushchev broke in to say he was talking about airplanes, not about satellites. He said any nation in the world who wanted to photograph the Soviet areas by satellite was completely free to do so.[7]

Thus, the world has lived since 1960 acknowledging as common law the legitimacy of a part, at least, of what Eisenhower proposed on July 21, 1955. And it has lived since 1992 with a formal Open Skies treaty, signed in Helsinki on March 24, 1992, by twenty-five states including Russia and the United States, but the Russians (along with some members of the former Warsaw Pact) have signed but not ratified the treaty.

Before turning to the considerations that took Eisenhower to Geneva and the intellectual and other controversies that suffused the six weeks or so preceding Eisenhower's thunderclap, it is worth noting that origins of the idea, so far as public policy was concerned, lay in concepts and proposals much broader than mutual aerial inspection. They were incorporated in the report of the Quantico Panel, June 10, 1955, an exercise organized by Rockefeller. Briefly, that report argued that the United States enjoyed as of

1955 a significant military advantage over the Soviet Union. The gap was narrowing and might close by, say, 1960 if present trends continued: "Because of the technological acceleration of the arms race and the nature of our adversary, we run the risk that he may, at some stage, achieve a technological breakthrough, and that at that time he would be prepared to exploit his advantage by initiating an attack on the United States. Or he might use his superiority for large-scale atomic blackmail, against the United States or other powers."

The Geneva summit should, therefore, be used as a test of Soviet intentions; the test should take the form of a series of proposals, each serious but representing a spectrum of degree of difficulty for the Soviet Union to accept unless its intentions were, indeed, pacific. The spectrum ranged from mutual aerial inspection and German unity to increased cultural and other East-West contacts. If it were established at the summit that the Soviet Union was interested in cooperation only at the lower range, that fact should be the signal for a much more energetic U.S. military and foreign policy, including enlarged assistance to developing countries. Only by frustrating in these ways the Soviet vision of closing the gap and, indeed, widening the gap to its advantage was Washington likely to persuade Moscow to undertake serious efforts toward peace as we understood it. That was the Quantico Panel's doctrine.

On Friday, July 22, Eisenhower did make a series of proposals at the lower, easier end of the spectrum, including expanded cultural exchanges and trade. But, in adopting the Open Skies initiative, there is no evidence that Eisenhower accepted the Quantico perspective as a whole. He was, of course, aware that the gap between U.S. and Soviet nuclear capabilities was narrowing. And it is difficult to reconstruct in the early years of the twenty-first century the anxiety and frustration felt by responsible American leaders in the 1950s at their ignorance of how far and how fast the USSR was moving toward nuclear parity or a superiority that might lead them to a first strike, or effective nuclear blackmail.[8] That anxiety and frustration underlay the Open Skies proposal as well as the balloons, U-2, and work on satellite photography. But Eisenhower did not view the presentation of the "hard" proposals at Geneva as a test where failure had urgent consequences for U.S. national security policy as a whole.

On the other hand, Rockefeller did accept the Quantico conception; he acted on it by organizing a second Quantico meeting in September 1955, which estimated the substantial budgetary requirements for a more vigorous U.S. response to the Soviet challenge in both military hardware and policy toward the developing regions. After his proposals were rejected by Eisenhower, Rockefeller resigned to set up the Rockefeller Brothers Fund

Panels, a bipartisan effort to establish a consensus in support of more effective domestic as well as foreign and military policy. In the wake of the Soviet launching of the first Sputnik (October 1957), a consensus of that kind did, indeed, emerge to which the reports of the Rockefeller Panels contributed. That consensus was the basis for a good many of the Kennedy initiatives of 1961–1963. But by that time the Soviet Union had narrowed much of the gap that existed in 1955 except for long-distance fusion-tipped rockets. In the post-Sputnik period the United States was psychologically on the defensive, abroad and at home.

The conflict over Rockefeller's views within the Eisenhower administration in 1955 involved elements that had little to do with concept and policy. Nevertheless, the conflict cannot be fully understood without an awareness of the larger issues—including budgetary issues—embedded within the matrix from which the Open Skies proposal emerged.

But, before dealing with these matters, it is necessary to explain briefly how the Geneva summit meeting came about.

THREE ROADS TO GENEVA: FROM MOSCOW, WESTERN EUROPE, AND WASHINGTON

As Chapter 4 made clear, a phase of postwar Soviet strategy was drawing to a close as Stalin died. For eight years Moscow had focused its external policy on maximizing the extension of Soviet power in the war-disrupted areas of Europe and Asia. Eastern Europe was consolidated, except Yugoslavia. In Asia, the Chinese mainland was under Communist rule, as was North Korea, while Communist power in Indochina was substantial. Mao was ready to turn to the tasks of his first Five-Year Plan; and there was danger that if Ho Chi Minh tried to push too far south from his northern base he might trigger American intervention—an outcome feared at the time in both Moscow and Beijing.

Only after Stalin's death did it become clear that an uneasy collective Soviet leadership was working on a new agenda, which came to rest on three questions. How should military force be reorganized in the light of fusion weapons and the possibilities of long-range missiles? What position should be adopted toward the governments and peoples of Asia, the Middle East, Africa, and Latin America as they pressed forward to assert themselves on the world scene and to modernize their societies? In the light of these two new elements, each of which profoundly affected the status of Western Europe, what policy should be adopted toward that area?

First, the new weaponry. From the moment at Potsdam in July 1945 when Truman told a well-informed Stalin that the United States had successfully tested a nuclear weapon, the Soviet Union adopted a posture of studied poise. Soviet military doctrine continued to rely on ground forces with tactical air support; and Stalin steadily reaffirmed the view—a mixture of the dogmas of a Communist and a Russian ground force soldier—that nuclear weapons had in no way fundamentally altered the "permanently operating factors" that determine the outcome of war: the stability of the rear, the morale of the army, the quantity and quality of divisions, the army's weapons, and the organizing ability of the commanding officers.

In diplomacy, the Soviets refused to entertain seriously any system for international control of nuclear weapons while the American monopoly held, and they were at a tactical disadvantage. In psychological warfare, through peace movements and other devices, by heightening the widespread sense of horror at the destructive possibilities of the new weapons, they maintained maximum political pressure on the United States not to bring to bear its briefly monopolistic advantage. Meanwhile there was feverishly intensive work to produce an atomic weapon.

There was thus virtually no overt change in the Soviet posture between September 1949, when the first Soviet nuclear weapon was exploded, and Stalin's death. The subsequent debate was accompanied, if not in fact initiated in its most serious phase, by the successful explosion of a Soviet fusion weapon in August 1953.

Fusion weapons suddenly opened up new possibilities in the field of long-range missiles. Soviet experts, like those in the United States, had been working since 1945 with German technicians and their V-2 rocket. But, until the fusion bomb was created, the long-range ballistic missile appeared as a relatively limited instrument of war. This was so primarily because the aiming error of rockets was so great and the destructive range of fission weapons so (relatively) limited that damage to chosen targets was problematic. Thus, the vastly enlarged area of destruction of the H-bomb, once its nose cone could be reduced in size to fit the nose cone of a rocket, elevated the military status of missiles. In the course of 1953 the long-range rocket for the first time became a weapon of self-evident and urgent operational interest.

At the same time, the pace of development of the Soviet strategic air command was reduced. A Ministry of Defense Production charged with the production of missiles was set up in 1953; a special Committee on Space Travel, at the highest scientific level, was set up in 1954; and the ablest minds in the four most relevant fields of basic science evidently turned with increased operational emphasis to the missile problem: fluid dynamics and heat transfer; fuel chemistry and combustion; structures and materials; electronics; and communication theory. In the course of 1954 the field of missiles technology invaded the Soviet engineering curriculum on a large scale.

This strategic decision undoubtedly appealed to Russian minds for several reasons. In the first place, although the Soviet Union had developed long-range aircraft and a long-range bombing force, it had not developed a strategic air command on anything like the scale of the American forces.

Moreover, the Second World War had not given the Russian air force experience in long-range mass flying, targeting, refueling, and navigation. Further, the American base structure and the air defense system rapidly building in North America during 1953 seemed to forecast a more or less permanent Soviet disadvantage. The Soviets may thus have felt that in relying for nuclear weapons delivery on a strategic air command they would be moving in behind a more experienced force and would be bound to remain somewhat inferior in this area. They may have felt in relation to the American Strategic Air Command somewhat as the Germans felt in relation to the British navy in the first decades of the twentieth century.

The 1953 decision to proceed at highest priority with missile development did not, however, settle post-Stalin military policy. The question arose: to what extent should the Soviet Union come to rely on the offensive and retaliatory power of ballistic missiles as opposed to modernized ground and naval forces? It is evident that in the course of 1954 the Soviet Union went through a major policy struggle in which the military fought against what they regarded as an excessive commitment of Malenkov to rely in the future on the ability to deliver nuclear weapons with ballistic missiles. Khrushchev openly argued against Malenkov on the balance of light versus heavy industry, in favor of the latter. And this abstract debate concealed an argument on the scale of the military budget and, especially, on the scale of allocations to more conventional military arms. Khrushchev's position on this matter may have gained him significant support from the military as he moved to dominance in the collective leadership.

But all this took time, and in nuclear delivery capabilities and in certain other fields the Soviet Union lagged considerably behind the United States. In the interval between the Soviet decision to give first priority to producing a missile delivery system and the time that operational tests were successfully completed—that is, from the end of 1953 to some time in 1956—Moscow pursued a policy designed to minimize the possibility of a major war. The missiles were not in place, the Soviet bomber force was under limited development at best, and American delivery capabilities remained very substantial. From the Soviet perspective this was a time for relative tranquillity on the world scene. Thus, the Indochina clash was settled on reasonable terms, and the Austrian treaty was at last signed on May 5, 1955.

On May 10 the Soviet delegation at a United Nations meeting in London proposed a phased disarmament scheme that contained a provision which would provide for an international control authority manning "control posts at large ports, at railway junctions, on main motor highways and in aero-dromes. The function of these posts shall be to ensure that no dangerous concentration of military land forces or of air or naval forces takes place."

The inspection feature represented something of a departure in Soviet policy and clearly required further exploration, although fixed inspection posts had been used in Korea and Indochina and proved a weak reed. It was in the relatively hopeful setting of the Austrian settlement and the Soviet in-spection proposals that a summit conference was finally agreed upon among the four powers.

From their point of view, the mood of relaxed tensions the Soviet nego-tiators wished to generate at the Geneva conference of 1955 had two major purposes. The first was to encourage complacency in the West and, in par-ticular, to allay anxiety concerning the Soviet maneuvers in Asia, the Middle East, and Africa, which were beginning to accelerate at just this time. The second purpose was to induce the West to diminish the attention and out-lays devoted to the arms race at a stage when the Soviets were pressing hard and hopefully to close the gap in weapons of mass destruction and to mod-ernize their ground forces as well. The published Soviet military budget of 1955 was increased from 18 to 19 percent of Soviet GNP; American military outlays for goods and services in 1955 were reduced from 11.2 to 9.6 percent of GNP.

A third element appears to have played a part in the Soviet desire for a summit conference in 1955. As leaders of their nation and, indeed, as human beings, the new Soviet rulers wished to come out onto the world stage, to demonstrate they could comport themselves appropriately, with dignity, and to be accepted as world statesmen.

This desire was, no doubt, heightened by memories of Stalin's interna-tional stature during the Second World War and of his view that his suc-cessors would be unable to deal successfully with "the imperialists." These strands clearly emerge in Khrushchev's memoirs in passages of considerable credibility:

> Right up until his death Stalin used to tell us, "You'll see, when I'm gone the imperialistic powers will wring your necks like chickens."
>
> After Stalin died it was an interesting challenge for us to try to deal with the foreign powers by ourselves. In 1955 we went abroad a number of times to meet with the representatives of the bourgeois states and to feel them out on various issues. Our trip to Geneva that year gave the bourgeois heads of state a chance to look us over. The Geneva meeting was a crucial test for us: Would we be able to represent our country com-petently? Would we approach the meeting soberly, without unrealistic hopes, and would we be able to keep the other side from intimidating us? [9]

And, again, Khrushchev recalled his reflections on the eve of his 1959 trip to the United States:

> It's not that I was frightened, but I'll admit that I was worried. I felt as though I were about to undergo an important test.
>
> We'd already passed the test in India, in Indonesia, and in England. [It was at Geneva that Khrushchev arranged with Eden to be invited to Britain.] But this was different—this was America. Not that we considered American culture to be on a higher plane than English culture, but American power was of decisive significance. Therefore our task would be both to represent our country with dignity, yet treat our negotiating partner with respect. You shouldn't forget that all during Stalin's life, right up to the day he died, he kept telling us we'd never be able to stand up to the forces of imperialism, that the first time we came into contact with the outside world our enemies would smash us to pieces; we would get confused and be unable to defend our land. In his words, we would become "agents" of some kind [10]

These symbolic and human objectives were, of course, framed by serious and more conventional considerations. Among them, as noted earlier, was the fact that in the mid-1950s Soviet policy toward Asia, the Middle East, and Africa was shifting onto a new long-term basis. The switch occurred between the time that truce negotiations began in June 1951 and July 1953, when the Korean War was brought to a close. The most corrosive dimension of the new policy, from a Western perspective, was the arms deals. It was on June 9, 1955—just before the Geneva summit—that the U.S. ambassador in Cairo informed Washington that "tentative agreements" had been reached on the Soviet sale of arms to Egypt. The deal was formalized in September. More generally, the summit conference, with its acknowledgment by the West of Soviet status as a world power, was seen in Moscow as an event strengthening its activities in the developing regions.

Soviet policy toward Western Europe in the wake of Stalin's death was, thus, to encourage European hopes about Soviet pacific intentions while the foundations of Western European strength and influence and the foundations of the North Atlantic Alliance were gradually eroded by the expansion of Soviet military strength and the disruptions induced or heightened in Asia, the Middle East, and Africa. Whereas Europe was the direct and primary focus of Stalin's offensive, Europe was a target at one remove in the Soviet policy that emerged in 1953.

The reader will recall from Chapter 4 that Malenkov made peace central to the posture of the new regime. A whole series of Soviet and Chinese Communist gestures followed. All this stirred a powerful desire in Western

Europe to enter promptly into negotiation with the Soviet Union on the abiding issues of Germany and the control of armaments, and in the summer of 1953 this desire was strongly enhanced by the explosion of the first Soviet fusion weapon. And then, in May 1955, Moscow made the most impressive gesture of all for Europeans by signing the Austrian treaty and launched its intriguing proposal for mutual inspection of disarmament agreements via fixed posts. The pressure of public opinion in Western Europe for a serious negotiating effort with Moscow mounted to a point, for example, where the British Conservatives felt it imperative to hold a summit meeting before they next faced their electorate.

As for the United States, the factors that led Eisenhower and Dulles to acquiesce in a summit meeting are tolerably clear. The completion in May of the Austrian State Treaty provided Eisenhower something of "the actual deeds giving some indication of a Communist readiness to negotiate constructively"; and, at home, support for such a gathering was on the rise, led by Walter George, chairman of the Senate Foreign Relations Committee.[11] Eisenhower concludes: "Because of the Soviets' action, and not wishing to appear senselessly stubborn in my attitude toward a Summit meeting — so hopefully desired by so many — I instructed Secretary Dulles to let it be known through diplomatic channels, that if other powers were genuinely interested in such a meeting we were ready to listen to their reasoning."[12] By June 13 formal agreement was reached, although it had been foreshadowed for some time. A week later the foreign ministers met in San Francisco on the occasion of the tenth anniversary of the signing of the United Nations Charter and went some distance in settling the procedures to be followed. Dulles' concept, as described by Eisenhower, was this: "He proposed a five-day meeting in Geneva, during which the heads of government would attempt only to define the crucial world problems and then issue a directive to the Foreign Ministers to work out the details and conduct negotiations."[13]

The notion of putting the president of the United States on the world stage for five days "only to define" the world's problems seemed neither sensible nor viable to one member of Eisenhower's staff — Nelson Rockefeller. Indeed, he had already proceeded, through correct bureaucratic channels, to set things in motion in another direction by a somewhat unbureaucratic device. We now turn to the consequences of this difference in view about what the president of the United States should do at Geneva.

THE QUANTICO PANEL: JUNE 5-10, 1955

Shortly after it was decided that a summit meeting was likely, Nelson Rockefeller and his staff organized a group of ten men to take stock of where the United States stood in the world and to recommend courses of action for the president at the summit. All were from outside the mainstream of the bureaucracies but professionally knowledgeable in one or another aspect of national security affairs. Rockefeller had succeeded C. D. Jackson as a presidential aide in December 1954. His status was somewhat more formal than his predecessor's. Rockefeller was not only a member of the Operations Coordinating Board, chaired by the undersecretary of state, Herbert Hoover Jr., but was also chairman of a special subcommittee designed "to exploit Sino-Soviet vulnerabilities." It was from this base that he launched, with Eisenhower's knowledge and agreement, the enterprise with which this chapter is mainly concerned.

Rockefeller also operated in a somewhat different way than had Jackson. He recruited a small staff, mainly within the government, headed by an army brigadier general of wide background, Theodore W. Parker. On the staff, and of considerable influence, was William R. Kintner, an army colonel also with broad experience and interests. He played a major role in suggesting the Quantico exercise, recruiting its personnel, and was present throughout.

Those participating in the Quantico venture were Frederick Dunn, director, Center of International Studies, Princeton University; C. D. Jackson, Time-Life; Ellis A. Johnson, director, Operations Research Office; Paul Linebarger, School of Advanced International Studies, Johns Hopkins University; Max Millikan, Center for International Studies, MIT; Philip Mosely, director, Russian Institute, Columbia University; George Pettee, deputy director, Operations Research Office; Stefan Possony, air intelligence specialist, Department of the Air Force; W. W. Rostow, Center for International Studies, MIT; Hans Speier, RAND Corporation; and Charles A. H. Thomson, the Brookings Institution. I was asked by Rockefeller to chair the meetings.

Jackson was present at the opening meeting on Sunday night, June 5. He returned to New York to reappear on June 8–9. A presentation of our conclusions was made to a considerable group of Washington officials on the latter evening, including Allen Dulles, Stassen, and, perhaps most important for later events, Andrew Goodpaster, Eisenhower's almost invisible but influential aide. Except for Walworth Barbour's appearance at the initial Sunday night session, no major State Department official attended.

What happened, as nearly as I can recall, was this.

After a typically discursive initial meeting on Sunday night, we spent Monday going around the table providing each member of the group an opportunity to state what he thought the report ought to contain. As one would expect, the participants brought to the occasion their accumulated intellectual capital, which proved both rich and diverse. Isolated as we were on a Marine Corps base, relatively few in number as such committees go, there was plenty of time; and, besides, it rained a good deal during the week. I believe we got through the individual statements on Monday. On Tuesday we began to weave them into the pattern of a report. Before dinner on Tuesday some clear notions had emerged, and I proposed the following.

1. The report should contain a terse summary and recommendations containing the major strategic conclusions at which we had arrived and, related to them, our proposals for the summit.
2. A relatively brief but longer text elaborating the bases for the strategy and summit proposals.
3. Appendixes underpinning major elements in the argument on which there was wide, if not universal, agreement.
4. Individual supporting papers in which each participant, in his own name, could file with the report a statement of his views on any subject he judged to be germane.

I volunteered to produce overnight a draft of the basic strategy and recommendations for the summit on which my colleagues could work the next day while I caught up on sleep. This procedure was possible because three basic ideas crystallized in the course of the Monday and Tuesday sessions.

First, a strategic conclusion. This was brought into sharp focus, in substantial part, due to the exposition of Ellis Johnson, director of the Operations Research Office, a unit working with the army in something like the way RAND worked with the air force. Johnson presented the results of a detailed study of relative U.S.-USSR technical military capabilities. It exhibited the leads and lags as of the mid-1940s and mid-1950s for types of aircraft, ordnance, tanks, electronics, and the size of the pool of scientific and technical personnel. In general, it showed a marked narrowing of the Soviet lags, where they existed, and the remarkable postwar buildup of highly trained Soviet scientists and engineers. It was the sort of analysis that was to become quite familiar later in the 1950s, notably in the wake of the launching of the first Sputnik in October 1957. Along with a good deal of other evidence laid on the table, including detailed analyses of the NATO–Warsaw Pact and the nuclear balance of forces, Johnson's exposition impressed us with the notion that the United States enjoyed, as of mid-1955, a net military advantage that was narrowing and would prove transient if current trends continued. We concluded that the summit should be used as a test of the seriousness of Soviet peaceful intentions.

Second, we hit on a method to make such a test and to do so in ways that both met the American interest in presenting itself as a power seriously interested in peace and gave the president scope for considerable personal initiative. The method was to have the president initiate during the week in Geneva a spectrum of proposals ranging from hard to soft; that is, proposals that the Soviet Union would accept only if its intent was substantially to liquidate the Cold War down to proposals that might well be accepted if Soviet interests in a pacific posture were merely transient and tactical.

At the hard end of the spectrum we suggested proposals for the unification of Germany and for graduated disarmament. It was in the latter context that the concept of mutual aerial inspections arose. The general concept behind it was that serious arms control agreements could not occur unless each side knew with some confidence the force structure of the other. Inspection had, therefore, to be tested before arms control agreements were finally concluded.

The other suggested proposals included the offer by the president of agreements to expand East-West trade, increase the freedom of persons to travel anywhere in the world for peaceful purposes, provide for free and un-hampered international communication of information and ideas, pool information and facilities for the exploration of peaceful uses of atomic energy, and generate a worldwide fund for the economic development of under-developed areas.

So far as the Quantico Panel was concerned, mutual aerial inspection was first proposed on Tuesday afternoon by Max Millikan as an element in our report. He later told Jackson that he heard the idea discussed at an arms control session in Cambridge. It was quickly seized upon and put into our spectrum of proposals. But one member of the group, Hans Speier of RAND, was disturbed. He took Possony and me aside and said that the proposal was dangerous and he would have to inform air intelligence immediately that we were thinking of putting forward the idea. (Possony was a civilian working for air intelligence and also closely associated with Rockefeller's staff.) Neither Possony nor I thought the idea dangerous, even if, as Speier guardedly implied, the United States might be generating plans for unilateral aerial photography of the USSR. I suggested that we append the following footnote at several points in the report when the proposal was mentioned: "Aside from our general assumption that before implementation all these suggestions will be considered carefully by the Departments, it is recommended that this proposal be examined with particular scepticism by the Department of Defense."

Here is the form in which mutual aerial inspection was proposed in the Quantico Panel report:

1. An agreement for mutual inspection of military installations, weapons, and armaments. Until experience has been developed on the feasibility of such inspection, this agreement would make no provision for arms

limitation. Its purpose would be to provide knowledge and evidence on the basis of which a control plan could be devised.

2. A convention insuring the right of aircraft of any nationality to fly freely over the territory of any country for peaceful purposes. The possibility of abuse of this right could be prevented by the establishment of safely located control points for the international inspection and registration of aircraft for flights across international boundaries.

The convention would be so drawn as not to interfere in any way with any nation's right to control for economic reasons commercial activities of foreign aircraft.

The third proposition on which we came to agreement followed directly from the assessment that the Soviet Union was narrowing the gap between its own and U.S. capabilities and from the notion of a spectrum of proposals to test the Soviet willingness to move forward on a peaceful basis. It was that, should the Geneva conference reveal Soviet unwillingness to deal seriously with the critical issues of arms control and Germany, as we expected it would, U.S. policy would have to face up to an enlarged military budget and a more energetic policy in other dimensions. This is how I concluded a personal letter to Rockefeller reflecting on the panel's report:

> Set this letter aside now. Perhaps Geneva will reveal that my timing is off and we can proceed directly and seriously to peace. But read it again if what we see is merely a clever playing for time, an effort to disrupt the unity and to diminish the effort of the West with gestures and blandishments. For then it will be the time to say to the American people that at the highest level we found no serious intent to end the arms race; and that the protection of our society requires a higher level of effort or sacrifice.

With these three propositions agreed to, it was not difficult to have a draft of the final report in the hands of my colleagues by breakfast on Wednesday. That morning the members of the panel refined the draft; in the afternoon, when I rejoined the group, we decided on and assigned drafting responsibilities for four major appendixes to be part of the report itself:

Appendix A — *Estimate of the Situation*
Appendix B — *Proposals to Test Soviet Willingness to Make Concessions and to Improve the U.S. Position* [including mutual aerial inspection]
Appendix C — *The German Question*
    1. — Preliminary Diplomatic Action in Preparation for the Summit Conference
    2. — U.S. Guidelines for a German Settlement
    3. — German Elections

4. — Possible Proposals for German Unity
Appendix D — *A Proposal for Graduated Disarmament*

Others went to work on their supporting papers.[14] By Wednesday evening, we were rolling along in pretty good shape.

On Thursday, the final substantive day of the conference, we worked on the drafts and prepared for the presentation of our results to Rockefeller and those who had accepted his invitation to attend the briefing. As noted earlier, Stassen, Allen Dulles, and Goodpaster were present. A good deal of time was spent on the proposal for mutual aerial inspection, which was, clearly, something of a surprise. Stassen, the senior arms control negotiator, appeared to have some difficulty understanding the rationale for the concept; but there was a general sense among our guests that, rather to their surprise, a reasonably coherent and substantive report had emerged. As we shall see, expectations had not been high in some quarters.

On Friday, July 10, the report, its appendixes, annexes, and a formal letter of transmittal to Rockefeller were duly completed, and the package went forward into the bureaucracy. The letter of transmittal included this passage: "We have no expectation that we have produced either a magic formula for positive U.S. action or a substitute for the staff considerations currently under way in the responsible Government Departments. We offer these recommendations and the papers that underlie them as a supplement to those considerations. It is our hope that responsible officials will find our efforts constructive and that use can be made of the many concrete suggestions included in the Panel results."

ACTION

FROM QUANTICO TO GENEVA: JUNE 10 TO JULY 21, 1955

The bureaucratic sequence from Quantico to Geneva, so far as the Open Skies proposal is concerned, is well set out in this chronology by Ted Parker (from papers personally released for publication by Nelson Rockefeller):

5-10 June   Quantico Panel. One of the most significant recommendations of their report was the one proposing mutual inspection, including overflight.

10-30 June   Efforts were made to generate interest in Quantico Report, particularly the mutual inspection proposal. No results. Wide distribution was made of the Report, including copies to the President, State Department, Defense Department, and Mr. Stassen.

30 June   Mr. Stassen reported to the NSC on the results of his disarmament study. No conclusion. The President

directed that an inspection system be carefully studied. [Rockefeller was not present.]

6 July

Nelson Rockefeller hand-carried to the President a memorandum strongly recommending approval of the mutual inspection proposal (as described in the Quantico Report) and use of it at the Big Four conference. The President called the Secretary of State on the telephone and expressed his interest. The Secretary said they were studying it.

11–13 July

In spite of opposition, Nelson Rockefeller arranged for himself and small staff to proceed to Paris for the period of Big Four conference (subject to call to Geneva). In preparation for the Conference, Nelson Rockefeller prepared a document, "Psychological Strategy at Geneva," copies of which were furnished the President, the Secretary of State, Mr. Dillon Anderson, and Colonel Goodpaster. The issue of disarmament was covered in this document, utilizing the mutual inspection proposal as the U.S. position. The strategy of handling the proposal was outlined, and a draft statement for use of the President drafted.

18 July

The mutual inspection proposal was discussed by Nelson Rockefeller in Paris in conference with Mr. Stassen, Mr. Anderson, Mr. Gray and Adm. Radford. Adm. Radford showed keen interest. The others showed interest, but with reservations.

19 July A.M.

Another meeting was held with Mr. Anderson, Mr. Stassen and Adm. Radford. Mr. Anderson and Adm. Radford, in a message of comments on the conference opening statements, addressed to the Secretary of State at Geneva, included a paragraph regarding the importance of the inspection issue. In the discussion following, Mr. Stassen concurred in a statement Nelson Rockefeller had drafted for the President on the subject, and suggested minor changes in the draft.

19 July

As revised, this statement was sent by Nelson Rockefeller to Colonel Goodpaster at 1315 hours. Later in the day Nelson Rockefeller and Mr. Stassen were directed to proceed to Geneva on 20 July.

20 July A.M.

The President discussed the mutual inspection proposal with Nelson Rockefeller and Mr. Stassen. He said that he had discussed the proposal at breakfast with Prime Minister Eden who was enthusiastic. The President stated that he wanted Adm. Radford to come to Geneva right away. He also said that Eden wanted Gen. Brownjohn to discuss the proposal with Gen. Gruenther.

20 July P.M.   Another meeting was held on the proposal. Present were the President, Nelson Rockefeller, Dulles, Merchant, Stassen, Anderson, Radford and Gruenther, latter three having arrived from Paris. A statement prepared by Stassen on Dulles' direction was used as basis of discussion. Dulles strongly supported proposal at this meeting.

21 July A.M.   Further conferences were held and the draft statement was polished. The tactics of presentation were planned by the President.

21 July P.M.   The President made the mutual inspection proposal in plenary session of the conference, using the prepared statement plus additional remarks along lines suggested by Nelson Rockefeller.

What the chronology does not capture is the curious bureaucratic and personal struggle that characterizes the story down to Geneva and beyond. Its central figure is Nelson Rockefeller and the opposition he generated within the Eisenhower administration in the course of 1955. There was also, as we shall see, a deep underlying anxiety on the part of John Foster Dulles about the summit meeting and what might transpire at Geneva. These had the effect of his seeking to narrow the president's role. Taken together, these concerns complicated the translation of the Quantico concept into a presidential proposal.

Dulles had been uneasy about the Quantico venture from the beginning. The beginning was in May, when agreement on a summit meeting was crystallizing. The OCB (Operations Coordinating Board), a committee at the undersecretary level in which Rockefeller participated, had approved the creation of the Quantico Panel, as had Eisenhower. The terms of reference of the panel, as understood by the president, were, however, somewhat vague. They related to the summit, but the task of the panel was defined somewhere in the ambiguous area of "psychological warfare." Rockefeller's memory of the Quantico framework, in an oral history interview, is fairly consistent with this ambiguity, although clearly the Geneva conference and what the president might do there were on his mind; and this dimension of our task was clearly transmitted to the members of the Quantico Panel. Dulles, however, defined the panel's function more vaguely: "So Ted [Parker] working with this colonel [Kintner] picked these people who were academicians and they went to Quantico for a series of sessions. Their assignment was: How do you view the world scene and world problems and what posture should the United States take? What can the President's position be?"[15]

The matter of terms of reference came to a head on May 25. The president's diary (kept from Eisenhower's dictation by his personal secretary, Mrs. Ann Whitman) includes this passage: "President said that Dulles at lunch had said that Nelson was calling a conference to determine policy to be followed at Summit Conference. President had defended Nelson saying that he had no such intention."[16] Eisenhower nevertheless called in Rockefeller, received assurances on Quantico, and called Dulles at 2:46 P.M. Notes on the conversation, made by Dulles' secretary, Phyllis Bernau, follow:

WEDNESDAY
May 25, 1955
2:46 P.M.

TELEPHONE CALL FROM THE PRESIDENT

The Pres. got Nelson in and re Quantico — it has nothing to do with the 4-Power Mtg. He has appointed himself a consultative body to study foreign reactions to things — heads of universities are on it. It advises on psychological warfare. (This sounds vague, but evidently they discussed it at lunch.)[17]

The vagueness noted by Dulles' secretary was, one can suspect, purposeful on the part of the president. On the one hand, he was not about to let the Quantico Panel or Rockefeller "determine policy," as Dulles had defined his concern at lunch; nor was he about to let Rockefeller supplant Dulles in his position of primary adviser in foreign affairs. On the other hand, he was looking for ideas and had found that the rubric of "psychological warfare" within which C. D. Jackson and Rockefeller worked in 1953–1955 could embrace the generation of some valuable substantive proposals, for example, the post-Stalin peace speech of April 16, 1953, and the Atoms for Peace proposal made at the United Nations on December 8, 1953. In short, Eisenhower was seeking to keep both men at work for him and reasonably happy. It proved rather difficult.

Rockefeller's problems with Dulles and Dulles' problems with Rockefeller were deeper than the Quantico venture. By May 25, in fact, Rockefeller indicated to the president, in response to a query from him, that in the light of his difficulties with the State Department he would consider taking the post of deputy secretary of defense. Robert Anderson had filled the job since May 1954 and indicated he wished to resign. Eisenhower had urged him to remain at his post. Here is the relevant note of May 25, 1955, from the Whitman diary:

> Later in the afternoon President asked Nelson if he had decided what to do about the job as Deputy Director of Defense. Nelson implied that it was so difficult to work with State that he might favorably consider, in case President did not urge Bob Anderson to reconsider [leaving].
>
> President didn't see how he could; later he said to acw [Mrs. Whitman] that he would write to some of his Texas friends if he knew how to put it on paper. May write, may not.[18]

In fact, Anderson stayed on until August 1955, and Rockefeller carried on as special assistant down to the end of the year.

From Dulles' point of view, Rockefeller represented an acute case of a general problem that Sherman Adams describes well in his memoir. After evoking Dulles' vivid memory of how his uncle, Secretary of State Robert Lansing, and Cordell Hull had been substantially bypassed by Wilson and Franklin Roosevelt, Adams goes on:

> Rockefeller's working methods, in contrast to those of Jackson, annoyed Dulles. Jackson had worked alone, with little or no staff. He formed his own ideas and put them to work in close collaboration with the Secretary. When Rockefeller, on the other hand, went to work on a dramatic peace plan that could be presented by Eisenhower at the 1955 summit conference at Geneva, he organized a large group of technical experts, researchers, and idea men and moved them into seclusion at the Marine Base at Quantico, Virginia, away from Dulles and the State Department. The air of secrecy around the Rockefeller operation and the number of people involved in it made Dulles apprehensive. "He seems to be building up a big staff," Dulles said to me suspiciously one day. "He's got them down at Quantico, and nobody knows what they're doing."
>
> Eventually the Quantico Panel, as the Rockefeller study group was called, came up with the open-skies inspection plan, which Eisenhower believed workable, not simply as a new weapon in the cold war, but as a possible breakthrough in the disarmament stalemate. Although Dulles would have been skeptical of any proposal coming from the Rockefeller operation, the lukewarm attitude that he took toward the open-skies plan was based mainly on his doubt that anything would come of it.[19]

Both at the time and in retrospect, Dulles' reaction to the assembly at Quantico of a rather harmless group of well-meaning characters seemed excessive, as was his reaction to Rockefeller's rather modest personal staff. But his concern was no doubt heightened by two other aspects of Rockefeller's performance. When Rockefeller decided an idea was sound and deserved advocacy, he plunged into the task of salesmanship with verve. He did, indeed, usually make sure that Dulles was informed; but he was never content to stop there.

Earlier on August 5, 1955, Dulles had raised formally with the president Rockefeller's status and method:

August 5, 1955

Personal and Private

EYES ONLY

MEMORANDUM OF CONVERSATION

WITH THE PRESIDENT

12:30

Subject: Nelson Rockefeller

I raised with the President the situation re Nelson Rockefeller, stating that I simply wanted the President to know at this stage that we were having a very difficult time working with him and that, although I was trying to work the situation out, I was not at all sure that I would be successful in doing so. I then described to the President briefly my own thinking as to the proper role that someone in Rockefeller's position should play. I said that I felt that his primary function was to screen the many ideas, written and oral, that came into the White House in the field of foreign affairs and to see to it that the worthwhile ones were put into proper Government channels for further consideration and followed up. I then showed the President the copy of the memorandum Governor Adams had given me from Nelson Rockefeller to the President outlining his staff requirements. The President expressed some surprise at the size and complexity of the proposed staff and said that he had been unaware of all these arrangements.

S RLO'Connor:mfl:ma[20]

And on August 11 Adams and Dulles discussed further "the cross they were bearing":

THURSDAY

August 11, 1955

3:05 P.M.

TELEPHONE CALL FROM GOV. ADAMS

A. asked if the Sec. had a satisfactory talk with Rockefeller. The Sec. said he didn't know — we didn't have a decisive talk. He told of some of his plans and I am not awfully happy with it. I can

live with it if it does not get any worse. It is a cross to bear. We can
get along for a while and see how it works out. The Sec. said he
does not know how long he can afford the time. A. said if the Sec.
thinks more therapy is needed, he better speak about it. A. would
like to keep it out of the boss' hair. The Sec. said he didn't mention it today to the Pres. The Sec. said he can get along until next
winter and see what happens. A. said if he thinks differently, to let
him know.[21]

Rockefeller was clearly not a man who would, in Dulles' phrase, confine
himself to "picking out nuggets from personal visits and letters"; but a more
important element in the conflict was, essentially, a matter of personality.
Rockefeller's style differed from C. D. Jackson's. Both were authentically
warm and considerate men. Both were capable of taking strong positions
and defending them before the president even against the views of the secretary of state. But Jackson dealt with Dulles (and others) with elements
of deference, compassion, supportiveness, and even flattery, all of which,
I suspect, Rockefeller felt were inappropriate between strong men bearing
serious responsibilities for public business. Rockefeller, who fought for his
ideas with exuberance, was, in his own phrase, "somewhat less than fully
restrained in my approach to life."[22]

All this helps explain Dulles' reaction to the Quantico exercise. Here, for
example, is a memorandum of a telephone conversation between Dulles and
his brother Allen (AWD) on the day of the final Quantico briefing (June 9):
"The Sec. asked if AWD is going to Nelson Rockefeller's show. Tonight.
The Sec. wants to play it down. Doesn't think much of it. AWD wondered
too. AWD did promise to go once and N. would be disappointed if he
didn't. They agreed nothing would probably come of it. The Sec. said he
[Rockefeller] went off on his own without any prior consultation. AWD will
report."[23] It also explains some of the odd situations that are outlined in
Parker's chronology given at the opening of this section.

First, there was a rather sterile interval (June 10–30) when, Parker notes
correctly, Rockefeller tried without much success to stir interest in the
Quantico report. He circulated it widely and enlisted C. D. Jackson to write
letters (on June 13) to Eisenhower and Dulles. Jackson's letter to Dulles
evokes rather vividly, in one passage, the inhospitable bureaucratic environment into which the Quantico report was inserted:

> I have just returned from the very interesting and exhilarating Quan-
> tico meeting set up by Nelson Rockefeller, and I wanted to send you this
> note to express the hope that the document produced there will not get
> too automatic a brushoff in the tepees.
> I can fully appreciate the instinctive irritation of a large number of in-

telligent, conscientious, seven-day-a-week fifty-two-weeks-a-year professionals at what may appear to them to be a one-shot, off-the-top-of-the-
head effort by some ad hoc enthusiasts.

I think the effort was considerably better than that, and merits your
personal perusal—at least the opening "Report" section.

On June 30 Rockefeller returned to his office, having, presumably, been
out of town and having thereby missed a rather important NSC meeting.
As a memorandum from Parker noted, the NSC session had been almost
wholly devoted to a discussion of a U.S. plan for disarmament. The upshot
was a directive to Stassen to come up with a "workable, satisfactory inspection system, if such exists." It was agreed that the work should not be hurried
and that results would not, therefore, be available for the Geneva summit,
less than three weeks away. Parker urged Rockefeller to recommend to the
president, Dulles, and Stassen that the Quantico mutual inspection proposal be considered in addition to the Stassen plan. About noon on July 6
Rockefeller acted on Parker's advice, hand-carrying to Eisenhower a two-
page memorandum, echoing in many respects the advice he had received a
week earlier from his staff.

Eisenhower reacted promptly, as he often did, by calling Dulles on the
telephone. Dulles' files contain the following report of the conversation:

> July 6, 1955
> 12:17 P.M.
>
> The Pres. said he just heard of an idea that might open a tiny
> gate in the disarmament fence. We set up two groups to study and
> develop a plan for immediately starting inspection of each other's
> armament now to determine the utility of the systems before we
> proceed. The Sec. said that is his idea—he told Stassen that was
> the way to get started. The Soviets so offered in their May 10 plan
> and the Sec. said we should take them up on it. It is not the last
> word but it is a beginning and would get us out of the realm of
> just thinking about it. The Sec. said he wanted to get it into our
> NSC paper. The Pres. wished he could have used it this morning
> [when disarmament came up at a press conference]. Nelson was
> in talking to him about it. The Pres. said as long as the Sec. was
> thinking of it, he was satisfied.[24]

Rockefeller's 1977 memory of the July 6 intervention with the president
is a bit more colorful:

> I went to President Eisenhower with this idea because I thought it
> was very good. The thesis was that he was going to have to take the ini-

tiative and it had to be bold and it had to be something that immediately electrified everybody because it was so conceptually sound and universal in its application and its appeal. He immediately reacted in favor of it.

And he picked up the phone which was a habit he had and said what he had said on other occasions which got me into similar trouble. He called up Foster Dulles and said, "Nelson is here and he has got a tremendous idea." He then described the idea. I couldn't hear but the President said that Foster Dulles said that they had already studied this and discarded it as being of no interest and the President should not consider it.[25]

It should be recalled that what Dulles had in mind was building on the Soviet May 10 proposal with its fixed inspection posts on the ground. On the basis of experience in Asia, Eisenhower had concluded these would be ineffective. He saw much greater opportunity in mutual aerial inspection. I would guess that it was Rockefeller's memorandum of July 6 that firmly fixed in Eisenhower's mind that there was a disarmament proposal available for him to use at Geneva, although he did not, of course, firmly decide to go forward with it until July 20–21.

As the Geneva conference came closer there were three matters for Eisenhower to settle: the strategy to pursue; the content of his talk to the American people before leaving and his opening statement at the conference; and who should accompany him to Geneva. Dulles had strong and lucid views on all of these points. He believed the president should offer no new initiatives but should confine himself to helping generate a spirit in which later detailed negotiations on such critical matters as Germany and disarmament might succeed; his preliminary talk to the American people should explicitly state that objective. Dulles' suggestions of July 13 for Eisenhower's tack on the eve of his departure for Geneva included this passage:

> . . . What is the purpose? It is not primarily to find quick solutions—quickies don't work out in these matters. They prove to be disillusioning. They give a superficial interpretation, which leads to differences in the future. These complex problems can only be finally resolved by painstaking effort, thinking out of every detail—that is the stage that has to be right. But during these ten years that have ensued since the end of the Second World War, there have been many conferences that have tried to solve problems as merely technical things. They have all been just frustrations, struggles for power, propaganda battles—to pursue the problems that way is barren.
>
> The purpose of this trip primarily is to see and help others, to generate new spirit, satisfy their longings and aspirations, demanding a way

that should be sound, sparing them and their children the devastations of another war.

Evidently, Dulles' image of the president's mission failed to answer a simple operational question: what should the president actually do in Geneva to generate a new spirit capable of suffusing subsequent technical negotiations with fresh vitality?

Given Dulles' limited view of the president's objective, only the secretary of state among the president's major advisers—not even Stassen the disarmament negotiator—was required to go to Geneva. Behind this impulse to narrow the president's role and his entourage lay not only a bureaucratic concern for the secretary of state's primacy but also deep inner fears, which he confided to C. D. Jackson at a private dinner on July 11.

After expressing some concern for the sturdiness of the British and French, Dulles, in Jackson's contemporary memorandum of conversation, went on as follows:

> "But what I am most worried about is the President. He and I have a relationship, both personal and operating, that has rarely existed between a Secretary of State and his President. As you know, I have nothing but admiration and respect for him, both as a person and as a man aware of foreign policy and conference pitfalls. Yet he is so inclined to be humanly generous, to accept a superficial tactical smile as evidence of inner warmth, that he might in a personal moment with the Russians accept a promise or a proposition at face value and upset the apple cart. Don't forget that informal buffet dinners will be the regular procedure every day, at which time I estimate the real work will be done, and it is at that time that I am particularly afraid that the Russians may get in their 'real work' with the President. . . .
>
> "The President likes things to be right, and pleasant, between people. He tires when an unpleasantness is dragged out indefinitely. . . ."

After rambling around on various details, Dulles said: "You know, I may have to be the Devil at Geneva, and I dread the prospect. . . .

> "To my mind this is much more serious than the way we have been discussing it. In fact, this is something that I have never breathed to a soul, or even intimated, and I suppose there is not anybody else I could actually say it to. My big problem is a personal problem. I am afraid that either something will go wrong in Geneva, some slip of the allies, some slip of the President's, which will put me in the position of having to go along with a kind of foreign policy for the United States which could be described as appeasement—no, appeasement is too strong a word, but you know what I mean—or, on the other hand, I may have to behave

in such a way at Geneva that my usefulness as Secretary of State, both domestically and abroad, will come to an end."

Rockefeller contested Dulles' view of the appropriate role for Eisenhower on the grounds that it was simply impossible for the president of the United States to appear passively on the world stage for five days, while leaders of other governments proposed all manner of initiatives. Here is how Rockefeller in 1977 recalled a critical confrontation on the matter:

> So at that meeting he [Dulles] said, "Now, Mr. President, the way we are going to handle this is you will go to the conference and you will identify the problem areas and then you will suggest that these be given to the Ministers of Foreign Affairs to come up with solutions for these areas."
>
> Being somewhat less than fully restrained in my approach to life I said, "Mr. President, you can't do that. This is an impossible position. Number one, the Soviets and probably the British and the French will already have come up with ideas for solutions so that you are going to be caught flatfooted and nobody is going to take seriously that General Eisenhower, President Eisenhower, comes all the way to Geneva to a summit meeting and says I am going to identify the problems and give them to the Secretaries of Foreign Affairs to solve." I said, "That is an impossible position psychologically for the world. They are all looking to you again in this time of tension for leadership."
>
> HM [Hugh Morrow]: What did Foster Dulles' face look like when you said that?
>
> NAR: I don't remember. But he said, "That is impossible, Mr. President. We have studied all these things and the way I have suggested is the way it should be." And the President said, "Nelson you have heard Foster. This is not acceptable and this is the way it is going to be."
>
> So I came back twice more at what I thought were possible openings and the third time he [Eisenhower] really got mad, as he could do, and said, "God damnit [sic], I have told you we are not going to do that. Now stop talking about it. We are not going to follow this course of action. We are going to do what Foster recommends." I said, "Yes, sir."[26]

Although this interview was evidently conducted without virtue of notes some twenty-two years after the event, it conforms closely in substance to Rockefeller's contemporary account to me of what was going on in the days before the president's departure for Geneva.

But Eisenhower didn't actually quite "do what Foster recommends." While backing Dulles formally, Eisenhower, at Rockefeller's urging, hedged his bet by sending Rockefeller, Stassen, Robert Anderson, and Admiral

Radford to Paris. Rockefeller took along to Paris several members of his staff and Possony. They were joined by George Pettee, a veteran of the Quantico Panel, who happened to be in town on other business. There is no direct evidence of which I am aware; but from the constitution of the Paris group it is possible, if not likely, that Eisenhower had in mind the Open Skies proposal as a contingency. It may be, even, that Eisenhower had quietly decided that he would make the proposal unless circumstances on the spot indicated otherwise.

Thus, the Open Skies issue was alive but unsettled as the two parties went to work in Geneva and Paris.

While decorous but sterile formal diplomatic and informal social exchanges proceeded in Geneva on July 18–19, things were a bit livelier at the Hotel Crillon in Paris, where the rear echelon was quartered.

On the eighteenth, Rockefeller, wasting no time, briefed Radford, Stassen, Anderson, and the rest of the Paris contingent on the Open Skies proposal.[27] Initially, Rockefeller made little progress, but, in the wake of an intervention by Possony, Radford firmly grasped the concept and approved it. Possony recalled for me when I was drafting this chapter, his trepidation: here he was, a modest civilian in the Pentagon, with a quite rich Hungarian accent, intervening to educate the chairman of the Joint Chiefs of Staff. As Possony remembers, Radford responded by saying: "It's a good idea. Let me take it from here."

Something almost equally important happened later on the eighteenth that is best recounted in Parker's words in a letter to me:

> Our game plan in Paris was to watch for the moment when the U.S. Delegation in Geneva ran out of ammunition. This moment came even earlier than we had anticipated. We had a staff level telephone conversation with Goodpaster late-evening (almost midnight as I remember) on Monday, July 18. I'm not sure now whether he initiated the call or me, probably the latter. We had an understanding with Andy that we in Paris would use him as our liaison in Geneva. Andy gave us the flavor of the opening day's exchanges, a sterile one as you recount, and painted a gloomy picture of the U.S. Delegation's prospects for injecting life in the proceedings. When we spoke of trying to be of some help in this respect by offering some input, he encouraged us, and we worked during the night. . . . [The drafting on the night of July 18–19 was mainly done by Kintner and Possony.]

With Radford aboard, Goodpaster encouraging, and a night of staff work in hand, things moved swiftly on the morning of Tuesday the nineteenth. Stassen and Anderson rallied in support of the idea; and a statement was drafted for the president to use on the twenty-first, formally scheduled for disarmament discussions. Two messages were then dispatched to Geneva: one from Anderson and Radford to Dulles underlined the importance of the inspection issue; the other from Rockefeller to Goodpaster, sent at 1:15 P.M., contained the agreed-upon draft statement for the president including this passage: "Inspection teams should also be free to overfly the territory of the nation being inspected, in order to determine by aerial observation the location and activity of military establishments in its territory and to make sure that none remains hidden." As the full text of that message makes clear, the proposal for providing information on the location of military establishments was less sweeping than that which Eisenhower, in fact, made on the twenty-first.

Later on the nineteenth Rockefeller and Stassen were ordered to Geneva, flying in a military aircraft. There was, apparently, no hotel space in Geneva that the American delegation could provide for Rockefeller's staff. Its members set up shop in Lausanne and commuted to Geneva in the final days of the conference.

On July 19–20, General Alfred Gruenther, commander of the allied forces of NATO, was brought into the act from two distinct directions. On the nineteenth, Radford and Anderson appear to have sought him out to brief him on what might be afoot, perhaps on Eisenhower's instructions, perhaps on their own initiative. In the wake of breakfast with Eden on the twentieth, Eisenhower asked Radford and Gruenther to come to Geneva immediately and reported that Eden wanted Gruenther and the senior British officer at SHAPE, General Nevil Brownjohn, to discuss the proposal. There was a technical problem to be resolved here: how would the proposal for exchange of information on military establishments and mutual aerial inspection relate to the existing operation of the so-called Potsdam teams? That is, representatives of the Warsaw Pact were currently permitted to travel anywhere in West Germany while reciprocal privileges were granted military teams from NATO in East Germany.

In any case, Gruenther was in Geneva for the critical meeting early on the evening of Wednesday, July 20, described at the opening of this chapter. Given his close ties to Eisenhower and the latter's respect for him, Gruenther's supporting voice was undoubtedly important. Next to Gruenther, the other most influential supporter of the proposal, apart from Radford, was probably Andrew Goodpaster. Although only a colonel in rank, Goodpaster served as a personal aide to Eisenhower with the passion for anonymity commended to Franklin Roosevelt when the concept of presidential aides was proposed by the Brownlow Committee in 1936. Goodpaster had been at the final formal session of the Quantico Panel on June 9, fully understood the

Open Skies proposal and the framework of thought that lay behind it, and had indicated his support to Eisenhower.

With all the relevant characters assembled events unfolded on July 20–21 as described at the beginning of this chapter. There was some difficulty in the drafting, which Eisenhower assigned to Stassen. Stassen appeared to resist the notion of exchanging blueprints of military establishments, but Rockefeller succeeded in restoring both elements in the Open Skies proposal. In a gracious letter of July 27, Stassen acknowledged Rockefeller's crucial role in the Open Skies initiative.

On the evening of the twenty-first, after Eisenhower's presentation, Rockefeller and his staff celebrated with, among other things, a bucket of caviar; but Rockefeller found time to dispatch cables to all members of the Quantico Panel who were not with him in Geneva.

THE AFTERMATH

Eisenhower's Open Skies initiative was generally regarded as a great success: it was concrete and understandable; it seemed to open a possible door to arms control at a time when the reality of fusion weapons had heightened anxiety; it dramatized effectively the authentic desire of the United States to move toward peace; as a piece of gamesmanship it laid before Moscow a tough question that would have to be answered; and as the French premier Edgar Faure said, Eisenhower "scored the first great victory over scepticism."

In a roundup of reactions, the *New York Herald Tribune* reported on July 22:

> Both the Senate and House, in an outburst of bipartisan acclaim, today welcomed President Eisenhower's Big-Four proposal for exchanging complete military information as a bold but practical diplomatic move sure of proving America's own peaceful intentions and certain of testing those of the Russians. . . .
>
> Bringing up a point that was frequently echoed elsewhere, Sen. [Lyndon] Johnson said the President's gesture "will test the good faith of the Communists and separate the warmongers from the peacemakers. The American people yearn for peace—peace that will maintain their traditional freedoms."

And, in general, reactions in politically open societies were similarly positive, the public enjoying what was clearly a coup de théâtre, an element in short supply at diplomatic conferences, even at the summit. And, after a brief delay, the Soviet press published the text of Eisenhower's proposal.

Approbation was, of course, by no means universal. Some of the more conservative Republican senators were clearly grumpy, as the *Washington Post* reported on July 23: William Knowland, Styles Bridges, and Eugene Millikan. Their dissidence stemmed in part from the fact that they had not been consulted. Indeed, no one in Washington was informed of the probability of the president's initiative until early in the morning of July 21 Geneva time. Given the time difference, they could, at best, have known about it only shortly before it was on the wire service ticker tapes. Senator Joseph McCarthy was openly hostile, but his day had passed by July 1955.

From a quite different perspective, James Reston of the *New York Times* was explicitly critical. Clearly the proposal had caught him by surprise. His dispatch from Geneva of July 20 portrayed accurately, no doubt from an authoritative source, the Geneva strategy as Dulles had initially defined it and which Eisenhower had formally approved over Rockefeller's objection before departure for Geneva:[28]

> The President, however, is doing precisely what he told his associates here Saturday night that he was going to do. . . .
>
> . . the President agreed with Mr. Dulles and the others that this was not the time or the place to try to get down to details. He insisted this was the place to encourage the new conciliatory line of the Soviet leaders and to try to establish personal relationships that would pay off in the later stages when the East and West were ready for detailed negotiations.
>
> He has stuck to that line all week. . . .
>
> Once in contact with the British, Soviet and French leaders, . . . he has shunned specifics like the plague and his only interventions in the debate today were general exhortations for everybody to get together.

Later in the same dispatch Reston noted the somewhat disconcerting arrival of the Paris contingent, finding different, specific reasons for the presence of each, including this for Gruenther: Eisenhower "wanted General Gruenther here for the simple reason that he likes him and wanted to play bridge with him tonight. Nobody quite believes the Gruenther story, but it's true."

His July 21 dispatch (headed "Change in Parley Course") was probably the most critical account of Eisenhower's initiative to appear in the Western press:

> The Big Four conference is declining fast. What was advertised for weeks as a realistic private discussion of conflicting national interests, and started this week as a determined demonstration of international chumminess, developed today into a propaganda battle between the United States and the Soviet Union.

There is nothing new about this so far as the Russians are concerned. They have been making propaganda since Monday.

The new thing is that President Eisenhower joined the propaganda parade today with a vengeance. He produced the only new dramatic proposal of the week. He suggested that the United States and the Soviet Union let each other know everything about each other's defense establishments. He proposed, further, that they, the Russians, fly all over the United States photographing our military establishments and that they let us do the same in the Soviet Union.

This was the surprise of the conference for a variety of reasons. In the first place it was generally regarded as unrealistic. As President Eisenhower himself said yesterday, the Soviet Union already knows almost everything it needs to know about United States defense arrangements. The Soviet leaders do not need to hand over their defense blueprints and let United States aviators photograph their country to find out what the United States is doing. . . .

Yesterday, however, a new flock of advisers arrived at the summit from Washington [sic] — Admiral Arthur W. Radford, chairman of the Joint Chiefs of Staff, Harold E. Stassen, disarmament assistant, and Nelson A. Rockefeller, White House propaganda chief. The President has been in conference with them ever since.

Whether they persuaded him to change his tactics or whether one or another of them merely threw out ideas he accepted was still a matter of speculation here tonight.

The fact is, however, that he changed his line. He is still saying that a new spirit and good faith may dissolve the contradictory East-West policies on German unity and European security but today's barrage of Soviet propaganda followed by President Eisenhower's improvisations have not improved the outlook.

There was a good deal of legitimate argument in Reston's July 21 dispatch, although one can't help feeling he was somewhat put out because, as a reporter, he had been misled unwittingly by his Geneva sources.

Eisenhower, in fact, was deadly serious about the Open Skies proposal; and his seriousness transcended Radford's perception that, if accepted, it would provide a net intelligence advantage for the United States. As Eisenhower had said to Dulles on July 6, he regarded the concept as "an idea that might open a tiny gate in the disarmament fence." And, like most serious professional military men who had lived through the transition from conventional to nuclear arms, he understood with authentic horror the meaning of the quantum jump in the powers of destruction. In a discussion about the

Atoms for Peace proposal on January 16, 1954, Eisenhower spoke in ways that clearly foreshadow the reasons for both his skepticism of the Soviet fixed-post inspection scheme of May 10, 1955, and the depth of his interest in mutual aerial inspection:

1. Meeting with the President on atomic disarmament between State and Defense. Foster Dulles, Beedle Smith, Roger Kyes, Admiral Davis, Lewis Strauss. No problems.

President very forthright and forceful making it all simple and clear, his central point being—The atomic weapon is the first weapon which ever really scared America, because for the first time American industry, which won previous world wars, could be crippled before war started. Therefore, if the atomic weapon could be completely outlawed, he would be for it, even though this would leave Russia with vast conventional superiority, because we could make up the difference through our industry ‸‸ ‸‸‸‸ ‸‸ ‸‸‸ ‸‸‸‸‸ ‸‸‸‸‸‸‸‸‸‸‸ ‸‸‸ ‸‸‸‸‸‸‸‸‸ ‸‸‸‸ ‸‸‸‸‸ ‸‸‸‸‸‸‸ ‸‸ ‸ ‸‸‸‸‸‸‸
outlawing of atomic weapons is impossible, because (a) we cannot believe the Soviets, (b) adequate inspection and control is impossible. If the Swiss and the Swedes cannot inspect North Korea, how can we inspect USSR? Therefore, argument is academic. However, let's go ahead with the atom-for-peace proposal, and if the Soviets wish to talk about atomic disarmament we will listen.[29]

In the wake of his Geneva proposal, Eisenhower knew his problem did not lie with the Senate conservatives or the *New York Times*. It lay with the Soviet leaders. He accepted the Soviet fixed-post proposal if it were combined with Open Skies; and he concentrated all his powers of persuasion in the final phase of the conference on Khrushchev, who had, in the end, agreed that the Soviet government would not "kick the idea out the window" but study it carefully, despite his (Khrushchev's) strong reservations.[30] Eisenhower's personal secretary, Mrs. Whitman, described to me, in the course of my research, a final desperate effort on July 23 after the formal adjournment. Eisenhower swept up Charles Bohlen, then ambassador to Moscow and Eisenhower's interpreter at the conference, and rushed down the corridors of the Palais des Nations to the Soviet delegation offices for one more try. The Soviet leaders had just departed.

Nevertheless, the U.S. government proceeded to follow up on the Open Skies initiative in a thoroughly professional way. At Geneva the various disarmament proposals of the four governments were referred to the United Nations Disarmament Commission, but the issue was also placed on the agenda of the meeting of the four foreign ministers scheduled for later in the year. The U.N. commission met from August 29 to October 7. Stassen presented a detailed version of Open Skies, including in his package the Soviet proposal for ground observers. On August 18, while the commission was at work, Bulganin sent a letter to Eisenhower formally confirming a position he had taken on August 4 when addressing the Supreme Soviet. Open Skies was set aside on three grounds:

1. The United States and the USSR were so vast that aerial inspection would not preclude concealment.
2. It did not provide for aerial inspection of troops and installations outside the two countries.
3. The U.S. proposals as a whole did not provide for prompt arms reductions.

Politely phrased, in the Spirit of Geneva as it was then called, the Bulganin letter did not rule out the possibility of mutual aerial inspection playing an ultimate role in arms control proposals; but it flatly rejected Eisenhower's fundamental proposition, that is, arms control measures required, as a prior condition, confidence that verification was possible and reliable. Bulganin's key passage was the following: "All this shows that the problem of aerial photography is not a question which, under present conditions, would lead to effective progress toward insuring security of states and successful accomplishment of disarmament."

Before Eisenhower could reply, he suffered a heart attack on September 24. He sent an interim response to Bulganin on October 11. The correspondence continued decorously but uneventfully into 1956, involving Germany and other matters including the Soviet offer of a bilateral Treaty of Friendship and Cooperation between the United States and USSR, offered on January 23, 1956, rejected with impeccable politeness on January 28.

For our limited purposes, the simple fact is that Open Skies was rejected by Bulganin, and his rejection was bluntly confirmed by Molotov at the sterile meeting of the foreign ministers that took place at Geneva from October 27 to November 16, 1955. Support for Open Skies (along with various other disarmament proposals) at the U.N. General Assembly gave little comfort to those who, like Eisenhower, took arms control seriously and saw in the Open Skies scheme a potential stabilizing device in a nuclear age that might, indeed, open the way for serious arms control agreements. Diplomacy having failed, aerial inspection was left to the intelligence services and the march of technology, yielding in the 1960s a tacit, but still fragile, common-law agreement that mutual satellite photography would be tolerated.

The foreign ministers' meeting in the autumn of 1955 was equally and even more unambiguously sterile on the issue of Germany, while events in the Middle East and other parts of the developing world stirred rising anxiety in Washington and Western Europe. It was increasingly clear that the Geneva summit of July 1955 had been, from the Soviet point of view, part of a strategy for quieting the West, increasing, if possible, tensions between the United States and its Western European partners, and pursuing an activist anti-Western strategy in the developing regions. The Council on Foreign Relations volume, *The United States in World Affairs, 1955,* published early in the next year, accurately summarized the state of affairs with a chapter entitled "Ascent and Descent of the 'Summit.'"

CONCLUSIONS

THE AFTERMATH — LONGER TERM

While formal U.S. diplomacy plodded its way to the end of the year with increasing disappointment, Rockefeller, who shared the Quantico Panel's view that the summit should be regarded as a test of Soviet intentions, drew immediately from the Soviet performance at Geneva the conclusion that peace was not about to break out and that the United States should begin to bestir itself. He gained Eisenhower's permission to mount a second Quantico Panel to take fundamental stock of the nation's military and political position on the world scene and to propose long-term policies to meet its weaknesses. The result is accurately described by James Desmond:

> The second Quantico conference was held September 25th to 29th. Again all the panelists were top men in their fields and in the government, and again all had to get security clearance to give them access to the top-secret material that comprised the working papers for the studies. But unlike the first meeting, which was concerned solely with preparing for Geneva, the later panel gave only incidental thought to the Foreign Ministers Conference, then being planned by the State Department, and spread its concerns over nearly all aspects of national and international affairs. Although some ideas generated at Quantico II went into the State Department hopper for use at the Foreign Ministers' meeting, the complete, 41-page, unanimous report of the panel wasn't published until December when Nelson was clearing up his desk to resign. Its circulation was restricted to government officials qualified to receive classified material.
>
> The Quantico II report was never acted on as a whole, perhaps because of its cost — $18 billion, in 1955 dollars, over six years to build up our military and economic strength around the world — but many of its concepts have since filtered into our policy. As an example, one may cite President Kennedy's buildup of conventional military forces to fight less-than-nuclear wars. The concept became commonplace by the 1960's, but

in 1955, despite the lesson of the Korean War, our military strategy was keyed almost wholly to atomic deterrence. The panel was clearly ahead of its time in this and other matters.

The report also enunciated four precepts that Rockefeller continued to regard as the cornerstones of foreign policy. These call for: full disclosure of the dangers confronting the country to rally the national will behind the government; military spending on whatever scale is necessary to make sure our defense never becomes second best; economic aid to build up the free countries so they can eventually contribute to the defense effort around the world; and constant pressure on the Communists to unmask the true intentions behind their propaganda and so-called aid programs. As a corollary to the military buildup, Rockefeller, both as Special Assistant and as Governor of New York, stressed the overriding importance of an adequate civilian defense program to impress on the Russians that our people will fight if forced to war.[31]

As 1955 wound down, Rockefeller was increasingly convinced he would have to resign. His budgetary proposals led Secretary of Defense Wilson to withdraw an offer for Rockefeller to take over as his deputy. But Rockefeller definitely made up his mind to resign after an hour's session on December 5 at Gettysburg, where Eisenhower was recuperating. The president clearly indicated that he would not act to implement the Quantico II budget recommendations. Reporting this conversation to me shortly thereafter at lunch in the MIT Faculty Club, Rockefeller noted that he found Eisenhower so restless, confined to Gettysburg, that he was sure he would run again in 1956. He also expressed a conclusion he conveyed to a good many others at that time: he would never again serve in Washington except as an elected official, a decision he was to violate by accepting the appointment in 1974 as vice president, albeit under unusual and unforeseeable circumstances.

Rockefeller evidently judged his best option was to challenge Averell Harriman as governor of New York in 1958, but he was not about to waste 1956 and 1957. Using as a base the Rockefeller Brothers Fund, over which he came to preside in 1956, he organized, with the active support of his brothers, a large-scale, public version of Quantico II, widened in scope to include education and domestic economic problems. There were six panels in all, involving almost a hundred substantive figures in American life, from both political parties: businessmen and labor leaders, foundation officials and academics, scientists and retired military men, lawyers and at least one cleric (James Pike). From the White House, Andrew Goodpaster participated. The secretariat was headed by Henry Kissinger, whom Rockefeller came to know through the Quantico II exercise. Here was the American establishment in its heyday.

The panel reports were influential to a degree in shaping policy in the late 1950s, but they were more strongly reflected in the party platforms of 1960 and in Kennedy's policies in the early 1960s. Their influence derived from two sources. First, timing was right. The launching of the first Sputnik by the Soviet Union on October 4, 1957, galvanized the country with a sense that the United States was, in some fundamental sense, falling behind the Soviet Union. In the wake of Sputnik, Rockefeller rushed to bring the interim conclusions of Panel II to Eisenhower's attention, publishing the report as a whole early in 1958 as *International Security: The Military Aspect.* The conclusions of Panel II constituted a thoroughly professional attack on the adequacy of Eisenhower's military policy and his budget. Second, and more profoundly, for reasons suggested below, a conviction gathered momentum among the leaders of American society during Eisenhower's second term that, over a wide front, the nation was not dealing adequately with its military, diplomatic, and domestic problems. The panel reports were part of a process of which the Rockefeller Brothers Fund enterprise was only one component.

So far as military policy was concerned, there had spread, by a curious and subtle process, both a knowledge of the essential military facts and a consensus on the directions in which the administration's policy ought to be changed. Leading businessmen, scientists, labor leaders, lawyers, foundation officials, military officers, journalists, professors, and unemployed politicians of both parties had begun to acquire a sufficiently firm and confident grasp on the facts to challenge the administration's policy and to formulate an alternative.

In different ways these converging processes came to a head in the Gaither Report and in the Rockefeller Panel Report II. From press accounts it would appear that those who prepared the Gaither Report had been assembled in the summer of 1957 to examine the question of whether the nation should invest large resources in the construction of shelters which would protect its citizens against fallout in case of nuclear attack. As is often the case with people engaged on a specific problem in a complex general context, their first impulse was to conclude that the narrow question could be answered only if placed in a broader setting. They sought a total picture of the existing and foreseeable Soviet threat and of American dispositions, current and prospective, to meet that threat; and they managed to act on this impulse and brought the camel into the tent.

Thus, by early October 1957, they had assembled from official sources an estimate of the total military situation and an array of recommendations for national security policy as a whole alternative to those on which the nation had been operating. The Gaither Report recommended a radical increase in military expenditure in a good many directions, and it challenged the administration view that the United States could maintain effective deterrence of Soviet military strength at the existing level and organization of the nation's military effort. In the wake of the launching of the second Soviet earth satellite, this view was laid before the National Security Council, an occasion of some historical moment since it represented in effect a charge by one wing of the Republican Party (symbolized, for example, by Robert Lovett, John McCloy, and William Foster) that those in command had not met adequately their first responsibility to the nation over the previous several years.

The substance of the consensus that had been developed on military policy in the two previous years was published shortly thereafter in the Rockefeller Panel Report II. Its conclusions reflect the precision with which a consensus had been reached outside the government on issues normally inaccessible to the democratic process unless the executive branch makes them so.[32]

Point by point, the Rockefeller Panel Report II was a public rejection of the Great Equation of 1953 — involving primary reliance on nuclear deterrence — and the specific policies that the Eisenhower administration had built upon it over the previous five years. The report rejected the notion that a healthy, recognizably American society required for the maintenance of its institutions a rigid limitation of budgetary expenditures. It rejected the concept that an ability to retaliate with nuclear weapons was a sufficient deterrent to Soviet strength. It rejected the continued denial to NATO of information about nuclear weapons and the weapons themselves. It rejected the notion that existing dispositions were sufficient to maintain American retaliatory power over the foreseeable future. It rejected the pattern of administration that had emerged during the previous five years in the Department of Defense, including the priority for and methods of handling research and development.

The clarity and detail with which these positions were articulated and the ability to get virtual unanimity on them in a group as diverse as the almost fifty signers of the Panel II report are to be understood only in the light of the process that had preceded the report over the previous three years.

In a sense, a representative group of leaders from both political parties had formed a kind of shadow cabinet in loyal opposition. With the help of experts inside and outside the government, they had done their homework on the nation's security problem; and they were able to persuade a kind of informal senate, made up of leaders from a wide range of American private institutions, to back this alternative program against the president. It is doubtful that unanimity around anything like such a program could have been achieved without the Soviet launching of the earth satellites, but the ground was well laid. There was already a substantial body of highly responsible American citizens prepared to commit themselves to an alternative program when the demonstration of Soviet capabilities was made.

It was, once again, the existence of a massive body of evidence that had been carefully analyzed before the event that permitted a unanimous report to emerge from Senator Johnson's Preparedness Subcommittee on January 7, 1958, with its fourteen-point program.

There was a similar emergence of consensus in other fields. Something clearly had to be done about the economy, which, in Eisenhower's phrase, "sputtered" during his second term, with recurrent recessions, low average growth, an emerging element of wage-push inflation, and a gold outflow reflecting a lag in U.S. productivity increase relative to Western Europe and Japan. There was similar soul-searching about the educational system, public services, and the beginnings of a consciousness that the problems of race were rising rapidly on the national agenda. And in foreign policy the concern about the military balance with the Soviet Union was matched, among a good many, by gathering awareness that we had no adequate policy to deal constructively with the developing regions, a process to be examined in the next chapter. In one way or another, Kennedy gathered all this under the spacious tent of "Let's get this country moving again" in 1960. But Nixon, mainly on his own but, as a working politician, also moved toward the new consensus as well.

This quiet crisis did not focus around one event. The Egyptian arms deal of 1955, successfully leapfrogging the Baghdad Pact, opened a phase of rolling crisis in relations between the Soviet Union and the West; but it was the related nationalization of the Suez Canal and the subsequent abortive Anglo-French effort to gain control of the canal that raised the curtain on the new period. Eisenhower wrote to a friend on November 18, 1957: "Since July 25th of 1956, when Nasser announced the nationalization of Suez, I cannot remember a day that has not brought its major or minor crisis. Crisis has now become 'normalcy.'"³³ And that was the way it was to be down to the end of his term. The major crises of the period included Sputnik and its shock waves within the Atlantic Alliance as well as at home, starting in October 1957; Lebanon-Jordan (May–August 1958); Quemoy-Matsu (August–October 1958); the revival of war in Indochina, starting in 1958; the Soviet threat of a treaty with East Germany, terminating Allied rights in Berlin, starting with a statement by Khrushchev on November 10, 1958; the emergence of Castro as a Communist closely allied to Moscow, in 1959; the breakup of the Paris summit over the U-2 incident, May 1960; and the revolt in the Belgian Congo and the struggle for its leadership, starting in July

1960. Aside from the launching of Sputnik, the related Berlin ultimatum, and the U-2 crisis, the Soviet role in these crises was marginal but significant. The Soviet leadership perceived correctly that the developing regions were in a volatile state and set out to exploit systematically the opportunities that volatility offered to diminish the power of the West and to expand its own influence.

The nuclear question was interwoven throughout that process in a quite particular way, notably after the test launching of a Soviet ICBM in August 1957 and the first Sputnik in October. Khrushchev encouraged the view that the Soviet ICBM capability was greater than it was; and this image was the backdrop to the Moscow conference, in November 1957, of the leaders of the twelve Communist parties that had achieved control over nation-states. Mao spoke for the mood of that meeting: "The superiority of the anti-imperialist forces over the imperialist forces . . . has expressed itself in even more concentrated form and reached unprecedented heights with the Soviet Union's launching of the artificial satellites. . . . That is why we say that this is a new turning point in the international situation." [34]

This was the perspective that inspired the Communist adventures which gathered momentum in Southeast Asia, the Congo, and the Caribbean and that lay behind Khrushchev's effort to translate the image of Soviet nuclear superiority into control over Berlin.

It was, of course, not quite that simple. The somewhat euphoric November 1957 meeting in Moscow also set in motion tensions between Moscow and Beijing that, from January to April 1958, brought on a definitive break over the nuclear question. [35] Moscow's differences with Beijing over nuclear matters, including the appropriate degree of risk to assume in Communist expansionist adventures, do not concern us here, but they help account for Khrushchev's maintenance of a continuing line of communication with the United States, his 1959 visit, and his efforts to keep things relatively quiet with Western Europe while he undermined the West's position in Africa and elsewhere.

What is clear in retrospect is that a good deal of the pressure on the West generated in the period 1958–1960, which presented President Kennedy with a rather formidable agenda of international troubles, stemmed from the psychological impact on both the Communist and noncommunist worlds of the Soviet launching of the first space satellite.

The U-2 did not cover enough of the Soviet Union to permit the U.S. government to be sure that Khrushchev's purposeful posturing about the Soviet ICBM capability was grossly exaggerated. As Paul Worthman observes (see note 3), the limitations of the U-2 effort are "almost shocking." Khrushchev was prepared to use to the hilt the image of the new Soviet nuclear delivery capacity, but he was under no illusion that his strength had surpassed that of the United States or—a quite distinct matter—had made war with the United States an acceptable risk. Moreover, his chosen arena for the application of Soviet nuclear leverage was Europe rather than Asia. He had real medium- and intermediate-range ballistic missiles (MRBMs and IRBMs) targeted on Western Europe rather than the fictitious ICBMs allegedly targeted on the United States.

The simple fact is that Moscow decided in 1957 not to produce ICBMs on a large scale until a more efficient model was available; but the Soviet leadership also decided that it would proceed to project to the world, for political and psychological purposes, the image of a rapidly growing, even massive ICBM capability. As the best historians of this strategy state: "Beginning in the late summer of 1957, the Soviet leaders, and chiefly Khrushchev, undertook to deceive the West regarding their strategic capabilities. The maneuver is remarkable for its deliberate and systematic character and for the relative consistency with which it was prosecuted over a period of five years."[36]

The ability of Moscow to conceal its military dispositions made this exercise conceivable. The character of the Western press and competitive American politics completed the conditions for making the exercise viable. Khrushchev was, of course, aware of the U-2 flights from 1956; but he did not think the limited U-2 routes would reveal how few ICBMs were, in fact, emplaced.

The first generation of Soviet ICBMs was clumsy. And a massive missile production effort would have interfered with the priority Khrushchev attached to rapid agricultural and industrial growth. Technology and economics argued for a delayed deployment of more efficient ICBMs while secrecy offered the possibility of deception.

The upshot was that by 1961—four years after Sputnik—only a "handful" of Soviet ICBMs had actually been deployed.[37] Yet, as of 1960, many of the world's people believed that the Soviet Union had outstripped the United States in strategic nuclear capabilities.

In August 1960 the United States Information Agency concluded: "While sophisticated political and press opinion tends to regard the current military situation as one of nuclear stalemate in which neither of the two super-powers has any material advantage over the other, the more impressionistic popular opinion has seemingly concluded from Soviet boasts of superiority and American admissions of a temporary "missile gap" that the United States is not only currently militarily inferior to the USSR but will continue to be so for the next decade or two as well."[38]

In early 1960, public opinion polls in five Western European countries showed that the following percentages of people believed the USSR to be ahead of the United States in military strength: Great Britain, 59; West Germany, 47; Norway, 45; France, 37; Italy, 32. Only in Italy did a higher percentage believe that the United States was ahead.[39] A good deal of the anxiety in the West and the high hopes generated in the Communist world could have been avoided if the United States had launched the first earth satellite, as it was quite capable of doing before the end of 1956.

The pre-Sputnik American space program was a limited affair, dominated by scientific rather than psychological and political considerations. On July 29, 1955, Eisenhower announced that the United States would undertake to orbit a satellite in connection with the International Geophysical Year—an eighteen-month period starting July 1, 1957, in which scientists would collaborate on a worldwide basis to advance knowledge of Earth and its environment.

Eisenhower notes (not quite accurately) that there was no appreciation in the United States government that the launching of the first Sputnik would have a major psychological and political effect;[40] and there was, objectively, no reason for surprise that the Soviet Union might launch the first satellite. The Soviets had made clear as early as April 1955 that they were working on a satellite; at an international meeting in June 1957, their scientists reminded their colleagues of their intention; and as early as November 1956 the American intelligence services estimated that a Soviet satellite could be launched after November 1957. When it was discovered in mid-1956 that the Jupiter booster had the capacity to launch a satellite before the end of the year, military leaders were divided but on balance wished to avoid diverting those at work on missiles. The scientists saw no reason to alter the Vanguard plan or contaminate their enterprise with a sinister military connection. Only a few sensed the emotions that would be stirred in observing for the first time a human-made object twinkling in orbit beyond Earth's atmosphere. Among them was Nelson Rockefeller. In May 1955, when the issue of a Jupiter or Vanguard missile for the first satellite launch was argued before the NSC, he circulated a memorandum throughout the government as well as to the members of the Council that included the following: "I am impressed by the costly consequences of allowing the Russian initiative to outrun ours through an achievement that will symbolize scientific and technological advancement to people everywhere. The stake of prestige that is involved makes this a race we cannot afford to lose."[41]

Rockefeller's advice was not taken. The NSC approved the Vanguard plan on the condition that it not interfere with urgent work on military missiles. The Soviets proceeded with a space program squarely based on military missiles.

CONCLUSIONS

SOME REFLECTIONS

The story of Eisenhower's Open Skies proposal of July 21, 1955, and its aftermath poses, among others, four issues of substance.

1. The role of mutual aerial inspection in U.S.-Soviet relations.
2. The problems inherent in the relations between the White House staff and the rest of the federal bureaucracy, notably the Department of State.
3. The problem of generating new ideas in a big bureaucracy.
4. The extent to which Eisenhower's failure to react vigorously to Soviet intentions, as revealed at the summit of 1955 and at the subsequent foreign ministers' meeting of October–November, contributed to the gathering crises of the late 1950s. Put another way, was the tense and dangerous phase in U.S.-Soviet relations in the six years from, say, the nationalization of the Suez Canal to the Cuban missile crisis avoidable?

Eisenhower's presentation of the Open Skies proposal in Geneva was certainly, in part, a political and psychological act. It was meant to be, and it was both praised and criticized as such. It was also a proposal that, if rejected, would make unilateral photographic reconnaissance more justifiable. And, from the perspective of Quantico I, it was part of a test of Soviet intentions. But it also raised and proposed answers to a fundamental and serious question: to what extent is mutual knowledge of military forces and dispositions of net advantage to both sides in a nuclear age? Despite Khrushchev's quick, understandable brush-off of Open Skies as an intelligence-gathering scheme of palpable net advantage to the West, there is considerable evidence that the Soviet government debated the matter seriously and over a considerable period of time; for Eisenhower's view that the proposal was, in the end, in the Soviet interest was correct in a longer-run perspective.

In the course of Bulganin's correct but sterile exchanges with Eisenhower in the wake of the summit, elements in that inner Soviet debate emerged and not always consistently. For example, Bulganin, on one occasion, evokes the danger that mutual aerial inspection would lead to unjustified complacency; on another, he considered the danger of heightened military competition:

> Finally, it is impossible not to stop and think about what would happen if we occupy ourselves with the questions of aerial photography and the exchange of military information without taking effective measures for reduction of armaments and prohibition of atomic weapons.

I have apprehensions which I cannot help but share with you. Would not such a situation lead to the weakening of vigilance toward the still existing threat of violation of the peace generated by the arms race?

It seems to us that in the present international situation and, moreover, under conditions of a completely unrestricted armaments race, the carrying out of such flights would not only fail to free the peoples from the fear of a new war, but on the contrary would intensify that fear and mutual suspicion. Judge for yourself, Mr. President: what would the military leaders of your country do if it were reported to them that the aerophotography showed that your neighbor had more airfields? To be sure, they would order an immediate increase in the number of their own airfields. Naturally, our military leaders would do the same in a similar case. It is not difficult to understand that the result would be a further intensification of the armaments race.[42]

One can be quite sure that there were a good many papers written and committee meetings held on Open Skies in Moscow. Undoubtedly, there were those who argued, simply, that the Soviet Union enjoyed a relative intelligence advantage in dealing with an adversary whose open society provided, through congressional hearings, professional journals, academic symposia, Soviet agents, and so on, such a massive and rich flow of military information. And they asked, as Khrushchev had from the beginning in Geneva, why the Soviet Union should surrender or radically reduce that advantage.

Others almost certainly argued a narrower, operational point: greater secrecy permitted the Soviet Union to pretend to greater military strength than actually existed, and this was both a deterrent to its adversaries and a pillar of support for its diplomacy. In the wake of the launching of the first Sputnik, with its astonishing and perhaps unanticipated global reaction, this argument no doubt gained ground. It is wholly understandable that, under such circumstances, Khrushchev was not anxious for the United States and the world generally to learn that Soviet ICBM capability was much less than his posturing suggested; and it is not surprising that during this period of deception the Soviet Union would seek to shoot down a U-2 on the first occasion its antiaircraft capabilities permitted it to do so.

There were, no doubt, others who understood the three fundamental arguments on the other side:

1. No serious arms control agreement was possible without reliable inspection, and aerial inspection was less intrusive than serious inspection (not fixed control points) on the ground.

2. Even without arms control agreements, mutual aerial inspection provided a means for avoiding excessive U.S. reactions to Soviet military

strength and dispositions based on ignorance and the fear that ignorance induced in a nuclear age inherently carried with it mortal danger to both sides.

3. Satellite photography provided a great deal of useful intelligence information beyond the territories of the two superpowers; and, as Sino-Soviet
relations progressively deteriorated from early 1958 forward, Moscow, no
doubt, was particularly interested in photographing China regularly.

Views on the first two of these propositions were temperately exchanged
between U.S. and Soviet officials, scientists, and others on many occasions
in the late 1950s and early 1960s. I was involved in one such set of exchanges
at a Pugwash meeting in Moscow in December 1960, with participants from
fifteen countries.

The formal position of the Soviet participants was quite clear: the degree
of inspection should be proportional to the degree of disarmament agreement. On both formal and informal occasions, some Americans present argued that a lack of information was inherently destabilizing in a nuclear age
and that even limited arms control agreements required a high degree of
confidence in their inspection provisions. If a government did not know
what its potential adversary was up to, it had, for the most primitive security
reasons, to assume the worst. In the course of a formal bilateral exchange of
views between the U.S. and Soviet participants, at the close of the general
session, Amrom Katz of the RAND Corporation engagingly made a case
for the pacifying effects of the U-2 and the destabilizing effects of its having
been shot down:

> About the U-2, much has already been said. Let me add only the fol-
> lowing—it is quite clear by now that Mr. Khrushchev and our Soviet
> colleagues knew much more about the U-2 during its entire history than
> did anyone sitting on the American side of the table. Did the U-2 fly over
> the Soviet Union for four years? Apparently.
>
> Which U-2 flights did the Soviets more damage by their standards,
> the U-2's which flew over and returned safely, or the U-2 which they shot
> down? Clearly it must be the U-2 that returned, not the one that was shot
> down.
>
> Yet I must point out that during this entire period the Soviet Union
> was engaged in serious negotiation and friendly conversation, and the
> spirit of Camp David was flying almost as high as the reputed height at
> which the U-2's flew. There is only one question I have then. Why did
> the Soviets shoot down the U-2 and spoil this nice situation and end this
> era of good will? [43]

The joke was too good not to be appreciated by the Soviet delegates, the
point too sharp to be accepted. The chief of the Soviet delegation replied,
in effect, that the USSR had to have irrefutable proof of the flights to force

the issue of their illegitimacy and, therefore, had to shoot one down at the first opportunity, meanwhile remaining silent.

In private conversations it was quite clear that some of the Soviet participants fully understood the case we were making and, in retrospect, it seems possible that they knew of and feared the playback effects on U.S. military policy of Khrushchev's propaganda projection of a Soviet ICBM capability far beyond reality. In addition, they may well have been conscious that Khrushchev's boasting generated pressures on the Soviet government from within the Communist camp to press harder against U.S. interests than was prudent from Moscow's point of view. I doubt if F. M. Cornford's minor classic, *Microcosmographia Academica,* was widely read in Moscow in the late 1950s; but one of its observations aptly matches one aspect of Khrushchev's ICBM deception: "Propaganda . . . [is] that branch of the art of lying which consists in very nearly deceiving your friends without quite deceiving your enemies."[44] In any case, some Soviet scientists and officials of the period avoided exaggerated claims of Soviet military progress and addressed the issues of arms control with evident seriousness. I do not know the weight given the judgment and advice of our more thoughtful Soviet Pugwash interlocutors in the decision finally made by the Soviet Union to accept as common law mutual satellite photography; but I can vouch that a number of Soviet officials and scientists fully understood the potentially stabilizing role of this form of inspection and the indispensable role of mutual inspection in any form of arms control, however limited.[45]

But, of course, mutual aerial inspection was no panacea. Aerial inspection proved capable of solving only one of four critical arms control inspection problems in the first twenty years of its use. It could monitor the installation of antiballistic missiles (ABMs), making SALT I possible; but it could not monitor underground nuclear testing, the installation of multiple independent reentry vehicles (MIRVs), camouflaged mobile missiles, or the degree of advance in antisubmarine warfare. I have no doubt that, for future arms control agreements to succeed, the United States and the Russian commonwealth will have to accept forms of mutual inspection that transcend satellite photography and provide much more flexible inspection on the ground than the "fixed control posts" of Soviet diplomacy of the 1950s.

Satellite photography was no panacea in another, quite different, sense as well. It did, of course, provide remarkable information to both sides on military production of certain kinds and order of battle; but rather full knowledge of Soviet military forces and dispositions did not guarantee an appropriate American policy. In the 1970s, for example, the United States government observed a rapid closing of the gap between U.S. and Soviet nuclear forces as well as a rapid and systematic expansion and modernization of Soviet conventional forces. The temper of the U.S. government and debates about the meaning of the Soviet effort delayed the beginnings of a serious response until the crises in Iran and Afghanistan, which, in the late 1970s, played, roughly, the role of the first Sputnik twenty years earlier.

Nevertheless, mutual photographic inspection remains an indispensable and stabilizing—if not sufficient—instrument of inspection if the worst is to be avoided in a nuclear age as well as the foundation for any progress that may be achieved in arms control and arms reduction in the future. Without doubt, Eisenhower understood all this and made his proposal in Geneva in deadly earnest, launching a debate in Moscow that, along with the development of the remarkable technology of satellite photography, yielded a limited but clearly salutary result.

Turning back to the curious story of how the Open Skies proposal came to life, there is embedded in it a problem that runs forward, more or less continuously, in the U.S. government from the 1950s to the 1990s. How should a member of the White House staff, engaged on aspects of foreign policy, with direct access to the president, relate to the secretary of state? As Dulles was acutely aware, the problem was much older, involving his uncle, Secretary of State Lansing, vis-à-vis Colonel House during and after the First World War, as well as Hull and Stettinius vis-à-vis Harry Hopkins and others outside the State Department a generation later. Indeed, one can trace the problem back with some legitimacy to Alexander Hamilton's challenges to Thomas Jefferson as secretary of state in the early 1790s. In the 1950s the tension centered around C. D. Jackson and, especially, Nelson Rockefeller; from 1961 forward, it centered around those who held the post of special assistant to the president for national security affairs.

A considerable literature explores this relationship, and this is not an appropriate occasion to review it. But the tension between Eisenhower and Dulles over the summit in general and, in the end, Eisenhower's need for what Rockefeller could provide do reveal, I believe, the nub of the problem: a president's role in foreign policy is, intrinsically, wider than, and in many ways distinct from, the conventional role of the secretary of state. It is not merely that the secretary of state is ultimately the president's agent; but both at home and abroad the president must be, finally, the initiator of policy. It is the president who must articulate policy in political language that effectively communicates to men and women everywhere; and who must also articulate, debate, and negotiate that policy face to face with other politically responsible chiefs of government. And that policy must embrace military and economic, psychological and political factors that transcend conventional diplomacy.

It follows that the secretary of state (and the State Department) should, ideally, fulfill three purposes: adviser to the president in these wider foreign policy functions the president alone can fulfill; coordinator of all forms of foreign policy; and conductor of conventional diplomacy. Few secretaries of state in the post-1945 era had more reason to be confident in the primacy accorded him by the president than John Foster Dulles; but, as the testimony of Sherman Adams and C. D. Jackson indicates, Dulles was an anxious man: anxious about the president, anxious about the right-wing Republican senators, anxious about those engaged in economic foreign policy and arms control, and, in this case, anxious about Nelson Rockefeller and his view of what the president confronted and the initiatives he ought to take at the summit.

Given Dulles' stature and the trust Eisenhower placed in him, it should not have been difficult for him to orchestrate the various actors over the full range of foreign policy; but, somewhat like James Byrnes, he appears to have preferred to operate with a small, intimate team rather than to reach out, exploit, and manage the foreign policy establishment as a whole, with its inevitable mixed bag of strong personalities.

Eisenhower could not wholly accept the construction of a foreign policy implicit in Dulles' conception. He brought other men into play and lived as best he could with the tensions this process set up with Dulles.

As for the summit, there appears to have been, in addition to Dulles' fears of Eisenhower's "human generosity," a simple failure of imagination on the part of the secretary. From his point of view and, apparently, the view of the State Department officers concerned, the summit was regarded as an unfortunate, unavoidable, no-win venture. The systematically negative tone of the staff papers prepared for the summit in the Department of State is illustrated by the following extract from an evaluation of Soviet prospects for achieving their objectives at the conference.

> 1. (Moral and social equality) The Soviets will probably make considerable gains in this respect. These gains can be minimized by the President avoiding social meetings where he will be photographed with Bulganin, Khrushchev, etc., and by maintaining an austere countenance on occasions where photographing together is inevitable. Also, the extent of Soviet gain could be limited by public knowledge that the occasion was being used by the U.S. to push for satellite liberation and liquidation of International Communism. Here we run into a conflict between a desire not to make the meeting into a propaganda forum and the fact that unless our position on these two topics is known, the Soviets will automatically gain very considerable advantage under this heading.

The concern reflected in this passage was by no means unjustified. It was, indeed, one of Moscow's purposes to gain increased respectability for the post-Stalin leadership at Geneva; and, once the summit was accepted, this cost to the West was unavoidable. Churlishness by the American delegation would not have helped, as Eisenhower perceived. He met the Soviet delegation with his usual human warmth. The problem with Dulles' defensive assessment lay elsewhere. It led Dulles to conclude that the best strategy was narrowly to restrict Eisenhower's role on issues of substance. He did not perceive that an American president could not spend five days as the central figure in a global drama, with his three counterparts laying on the table a wide range of more or less serious substantive proposals, and confine himself to defining problems to be negotiated down the road. This was Rockefeller's basic, correct insight. He gambled on it; and, so far as Geneva was concerned, he "won." After recounting his "defeat" on summit strategy as a whole Rockefeller goes on:

> So I went ahead with Lloyd Free and prepared the President's speech to make at the Geneva Conference. We got all the papers ready because I knew he would get into this bind and then he would have to come to this because after the others had made proposals and he was flatfooted he would be in an intolerable position. He would then remember this just as Harry Truman did on Point Four.
>
> It was written by somebody out of my office as Coordinator and Dean Acheson took it out of his acceptance [Truman's inaugural] speech. Then Clark Clifford, when the State Department had finished and there was nothing left in it, said, "Let's put that idea about Point Four of aid to other countries back in the speech. That has got more sex appeal than anything else." So the President put it back in and never told Acheson. And Acheson heard it when the speech was made.[46]

To what extent could Rockefeller have conducted his business in ways that would have served Eisenhower's purposes but avoided tensions with Dulles? Obviously, Rockefeller's sturdy exuberance did not make matters easier. Nor did the fact that, unlike C. D. Jackson, Rockefeller was evidently a man with further ambitions and potentialities for public service. And Eisenhower's reaching for the telephone and telling Dulles that Rockefeller had just come into his office with an interesting idea was not the most felicitous way to handle the evidently sensitive relationship between the two men. The root of the matter, however, lay in Dulles' unwillingness or inability to absorb and coordinate in a confident way the talents throughout the foreign policy establishment. As a number of analysts have observed, Dulles operated as a lawyer with Eisenhower as his client rather than the orchestrator of U.S. foreign policy as a whole. He intended to stay very close to his client and keep others from diluting or confusing his line of communication. But it is significant that he seriously considered asking for the post of special presidential assistant on foreign policy rather than secretary of state. And behind all this there may have been, as one element, a trait of personality that Gerard Smith captured in his oral history interview: "He was much happier with just three or four people, because I think basically he was a shy man. As far as I was concerned, I felt that it took me years to get really in his confidence. And after that, I was amazed how frank he was." [47]

It is also, perhaps, worth asking why Eisenhower did not take greater pains to organize the men he put to work in ways that avoided this kind of bureaucratic difficulty. Here, quite particularly, we come back to the problem that emerged in the wake of Stalin's death and that I summarized in these terms: despite the almost compulsive detail of the communications between Eisenhower and Dulles, their minds did not quite meet, as Dulles' anxieties about the summit suggest. Eisenhower responded to Dulles' concern about potential competitors, Rockefeller and the others; but he went on using such supplementary characters. The president and his secretary of state could never quite talk the matter out and come to a definitive understanding about it.

More broadly, Eisenhower, notably after his experience in managing the collection of semi-independent Allied ground, air, and naval commanders in the final stages of the Second World War in Europe, tended to take his subordinates as he found them, shrewdly assaying their strengths and weaknesses, keeping them in harness as best he could, and accepting as a fact of life that the relations among them would not always be a model of harmonious fraternity.

The underlying problems illustrated by this episode are, as noted earlier, by no means a unique result of Dulles' somewhat limited but monopolistic image of his mission; for example, the real or believed tensions between the president's assistant for national security affairs and the secretary of state became in the 1970s an endemic feature of bureaucratic life and gossip.

It is not impossible for the closely related but distinct sets of functions of the secretary of state and the special assistant to be performed in reasonable bureaucratic and human harmony. It requires, however, that the major actors understand that they are all agents of the president, who, alone among them, is an elected official; that they understand with sympathy the legitimacy of their respective chores; and that the president articulate and conduct with constancy policies that impart a sense that the lines of action being pursued in the various parts of government converge to well-understood purposes. But, in the end, the coherence and collegiality of the team managing foreign affairs are determined by the personalities of those whom the president chooses and by his capacity, as a leader, to keep them effectively in harness. Truman's administration was one thing when Byrnes was secretary of state, quite another when Marshall and Acheson held the post; it operated in a tense and acrimonious way with Louis Johnson as secretary of defense, but as a model of inner harmony with Robert Lovett presiding at the Pentagon.

The Eisenhower first term was not marked, as post-1945 administrations go, by particularly acute inner tensions in the conduct of its foreign policy. In part, this was the case because, relatively speaking, the period from Stalin's death in March 1953 to the nationalization of the Suez Canal in July 1956 was an interval of pause and calm in the Cold War. It was also the result of Eisenhower's political popularity and working style, which fitted well such a relatively quiet time. Nevertheless, the story of the 1955 summit and Open Skies suggests that State Department–White House relations were rather awkward despite the formidable machinery of interdepartmental staff work and cooperation that Eisenhower initiated in 1953.

Open Skies also illustrates a narrower endemic problem in the American bureaucracy that is worth noting because Dulles was conscious of it. It will be recalled that in his complaint to Eisenhower about Rockefeller on August 5, 1955, Dulles said, in his memorandum of conversation: "I recognized that the regular departments were often so tied to daily routines that they did not have time or resourcefulness in dealing with new ideas." In his oral history interview William Macomber addressed himself at some length to Dulles' view of this problem: "He [Dulles] worried a great deal about the lack of ideas in the Department. I remember one time, some people came running in. There was an international meeting coming up, and the task force had been set up in the White House to prepare for this meeting. . . . He said, 'I don't get the impression that we're coming up with the ideas. And if we don't, this Department is not going to stay on top of things.'"

Six

EISENHOWER AND KENNEDY
ON FOREIGN AID, 1953-1963

THE WHITE HATS TRIUMPH
AFTER A FASHION

INTRODUCTION

The analysis of economic development in the underdeveloped regions and participation in the formation of public policy to achieve it was a gratifying endeavor — one of the great rewarding tasks of the 1950s and 1960s. It engaged many men and women in the governments, universities, in private sectors of Western countries to lay a firm foundation for systematic aid to the developing nations.

First, there was the moral claim upon us which a good many felt as we contemplated men, women, and children caught up in poverty. We imagined what was possible if poverty was lifted from them: longer life, proper medical care, the widening of choice and fulfillment of talent and ambition that education could provide. Adam Smith said it well in the opening sentence of *The Theory of Moral Sentiments:* "How selfish so ever man may be supposed, there are evidently some principles in his nature, which interest him in the fortune of others, and render their happiness necessary to him, though he derives nothing from it, except the pleasure of seeing it." In the highest sense, the one thing economic development cannot provide is happiness; but there is enough satisfaction in seeing brought about what economic development can grant.

Second, knowledge of the process of growth made it possible to mobilize ideas and evidence to help those politicians or citizens so minded to make their case. Max Millikan and I with our colleagues at MIT once wrote a book (*A Proposal: Key to an Effective Foreign Policy,* 1959) that had some impact on policy. And we were otherwise active in policy advocacy for most of the 1950s.

Third, as a historian as well as an economist, it was natural for me to view economic development as a process that takes time — not much time once it starts, but more time than politicians, who in the normal course have to think of reelection, usually take into account. I remember arguing with members of Congress in the mid-1950s that once sustained growth began in underdeveloped countries, helped by foreign aid, in a generation or so most of these countries would be borrowing in private markets and moving off the foreign aid rolls. The congressmen did not believe me; but they grudgingly went along because other industrial countries and the World Bank were willing to try, and the Soviet Union was obviously competing with the West in Asia, the Middle East, Africa, and Latin America; but more often than not, I am bound to say they were drawn—in part of their minds—to the spirit of Adam Smith's observation about human concern for the less fortunate.

In short, foreign aid to the world's developing countries to me was worth a crusade, as was, much later, the problem of the disadvantaged in American cities (see Chapter 10).

THE KENNEDY-COOPER INITIATIVE AND ITS BACKGROUND

In the autumn of 1957 Senator John Kennedy decided to generate a bipartisan initiative that would lead to enlarged immediate and long-term international support for the economic development of India. Kennedy sought and easily achieved the collaboration of Senator John Sherman Cooper, a Republican from Kentucky who had been ambassador to India in 1955–1956. He was an older man, courteous and well mannered, but also wise and determined. From his post in New Delhi and subsequently, Cooper was a steady advocate of larger and more flexible American economic aid to India. Over the winter of 1957–1958 Kennedy consulted a variety of people knowledgeable in Indian affairs, while he and Cooper devised a formula that might permit two senators of only modest power and influence in the legislative branch to set in motion a process that might, in time, achieve their objective. The initial method chosen was a concurrent resolution of the Senate and the House of Representatives.

On March 25, 1958, Kennedy introduced to the Senate the resolution in the context of an elaborate speech of some 8,000 words on which I was privileged to help.[1] Kennedy's speech, made in the rather anxious post-Sputnik setting of American politics, with China apparently forging ahead in the Great Leap Forward, contained the following major points:

1. U.S. and Western policy is adrift, focused on Soviet and Chinese Communist achievements and initiatives, not on our own capacities and objectives.

2. As members of the opposition, many Democrats are properly searching for and proposing new initiatives related to the military balance and space (e.g., Lyndon Johnson), disarmament (Hubert Humphrey), our international role in education (William Fulbright), and other fields.

3. We lack, however, a policy to associate the West constructively with the uncommitted world "from Casablanca to the Celebes." A military response is inadequate given the fundamental economic and social problems these nations confront and their anxiety to assert their nonalignment in the Cold War.

4. India is a critically important case: it is an authentic democracy; it is seriously committed to economic and social development; its First Five-Year Plan (1951–1956) has demonstrated a capacity for progress; its performance relative to that of Communist China will have great political and ideological significance in the developing regions.

5. India's Second Five-Year Plan (1956–1961) is in danger of collapse because of a foreign exchange shortage induced, in part, by bad harvests; in part, by the import requirements for industrial expansion. U.S. assistance is far below the minimum necessary to permit the plan to be fulfilled. The question arises, therefore: "Is it not time that India and its foreign friends reach an understanding about the real scope of need?"

6. There are certain immediate, emergency measures the United States might undertake to prevent a gross failure of the Plan, but this country and India's other friends should gear their efforts to the full life of the Plan much as the United States did in relation to the process of reconstruction of Western Europe through the Marshall Plan. The concurrent resolution aims to achieve this result. Required external assistance might be of the order of magnitude of $3 billion for the three remaining years of the Plan.

7. To establish more firmly the order of magnitude of India's external needs over the life of the Second Five-Year Plan, a subcommittee of the Organization of European Economic Co-operation (OEEC) should at once be designated to go to India and "to recommend plans by which long-term assistance could be given by all member nations through an international consortium. . . . An OEEC committee, if it could include among its members persons of broad experience such as John McCloy of the United States, Sir Oliver Franks of Great Britain, Professor Tinbergen of Holland, Albert Kervin [Kervyn] of Belgium, or Erland Waldenström of Sweden, could give a powerful impetus to such an international consortium." It could also provide a model for other, later efforts, perhaps including Pakistan.

8. Kennedy then responded to four criticisms of special action for India: (a) private investment could and should do the job; (b) the program should be a joint effort for India and Pakistan; (c) the recession in the United States precluded such an effort; (d) Indian acceptance of Soviet economic assistance was problematic.

Kennedy's conclusion, incorporating the large framework in which he set the Indian problem, was as follows:

Mr. President, let us recall again the profile of the Asian continent. India, with its nearly 400 million souls, and China, a country in the neighborhood of 600 million. India contains nearly 40 percent of all the free peoples of the uncommitted world. Let us not be confused by talk of Indian neutrality. . . . Nothing serves the ultimate interests of all of the West better than the opportunity for the emergent uncommitted nations of the world to absorb their primary energies now in programs of real economic improvement.

. . . Our friendships should not be equated with military alliances or "voting the Western ticket." . . .

. . . They [the Russians] are counting on the Indian disenchantment with the inadequacy of Western assistance and democratic methods of planning and economic life.

. . . No greater challenge exists in the future than the peaceful organization of a world society which includes not only the wealthy industrial states of America, Western Europe, and Russia, but also powerful new industrial states in Asia, Latin America, Africa, and the Middle East. How these states emerge from their period of economic transition will not only color but quite likely cast the historic setting of the next generation. . . .

There is no visible political glory for either party in coming to the aid of India, particularly at a time of high taxes and pressing defense needs. . . . India today represents as great a hope, as commanding a challenge as Western Europe did in 1947 — and our people are still, I am confident, equal to the effort.

Cooper then spoke more briefly in support of Kennedy's initiative. He restated in his own way some of Kennedy's basic propositions but concluded on a distinctive note:

I have dealt chiefly with the self-interest of the United States. But I do not want to overlook the deep humanitarian impulses of our people which have led us throughout our history to help peoples throughout the world. We cannot help but know that it is inequitable if democratic countries will not move toward correcting the imbalance of opportunity and living standards which exist in different areas of the world. Humanity and justice dictate the responsibility of the United States, as a favored nation, to do its part to correct this imbalance. . . .

I should like to say, also, that I know, from personal experience, that the President of the United States, and the Secretary of State, Mr. Dulles, have continually shown their deep interest in the problems of India and Asia, and have taken the initiative in supporting their democratic efforts. And it has been evident to all that Mr. Christian Herter and Mr. Douglas

Dillon, in their positions of leadership in the Department of State, have given strong and effective support to this aspect of our foreign policy.

In our preoccupation with world communism, we may forget at times the powerful drive for freedom and independence which has swept from the Philippines, across Asia, into Africa. It offers great opportunities. It also offers some dangers. We believe that freedom will prevail, but we know that its spirit is not constantly and uniformly irresistible. The great Justice Holmes said: "The irresistible comes to pass through effort." We have submitted this concurrent resolution to suggest that the United States make its greatest effort for freedom, and in the hope that it may prevail in Asia.

The concurrent resolution was attached to Section 2 of the Mutual Security Act and thus entered formally into the congressional foreign aid debate of 1958.

As Kennedy's speech of March 25 suggested, he was quite conscious that 1958 appeared to be a difficult year for foreign aid in general and for aid to India in particular. Indeed the *New York Times* account of the Kennedy-Cooper initiative published on March 26 concludes:

> The Kennedy-Cooper resolution's chances of approval by Congress are rated slender for three reasons.
>
> First, Congress has grown increasingly hesitant about making long-term advance commitments on foreign aid.
>
> Second, the Kennedy-Cooper resolution has neither strong Senatorial backing nor a national sense of crisis about India to aid it.
>
> Third, Senatorial opinion is becoming increasingly hostile toward aid to neutralist nations like India and is generally antipathetic to all forms of foreign aid this year.

The debate is a vivid and faithful reflection of the conflicting views of the time on foreign aid in general and aid to India in particular. Although the arguments against the Kennedy-Cooper resolution were more deeply rooted, some opponents echoed the formal position taken by the Department of State in a letter of May 1, 1958, from Assistant Secretary for Congressional Affairs William B. Macomber Jr. to Senator Theodore Francis Green, chairman of the Foreign Relations Committee. Macomber expressed general support for aid to India, but concluded: "We wish to note additionally that these objectives [incorporated in the Kennedy-Cooper resolution] apply equally to many other Free World countries. As a general rule, therefore, the Department believes it desirable to avoid resolutions limited to individual countries."

In the spirit of this dictum from the Department of State Senator Bridges opposed the resolution and was, to his surprise, defeated on June 6 by a vote of 35-47 with 14 paired or not voting. The Kennedy-Cooper resolution was supported by a coalition of Democrats and liberal Republicans, opposed by a coalition of right-wing Republicans and conservative Democrats, mainly Southern Democrats. Lyndon Johnson, Senate majority leader, however, supported the resolution.

Things did not go so well in the House of Representatives. The issue had not been systematically debated on the floor; and, for a variety of reasons, the House was less sympathetic to development aid than the Senate. In the conference on the somewhat different versions of the 1958 aid bill, which concluded on June 17, the House members rejected the concurrent resolution on three grounds: lack of a House debate; their belief that existing legislation provided an adequate framework for aid to India; and reluctance to single out a particular country. Kennedy and Cooper filed formal statements regretting and rebutting the House position of substance, and chairman Green of the Senate Foreign Relations Committee, in presenting the report, noted: "[I]t was the opinion of most of the conferees on both sides that Indian economic development is of the utmost importance and the act should be administered in a manner which recognized this fact."

Thus, by mid-1958, Kennedy and Cooper had managed to carry the Senate and to heighten somewhat the priority for Indian aid in U.S. policy and public opinion. They had heartened supporters of enlarged aid to India in the executive branch and the international community, including the World Bank; they had provided an element of hope to somewhat gloomy Indian leaders; but they were a long way from their objective of creating an international consortium capable of supplying the foreign exchange required to assure the success of the Second Five-Year Plan and to grubstake the Indian development effort in the decade ahead.

THE COMMUNIST CHALLENGE, 1953-1958

It is evident that the Kennedy-Cooper initiative launched on March 25, 1958, was, in part, the product of a gathering uneasiness in American political life about both Communist policy toward the developing regions of the non-Communist world and the apparent economic momentum of Communist China. This uneasiness was heightened, as it was in military policy, education policy, and other fields, by the launching of the first Soviet Sputnik in October 1957.

A distinct and explicit Communist policy toward the developing regions had, in fact, begun to take shape as early as 1947, as prospects for a further extension of Soviet power in Europe dimmed and Stalin concluded, rather to his surprise, that Mao was likely to triumph in the Chinese civil war.

Soviet strategy appears to have had three major objectives: to buy time for the Soviet Union to develop fusion weapons and missile delivery capabilities; to weaken the ties between the United States and Western Europe (and to reduce Western allocations for military purposes) by apparently peaceful initiatives; and to expand Soviet influence in the developing regions through increased trade, loans, and technical assistance as well as more conventional forms of political penetration.

It was also a strategy that held some promise of leapfrogging or diluting the cohesion of the new military pacts formed around the periphery of the Communist world to deter another Korea-like adventure: the Southeast Asia Treaty Organization (SEATO) and the Baghdad Pact. In a larger sense, the new strategy marks the beginning of the Soviet move from status as a Eurasian power to a sustained bid for global power and influence. In 1954 the Soviet Union, in addition to expanded trade, began to offer credits and technical assistance to certain selected nations in Asia, the Middle East, and Africa. The scale and spread of Communist bloc credits and technical assistance agreements was fairly impressive, exceeding U.S. aid in a number of cases.

In general, the Soviet Union placed its credits with an eye to concrete specific advantages, both short- and long-run in character. Like military policy as reformulated after Stalin's death, Soviet economic policy toward the developing countries had the earmarks of a program mounted step by step for the long pull.

The Soviet program was conducted against a background of policy and propaganda designed to impress the governments and peoples of these areas with the rapid growth in Soviet military and technological strength vis-à-vis the United States. It was typical of this strategy that when Khrushchev and Nikolay A. Bulganin barnstormed through India in 1955 a fusion weapon was test-exploded in Central Asia.

However much Beijing may have disliked this effort to assert Soviet primacy—particularly in Burma, Indonesia, and the other areas close to China's borders—the hard facts of relative military and economic power at this period of history were accepted by Beijing up to 1958. Meanwhile, Beijing maintained its own ties and apparatus of influence in North Korea, Malaya, and Indonesia, while contesting Moscow for influence in Hanoi.

The whole communist enterprise could be presented to the developing world in what Douglas Dillon described in 1958 as a "most attractive and colorful wrapping," while the contrast with then current U.S. policy could be drawn by Soviet speakers in passages like these:

We do not seek to get any advantages. We do not need profits, privileges, controlling interest, concessions or raw material sources. We do not ask you to participate in any blocs, reshuffle your governments or change your domestic or foreign policy. We are ready to help you as brother helps brother, without any interest whatever, for we know from our own experience how difficult it is to get rid of need. Tell us what you need and we will help you and send, according to our economic capabilities, money needed in the form of loans or aid . . . to build for you institutions for industry, education and hospitals. . . . We do not ask you to join any blocs . . . our only condition is that there will be no strings attached.[2]

To the extent that the Kennedy-Cooper resolution of 1958 was a response to Communist policy, it was affected not only by Soviet and Eastern European aid and trade initiatives but also—and perhaps even more—by the image in the West of what was transpiring in the People's Republic of China in the period 1953–1958. Statistical estimates of the year by year course of the Chinese economy are difficult to construct for this period, and experts differ to a degree. But the simple, universally recognized fact is that the years 1953–1958 witnessed a surge of agricultural and industrial output, which, for complex reasons, Chinese society proved incapable of sustaining.[3] However, to a degree, the short-run momentum of the PRC was real and suggested to some that the Chinese Communists had hit upon a formula for the rapid modernization of poor, underdeveloped nations that might exert great attractive power as a model to be emulated throughout Asia, the Middle East, Africa, and Latin America.

The first Chinese Five-Year Plan was modeled on the Soviet Union's First Five-Year Plan (1928–1933). It centered on rapid expansion of heavy industries as the basis for the modernization of the Chinese armed forces; and, as in the case of the USSR, capital resources were to be extracted from a rapidly collectivized peasantry. The Chinese Communist cadres were, quite literally, instructed to take their guidance from Chapters 9–12 of Stalin's short course *History of the All-Union Communist Party,* covering both the NEP (New Economic Policy) and the Soviet First Five-Year Plan.[4]

The analogy was inexact. China as of 1952 was a much less industrialized nation than the Soviet Union of 1928; its highly labor-intensive agriculture was of a quite different character; and its people lived closer to the margin of subsistence.[5]

Mao decided in 1955 to move firmly in a quite different direction: to mobilize, motivate, and lead China's great abundant resource—its manpower— in a maximum collective surge of human effort in both industry and agriculture to compensate by political means for the nation's lack of capital. A poor harvest in 1956–1957 slowed things down but, against the background of an abundant harvest in 1957–1958, the Great Leap Forward—an effort to get the peasants to produce iron in backyard kettles—was in full cry. But the application of Mao's political and psychological theories of guerrilla war to economic development proved wasteful of resources, extremely counter-productive, and literally deadly. Perhaps 30 million Chinese may have died as a result of the Great Leap Forward. The point is that as of early 1958, when the Kennedy-Cooper resolution was launched, the Chinese economic development effort appeared to most observers a formidable, original, and apparently successful enterprise. It took several years to appreciate in the international community that Chinese development in its first phase under Mao had been a disaster.

As of 1958, however, Indian economic development since independence (1947) was much less glamorous. For one thing, India did not experience the expansion that came, as it were, automatically to China from the ending of civil war, the relinking with Manchuria, and the reactivation of idle industrial capacity. On the contrary, there were some significant economic as well as human costs to the separation of India and Pakistan on the previously unified subcontinent. Moreover, all the imperfections of the Indian development effort were open to view and, indeed, debated vigorously in the Indian press and parliament.

Conservatives (including many Southern Democrats) were largely content with the military and foreign policy posture that had emerged from the Eisenhower administration's dispositions of 1953: overwhelming reliance for deterrence on the nation's nuclear delivery establishment; emphasis on military pacts, and military aid and support as reinforcement for those pacts, to enlarge and strengthen local ground forces in sensitive strategic areas; a commending of private foreign lending as the principal source of capital from abroad; and a reserved or negative diplomatic stance toward those governments adopting a neutralist position in the Cold War. The conservative credo was framed by a general view coloring domestic as well as military and foreign policy: that budgetary restraint was a fundamental, overriding imperative.

The sufficiency of these dispositions was questioned from within, as well as outside, the Eisenhower administration from its early days. And, by the autumn of 1957, the activists, including the proponents of development aid, had, piecemeal, gained some ground. Their hand was strengthened on all fronts by the Soviet launching of *Sputnik 1* in 1957—a fact of which Kennedy was quite conscious as he began the India initiative on March 25, 1958.

IDEAS

THE GREAT DEBATE OF THE 1950S ABOUT
DEVELOPMENT AID POLICY

U.S. policy toward development aid in the 1950s evolved not only in response to policies and events in the Communist world but also, to a degree, in response to a searching debate in the advanced industrial countries on three quite complex matters: the nature of the process of modernization in developing countries; the relation of external assistance to it; and the U.S. (and Western) interest, if any, in the success or failure of the developing nations to achieve sustained growth.

It may be well to begin with the arguments against U.S. development aid; that is, aid outside the framework of U.S. military security arrangements. These arguments represented, on balance, the majority view within the Congress and the executive branch for most of the 1950s.

One version of the opposition to development aid was, in its own way, positive. It suffused, for example, the 1954 Randall Commission report on foreign economic policy—a commission made up mainly of businessmen and conservative politicians. It took the view that the task of U.S. policy was to lead the world economy, as rapidly as possible, back to an approximation of the world before 1914: liberal if not free trade; unrestricted movement of private long-term capital; convertible currencies. The pre-1914 world economy did not, in fact, operate in such an engagingly uninhibited way, but the romanticized memory of that era exercised a powerful hold over many minds. And the influence of that memory had some positive consequences; for example, it encouraged those who accepted the concept to struggle against protectionist impulses in the United States and helped set in motion the succession of global negotiations to reduce trade barriers. But, implicitly at least, this vision of the task did not recognize that distinctive and difficult problems existed in the developing regions for which free trade, free private capital flows, and convertible currencies were not sufficient immediate answers. The case for development aid was not among the Randall Commission's recommendations.

Among those who recognized the distinctive problems of the developing regions, P. T. Bauer was, without doubt, the most sophisticated analyst who took a reserved stance toward development aid and set explicit, highly restrictive economic and political criteria for expanding such aid. A Hungarian-born British academic at the London School of Economics, Bauer wrote, among other things, a short book analyzing the development process in India and urging, explicitly, the rejection of the Kennedy-Cooper resolution.[6]

Bauer argued that the West should not support the Indian Second Five-Year Plan on the dual grounds that the Indian development strategy was technically ill-conceived and that the ultimate domestic political objectives of the Indian government were contrary to Western interests.

He attacked the bias of the Indian Second Five-Year Plan toward development of heavy industries, on the one hand, and inefficient cottage industries, on the other. In his view, India, as of the mid-1950s, should have concentrated its efforts on agriculture, education, transport and other infrastructure while creating a setting in which the private sector (mainly, but not exclusively, light industry) was encouraged to expand as higher incomes in agriculture, improved transport, etc. enlarged the domestic market.

The opposition argument—notably Bauer's—was not trivial; and, indeed, certain aspects of it were shared by some who, on balance, disagreed with his conclusions. Some of his strictures on Indian agricultural policy, for example, hold up quite well in retrospect. But there was an alternative perspective on India and the developing regions as a whole in the 1950s, and alternative criteria for U.S. and Western assistance. In presenting that perspective, I shall confine this exposition mainly to work of the Center for International Studies at MIT (CENIS). It should be said immediately that the interest of CENIS in economic development analysis and policy was by no means unique. On the contrary, as the 1950s wore on, development analysis and even aid to India became something of an intellectual fad in American academic life. The policy debate on these matters was conducted on an increasingly crowded stage, including persons of experience, judgment, and sophistication that certainly matched the MIT team.

Although I am not a wholly objective judge of the matter, in retrospect I would guess Russell Edgerton's observations on the Millikan-Rostow (i.e., CENIS) proposal are more or less correct: "Nothing else on the scene in Washington rivaled the grand scale of the Millikan-Rostow proposal nor the sophistication of its presentation. . . . As the different parts of the Executive and Congress launched reappraisals of aid in different directions with different motives, Millikan and Rostow supplied them all with a common theme."[7]

The central, distinctive feature of our approach was that we placed economic growth and foreign aid systematically within the framework of the process of the modernization of societies as a whole. With some oversimplification of a reasonably complex exposition, the argument of *A Proposal,* can be paraphrased as follows:

1. The bulk of the world's population, for the first time in history, is caught up in a revolutionary transition which is "rapidly exposing previ-

ously apathetic peoples to the possibility of change." The transition presents the United States "with both a great danger and a great opportunity."

2. U.S. assistance should not aim "to insure friendship and gratitude," or "to enable the recipient countries to carry a much larger burden of military buildup against Communist armed forces," or "to stop Communism by eliminating hunger." U.S. assistance should contribute to "the evolution of societies that are stable in the sense that they are capable of rapid change without violence."

3. External economic assistance can be effective only if it is meshed with and designed in ways which contribute to the society's own efforts to move toward "political maturity."

In its widest sense, economic development is seen as a potentially constructive outlet for nationalism, a social solvent, a matrix for the development of new leadership, a means for generating at the grass roots confidence in the democratic process and for imparting a strand of reality to the concept of international solidarity.

Against this background, the proposal consisted of an international plan to generate sufficient resources to meet all requirements for external assistance which could be justified by absorptive capacity plus enlarged technical assistance to accelerate the increase in absorptive capacity. The plan was estimated to cost some $3.5 billion ($10.5 billion in 2001 dollars); that is, the receiving countries estimated ability to absorb efficiently the technology involved. It would require an extra $2 billion per annum appropriation by the American Congress for foreign aid. In mid-1950s prices the extra burden per annum would be about 0.5 percent of GNP.

Administratively it was proposed that the program be conducted mainly by existing institutions, but that the World Bank create a special instrument "to co-ordinate information, set the ground rules, and secure acceptance of the criteria for the investment program."[8]

India seemed particularly important in this context because its government, under Nehru, had decided in the wake of independence and the division of the subcontinent to accord economic and social progress an extremely high priority. And, by a kind of miracle, this vast, complex, impoverished society began its national life with an extraordinarily strong commitment to the democratic political process. Rightly or wrongly, we believed the success or failure of India with respect to both its development and its politics would be widely influential.

As for the linkage between economic development and the emergence of stable political democracies, we may, in retrospect, have been a bit too hopeful, but we were by no means naive. One CENIS publication of 1955 posed and answered bluntly the question of linkage: "Is there any guarantee that the free Asian nations will emerge from rapid economic growth politically democratic? No such guarantee can be made. The relation between economic growth and political democracy is not simple and automatic. More than that, the decisive takeoff process involves complex and often unsettling effects on societies, which must transform their institutions and ways of doing things."[9] Our consciousness of the lack of automatic linkage was heightened by knowledge of the troubled political evolution of Latin America where, on the whole, the major countries were more economically advanced than in the other developing regions.[10] Lucian Pye's work on Malaya and Burma, Dan Lerner's on the complexities of modernization in the Middle East, Ithiel Pool's on communications, James E. Cross' on guerrilla warfare in the Philippines and elsewhere also widened the perspective of CENIS' economists. Similar academic work going forward in CENIS and other institutions in the 1950s impressed on us the truly revolutionary character of the modernization process, the length of time it was likely to take, and the unlikelihood that Western-style democracies would inevitably and universally soon emerge.

On the other hand, we were firmly convinced that a concentration of scarce resources, talents, and political energies on the tasks of development was likely to maximize the chance that societies would move through the modernization process with minimum violence and human cost. The obverse of this proposition was impressed on CENIS rather directly through its short-lived Indonesia project. Sukarno was a leader who dissipated his own and his nation's resources in many directions. When Kennedy offered to support him in a World Bank consortium support for Indonesian development he said: "Development takes too long. Give me West Irian." We soon concluded that no useful purpose was served by continuing the CENIS program on Indonesia at that time.

The differing views summarized here were part of an insiders' debate among those who felt that the destiny of the developing world mattered to the West. A great many political figures (and, indeed, economists), implicitly or explicitly, simply ignored the long-run issues involved; and when politicians of negative bent were forced by events to take a position, they reached out for the kind of rationale Bauer formulated.

Nevertheless, the underlying question was serious and fundamental, and it has proved to be an abiding question: What interest did the United States and the West, as a whole, have in the fate of the developing regions which was worth the allocation of scarce resources painfully extracted from the taxpayer? After all, if one felt human, moral, or religious concern for the poor, aspiring people of the South, institutions of charity existed to which one could contribute. And if one commanded economic or other training and talents, one could go as an individual and, if accepted, work side by side with the men and women in a developing country. In the old missionary tradition, some citizens in the North during the 1950s and 1960s did these things; that is, gave money through their churches or other institutions or went to work in developing regions in the Peace Corps or similar organizations. And others turned their professional talents to the analysis of and prescription for problems in the developing regions.

These impulses, rooted in the values and culture of the West, were strong enough to constitute one strand in the effective political support for foreign aid; but, by themselves, they were clearly insufficient. The problem was to make a case for steady, long-term development aid in terms of the abiding vital interests of the United States and the West, without the spur of short-term strategic interest against the Communists.

ACTION

JFK AND THE DEVELOPING WORLD, 1951-1958

We turn now to a much narrower element in the background to the Kennedy-Cooper Resolution of March 1958: how it came about that John Kennedy, a promising young politician, decided to launch this somewhat unlikely enterprise in support of Indian economic development.

In fact, I believe it is fair to say that, to date, Kennedy and Lyndon Johnson have been the only two post-1945 presidents who not only believed that the security of America and the whole advanced industrial world was bound up in a fundamental way with the path those regions would follow, but also acted systematically on that judgment. When, for example, Kennedy defined in ten chapters of *The Strategy of Peace* (1960) the "Areas of Trial" ahead in foreign policy, eight focused on specific problems in Asia, the Middle East, Africa, and Latin America.

What accounts for this emphasis on the importance of the developing regions? On a matter of this kind one cannot be dogmatic.[11] I would guess that the following four factors are a significant part of the background to his decision to launch the 1958 resolution:

First, in the fall of 1951, he took a trip with his sister Patricia and his brother Robert, to the Middle East and Asia. This included stops in Israel, Pakistan, India, Indochina, Malaya, and Korea. This experience was clearly a benchmark shifting perceptibly Kennedy's view of the world. In his first five years as a congressman (1947-1951), Kennedy was a somewhat erratic supporter of Truman's foreign policy. He voted for most of the administration's measures (except, initially, Point Four), but he was also a rather sharp critic. The Communist takeover of China led him to attack head-on Roosevelt's decisions on Asia at Yalta as well as Truman's policy toward China. He attacked Truman's pre–Korean War military budgets as inadequate. After the Korean War began, however, he expressed fear that the United States might be so diverting forces to Asia as to be unprepared to deal with a military crisis in Western Europe, which he predicted was on its way. After a trip to Western Europe early in 1951, he gave testimony in the Senate in support of the Vandenberg Resolution assigning U.S. forces to NATO.

Although political labels often conceal as much as they illuminate, it is roughly fair to categorize Kennedy's initial positions in foreign policy as non-isolationist conservative but colored, especially in the period 1949–1951, by a fear that the 1930s were about to be replayed with Stalin in Hitler's role and the United States as inadequately prepared as pre-1939 Britain. In all this there were echoes of his experience of living in Britain during part of the 1930s and his reflections as set down in the book derived from his undergraduate thesis, *Why England Slept.* He initially felt the attack on South Korea was a feint to be followed swiftly by an attack on Western Europe by a Soviet Union which already had nuclear weapons as well as many well-placed divisions.

In 1952, after his trip to the Middle East and Asia, Kennedy's position sharply reversed. He supported assistance under the Point Four program and expressed the view that the United States had concentrated its attention excessively on Western Europe at the expense of the two-thirds of the world beyond. His statement in the House on June 28, 1952, reversing his previous position on technical assistance, is worth quoting among other reasons because it already reflects a concern for India:

> Mr. Chairman, last year when this bill was before the House, I offered a motion to cut technical assistance. But, this fall, I had an opportunity to visit southeast Asia and I think we would be making a tremendous mistake to cut this money out of the bill. . . . Asia [is] where the Communists are attempting to seize control, where the money is to be spent among several hundred million people, and where the tide of events has been moving against us. . . . The Communists are now the second largest party in India. The Communists made tremendous strides there in the last election. What weapons do we have that will stop them? The most effective is technical assistance. The gentleman from Michigan [Mr. Crawford] is right, that the amount of money involved here is not sufficient to prevent their being attracted to the Communists, but it gives them some hope, at least, that their problems can be solved without turning to the Communists. We are planning to spend a very large amount of money in this area for military assistance, which is of secondary importance compared

to this program. To cut technical assistance when the Communists are concentrating their efforts in this vital area seems to me a costly and great mistake.[12]

Robert Kennedy observed that the trip, including the visit to Indochina, had made "a very major impression on his brother,"[13] but something else had happened of importance in 1951. The widespread fear in the Atlantic world that the Korean War was a prelude to a Soviet attack in Europe had dissipated.

The second relevant factor is that the seriousness with which Kennedy began to take the developing regions after his trip in the autumn of 1951 was increasingly vindicated as the 1950s wore on. As noted in Chapter 4, the period after Stalin's death saw the emergence of a new Communist strategy addressed to the developing regions. From the Suez crisis in the autumn of 1956, that strategy, interacting with the inherent volatility of the developing regions and the inadequacy of U.S. and Western European policy yielded a succession of substantial crises. Third, quite particularly, the visit to Indochina impressed indelibly on Kennedy the corrosiveness of the French effort to maintain an imperial position against the will of the people and the opportunities French policy afforded the Communists.[14]

With respect to Algeria and North Africa, he again called on July 2, 1958, for a U.S. willingness to undertake sustained economic support for development.

The need for Kennedy to formulate and articulate a coherent foreign policy position was heightened by his assignment in January 1957 to the Senate Foreign Relations Committee. With Lyndon Johnson's support he won out in the Senate Democratic steering committee over the more senior Estes Kefauver for the seat vacated when Walter George retired.

He soon took the occasion to publish a piece in the October 1957 issue of *Foreign Affairs*, "A Democrat Looks at Foreign Policy." The article dealt with a good many matters: Germany, East-West relations, military policy, the organization of national security affairs, the role of the Congress, and the potentialities and limits of bipartisanship in foreign affairs. But nearly three-fourths of the text concerns the inadequacy of policy toward the developing regions.

Thus, as he found his feet as a senator and member of the Foreign Relations Committee in 1957, Kennedy was looking for some concrete things to do which advanced broad policies in which he believed. Chet Bowles, Hubert Humphrey, and others were talking about a Marshall Plan for India, but the political facts of life in the executive branch and the Congress made an immediate radical enlargement of long-term aid to India unrealistic. On the other hand, Kennedy perceived that the situation might be quite different if it were clear from the beginning that the United States was entering a commitment to support India shoulder-to-shoulder with the major countries of Western Europe and Japan. Multilateralism appealed to JFK—and to other senators. A communal venture looked less like a unilateral giveaway. And, besides, it eased some of the inevitable frictions between borrower and lender. Thus, as a concrete initial move, the notion of a high-level international team to survey India's needs appealed to him as a double step in a direction he wished U.S. policy to go.

What part did politics play in Kennedy's decision to use up some of his political capital in support of Indian development? I have no doubt that every substantial decision Kennedy made from, say, January 1957, forward took into account, among other things, his probable bid for the presidential nomination in 1960. As one of Kennedy's advisers, Fred Dutton, wrote: "Support for India was a cause with which "liberals" identified and that was an uncertain and inconstant constituency for him at that time. Conversely those who were opposed would have been opposed to him in any event for a host of reasons."[15]

Early in 1959 I visited Oliver Franks in Oxford. I had been a fellow of The Queen's College in 1946–1947 when he was provost. He had gone on from being an academic logician to being perhaps the most distinguished man in the civil service during World War II. I had corresponded with him from MIT about CENIS' views on foreign aid in general and on India in particular in 1956. A year later, I explained to him in Oxford the circumstances that had led to his name emerging on the floor of the Senate in the context of a speech about India. He asked why an evidently ambitious young politician was spending so much time on the Indian aid program. It did not seem to Franks a vote-getting issue. I replied that, while marginally it might help Kennedy alter his image favorably among the Democratic liberals who were giving him considerable trouble, it was basically because the question of aid to India was something important and creative that he could influence from where he was. Politics was his chosen medium; he was a senator, and this was something a senator could do that might not otherwise get done.

Once Kennedy came into focus on India, toward the close of 1957, he looked for technical help. At that time Kennedy's staff was not large, and his ties to the academic community were rather limited. Theodore Sorensen evokes lucidly how he sought supplementary assistance on substantive issues:

> The Kennedy Senate staff, even when supplemented in later years by the part-time or full-time efforts of Fred Holborn, Harris Wofford and Richard Goodwin, could not keep pace with his demand for new speech ideas and material. Professor Archibald Cox of the Harvard Law School

(later Solicitor General) headed a team of outside experts on labor reform. Professors Max Millikan and Walt Rostow of the Massachusetts Institute of Technology (the latter was later Assistant Secretary of State) were among many advisers on foreign policy. For material on a speech on nuclear tests, he directed me to call his friend Sir David Ormsby-Gore (later U.K Ambassador to the United States) in the British UN delegation. His 1954 speech on Indochina was checked with Ed Gullion of the Foreign Service (later his Ambassador to the Congo) and with an old family friend, Arthur Krock of the *New York Times* (later the chief critic of his policy in the Congo). Columnist Joe Alsop helped on a defense speech. Jacqueline translated French documents for his Vietnam speech. Law professors Freund and Howe were consulted on civil rights. Occasionally he would turn to his father's associate, New Dealer James Landis. In short, while the Senator was a brainy man, his intelligence included the ability to know his own limitations of time and knowledge and to draw on the brains of others.[16]

CENIS became Kennedy's major, but not unique, source of staff work and advice on the India resolution in November 1957. Frederick Holborn, who had joined Kennedy's staff a few months earlier, came to visit us at MIT. I remember meeting him in an office where he was already talking with Paul Rosenstein-Rodan and Wilfred Malenbaum. I joined in the discussion that went on for some time. We offered our assistance. Holborn later called to say Kennedy wished to meet me on my next trip to Washington. We had lunch on February 26, 1958, with Holborn, the day before I gave testimony before the Senate Foreign Relations Committee. Among a good many other things, we discussed the kind of questions he might raise at the Senate hearing to elicit material on India relevant to his planned initiatives with Cooper. From that time, my tie to Kennedy gradually expanded to issues beyond India and development aid.

Toward the close of 1957, Kennedy decided to commit a limited but not trivial part of his political capital to the cause of Indian economic development. Kennedy carried through, without loss of momentum, after his rather limited success in 1958, to renew the struggle in 1959.

FOREIGN AID, 1945-1952

The Kennedy-Cooper initiative was a part of the larger process, by which American foreign aid was institutionalized in a more or less stable way in the period 1945 to 1952.

The proximate beginning of the process was the agreement at Bretton Woods in July 1944 to create an International Bank for Reconstruction and Development (IBRD).[17] Behind its creation were memories of the interwar uncertainties in the flow of U.S. long-term capital exports, and the patent future capital requirements of nations damaged or disrupted by the war.

The early days of the IBRD were a study in slow motion. Its first loans were thus made to four European countries in 1947: France, Netherlands, Denmark, and Luxembourg. Its first loans to less developed countries were to Chile in 1948; Mexico and Brazil in 1949. But an institution had come to life capable of evolution in directions not initially envisaged; by 1980 the World Bank was lending some $12 billion annually for development purposes.

So far as American policy was concerned, Truman's enunciation of his fourth point, on U.S. technical and capital assistance to the developing world, in his inaugural address of January 20, 1949, was the next benchmark.

The Point Four program reflected two facts aside from a typically presidential impulse to make a mark in history in an inaugural address: the evident progress in European reconstruction as the Marshall Plan took . hold; and the gathering pressure of the less developed nations for assistance, which they came to feel was being allocated rather inequitably to the more advanced nations. The emergence from colonialism of a number of nations, including India and Pakistan, played an important role in the process, yielding also the Colombo Plan, a modest but efficient technical assistance program.[18]

The importance of the underdeveloped areas of the world to the American interest was increasingly appreciated in 1949–1950, as European recovery gathered momentum and the military position there appeared to be stabilized, while communism moved to victory in China, shaking the fragile foundations of non-Communist Asia. Acheson's speeches on Asia of January and March 1950, Gordon Gray's report in November 1950, and Nelson Rockefeller's "Partners in Progress" report of March 1951 all reflected a gathering awareness of the strategic importance to the United States of long-run development in the underdeveloped areas.[19] And in October 1951 Chester Bowles went as ambassador to India and plunged wholeheartedly into the adventure of the First Indian Five-Year Plan.

Such efforts were treated by the Congress as a low priority matter in the first half of 1950, and then they were all but overwhelmed by a short-run reality: the Korean War. For the next two and a half years, the dominant problem in Washington was the building a structure of military alliances calculated to prevent another Korean War. Included in that effort was the creation of SHAPE, which gave operating military substance to NATO. But, as Chapter 3 indicates, it was at just this time that Communist strategy and tactics began to move toward alternative, and less overtly military, means for advancing the power and influence of Moscow and Beijing. Thus, the creative and anticipatory dimension in foreign policy, symbolized by Point Four, was throttled back while the nation continued in its familiar style to institutionalize its emergency response to the current crisis.

THE FAILURE OF THE WORLD ECONOMIC PLAN, 1953–1954

Thus, the avoidance of another direct engagement of American ground forces was central to the Eisenhower administration's domestic political strategy as well as to its foreign policy. The American government after 1953 became deeply committed, in effect, to defend the national interest within the limit, if possible, that no American soldier again fight in Asia or elsewhere along the non-European periphery of the Communist world. And given the raw political effect of the Korean War, this stance of the Republican Party was quite understandable.

The Korean War had, then, a curious, paradoxical effect. The success of the American Eighth Army and its associated forces in the spring of 1951 in decimating the massed attacking armies of Communist China convinced Moscow and Beijing that the military phase of the exploitation of postwar instability was about at an end, and that a sharp shift in tactics toward diplomatic, economic, and ideological competition was called for. On the other hand, the heavy casualties, indecisiveness, and controversies of the Korean War launched the United States into a protracted phase during which, with almost obsessive single-mindedness, American diplomacy and resources were devoted to creating the kind of military arrangements around the periphery of the Communist bloc that were judged by Eisenhower most likely to discourage a second Communist venture along the lines of the Korean War.[20]

The adequacy of this policy was challenged within the Eisenhower administration as well as without from 1953 forward. The protracted debate on foreign aid for development purposes was, in a quiet way, one of the most dramatic strands in the Eisenhower administration. The unfolding of this inner struggle—in part a struggle within the minds of some of the key participants—is, perhaps, best illuminated by outlining its chronology.

Eisenhower's first articulation of a policy embracing the developing regions as a whole came in his speech of April 16, 1953, in the wake of Stalin's death: "This Government is ready to ask its people to join with all nations in devoting a substantial percentage of any savings achieved by real disarmament to a fund for world aid and reconstruction. The purposes of this great work would be: To help other peoples to develop the undeveloped areas of the world, to stimulate profitable and fair world trade, to assist all peoples to know the blessings of productive freedom."[21]

Safely protected by the caveat of prior "real disarmament," this statement had no operational consequences whatsoever. The administration proceeded to reorganize the foreign aid program in a new Foreign Operations Administration, headed by Harold Stassen. The foreign aid program, as it emerged from the Congress, consisted of appropriations of about $4.5 billion, of which 70 percent was direct military assistance, 20 percent defense support. There was a marked shift in allocations from Europe to Asia. The sums available for development assistance outside the structure of military pacts were exceedingly modest and thinly spread, as Dulles acknowledged in an address on June 1, 1953.[22]

Outside the administration, the inadequacy of these dispositions was articulated by a good many figures, including Adlai Stevenson and Chester Bowles, and within the administration, by Milton Eisenhower (for Latin America) and many of the professionals in the State Department, notably those working on Asia. As often happens in such circumstances, a presidential commission was appointed, headed by Clarence B. Randall, an articulate steel executive. It contained members of Congress as well as a representative group of citizens. Their report, which broke no new ground, was filed with the president and the Congress early in 1954.

Reflecting the balance of opinion in the Randall Commission report, Eisenhower tersely summarized his views in a March 30 message to Congress on foreign economic policy:

> Aid—which we wish to curtail;
> Investment—which we wish to encourage;
> Convertibility—which we wish to facilitate;
> Trade—which we wish to expand.

The focus was on the rapid movement of the world economy toward liberal goals in which U.S. private investment and expanded imports would permit the still present element of dollar shortage to be ameliorated and currency convertibility attained.

Congress appropriated only $2.4 billion in 1954, of which 86 percent was for military assistance and defense support. So far as the formal record showed, the only aberration was Stassen's initiative for a regional development program in Asia, the rise and fall of which was well chronicled by Richard Stebbins in his 1954 annual review of American foreign policy:

> . . . Mr. Stassen became the principal exponent of a new concept of the "Arc of Free Asia" which was said to extend from Pakistan around to Japan and to afford a possible basis for a cooperative organization like the OEEC in Europe—one in which Japan's industrial and technological preeminence would play a particularly vital role. . . .
>
> But the bold scope of these proposals aroused considerable misgivings

both in Congress and within the administration, and the scale of the proposed assistance began to be whittled down even before work on the new Mutual Security appropriation got seriously under way. . . . By the end of the month it was apparent that the overall Mutual Security request for fiscal year 1956 would be further reduced as compared with the year preceding.[23]

Stassen was not acting irresponsibly. The administration did, indeed, formally staff out and approve, with Dulles' support, the concept of a special Asian development fund. Stassen's concept of the scale of such a fund exceeded that of some of his colleagues, notably the profoundly conservative undersecretary of state, Herbert Hoover Jr.; and Stassen's advocacy was judged excessively ardent. His bit of enterprise helps explain the creation, at the end of 1954, of a new Council on Foreign Economic Policy, headed by a rather tight-fisted former director of the budget, Joseph Dodge, and Stassen's subsequent transfer to the less budgetary field of disarmament negotiations.

Beneath the surface, however, 1954 was the year in which a little-known, major, head-on confrontation occurred on the issue of development aid at the highest level of the Eisenhower administration.[24]

The battle began on March 25. John Foster Dulles invited to lunch C. D. Jackson, with whom Millikan and I had been in touch on a number of matters, including foreign aid policy. Jackson, after service on the White House staff since January 20, 1953, was about to return to a post in the Luce magazine empire. Robert Bowie, head of the State Department Planning Staff and one of Dulles' closest advisers, was also present. In his diary Jackson made the following terse entry:

> JFD asked me to lunch with him and Bowie [a trusted aide of Foster Dulles and a fellow conspirator on behalf of foreign aid]. Discussed sad state of affairs. He repeated the statement that only real things done in foreign policy had been April and Dec. speeches [Eisenhower's April 16, 1953, speech in the wake of Stalin's death and his Atoms for Peace speech of December 8, in the design of which Jackson was a central figure]. Asked for a new idea. Uncorked world economic plan and new Princeton Conference.[25] Very enthusiastically received. Later went over possible names with Bowie.[26]

As I recall Jackson's contemporary account of the lunch, Dulles was deeply depressed by the impending setback in Indochina and the gathering momentum of the Soviet economic and political offensive in the developing regions. He said that, as secretary of state, he was being forced to defend the interests of the United States with one arm tied behind his back; namely, the nation's economic strength. U.S. military power—the other arm—was not enough and was, indeed, largely unusable. Dulles asked for Jackson's help.

On March 30 Jackson had lunch with Millikan and solicited his assistance in organizing the proposed Princeton meeting.

In the peaceful setting of Princeton Inn a rough-and-ready consensus did emerge that an enlarged global initiative by the United States in support of development was required. Among those present from inside the government were Allen Dulles, chief of the CIA; Robert Cutler, the president's special assistant on national security; and officials of the Treasury and foreign aid. From outside, David Macdonald, head of the steelworkers union; Edward Mason of Harvard; and Max Millikan and I of MIT. On the basis of some preliminary drafting on the night of May 15, Millikan and I were commissioned to produce a coherent proposal. A paper of fifty-two pages, entitled "A Proposal for a New United States Foreign Economic Policy," was finished by July 23. This essay contained essentially the same calculations on the order of magnitude of required development aid as those published three years later in Millikan's and my book, *A Proposal*. It was the July 23 draft that circulated widely through the executive branch in the summer of 1954 and became the focus of intense debate. Jackson, with the assistance of John Jessup of *Life* magazine, Millikan, and myself, drafted, early in August, a speech for Eisenhower that might have launched the enterprise.

The speech draft and the text of the proposal on which it was based were sent to Robert Cutler, director of the NSC staff, Brigadier General Paul ("Pete") Carroll, a presidential aide, as well as to Allen Dulles. Cutler, who attended the Princeton meeting, appeared to be in strong support and passed the documents to John Eisenhower "to interest his father."[27] On August 7 Jackson had a long session with John Foster Dulles in which the difficulties began to emerge:

> Two and a half hours with Foster, starting with Beaver [World Economic Plan], which he is all for although had not given it full reading yet, but promised to do it over the weekend. . . .
>
> Raised difficulties regarding presenting such a package while Congress was away, and without pre-conditioning. Also difficulty of economy-minded Congress against further grants. Countered by telling him that if President wanted to he could call in carefully selected group of Congressmen and Senators before adjournment and tell them what he proposed to do. . . .
>
> Argued back and forth with Foster repeatedly saying, "Don't misunderstand me, I am for this, not against it."

Then got into real hair-down session on Administration, Prexy [the president], and foreign policy. . . .

JFD is sincerely devoted to Prexy, but makes two important points:

1. When JFD is away, Prexy falls apart from other pressures;

2. His exaggerated desire to have everybody happy, everybody like him, prevents him from making clean cut decisions and forces him to play ball with the last person he has listened to.

Conclusion: Is wonderful man, every right instinct, the man to fulfill Arthur Vandenberg's 'bipartisan leadership America-out-of-crisis' dream. May well go down to ignominy and defeat."[28]

On August 11 Jackson spent three quarters of an hour with Eisenhower. The meeting reveals clashing concepts of leadership and administration. Jackson's account is worth quoting at length:

. . . I have lived through fifteen months of what I would call foreign policy by Presidential speech, with no follow-through afterwards, and I know it doesn't work. . . .

For instance, you will be told that it will be difficult to put this plan across with Congress. All right. Difficulty with Congress is an occupational hazard for the President of the United States. It is built in. For me or anybody else to propose something to you that was NOT going to make difficulty with Congress would be to suggest something ridiculous or innocuous that no one will pay any attention. . . .

What you need is something that will capture the imagination. The prestige of the United States is at a low point today, and will not be captured or enhanced by dribbling out little bits and pieces. . . .

If there is action and follow-through, then the psychological warfare boys can do things. But if they are expected to do things in a vacuum and then nothing happens, you might as well not have them around.

The President seemed to take it all right. . . . We fenced around for a bit, and then the President said, "Look, I don't want to force you to come down here. You have been here for more than a year, more than you agreed to originally, and I am grateful for that, and I certainly don't want to drag you away from anything. But what happens in this Government is that unless there is one person in the setup who is really concerned about these things and pulls the others together, things just simply don't get done—and that is the lack and that is what I would like to have you do . . . then I would relieve Pete Carroll of his present duties and he would be sort of in residence and be able to follow through, and you and he could check with each other, and I think we could get somewhere."[29]

In terms of style the clash of conceptions is clear: Jackson requested an unambiguous command decision from the president that would force unified action; Eisenhower envisaged a subordinate who would "pull the others together" into consensus.

By August 16, Eisenhower, having read the speech draft and the supporting papers, sent Jackson the following serious but troubled reply:

> The new concept in your paper is the breadth and depth of your attack; but that these factors make the entire project something new and different will be difficult to sell.
>
> The question in my mind is whether these two considerations — (a) to educate our own people, and (b) to have a dramatic effect upon the world — do not create considerable difficulties in the exact terminology of the initial speech.[30]

Jackson responded, in effect, to Eisenhower's concerns in a letter to Dulles with a copy sent to Carroll at the White House.[31] A letter from Dulles to Jackson of August 24 clearly revealed his fundamental dilemma: Dulles' strong support for the plan on anticommunist grounds and his determination not to lead the battle against its opponents in the administration and the Congress.[32]

By the autumn, the defeat of the proposal became increasingly clear. A Millikan note to Jackson on October 1 reported his impression, while in Washington, that "something would definitely be done for Asia; but that there was an almost equally definite decision not to launch anything on a broader geographic scale." Then, again, Millikan wrote on October 28:

> . . . My conversations (in Washington) depressed me profoundly as it was quite apparent to me that the Treasury has skillfully and effectively sabotaged all efforts to produce a program which will cost anything. In addition to this effective sniping from the economy boys the lack of any high-level energetic leadership has led to just what we were afraid it might lead to, namely a set of bureaucratic squabbles at a relatively low bureaucratic level as to who should handle any program that might be launched and how it should be organized.[33]

To which Jackson replied on November 2:

> . . . Your advice on the corridor status of the World Economic Plan is terribly discouraging, particularly as it pretty well confirms what my grapevine was carrying. . . .

Before the year was out, Jackson made several further efforts. He wrote to Herbert Hoover Jr., a determined, even ruthless opponent of the proposal.

This venture yielded an impeccably correct reply of December 10, with Hoover saying, in effect, that there might be a U.S. program for Asia "appropriate to our responsibilities and capabilities" but not a global effort.[34]

On December 13, the editors of *Time*, with Jackson's encouragement and Henry Luce's support, had laid out in some detail the case for a global plan; but 1954 was a year when we who believed in such a program tried hard but clearly failed. But Eisenhower was not prepared to overrule its opponents within the administration — notably Humphrey, Hoover, and Dodge; and he was not prepared to take on the opposition in the Congress, much of it within his own party. Moreover, he was honestly concerned about the cost of the effort. And so 1954 ended with foreign economic policy firmly in the grasp of the opponents of any large-scale U.S. effort in support of development.

FOREIGN AID DOLDRUMS, 1955–1956

Dodge's assessment that Eisenhower's State of the Union message of 1955 would be "rather restrained" on the subject of foreign aid proved prescient. Eisenhower's address of January 6 and a special message on foreign economic policy of January 10 focused, in the spirit of the Randall report, almost exclusively on lowering barriers to trade and investment and moving toward convertible currencies.

The previous pattern of military assistance and defense support continued, increasingly focused on a few parts of Asia: Korea, Taiwan, and Indochina. Stassen's large vision of a program for "the Arc of Free Asia" emerged as an exceedingly modest Fund for Asian Economic Development of $200 million to be used over a three-year period.

Although the Democrats had regained control of the Senate and House in the congressional elections of 1954, this fact did not significantly affect the congressional dispositions of foreign aid in 1955, which remained cautious, skeptical, and pretty much in harmony with the proposals laid before Congress in that year. Once again, however, there was an unpublicized battle within the administration on foreign aid. This one was brief and decisive, but the stakes were high.

As Chapter 5 details, the Quantico Panel dealt also, in its background analyses, with larger issues of military and foreign policy. These included the possibility of mounting "with NATO countries a joint policy for accelerating economic growth in the underdeveloped countries of the free world" including a special development program for Asia. These passages had, I suspect, little impact.

The report of a second Rockefeller-led meeting at Quantico in September 1955 focused more sharply on foreign aid. Millikan, who played a major role in Quantico II (as well as Quantico I), provided a substantial supplementary paper for the report entitled "Economic Policy as an Instrument of Political and Psychological Policy."[35] It reflected explicitly the paper we had developed in the wake of the May 1954 Princeton meeting, focusing, in particular, on what a global development plan could be expected to accomplish and not accomplish. It incorporated an estimate that a concerted program, looking ahead ten years, and matching the absorptive capacity of the developing world, might involve additional annual investments of $2–3 billion, of which the U.S. budgetary share might be $1.5–2 billion. These figures were included in the final report, backed by Rockefeller, and they were met with the same frigidity they generated when presented earlier by Jackson. At a climactic meeting at Eisenhower's earlier office in the Post Office at Gettysburg on December 5, 1955, it became clear to Rockefeller that Eisenhower would not advocate substantial increases in either military expenditures or foreign aid. Rockefeller decided to take his case to the public through the panels organized by the Rockefeller Brothers Fund.

While the 1955 debate within the administration was kept quite firmly within the family, the basic issues were widely discussed outside. There was, for example, a proposal by Christian Herter, then governor of Massachusetts, that the United States offer to join with the Soviet Union in a common program of assistance to developing nations, thus removing the issue from its Cold War environment.

In 1955 CENIS published its recommendations for *An American Policy in Asia* in the wake of its study of *The Prospects for Communist China*.[36] One of the basic conclusions of the latter book was the following:

> The effectiveness of this [the Chinese Communist] program obviously hinges on the military and political performance of Free Asia. . . . if Free Asia does not substantially improve its performance, an indifferent outcome on mainland China could still represent an important relative achievement both to the Chinese and to Asians generally.

> On the other hand, the evolution of solid military, political, and economic policies in Free Asia could deny Peking its claim to military and ideological primacy in Asia, and help force, over a period of time, a fundamental re-evaluation of the Chinese Communist regime's domestic and foreign policies.[37]

In the policy volume, we applied to Asia the criteria of the proposal developed in 1954 out of the dynamics set in motion by the Princeton meeting. The operational conclusion was that "the United States should consider enlarging its program of technical assistance and loans to Asia, looking ahead at least five years, at a rate of about $1.3 billion per year; and the other industrialized areas of the Free World should put up about $0.7 billion."[38]

But undoubtedly, the most important events of 1955, so far as aid policy was concerned, were the Soviet (nominally Czech) arms deal with Egypt and the barnstorming, month-long visit of Bulganin and Khrushchev to Afghanistan, India, and Burma in November–December. Referring to Western claims that Soviet aid offers were without substance, Khrushchev said in India:

> To those who write this, we say: Perhaps you would like to compete with us in establishing friendship with the Indians? Let us compete. (Applause.) Why have we come here? We come with an open heart (applause) and with honest intentions. We are glad of it. Perhaps you have not sufficient experience? Then apply to us, and we shall help you. (Applause.) You want to build electric power stations? If you have not the necessary know-how, if you need technical assistance, apply to us and we shall help. (Applause.) You want to send your students, your engineers to our country for training? Please do so. (Applause.)[39]

And a considerable array of Soviet-financed projects, including a steel mill, were set in motion in India early in 1956.

These and other similar events, rather than the arguments of Quantico II and CENIS, led Eisenhower in a letter to Dulles sent from Gettysburg on December 6, 1955, to observe: "I am delighted that you are calling attention to the economic phase of the Cold War"; and to note in his May 3, 1956, report to the Congress on the Mutual Security Program: "The last six months of 1955 saw Soviet tactics shift increasingly from threats and violence to more subtle methods for extending Communist influence across new borders. The underlying purpose of this shift requires careful study."[40]

The fact is, however, that, despite Eisenhower's and Dulles' increasing awareness that U.S. policy was deficient, 1956 was another year in which nothing much of substance happened in the field of U.S. foreign aid policy; however, "the implications of Soviet tactics as they bear on the conduct of the Mutual Security Program" were carefully studied both within the executive branch and in the Congress.

In a letter to Jerry Persons, an Eisenhower aide with responsibility for liaison with Congress, Jackson evoked the reasons for this stance as articulated by a senator's assistant:

> Politically it is very simple. The House is simply trying to wash its hands of the whole business, and go to its constituents on strictly domestic affairs. There was a time when they would have found it difficult to go through this hand washing act, but as they look around today, what do they see?
>
> The first thing they see on foreign aid is that the Administration has

selected a man, Hollister, to head up the non-military aspects, who by his own admission does not believe in the thing itself. In the second place, neither the President nor the Secretary of State have evidenced, in public, anything but the most routine pressure on this subject—no new ideas, no new words, no drive. So the House says to itself, "Why the hell should we be front man for carrying this torch, particularly as we are not at all sure that our own people back home give much of a damn."[41]

There may well have been another factor at work in the House as opposed to the Senate. The Democratic leaders and their staffs in the Senate were, by and large, authentically sympathetic to development aid and responsive to the arguments for its expansion. Influenced by Otto Passman and others, the mood was, for the most part, quite different in the House. As Russell Edgerton observed: "The hearing rooms of the Senate Foreign Relations Committee and the House Foreign Affairs Committee are not physically very far apart. But the mental distance between the two committees is considerable. . . . The staff of the Foreign Affairs Committee privately referred to Millikan and Rostow as the 'cloud nine boys.'"[42]

In the spring of 1956 CENIS produced a further draft of its proposal which received widespread public attention in May and June with articles in the *New York Times, Washington Post, Washington Star, St. Louis Post-Dispatch, Christian Science Monitor,* and other journals. It circulated widely in both the executive branch and the Congress, finding a supporter, among others, in Robert Jackson, who had succeeded Nelson Rockefeller on the White House staff. The special Senate committee on foreign aid asked CENIS to submit, under contract, a paper on "The Objectives of United States Economic Assistance Programs." Millikan, in fact, was the lead witness when public hearings opened under Fulbright's chairmanship on March 20, 1957.

In counterpoint to the CENIS effort, C. D. Jackson kept up a flow of letters to Dulles urging, among other things, that the U.S. approach to foreign aid be positive, in terms of its own plan, rather than responsive to Soviet initiatives; and he offered to mobilize citizen support if the administration should be serious. And there was a good deal stirring elsewhere in the administration that George Humphrey, the secretary of the treasury, sensed. He tried to warn Dodge on the telephone; but the latter's departure on a trip outside Washington led Humphrey to drop him a note on April 27, 1956, which records for history something of the flavor of the opposition:

> I had a talk with Foster this morning about multilateral aid. He says he has no idea of getting into anything of the kind at the present time; yet in his conversation it is perfectly plain that it keeps recurring to his

mind. He is sending me a note about his views and when it is received, I will send a copy to you.

With Hoffman, Lodge, a whole small coterie in the State, and most of the foreign countries all promoting the project, we are going to have to be pretty agile or we will wind up with both feet in the trap.[43]

The reference to Paul Hoffman and Henry Cabot Lodge stems from activity in New York, where Hoffman had taken on the administration of the technical assistance work of the United Nations and Lodge was the U.S. ambassador. A proposal for a Special United Nations Fund for Economic Development (SUNFED) had been formulated to supply additional capital for developing countries on attractive terms.

On May 7 Humphrey addressed himself directly to Eisenhower in opposition to SUNFED and all other multilateral soft lending schemes in perhaps the most full exposition of his views available:

These are a few thoughts to have in mind in considering the relative advantages and disadvantages of new proposals for multilateral aid.

. . . Despite these very substantial provisions for multilateral lending, there are several current suggestions for new organizations. . . .

[Humphrey then cites SUNFED at the United Nations and proposals for Asia and South America.]

If we engage in any one, we will be set upon immediately for the others, and unless we join with them, we will make more enemies than friends.[44]

Meanwhile, out of his contacts with Dulles and others, C. D. Jackson had generated (with John Jessup of *Life* magazine drafting) yet another possible speech for Eisenhower on a world economic plan. Jackson described the mixed and indecisive reaction on May 22, 1956, to the draft in a memorandum to Luce, concluding that any new initiatives would have to wait until "next year." The fact was that Eisenhower had decided early in 1956 that he would undertake no major divisive initiative until after the presidential election.

In the midst of his fruitless activism within the administration in the spring of 1956, C. D. Jackson spent an hour and a half with Dulles on a Saturday afternoon (April 14). He reported the meeting in a letter to Henry Luce. It is a rare portrait of Dulles' view of the Soviets as of the mid-1950s, of Eisenhower, the state of the bureaucracy, and C. D.'s frustration by the Humphrey-Dodge-Hoover axis.

Nevertheless, by September the indefatigable Jackson was already focusing on Eisenhower's January 1957 State of the Union message. He wrote to Emmet Hughes, who had been brought back to the White House for speech writing during the campaign, providing him material to buttress his recommendation that a world economic plan be a major focus of the State of the Union address; and on December 27 Jackson addressed Dulles, who was recovering from a cancer operation, recapitulating the long road since 1954 and urging that the State of the Union message of 1957 at last launch the global development plan.

THE LOGJAM BREAKS: THE DEVELOPMENT LOAN FUND, 1957

For the development crusaders, 1957 began with a bang. Eisenhower's second inaugural address included the following rousing passage:

> We must use our skills and knowledge and, at times, our substance, to help others rise from misery, however far the scene of suffering may be from our shores. For wherever in the world a people knows desperate want, there must appear at least the spark of hope, the hope of progress — or there will surely rise at last the flames of conflict. . . .
>
> . . . We do not fear this world of change. America is no stranger to much of its spirit. Everywhere we see the seeds of the same growth that America itself has known. The American experiment has, for generations, fired the passion and the courage of millions elsewhere seeking freedom, equality, opportunity. And the American story of material progress has helped excite the longing of all needy peoples for some satisfaction of their human wants. These hopes that we have helped to inspire, we can help to fulfill.

In the wake of this pronouncement C. D. Jackson was invited on February 6 to present the World Economic Plan to a meeting organized by Clarence Randall. (Randall had succeeded Dodge as coordinator of foreign economic policy and had moved beyond the position taken in the report of the commission he chaired toward support for development aid.) Here are the key passages from Jackson's vivid, somewhat disabused account of the session as reported to Luce the next day:

Report on Meeting Organized by Clarence Randall
for me to present World Economic Plan
Washington, Feb. 6, 1957

Around the table, chaired by Clarence Randall, sat John Foster Dulles, George Humphrey, Sinclair Weeks, John Hollister, Gabe Hauge, Robert Cutler, True Morse (Agriculture), Steve Saulnier (successor to Arthur Burns as Chairman of the Council), C. D. Jackson.

Although it was never asked in terse Gallup fashion, the question "Do you or do you not propose to do anything to follow through (implement) the promise in the President's Inaugural address?" would have received the following vote:

YES—1 (Randall)

NO—9 (all the others).

These negative votes ranged all the way from really closed minds like Humphrey and Hollister, through the Hauge, "Well, we really are doing quite a lot of this sort of thing, you know; in South America we discovered that twenty beggars don't make a bank, but I for one am very hopeful about the Colombo Plan," to a kind of groping hopelessness voiced by John Foster Dulles. . . .

The Millikan-Rostow book, which I did not mention, also came in for a panning. At one point, Saulnier said, "I have just finished reading that book by Millikan and Rostow. I didn't find anything new or interesting in it. It is just some more of the same kind of thing we have heard so often before."

I had been told by Randall that the session had to wind up in an hour. When everybody had had his say, it was five minutes past the hour. . . . Therefore, I proposed to have a brief and strictly nuts-and-bolts paper in their hands before the end of the month. Randall assumed responsibility for distribution.

At that, the meeting broke up, I crawled onto my shield and was carried out.

———

One way of analyzing the above is to say that, given a golden opportunity, I did a lousy job. Maybe so.

But I don't think it is just vanity which makes me add that I do not think anyone short of the President, in a command decision mood, could have made a real dent on that group. Although there were three different types of minds present, they all formed an instinctive alliance.

One type, led by George Humphrey, does not believe that we should do anything beyond strictly military defense unless the proposed recipient country promises to behave like a God-fearing Middle Western businessman.

A second type, led by Foster Dulles, will take no initiative, won't even approve in principle, unless his client, the President of the United States, tells him to damn well pick up that ball and run with it.

The third type, part Hollister, part Hauge, thinks that actually we have not done too badly, and is mildly irritated that someone should suggest something more, given the difficulties on Capitol Hill, the problems of the budget, and the difficulty of coordinating so many divergent and Departmentally protectionist points of view.

As I said, although their attitudes were quite different, they easily formed an instinctive alliance against W. E. P.

———

I should be discouraged to the point of "To hell with it." But I am not—quite. . . .

As a matter of fact, I have great sympathy for all of those guys who gave me my lumps yesterday afternoon. They are so overwhelmingly beset with the daily crisis requiring an ad hoc decision that they can't help an "Oh my God, as though I didn't have enough already!" when some cheerful world saver comes down from New York and starts talking about a *World Economic Policy.*

This has got to be brought down to pilot project size, and then let it spread.[45]

That is what began to happen in 1957. But it may not have happened if two men had not left the administration: Herbert Hoover Jr., on February 21, succeeded by Christian Herter; and George Humphrey, on July 28, succeeded by Robert B. Anderson. Herter was genuinely pro–development aid and quite knowledgeable about the situation in Washington, as Millikan and I discovered when briefing him on our proposals in Boston before he took up his new post in the State Department. Anderson was, by and large, a conservative political figure, in conventional parlance; but he proved to be considerably less rigid than his predecessor and, indeed, on several occasions, constructive and resourceful. In addition, the balance on foreign aid policy was shifted significantly by the return to Washington from his ambassadorial post in Paris of Douglas Dillon as deputy undersecretary of state for economic affairs.[46]

So far as U.S. foreign aid policy was concerned, the intellectual, ideological, and political debate over the period 1954–1957 came to rest operationally on the question of whether tax resources should be explicitly set aside in support of economic development in countries not allied with the United States in military pacts. The scale of such a program and whether it should take the form of a multiyear fund or annual appropriations were also involved; but the issue of principle had become quite clear.

The foreign aid Special Committee of the Senate, led by Fulbright, had emerged in 1957 in support of such a program. Two citizens' committees, both linked to the Eisenhower administration, split cleanly on the issue. The International Development Advisory Board (IDAB), chaired by Eric Johnston, was strongly in support. Millikan and I, as well as various other like-minded characters, worked closely with the IDAB. The President's Citizen Advisers on the Mutual Security Program, chaired by Benjamin Fairless, was against such an innovation. The latter was, at the time, the more prestigious effort—in effect, a well-publicized counterweight to the Senate Special Committee. The IDAB had been in existence since 1950. Its report on foreign aid had been initially envisaged (in September 1956) as a private communication to the administration. On the other hand, Eric Johnston had good ties to the White House and was a strong, articulate personality when fully committed to a cause.

The Fairless report was delivered to the White House on March 1, and released to the press on March 5. The Johnston report, although dated March 4, was delivered earlier and had, in fact, been made available to the Fairless committee. When Sherman Adams learned of the substance of the Johnston report, he ordered all copies locked up to avoid undermining the Fairless report. The device did not work. Johnston saw Eisenhower on March 4 and, perhaps with Dulles' backing, persuaded him that the IDAB report should be released by the administration. On March 7, Johnston held an effective press conference as his report was released. It proposed a fund that would operate for a minimum of three years without requiring additional financing; appropriations would be substantial and would include the developmental portions of defense support; the major emphasis would be on loans, many of which would be soft; and the administrator of the fund would be given broad discretionary powers in setting interest rates. The fund would not meet requirements that could be filled by private investors, the IBRD, or other institutions lending in hard terms, but would participate with these institutions in joint financing arrangements. The IDAB recommendations were well reported in the press, which contrasted its findings with those of the Fairless committee. Johnston appeared before the Senate Special Committee on April 13, Fairless on April 5.

This was the schizophrenic background against which an administration, long split on the subject, made its 1957 dispositions on the question of development aid and a U.S. fund to support it. The heart of the inner battle centered on a quite specific proposal arising from the policy planning staff, headed by Robert Bowie, who took development aid very seriously indeed. Two members of his staff, Henry Owen and Philip Tresize, had generated by May 1956 a proposal for an Economic Development Corporation with about $5 billion in initial capital, which would operate on strict development criteria but would be empowered to make grants and soft loans. It would take over both existing technical assistance and defense support programs. As Soviet diplomats were wont to say, it was not accidental that the IDAB recommendations of March 1957 greatly resembled the Owen-Tresize proposal. The latter had worked closely with the IDAB staff, which was headed by Alfred Reifman, a State Department economist; and it was not accidental that Millikan and I were in close touch with Bowie and Owen as well as with the IDAB, although it should be underlined that they were all strong-minded men quite capable of formulating their own views.

As deliberations moved forward in the State Department in the late winter of 1956–1957, under the supervision of Herter, the fund became the central issue; and a good many conflicting views and interests came into play.[47] The upshot, on March 15, was Herter's approval of a development loan fund.

The prospects for a large increase in total aid appropriations to support such a fund were, however, firmly deflated two days earlier. Eisenhower, at a press conference, was asked: "Well, is there any intention to increase the economic aid, as Mr. Eric Johnston recommended?" He replied: "Not in any great amount over what we have already recommended." Behind this response was Eisenhower's curious approval of Humphrey's denunciation of the president's budget message of 1957 as involving tax burdens that would lead to "a depression that will curl your hair." Eisenhower, defending Humphrey, had urged Congress to find ways to cut the budget. It was not an optimum setting in which to launch a grand new initiative in development aid.

On the other hand, after Eric Johnston's Senate testimony on the morning of April 3, Fulbright told the State Department's liaison officer, Philip Claxton (who worked closely with Owen and Tresize), that he could support the Johnston proposal. Dulles met that afternoon to consider the testimony he was scheduled to deliver five days later before the Senate Special Committee, having been told by Herter of Claxton's conversation with Fulbright. He decided to support the fund and saw Eisenhower on April 4 with Herter. The upshot was Eisenhower's agreement to shift some defense support funds to a new development fund. Once Eisenhower's agreement was obtained, Dulles, with one exception, apparently informed none of his cabinet colleagues, most of them dissident. He did tell Hollister, who was his subordinate in charge of foreign aid, on Friday, April 5; but Eisenhower was already in Gettysburg for the weekend and inaccessible. On Sunday, April 7 Dulles prepared his testimony, delivering it the next morning:

> We believe that all economic development, including that which goes to countries with which we have common defense, should be considered together. We also believe that more emphasis should be placed on long-term development assistance.
>
> It is true that our economic aid cannot be more than a marginal addition to any country's development efforts. This addition can, however, be significant and even determining. It can break foreign exchange bottlenecks and it can be a key factor in stimulating a country to a more effective development program of its own. If our development aid is to have this effect, however, we must do two things: (i) break away from the cycle of annual authorizations and appropriations, and (ii) eliminate advance allocations by countries.

Economic development is a continuing process, not an annual event. . . .

. . . To be effective, such a fund would need continuing authority and a capital authorization sufficient for several years, to be renewed when needed. . . .

We believe that the proposals I have outlined this morning are "adapted to meet the new circumstances."[48]

Dulles' testimony, his evident commitment to new aid principles, and his prior understanding with Eisenhower created a new situation. But the dissidents were not wholly defeated. The battle came to center not on the fund, but on multiyear financing, which would bypass the congressional appropriations committees. Dulles was at a NATO meeting in Paris during the most intense phase of the counterattack; and Herter appeared to be losing ground to Humphrey. On May 7, Dulles, back from Paris, confronted Humphrey and arrived at a compromise: the administration would request appropriations for the first year of the fund and, at the same time, ask for an additional two years of borrowing authority. This deal was cut without consultation with Eisenhower; but the president, refreshed by a two-week vacation, threw himself with vigor into the battle for the new approach to foreign aid, including a nationally televised address on May 21 wholly devoted to the subject.

Clearly, a corner had been turned in policy conception, institutionally, and in the balance of power within the administration. And the turn in the road was consolidated bureaucratically at the end of the year with Douglas Dillon's becoming chairman of the loan committee of the Development Loan Fund (DLF).

But the initial upshot was modest. The Senate supported the DLF as presented by the administration; but the resistance in the House was considerable. Its members had not shared, like the Senate, in bringing the DLF to life; the House, as the ultimate constitutional appropriating body, was more sensitive to even a limited bypassing of the appropriations process; and then there was Otto Passman, the sadistic enemy of foreign aid. Passman, as chairman of the Subcommittee on Foreign Operations, enjoyed greatly his quasiregal authority over the whole field. He ultimately took the position that unless the DLF was limited to a one-year appropriation there would be no appropriation for the first year and, indeed, appropriations would be withheld from all other aid categories. The blackmail worked, but a step had been taken. The DLF was clearly not the grand long-term commitment of an additional $2 billion a year as the American component of a global program of $3.5 billion envisaged in CENIS' *Proposal* and C. D.

Jackson's World Economic Plan. But it was the pilot project Jackson had reluctantly concluded was the only realistic way to move forward, given the curious mixture of attitudes at the top of the Eisenhower administration.

Jackson promptly recognized that Dulles had created a new situation, and the pilot project was only a first step. On April 11, he wrote to Eisenhower noting Dulles' "most rewarding" statement before the Senate committee on the 8th. He suggested that the president be "publicly and strongly identified with this proposal," and that the "large national citizen's organizations" be mobilized as a method for both "grassroots education" and political support. On April 18, Eisenhower agreed but said the organization should not have "a Congressional—or White House—character." In a letter to Eisenhower of April 9 Jackson, having been drawn by Sherman Adams and Herter into the design of a presidential speech as well as the mobilization of citizens' groups, strongly objected to dealing with both the budget and mutual security in the same address: "[I]t will inevitably link in the public mind a nasty political fight—the budget—with an imaginative, positive, 'happy' program." On April 30 Eisenhower replied in a rather vivid letter, which, after discussing the linkage, agreed to two speeches, if necessary; but he did make the linkage, in his own way, quite effectively, and much in the spirit of his April 30 letter to Jackson. The occasion was his May 21 "Address to the American People on the Need for Mutual Security in Waging the Peace":

> We live at a time when our plainest task is to put first things first. Of all our current domestic concerns—lower taxes, bigger dams, deeper harbors, higher pensions, better housing—not one of these will matter if our nation is in peril. For all that we cherish and justly desire—for ourselves or for our children—the securing of peace is the first requisite. . . . I am convinced of the necessity of these programs of Mutual Security—for the very safety of our nation. For upon them critically depends all that we hold most dear—the heritage of freedom from our fathers, the peace and well-being of the sons who will come after us.[49]

Eisenhower asked for $500 million for the DLF, by switching funds already requested, plus authority for $750 million for each of the two succeeding years. Congress granted him $300 million for one year only; and the total aid appropriation came to $2.8 billion as opposed to the $3.4 billion requested. Congress acquiesced in the DLF, the Senate with reasonable enthusiasm; but neither house was in what might be called a generous mood.

Against the background of this story a central question is evident: Why was Dulles prepared in 1957 to confront Treasury Secretary George Humphrey and to throw his weight behind a development aid proposal, when he was not prepared to do so in the three previous years? One cannot answer with confidence that kind of question about the balances at work in another man's mind. But I would guess that these four circumstances mainly explain the change:

1. Dulles was committed to presenting proposals to a Senate committee of considerable power, clearly demanding substantial change in the foreign aid program, clearly leaning to Eric Johnston's view rather than that of the Fairless committee. Inescapable commitments of this kind are, quite often, a forcing mechanism in policy-making, concentrating the minds of political leaders wonderfully, like Dr. Samuel Johnson's sight of the gallows. Dulles would have been in an awkward position, indeed, taking, say, Humphrey's or Fairless' position on April 8, 1957, before the Senate Foreign Relations Committee; and besides, he did not believe in it. Thus, Fulbright's support for the Johnston proposal gave Dulles an opportunity he seized.

2. There was, also, ready-to-hand a well-staffed, concrete proposal available within the State Department, backed by a highly trusted aide, Robert Bowie.

3. The proposal was capable of being launched on a relatively modest scale by switching the allocation of foreign aid funds already submitted to the Congress—the condition for acquiring Eisenhower's support.

4. Christian Herter, rather than Herbert Hoover Jr., was now the undersecretary of state charged with overseeing the day-to-day process of formulating the State Department's foreign aid position.

The real, if limited, success of the venture also required that the intellectual architects of the DLF within the State Department—Owen, Tresize, and their coconspirators—be formidably competent, energetic, and dedicated bureaucratic infighters.

Thus, Dulles was at last permitted to move in a direction he had wished to move for at least three years.

The last months of 1957 were colored, of course, by the psychological, diplomatic, and political forces set in motion by the launching of the first Soviet satellite. On October 31, Dulles sent a memorandum to Eisenhower expressing concern that "Sputnik will lead Congress to be liberal with military appropriations, perhaps even with the military aspects of mutual security, but will offset this by cutting down on the economic aid. This seems to us of at least equal importance."[50] He suggested that this point might be introduced into presidential speeches.

Dulles' anxiety was shared at just this time—and his perspective supported—from an unlikely quarter: Adlai Stevenson. The Democrat was asked to consult with Dulles in formulating a bipartisan post-Sputnik policy in general and, specifically, on a position for Eisenhower to take at a NATO Heads of Government meeting scheduled for mid-December in Paris.[51]

In a session on November 6, 1957, with members of the State Department and outside consultants (but not yet Stevenson), the official Memorandum of Discussion reports: "The Secretary said that the prospect was that we would get more money for outer space than we need and that we would then lose the war which really counts—which is the economic war."[52]

Both Nelson Rockefeller and Stassen, who were present, urged that, in the former's phrase, "We should institutionalize our economic effort in support of the uncommitted areas," including such regional groupings as the Colombo Plan. Stassen cited the OEEC as the appropriate instrument for this purpose.

NATO was a narrowly military grouping. It had, as it has today, difficulty in finding concert on political problems outside the NATO area. Moreover, it was seen around the world as a military enterprise from which neutral nations wished to keep their distance. The OEEC, derived from the Marshall Plan organization, was evidently a possible instrument for mobilizing a concerted aid policy; but it excluded Japan, which, from about 1955, had not only fully recovered from the war but had moved into an extraordinary surge of growth, which made it a potential donor rather than recipient of foreign aid.

Stevenson asked me to have breakfast with him at a Cambridge (Massachusetts) hotel, where he requested that I help him in his task as consultant on the NATO meeting, which I was pleased to do.[53] We easily agreed that in addition to whatever new military measures or improved methods of political consultation might be canvassed, the United States should press hard at the forthcoming NATO meeting for a new, enlarged, and concerted program of development aid. This view was incorporated in a fifteen-page memorandum to Dulles from Stevenson of November 29. Stevenson then put in a week's hard work in the State Department, where he was in close touch with all the relevant staffs. Stevenson suggested the OEEC as the appropriate coordinating mechanism. On December 4, Dulles asked Stevenson to develop his ideas on alliance economic policy in more detail, which Stevenson did in a second memorandum of December 5, which began rather tartly as follows:

> The suggested U.S. position that has gone forward to Ambassador Burgess is all right as far as it goes, but it does not go anywhere—beyond expression of "interest in an enlargement of the resources available to the less developed areas." The *action* portions which I suggested have been deleted.
>
> I have urged that we

(1) Announce that we are asking Congress for a substantial increase of our foreign development funds;

(2) Call upon the other NATO countries to make increased resources available for underdeveloped countries;

(3) Propose a special meeting of the OEEC to be held in January to (a) determine a scale of effort for foreign economic development; and (b) improve coordination among the participating countries.[54]

He then argued his case in tight, substantive style for five further single-spaced pages. But the fact was that Eisenhower, despite the sensitivity of Dulles, Herter, Dillon, and others to the importance of the issue, was in no mood for a "serious" concerted development effort, and the Europeans were not about to take the lead. The American delegation raised the problem in Paris in general terms; but it was alone, as Stevenson reported in a letter to me of December 23 after a debriefing by Dulles: "Foster Dulles called me this morning, and among other things said that the only NATO country that talked about economic development at all at Paris was the United States. I got the impression that we have a lot of work to do with our Allies if there is going to be any progress toward coordination, let alone enlargement. But I quite agree that we should go on talking about it, and all the more so!" Only a prior, major surge in U.S. development aid policy might have made concerted action at the summit meeting possible; Eisenhower was not prepared to initiate such a change; and, besides, time was short.

There may have been one constructive long-term result of Stevenson's exercise. It may well have heightened a consciousness in the U.S. government of the need to transform the OEEC into a coordinating instrument for development assistance. That transformation was achieved, under the leadership of Douglas Dillon, by December 1960 when the OEEC was converted into the Organization for Economic Cooperation and Development (OECD), whose Development Assistance Committee (DAC) has subsequently monitored and, to a degree, fostered coordinated action in support of the developing countries.

THE FOUNDATIONS FOR DEVELOPMENT AID
ARE LAID, 1958–1960

In the history of development aid, 1958 was an important year. As already detailed, Kennedy and Cooper got their resolution through the Senate and girded for a second round in 1959. Of more immediate importance, the World Bank presided over a path-breaking ad hoc short-term consortium that bought time for the failing Indian Second Five-Year Plan. The DLF survived a second congressional year and began to operate in concert with other sources of development assistance. An initiative by Senator Mike Monroney in 1956 led, via a Senate Resolution passed in July 1958, to the creation in 1960 of the International Development Association (IDA), a soft-loan window in the World Bank. In a speech of August 13 before the United Nations General Assembly, Eisenhower offered U.S. support for a regional development program in the Middle East; and in "a sweeping change in United States policy toward Latin America,"[55] Eisenhower announced on August 27 U.S. willingness to participate in the creation of what was to become the Inter-American Development Bank (IADB).

Before seeking to explain this burst of institutional creativity in the field of development policy in 1958, I note that virtually none of this new enterprise was reflected in current U.S. budgetary outlays or in the aid dispositions of the Congress. In what was now a stylized, repetitive exercise, the administration asked for about $4 billion in military and economic aid; the Congress pushed it back to just about the level of the previous year ($3.3 billion), of which 68 percent was military aid and defense support. When I gave testimony before the Senate Foreign Relations Committee on February 27, 1958, in support of development aid in general and for India, in particular, Fulbright evoked vividly the recalcitrant mood of the Congress as well as an honest but not wholly germane response from his witness:

> SENATOR FULBRIGHT: . . . You have had a year now to reflect upon the failure of the Congress to adopt a long-term program of funds for loans for economic development, the program which this committee recommended almost in the precise form which you recommended. Are you optimistic, in view of the experience of the last year, that your ideas will be followed by this Congress?
>
> MR. ROSTOW: I have had to pose, sir, as an expert on many things, but I would not pretend to judge the mood of Congress or the political forces at work in the country.
>
> SENATOR FULBRIGHT: . . . You have indicated an understanding of the problem. Do you have any reason to believe that this Congress will respond to your proposals? I see no reason to believe there will be any more response now than there was last year. This matter was examined in great detail. This committee spent practically a year examining the foreign aid program from every point of view. As I said, the committee really, to a great extent, agreed with your proposals, and so did the Senate. But the matter got nowhere; the proposal was completely emasculated.
>
> MR. ROSTOW: Yes.
>
> SENATOR FULBRIGHT: Now, it is obvious that we are greatly concerned, but I don't think the United States will now have such a program as you recommend. . . . I do not know why you hesitate to give your

own personal opinion. Do you feel optimistic about it, or not? That is all I am asking.

MR. ROSTOW: I will tell you why —

SENATOR FULBRIGHT: Do you have a feeling, either one way or the other? I don't know why you should hesitate. I don't want to push you.

MR. ROSTOW: I will tell you why I hesitate. It is not that I fear to give you a judgment. It is because, as a citizen who is interested in these matters, I am in a fight.

SENATOR FULBRIGHT: Yes.

MR. ROSTOW: I may be the smallest fellow in the fight, but when I am in a fight I don't generally ask as my first question: What are the odds? Am I going to succeed or fail? I ask: What is the problem, and what can I do before the options are closed? That is why I came back at you; because the books are not yet closed on how the Senate responds, or (how) the Nation's leaders and the public as a whole respond.

SENATOR FULBRIGHT: Well, I withdraw the question. Perhaps it is premature to ask it. I think your thinking about what is involved here is extremely interesting.[56]

The chronic dissidence about foreign aid in the House was heightened in 1958 by the state of the economy: a sharp rise in unemployment to 6.8 percent for the year; a rapidly rising federal deficit; and the emergence, for the first time in the postwar years, of anxiety about the U.S. balance of payments as the balance on current account shifted unfavorably by $4 billion. For most politicians seeking reelection in November this was not a setting in which it was judged helpful to have to defend a vote for a large increase in foreign aid. Why and how, then, did an administration that, excepting the DLF, had exhibited for four years (1954–1957) little effective will to innovate in development policy move forward in four areas in 1958? Each of these areas carried with it large potential future claims on the federal budget as well as quite radical shifts in the direction of foreign aid.

The answer in each of the four cases differs, but they had these things in common:

1. 1958 was a year of multiple crises heightening strategic as well as diplomatic concern about the trends at work in the developing regions.

2. The team at work in the executive branch beneath Eisenhower was either eager to move forward in development policy (e.g., Herter and Dillon) or willing if the case was strong (Anderson). Moreover, Humphrey, Hoover, and Dodge had gone; and Dulles, by and large, viewed benignly the changes that went forward.

3. Despite Fulbright's apparent discouragement about the congressional process in February, the Senate, on balance, remained pro-development aid and supportive of its innovators: Fulbright himself, Monroney, Kennedy, and Cooper, as well as the staff of the Senate Foreign Relations Committee.

4. As noted earlier, the initiatives could be taken without increasing current appropriations.

Of these factors, the sense of gathering crisis in the developing regions was, I would guess, the most important single force at work. It was least explicit in the successful passage of the Monroney Resolution on July 23, 1958, which laid the basis for the IDA.[57]

Monroney hit on the idea of converting the counterpart funds into a pool for productive investment. Superficially, it appeared a quite painless way for the American taxpayer to increase development assistance. He was only to discover later that the capacity of these funds to substitute for new soft loans from abroad was rather limited.

The hearings on March 18–20, 1958, were stormy, and the outcome of Monroney's initiative was clearly in doubt. Quiet diplomacy, in which Dillon played a key role, finally yielded Senate Resolution 264, which passed 62–25 on July 23, though not without some last-minute fireworks. The text of the basic compromise reflects clearly the critical shift from local currencies to low-interest long-term loans to be financed by governmental contributions on a multilateral basis.

The other three development initiatives were clearly linked to situations of heightened anxiety or crisis. The launching of the Kennedy-Cooper resolution on March 25 related explicitly, as we have seen, to Indian difficulties with the Second Five-Year Plan against the background of the apparently exuberant success of Mao's Great Leap Forward of 1958. Never was a complete misunderstanding of what was happening in China of greater help in American politics. In May the Indian government felt impelled to reduce its planned scale of investment by about 15 percent as it searched for supplementary sources of foreign aid.[58]

Meanwhile, the Inter-American Development Bank (IADB) was detonated into life—and, indeed, a new phase in U.S. policy toward Latin America was launched—by a more dramatic event. The event occurred against a background of strong Latin American dissatisfaction caused by a relative fall in the region's export prices since 1951. On May 8,1958, Vice President Nixon was roughed up by a mob in Lima; on May 13, he had an even more difficult time in Caracas. Eisenhower alerted naval and marine forces in the Caribbean against the possibility that Nixon would have to be rescued by force of arms. With Castro moving toward power in Cuba, the administration became convinced that communism was a clear and present danger in the hemisphere, although it was not until the end of 1958 that Castro's tilt to communism was fully appreciated in Washington.[59]

In the wake of Nixon's vicissitudes in Latin America, President Kubitschek of Brazil addressed a letter to Eisenhower calling for a restoration of "Pan American ideals in all their aspects and implications," which, he said, had "suffered serious impairment." The administration understood that what Kubitschek had in mind was, above all, the need for a more forthcoming policy of U.S. economic support for Latin America, which had experienced a 34 percent deterioration in the terms of trade (excluding petroleum) between 1951 and 1958 and a consequent deceleration in economic growth. In fiscal year 1958, U.S. economic aid commitments to Latin America were only $88 million out of a total of $1.46 billion (6 percent); and as late as September 1957 the United States continued its long-standing opposition to the concept of an Inter-American Bank, which was being pressed forward by Latin Americans with vigor at an Organization of American States meeting in Buenos Aires. But in the wake of Nixon's troubles, ideas that had been advocated for some years by Milton Eisenhower, Nelson Rockefeller, and some who currently held posts in the administration received a more favorable hearing than they had earlier. In June 1958, in a reversal of previous policy, the administration participated in the first of a number of commodity study groups, which led in September to an agreement designed to stabilize coffee prices. In July, the U.S. government decided to support the creation of the IADB, a decision formally announced on August 12, 1958.

The year 1958 was also marked by back-to-back crises in the Middle East and the Formosa Straits, running, respectively, from May to August and from August to October. The latter generated no new initiatives in development policy, the former did; namely, Eisenhower's proposal for a Middle East regional development plan. Although that proposal was not taken up, it is useful to examine its origin because it illustrates even more fully than the difficulties in India and Latin America the complexity of the setting in which the priority for development policy rose in the late 1950s.

On the morning of July 15, 1958, American forces landed unopposed in Lebanon. This move was rooted in the Middle East Resolution signed by Eisenhower on March 9, 1957. After the Suez crisis, Eisenhower concluded: "The existing vacuum in the Middle East must be filled by the United States before it is filled by Russia."[60] A new basis had to be found to protect "Western rights" and disabuse Moscow and others of the notion that the West was in permanent disarray and the United States was neutralized in that area by vague nuclear threats.

In the spirit of Truman's 1947 Doctrine, the Middle East Resolution authorized American cooperation with and assistance to any nation or group of nations in the Middle East "in the development of economic strength dedicated to the maintenance of national independence." To that end, it authorized upon request programs of military assistance and military aid against armed aggression from any nation "controlled by international Communism." One problem for the United States in the Middle East during the mid-1950s was the difficulty in defining the phrases "armed aggression" and "controlled by international Communism."

Moscow and Washington were operating in a region with its own churning dynamics that involved a number of elements: the Arab struggle with Israel; the rise of a new generation of Arab radical leaders; Nasser's effort to encourage the rise of such leaders (notably in Syria, Saudi Arabia, Iraq, and Jordan) and the nationalist resistance to Nasser's domination; the Bedouin-Palestinian schism in Jordan; the Muslim-Christian schism in Lebanon; and the tensions between the Arabs and the non-Arab Muslims in Turkey and Iran. In this turbulent modernizing region Moscow and Washington were dealing with situations where their control over events was diluted, and where national and regional objectives were, in the end, paramount.

On July 14, 1958, however, the unstable status quo in the Middle East was clearly challenged. The Hashemite monarch of Iraq was overthrown and murdered, along with the crown prince and the prime minister, Neuri es-Said. This broke the Baghdad Pact. The revolution was led by young military officers, Nasserite and anti-Western; but there was no firm public evidence of Cairo's hand in the enterprise, let alone Moscow's. The acute anxieties of Jordan and Lebanon led Hussein and Chamoun to request British and American armed intervention to protect their independence under the Middle East Resolution of 1957. United States seaborne forces began to move unopposed across the Lebanese beaches the day after the coup in Iraq. On July 17 British paratroopers moved into Jordan, where a plot against Hussein had failed.

It is the cumulative buildup of tension and trouble in the Middle East that explains Eisenhower's instant response to the Iraq coup of July 14: "That morning I gathered in my office a group of advisers to make sure that no facet of the situation was overlooked. Because of my long study of the problem, this was one meeting in which my mind was practically made up regarding the general line of action we should take, even before we met."[61]

Eisenhower's decision to move on July 15, before the meaning of the Iraqi coup could be fully assessed, was based on an instinctive judgment that the Middle East was getting out of hand, rather than on precise evidence that "armed aggression" from a nation "controlled by international Communism" had occurred or was about to occur.

Robert Murphy, a senior foreign service officer, was promptly launched into the Middle East along with the U.S. Marines. His mission was to comfort a harassed and ill Chamoun; to commit him to the early election of a successor; and to explain to the new leader in Baghdad, Abdul Kassim, and to Nasser the limited objectives of the American initiative.

The operation stabilized the Middle East for some time. There was no U.S. move against the new government of Iraq, as Moscow and Beijing feared. American influence was not used to keep Chamoun in power, as he may have hoped. Nevertheless, the Anglo-American landings strengthened Jordanian, Lebanese, and Saudi confidence in their ability to survive against radical nationalists backed by Moscow and Cairo. The military operations also provided a demonstration that, in the face of threats issuing from the Moscow press, the United States was prepared to move military forces in defense of its interests. That demonstration increased the degree of independence even radical Arab nationalists felt they could assert against Moscow.

With Beijing pressing its flank, Moscow had to react. It did so by demanding a high-level meeting of heads of state. It hoped to bring Britain and the United States to the bar as opponents of nationalism. As during the Suez crisis, the threat of missiles and "volunteers" was also invoked, but in ways that did not commit Moscow to act. Moscow resisted Beijing's pressure for what it regarded as an excessive reaction. A series of exchanges between Eisenhower and Khrushchev on the forum in which the matter should be debated led finally to the convening of the United Nations General Assembly, which Eisenhower addressed on August 13. By this time the Middle East was relatively calm, the presidential election in Lebanon having taken place at the end of July.

Dulles initially urged a narrow focusing on the question of indirect aggression. He left Washington for a conference in Latin America, to return late on August 8; but before leaving town he had asked C. D. Jackson and me to come to Washington to develop materials for Eisenhower's speech before the United Nations. Our inclination was to put the question of indirect aggression in the larger context of the rise of radical Arab nationalism and to focus on the possibility of regional development in the Middle East. In addition, we wanted to counteract the image in the Middle East and elsewhere evoked by Moscow's use of nuclear threat during the Suez crisis.

We arrived in Washington in the late afternoon of August 7 and were whisked to the home of Allen Dulles. We met there not merely the director of Central Intelligence but some of his senior aides with knowledge of the Middle East. When asked what line we planned to take in drafting the president's speech we outlined our views. Allen Dulles said he strongly agreed and went on to explain that if the president took his brother's idea and attacked covert operations by radical Arabs—he (Allen D.) might have to resign. The CIA also had covert operations in the area and the General Assembly of the United Nations was so constituted that small powers would win over large powers.

On Friday morning, August 8, C. D. Jackson and I were installed in a large State Department office normally used by ambassadors on leave in Washington. We assembled our thoughts and drew ideas from many parts of the bureaucracy. These included Lewis Strauss and his Atomic Energy Commission's water-desalting crusaders and the State Department policy planning staff then headed by Robert Bowie. We talked at length with Vice President Nixon, who appeared to agree with the line we were about to take; but who also told us that his influence in the White House was virtually nonexistent. Jackson and I worked together most of the night, aided in the frenetic effort by Henry Owen of the policy planning staff. Jackson was able to hand a draft to Dulles during breakfast at Dulles' home the next morning, August 9. With a nod of approval in principle, the draft was then given to those bearing operational responsibility in the government. At the Treasury, Robert Anderson made sure that resources, including a diversion of oil revenues by the American private oil firms, would be available for Middle East development if the Arab world responded positively. The document moved forward, after the usual redrafting, to Eisenhower, its essential structure unchanged.

The whole program was framed by the demonstration that the United States and Britain were not prepared to abandon their vital interests in the face of Soviet missile and "volunteer" threats.

The broad objective of the speech was not merely to reaffirm American opposition to direct and indirect aggression but also to hold up a vision of American support for a constructive expression of Arab nationalism—and the nationalism of others in the developing world.

In *Waging Peace,* Eisenhower quotes this passage from his August 13 speech:

> The world that is being made on our planet is to be a world of many mature nations. As one after another of these new nations moves through the difficult transition to modernization and learns the methods of growth, from this travail new levels of prosperity and productivity will emerge.
>
> This world of individual nations is not going to be controlled by any one power or group of powers. This world is not going to be committed to any one ideology.
>
> Please believe me when I say that the dream of world domination by one power or of world conformity is an impossible dream.

So far as doctrine was concerned, the need to deal with Arab radicalism accelerated the shift in Eisenhower's initial stance toward the developing world as a whole. His August 13 speech acknowledged, in effect, that what the United States was prepared to do for radical Arabs in their most disruptive mood, the United States must be prepared to do in Latin America, Asia, and Africa as well. The criterion that economic aid should be an instrument of support only for those joined with the United States in military alliance against the Communist bloc was, evidently, gone. The objective of economic assistance as a means for supporting the emergence of independent states, and for focusing their ardent nationalism increasingly on the modernization of their societies, had been enunciated under circumstances likely to commit the United States over a long future. In the context of American economic foreign policy since the Korean War, this was a radical departure.

But the churning ambitions, conflicts, and anxieties of Middle Eastern political and diplomatic life did not permit a united, positive regional response to Eisenhower's August 13 offer. Nevertheless, the environment in which Kennedy, Cooper, and others of like mind carried forward their assorted development crusades in 1959 was somewhat different — and a bit more congenial — than that which prevailed a year earlier. And for this fact the crises in India, Latin America, and the Middle East were primarily responsible.

THE KENNEDY-COOPER RESOLUTION SUCCEEDS, 1958-1961

We return now to the Kennedy-Cooper enterprise, which we left with passage in the Senate on June 6, 1958, but rejection in conference with the House on June 17. As the two senators looked forward to resuming their effort in the next session of Congress, they continued to keep the issue alive by arguing their case in the media and urging that existing resources and mechanisms be used to provide immediate assistance to permit India to avoid a drastic cutback in the objectives of the already reduced Second Five-Year Plan.

Meanwhile, the World Bank moved effectively onto the scene in August. The Bank's president, Eugene Black, called a meeting, attended by five countries, to deal with India's immediate foreign exchange crisis. Here is how the Bank's historians describe the occasion:

> The first consortium, the one for India, was not organized initially for the purpose of mobilizing and coordinating external financing for India's five-year development plans. Rather, it was originally conceived as a temporary rescue operation that came into being in 1958, after it had become apparent that India's rapidly shrinking holdings of foreign ex-

change would be wholly insufficient to finance the second five-year plan, which was then under way.[62]

B. K. Nehru, a high official appointed to deal with aid from abroad, took this view:

> It was decided that this immediate rescue operation should not be handled through diplomatic channels in order to avoid any political flavor being brought into it but should be regarded as a simple banking operation. The World Bank was our international banker. We were to go to it and place our difficulties before it, tell it that we wanted a large loan and ask it to raise the finance for us from whatever sources it thought proper in a manner similar to what a commercial concern would do *vis-à-vis* its own bankers, if it got into financial difficulties. . . .
>
> The first meeting of what subsequently became the Aid-India Consortium was held in Washington in August 1958 and agreed to give us to the last cent the money we said we would need which was over a billion dollars. There were no political conditions attached nor any economic ones beyond our undertaking to complete the (reduced) Plan as presented to the World Bank.[63]

On August 29, 1958, the *New York Times* could report that the World Bank, the United States, Britain, West Germany, Japan, and Canada had generated "the largest multi-nation economic aid plan ever arranged for an under-developed country": $350 million in immediate emergency assistance plus, less firmly, the prospect of an additional $600 million over the period running to the end of 1961.

When Kennedy and Cooper returned to their self-imposed task in 1959, a good deal had changed—quite aside from the time-buying initiative of the World Bank. First, the Democrats had won a major victory in the congressional elections of November 1958, gaining thirteen seats in the Senate, forty-eight in the House of Representatives. From the point of view of foreign aid politics, the departure from Congress of a good many opponents of development aid was more important than the statistical outcome. In the Senate, for example, Knowland had retired to run, unsuccessfully, for governor in California. His successor (Claire Engel), like the successors to William Jenner (Vance Hartke) and Edward Martin (Hugh Scott), were also figures more sympathetic to foreign aid. Of the ten defeated Republican senators, nine were replaced by men less conservative on the foreign aid issue. The congressional landslide also had the effect of appearing to increase the likelihood of Democratic victory in the presidential elections of 1960, and thus somewhat heightened the stature in Washington of Kennedy, who was clearly one of the possible candidates after his not unexpected, but nevertheless overwhelming reelection to the Senate with 73.6 percent of the total vote.

Second, and more narrowly, Kennedy and Cooper were strengthened by the recruitment of two members of the House of Representatives who joined in presenting a fresh version of their concurrent resolution: Democrat Chester Bowles (D-Conn.), one of the earliest American crusaders on behalf of Indian economic development, and Chester Merrow (R-N.H.).

Third, the World Bank was now a central actor in the drama and Kennedy was in close touch with both Black and one of the Bank's vice presidents, Burke Knapp. The World Bank emerged as an operational substitute for the OEEC as the possible sponsor of an international mission to India.

Fourth, the acute foreign exchange crisis and the pessimism in New Delhi about India's prospects had considerably eased. A memorandum of B. K. Nehru to his staff of June 1959 indicates that the ad hoc assistance organized in August 1958 by the World Bank, a bumper harvest, and the discovery of oil in western India mainly account for the change. (The collapse of Mao's Great Leap Forward and the growing tension between Moscow and Beijing would have further heightened the mood if they had been fully understood at the time.) Thought in India turned increasingly to the design for the Third Five-Year Plan to cover the period 1961–1966.

Finally, the case for large-scale, sustained economic assistance to India, if not quite the conventional wisdom in Washington, was much more widely accepted than a year earlier, in part because it had been demonstrated at the World Bank meeting in August 1958 that other countries were prepared to join the United States in aid to India on a significant scale; in part because of the expanding activities of the DLF, the movement toward the IDA and IADB, and the altered stance of the Eisenhower administration toward development lending as reflected in its August 13, 1958, offer of a Middle East regional development plan. The older emphasis on military aid and support plus private international investment had been breached on many fronts.

Nevertheless, in 1959, even India's short-run problems were not at an end. India confronted a heavy repayment burden on international loans already contracted; a good deal of emergency aid had to be allocated to meet unpaid bills and existing shortages rather than to finance new projects; export prices were declining; and the pressure of rising population on the food supply was still acute. All this was reflected in the presentations to the Senate by Kennedy and Cooper of their revised concurrent resolution on February 19, 1959.[64] Bowles briefly presented the resolution in the House on the same day, on behalf of himself and Merrow.

Kennedy's speech was entitled "The Economic Gap," which he contrasted with the "missile gap":

> *It is this [economic] gap which presents us with our most critical challenge today.* It is this gap which is altering the face of the globe, our strategy, our security and our alliances, more than any current military challenge. *And it is this economic challenge to which we have responded most sporadically, most timidly and most inadequately.*

After making once again the case for the importance of India, Kennedy argued that 1958 was "their"—the Communists'—"round"; 1959 should be "our round":

> During the past year India has had a national growth rate of only three percent and two percent of this is largely dissipated by population increases. . . .
>
> But 1959 could and should be our "round," our year. We have, in this Congress, in these next few months, a moment of opportunity which may never come again. If we act now, on the right scale, in the right way, we may reverse the ever-widening gap. This year, 1959, could be the year of their economic downfall—or the year of their economic "take-off," enabling them to get ahead of their exploding population, to stabilize their economies and to build a base for continuing development and growth.

Kennedy then focused sharply on the need to expand the resources available in the DLF, the major potential U.S. source of long-term low-interest loans: "When this body decides the future of the Development Loan Fund this year, it will also in large measure be deciding the future of India." He went on to urge an international mission to India citing Escott Reid of Canada (as well as McCloy and Franks) as illustrative of the stature required, reflecting the rather generous role of Canada in the August 1958 World Bank barn raising for India as well as Reid's personal advocacy of aid for India. In short, Kennedy looked to the emergence of "a donor's club, under the sponsorship of the World Bank rather than the OEEC."[65]

The proposed concurrent resolution now read as follows:

> Whereas the continued vitality and success of the Republic of India is a matter of common free world interest, politically because of her four hundred million people and vast land area; strategically because of her commanding geographic location; economically because of her organized national development effort; and morally because of her heartening commitment to the goals, values, and institutions of democracy: Now, therefore, be it

> *Resolved by the Senate (The House of Representatives Concurring),*
> That it is the sense of Congress that the United States Government should
> invite other friendly and democratic nations to join in a mission to consult
> with India on the detailed possibilities for joint action to assure the fulfill-
> ment of India's second five-year plan and the effective design of its third
> plan. And that the Secretary of State report to the Congress on the fea-
> sibility of such a mission after consultation with interested governments
> and with the Republic of India.

The shift of emphasis to the emerging Indian Third Five-Year Plan is
evident.

Again Cooper spoke more briefly in support, making the case in general
terms and citing the role of Eisenhower, Dulles, Herter, and Dillon in working, over the previous year, "with other countries to provide substantial aid
to India's economic development."

On May 4-5, 1959, as foreign aid legislation moved forward in the Congress, a rather remarkable event occurred in Washington—a "Conference
on India and the United States—1959." It was sponsored by a bipartisan
citizens' group, the Committee for International Economic Growth (CIEG).
Its chairman was Eric Johnston, a Republican liberal who had played a
significant role in the emergence of the DLF in 1957. A year earlier the
CIEG had mobilized an impressive array of speakers at a Washington conference in general support of development assistance, among them President Eisenhower, former President Truman, Vice President Nixon, Allen
Dulles, James Killian, Dean Acheson, and Adlai Stevenson, as well as a distinguished baseball player of the time, Stan Musial, and the actress Myrna
Loy. (I wrote three of the speeches delivered at this Conference.) The 1959
conference was less glamorous, narrower, and more professional. Indian as
well as American officials participated, as well as American business leaders,
academics, and Barbara Ward. She had written a widely read twenty-page
special supplement on India for the January 22, 1955, issue of the London
Economist and was an effective and indefatigable crusader for aid to India
and the developing nations generally.

Behind the conference lay not merely a convergence of India's needs and
U.S. interests, as they came increasingly to be defined, but also the emergence of a corps of Americans (and others) who had entered during the
1950s into the study of India's problems with such patent objectivity, human
sympathy, and enthusiasm that, as I. G. Patel was later to write, "we should
be privileged to count them as honorary citizens of this ancient land."[66]

While things were moving forward in Washington, Kennedy, conscious
of the importance in U.S. politics of aid contributions by other nations, en-

gaged in a bit of lobbying overseas. I had worked with him on the project, along with other members of CENIS, since November 1957. In September 1958 I left on a year's sabbatical to Cambridge, England, but I kept in touch with Kennedy, both directly and through Holborn; and, in particular, I discussed the project with British Treasury and Foreign Office officials and journalists. My central theme was this:

> [W]hat emerges from the Congress in the coming session may well depend substantially on what, at the right time, appears to be the scale and willingness of European nations, Canada, and Japan to enlarge and, especially, to extend the time period of their commitments to aid the underdeveloped areas. And I suggested that Britain might have a role to play — in both the Commonwealth and the OEEC — in exploring what those contingent commitments might be.[67]

I also kept in touch with B. K. Nehru when he was in England. To assess prospects on the spot, Kennedy also sent Holborn to Europe in December 1958. Holborn and I conferred at some length in Cambridge. In May 1960, while in Germany on academic business, I sought to stir up the German Foreign Office in Bonn. The German officials courteously heard me out at a lunch in a hotel overlooking the Rhine, but it was a moment when they were more immediately concerned with the quadripartite negotiations on Germany then under way. In Paris I also saw Jean Monnet, whose Action Committee in support of European unity was already advocating greatly enlarged European support for the developing countries. Monnet immediately saw in the Kennedy-Cooper resolution a way not only of helping India, but also of tightening the bonds across the Atlantic by engagement in a common enterprise. He wrote to Kennedy on June 10, 1959, forwarding the latest Action Committee documents relevant to Kennedy's enterprise.

On the whole, things fell into place rather well in 1959 for the Kennedy-Cooper enterprise. In March, Kennedy talked to Dillon at the latter's request on the India resolutions, and in a subsequent letter to Dillon of March 21 Kennedy asked if there was a form for the India resolution that might meet State Department objections. Those objections centered on two points: the fact that Pakistan was excluded; and the judgment that a mission dispatched by a congressional committee was preferable to one made up of even distinguished private citizens from different countries. Holborn, in a memorandum to Kennedy of April 6, 1959, argued that if the resolution were broadened to include Pakistan, the State Department might accede in time to launch the international mission.[68]

Holborn proved to be correct. Differences with the State Department were resolved after a letter from Macomber to Fulbright of May 4 indicated that the administration might support the resolution if its terms were modified to embrace all of South Asia. Kennedy and Cooper agreed to the change, and the revised resolution was presented to the Senate Foreign Relations Committee, with Bowles appearing from the House, on July 14. Executive sessions were held on July 21 and 23. A representative of the Treasury expressed cautious administration support, characterizing the revised resolution as "a purely exploratory measure and a useful one."

At this time it also became clear that the World Bank would be the best sponsor of the mission, especially if its plans for the IDA came to fruition.

B. K. Nehru reported, in a letter to me of August 5, 1982, about the final drafting of the resolution in early September 1959. "He [Kennedy] asked me if I would help in amending the Resolution. I say it must have been September because Morarji Desai was then in town which he usually was only for the Bank-Fund meetings. Max Millikan and Paul Rosenstein-Rodan were also in town and after consulting Morarji we (principally I. G. [Patel] and Max) worked on the Resolution and sent it back to Kennedy through Patel and Holborn."

On September 10, 1959, at the instigation of Lyndon Johnson, the amended resolution was agreed to in the Senate by voice vote, without dissent.

In the early autumn, a not trivial obstacle emerged: the Indian government appeared to resist the idea of the international mission. Indians had, of course, followed the Kennedy-Cooper enterprise from the beginning and with implicit support. But as it moved toward reality, the problems it might raise, as well as solve, became more vivid. After all, there was something odd about the legislature of one country generating a resolution that an international mission be sent to another, even if the latter was rather hard-pressed.

The issue was resolved early in October when Morarji Desai, the Indian finance minister who was then in the United States, agreed that India would receive the mission early in 1960, on the assumption that it would visit other countries as well. As we shall see, Indian nervousness was not wholly dissipated until the mission's work was completed.

As 1959 drew to a close, the attention of those concerned with this matter shifted toward the membership, exact status, and sponsorship of the international mission. Despite his increasingly evident decision to seek the Democratic nomination in 1960, Kennedy followed these matters in detail and helped sort them out in close collaboration with Dillon. The remaining problems were resolved with some elegance by having Eugene Black, president of the World Bank, "suggest" in his personal capacity that three distinguished men, "as independent private individuals," undertake the mission. They were Hermann Abs, chairman of the Deutsche Bank of Frankfurt; Sir

Oliver Franks, chairman of Lloyd's Bank of London (but also a philosopher of distinction as well as a former ambassador to the United States); and Allan Sproul, former president of the New York Federal Reserve Bank.[69]

Their appointment was announced on December 19, 1959. Their report, after a six-week visit to India and Pakistan, took the form of a letter dated March 19, 1960, from New Delhi, addressed to Black, later published as *Bankers' Mission to India and Pakistan* by the World Bank.

The report, which owed a great deal to Franks' leadership and lucid drafting, dramatized the reality of poverty in the two countries, the pressure of rapid population increase, the seriousness of the development efforts undertaken by the governments, the modesty of their targets, and the need for long-term, low-interest, official loans as well as private capital imports. It touched in temperate, well-modulated language on a number of sensitive points: the requirement for mutual understanding of the political imperatives operating on borrower as well as lender; the need for higher priority for agriculture and for nurturing a diversified private sector in the borrowing countries; and the need for a liberal trade policy in the lending countries to permit additional foreign exchange to be earned. Read in retrospect, this brief, unpretentious but unambiguous report deserved I. G. Patel's high praise: "one of the most heart-warming documents in the annals of international relations."[70] It also performed precisely the function Kennedy and Cooper had envisaged: it rendered politically respectable long-term development aid to India in an international setting.[71]

In the wake of the report, the World Bank dispatched a technical study mission to India, headed by Michael Hoffman, a former *New York Times* economic reporter who went to work for the Bank. And in the autumn of 1960 the two-phase rhythm of the India and Pakistan consortia formally began: a session of economic analysis followed in the spring by a pledging session. India's Third Five-Year Plan was reviewed in Paris in September 1960; and in April 1961 the first pledging session took place. By that time Kennedy was president; and he had the satisfaction of rounding out the effort launched in March 1958 by committing the United States to make a major contribution at the first pledging session of the India consortium in April — a constructive act that gave Kennedy some comfort, coming as it did amidst the painful process of cleaning up after the Bay of Pigs fiasco. The United States was prepared to lend $500 million to India for each of the first two years of the Third Plan if the other members of the consortium would match the American figure. They failed to do so in April, but they came close enough in a special meeting in May for the Third Five-Year Plan to be launched with a fairly solid and reasonably adequate base of international support.

As Kennedy's aide with responsibility to follow this among other matters, I was able to send him a memorandum on June 1, 1961: "Herewith a report on the second Consortium meeting on India, which represents a major success. There is no doubt that your boldness in putting up the $500 million [for fiscal year 1962] has jacked up everyone's contributions. We all agree this should help us on the Hill. Those dealing with the Hill have already been alerted as to the result."

The India consortium was under way and the Pakistan consortium as well; but, of course, economic and social development in the subcontinent did not unfold smoothly. Over the next twenty years the two countries confronted many vicissitudes as they made their ways forward carrying the burdens of excessive rates of population increase and vast, low-productivity rural sectors. Moreover, economic and social development does not take place in a vacuum. The two nations confronted political crises, including conflict with each other and the division of Pakistan into two states. Nor did the sense of convergent interests between Washington and New Delhi that marked the late 1950s and early 1960s prove stable; and the common-law marriage between India and the consortium, presided over by the World Bank, was not always smooth and easy. But the consortium survived, played on the whole a constructive role on the world scene, and created a model for at least sixteen similar arrangements over the next decade.

THE INSTITUTIONALIZATION AND VICISSITUDES OF DEVELOPMENT AID IN THE 1960S AND BEYOND

The focus of this chapter is the Kennedy-Cooper initiative of 1958–1959 and its place as the turning point in U.S. and international development policy toward the close of the 1950s and in 1961. It may be useful, therefore, to provide in this chapter a brief sketch of how development aid was consolidated and institutionalized in the course of the 1960s.

Kennedy, as president, did not delay long before translating his views on development aid, generated while he was in the Senate, into executive initiatives. On March 1, 1961, he sent to the Congress a message on the Peace Corps established by executive order that day; on March 13, he launched the Alliance for Progress in an address to the assembled diplomatic corps of the Latin American republics; and on March 22 he sent to the Congress a special message on foreign aid embracing the concept of the Development Decade. Acknowledging a continuity with Truman and Eisenhower—and thereby reaching out for bipartisan support—Kennedy nevertheless opened and closed his message with rhetoric of a distinct and positive cast.

Specifically, Kennedy sought to shift the existing aid program in the following directions:

(a) a unification of technical assistance, development lending, Public Law 480, and other scattered activities;

(b) a concentration on national development plans as opposed to specific projects, with priority for nations making serious and coherent self-help efforts "to reach the stage of self-sustaining growth";

(c) a multilateral approach, designed to draw other industrialized nations systematically into the effort on a larger scale; and

(d) authority from the Congress for long-term (five-year) authorization and borrowing authority to make dollar-repayable loans.

Eisenhower's final aid request of the Congress was high: some $800 million more than the sum actually voted in the previous year.[72] For his first year, Kennedy therefore stayed with Eisenhower's request for a $4 billion economic and military authorization, but proposed to shift allocations toward development loans, repayable in dollars over long periods.

Even this aid increase appeared difficult to get from a Congress more conservative than that elected in 1958. Sorensen's low-key first draft of the aid message was geared to the rather gloomy prospects on Capitol Hill. Kennedy evidently wished to aim somewhat higher. He had Sorensen send the draft to me for revision. My suggestions were radical and extensive but wholly consonant with Kennedy's views as I had known them over the previous three years. And, when Kennedy approved the new directions suggested by me (and, perhaps, by others), Sorensen, in typical fashion, carried forward in a more heroic direction with verve and elegance.

In 1961 Kennedy moved the foreign aid program some distance toward the goals he had formulated in the late 1950s; although its momentum was damped by initial administrative problems and then, in 1963, by increased congressional resistance in the post–Cuban missile crisis letdown of anxiety about the Cold War. Other forces operating later in the 1960s further diminished U.S. support for development aid.

Nevertheless, Kennedy achieved a good deal. He got from Congress the authority to make long-term commitments; however, he did not get the borrowing authority for aid lending he sought. The latter would have been a bold innovation, relieving development lending (not grants) from the annual appropriations cycle. It might have helped sustain the level of American capital flows to the developing world later in the 1960s. But it was rejected as "back-door financing" and a dilution of congressional power over the purse strings. He completed the initiative he undertook as a senator, launching the India and Pakistan consortia arrangements in the World Bank with a strong U.S. contribution, inducing proportionate contributions from others. This not only strengthened development programs potentially affecting the lives of some 40 percent of the people in the noncommunist portion of the developing world, but also set a pattern for multilateralism that was rapidly extended in the 1960s. He launched the Alliance for Progress as well as the Peace Corps. When the American contribution to development is measured as a whole (including the World Bank, IDA, IADB, etc.), the lift in resources made available in the early 1960s is impressive: an increase of one-third. And there is a major element reflected in the data on U.S. development aid that reaches beyond Kennedy's time. His strong advocacy of international support for serious development efforts helped induce other nations to expand their contributions, a trend that continued as the 1960s wore on.

CONCLUSIONS

The process of linking ideas and action with respect to foreign aid in the 1950s occurred in a rather curious triangular way. The ideas were generated in universities and research institutions, of which CENIS was a significant example but by no means unique. These ideas flowed in two important directions: to sympathetic members of Congress and their staffs, and to sympathetic members of the executive branch at both high and working levels. They flowed also to the World Bank and other international institutions, and, of course, to other academics and interested laypersons in the United States and abroad.

Those working in the public service were by no means merely passive recipients and a transmission belt for the ideas generated outside; and the ideas that flowed to them, while based on intellectual concepts, were at least quasioperational in form. CENIS, for example, felt that part of its duty was to understand the political context of action well enough to present its notions in ways that working politicians and bureaucrats could recognize as potentially realistic. There was thus an interacting osmotic process between those conducting academic research and those charged to act.

The triangle was closed by the quiet, faintly conspiratorial collaboration between sympathetic members of the Congress (and their staffs) with sympathetic officials of the executive branch (and their staffs).

The triangular process was framed by considerable propaganda activity conducted by both political and academic figures: books, articles, and letters to assorted editors; speeches and symposia; appearances before congressional committees. This protracted effort, conducted from 1954 to, say, Kennedy's election as president, was a kind of substitute for the clear presidential command decision C. D. Jackson and Rockefeller sought from Eisenhower and were denied.

Looking back at the intellectual struggle for development aid of the 1950s and 1960s and at the political figures who joined early in the campaign, I would underline a chastening fact. The pathbreaking victories won in the form of IDA, the IADB, the India and Pakistan consortia, the Alliance for Progress, and the Development Decade did not come about because, at last, we persuaded the opposition that our long-term arguments were right. They came about because a series of short-term crises emerged in the developing regions, which forced on responsible politicians an acute awareness of the political and strategic danger of not assisting the process of development in Latin America, Africa, the Middle East, and Asia. In fact, the whole critical period when the long-run foundations for development assistance were laid was framed by the protracted short-term anxieties, in the United States and elsewhere, that followed the Soviet launching of the first satellite in October 1957. The story of the transition to large-scale sustained development aid is, thus, a vivid illustration of Jean Monnet's dictum: "People only accept change when they are faced with necessity and only recognize necessity when a crisis is upon them."[73]

Nevertheless, the work of the development crusaders was not irrelevant. When governments in the advanced industrial world were forced by events to turn to the tasks of development, there existed a body of thought and doctrine, based on research, debate, and some practical experience, that permitted reasonably sensible courses of action to be fashioned quickly. And, perhaps most important of all, development thought and doctrine had been thrashed out on a global basis between economists of the North and South. This lively process proceeded not only in universities, but also on the occasion of research and aid missions to developing countries and within the secretariats of the World Bank, the United Nations, and the regional banks and economic commissions. It was, clearly, a two-way process of mutual education. The existence of this common framework of reference, often underpinned by close personal ties, rendered North-South collaboration much easier than it would otherwise have been once the institutional framework for development assistance was built and put to work in the late 1950s and early 1960s.

But the arrival at the White House of John Kennedy, with his whole-hearted and deeply rooted acceptance of the doctrines of the development crusaders of the 1950s, did not launch a long era of expanded development assistance and amicable North-South relations. There was, it is true, a brief interval of relative harmony with India and Latin America on which some still look back with nostalgia. So far as India was concerned, three factors account for this transient passage of amity: the consolidation of the World Bank consortium arrangements behind the Indian Third Five-Year Plan; the prompt U.S. logistical support for the beleaguered Indian forces at the time of the border clash with China late in 1962; and the human ties that developed between Indian and U.S. officials symbolized by Mrs. Kennedy's visit to India. These strands in U.S.-India relations were not trivial. But beneath the surface there were, quite naturally, fundamental unresolved differences in perspective. By far the most important was the clash between the U.S. interest in a settlement between India and Pakistan and Nehru's determination to offer no concession whatsoever on Kashmir. From an Indian point of view, the continuing U.S. insistence on maintaining friendly links to Pakistan, including some elements of military assistance, complicated relations. Of lesser importance were India's relations with the Soviet Union and the gap between the private and publicly stated views of Indian officials on Southeast Asia. But it was the incapacity of India and Pakistan to resolve their problems that was, above any other factor, to shadow U.S. relations with India in the post-Kennedy years. Kennedy, although skeptical that an outsider could be effective, did all he could do to induce an India-Pakistan agreement on Kashmir; but he failed.[74]

Despite the real enough complications of the Bay of Pigs, three rather different important factors in U.S. relations with Latin America were: the launching of the Alliance for Progress; the extraordinary unforced hemispheric consensus that Khrushchev's missiles in Cuba were unacceptable; and Kennedy's charismatic appeal to Latin Americans. Again, beneath the surface, even in Kennedy's time, there were abiding unresolved problems that indicated U.S.-Latin American relationships were, in fact, suffused with latent elements of friction. There was, for example, the unwillingness of the Latin American countries located at some distance from the Caribbean to accept the domestic political tension of joining those closer (most notably, Venezuela) in combined efforts to limit Cuba's capacity for troublemaking across borders. This was the central issue at the January 1962 Punta del Este conference. And there were recurrent problems for Kennedy in the instability of domestic politics in Latin America yielding more military regimes than the common hemispheric aspirations for democracy would decree.

And beyond India and Latin America, Kennedy's wholehearted support for development assistance did not prove to be a panacea. He had difficulties with, among others, Sukarno, Nkrumah, and, after a promising start, Nasser.

The reason for those difficulties goes to the heart of what development aid could and could not accomplish in the context of U.S. foreign policy as a whole. Politicians in developing countries faced, like politicians everywhere else, difficult choices. The endemic raw material of politics was nationalism—in fact, a reactive nationalism—reacting against the memory of past intrusions, current intrusions, or feared intrusions from more advanced nations.[75] A reactive nationalism has been, in fact, the most powerful single force driving forward (and, at times, backward) the process of modernization.

But nationalism can be turned in any one of several directions. It can be turned outward to right real or believed past humiliations suffered on the world scene, or to exploit real or believed opportunities for national aggrandizement that appear for the first time as realistic possibilities once the new modern state is established and the economy develops some momentum. Nationalism can also be held inward and focused on the political consolidation of the victory won by the nation over the colonial power; or it can be turned to the tasks of economic, social, and political modernization, which have been obstructed by the old regionally based, usually aristocratic societal structure, by the former colonial power, or by both in coalition. And then there is in colonial states (or quasicolonial states like pre-1949 China) an understandable priority for "throwing the rascals out."

Once modern nationhood is established, different elements in the coalition press to mobilize the newly triumphant nationalist political sentiment in different directions: the soldiers look to the redress of past grievances or to the exploration of opportunities for expansion; the professional politicians, to the triumph of the center over the regions; the merchants, to economic development; the intellectuals, to social, political, and legal reform. And there is often the wild card of ethnic conflict.

The cast of policy at home and abroad of newly created or newly modernized states hinges greatly, then, on the balance of power within the coalition that emerges and the balance in which the various alternative objectives of nationalism are pursued. Quite often the critical balance is determined not by a clearly definable, stable coalition but by the character of the leader who happens to emerge out of the dynamics of early postcolonial politics.

In such settings — say, Indonesia, Ghana, and Egypt of the 1960s — where passionate domestic politics enjoyed an evident primacy, and external ambitions or anxieties sometimes outranked economic progress at home, development assistance could play only a limited role. It could strengthen the hand of those who, for their own reasons, sought to move their countries forward in a serious sustained effort at economic and social development. What it could not do is to force, say, a Sukarno, an Nkrumah, or a Nasser to concentrate in a steady way his political energies and economic resources on development as opposed to other objectives to which he accorded, for his own reasons, a higher priority. Nor, evidently, could the existence of a flow of development aid guarantee that politics in developing countries would automatically assume democratic forms.

In short, the story of foreign aid in the second half of the twentieth century is crosscut at many points by disruptive crises and other circumstances that, for a time, lowered the legitimate claim of some developing countries for assistance and discouraged donors.

In this setting the major achievement of the 1960s—and Kennedy's in particular—was to institutionalize a substantially larger share of development aid around serious, internationally recognized criteria, so that collaboration for development could proceed, damped, in part at least, from the oscillations in the mood of donors induced by the erratic course of North-South relations or changes in their own domestic and foreign policy preoccupations.

Up to this point, the story of foreign aid has been told from a partisan point of view; that is, the author's frankly acknowledged biases and involvement have been permitted to shape the analysis, defining heroes and villains, successes and setbacks. But it is time now to ask skeptically two questions, the answers to which have been thus far assumed: Were Soviet aid policies in the developing world, in the 1950s, as significant a challenge as Eisenhower, Dulles, and others judged them to be? And, more fundamentally, looking back from the early twenty-first century, were the long-range programs of development aid launched by the advanced industrial countries in the 1950s and 1960s worth the effort?

Like all counterfactual questions in history these are difficult to answer with a high degree of confidence. This is peculiarly true of the question of Soviet aid because Soviet and U.S. policies, in this domain as in others, were interactive; that is, the Soviet aid and trade policies launched after Stalin's death were, in part, a response to Point Four and subsequent U.S. initiatives of the early 1950s just as later U.S. aid policies responded, in part, to the perceived challenge of Soviet policies in India and elsewhere. It is, therefore, impossible to predict what policies Moscow would have pursued if the United States, along with Western Europe and Japan, had not launched the policies it did starting in the late 1950s. There are, nevertheless, a few observations that can be made with reasonable confidence.

First, the bulk of Moscow's economic aid to noncommunist countries in the 1950s was concentrated at a relatively few points of serious strategic interest to the Soviet Union. For example, as of February 1, 1958, 87 percent of Soviet bloc economic aid went to Afghanistan, Egypt, India, Indonesia, and Syria. In ten other countries Moscow kept its hand in with small or modest loans or grants.

The Communist aid effort in the non-Communist developing world was evidently serious, long-term in character, and backed by an impressive flow of resources. But what would it have been if the OECD shift to development aid had not occurred in the late 1950s? One can only guess at an answer. One clue is that the Communist effort was notably enterprising, alert to

Western vulnerabilities, energetic in its exploitation, and undiscouraged by the need to write off failures from time to time; for example, in Indonesia and Egypt. It is therefore reasonable to assume that if the United States and other advanced countries had not responded to, say, Indian and Latin American needs in the late 1950s, the Soviet Union might well have done so with greater vigor; and that Moscow's political and strategic influence and authority in the developing regions would probably have been considerably greater than it was when the Soviet Union came to an end.

There is, however, a significant caveat to be made on this point. The driving political force in the developing regions is, palpably, nationalism. To estimate that enlarged Soviet economic aid, without an answering U.S. effort, would have increased Moscow's influence in the developing regions is *not* to conclude that many more countries would have been brought directly under Soviet control. In fact, military assistance has been a more powerful lever in that respect than economic aid because of the dependence on spare parts and replacements it creates. Even then, several countries have broken out of spare-parts dependence when their national objectives clashed starkly with those of the USSR—for example, Egypt and Indonesia.

Put another way, the fact that the United States did commit itself seriously to programs of development aid did not increase the number of U.S. military and political allies; but it probably did create a better balance between U.S. and Soviet political influence than would have otherwise existed. Beyond that one cannot safely go.

This brings us to a larger question: Has development lending been a good thing? Are the lives of men, women, and children in the developing regions better off than they would be if, say, the doctrines of the chairman of the Randall Commission had prevailed and the advanced industrial countries had confined themselves to technical assistance or no aid whatsoever in their relations with the developing regions?

First, some background facts. Supported by external aid, the aggregate average performance of the developing regions down to the Asian Crisis of the late 1990s approximated or exceeded our earlier hopes, falling in the range of 4–5.5 percent per annum, yielding an average increase in GNP per capita of 1.6 percent for low-income countries and 3.8 percent for those in the World Bank's middle-income range (generally, in what I define as the drive-to-technological-maturity phase). The former figure approximated the nineteenth-century performance of the presently advanced industrial countries during takeoff (1.7 percent); the latter substantially exceeded the earlier performance during the drive to technological maturity (2.1 percent).[76] And these aggregate growth rates were strongly reflected in such basic social indicators as length of life, literacy, and level of education. By

World Bank calculations life expectancy increased from 42 to 57 in low-income countries between 1960 and 1979, from 53 to 61 in middle-income countries. Population per physician more than halved in both categories; adult literacy rose from 27 to 43 percent in low-income countries; between 1960 and 1976, from 53 to 72 percent in middle-income countries; the numbers enrolled in secondary school and higher education about doubled for both income categories. Clearly, there is a long way to go; but sustained economic growth in the third quarter of the twentieth century was not a statistical artifact nor a process insulated from the life of the average citizen.[77]

But I am skeptical that any kind of satisfactory approximation of an answer can be established by argument, one way or another, in these economic and social terms. Moreover, none can deny that economic modernization has costs as well as benefits. I would judge the decisive considerations to be four; and they are all political.

First, the existence of institutionalized development aid elevated the stature of the men and women in the governments of developing countries who were seriously committed to economic and social development and capable of formulating the case for assistance in terms of internationally recognized standards. After all, external resources are, in the short run, extremely important to hard-pressed governments in developing regions; and those individuals capable of negotiating successfully for such resources become important national assets. From close observation of many developing countries, I have no doubt that the domestic priority of development was thus heightened.[78] And I would take that to be, on the whole, a good thing.

Next, in an inherently divisive world, with ample capacity to generate international violence, institutionalized development aid has been perhaps the strongest tempering force, quietly at work, giving some operational meaning to the notion of a human community with serious elements of common interest and common action.

Further, the existence of institutionalized development aid helped dampen, to a significant degree, the domestic conflicts inherent in the modernization process in those countries that pursued reasonably balanced, purposeful, and sustained development programs; and that, rather than the prompt adoption of the institutions of Western democracy, was a critical part of the case for foreign aid.

Finally, institutionalized development aid, when combined with national measures of self-help, has lifted many nations and their citizens from the sense that they are weak and vulnerable to external intrusion. After all, the most common impetus to modernization of economies was articulated a long time ago by Alexander Hamilton: "Not only the wealth but the independence and security of a country appear to be materially connected with the prosperity of manufactures." The dignity of individuals and human communities are at stake in moving successfully through the stages of growth.

My reflection concerns a still larger issue: is regular growth still a legitimate objective for the developing regions? Do global resource and environmental limitations decree that the old devil, diminishing returns, will soon generate a global crisis unless the developing regions and the advanced industrial countries level off promptly, adopt new, less materialistic criteria for the good life, and even things out within the human family by drastic redistribution of income and wealth within national societies and among nations? This was, of course, the theme of *The Limits to Growth,* and since its publication by the Club of Rome in 1972 its central thesis has been both elaborated and denied.

But quite aside from the potentialities for continuing to fend off diminishing returns through human ingenuity — as we have done for two centuries — there is no evidence that *The Limits to Growth* prescription is politically, socially, and psychologically viable. On the contrary, the thrust for higher real incomes by less advantaged groups and nations is one of the most powerful forces operating on the world scene; and so is the determination of advantaged nations and social groups to sustain and even improve their material status. Thus far the tensions generated by these ambitions have been softened because the pie to be divided was expanding. It is one thing to quarrel about fair shares when all are gaining in real income; the struggle for fair shares is a more dour matter in the face of a static or low growth rate in real income per capita.

But trees do not grow to the sky. It is wholly possible, even certain, that, with the passage of time, our perceptions of affluence will change; or change will be forced upon us. More than four decades ago, in writing *The Stages of Economic Growth,* I raised the question of what would happen in the richer societies when "diminishing relative marginal utility sets in, on a mass basis, for real income itself." The problem was much discussed in the 1960s. A margin of the more affluent young went into revolt against the values of material progress and the consequences of those values as they perceived them. They sought nonmaterial objectives. And a no-growth strand exists in the politics of most advanced industrial countries today. But it is not a majority view. The fact is that among both early- and late-comers to industrialization, we must count on a protracted period of effort to continue to grow. Right or wrong, the odds are that the effort will be made; and serious policy-making should be based on that probability. As an African American colleague of mine once said, the disadvantaged of this world are about to buy tickets for a film; they are quite unmoved by the affluent emerging from the theater and pronouncing the movie a flop. They are determined to find out for themselves.

That determination underlines the urgency of the kind of North-South functional cooperation to deal with the problems of energy, food, raw materials, and the environment that we confront in the world economy. These problems if unattended may decree an end to industrial growth after, say, a run of two hundred fifty years from the late eighteenth century.

Moreover, history has also decreed that the human community also faces the decline in fertility—and, unless humanity changes its ways, a corrosive decline of population—a topic to be explored in Chapter 11. Those problems are real and still degenerative; that is, they will worsen with the passage of time unless national and international policies change. We shall have to work together on a global basis to produce both a static global population and a steady improvement in the quality of life and real wages, which continued technological progress will help make realistic.

In the end, those policies should reflect the universal stake, shared equally between the North and South in the continuity of industrial civilization. To that future challenge the story of development in the 1950s and 1960s may not be wholly irrelevant.

Seven

THE REPUBLIC OF KOREA

MY MARGINAL ASSOCIATION
WITH A MIRACLE

INTRODUCTION

The crusading on foreign aid recounted in Chapter 6 was conducted at a
rather abstract conceptual level typical of a struggle over policy in Washington and elsewhere. There was, however, another level of direct contact with
the men and women actually engaged in development in the countries with
which we were dealing. These human contacts cannot be weighed in their
full consequences. But surely—whether they consisted, say, of an informal
conversation with a foreign head of state in a capital city, or the support
given by David Bruce and William Tomlinson to Jean Monnet during the
implementation of the French Modernization Plan,[1] or a Peace Corps member sweating side by side with local people building a tube well in India—
they were part of the story.

Illustrative of both levels of action is the story of my ties with South Korea.

THE HAY-ADAMS BOYS: APRIL-MAY 1961

I was called at the White House by the deputy chief of mission of South
Korea on Wednesday, May 31, 1961. He said that he had three young economists in town. They said they would not go back to Korea until they had
talked with me, and they were using up scarce foreign exchange staying in
America. They had read *The Stages of Economic Growth* and had some questions. I said I was used to students and questions, and suggested we meet
for lunch across the park at the Hay-Adams Hotel on the next Saturday.
Their names were Hahn Been Lee, later deputy prime minister of South
Korea and my major contact over subsequent years; Daniel Kie Hung Lee,
later editor of a Korean equivalent to *Time;* and Kim Young Rok, who died
relatively young but was at that time head of the Bureau of Financial Institutions at the Ministry of Finance. In fact, all three were then chiefs of
important economic bureaus despite their relative youth.

They did, indeed, have a good many questions to ask, and so did I. We talked at length about where South Korea was in its development and its prospects for the future—so long, in fact, that we were politely thrown out of the Hay-Adams at about four o'clock because they had to prepare the dining room for dinner.

Out of that lively occasion I formed the view that South Korea had a well-trained generation of economists who wanted their country to develop rapidly not simply for human welfare but to stand on its own feet against a former colonial power, Japan, a hostile Soviet Union, a hostile China, and a hostile North Korea, the source of recent military attack. They were classic adherents of Alexander Hamilton's case for economic development for security as well as welfare purposes.

At just that time, great political unrest swept through Seoul, which, among other things, overthrew the Chang Myon regime and installed a military dictatorship. Major General Chung Hee Park emerged on top on June 9, 1961. There was some uncertainty in Washington about what sort of political dictator Park was. It turned out that the model for the military revolt was Kemal Atatürk, who took over Turkey, after four years of turbulent struggle (1919–1923), following the collapse of the Ottoman Empire. Incidentally, Park believed, like Atatürk, that modernization required his country to move toward democracy in time, which South Korea did as had Turkey. American generals in South Korea at first took a dyspeptic view of Park because they thought colonels (which Park was initially) should not go about overthrowing generals. (The revolt of the young colonels, whom Park initially led, was triggered by the fact that Korean generals were having soldiers cut down timber in the national forests to sell on the black market.)

Kennedy called in the top American military and civilian leaders in Korea to clarify the situation after the coup. They met around the cabinet table on June 13, 1961.

They presented a rather dismal picture of the prospects for the South Korean economy. Kennedy put to them a sharp quantitative question: "By the end of the decade how much will South Korea need in foreign aid?" The answer from the military men and civilians was: "Roughly the same as in 1961." In short, no progress.

Although I didn't think it appropriate for a presidential aide to debate with cabinet members on formal occasions, I asked the president if I might speak as an economist rather than a public servant. He nodded assent. I said I thought the estimate we had heard was too pessimistic. Park was young and, I thought, would gather around him some young economists who wanted, without prodding from Washington, for their own reasons to

TABLE 7.1 INCREASE IN SCHOOL POPULATION: SOUTH KOREA,
1935–1964 (in thousands)

	1935[a]	1945	1955	1964
Elementary	840	1,382	2,959	4,744
Secondary	38	85	748	1,066
Higher	5	8	87	143
(a) Total school population	883	1,475	3,794	5,953
(b) Total population	22,000	16,000	21,500	28,000
(a) as % of (b)	4	9	18	21

Source: Adapted from Hahn-Been Lee, *Korea: Time, Change, and Administration* (Honolulu:
East-West Center, 1968), p. 49, and from Ministry of Education, *Annual Survey of Education,
1964* (Seoul), p. 2.
   [a] All Korea.

lift the rate of growth, increase exports, and reduce the level of U.S. subsidy. Such economists existed in South Korea, and we should back them.
We would find we were not pushing on a string.

The meeting soon broke up. The president came around to my side of
the table and said in a low voice: "I'll remember what you said. Last year
you thought I could beat Nixon."

I hoped I was right; but the Hay-Adams boys (and other evidence) did
convince me that the post–Syngman Rhee generation would move things
forward. And they did. Even during the Korean War South Koreans' hunger for education, largely denied them by the Japanese occupation, asserted
itself (see table 7.1).

THE BLUE HOUSE CONVERSATION WITH PRESIDENT PARK AND THE MAY 3 SPEECH AT SEOUL NATIONAL UNIVERSITY

It was Dean Rusk who suggested that we open a bilateral meeting with Japanese foreign policy planners parallel to NATO's Atlantic Political Advisory
Group (APAG). We both felt that Japan had passed far beyond the tutelage
of occupation and ought to take its place on the world scene as a major,
industrial country. It was suggested that, as head of the planning staff at
State and U.S. member of APAG, I might open the sessions with Japan if
they agreed that an informal bilateral exchange of views would be useful. In
talks in Washington with the Japanese they agreed, and asked that they host
the first meeting.

I took the view that the meeting should be somewhere in the countryside,
remote from the capital city, which did not lend itself to serious discussion.

We had found in APAG that planners needed to go for walks together and not be bedeviled with complicated diplomatic meals, the theater, and so forth. After APAG's first meeting in Paris, we met subsequently in various estates and castles in the European countries. The Japanese said they would find a comparable setting. After exchanges with Seoul, it was also agreed that I would spend a few days in South Korea and give a talk at the Seoul National University.

The Japanese reassembled the bipartisan senior and junior teams which had arranged Robert Kennedy's trip in 1964. I experienced intensive meetings with groups from virtually every element in Japanese society, in addition to the planners' talks.

After ten fairly exhausting days, I was at the Tokyo airport on Saturday, May 1, 1965, en route to Seoul when a courier arrived from the American Embassy in Tokyo. He had a telegram from Seoul that said my planned talk on Monday, May 3, on Asian regional economic co-operation was too general. The only subject they expected of me was — "Where does South Korea stand in the stages of growth?" — an echo of my book with that title, which was widely read by Korean students.

I signaled my assent; and on the flight to Seoul I began to outline the talk.

On Monday, I met with President Park before I went to Seoul National University. He plunged immediately into the most sensitive current issue — the normalization of relations with Japan. There were in Seoul persistent large-scale riots, including many students in opposition. Park said President Johnson had enough problems in Asia without being concerned with normalization. He then gave me a charge: "I'd like you to give President Johnson this message. 'I have not been in politics long, but I have already learned one lesson. It is easier to keep a quarrel alive than to settle it. Nevertheless, I shall settle our differences with Japan.'" And he did.

Picking up from what he had said, I pointed out that the United States was familiar with this problem. The Mexican government, for example, felt the weight of American economic power severely before 1940. Even the electric power station in Mexico City was owned and run by Americans, and resented by the people of Mexico. Mexico had an old engineering tradition. That changed after 1940 when the takeoff of the Mexican economy began. The Mexicans nationalized the power station. They paid the former American owners in Mexican pesos because they were short of dollars. The Americans invested their money in higher technology fields, in which Mexico needed foreign help, rather than repatriating that sum. Everyone gained.

Park was interested in my SNU speech — how would I deal with the question of Korea's place in the *Stages*? I responded that South Korea, in my view, had begun its takeoff. It had begun to achieve high momentum. It was my conclusion as an American planner that South Korea was in the early phase of takeoff, and it could look forward to a high rate of growth. Korea could now work out with the Japanese what sectors would gain technological advantage and hasten the process of Korean modernization. Just as when Mexico entered takeoff in about 1940 its relations with the United States began to change, so too would Korea's relations with Japan begin to change as its economy took off.

President Park asked if I would tell that story in my talk at Seoul National University. I agreed to do so. (That talk is reproduced as Appendix B).

The speech attracted an overflow crowd, and drew media attention. My conclusion about where South Korea stood in terms of the stages of growth was picked up by the Korean press. A considerable public debate followed. The original reaction was negative. Rostow, they said, was a well-meaning foreigner who obviously did not understand how poor and badly organized South Korea was. After some three weeks of debate, the press came to a more optimistic view of their nation's prospects.

A BRIEF STOP IN SEOUL, OCTOBER 31, 1966

President Johnson made a three-week tour of Asia in the autumn of 1966. The principal subject was not Vietnam but Asian regional cooperation. Seoul was our last stop before returning to Washington via Alaska. Although President Johnson was somewhat tired, the stop in Seoul buoyed him up. Several South Korean divisions were fighting with distinction in Vietnam, and the war in Korea was no distant memory. In addition, a substantial body of U.S. military forces was still stationed in South Korea. We were greeted unambiguously as allies.

Driving in from the airport, the streets were lined by families and their children. The schoolchildren had obviously made the signs they held. One had a picture of President Johnson, with a big Texas hat, inscribed "Welcome to the Cowboy President." On his travels President Johnson was used to manufactured flags and signs. He was delighted with the homemade greetings and got out of his car and returned the greetings by shaking many hands.

This gave me a chance to observe a remarkable phenomenon: the children, who averaged about twelve years old, were systematically several inches taller than their parents. I later sought out one of my economist friends in the South Korean government who confirmed that the younger generation was, indeed, a much taller crop than their parents. He attributed this to improvements in diet.

The cavalcade proceeded to the center of the city. We assembled on a platform that had been prepared for the visiting party and for President Park's entourage.

President Johnson noted the enormous size of the crowd, which stretched as far as the eye could see in all four directions. He asked President Park how many he thought were out there. President Park replied: "That's all we got."

A SOMBER BREAKFAST WITH DR. KIM JAE IK: 1983

Elspeth moved over from deanship of General and Comparative Studies to deanship of the LBJ School of Public Affairs, at the University of Texas in Austin, in 1977. After six years as LBJ School dean, she proposed that we both take a year off. I agreed. And so we went round the world in 1983–1984 under U.S. Information Agency and Fulbright auspices, visiting thirty-two countries, giving one-hundred-plus speeches between us, and, for the most part, having a ball. We included South Korea in our itinerary and saw a number of old friends.

I was urged to meet Kim Jae Ik who was already, as a young man, a high economic official in the South Korean government and universally respected. A breakfast meeting was arranged.

Dr. Kim and I found a good deal to talk about, recalling both the history of economic policy in South Korea and current problems. As our conversation drew to an end, I asked him: "Thinking of your job, what is on your mind when you go to bed at night?"

He took the question seriously, paused, and said: "I worry most about the younger generation. The civil war and years of poverty are far behind them. They take our relative affluence for granted. I don't know if they will rise to the occasion should we hit hard times or great challenges again."

I recalled, in reply, that the young in British and American societies performed well in the Second World War despite somewhat ambiguous interwar behavior.

Dr. Kim Jae Ik, whom I found exceedingly impressive, was killed in Burma by North Koreans a few days later with most of his cabinet colleagues. We learned of this loss en route to Calcutta from Seoul. If I were to respond to Dr. Kim's observation as of 2002 I would say: South Korea did a good job of dealing with the Asian monetary crisis of 1979–1980, but its next crisis will be an awareness of its aging population and its imminent decline. South Korea's fertility rate is now far below replacement at 1.5. To bring the society back to a 2.1 replacement rate and long-term viability will require radical change and a united effort by the South Korean people (see Chapter 12).

TABLE 7.2 SOUTH KOREA'S STATUS IN THE STAGES OF GROWTH, 1980–1997

Economy	Public expenditure on health (% of GDP) 1990–1997	Access to safe water (% of population with access)		Access to sanitation (% of population with access)		Infant mortality rate (per 1,000 live births)		Total fertility rate (births per woman)	
		1982	1995	1982	1995	1980	1997	1980	1997
Korea, Republic of	2.3	83	83	100	100	26	9	2.6	1.7
Upper middle income	3.0	78	79	52	75	57	27	3.7	2.4
High income	6.0	98	..	..	..	12	6	1.8	1.7

Source: World Bank, *Entering the 21st Century, World Development Report* (Washington, D.C., 2001), pp. 242–243, table 7.

THE HAY-ADAMS BOYS THIRTY YEARS LATER: 1991

In the spring of 1991, Hahn Been Lee thought we ought to celebrate our lunch thirty years before. He invited me to Seoul and said he would assemble a group of public servants who had lived through the heroic early stage of Korean economic development. There was an elderly gentleman among them who was evidently a leader of the economists in the 1960s. He was In Sang Song, a Minister of Planning in Rhee's cabinet who had studied development at a World Bank seminar in the United States. Park had kept him on as he had the Hay-Adams contingent.

The occasion was a late dinner at one of Seoul's modern hotels. After dinner Lee went around the table asking for reflections on the past three decades. The discussion was leisurely, as if all understood it was a rare moment. I wished the talk after dinner had been taped because among those who spoke were major figures in the remarkable evolution of the South Korean economy since, say, 1961. When I first rode from the airport to the center of Seoul in 1965, the most memorable feature of the ride were the long rows of small industrial plants throwing long plumes of steam into the air. These small plants were processing Indonesian hardwood logs into plywood for export. Some quarter century later Seoul was a truly modern city, with a handsome skyline. It was backed by a diversified up-to-date industry staffed by men and women who were well educated by high international standards. The city contained banks, insurance and investment companies, as well as excellent hospitals, universities, and restaurants.

In terms of World Bank criteria, South Korea had sustained a rate of growth since 1965 of about 9 percent per annum and had achieved in some thirty-five years a movement from status as a war-torn low-income economy to a status somewhere between an "upper-middle-income" and a "high-income" country (see table 7.2).

South Korea remains an example of how rapidly the technological tricks of modern life can be picked up by a highly educated and motivated people.

Eight

THE EISENHOWER, KENNEDY, AND JOHNSON EFFORTS TO CONTROL INFLATION, 1957-1972

INNOVATIONS SHOULD BE INSTITUTIONALIZED

BACKGROUND

INTRODUCTION

Economists, as usual, were in disarray in the 1960s. To control inflation, some economists thought that short-run demand analysis was a sufficient framework for policy; others like myself believed long-run productivity factors should immediately be part of the mix. My stress on these factors begins with my academic commitment to the Marshallian long-period. In plain English this means a commitment to take account of the supply as well as the demand factors in the life of economies. This includes changes in the population and the workforce as well as technological change, which lies at the heart of expanding economic growth and productivity.

The 1980 preface of the second edition of the Gayer study (see Chapter 1) enunciates clearly the theme of this chapter:

> Chronicles also drive home a general lesson easily forgotten in a world of neo-classical growth models and micro-economic theory: in real life, historical or contemporary, one cannot safely separate the Marshallian short-period from the Marshallian long-period.

Short-run theorists have, of course, been aware of the long-run problem. One device has been to make long-run factors exogenous to the system; that is, subject to forces not taken into account in the theory itself. Conventional modern theorists, for example, treat certain grand inventions, like the railroad, the automobile, and the computer as exogenous.

Before turning to the Action portion of this chapter,[1] I should emphasize a point that plays a significant role in what lies ahead: namely, institutional change is a form of innovation and therefore a long-period force.[2] Institutional change is, as we shall see, peculiarly important in public affairs. Through competition, technological innovation in business usually carries with it—sometimes with a time lag—changes in organization; but innovation in government does not happen unless it is codified in law and organization, decreed by legislation. This explains the paradox of Jean Monnet. He at once believed that his many innovations in public policy had to take institutional form before they could become a long-run reality; on the other hand, he, an innovator, was personally bored once a goal for which he fought assumed institutional form.[3] The paradox is captured in an anecdote as told by Richard Mayne:

> One spring day in 1973, the Action Committee was meeting in the Berlaymont, the massive steel, glass, and concrete headquarters of the European Community's executive arm. As I guided Monnet through the labyrinth, I gestured at all the rows of offices and the functionaries hurrying to and fro. "Isn't it odd to think that all this was once just a piece of paper on your desk?" Monnet's eyebrows rose, "Yes, it's extraordinary." I th... then a pause, "it's appalling." [

Whatever his reaction to Berlaymont and its bureaucrats, Monnet's talk to the first meeting of the Assembly of the Coal and Steel Community gathered in Strasbourg on September 10, 1952, was nearer to his considered thought on this matter:

> The Union of Europe cannot be based on goodwill alone. Rules are needed. The tragic events we have lived through and are still witnessing may have made us wiser. But men pass away; others will take our place. We cannot bequeath them our personal experience. That will die with us. But we can leave them institutions. The life of institutions is longer than that of men; if they are well built, they can accumulate and hand on the wisdom of succeeding generations.

This stricture ultimately bears on the story told in the chapter that follows.

ACTION

THE EISENHOWER SECOND TERM

The setting for the debate in the Kennedy administration about unemployment, growth, and the balance of payments had its origins in Eisenhower's second term. Eisenhower described the period from 1958 to 1961 as "Sputnik and a Sputtering Economy."[5]

The USSR was proceeding (by Soviet statistical methods) at an annual growth rate of about 6 percent, more than twice the U.S. rate. The awkward performance of the American economy in these years reinforced Khrushchev's image as an ardent Avis trying harder and closing fast on a be-deviled Hertz.

In the face of pressures on the balance of payments and high unemploy-ment Eisenhower cut the domestic budget and carried out a policy of mone-tary limitation. Meanwhile, however, he carried out a verbal policy of re-straint of wages and prices by industry and labor. In a summing up H. Scott Gordon, a somewhat disabused historian of policy in this period, has this to say:[6]

> The history of the Eisenhower administration does . . . have something more definite to contribute to our understanding of the politics of stabi-lization policy. It supports a thesis, which could be documented as well from other periods in American history, that the political benefits of an anti-inflationary policy are derivable only from its verbal aspect. An ad-ministration gains public support and favor by expressing a firm resolve to fight inflation and by exhorting others to do likewise. But to act against it with any of the weapons in the stabilization armory, whether fiscal policy, monetary policy, controls, or intervention in labor and other markets, will surely bring a net political loss. In these terms, the Eisenhower admin-istration's policy of exhortation was politically optimal (or nearly so); it preached against evil, and even evildoers have no great objection to that.

Whether Gordon's sardonic conclusion is correct remains to be seen. But, in any case, Kennedy inherited an economy with 5.1 percent unem-ployment (1961), a budget deficit of nearly $4 billion (1961 or some $40 billion in 2000), and an overall balance of payments deficit of about $600 million. These dollar deficits are low, even if inflation since 1961 is taken into account; but, as we shall see, they were a not unimportant part of the Kennedy-Johnson agenda.

SHORT-RUN AND LONG-RUN FORCES

The central intellectual issue was exceedingly simple. There were those who felt that it was legitimate and right to act on the short-term (demand) fac-tors affecting the economy, notably fiscal and monetary policy. There were others who felt that it was legitimate and right to act in addition to make the average increase in wages equal to the average increase in productivity—a long-run factor. And, indeed, they sought to raise the average increase in productivity.

But this simple intellectual issue was by no means simple when it came on the agenda of the Kennedy-Johnson administrations, for they did not merely "preach against evil" but tried to do something about it.

IDEAS

THE "GREAT SAMUELSON-ROSTOW DEBATE" OF 1960

Following Kennedy's successful campaign the public debate began in late 1960 with two MIT economists blowing their respective trumpets loud and clear.

First, there was Paul A. Samuelson who was charged by President-elect Kennedy to do a report on economic policy.[7] Samuelson made an all-out case for an expansionary, short-run, Keynesian policy, financed in part by a deficit, which would return the economy to full employment with industry at an approximation of full capacity. He concluded, however, with "A Final Caution," in the spirit of the long run:

> If there is indeed a tendency for prices and wages to rise long before we reach high employment, neither monetary nor fiscal policy can be used to the degree necessary to promote desired growth.
>
> What may then be needed are new approaches to the problem of productivity, wages and price formation. Will it not be possible to bring government influence to bear on this vital matter without invoking direct controls on wages and prices? . . . Just as we pioneered in the 1920s in creating a potent monetary mechanism and in the 1930s in forging the tools of effective fiscal policy, so may it be necessary in the 1960s to meet head on the problem of a price creep.[8]

A "second perspective," for which I was taken as "a representative spokesman," was put forward as follows:

> I cannot emphasize too strongly that the capacity of the new Administration to do what it wants to do at home and abroad will depend on promptly breaking the institutional basis for creeping inflation, notably in the key steel and automobile industries; and on driving hard to earn more foreign exchange and to increase domestic productivity over a wide front. Without determined action in these areas it will be extremely difficult to bring the domestic economy back to reasonably full employment without inflation; and this means that we shall not have the federal revenues to give extra needed thrust in military and foreign policy. If we do not evoke American effort and sacrifice for communal goals at home, we run the danger of being forced by the balance of payments position and inflation into substituting rhetoric for action abroad.[9]

For some time I had argued to the candidate that he would be merely a "rhetorical Eisenhower" if he permitted himself to be hemmed in by mere exhortation of "shared responsibilities" on the part of capital and labor while the reality of institutionalized inflation, a balance of payments deficit, and the loss of gold reserves forced on him, as on Eisenhower, a sluggish economy.

I also crusaded in public. I earlier used the occasion of a commencement address at the Harvard Business School in June 1960 to propose a series of wage-price "treaties" in which labor would agree to forgo increases in money wages on the understanding that productivity gains would be converted into price reductions.

Evidently, decision on which of these policies to pursue immediately after January 20, 1961, transcended economics narrowly interpreted. It touched on how serious the economic impasse of the Eisenhower administration was judged to be. A conservative task force on international economic policy headed by Allan Sproul (former president of the Federal Reserve Bank of New York) that Kennedy appointed was not of much use, advocating a continuation of "quiet explorations" with capital and labor much in the spirit of those undertaken by the previous administration.

When I came to write of this problem in *The Diffusion of Power* (1972) I entitled the section "The Complexities of Keynesianism in the Real World." Above all, there was nothing in the advice given by either Samuelson or the Sproul committee that dealt with the ominous decline in the nation's gold reserves—a fact impressed on the president-elect by his father. This view was heightened on January 19 by Kennedy's final substantive meeting with Eisenhower as president. Surrounded by Kennedy's three senior advisers (Rusk, McNamara, and Dillon) Eisenhower impressed on Kennedy and his aides that he was leaving them with two overriding problems: the position in Laos, which was then under attack by the Pathet Lao and the North Vietnamese, backed by Soviet aircraft; and the balance of payments deficit. Eisenhower later pronounced himself, to his surprise, as pleased by Kennedy's detailed knowledge of the inflation problem.

Despite his amiable, self-deprecatory stance as only a moderately good student of undergraduate economics at Harvard, Kennedy had long understood the pure Keynesian case for lifting the level of employment and the rate of growth by unbalancing the federal budget, grossly if necessary. In all conscience this was not a very complicated argument. But Kennedy knew his task was more subtle and complex than pure Keynesian doctrine allowed: to lift productivity for the long pull; to cushion pressures on the balance of payments by shorter-run devices; to achieve wage-price understandings from labor and industry that would permit expansion without inflation; and, on these foundations, to persuade the business and financial communities that a large, purposeful deficit — a tax decrease without an expenditure cut — was sound economic policy. He saw all this as a policy to be achieved through time, not instantaneously.

In human and institutional terms, the execution of this policy required the orchestration of Walter Heller and the Council of Economic Advisers; Kermit Gordon of the Budget Bureau; Douglas Dillon at the Treasury; Arthur Goldberg at Labor; Luther Hodges at Commerce; and in the end, it was critically important that William McChesney Martin at the Federal Reserve also be aboard. Under Kennedy's leadership this team came to an effective working consensus with the passage of time. Those who would have preferred the Samuelson policy initially soon rallied around the more difficult path Kennedy had chosen.[10]

ACTION

THE FIRST SOCIAL CONTRACT

In the historical and analytic literature on wage-price guideposts, the story usually begins with Kennedy's letters of September 6 and 14, 1961, to the steel industry and the steelworkers union urging, respectively, price and wage restraint as the agreement of January 1960 came to an end and negotiations for a new contract had to be undertaken. These exercises in jawboning were then followed by the formal enunciation of wage-price guideposts in the *Economic Report of the President* of January 1962, and notably, the *Annual Report of the Council of Economic Advisers* dispatched with it to the Congress. By January 1962 Kennedy was so deeply committed to affecting the outcome of the steel negotiations that he and the Council of Economic Advisers felt it wise to articulate the principles emerging in more general terms.

Interwoven with the formulation and public projection of the guideposts, however, was a rough-and-ready understanding that laid the foundations and provided legitimacy for the jawboning about steel wages and prices. This process reached its climax in the Kennedy–Roger Blough confrontation of April 10–13, 1962. This crude social contract was the forerunner of what ultimately will be required if high and steady rates of growth are to be reconciled with relative price stability. And the hinge on which the enterprise turned was automobiles rather than steel.

But first Kennedy instructed me to talk with Secretary of Labor Arthur Goldberg about the possibilities of inducing both labor wage restraint geared to productivity increases and appropriate price restraint by industry. Guideposts along these lines were evidently required if the Labor-Management Council, already envisaged, was to have substance. Goldberg and I had lunch together at his office on February 1, 1961, the day after a vigorous but inconclusive discussion in the Cabinet Room on wage-price policy.

I put the case to Goldberg in much the same strong terms I had to the president. Goldberg, of course, understood the concept fully. Out of his hard-won experience in labor negotiations he also understood vividly a dimension of the problem to which the economists were initially less sensitive: the human and institutional difficulties involved in bringing a fragmented labor movement, with lively competition among its leaders, negotiating their contracts at different times under different economic circumstances, to effective agreement on wage-price guideposts. He was skeptical the job could be done without legislation. Nor did he believe an immediate voluntary price-wage agreement was possible. But since the stakes for domestic and foreign policy were high and urgent, and legislation was beyond the range of practical politics, he agreed we would have to try with the tools of presidential leadership and executive branch persuasion. We frankly considered the difficulties. In particular, we agreed the construction unions would constitute a major obstacle, and this would prove peculiarly important in a decade when a high rate of growth required enlarged outlays on housing and urban redevelopment.

Having reported this exchange to Kennedy, I returned to the crisis-filled world of foreign policy that kept all of us busy at the White House in early 1961: crises in Berlin, Southeast Asia, the Congo, to say nothing of the Bay of Pigs. On April 5, I came back to Kennedy on the wage-price issue, focusing, in particular, on the critical role of the coming automobile negotiations:

> The negotiations of the wage contract in the automobile industry will be a crucial event for both our domestic and foreign policies. The Big Three contract expires on August 31; and the Union [UAW] will have a major strategy meeting on April 27. . . .
>
> We should, I believe, use every device at our command to persuade the two parties to go for a wage freeze and price cut. . . .
>
> Although we cannot be sure that the auto contract will set a voluntary national pattern, we can be sure that the national pattern will go against us if the auto settlement is inflationary. . . .
>
> A good auto settlement would only be the beginning, of course. The pattern would have to be worked out by industries — construction, steel, textiles, etc. But it is the proper place to begin. And if we don't begin here, we may not begin at all.

Even without a wage freeze, an automobile price cut was possible. Productivity increases in the industry were sufficient to permit both a wage increase equal to the average national increase in productivity (say, 2.5 percent) and a price cut, without reducing profits.

I raised the issue again briefly at the close of a memorandum of April 28 on foreign policy strategy:

> We shall need more money for these purposes, among others: increased military aid; increased assistance in the struggle against subversion; some enlargement in the American military establishment; probably some increased assistance to NATO; an acceleration of the space effort. These expenditures, if they are not to be wholly matched by an increase in tax revenues, require policies which assure the country that inflation will not promptly result, bringing with it a deterioration in our balance of payments. We must, therefore, proceed with urgency—starting with the auto negotiation—to get voluntary price and wage control.

On June 5–6, I was asked to chair a session of the Advertising Council briefings by administrative officials.

The senior speaker at these sessions was Vice President Johnson, who, in the wake of his trip to Asia, made a powerful and moving appeal in support of Kennedy's foreign aid proposals. With Kennedy's approval, I took the occasion to outline the case for wage and price restraint as fundamental to the national effort abroad as well as at home. These remarks were reported to Walter Reuther by his aide Stanley Ruttenberg, who attended the Advertising Council sessions. Reuther called Kennedy and expressed his objections in strong terms.

Kennedy, quite typically, was prepared to encourage his aides to explore a new line of policy, but wished to feel firmer ground under his feet before he became fully committed. He therefore told me to call on Reuther and see if I could persuade him. He said: "You've convinced me. You've convinced Goldberg. Now convince Reuther." On June 20 I went around to his rather grand office in the steel and glass UAW building near the Union Station, noting to myself that the labor movement had come a long way since my parents met, I believe, in a pre-1914 socialist Sunday school.

Ruttenberg was also present but silent. Reuther took the offensive. He addressed me first: "Why you son of a bitch." In lively language he went on to suggest that it was inappropriate, as the first initiative of the Democratic administration, for "White House professors" to throw their weight against a labor movement whose efforts had elected the first Democratic president in eight years. He expressed at some length and with a certain vividness the view that my proposition, as reported to him, was naive as well as inequitable.

I responded that by upbringing and political persuasion I too was rooted in the social democratic tradition and did not require instruction on the rights and virtues of labor. There was nothing in that tradition that required labor leadership to contribute to inflation, which always worked against the interests of labor as a whole; to force stop-and-go policies and low rates of growth on the administration; to deny public authorities the tax resources required for expanding welfare outlays; and to attenuate the nation's capacity to meet its military and foreign aid obligations in a dangerous world.

I then explained, with less color and more technical detail, why I believed it was in labor's interest, as well as in the national interest, to accept a wage increase of only 2.5 percent in the forthcoming negotiations with the automobile industry as well as a price decrease.

Reuther took all this well. There was the beginning of a twinkle in his eye as he turned to the business at hand.

Conscious that his negotiations preceded those in the steel industry, he asked if he were damn fool enough to agree, could Kennedy assure that David McDonald, the steel labor negotiator, wouldn't do better?

I said this was a reasonable condition.

He then asked that if they were both damn fools enough to agree, could Kennedy assure that their restraint would not be exploited by a rise in steel prices?

I said my proposition assumed no exploitation by the steel industry of labor restraint with respect to both auto and steel prices. Auto prices could fall given productivity and profits in the industry. Steel prices could remain steady. There was no intention to shift the distribution of income in favor of profits. He said we shouldn't worry about auto prices. He would look after them. (He didn't.) The price of steel, however, was crucial. He expressed some doubt that "White House professors" could deal effectively with the leaders of the steel industry.

I feared he would raise the question of construction wage rates, for which I had no credible answer. But he did not.

I then summarized what seemed to emerge: auto and steel wage negotiations geared to the average increase in productivity with no exploitation by the steel industry of labor restraint through price increases. I asked if I could inform the president that he agreed to this position. He said he did not agree; but I could tell the president that Reuther would consider it.

I reported back to Kennedy, who chuckled and said I was a pretty good negotiator for a professor. After that, I withdrew from domestic crusading, leaving matters in the hands of thoroughly capable colleagues.

This story is told because Kennedy, in fact, acted in terms of the proposition that emerged from the June 20 talk with Reuther. What subsequently transpired between them I do not know; although Kennedy saw Reuther on August 4 and August 16, on the latter occasion alone and off the record. (Reuther was simultaneously engaged on behalf of the White House in negotiations with Castro on a deal for Bay of Pigs prisoners in exchange for American wheat and tractors).

The key actor for Kennedy in this phase was Arthur Goldberg. He monitored the automobile negotiations during the spring and summer and entered even more deeply into the steel negotiations.

Negotiating habits and traditions differed in the two industries. The automobile union and industry leaders had hammered out, over the years, rather sophisticated and civilized criteria for negotiation, centered on the course of productivity in the industry. Government intervention in these negotiations was rare. Goldberg was, however, in occasional touch with Reuther. His past close connections with Reuther as automobile labor negotiator and current responsibilities as secretary of labor permitted and required a somewhat elliptical and diplomatic approach. In language less blunt than my exchange with Reuther of June 20 (of which Goldberg was not then aware), Goldberg, with Kennedy's support, communicated the rationale for the administration's policy of linking wage increases to the average level of increase in productivity; and he assured Reuther that he could assume that the steel settlement would match the restraint Goldberg was urging upon him. Goldberg acknowledged the difficulties in the construction industry but said Reuther's problem as a labor leader lay in the manufacturing sector.

Kennedy also discussed the negotiations several times with McNamara; but they proceeded to the final phase without deep government intervention, although Goldberg assisted in finding a formula for certain narrow but sticky issues at the very end.

In steel, the tradition was one of strikes leading to one form or another of government involvement — or even dictation of settlement — under crisis conditions. Kennedy and Goldberg were, therefore, sensitive to three major considerations: the possible consequences for the whole economy of the shock of a major strike; their implicit commitment to Reuther concerning the steel wage settlement; and the critical importance of the wage-price outcome in steel for the president's economic policy as a whole. Goldberg was, for all these reasons, deeply involved in the steel negotiations from beginning to end.

Over the summer of 1961 the Bureau of the Budget, the Council of Economic Advisers, and a group of Democrats in the Senate also took a hand. Kermit Gordon called to Heller's attention rumors in the business and financial press that a price increase was contemplated in the steel industry. Acutely aware of the substantive and symbolic role of steel prices in the economy, they called the possibility of an increase to Kennedy's attention.

A group of somewhat frustrated liberal senators was enlisted to apply some heat to the steel industry. Led by Senator Albert Gore, they had themselves quite a day on August 22, 1961, urging the president to use the full powers of his office to prevent a rise in steel prices. Roger Blough was to regard the Senate onslaught as the beginning of the steel-price war of 1961–1962.

THE PUBLIC RECORD

On September 5, as Reuther's negotiations with General Motors moved toward a climax, Kennedy sent telegrams urging a settlement fair to both parties "which preserves price stability in the industry."

On September 6, as the outlines of a restrained auto settlement emerged (about 2.5 percent wage increase, including fringe benefits), Kennedy addressed himself immediately to the leaders of the steel industry. He cited the satisfactory state of profits in the industry and asked them to absorb the wage increases (scheduled under the 1960 agreement to go into effect October 1) without raising prices. Looking forward, he said:

> If the industry were now to forego a price increase, it would enter collective bargaining negotiations next spring with a record of three and a half years of price stability. It would clearly then be the turn of the labor representatives to limit wage demands to a level consistent with continued price stability. The moral position of the steel industry next spring—and its claim to the support of public opinion—will be strengthened by the exercise of price restraint now.

On September 8 McDonald, knowing where Reuther was coming out and with the president's appeal to the steel industry leaders on the public record, pledged to Kennedy his cooperation in assuring that the public interest would be recognized in the 1962 steel negotiations. On September 14 Kennedy responded to McDonald that the public interest in price stability "implies a labor settlement within the limits of advances in productivity. . . . The whole nation has benefited from the price stability in steel for the last three years. We count on all concerned to maintain this stability."

As the president moved toward deep personal commitment in the steel wage and price settlement, the Council of Economic Advisers addressed themselves to the complex principles involved in applying wage-price guideposts to the economy as a whole, to achieve "non-inflationary wage and price behavior." In a full exposition, the council was admirably candid about the intellectual complexities and practical difficulties their policy entailed.

As the narrow community of those interested in technical economic matters was absorbing and debating the guidepost formulation, Kennedy's operational scenario, managed vigorously by Goldberg, unfolded in good order down to March 31, 1962. He was then able to telephone messages to the steel industry and labor leaders in steel, congratulating them on a settlement that was "obviously non-inflationary." Wage rates remained constant, but fringe benefits yielded the same kind of 2.5 percent hourly increase Reuther had negotiated in September 1961. It was also the first steel settlement negotiated without a strike since 1954.

Then came the fateful request of Roger Blough to see the president at 4:40 P.M. on April 10. Blough read the announcement scheduled for public release at 7:00 P.M. of an across-the-board increase in steel prices of $6 per ton: a 3.5 percent price hike. The government felt that productivity and profit prospects in steel justified no increase in prices.

The seventy-two hours that followed have been documented almost as exhaustively as the Cuban missile crisis. Blough was quite clear that Kennedy had persuaded McDonald to accept a settlement in accordance with the wage-price guideposts on the assumption of no price increase in steel; but he was not legally bound to the semi-explicit social contract that had unfolded in the wake of the automobile settlement—a contract without a clear constitutional precedent.

To some extent Blough's action in raising steel prices was an effort to defeat what he regarded as dangerous constitutional precedent. Looking back on the Senate debate of August 22, 1961, he later said: "To my knowledge this is the first time any president has been publicly called upon to exercise control without authority of law—over the price of an entire industry—and initiate or participate in a whole series of administrative and legislative actions of a punitive nature if that control were not accepted." And so he let Kennedy move to hold down the steel wage increase and link it publicly and privately to steel price restraint, without formally committing himself to price stability or otherwise showing his hand. Then he challenged the whole enterprise with his six-dollars-per-ton rise in the steel price.[11]

Kennedy had found and then seized on a remarkably fortunate moment. The economy was in recession. The depressed economic environment since 1958 left a legacy of muted expectations with respect to wage increases as well as anxiety within labor about the level of employment. The accidental sequence of the automobile and steel negotiations provided a unique opportunity to nail down the pattern of a wage-price policy Kennedy needed, aided by two labor leaders who combined a lively competitive sense with considerable statesmanship, by a secretary of labor who had earned over the years the confidence of both, and by an ardent team of first-rate economists.

There was also the fact that neither market conditions nor equity required an increase in steel prices; and that the structure of the steel industry was not only imperfectly competitive but imperfectly monopolistic: it was indicated to Bethlehem Steel that its naval orders, on which it depended, were at stake; and Inland Steel, which had modernized its operations, did not go along with the price increase announced by Blough.

The fate of the guideposts, defined in general terms early in 1962, obviously hinged on the de facto success of the automobile and steel negotiations and on the effort to hold the steel price. The emergence of Kennedy's rough-and-ready social contract demanded that Blough and the steel industry rescind the price increase of April 10. The president would have been in an impossible situation with respect to Reuther and McDonald in particular, and the labor movement in general, if the steel price increase had stayed on the books: the recently proclaimed wage-price guideposts would have been without force.

Kennedy's massive offensive against Blough and the price increase was, therefore, an essential act of policy, as well as the reaction of a man who felt that, as the president of the United States, he had been double-crossed.

On the other hand, lacking a formal legal or constitutional basis for forcing rescission, the president had to improvise a series of ad hoc pressures on United States Steel, which alarmed some critics who thought it an excessive use of the executive power. Kennedy's battle with Blough was imperfectly understood. This happened in part because the underlying linkage of steel-price stability to the prior auto wage negotiations was not widely appreciated, even within the government.

THE UPSHOT

With respect to steel prices, the outcome was salutary. John Sheahan concludes:

> Either the emotional costs of the 1962 conflict with the steel industry were so great, or the lesson so firmly driven home, that no further conflicts over price increase occurred during the next two years. The steel firms did not hesitate to raise some prices in 1963 and subsequently, but they no longer tried to repeat the practice of across-the-board increases on all products by all firms. Instead, some products went up and others down, with different patterns among companies, suggesting careful study of differential costs and competitive conditions rather than a mechanical upward march.
>
> The net result of these more discrete price changes in the steel industry was to accomplish quietly what had been blocked publicly. The wholesale index of iron and steel prices at the end of 1963 was exactly where it had been at the end of 1961.[12]

The outcome in the automobile industry was less satisfactory. Given the higher productivity increase in the automobile than in the steel industry, the correct guidepost outcome for prices, given the 1961 wage settlement, should have been a decline. In the course of the early 1960s this price reduction was not, in fact, brought about. There was, therefore, a disproportionate rise of profits in the automobile industry; and this contributed, along with other factors, to the later breakdown of wage-price guidelines.

In the fragmented construction industry, as expected, the low productivity increase was combined in subsequent years with disproportionately high hourly wage increases: above 4 percent. The bringing of the construction industry into the social contract remains a major unresolved problem of American society.

But, overall, the price performance of the American economy under Kennedy was remarkable by previous standards and, in the short run, roughly met the objectives he had set, as the following table suggests (see table 8.1).

CONCLUSIONS

My direct involvement in the wage-price-productivity problem was limited in time and scope largely to what is reported here. What follows are a few observations that will seek to put in perspective—the problem of reconciling in democracies relatively full employment and relatively stable prices.

1. The effort of the Kennedy-Johnson experiments of the 1960s is part of a long series of formulas for achieving this reconciliation. Aside from the full price and wage controls imposed and accepted by the American public during World War II, there were the short-lived efforts to continue some wartime controls in the immediate postwar period; the full price and wage controls during the Korean War; and the August 1971–April 1974 Nixon-Connally sequence of a freeze and then increasingly selective controls. There have also been phases of exhortation and the Kennedy-Johnson guidelines, which went further than any other effort in the spectrum between *laissez-faire* and full control of wages and prices.

2. On the whole the Kennedy-Johnson guidelines only fell apart in 1966; but the period of uneasiness reaches back into the latter days of Kennedy's presidency.

3. It is wholly explicable in terms of the real enough problems that Kennedy faced as a chief executive; but he did not set up, as Monnet counseled, an institutional structure that would overcome in the Congress, in public opinion, and even within the executive branch the special interests that had to be overcome if the policy were to succeed in the long run. In a memorandum to President Johnson of June 14, 1966, I said, *inter alia:*

> The battle we are now engaged in to hold both prices and the wage guidelines is *not* a battle merely for the next six months until we have a

TABLE 8.1 SOME ECONOMIC INDICATORS FOR THE UNITED STATES, 1957-1965

Year	Consumer Price Index	Av.	Wholesale Price Index	Av.	Implicit Price Index GNP	Av.	Industrial Production	Av.
1957	3.5		3.6		3.7		0.9	
1958	2.7		2.3		2.5		−7.0	
1959	0.8	2.1	−0.2	1.6	1.7	2.4	12.6	2.4
1960	1.5		0.8		1.6		3.0	
1961	1.1		0.0		1.3		0.9	
1962	1.1		0.3		1.0		7.8	
1963	1.3	1.3	−0.3	0.4	1.4	1.4	5.1	5.7
1964	1.4		0.4		1.6		6.4	
1965	1.6		1.8		1.9		8.3	

Source: W. W. Rostow, *The Diffusion of Power* (New York: Macmillan, 1972), p. 146.

political base for a tax increase. It is the kind of battle that will have to be fought on a systematic basis for the long pull, if we are to hold this economy up close to full employment without inflation. I don't think this is clear to [Secretary of Commerce] Connor and [Secretary of Labor] Wirtz—or only half-accepted, if it is clear. . . . I think we shall have to accept this as a normal part of trying to keep full employment without inflation. And we need a general staff operation, focused on each battle-front, sector by sector, as a regular part of our business. Commerce and Labor must become part of a strongly led team. We shall have to work hard to generate public (business, labor, consumer) understanding of what we are doing; why; and what the stakes are for each group and the nation as a whole. . . . Therefore:

—I see no way forward except to refine the guidelines and make them stick; the alternative is inflation or a return to boom and bust.

4. The responsible figures in the Kennedy-Johnson (and other) administrations were able, intelligent men. Their reflections on this problem and how to solve it institutionally covered a wide spectrum of possibilities both at the time and in retrospect.[13]

5. Price control tends to go on the back burner in periods when basic commodity prices are falling for other reasons—as during 1815-1848, 1873-

GNP in Constant Prices	Av.	Per Capita GNP in Constant Prices	Av.	GNP per Person Employed in Constant Prices	Av.	Hourly Earnings	Av.	Unemployment Rate	Av.
2.1		0.6		2.0		5.8		4.3	
-1.6	3.0	-3.2	0.9	0.0	1.8	2.2	3.9	6.8	5.5
6.6		4.6		4.0		4.3		5.5	
2.7		1.4		1.0		3.1		5.6	
1.6		-0.2		1.4		3.0		6.7	
6.1		4.8		4.5		2.9		5.6	
9.0	4.5	2.3	3.0	1.3	2.0	1.0	1.0	5.7	5.0
5.6		3.5		2.7		2.8		5.2	
5.5		4.5		2.9		3.6		4.6	

1896, 1920–1933, 1951–1958 and 1982–2000. Such long swings in relative basic prices are an international phenomenon since 1790; but they have generally been dealt with by mainstream economists as an exogenous rather than an endogenous long-period recurring factor.[14] Therefore, it is the conventional reaction of economists to regard periods of falling prices either as requiring no action or comment or as a major depression (1873–1896); and periods of rising prices as *ad hoc* affairs.

6. In coming to his recommendations at the end of his final essay Arnold Weber says: "First, there has been a consistent failure to develop a national consensus on the objective and rules of wage price policy."[15]

This implies that a national consensus is there to be found or created. Fortunately, there is. It has been found and built upon for considerable periods of time in a number of highly capitalist countries. The consensus has consisted in the overriding interest of the vast majority of people in reconciling a low level of unemployment with a low (or negative) rate of inflation; a sense of equity in the distribution of income among sectors; and a balance of payments that does not threaten to force the nation into depression or devaluation of its currency. The trick is to make these common interests override the inherently competitive nature of the struggle for maximum shares of the national income — capital against labor, union against union — in a fragmented system.

7. This has been done successfully for considerable periods long enough to give us hope that a reconciliation is possible if three rules are applied:

- First, wage changes are synchronous (i.e., made at approximately the same time);
- Second, changes are centralized in the sense that wage changes throughout the economy are related to those in a sector or small group of sectors;
- Third, if the labor force attempts to achieve wage increases in excess of productivity increases, it is understood that the authorities will invoke as a last resort monetary deflation and a rise in unemployment. Some such rules have worked for considerable periods in Japan, Germany, Austria, Switzerland, and the Netherlands.

8. As the 1962 Council of Economic Advisers' formulation of "Guideposts for Non-Inflationary Wage and Price Behavior" indicate, their actual application is more complex than these three rules would suggest. But at the core the institutionalization of an incomes policy in a capitalist society like ours requires that they be honored. Indeed, the success of the common currency in Europe will, in the end, depend on an acceptance of these rules.

My mother's family. Lillian is standing at far right. 1900 or 1901.

My father's family in Arechov (near Ykayernislav), Russia. Victor is standing at far left, in Napoleonic stance. 1900 or 1901.

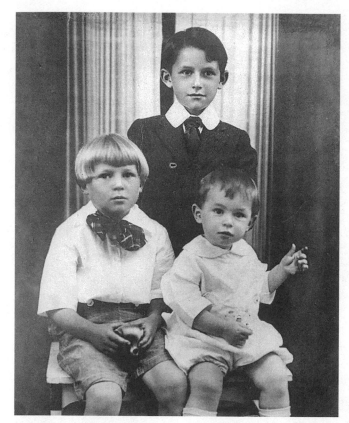

The three Rostow boys: Eugene (standing), Walt (seated, left), Ralph (seated, right). April 1923.

Lillian and Victor, with their three sons, Ralph, Eugene, and Walt. Circa 1931.

The three Rostow men: Ralph, Walt, and Eugene (seated). 1990s.

WWR as camp counselor in Maryland Point. Summer 1933.

Geneva. WWR (standing in back right corner), Elspeth (seated, front left, in saddle shoes). 1937.

Wild Bill Donovan pins a medal (Legion of Merit) on WWR. 1945.

Harmsworth Visiting Professor, Queens College, Oxford. WWR (second row, second from right), Oliver Franks (center, front row). May 1947.

Left to right: unknown, Gunnar Myrdal, WWR, Albert Kervyn (head turned), Nicky Kaldor. Between 1947 and 1949.

Gunnar Myrdal at a trade meeting with his two special assistants: *left,* Albert Kervyn; *right,* WWR. February 1949.

First visit to the Oval Office with Eric Johnston and Executive Committee for International Economic Growth. Johnston is next to Eisenhower. WWR is standing in back, fourth from right. April 8, 1958.

THE KENNEDY "BRAIN TRUST"

Archibald Cox— age 48—Harvard

A Harvard law professor, specialist in labor affairs, with a reputation as a "liberal." Many of his ideas on revising labor laws have won AFL-CIO endorsement. The Supreme Court recently quoted Mr. Cox in an opinion regarded as curbing the powers of business management. If Mr. Kennedy wins, Mr. Cox is expected to get a key position in the Administration. He previously worked in both the Labor and Justice Departments under President Roosevelt.

Walt Whitman Rostow— age 43—M.I.T.

A professor of economic history at Massachusetts Institute of Technology whose theories on economic growth recently attracted international attention. Mr. Rostow discounts, as exaggerated, reports of rapid growth in Soviet Russia. He says the main danger to U. S. is not Soviet growth but American policies. He calls for more Government spending on such things as education, research, missiles and foreign aid.

John Kenneth Galbraith— age 51—Harvard

An economics professor and prolific writer who advocates increased Government spending for public services, less emphasis on production for consumers, and some Government control over wages and prices to curb inflation. He was a wartime director of price controls and a frequent consultant to Government agencies in the Truman Administration. In the presidential campaigns of 1952 and 1956, he was an adviser and "ghost writer" for Adlai Stevenson.

Arthur M. Schlesinger, Jr.— age 42—Harvard

A history professor at Harvard and author who says U. S. overspends for private purposes and underspends for public purposes. He predicts that this country is heading into a new era of "progressivism" and "growing idealism." From his writings, he has become known as historian of the New Deal. He was a speech writer for Adlai Stevenson in his presidential campaigns.

The Kennedy "Brain Trust." *U.S. News & World Report*, July 25, 1960.

Signing in at the State Department, with Elspeth, Peter, Dean Rusk, and Ann.
December 1961.

Berlin. WWR confers with Governing Mayor Willy Brandt in mayor's office in
Schoenberg Rathaus. October 18, 1962.

Peter, Elspeth, and Ann. 1960s.

Opposite page, top: Henry Owen, deputy to WWR in the Planning Council.
December 2, 1962.

Opposite page, bottom, left to right: WWR, Dean Rusk, Bob Bowie, Carleton
Savage, George McGhee. December 28, 1962.

Henry Owen, WWR (back row, second and third from left), and Policy Planning
Council. 1965.

WWR, Dean Rusk, and LBJ. 1966.

Washington, D.C. Elspeth, Harriet Davies (Elspeth's mother), Ann, WWR, and Peter. Mid-1960s.

WWR and EDR. 1970s.

The "Great Samuelson-Rostow Debate," George Kozmetsky as moderator. April 1977.

Tokyo, Japan. May 22, 1980.

WWR, tune writer, with Gordon Craig, lyricist, historian of modern Germany, and professor at Princeton and Stanford Universities. 1990s.

WWR with Arthur Schlesinger (left) at LBJ boyhood home. 1990s.

Nine

CHINA, 1949-

WAITING FOR A DEMOCRATIC REVOLUTION

INTRODUCTION

There is a considerable literature that covers the contentious issues affecting engagement versus confrontation in U.S.-China relations. They embrace, for example, Taiwan, Tibet, and Hong Kong: security problems in Asia as seen from the various capitals; civil rights; the WTO and commercial diplomacy in general.[1] These are immediate and inescapable issues that belong legitimately on the current agenda of dialogue or negotiation between the United States and China. I shall deal here with some longer-run but relevant issues.

QUALIFICATIONS: LIMITED AND UNORTHODOX

But first my qualifications in this field and lack of qualification.[2] The Center for International Studies (CENIS) at MIT was asked by the government in early 1953, only a few years after the Communist takeover, to undertake a study of the prospects for Communist China. Max Millikan, head of CENIS, was consulted and turned to me to lead a CENIS team on China. My previous CENIS study of *The Dynamics of Soviet Society* had proved useful in Washington at the time of Stalin's death.[3] I said that, following the Soviet study, done while I was teaching at MIT, I wanted to concentrate on writing about economic history and development, and that he should get an authentic China expert to do the job. Millikan, however, was turned down subsequently by a considerable number of China experts and general social scientists, at least in part on the grounds that they did not wish to be the targets of Senator Joseph McCarthy and the China Lobby; and this would be the inevitable result of leading the enterprise. So Millikan turned back to me.

Elspeth and I discussed the second invitation. She pointed out *(a)* that my knowledge of China was limited to a bit of its economic history, and that I lacked the language: but *(b)* that China would be important in our lifetime and the lives of our children; *(c)* that I had no left-wing past to hide from Senator McCarthy or anyone else; and *(d)* as a clincher, Elspeth pointed out that I had written extensively about the British nineteenth century without going there or mastering the dialect. So I said yes.

I assembled and took away in the summer of 1953 to Peterborough, New Hampshire, about a hundred books in English about China from the MIT and Harvard libraries. They were not mainly about the modern period, but about the, say, three thousand years of the undulating Chinese dynasties, about the religion, philosophy, art, science, novels, and poetry of traditional China. This enjoyable summer's work was not only an effort to make up after a fashion for my lack of background on China but also reflected an awareness that I was about to deal with a country that had a unique, long, and continuous culture. It was only when I felt I was reasonably familiar with the various facts and interpretations of Chinese history and culture that I turned to the modern period, which I would date roughly and arbitrarily from the Opium Wars (say, 1840–1842).[4]

Although I headed a collective study, I was alone responsible for the conclusions. We set out to answer these questions:

1. What are the operative motivations of the Chinese Communist regime?
2. What are its current intentions with respect to both the society of the mainland and to the external world?
3. What problems does it confront in achieving its purposes?
4. What is the likelihood of Chinese Communist success or failure, in terms of the regime's apparent objectives?
5. What are the prospects for change in Chinese Communist society over the foreseeable future?[5]

The book that resulted came out in 1954. In it, I concluded that (1) the agricultural policy of the regime would not meet China's requirements and the government would have to change that policy; (2) the close Sino-Soviet alliance would not last; and (3) China would be more influenced by the success or failure of efforts in non-Communist Asia than the Soviet Union would be influenced by developments in Western Europe. I discussed Mao and the veterans of the Long March as the first generation of Chinese Communist revolutionaries and speculated a bit about what the second generation would be like. But there was not enough evidence to be dogmatic about them or their successor generation.[6] However, my main points proved out as Mao's people starved, China and the Soviet Union split apart, and China's worldview became more pronouncedly Asian.

In the 1960s, I followed the course of events in China quite professionally as head of the State Department's Policy Planning Council and as national security adviser to two presidents. (As for going there, I got no further than a brief visit to Hong Kong in 1961 on the Maxwell Taylor mission.) This political landscape early in the decade included the Sino-Soviet split (which had actually begun in 1958); the failure of the Great Leap Forward (which had its major impact in 1959–1961); and, after a short period of recovery, the Cultural Revolution, which Mao once described quite exactly as a campaign "to stimulate the masses to dismantle the . . . party bureaucracy."[7]

The final year and a half of the Johnson administration saw signs of a return to rationality in communications between Washington and Beijing, which I described as follows in *The Diffusion of Power:*

> Perhaps the most important diplomatic communication between John-
> son and Beijing . . . took place in the summer of 1967, through the visit of
> the Romanian Foreign Secretary, Ion Gheorghe Maurer. He called on the
> President on June 26, just before going to mainland China. [Maurer asked
> if Johnson had any message to China's leaders.] Johnson told Maurer that
> he wished neither war with China nor to change its form of government.
> He hoped to see Communist China join the society of nations. He be-
> lieved the two countries should discuss the nonproliferation treaty and
> work out ground rules for avoiding nuclear war. He made clear to Maurer
> that he was at liberty to express his view to other governments.
>
> The message was undoubtedly recorded in Beijing, which had then
> not wholly emerged from the convulsion of the Cultural Revolution.
>
> On May 28, 1968, the Chinese Communist Embassy in Warsaw an-
> nounced it wished to postpone the 135th ambassadorial meeting until
> mid or late November, evidently to await the outcome of the American
> election.[8]

The only reply we received to Johnson's message was that the dialogue — which had consisted of mainly propaganda lectures by the Chinese team — would be moved from the virtually public locale of the Polish Palace of Culture to the privacy of the Chinese and American Embassies in rotation.[9] Then came the Chinese communiqué of May 28, 1968, which arrived, of course, after the March 31 announcement by Johnson that he would not run for reelection. It stated that talks between the two countries would start after the American election. We were glad, however, to turn this new arrangement over to President Nixon, who had indicated in a 1967 article in *Foreign Affairs* that he believed a new relationship with China should be established.[10]

Returning to academic life early in 1969 I kept up my interest in China through the teaching of Chinese economic history and a reading of the newspapers and periodicals. In 1984 Elspeth and I spent some weeks in China talking at universities and think tanks in several cities. This procedure was heightened by the fact that the spring term of my seminar not only covered the twentieth century but also speculated about the economic problems of the twenty-first. This led, in turn, to the considerable discussion of current population trends on the Chinese mainland and in Taiwan in *The Great Population Spike and After: Reflections on the 21st Century* (New York: The Oxford University Press, 1998).

Out of this somewhat unorthodox background as a "new China hand" I have emerged with six factors that I would add to the current discussion. Each of them, I believe, should govern an important long-run element in the Sino-American dialogue.

IDEAS

CHINA'S FEAR OF DISINTEGRATION

Some time during my period in Washington, probably in 1967, we received a report that a group of senior regional military commanders called on Mao uninvited, in Beijing; they said that it was their considered opinion that if the Cultural Revolution went on it would result in a Civil War they could not control; and Mao should, therefore, bring the Cultural Revolution to an end if he was to avoid the fate of Sun Yat-sen.

Every Chinese leader, military and civilian, knew of the fate of Sun Yat-sen: although formally proclaimed president of the Chinese Republic in February 1912 after the collapse of the Manchu dynasty in the previous year, he was never able to establish effective central rule. His appeals for assistance to Great Britain and the United States went unanswered. Power fell back into the hands of the regional warlords. In 1923, Sun appealed to the Soviet Union for help. As a result, Mikhail Borodin was appointed to help reorganize the Kuomintang Party (KMT). Chiang Kai-shek went to Moscow to study the organization and tactics of the Communist Party in administration of its sprawling territory.

In 1925 Sun Yat-sen died and was succeeded by Chiang. After consolidating his effective rule of the KMT, Chiang purged the Communists, who had formed the left wing of that party, and launched the Northern Military Expedition. This operation established the Nationalists' rule of China with the significant exception of the Communist escape via the Long March to Shaanxi Province in 1935.

Although the subsequent history of the KMT and the Communists until the latter's ultimate victory in 1949 is not relevant to this chapter, what is relevant is that both the Communists and the KMT built their initial administrative structures on the Soviet model. In fact, what interested the Chinese about the Soviet Union was not primarily Communist ideology but the fact that Lenin had managed to create effective central rule of a large continental landmass.

For the Chinese this was impressive not only because of their experience since 1912 but because, for several thousand years, Chinese dynasties, sooner or later, had fallen into a stage of ineffectual, fragmented rule and were superseded by a band of brothers from the hills who were victorious in internecine struggle. They produced a new dynasty, and effective rule — for a time. The time was usually long in the Confucianist dynasties. But deep in Chinese history as well as in the evolution of communism in the twentieth century there was a concern about the staying power of the center's ability to govern such a vast territory. Perhaps it was a shadow of these fears that played a part in the tragedy in Tiananmen Square in 1989.

Moreover, if the PRC were to take over Taiwan peacefully, it seems likely that Sun Yat-sen's name and memory would play a significant part. Both Communists and the KMT trace their legitimacy from him. The Chiang Kai-shek Museum in Taiwan is, in fact, largely a Sun Yat-sen Museum. It would be easier to unite Taiwan with a democratized mainland in the name and memory of Sun Yat-sen than of Karl Marx, who was not cited often in Mao's works.[11]

THE POSSIBLE RELEVANCE OF THE AMERICAN CONSTITUTION

If the precarious maintenance of unity has been and is now an abiding problem on the mainland, and if there are growing impulses within China to find a path from autocratic to more democratic rule, the example of American federalism may be relevant. After all, American federalism had two distinctive roots:

First, the U.S. Constitution gives residual powers to the states and to the people, after specifying those powers that are assigned to the central government.

Second, in a pragmatic antidemocratic deal, the framers of the Constitution provided that each state, regardless of size, would have two senators each: guaranteeing that in time Rhode Island and (in time) Texas would have formal equal power in the upper house. If that reassuring deal had not been made, the small states may not have agreed to ratification. The unbalanced power on which unity was achieved was exacerbated by the central role of the electoral college in presidential elections, which, again, gives the small states a disproportionate voice.

Most early Americans had an abiding respect for power, yet they did not believe the average human being had the capacity to handle much power with restraint and grace. As James Madison wrote in *Federalist Paper* No. 47: "The accumulation of all powers, legislative, executive, and judiciary, in the same hands, whether of one, a few, or many, and whether hereditary, self-appointed, or elective, may justly be pronounced the very definition of tyranny."[12]

Thus, the deal on the Senate was surrounded in time with other safeguards; that is, the separation of powers, the Bill of Rights, the other amendments to the Constitution, later the Sherman Act of 1890, and other protective features of American democracy. But the structure of the Senate was one of the critical decisions.

The course of the Chinese dynasties confirms the importance of this skepticism of concentrated power. Without a gross violation of Chinese history, there are two strands in the Chinese political tradition: The Legalists and the Confucianists.[13] The longer Chinese dynasties were governed by the fairly permissive Confucianist rules. The Tang, Ming, and Manchu (Ch'ing) dynasties were, for example, among these longer dynasties. This did not exempt them from demographic crises or from crises of morality and morale (see note 2).

The Confucianist dynasties were marked by a willingness of the central authority to avoid interference in detail below the level of the *hsien,* or county. They counted on the citizens of the *hsien* to pay taxes and supply manpower for the army or physical infrastructure; but it was up to the rulers of the *hsien* to deliver the taxes and the manpower requirements of the central authority. By contrast the Legalists sought to impose their authority directly within the *hsien.* They lived by the Machiavellian statement from Shang Yang, fourth century B.C., quoted at the beginning of *The Prospects for Communist China:* "Therefore, in general, an intelligent prince in his administration relies on force and not on virtue." Traditionally, Legalist dynasties lasted only thirty years.

The Communists of the first generation led by Mao belong with the Legalist dynastic tradition. Their first phase, for example, clearly involved the imposition of policy in the villages by Communist cadres who received their orders directly from the center.

It was twenty-seven years from Mao's assumption of power in China until his death. A new dynasty began with Deng Xiaoping's elevation. In many ways his role, including the Family Responsibility policy in the countryside and other elements of the diffusion of power, was that of a somewhat more Confucianist dynasty than its predecessor. But his partial liberalizing moves were accompanied, like other transitional regimes, by simultaneous loyalty to the first generation's form of rule.

The important point, however, is that there is in the Confucianist political tradition a rough equivalent of federalism on which to build in the future. Perhaps Deng's reforms and the pace of Chinese industrialization may have moved China in this direction, as will be shortly considered. Without taking the American solution too literally—after all, there are a good many examples of federalism—perhaps the Chinese should read Madison's notes on the debates at the Philadelphia Constitutional Convention of 1787.[14]

THE SOCIAL DYNAMICS OF CHINA

The triumph of a Chinese version of federalism would not, in itself, constitute movement toward democracy in general; that is, a system that is likely to contain a reliable, independent legal system within which competitive parties work; the substitution of these parties for single-party, Communist rule; and protection of human rights by law, including freedom of speech. Reports from China chronicle in degree the democratic reforms under Deng or his successors without asking how far the process is likely to go or when. Thus, in talking about China one is considering a dynamic society—a society in motion; with an obvious ferment of technological, generational, and even ideological change; dominated by the inescapable responsibility for managing a large country of great diversity.

The process of political change will be accelerated by the likely course of economic events and policies in the generation ahead.

I would certainly not take the view that social, cultural, and political change is a simple function of a superstructure determined by economic and technical change. I take it that the course of events is the result of a complex interactive process in which economic change is only one element in the path taken by societies as they move through history. Nevertheless, the death of Mao unleashed a profound set of changes in Chinese society in which economic change evidently played an important part; and the change in perspective, transcending economic affairs, has been more marked among the young than among the older citizens of China.

The point is implicit in the elaborate essay *China 2020*, put out by the World Bank.[15] The book is more coherent than its complex authorship would suggest. It leaves out many—not all—the issues in contention with the world beyond China; however, it is a remarkable survey of the past twenty years and a candid view of the possibilities and difficulties ahead.

Chinese development since the death of Mao in 1976 is markedly different than before. As the accompanying Figure 9.1 indicates, Mao's rule was marked by two severe setbacks.

Figure 9.1 reflects the romantic but bloody adventures of Mao in the Great Leap Forward, in which perhaps thirty million people died of malnutrition, and in the Cultural Revolution: the former designed to create out of abundant manpower and backyard iron ore the backbone of an industrial revolution; the latter to overthrow the bureaucracy Mao had created since 1949 with the aid of ardent young revolutionaries. Both efforts failed but

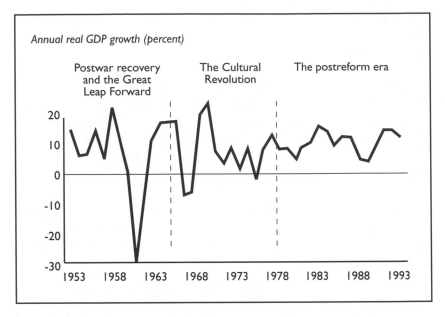

9.1. The Ups and Downs of China's Growth, 1953–1993
    Credit: The International Bank for Reconstruction, *China 2020: Development Challenges in the New Century* (Washington, D.C.: World Bank, 1997), p. 4, figure 1.3.

bore a family relation to Mao's more effective tactics in the preceding civil war in which he mobilized an effective rural-based army.

The Deng Xiaoping era that followed exhibited no equivalent breaks in the continuity of growth, although it was marked by several moderately acute political crises and milder cycles of greater and less inflationary pressure. Nonetheless, in some twenty years China managed to quadruple its GNP, a performance matched only by much smaller South Korea and Taiwan.

The Chinese effort was marked by an increased high rate of domestic savings and investment, an inflow of investment and technology from overseas, and rapid industrialization and urbanization. Behind this authentic great leap forward was the rural household system, which, according to *China 2020,* "went on to become the cornerstone of reforms in agriculture and arguably in the whole economy."[16] This system was launched with large increases in the procurement price for grains. The Communist cadres lost much of their power as the farmers were allowed to sell at market prices all they produced above the rent owed to the government. By 1984, six years after the program was launched, 99 percent of Chinese agricultural households were operating under this system in which they produced, earned, and saved more. There was a similar transfer of responsibility in the many government-owned industrial plants to new industrial managers whose authority to make decisions was enlarged. The results in state industries were salutary but did not match those in agriculture.

All together the results achieved in these two decades reflected the rebound of human beings released in important degree from some of the inhibitions that had bound them tightly in Mao's more Legalist system. China cannot be counted on to maintain this momentum in the time ahead. The history of recurrent chaos still hangs over China's rulers. Speaking in early August 2001 President Jiang Zemin said this: "I am seventy-five years old now and I can tell you with certainty: Should China apply the parliamentary democracy of the Western world, the only result will be that 1.2 billion Chinese will not have enough food to eat. The result will be great chaos."[17]

To dramatize its perspective *China 2020* contains the chart set out below. Specifically, it counsels a threefold development of reforms:

First, the spread of market forces must be encouraged, especially through reforms of state enterprises, the financial system, grain and labor markets, and pricing of natural resources. Second, the government must begin serving markets by building the legal, social, physical, and institutional infrastructure needed for their rapid growth. Finally, integration with the world economy must be deepened by lowering import barriers, increasing the transparency and predictability of the trade regime, and gradually integrating with international financial markets.[18]

In short, *China 2020* recommends strongly that the reforms launched by Deng be carried through along with the buildup of the infrastructure of a market economy and measures that would narrow the gap between a relatively wealthy emergent middle class and a great many others who have not benefited equivalently from the remarkable economic surge of the 1980s and 1990s (see figure 9.2). These developments would strike also at one of China's great current weaknesses: widespread corruption.

Although, technically, China has many of the essentials for high continuous growth along the path Deng pioneered, it is likely to conform to the experience of other countries where growth somewhat slowed with the passage of time and the natural retardation of the sectors that led the way in the previous generation.[19]

This technical retardation may be heightened by the potential clash between the emerging new social structure accommodating to an expanding private sector versus a self-perpetuating dictatorship of single-party rule.

I would certainly not predict that the Communist system in China would change as radically as the Soviet Union has in the third generation after revo-

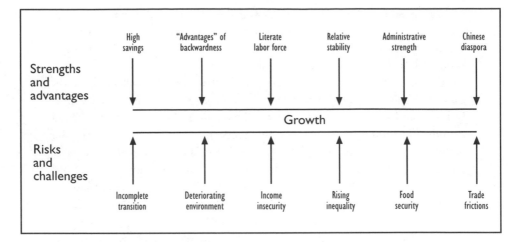

9.2. China's Opposing Forces
Credit: The International Bank for Reconstruction, *China 2020: Development Challenges in the New Century* (Washington, D.C.: World Bank, 1997), p. 19, figure 2.1.

lution. But the pace of economic and social change in China argues that radical political change is possible, and China has proved not wholly insensitive to currents in the rest of Asia that have broadly been in the direction of democracy.

It should be noted that Lucian Pye, at the end of his splendid biography of Mao Zedong, quotes a poem written by Mao early in 1975, a year before his death. It was addressed to Chou En-lai and was entitled "To Reveal One's True Feelings":

> Loyal parents who sacrificed so much for the nation
> Never feared the ultimate fate.
> Now that the country has become red, who will be its guardian?

> Our mission unfinished may take a thousand years.
> The struggle tires us, and our hair is grey.
> You and I, old friends, can we just watch our efforts be washed away?[20]

I doubt that Mao's and Chou's efforts will be totally "washed away," but Mao foresaw correctly that the China that will emerge will be quite different than the one they built.

THE POSSIBLE IMPACT OF DEPRESSION

Deng's rule was accompanied until 1997 in Asia by a sustained period of relative prosperity in the world economy in which China fully shared. It was as if Deng had released at last the natural gifts of the Chinese already exhibited on a smaller scale in Taiwan, Hong Kong, and Singapore—and one could add Thailand and Indonesia—for development and making money.

This boom was featured by—and, to a degree, made possible by—a remarkable increase in Chinese exports and Chinese imports of goods and capital. There is also no doubt that a part of the progress in the field of civil rights was caused not only by the boom itself, which enlarged the size of the Chinese middle class, but also by the human contacts that accompanied expanded foreign trade and capital imports. There was a real sense in which China as a country became for the first time since 1949 a vital part of the world trading system. This movement was enhanced on the social and political as well as the economic side by the absorption of Hong Kong and the need to formulate policy toward a now democratic Taiwan. Similarly, there has been a vast increase in Chinese participation in international organizations and agreements, symbolized by the vote by the American Congress to support Chinese membership in the WTO.[21] There has also been an extraordinary increase of attendance by Chinese students at universities in the West, of which the long-run consequences for China are bound to be considerable.

There are thus strong vested interests in China as well as outside to carry forward this engagement with the rest of the world. But what happened on a global scale in the 1930s is a reminder that the policy of constructive engagement can be reversed. If, for example, the world economy falls again into a protracted depression, China might turn inward to solve its economic problems; and that economic turn might be accompanied by a much more aggressive and nationalistic policy than at present. The fairly democratic regime in Tokyo in the 1920s was succeeded by a nationalist military regime when the world economy, run, in effect, by the democratic regimes in London, Paris, and Washington, fell apart. Hitler, too, was a product of the Great Depression and its weakening of the Western world.

Aside from the future political orientation of China, there are many other reasons for the United States and its fellow democracies to avoid a major protracted depression. But as of the year 2002 we are close enough to a global catastrophe that we should not take it for granted that the world economy is indefinitely immune from such an event.

THE AMBIGUITIES OF DETERRENCE

The record of the United States during the twentieth century, in the matter of actually fighting in war, is quite good. However, in signaling to our potential enemies how we would actually regard their military adventures, our record is quite bad. Dean Rusk reported a statement of Andrei Vishinsky after we had gone to war in Korea despite every sign that we did not regard South Korea as a primary American interest: "The Americans deceived us." In this sense, we deceived the Germans twice (1916 and 1940) and the Japanese once (1940). And in the dishevelment of 1946 we may have deceived Stalin too.

As the First World War opened, the United States seemed to be firmly committed to isolationism. We sold supplies to the Allies on credit, but we did not rearm or acknowledge that we had a serious interest in the outcome of that war. The Central Powers had every reason to take the United States at its neutral word, which was consistent with our lack of preparedness.

Then Germany took two actions that galvanized the United States into action: it adopted in the Atlantic a policy of unrestricted submarine warfare; and it had its Foreign Minister, Arthur Zimmerman, send to Mexico a cable offering that country land ceded in the nineteenth century to the United States if Mexico supported Germany. The presidential election of 1916 sent our potential enemies an ambiguous signal. On balance, Germany expected its actions might lead to war, but judged the United States would not be able to contribute to the Allied cause significantly in the relevant period of time. The long and short of it was that the United States declared war on Germany in April 1917 and tipped the balance in the campaign of 1918 in favor of the Allies.

In the Second World War America was even more unprepared than a quarter century earlier. The Congress had seemingly drawn the firm conclusion that participation in the First World War was a mistake. In 1940, however, there was a radical change. German submarine pens appeared in French ports and submarines sank ships off the American coast; Britain miraculously rescued some 200,000 British troops from Dunkirk as well as 120,000 French. Britain's RAF barely won a defensive battle — but it won — against the German Luftwaffe; Hitler turned east; and both Roosevelt and Willkie backed the Lend-Lease legislation in the election of November 1940.

At the end of the "phony war" (May 10, 1940), some 65 percent of American people felt that the Allies should be aided but that, more important, war with Germany should be avoided. At the end of 1940, the figures had virtually reversed: almost 70 percent of Americans thought it was more important that Germany should be defeated.[22] But the United States did not enter the war until the Japanese, similarly deceived about U.S. attitudes and industrial capacities, bombed Pearl Harbor in December 1941; and Hitler declared war on us.

In 1945–1946 we gave Stalin every reason to think that he had a free hand to make an empire in Eastern Europe. As late as Yalta, Roosevelt told his wartime colleagues that they should not expect the United States to take part in German occupation for more than two years. We unilaterally cut our armed forces and showed other serious signs of restricting our role in the world until the Truman Doctrine and Marshall Plan offer of 1947. But by that time Stalin was already committed to his effort to create a Soviet bloc.

We know little at this point from Chinese documents about what Beijing had in mind when its ships launched missiles in the direction of Taiwan in 1996 in the course of Taiwan's election period. But it was of some importance that two American carrier task forces were promptly sent close to Taiwan without fanfare. It signaled that the United States took seriously the Nixon pronouncement at Shanghai in 1972 that the uniting of China and Taiwan should only come about peacefully.

Perhaps Ezra Vogel's summary in the Introduction to his *Living with China* is the best we can now do:

> Chinese officials became more worried that with support from the American nation, especially from the newly elected 1994 Republican Congress, Taiwan might move more boldly toward independence. When a buoyant President Lee Teng-hui returned from the United States amid growing popularity, China's leaders believed that they could no longer count on the United States to maintain a one-China policy. Chinese explained to Western visitors that they believed strong action was required to counter Taiwanese momentum toward independence, and China fired missiles off Taiwan's shores.
>
> Many members of Congress and administration officials who had criticized mainland China's human rights actions and praised Taiwan were nonetheless sobered by the prospect that the United States might easily become involved in a war with a resolute China prepared to risk millions of lives to ensure that Taiwan and Tibet remained part of China. Beijing was sobered by the negative reactions it evoked with the use of force near Taiwan, not only from the United States but from its Asian neighbors. Hence both China and the United States recognized the desirability of avoiding conflict, thus creating a window of opportunity for meaningful dialogue about long-range interests.[23]

It is likely that in Beijing there are those advocating (at least for the time being) a harder line in relations with both the United States and Taiwan and those advocating a softer line in the interest of Chinese domestic development. In any case the outcome of the 1996 incident off Taiwan was the emergence of an increased willingness of both sides to talk seriously.

The 1996 incident underlined not only the importance of a continuous dialogue about the basic national interests of both parties but also the special responsibilities that they bear as nuclear powers. The nuclear burden

has preoccupied me—as well as many others—since Hiroshima. For example, in November 1946, in my Inaugural Lecture at Oxford, I made the
following observations on the new weapons:

> The great cheapening which has come about in the cost of inflict-
> ing human and physical destruction has thrown in doubt whether, in a
> future war, the total amount of resources commanded on either side will
> in fact be relevant. The atom bomb is not only a weapon of great efficiency
> against concentrations of human beings: it is also capable of destroying
> industrial facilities and stopping production with a thoroughness, and
> for periods of time, far beyond the capabilities of any air weapon of the
> Second World War. After a thousand atom bombs have been delivered,
> what significance has the second thousand? Professional soldiers may
> still be capable of envisaging the need to land and to deploy armies in the
> wake of such attack; and professional sailors may well look to their trans-
> port and supply. But there is probably military wisdom in the laymen's
> suspicion that the new powers of destruction have caused not simply a
> relative change in the nature of war, but an absolute change. In a happier
> day students of history may be entertained by the irony of America's final
> acts in a victorious war, which compromised perhaps fatally the two great
> props of military security—distance and a preponderance of economic
> resources.[24]

In the twenty-first century China will reach a population of, say, a billion
and a half as well as possess a nuclear force of considerable size and range.
Its population may be five times that of the United States and it will be operating a mature industrial economy. The odds, however, are that China will
face the same inhibitions as did the contestants in the Cold War; that is,
a nuclear force is only useful to deter others from using nuclear weapons
against you; and there is no simple proportion between industrial and military capability.

More generally, by the middle of the twenty-first century, the diffusion of
power will produce industrial states in all the continents. The notion of explicit or implicit colonial dependent relationships will narrow or disappear.

In a way, this is unfair. A nation like China, which has experienced a long
passage of poverty, dependence, and civil war, should, by some calculation
of fairness, enjoy a time of glory as it achieves affluence, independence, and
unity. But the panorama of the twentieth century has indicated that the days
of regional hegemony or colonialism have passed. Germany twice, Japan,
and Russia have discovered this fact the hard way. China should find its
satisfactions as a recognized major power in a more benign manner. A mutually transparent relationship between Washington and Beijing—difficult as

TABLE 9.1 SOME DEMOGRAPHIC FACTS ABOUT INDIA AND CHINA

	Population (in millions)	Natural Increase of Population (%)	Fertility (2.1 = replacement)	Est. Population, 2050 (in millions)
India	1,033	1.7	3.2	1,628
China	1,273	0.9	1.8	1,369

Source: Population Reference Bureau, *2001 World Population Data Sheet.*

its politics would be—would not guarantee such an outcome, but it would help, as would a common historical view of the hard road both nations have traveled in the past two centuries.

CHINA AND INDIA

One long-run factor should be defined at this stage even if no dogmatic conclusion can be stated:[25] In the course of the first half of the twenty-first century, the population of India is now projected to exceed that of China. By 2050 China is calculated to contain 1.37 billion; India, 1.63 billion (see table 9.1).

The Chinese natural increase is half the Indian figure, and fertility is almost half; Indian population will begin to exceed the Chinese figure about 2020; the Chinese total population will begin its decline about 2040: Indian population will begin its decline some years later, probably early in the twenty-second century.

The working population of India will exceed the Chinese working population about 2030; the dependent population of China will exceed that of India from about 2020; the draft-age Indian males will exceed the draft-age Chinese males from about 2010; the proportion of fertile-age Indian women will be approximately the same as the Chinese (25 percent) until about 2010, after which the Indian proportion will exceed the Chinese.

These demographic forces will begin to assert themselves in the course of the next twenty years. They stem from China's "success" in the one-child-per-family policy combined with the "failure" of Mrs. Gandhi's effort to impose a similar population-control policy on India. There was a greater surge of economic growth in China than in India from, say, 1980 to 2000. This may also have played a part because affluence is the enemy of fertility.

The government of China has already published its estimates of the rapid rise of the dependent population: from 10 percent in 1997 to 21 percent of the population in 2030, when the figure will reach an astounding 339 million.[26]

In short, after a long period during which China has enjoyed the position of having the largest population in the world, it will be overtaken by India. Both are moving toward command over the major technologies, military and otherwise; but on present estimates, China's population will enter decline perhaps fifty years before India's and will experience the symptoms of rapid aging of the population before India's, with the consequent simultaneous decline in the proportion of the labor force to the dependent population.

The strategic forces that will operate on both governments and societies cannot now be confidently predicted; but this surprising demographic turn of events should evidently be carefully watched and taken into account, for it may improve the odds for engagement rather than confrontation. These deeper long-run questions — rather than the necessary short-run questions alone — are likely to shape long-term Sino-American relations.

Ten

VIETNAM AND SOUTHEAST ASIA

SHOULD THE HO CHI MINH TRAIL HAVE BEEN CUT?

INTRODUCTION

Much has been written about Vietnam. I have contributed something to that literature.[1] What is the case, then, for penning yet another essay on that subject? Two considerations led to my inclusion of this chapter.

First, I was involved in Vietnam planning and policy toward Southeast Asia in part of the 1960s (1961 and 1966–1969). It would have been wrong to have left out the subject in an account such as this.

Second, the voluminous literature on Vietnam has certainly permitted a large number of people to vent their feelings, offer insights, and pronounce judgments. But there is no agreed-upon framework for looking at the debates and defining the central issues. There is a dialogue-of-the-deaf quality to the often impassioned writing on this subject. People tend to talk past each other. Now, more than twenty-five years after the withdrawal of American military forces and the fall of Saigon, I shall attempt here a brief analysis of what I regard as the central issues. Vietnam and Southeast Asia will not go away; we shall have to make American policy there for as far ahead as any of us can peer. And our engagement from the Southeast Asia Treaty (1954–1955) to the fall of Saigon (1975) is a crucial part of American history.

Three issues are taken as central to this debate:

- Over what basic matters did President Johnson and the American military clash as to how the war should be conducted in Vietnam?
- What significance should be attached to Southeast Asia as a whole in the American interest, and what did we do about that region?
- Were the extent of American casualties in Vietnam and civilian suffering in the region and at home disproportionate to the interests at stake in the military conflict in Southeast Asia?

I. THE CONFLICT OVER MILITARY STRATEGY

Until President Kennedy's administration, the foreign policy of the U.S. government in Southeast Asia, including military policy, was governed by SEATO Plan 5. This plan called for the defense of Southeast Asia in alliance with Laos. Put another way, the Eisenhower administration envisaged a thrust south by North Vietnam through Laos toward Thailand, Malaya, Singapore, and Indonesia, backed by the USSR and Communist China together or in competitive parallel. In the gathering in Moscow of heads of state of Communist governments, in the wake of the October 1957 launching of the first Sputnik, it was jointly agreed by Moscow and Beijing that Hanoi would relaunch its offensive against its neighbors after four relatively quiet years (1954–1958). The deep split between the USSR and China occurred in 1958 over the terms on which the USSR would transfer nuclear weapons to China. The Soviets insisted on their control over nuclear warheads; and Mao told them to go to hell.

In a conference with the outgoing president the day before his inaugural, Kennedy was told by Eisenhower that, with the help of a Soviet airlift, the Lao Communists and North Vietnamese cadres were moving into the Plaine des Jarres and toward the Mekong River and Thailand. According to Eisenhower's prediction, Kennedy would probably have to put troops into Laos, if possible with those of other nations, if necessary alone. Eisenhower considered the situation in Laos to be one of two major corrosive issues he was passing along to his successor. The other was the weak U.S. balance of payments and the loss of gold to foreign countries. It was agreed that the United States alone would trade other currencies into dollars (see Chapter 8). As Kennedy later noted, Vietnam was not mentioned.

The first days of the Kennedy administration were taken up with the Communist attack in Laos. The defense of Laos did not go well. At the same time, Kennedy read Edward Lansdale's report after a trip to Vietnam. Lansdale was a wise and effective American adviser to chiefs of government engaged in defending against guerrilla warfare. He had, most recently, advised Magsaysay in the Philippines. In his report on Vietnam, Lansdale noted the increasing pressure being exerted by the North Vietnamese cadres and South Vietnamese Communist infiltrators, and the political as well as military difficulties of Diem. After reading Lansdale's grim report on the afternoon of February 2 Kennedy said: "This is the worst one we've got."

As for Laos, the upshot was the conference in Geneva that aimed at the neutralization of that country. This was achieved by Kennedy's loading Marines in Okinawa, which made the Communists pause in their movement south toward the Mekong; and in Geneva the agreement of Averell

Harriman and Soviet Ambassador Georgy Pushkin that the USSR and the British would guarantee that Laos would not be violated by Communist or noncommunist forces, respectively, en route to North Vietnam or South Vietnam. A control commission of India, Poland, and Canada was also supposed to look after the terms of the Laos agreement, but did not. The Laos agreement went into effect early in October 1962. The North Vietnamese did not obey the Laos Accords for even one day. Infiltration continued.[2] But after a fashion, with that significant exception, the neutralization of Laos was accomplished.

In the wake of the Laos Accords Kennedy turned to Vietnam. One of the measures taken was to send General Maxwell Taylor and me on a mission to Southeast Asia, including Vietnam. By this time Kennedy had decided to alter SEATO Plan 5. If he had to fight in Southeast Asia, Kennedy decided he would fight in Vietnam rather than Laos. He took this step for three reasons:

- Vietnam had a bigger, more mature and effective military establishment. It was a more advanced but still underdeveloped country;
- The logistics of supplying forces on the Mekong from Thai ports required longer and more complex lines than supplying through Saigon;
- Vietnam was a better base to bring American naval and air strength to bear.

General Taylor advised Kennedy that he should formulate his strategic outlook before Taylor headed out on a mission to Asia. After a long session with Kennedy, this is how Taylor and I set down the president's view on August 4, 1961, in a joint memo to him:

As we understand your position: you would wish to see every avenue of diplomacy exhausted before we accept the necessity for either positioning U.S. forces on the Southeast Asian mainland or fighting there; you would wish to see the possibilities of economic assistance fully exploited to strengthen the Southeast Asian position; you would wish to see indigenous forces used to the maximum if fighting should occur; and that, should we have to fight, we should use air and sea power to the maximum and engage minimum U.S. forces on the Southeast Asian mainland.

The Taylor mission resulted in a considerable increase in American advisers to the South Vietnamese; but Kennedy was not prepared at that time to put formal U.S. military units in Vietnam although he stationed a battalion of marines offshore in case of an emergency.

On the whole, 1962 was a relatively good year for South Vietnam. In 1963, however, things went bad politically. In 1964 things went bad militarily.

Buddhist protests began on May 8, 1963; important differences surfaced between Washington and Diem on the handling of the Buddhists. This led to the South Vietnamese coup against and the assassination of Diem and his brother Nhu on November 2. Kennedy, much troubled by the manner of Diem's removal from power, was himself assassinated some three weeks later.

Between General Minh's assumption of responsibility after the assassination of Diem in November 1963 and Prime Minister Quat's turning over the power of the state to the Armed Forces Council at the end of June 1965 — a nineteen-month period — there were some eleven changes of government or attempted coups in South Vietnam. The military situation deteriorated. With Thieu as chief of state and Ky as prime minister, however, a substantial period of relative political stability and peaceful evolution was launched, marked by a series of well-inspected elections.

But the period of instability (which began, of course, prior to Diem's assassination) was as costly a passage in postcolonial political history as the world has seen; for it reignited Hanoi's hopes for victory and led to a decision, probably in the summer of 1964, to introduce regular North Vietnamese units into the battle for South Vietnam in the winter–spring offensive of the 1964–1965 dry season.

On January 27, 1965, two of the senior officials carried over from the Kennedy administration, Robert McNamara and McGeorge Bundy, sent President Johnson a joint memorandum, which the latter described as follows:

> On January 27, 1965, Mac Bundy sent me a memo saying that he and Bob McNamara were "pretty well convinced that our current policy can lead only to disastrous defeat." They had reached a critical moment in their thinking and wanted me to know how they felt. They argued that the time had come to use more power than we had thus far employed.
>
> As Bundy put it:
>
>> The Vietnamese know just as we do that the Viet Cong are gaining the countryside. Meanwhile, they see the enormous power of the United States withheld, and they get little sense of firm and active U.S. policy. They feel that we are unwilling to take serious risks. In one sense, all of this is outrageous, in the light of all that we have done and all that we are ready to do if they will only pull up their socks. But it is a fact — or at least so McNamara and I now think.
>
> Bundy and McNamara saw two alternatives: either to "use our military power in the Far East and to force a change of Communist policy or to deploy all our resources along a track of negotiation, aimed at salvaging

what little can be preserved with no major addition to our present military risks." They said that they were inclined to favor the first alternative — use of more military power — but they believed that both courses should be studied carefully and that alternative programs should be developed and argued out in my presence.[3]

In the six months between this joint memorandum and Johnson's decision of July 28, 1965, when substantial American forces were committed to Vietnam, the North Vietnamese applied maximum pressure to South Vietnam. But by the end of 1965 the tide had slowly turned and the long slow process of wearing down the North Vietnamese and Vietcong forces and building an infrastructure for the American military was begun.

This was the background to a fundamental decision made by President Johnson when he decided to put substantial U.S. forces in Vietnam. As commander-in-chief he decided that U.S. forces would not move outside the borders of South Vietnam. That rule did not apply to air power nor to covert operations. It was nevertheless a momentous decision. (I was over in the State Department and did not participate in it.)

Johnson's rules of engagement determined how U.S. forces would be used. It decreed that the battle would be fought as a series of attritional engagements inside South Vietnam with implications for the casualties inflicted on U.S. and Allied forces, North Vietnamese forces, Vietnamese civilians on both sides, and for the length of the war. The Communist forces had the advantages of sanctuary to which they could withdraw. Above all, they had a protected line of supply from North Vietnam down the Ho Chi Minh Trail through Laos to South Vietnam and Cambodia. There was not even a Saturday Night Special produced in North Vietnam or South Vietnam.

The critical role of a sanctuary for supply lines in a guerrilla war was raised before we put a large number of American troops in Vietnam. Here, as of the early 1960s, is the analysis of James E. Cross, my colleague in CENIS, starting with the communist guerrilla offensive in Greece, and ending with a prescient comment on Vietnam:[4]

> There, in the years immediately after the war, Communist-led guerrillas had received massive aid and reinforcement from across the Yugoslav and Bulgarian borders and were well on the way to overthrowing the government by the spring of 1948. Then, following Tito's break with Moscow, the Greek-Yugoslav border was closed, and the guerrillas in Greece, deprived of well over half their support and barred from their most valuable bases, became gradually weaker. The Greek government was able to assume the offensive, and the threat of a Communist take-over by guerrilla action was past.[5]

The evident conclusion of these campaigns was that unconventional offensives built around guerrilla operations and mounted against reasonably responsive and competent governments have little chance of gaining national victory unless they receive sustained and large-scale support across a contiguous border and can look to the Communist side of that border as a sanctuary and base as well as a source of supply. These were the conditions under which the Vietminh were able to defeat the French in the long Indochina war, and it is precisely this situation that obtains, at this writing, in South Vietnam.

The costs of this policy were not lost on the American military. General Taylor cabled from Saigon near the close of 1964:

> [Hanoi] enjoys the priceless asset of a protected logistic sanctuary in the DRV and in Laos. I do not recall in history a successful anti-guerrilla campaign with less than a 10 to 1 numerical superiority over the guerrillas and without the elimination of assistance from outside the country.[6]

Senator John Stennis echoed this point in August 1967: "The question is growing in the Congress as to whether it is wise to send more men if we are going to just leave them at the mercy of the guerrilla war without trying to cut off the enemy's supplies more effectively."

And McNamara himself quotes General DePuy, General Westmoreland's planner, in a 1986 interview: "It turned out that [search and destroy] was a faulty concept, given the sanctuaries, given the fact that the Ho Chi Minh Trail was never closed. It was a losing concept of operation."

I had secondhand reports of the North Vietnamese military view that the Ho Chi Minh Trail was decisive to their military victory, but never had direct evidence. While writing this chapter, I ran across the following report in Richard H. Shultz Jr.'s *The Secret War against Hanoi,* which I quote in detail:

> Finally, there were the peace activists. While they had opposed U.S. involvement in the war, few had the opportunity to meet face-to-face with North Vietnamese leaders. This began to change in the 1990s, as such encounters took place in Hanoi and elsewhere. Other political activists likewise were involved in such meetings.
>
> One such session took place in 1995 between a human rights activist from Minnesota and a retired NVA colonel. A hardened veteran who had fought many battles against American soldiers, Colonel Bui Tin was no ordinary NVA commander. On April 30, 1975, Hanoi had given him the honor of receiving the unconditional surrender of the South Vietnamese regime. Earlier, in December 1963, he had been involved in the decision

by the North Vietnamese Politburo to expand its use of the Ho Chi Minh Trail. As they chatted, the human rights activist asked many questions about the war. Toward the end of the meeting, he came to the heart of the matter. "Colonel, was there anything the United States could have done to prevent your victory?" he asked. In the dogmatic canon of the antiwar movement, the answer has always been an unequivocal "No." After all, they believed, North Vietnam had the "mandate of heaven" on its side. There was nothing the United States and its military machine could have done. Hanoi's victory was in the stars.

The colonel's answer was a devastating refutation of this protest-movement orthodoxy. To prevent North Vietnam's victory, Bui Tin observed, the United States would have had to "cut the Ho Chi Minh Trail." The human rights activist queried, "Cut the Ho Chi Minh Trail?" "Yes," he repeated, "cut the Ho Chi Minh Trail inside Laos. If Johnson had granted General Westmoreland's request to enter Laos and block the Ho Chi Minh Trail, Hanoi could not have won the war." He then explained the strategic importance of the trail for Hanoi's escalation and conduct of the war. It was the only way "to bring sufficient military power to bear on the fighting in the South. Building and maintaining the trail was a huge effort, involving tens of thousands of soldiers, drivers, repair teams, medical stations, and communications units." If it had been cut, Hanoi could not have intensified the fighting with NVA regulars, as it did in 1965. This did not mean that the United States and its South Vietnamese client would automatically have won. No, they still had to defeat the Viet Cong and win the support of the people. Nevertheless, cutting the trail would have made those tasks significantly easier.

It was a telling revelation from one who should know. As the discussion unfolded, Colonel Bui Tin's observations became more and more convincing—they actually made sense. This raises a fundamental question. If this made such obvious sense, how is it that the "best and the brightest" didn't figure it out during the war? It is a good question.[7]

Thus, the sanctuary granted Hanoi was historically incompatible with American and South Vietnamese victory in a time span consistent with American patience as a nation; and the bombing of the supply trails or other devices to reduce the flow from North Vietnam were demonstrably inadequate.

This was the lesson of guerrilla warfare all the way back, at least, to the Peninsular War of the Napoleonic era.

The American military formally presented to President Johnson a plan on April 27, 1967, to put some 200,000 additional troops across the Ho Chi

Minh Trail in Laos roughly opposite the Seventeenth Parallel across from the truce line dividing Vietnam. Since July 1965 the military had built the infrastructure for the enlarged Allied forces in Vietnam. They had made steady but slow progress in 1966. They were ready in 1967 for a decisive battle to end the sanctuary provided to the North Vietnamese. They had behind them the Soviet violation of their undertaking at the Laos Conference at Geneva in 1962.

In the wake of a military exposition on April 27, 1967, I indicated my support, which Johnson already knew. The military and I were turned down by the president, Rusk, and McNamara.

We advocated a decisive engagement, in Laos where the Ho Chi Minh Trail entered South Vietnam, where the North Vietnamese would be forced to fight for their vital supply lines and for the sanctuary they enjoyed. It would not be an attritional engagement from which they could withdraw as in the past. They would have to stand and fight our kind of war against the massive artillery and air power we commanded and they did not. We envisaged the kind of battle fought at the thirty-eighth parallel in Korea, which General Matthew Ridgeway organized and which stopped the retreat from the Yalu in 1951 and led ultimately to the truce in Korea.

Why did the president hold to his rules of engagement? The answer is simple. He knew that the Soviets and Chinese were both nuclear powers. He was determined to defend Vietnam and Southeast Asia without at his initiative bringing on the United States and the world a much larger war and perhaps a nuclear war. He (and Rusk) never forgot the traumatic entrance into the Korean War of the Chinese Communists. Both men bore serious responsibilities in 1950–1951, in the Congress and executive branch, respectively.

I believed then—and believe now—that those fears were exaggerated, but in a matter of this kind I felt a profound reticence in pressing the case. First, in a nuclear age the margins of error should not be estimated too fine. Second, Johnson had an acute ear and a remarkable memory: repetition was not required. Third, and above all, the positions of a president and an adviser are quite distinct. The best formulation of the problem was Rusk's. He used to say: "If I urge a course of action on the President, he adopts it, and things go wrong, I can call up and say 'Sorry, sir,' resign, and disappear. The President must live with his decisions and their consequences." He, not I, had been chosen by the American people to make decisions involving nuclear weapons. I owed him my best prayerful advice. But I did not owe him my public opposition.

I agreed on the whole with the domestic and foreign policies of the president. So I stayed with Johnson to the last day, while steadily but quietly opposed to the way the war was being fought. This he knew; but it did not affect our mutual trust or our friendship.

Speaking at San Antonio on September 29, 1967, Johnson replied, in effect, to McNamara and others and explained his position. It was a rare presidential statement that reveals the uncertainty that lies inevitably behind a decision.

> I cannot tell you tonight as your President—with certainty—that a communist conquest of South Vietnam would be followed by a communist conquest of Southeast Asia. But I do know there are North Vietnamese troops in Laos. I do know that there are North Vietnamese trained guerrillas tonight in Northeast Thailand. I do know that there are communist-supported guerrilla forces operating in Burma. And a communist coup was barely averted in Indonesia, the fifth largest nation in the world.
>
> So your American President cannot tell you with certainty that a Southeast Asia dominated by communist power would bring a third world war much closer to terrible reality. One could hope that this would not be so.
>
> But all that we have learned in this tragic century strongly suggests to me that it would be so. As President of the United States, I am not prepared to gamble on the chance that it is not so. I am not prepared to risk the security—indeed, the survival—of this American Nation on mere hope and wishful thinking. I am convinced that by seeing this struggle through now, we are greatly reducing the chances of a much larger war—perhaps a nuclear war. I would rather stand in Vietnam, in our time, and by meeting this danger now, and facing up to it, thereby reduce the danger for our children and for our grandchildren.

Perhaps the last word is that of General William Westmoreland, speaking with hindsight on March 10, 1991:

> The geographic restraints on the ground war were very real, and understandable.
>
> Yet if you'll look at the situation as it's turned out, we basically attained our strategic objectives. We stopped the flow of communism. . . . I conclude that by strength, awkwardness, and good luck, most of our strategic objectives have been reached. I also say that we have to give President Johnson credit for not allowing the war to expand geographically . . . he was quite fearful that this was going to escalate into a world war. One of his main strategic objectives was to confine the war. He did not want it to spread. . . . Having said that, that's not the way I felt at the time. I felt that our hands were tied.[8]

II. SOUTHEAST ASIA: ITS STRATEGIC POSITION

Having failed to convince President Johnson of my notion of how the war in Vietnam should be fought, I did not campaign for my view inside or outside the government. But I did throw my weight into the other part of the job accelerating economic growth and encouraging regional cooperation in Southeast Asia as a whole. Southeast Asia together with Japan, South Korea, and Oceania now contain almost a billion people. If mainland China and India are included, add another 2.2 billion. About 40 percent of the world's population lives in Asia including China. Despite the economic crisis from which the whole area is now recovering, Asia is likely to be the most economically dynamic part of the world in the twenty-first century. Virtually all of its countries have moved into takeoff or gone beyond: Japan is roughly as rich per capita as Western Europe and is the second-largest economy in the world—a status now endangered by its precarious demographic position. In the twenty-first century a number of its countries will command all the then-current military technologies. China is a nuclear power and both India and Pakistan, nearby in South Asia, have crossed the nuclear weapons' threshold.

Incidentally, I should perhaps indicate here that the American government, at no time in my experience, ever lacked knowledge of Asia or Asians —and that includes Vietnam and the Vietnamese. Our ties to that part of the world go back a long way in our history, ties of commerce and, in the case of Korea, of war. There were in the American government authentic experts on the individual countries of Asia—and they were regularly consulted. Whatever mistakes may have been made in our dealings with Asia did not stem from ignorance.

Aside from Asia's population, economic and technical momentum, the United States gradually demonstrated in the twentieth century a calculus there symmetrical to that in Europe: it opposed any nation that threatened to take over the balance of power in the region. It opposed, in turn, Japan, Communist China and the Soviet Union (when they worked together or in parallel), and Communist China when it moved ambitiously on its own.

As in Europe, America encouraged the regional organization of power in Asia, which elevated for the long pull the collective power of the smaller nations behind which was thrown implicitly or explicitly the support of the United States. As for Southeast Asia narrowly conceived (including the so-called protocol states: South Vietnam, Cambodia, and Laos) the United States was committed formally by the SEATO treaty since 1955 and the article of the U.S. Constitution that regards treaties as "the law of the land." In short, the United States declared formally that holding the balance of power in Southeast Asia was part of the task of holding the balance of power in Asia.

Dwight Eisenhower, John Kennedy, and Lyndon Johnson came to hold this treaty as a correct expression of U.S. interests although they had quite different experiences of Asia. Only the victory of the United States at Midway had prevented us from being forced by the Japanese to abandon all positions west of the continental United States. Subsequently, China emerged as the potential Japan of this region. Aside from the control of the Pacific, the control of the Strait of Malacca would cut off Russia, Japan, and all of Southeast and East Asia from normal shipping routes to Europe and the West and would almost certainly detonate a major war. It is by no means inevitable that China will pursue these expansionist objectives, but it is evident that some such goals have already tempted some in Beijing.

U.S. engagement in Vietnam was rooted, as we have seen, in the Southeast Asia Treaty. This involvement, lasting some twenty years, was conducted at various levels by the Eisenhower, Kennedy, Johnson, and Nixon administrations. Perhaps most striking of all, when President Johnson spent some three weeks touring Asia in the autumn of 1966 (October 17 to November 2) he spoke almost exclusively about the need for a cooperative economic organization in Asia, explicitly including, in the long run, China. On this trip there was a conference in Manila of the nations contributing troops to the struggle in Vietnam. The Manila Declaration of October 25, 1966, emerged. An excerpt from its communique demonstrates its thrust:

> We, the seven nations gathered in Manila, declare our unity, our resolve, and our purpose in seeking together the goals of freedom in Vietnam and in the Asian and Pacific areas. They are:
>
> 1. To be free from aggression.
> 2. To conquer hunger, illiteracy, and disease.
> 3. To build a region of security, order, and progress.
> 4. To seek reconciliation and peace throughout Asia and the Pacific.

Johnson exploited his travels to drive home at virtually every stop the theme of Asian regional cooperation, notably, in his speeches at the East-West Center in Honolulu; at a parliamentary luncheon in Wellington, New Zealand; at a similar occasion in Canberra; at the Manila Conference; at a state dinner in Kuala Lumpur; in his joint statement after discussion with President Park in Seoul; and in the rain at Dulles Airport on the night of November 2. The emphasis was uniformly on his faith, in the end, that Asia and Asians would shape their own destiny and that the role of the United States and others willing to help was to assist in a critical transitional period, "when needed and when invited." For example, in Wellington on October 20, 1966, Johnson stated:

> The key to Asian peace in coming generations is in Asian hands.
> For it is Asia's initiative that will found the institution of progress.
> It is Asia's example that will inspire its people to build on the bedrock of social justice.
> It is Asia's dream that will determine the future for three of every five human beings on earth.
> And I know that your nation and my nation will respond to that dream and will respond willingly and will respond generously.

As nearly as one can make out in retrospect, Johnson's emphasis during this trip on the future organization of Asia had little resonance in the United States. The Johns Hopkins speech of April 1965 had been widely reported and supported. But this was a year and a half later, and the United States was now directly engaged in a difficult war. Approval for Johnson's handling of the war had dropped in the polls from its peak of 57 percent in January 1966 to 43 percent in October of that year. A substantial part of that decline consisted of self-designated "hawks," who remained a majority in the polls until the spring of 1968. They felt that Johnson was not pursuing a sufficiently decisive military strategy. In this setting press coverage of the Manila Conference concentrated on the continuing struggle in Vietnam, including especially a formula agreed to at Manila for the withdrawal of all foreign troops within six months of a North Vietnamese withdrawal from South Vietnam. The major exceptions were an article in *U.S. News and World Report,* October 31, 1966, headed "Asia: World's New Frontier" and a piece in *Fortune* (December 1966) entitled "New Building Blocs for Asia," which began as follows:

> It's too bad that the news reporting of the Manila Conference left the impression that it was principally concerned with cooking up a political formula for inducing Hanoi to negotiate the Vietnam war. The deepening American involvement in that war unavoidably overshadowed all other considerations at Manila, but war-waging did not dominate the agenda by any means.
> The principal discussions concerned the future shape of the Pacific Asian world. In a quiet way, there was a good deal of talking back and forth about economic and social development, and about how various difficulties might be overcome on a collective basis. In these matters, President Johnson and Secretary Rusk deliberately retired into the background. The Asian and Pacific statesmen did most of the talking, and it was clear

that they had their own ideas about how they and their neighbors might best begin to work together on affairs of common value. This preliminary search for common ground is what made the Manila meeting a genuine turning point in the relations of East and West.[9]

Although thought in the United States about Asia continued understandably to focus on a protracted, slow-moving attritional war, in which Americans died and were wounded every day, Asians continued to act in 1967–1968 as if they shared Singapore prime minister Lee Kuan Yew's judgment of the American role in Vietnam. On June 15, 1966, Lee said that the United States was "buying time" for the nations of Asia and "if we [in Asia] just sit down and believe people are going to buy time for ever after for us, then we deserve to perish."[10]

On April 7, 1965, in Baltimore, when Johnson was considering the introduction of large forces in Vietnam, he first outlined his views on Asian regionalism. Johnson was responding to a deep American instinct and pattern of behavior. When confronted with the ugly reality of war or its likelihood—as Johnson was in the spring of 1965—Americans have instinctively reached out to give active expression to the large ideals in which our sense of nationhood is rooted. Thus, for example, the transcendent terms of the Declaration of Independence and the Gettysburg Address, of Wilson's Fourteen Points and the Atlantic Charter. A similar impulse underlay the balancing of the Truman Doctrine with the Marshall Plan, the confrontation with Cuba and support for Latin American economic and social development in both the late Eisenhower and Kennedy periods. And so it was with the image of Asia's future evoked by Johnson as he came to his critical decision on Southeast Asia.

The great positive purposes articulated on these occasions were, in each case, both a reflection of our operating style and a legitimate part of the struggle under way. Their evocation not only widened the basis for public support in the United States but also, to the extent that they were judged credible by those engaged outside the United States, rallied support abroad. On this occasion Johnson not only held out the hope of the United States contributing to the construction of a dam on the Mekong but he unleashed a somewhat reluctant Eugene Black, anxious about his health, to consult with Asians about the setting up of a regional bank to support development. As it turned out, Black was remarkably effective and the Asian Development Bank came to life with Japanese, American, and other initial contributions.

But the most important result of the crusade for Asian regionalism was the emergence of the Association of Southeast Asian Nations (ASEAN) on August 8, 1967. ASEAN was, in fact, the product of a long history. Its origins reached back to the Association of Southeast Asia (ASA) established on July 31, 1961, by Malaya, the Philippines, and Thailand, whose impulse to move toward association had been still earlier foreshadowed in the diplomatic initiatives referred to as Maphilindo. ASA's activities were confined to economic, social, and technical fields; but its creation reflected an uneasiness about the security of the region. Specifically, there was dissatisfaction with the weakness of SEATO in the face of the Communist incursions into Laos, notably the ambivalent policies of Britain and France. This was compounded by the pursuit of a neutral Laos in U.S. negotiations with the USSR and uncertainty about what stance the United States would ultimately take toward the gathering Communist pressure on South Vietnam. In addition, ASA responded to a shared desire of these intensely nationalistic but vulnerable states, freshly emerged from colonialism, to begin to reduce their dependence on external powers and to take more of their destiny into their own hands. Thus, the major themes of ASEAN as of 1965 included a common preoccupation with the independence of the Indochinese states, which were present in ASA more than twenty years earlier.

The emergence of post-Sukarno Indonesia provided a practical basis for the creation of ASEAN. The discussions between the Indonesian foreign minister Adam Malik and the Malaysian deputy prime minister Tun Abdul Razak, which ended the confrontation and normalized relations, led directly to the notion of establishing a grouping wider than ASA. A series of meetings at the Thai seaside resort Bangraen yielded ASEAN, in which Singapore as well as Indonesia joined the original ASA members; but the settlement between Djakarta and Kuala Lumpur was a necessary prior condition.[11] The first operating tasks referred to the ASEAN Standing Committee, located in Djakarta, were in the fields of tourism, shipping, fishing, and intraregional trade. But beneath the surface were the security concerns of the region reflected in this statement of the founding declaration: "Considering that the countries of South-East Asia . . . are determined to ensure their stability and security from external interference in any form or manifestation in order to preserve their national identities in accordance with the ideals and aspirations of their peoples." ASEAN was built slowly but quite solidly from 1967 forward.

Speaking in Boston on November 11, 1981, the Malaysian foreign minister, Tan Sri M. Ghazali Shafie, reflected thoughtfully on the significance of this phase of ASEAN's evolution in relation to the 1975 debacle in Indochina.

In its early years, specifically between 1968 and 1975, ASEAN activity was conducted through eleven Permanent Committees which encompassed the social and economic goals of the Association. Basically this was a learning stage of getting to know each other's systems, their strengths and weaknesses and their procedures. The going was slow, because each party was treading gingerly along so as to avoid sensitivities which were generally created by different colonial pasts, or to avoid disrupting a basic process so critical to the strength and resilience of the other.

They were very useful years to further bind the member countries together. Besides, in the less sensitive areas of culture exchanges, tourism, research and development, and training on existing institutions, major advances were made. Travel controls within ASEAN were relaxed, special ASEAN package tours were developed—harmonisation of port procedures were initiated; radio and television programmes were exchanged; several festivals of the mass-media were launched. Indeed, a popular movement on ASEAN was launched to emphasise the strength of the Association and to relate its activities with the daily life of the people—so as to break down the ramparts of history and of prejudice. It was important that our peoples understood the need for togetherness so as to garner support for our efforts to strengthen the system of free enterprise which was serving them well. Indeed one of the earliest results and heartening features of ASEAN are the growing number of conferences and projects undertaken by private organisations and the business community.

In 1975 North Vietnamese tanks rolled past Danang, Cam Ranh Bay, and Ton Son Nut into Saigon. The United States withdrew their last soldiers from Vietnam, and the worst of ASEAN's fears which underscored the Bangkok Declaration of 1967 came to pass. But ASEAN by then had seven solid years of living in neighbourly cooperation. Call it foresight, or what you will, the fact remains that with ASEAN solidarity there were no falling dominoes in Southeast Asia following the fall of Saigon to the Communists, and the United States withdrawal from Southeast Asia.[12]

Something else was happening in the first decade of ASEAN's existence: extraordinarily high rates of economic growth were sustained throughout the region (see table 10.1).

There was some retardation under the impact of the global recession of 1974–1975, but a sharp rebound in 1976.

The expansion of real GDP and GDP per capita was accompanied by a shift to manufactures and manufactured exports, which expanded unevenly but generally, at even higher rates (see table 10.2 and figure 10.1).

In all cases, for example, there was a rise in per capita caloric and protein supply between 1967 and 1974.[13] Education levels and indicators of health

TABLE 10.1 PATTERNS OF GROWTH PERFORMANCE IN ASEAN (per Capita GDP and Real GDP Growth)

| | GDP at Market Prices | | Per Capita Growth Rates | | Real per Capita GDP in 1970 Constant U.S.$ | | | GDP Growth Rates at Constant Prices (%)[a] | | | | | |
	Per Capita (U.S.$) 1975	Index	1960–1974	1965–1974	1970	1974	Compound Growth Rates (%) 1970–1974	1969–1973	1972	1973	1974	1975	1976
Indonesia	260[b]	32	2.4	4.1	77	140	12.3	8.7	8.2	12.8	6.6	5.2	(7.9)
Malaysia	750	91	3.9	3.8	320	380	4.4	7.8	6.7	11.3	8.0	3.5	8.5
Philippines	350	43	2.4	2.7	175	200	3.4	6.5	4.2	10.1	4.8	6.6	6.4
Singapore	2,500	292	7.6	10.0	930	1,320	9.1	12.8	11.3	11.1	6.8	4.1	6.8
Thailand	350	43	4.6	4.3	180	210	3.9	7.2	4.3	10.3	4.6	5.5	6.3
ASEAN Average	842	100	–	–	–	–	–	–	–	–	–	–	–

Sources: *World Bank Atlas 1976*, supplemented by national sources: for Indonesia, Biro Pusat Statistik, *Statistik Indonesia, 1974–1975* (Jakarta, 1976), and *Bulletin of Indonesian Economic Studies*, March 1977; for Malaysia, The Treasury of Malaysia, *Economic Report* (Kuala Lumpur, various years), and Bank Negara Malaysia, *Annual Report and Statement of Accounts, 1976* (Kuala Lumpur, 1977); for the Philippines, National Census Statistics Office, *Philippine Yearbook 1975* (Manila, 1976), and NEDA, *Philippine Economic Indicators*, September 1976; for Singapore, Ministry of Finance, Singapore, *Economic Survey of Singapore, 1976* (1977); and for Thailand, Bank of Thailand, *Monthly Bulletin*, March 1977.

Secondary Source: John Wong, *ASEAN Economies in Perspective* (Philadelphia: Institute for the Study of Human Issues, 1979), p. 135.

[a] The starting levels for constant market prices differ for individual ASEAN countries: Indonesia, 1973; Malaysia, 1970; Philippines, 1972; Singapore, 1968; Thailand, 1962. The growth series for each country is indicative of the historical growth performance of that country, though it is not quite so useful for intercountry comparison.

[b] It has become known that previous national income estimates were understated by over 20 percent. The figure here is based on the "input-output table 1977." See Olch Nugroho, "Table Input-Output Indonesia, 1971," *Ekonomi dan Kellangan Indonesia*, June 1977.

TABLE 10.2 PERCENTAGE OF GROWTH OF MANUFACTURING PRODUCTION IN ASEAN (at Constant Prices)

	Value added 1960–1969 (average)	Manufacturing and Production 1960–1969 (average)	1969	1970	1971	1972	1973	1974	1975	1976 (first half)
Indonesia	5.9	2.8[a]	—	15.0[b]	10.1	—	15.2	16.1	—	—
Malaysia (West)	10.4[c]	—	15.6	12.3	6.2	22.8	21.0	15.3	0.0	18.5
Philippines	4.6	5.9	3.0	1.5	10.6	9.3	10.7	-2.2	-0.8	3.1
Singapore	19.5	12.7	52.7	7.8	14.3	15.8	17.0	4.2	-2.3	7.7
Thailand	10.9	—	—	12.1	10.8	9.7	13.8	4.2	6.9	7.5
ASEAN	10.3	—	—	—	—	—	—	—	—	—
For comparison										
All developing countries	—	—	—	—	6.6	9.2	10.0	6.4	3.9	—
World	—	—	—	—	4.0	7.5	9.6	3.7	-2.2	—

Sources: UN ESCAP, Mid-term Review and Appraisal of the International Development Strategy in the Second United Nations Development Decade in the ESCAP Region, 1974, p. 83; Economic and Social Survey of Asia and the Pacific, 1976, March 1977; UN, World Economic Survey, 1975.

[a] 1960–1968.
[b] Value added.
[c] 1960/1961–1969/1970.

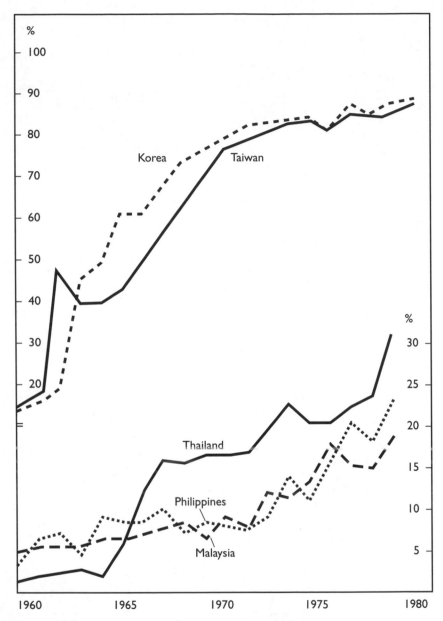

10.1. Percentage Shares of Manufactures in Total Exports of ASEAN and Asian Newly Industrialized Countries (NICs), 1960–1979

Credit: W. W. Rostow, *The United States and the Regional Organization of Asia and the Pacific, 1965–1985* (Austin: University of Texas Press, 1986), p. 72, chart 1.

and health services also generally responded positively (see tables 10.3 and 10.4).

This kind of sustained, palpable progress, experienced in a region that also contained parallel examples of high growth and modernization in South Korea, Taiwan, and Hong Kong—let alone the continuing momentum of Japan—strengthened the sense of confidence among the members of ASEAN. They concluded that history had not automatically destined them to fall under one kind or another of Communist dominance. The economic and social viability of the individual countries also contributed to the will to assert certain shared diplomatic positions through ASEAN.

In addition, it was during the 1960s and 1970s that the seriousness and depth of the economic problems confronted by the PRC became increasingly clear and were, indeed, acknowledged with admirable candor by the authorities in Beijing. In fact, looking about on the world scene, the members of ASEAN had no reason to believe that models for economic and social development existed better than those they were evolving on their own.

One other regional institution moved forward with élan in these years: the Asian Development Bank (ADB). Corrected for the approximately 45 percent price increase between 1969 and 1975, average annual lending, in real terms, increased by three and a half times in the first phase of the ADB's history. Like the region it served, the ADB was a going concern by 1975, an instrument of multilateral cooperation respected widely within Asia and beyond.

Thus, the ten-year interval between Johnson's decision to introduce American troops to Vietnam and the fall of Saigon was well used by the peoples and governments of the Western Pacific and their friends. This development—often ignored by critics of Johnson's policy—engaged much of the president's time and attention, and was an integral part of his strategy.

III. WERE U.S. AND VIETNAMESE CASUALTIES DISPROPORTIONATE TO U.S. INTERESTS IN SOUTHEAST ASIA?

The official U.S. casualty figures in Southeast Asia from 1965 to 1975 are roughly 47,000 killed in action; nearly 11,000 died of other causes; and 303,000 wounded. To these should be added the casualties of our allies and Vietnamese, South and North, which are estimated to have run, respectively, to 200,000 and 900,000 killed, or about four and eighteen times the American figure. The number of Americans killed in the more intense but shorter engagement in Korea (1950-1953) is about the same: 54,000. These figures tell us nothing of the pain and disruption suffered by those caught in the wars, including their families and other civilians. There is, of course, no way

TABLE 10.3 INDICATORS OF EDUCATION LEVELS: ASEAN, 1960, MID-1970S, AND 1981

| | Number Enrolled as Percentage of Age Group | | | | | | Number Enrolled in Higher Education as Percentage of Population Aged 20-24 | | | Adult Literacy Rate (%) | |
| | Primary School | | | Secondary School | | | | | | | |
	1960	1977	1981	1960	1977	1981	1960	1977	1981	1960	1975
Indonesia	71	86	100	6	21	30	1	2	3	39	62
Malaysia	96	93	92	19	43	53	1	3	5	53	60
Philippines	95	105	110	26	56	63	13	24	26	72	87
Singapore	111	110	104	32	55	65	6	9	8	—	75
Thailand	83	83	96	13	27	29	2	5	20	68	84

Sources: World Bank, *World Development Report, 1980* (Washington, D.C., 1980), table 23, pp. 154–155; *World Development Report, 1984* (Washington, D.C., 1984), table 25, pp. 266–267.

TABLE 10.4 HEALTH-RELATED INDICATORS: ASEAN, 1960 AND 1977

| | Population per: | | | |
| | Physician | | Nursing Person | |
	1960	1977	1960	1977
Indonesia	46,780	11,530	4,520	2,300
Malaysia	7,060	7,910	1,800	940
Philippines	6,940	7,970	1,440	6,000
Singapore	2,380	1,150	650	320
Thailand	7,900	7,100	4,830	2,400

Source: World Bank, World Development Report, 1984 (Washington, D.C., 1984), table 24, pp. 264-265.

to measure the death and human suffering caused by the war in Southeast Asia — or, indeed, any war — against the issues at stake in that conflict.

Lyndon Johnson believed with absolute sincerity that the alternative to holding the line in South Vietnam was the risk of a much larger war engulfing all of Southeast Asia at least and quite possibly a nuclear war. That was the meaning of what he said at San Antonio and the final temoinage of General Westmoreland.[14] The alternative that Johnson stated at San Antonio would clearly have brought with it more casualties and human suffering than the war in Southeast Asia as it ground on.

I must return to the wild card in this story: the manner in which the United States was driven into painful controversy over the war. And that is a part of the equation for all Americans. With the exception of the Second World War, every conflict in which Americans have been engaged has involved major public controversy. And this is to our credit, for who wants war? In the Revolutionary War, perhaps one-third of the people wanted independence; one-third were pro-British; and one-third awaited the outcome more or less passively. In the War of 1812, the New England states, in the Hartford Convention, passed a resolution calling for withdrawal from the Union rather than joining in the war against Canada. The Mexican War stirred great controversy in the United States. The Civil War, of course, split the nation—with divisions lasting for more than a generation at least. The Spanish-American War was followed by the unpopular conflict with Philippine guerrillas. The First World War, like the Civil War, touched off draft riots. The Korean War left Truman more unpopular than either Nixon at the nadir of his fortunes, or Lyndon Johnson at his lowest point in the polls.

No one has promised that American independence itself, or America's role as a bastion for those who believe deeply in democracy, could be

achieved without pain or loss or controversy. The pain, loss, and controversy resulting from engagement in Vietnam were accepted for ten years by
the American people. That acceptance held the line so that a free Asia could
survive and grow; for, in the end, the war and the treaty that preceded it were
about who would control the balance of power in Asia, an issue that was evidently at stake in the Asian crisis of 1965 and thereafter. Those who died or
were wounded in Vietnam or are veterans of that conflict were not involved
in a pointless war. As General Westmoreland wrote in the *New York Times*
of May 28, 1990: "The wisdom of President Johnson's strategy of avoiding
a larger and possibly uncontrollable war and at the same time protecting our
strategic interest has been sustained by history" (see note 12).

I once put the issue differently. Elspeth, who continued to teach at American University throughout our time in Washington, once asked me: "Have
you ever thought that you might be wrong on Vietnam?" I can remember
looking at her in some amazement: "Of course!" I replied. "Often. But I've
gazed like hell at the alternatives and this is the painful best choice."

Eleven

THE URBAN PROBLEM, 1991–

PREVENTION VERSUS DAMAGE CONTROL

WHERE DID THE AUSTIN PROJECT COME FROM?

When my family (wife, two teenage children, mother-in-law, standard poodle) moved to Austin in early 1969, my personal agenda was to teach and to write a series of books, the last of which was *Theories of Economic Growth*. As I pursued this congenial line of work, I became aware of an interesting transition with which all of Texas was grappling. The 1970s was both the last stand of Texas as a major source of oil and gas for the country and its dawning as one of the nation's major centers of high-tech industry—the Lone Star Silicon Hills. I had a chance to observe both sides of this transition. On the one hand, I was part of the Texas team that helped the governor of Texas speak on energy in Texas and Washington, during the energy crises of the 1970s; on the other hand, I was on the outer fringe of the group encouraging the coming to Austin of MCC (Microelectronics and Computer Technology Corporation) in 1983.

What struck me was a simple, brutal fact. In the oil and gas windfall of the 1970s and the gathering momentum of high-tech in the 1980s what I learned to call the Anglos were reaping the main rewards of prosperity and the Hispanic and black communities much less. For example, when the team working on the plan for the Austin Project (TAP) took stock in 1994, using the 1990 census as the base, we found that unemployment averaged 6 percent in Travis County as a whole, 13 percent in the eastern part of the city, where most Hispanics and African Americans live. Durable manufactures, then Austin's leading sector, employed 17 percent of the population of Travis County, but minorities held less than 4 percent of the jobs in that vital sector. One can multiply such statistics indefinitely, but these figures from Austin's submission for an Empowerment Zone (June 8, 1994) are typical:

The median family income within the nominated Empowerment Zone [the poorest part of Austin] is less than half that for Travis County: $17,700 versus $35,931. The per capita income of the Zone residents is approximately 40% of all residents of the county. Almost four times as many people in the nominated Empowerment Zone live in poverty as compared with the county as a whole. Within the Zone, the poverty rate is 36.7%; for the county, it is 9.6%.[1]

If we traced back these income figures into low-weight births, school dropouts, incarceration, gangs, level of educational attainment, it was clear that a vicious circle was at work. Minority children started life on a perilously unequal playing field.

The first plan of what was to be the Austin Project was quite specific:

> [The reality is] low incomes; severe chronic unemployment; humiliating dependence on welfare; anxiety about the children and their fate; nights suffused with the fear and sometimes the reality of crime and violence that isolates many behind doors of their houses; and a pervasive sense that their neighborhoods are cut off from the affluence [of their Anglo fellow citizens].
>
> If that is all there was to life in the neighborhoods there would not be much hope. But there is, in both the Hispanic and African American communities, pride in their cultures; an abundance of creative, intellectual, and administrative talent; men and women who hold their families together against tough odds; leaders at every level — in the blocks and neighborhoods, churches and schools, business and professions — who every day strive to build a future in which the men, women, and children of their neighborhoods take their just place in American society with a heightened loyalty to their cultural roots.[2]

Roughly, this vision of Austin's missing potential gradually formed up in the 1970s and 1980s when I was writing *Theorists*. When that book went to the printer, I began to outline with my wife what became the Austin Project, which was initially presented and published in its *Proceedings* by the American Philosophical Society at Philadelphia.[3]

Bruce Todd was elected mayor of Austin in 1991. Shortly after his election we met for the first time at a reception at a local club. The new mayor asked casually what I was doing these days. To his surprise I launched into an exposition of the paper we were working on about the urban problem with special reference to Austin. Probably to be polite, Todd asked to see the paper when we finished it. I agreed. It turned out that he cared deeply about the people on the east side of town; and, without publicity, had visited most of the schools in that area.

From that time forward we have been colleagues in bringing the Austin

Project to life: first when Bruce Todd was mayor; then when he stepped down, as my successor as chair of the board and CEO at TAP. (His able successor is Wayne Holtzman, former head of the Hogg Foundation.) I remain on the board.

Mayor Todd and I began in 1991 by trying to sell the idea of an "Austin Project" to members of the Austin City Council, the Travis County Commissioners Court, and the school board, as well as to leaders of both minority communities and majority communities, philanthropic agencies, religious leaders, leaders of the private sector, the Chambers of Commerce, and so on.

This was an exhausting, often frustrating, but overall rewarding enterprise. I often returned home to be greeted by Elspeth as the Willie Loman of urban renewal. Todd and I spent time listening as well as talking. But we *did* talk!

We stressed the importance of preventive action, from prenatal care to the workforce and the professions; indicating that, after small-scale experiments, we would try to take the whole enterprise "to scale." By that phrase we meant to match the scale of the Austin community's efforts with the scale of the city's problems. Never, however, did we attempt to be a service provider. Instead, we hoped to act as a catalyst to bring together the many agencies in Austin into a common effort. I told the mayor that I intended, if we succeeded, to put ourselves out of business by having the task taken over by the city, county, and the school board as well as by, above all, the citizens of the neighborhoods. His reply "Not so fast!" probably reflected some skepticism of academics as practical politicians.

The splendid bishop, John McCarthy, expressed well the mixture of goodwill and skepticism with which we started: "God bless you. I don't know whether you'll succeed, but it is worth trying."

Some people wondered why I was apparently suddenly turning from national and international issues to focus on urban issues. To me the transition was obvious. As an economic historian I had long been concerned with economic development, tracking developing countries closely from my years at MIT to my time in government service. There was—and is—a certain parallel between urban problems and those confronting an underdeveloped country. On the positive side, disadvantaged sections of modern cities are physically close to vital communities and economies that could (in theory at least) help them. They also have had higher incomes per capita than most underdeveloped countries. On the negative side—and much more serious—the urban poor exhibit progressive weakening of family structures, which gravely inhibits their capacity to develop. They can accept assistance; but they frequently have great difficulty developing on their own.

There turned out to be another basic difference between a typical developing country and the typical disadvantaged section of an American city. The typical developing country had a more or less coherent government that was led by its own dynamism, by the example of other more advanced developing countries, by the fads or wisdom of its economists, or often by the terms on which it could get money from the United States, the World Bank, or other bodies — it was led to consider its development as a whole, as an interconnected system. Sometimes the plans that emerged from these pressures were initially dreadful. For example, some economists from MIT's Center for International Studies were sent out early in the 1950s to help Sukarno's Indonesia with its Five-Year Plan. Before long they found it impossible to work constructively, and they were withdrawn. Later I had occasion to see the completed plan and found it a rather shapeless compendium of statistics. In fact the Indonesian economy did not begin to develop until Sukarno had been deposed in 1965. In other developing countries — for example, South Korea after 1961 (see Chapter 7) — the national plans were coherent, the parts fitted, and development proceeded in a reasonably orderly way, with roles for the expanding private sector as well as for the public sector. Top-down planning? Yes, but at least it was effective; and in the early stage there was no center of initiative if the government did not lead.

There was no equivalent in the disadvantaged American neighborhoods of this sequence that occurred naturally among developing countries as they made their way from traditional to modern societies. The communities were governed as part of a larger city; and the city governments themselves, the churches, the foundations, and the welfare agencies usually had no workable plan for their underdeveloped neighborhoods taken as a whole. State governments, the Congress, and the federal agencies were equally frustrated in dealing with those trapped in urban poverty.

The result was a pattern of fragmented, reactive efforts. More often than not, in effect, fires were being put out rather than fire-preventive policies being put in place. City governments tended to deal with the most flagrant symptoms of urban problems; churches to do something helpful about the symptoms of a problem too big for a church to handle. Foundations tended to do something constructive about one particular facet or another of the urban problem (pregnant teenagers, family violence, dropouts, medical abnormalities, etc.), in part because they did not wish to tie up their limited funds for a long period, which any generous plan would do. State governments could only act in a limited way on the cities, and tended to stick with what was familiar (education, although that was largely assigned to local school boards; public health; police; etc.). Congress, meanwhile, was ill-constructed to deal with urban problems except by fragmentation in which each of the various committees was sovereign in its own narrow domain. As for the executive branch, it had its own inherent fragmentation to overcome, though the urban problem as a whole was finally handed to the Department of Housing and Urban Development.

Thus, America's urban problem as a whole systematically clashed with the nation's political process. Despite the many people of skill, devotion, and goodwill long engaged with the problems of the disadvantaged areas of the cities, their efforts by the end of the twentieth century had neither resolved the issues separately nor resulted in any consensus approach.

1992: THE AUSTIN PROJECT BEGINS

The Austin Project was formally announced on May 6, 1992, by Mayor Bruce Todd, supported by the county judge, and the president of the school board.

By this time, I had set up a task force to flesh out a coherent and consistent plan for Austin. This group of some twenty-five members from the public sector, the University of Texas, and the world of service providers agreed on the basic premise of preventive action, stretching comprehensively from prenatal care to the workforce and the professions. After a lively set of sessions, the task force produced a 350-page report that constituted the basic framework for TAP.

By a conservative estimate, the problems facing East Austin at that time cost the Austin community as a whole some $390 million per annum in 1992, when measured against the average cost of services for Travis County. I would guess the figure is now at least $450 million (2002).

The report, entitled *An Investment Plan for the Young: The Austin Project First Phase,* was presented to the newly named board of directors in September 1992.

In a national framework, the present deteriorating state of America's inner cities, like many major phenomena, results from the convergence of a number of independent powerful forces, in particular the following:

- The World War II and postwar large-scale migration of African Americans from the rural South to northern cities and an accelerated flow of immigrants from Latin America. On the whole, both groups were initially poor and not well educated.
- Nevertheless, until the coming of the microelectronics revolution in (approximately) the mid-1970s, a good many migrants commanded sufficient skills to find places in the manufacturing workforce. The new technologies widened the gap in required areas of competence (and in wage rates) between skilled and unskilled labor and raised the skill requirements for many service as well as manufacturing jobs.

- As this process proceeded, the average level of unemployment in the United States rose from 4.7 percent in the 1950s and 1960s to 7.1 percent in the 1970s and 1980s. "Black" unemployment ran at about twice the level of "White." (See table 11.1.) For males 16–19, the "Black and Other" proportion of unemployed in the United States more than doubled during this period relative to "White."

- The adjustment of the inner-city workforce to the imperatives of the new technologies from the 1970s forward was gravely impeded by the sluggish response of the public-school system to the new environment and by the almost equal sluggishness of private and public employers in cooperating intimately with the school systems in training the young for good entry-level jobs upon graduation from high school. Under these circumstances, the verdict of inner-city youth was overwhelmingly that their schooling was unrelated to any credible path to an attractive future. The adjustment to the realities by both public schools and employers is slowly changing, but change does not yet match the scale of the problem.

- This complex of circumstances heightened in the inner city the endemic pressures on conventional family life. In fact, these pressures were induced throughout the advanced industrial world by a change in sexual mores and the increased role of women in the workforce. In different ways, these circumstances in the inner city tended to reduce the inhibitions against teenage pregnancy and increased the attractiveness of gangs as a substitute for gravely weakened or nonexistent families.

- To an extent difficult to measure when multiple forces are at work, welfare policies might have compounded inner-city problems (as well as cushioning their impact) by providing what appeared to some a subsidy for creating a single-parent household and, more generally, by strengthening a sense of neocolonial dependence, humiliation, and bitterness, thus weakening a view that greater control over one's destiny was possible. That, too, might be changing, but not rapidly enough to undo the vicious circle. The welfare-reform legislation of 1996 might alter this situation; but this is still to be seen, and progress may have been reversed by the recession that began in 2001.

- The dynamics at work in the inner cities were exacerbated greatly by drugs and the fact that dealing appeared to be a realistic alternative to the more conventional career pathways, even though it carried a high risk of incarceration or early death.

Looked at in this way, the problem can be stated as follows: A powerful converging set of economic and technological forces sharply raised the

TABLE 11.1 CYCLICAL BEHAVIOR OF BLACK AND OTHER CIVILIAN
UNEMPLOYMENT RELATIVE TO WHITE, 1948-NOVEMBER 2000

	All Workers %	White %	Black %	Black and Other White %
Peak 1948	3.8	3.5	5.9	1.7
Trough 1949	5.9	5.6	8.9	1.6
Peak 1953	3.0	2.7	4.5	1.7
Trough 1954	5.5	5.0	9.9	2.0
Peak 1956	4.1	3.6	8.3	2.3
Trough 1958	6.8	6.1	12.6	2.1
Peak 1960	5.5	5.0	10.2	2.0
Trough 1961	6.7	6.0	12.4	2.1
Peak 1969	3.5	3.1	6.4	2.1
Trough 1971	5.9	5.4	9.9	1.8
Peak 1973	4.9	4.3	9.0	2.1
Trough 1975	9.5	8.9	13.8	1.8
Peak 1979	5.8	5.1	11.3	2.2
Trough 1982	9.7	8.6	17.3	2.0
Peak 1989	5.3	4.5	10.0	2.2
Trough 1992	7.5	6.6	14.2	1.9
Peak November (2000)	4.0	3.5	7.6	2.2

Sources: Economic Report of the President (Washington, D.C.: GPO, 2001); *Economic Indicators* (Washington, D.C.: GPO, February 2001).

level of unemployment in the inner city and simultaneously reduced in the minds of young men and women future prospects for good jobs. This perceived narrowing of realistic options had important social consequences. It led many young people to accept life on the streets. This led, in turn, to an increase in teenage pregnancies, often associated with low-weight births. More generally, many inexperienced and hard-pressed young mothers did not provide their children with the physical care, continuity of affection, and stimulus required for proper development in the critical early years. As a result, the children often entered school with little self-esteem or confidence. They often regarded themselves as losers.

In schools dominated by the principle that time should be the independent variable and learning the residual, many students fell behind as problems of discipline ate up the time available for teaching. This lag, plus the gathering sense that school offered no credible, attractive future, yielded a decision to drop out and surrender to the real enough attractions of the streets: gangs, crime, sex, drugs. For some the attractions included money. The surrender to street life, in turn, constitutes a powerful negative feedback. It not only adds to the number of teenage mothers but also enlarges the pool of young people ill-equipped for decent entry-level jobs in an increasingly high-tech world.

As earlier suggested, our present social policy organized by public and private agencies is primarily reactive, not proactive. This kind of primarily remedial social policy would only be acceptable for the long run if some other forces were bringing forward the young out of inner-city poverty into the mainstream. For previous generations of immigrants, there were three such forces: the family, the churches and other religious institutions, and an educational system (and settlement houses) that effectively equipped students for a workforce demanding only modest skills. Some schools of an earlier era did prepare many immigrant children for business and the professions. But these institutions have, to an important degree, operated with diminished powers.

As a matter of long-term trend, the old dynamics do appear still to be working; that is, the proportion of African Americans and Hispanics entering the middle and white-collar classes appears to be slowly rising. But for a large number of minority children, men, and women, the system of institutions from prenatal care forward fails, tragically wasting human potential.

In the short run, society is protected from the full, potentially disruptive consequences of this failure only by enormous safety-net and remedial expenditures that mitigate, but do not solve, the urban problem. Something like 40 percent of the entrants into the workforce are minorities, and this proportion is rising. In the longer run, the size and productivity of the effective workforce will be reduced, and the unity of our communal life placed at risk.

TEXAS: AN EXAMPLE

This point can be driven home by examining a 1996 Texas A&M study of prospects for Texas, where the proportional rise of the Hispanic population is substantial.[4] First, the pessimistic base projections: If the trends of 1980–1990 persist, by 2030 the total population of the state would increase by 99 percent to 34 million. This increase, however, would be dominated by minorities, Hispanics above all. Anglos would increase by 20 percent, Hispanics by 258 percent. The Anglo population, almost 60 percent in 1990, would fall to 37 percent, while Hispanics would account for 46 percent of the population in 2030.

Under the rigid and linear assumptions used in this exercise in forecast-

TABLE 11.2 COMPOSITION OF TEXAS POPULATION BY RACE, 1990–2030

Anglo		Black		Hispanic		Other	
1990	2030	1990	2030	1990	2030	1990	2030
64.6%	37.5%	10.8%	9.1%	22.3%	45.6%	2.3%	5.2%

Source: W. W. Rostow, *The Great Population Spike and After: Reflections on the 21st Century* (New York: Oxford University Press, 1998), p. 217.

ing, the shift would profoundly affect the structure of the workforce as well as levels of expenditure on TANF (cash assistance to mothers with pre-school children), Medicaid, and food stamps. The proportion of Texas citizens below the poverty line would rise, average household income would fall, and total state tax revenues would increase by less than the population. A marked further polarization of incomes between the minorities and the Anglos would take place. Texas would contain, in this scenario, a somewhat poorer population in 2030 than in 1990, with a larger proportion of its people ill-trained.

For comparison, the labor force on a national basis would undergo the change shown in note 5, and Table 11.2.[5]

The Texas A&M authors then make an alternative optimistic linear assumption. They assume that between 1990 and 2020 there is "total closure in the difference in rates" among its more- or less-advantaged citizens. This hopeful calculation demonstrates the cost to the community of the degree of its poverty.

- Public-school enrollment increases by 59% from 1990 to 2030, compared to 61% under the base projections. College enrollment increases by 103% from 1990 to 2030, compared to 61% under the base projections.
- Aggregate income would increase by 151% versus 99% from 1990 to 2030.
- Poverty would be reduced by 165% from 1990 to 2030 as opposed to an increase of 44%. The number of Texas Youth Commission enrollees (youthful first offenders) would decline by 22% rather than increase by 81%. The number of persons in prison would decline by 21% from 1995 to 2030 instead of increasing by 68%.
- AFDC would decline by 21% from 1990 to 2030 rather than increase by 131%.
- The number of food-stamp recipients would decline by 26% to 2030

rather than increase by 109%. Medicaid enrollees would decline by 1% from 1995 to 2030 rather than increase by 102%.

- Average household income would increase by 14% rather than decline by 9%.
- Consumer expenditure would increase by 133% from 1990 to 2030 rather than increase by 106%.
- State tax revenues would increase by 139% rather than increase by 98%.[6]

It should be emphasized once again that these two projections are linear—that is, they blindly project forward, respectively, the present distinctions between the advanced versus disadvantaged parts of the state and a complete achievement of a level playing field. Specifically, our analysis would take into account the extent of intermarriage among the young in the presently minority populations and the possibility that the demographic situation in Mexico and the rise there in real income per capita might lessen the pressure to migrate to the United States.

But these two linear projections do reflect an authentic challenge. Just as the current differentials between minority status and socioeconomic resources might lead to increased dependence and poverty in the underclass, so an alteration of such patterns could lead to enhanced socioeconomic conditions and increased independence. It is obvious that addressing such differences is critical to the state's long-term economic and social well-being. Specifically, the systematic exploitation of these possibilities would have a high rate of return.

1993-1994: A FAILED HOPE

Returning to this brief history of the Austin Project, I thought President Clinton began well in presenting a plan for empowerment and enterprise zones on May 7, 1993. "Our proposal recognizes that long-term, stable economic growth in severely distressed areas must be achieved through a coordinated plan of economic, human, and physical development. And it recognizes that the answers to a community's problems must be generated by that community. Under our program, not a single dollar will go out without a coordinated strategy developed at the grassroots level."[7] This bold statement seemed, with a few words, to change fundamentally the whole nature of urban policy in Washington from fragmented categorical grants to comprehensive urban plans.

We therefore turned in good heart to preparing a detailed plan that would have fulfilled our hopes for Austin. This drew on information from all the relevant sections of the city, county, and state governments. The federal government asked for a "comprehensive" plan. This was such a plan. We were heartened when we were asked to go to Washington to present our plan.

Austin's application for an empowerment zone was well crafted and, I felt, a strong contender. I was astonished, therefore, when Mayor Todd telephoned me in December 1994 to say that we had been totally rejected. However, Austin's situation, with all its problems, remained unchanged. So we decided to go ahead, with diminished resources, along the lines we had originally outlined. Two elementary schools, Andrews and Ortega, were chosen as our experimental models, in hopes that the strategies we would develop there could in the end be replicated on a larger scale. Both schools had strong principals and neighborhoods with promising potential, but the children were overwhelmingly "at risk."

While we were getting under way, a transition was taking place in Austin: the municipal airport was moving to a former air force base, leaving a fairly large officer's house scheduled for demolition. Instead, we decided that the house, once rehabilitated, would serve admirably as a "Family Resource Center." So the building was split in two and transported in the middle of the night to a vacant lot near the Ortega school. Remodeling—made possible by supplies from friends of TAP such as Dell Computer—went smoothly. Andrews, for its part, improvised a Resource Center from nearby Quonset huts.

And so we carried on and slowly expanded our functions—our ideology and long-term goals intact.

THE MEXICAN CONNECTION

The work in East Austin related to the flow of immigrants from Mexico, and the future of this flow should be made explicit here. As of 2002, gross fertility in the United States is 2.1, which is also the replacement figure for the long run. The United States is the only major industrialized nation whose fertility rate is not below the replacement rate. In the United States, however, the Anglo figure for fertility is below 2.1, at 1.7. The national rate is elevated thanks to a higher Mexican/Hispanic figure of 2.3 fertility. Many population analysts tend to regard the American case casually. They simply assume that total immigration from Mexico will remain at its present high figure, and that Anglo fertility north of the border will remain steady, leaving overall fertility in the United States constant at the replacement rate of 2.1. There are reasons to be skeptical.

First, if Europe is a likely model, the forces arguing for a reduction in immigration may grow stronger with the passage of time. Political opposition to a continued high level of immigration has been increasing in virtually every European country where the fertility rate is below the replacement rate. The trend may take hold in the United States despite our tolerance for immigration in recent decades. There have, of course, been periods in our history of severe reaction against immigration.

Second, much more certain is that the pressure for migration to the United States from Mexico will diminish with the passage of time as real wages there rise and as the Mexican population ages. Mexico's fertility rate has fallen from 6.3 in 1974 to 3.1 in 2000. That remarkable decline will almost certainly continue and the pressure to come north will gradually diminish. In talking to the U.S. Congress on September 7, 2001, Mexican president Vicente Fox said Mexicans now desire to come north, and that this immigration is now to mutual advantage; but that in time these immigrants will be needed back in Mexico. President Cardoza of Brazil is reported to have said, "Now we are worried about sufficient schoolrooms. In a little while we'll be worrying about sufficient old-age homes." Mexico, like Brazil, is rapidly aging. The average rate of increase in real wages in Mexico is over 2 percent per annum; and the decline in fertility in all countries has been a function of rising real wages, rising urbanization, rising educational standards, and rising use of modern methods of birth control. All are true of Mexico. That is why in Chapter 12 I treat immigration as a time-buying factor, not a means of ultimate solution of our population problem. And that is the view taken in the Austin Project.

WHAT THE AUSTIN PROJECT HAS DONE SO FAR

Against this background, the Austin Project has engaged thus far in three enterprises. First, we have established in two communities containing some seven thousand men, women, and children, Family Resource Centers linking the neighborhoods and their elementary schools. Andrews and Ortega Elementary Schools bring health services, computer training, legal support, supplementary educational support, information about training and jobs, and other services to their neighborhoods. There has been a marked improvement in standard test scores, discipline, and other measures of progress, attested by objective criteria and by the principals of the two schools (see Appendix D).

Ortega has already been defined as a "Recognized School," one that has come forward radically on the standard tests set by the Texas Educational Agency and Andrews has exhibited comparable improvement so that this designation is almost within reach. The bulk of the children at these two schools are formally defined as "at risk." The following summary figures give some idea of the progress made at these two schools in the course of the 1990s:

TAAS SCORES (ALL TESTS, AVERAGE)

Economically disadvantaged schools	1994–1996	1998–2000
Ortega	47.1	61.5
Andrews	40.5	52.2

The principals at Andrews and Ortega, Betty Jo Hudspeth and Martha Garcia, respectively, are among those to whom this book is dedicated. While helping design the Link system described below, the Austin Project has carried forward the agenda at Andrews and Ortega, working with relevant faculty to enrich the teaching of mathematics, the sciences, and technology.

Meanwhile, a second branch of the Austin Project, the Capital Area Training Foundation (CATF), has established career awareness planning and internships within the school system. The CATF has been working with seven industries and other nonprofit organizations to support the establishment of career opportunities in those industries. This has required cooperation of the high schools, the community college, and the private sector.

Some three hundred students have moved over from Career Planning to the internship program in which, once again, the CATF and the private sector have played an important role. Private companies are financing these internships.

Meanwhile, with Austin Community College, the CATF, and the private sector playing central roles, training operations are being conducted that lead to entry-level jobs. By 2001 the resultant Gateway Program was turning out some eighty-five construction workers a year. The Capital Area Training Foundation now works with the private sector on computer-telecommunication training as well, serving some two hundred students on their way into the labor force.

The third and most recently inaugurated part of the Austin Project is the *Link system,* an experimental effort to deliver social services to families. It puts the families at the center of the process of deciding which services the children need and which agencies will supply them. Seven schools and their neighborhoods are involved: Johnson High School, Kealing and Martin Middle Schools, and Blackshear, Allison, Oak Springs, and Zavala Elementary Schools.

The Austin Project has been chosen to play a catalytic role in this enterprise, bringing the service agencies and the families together and arranging for an evaluation of the results by the University of Texas School of Social Work and the Hogg Foundation. The experiment has the support of the city and the county, as well, of course, as the schools involved. We are all trying to find out if services can be delivered more efficiently and with greater involvement of the families in making the critical decisions. During the start-up period, August 1–December 31, 2001, seventy-eight children and their families participated in the Link system.

The city and the county intend to support this experimental procedure for three years, at which time they will decide whether its results justify application to the whole disadvantaged community.

In coordination with the Link system, we are most recently engaged in efforts to increase early literacy for preschool children and to strengthen math, science, and technology instruction in the early years of elementary school. Some two-thirds of the funding for these programs will be provided by foundations, with the other third coming from the city and county. These efforts to strengthen academic programs will be evaluated by the Link Center.

These programs have a special meaning for the Austin Project. We have never forgotten the advice given to us by Barbara Jordan, who was a friend of the project in its early days: "If you don't begin at the beginning, you'll never get there."

As a set of substantial preventive experiments, TAP thus constitutes one approach to the urban problem seen as a systematic vicious circle that must be reversed by a coherent investment program if we are to make progress toward a solution. The next phase is to go to scale. This requires the city, county, school board, and the community at large to work in concert to move the successful experiments to an enterprise covering the entire disadvantaged part of the city. This, we estimate, will take an additional five years if the task is, in fact, undertaken. To bring the disadvantaged neighborhoods up to the average level of preparation for the workforce or higher education of the surrounding county will require, perhaps, an additional fifteen years.

CONCLUSIONS

I came to Austin over thirty years ago, knowing something about development problems worldwide but next to nothing about Central Texas. Although I still speak like an East Coast type (our daughter speaks Texan as a second language), I've learned a lot in a third of a century. Here are some conclusions.

Comprehensive investment in young people is a good first step in urban planning. To maximize resources from foundations and the public sector, there must be a unified approach by the city, county, and school boards, with community colleges, universities, and the private sector contributing where relevant to the common effort.

Planning is a tough business: too many urban scenarios have cratered — or have died on the shelf. However, a coherent approach can be translated into a set of reachable targets stretching over the whole span from prenatal care to the workforce and the professions. With prodding and good luck, each of the public programs and private agencies will then find it expedient to make a contribution to the plan as a whole. The challenge is to establish entitlement: once the fragmented agencies, public or private, see that they are making a contribution to a larger effort, the greatest barrier to progress will diminish. That barrier is the widespread belief that "the urban problem" cannot be solved. That is wrong. It can be solved. And it must be solved not merely for moral reasons, not merely because the underprivileged parts of cities waste a great deal of the community's money and human talent, but because they contain an underutilized, badly needed part of the local workforce. In the years ahead, we shall need a coherent and intelligent urban policy to buy time to bring our population into stable equilibrium (see Chapter 12).

Cities may anticipate some (probably diminishing) financial help from national and state governments, but essential initiative and resources must come primarily from local communities.

The heart of progress lies in increased investment in prevention. Work on damage control and compassionate programs will and should go on: for example, hospices for the very ill; meals-on-wheels for the elderly and those lacking mobility; help and a safe haven for battered women and abused children; incarceration for those who commit crimes, and so on. Every civilized community will provide such services. But those services will not provide a solution to the urban problem.

On the other hand, we in the Austin Project, after more than a decade of hard work, are by no means naive; but we are convinced that a solution is possible and that a level playing field can be provided to all our young.

Twelve

POPULATION, MODERN JAPAN'S
FOURTH CHALLENGE

THE CENTRAL PROBLEM OF THE
TWENTY-FIRST CENTURY

PREFATORY NOTE: My work on the world's population in the twenty-first century has had three stages. First, I surveyed the global population scene in *Theorists of Economic Growth* (1990) mainly to capture the extent to which population growth in the years ahead would radically increase the proportion in the developing regions: from 71.5 percent in 2000 to an estimated 87.1 percent in 2100.[1]

After the population analysis of that book I continued to work on population and focused on the fall in gross fertility below the replacement rate. This forecast of a fall in population was not confined to rich countries but had spread to the more precocious developing countries. South Korea, Taiwan, mainland China as well as Hong Kong, Singapore, and Thailand were already below the replacement rate. Fertility was falling rapidly, although still above 2.1, in India, Brazil, Mexico, and Indonesia, and in other developing countries with large populations. The decline in fertility except in sub-Saharan Africa between 1970 and 2000 was of the order of 50 percent — a truly major historical development. I tried to put this turn of events in historical perspective in *The Great Population Spike and After: Reflections on the 21st Century* (1998).

As I continued to work on this problem I concluded that, although I had discussed some of the policy problems that were raised by these developments, I had nowhere lucidly and tersely answered the question posed by the two presidents for whom I had worked in the 1960s. When one of their assistants advanced an idea, they said: "What do you want me to do about it today?" (JFK); "Therefore?" (LBJ). This chapter is designed, in part at least, to answer these fundamental operational questions. The bulk of this chapter is reproduced by the kind permission of *The Japanese Economic Review,* September 2000.

I will consider the three major policy issues raised by the population situation that lies ahead for most of the advanced industrial and developing countries. Sub-Saharan Africa is something of an exception. Its total fertility level, in 2000, was 5.6, near the human maximum, although now shadowed by the AIDS epidemic. Elsewhere, the fall in fertility associated with the takeoff stage of growth has begun, and will be followed by a fall in population. And I do believe population will be the central issue of the twenty-first century.

The fall in population has begun in all of the European portions of the former Soviet Union, and it will start in Japan fairly soon—say, 2007 for the general population, 2001 for the workforce. Japan's postwar "baby boom" lasted only to 1949; therefore, there is no backlog of a large young population, nor of a large flow of immigrants, to lengthen the time between fertility decline and population decline. We shall all, sooner or later, be confronted by the issues now faced urgently in Japan.

INTRODUCTION

Japan now faces the fifth phase in its modern history. The first phase was the Tokugawa era, which ran from 1603 to the Meiji Restoration of 1868. In this first period Japan cut itself off from the West. After 1868, Japan entered gradually into the Western game of imperialism, and this second phase ended with the Japanese defeat in the Second World War. The central theme for both periods: how should Japan relate to the West?

Before 1603 there were sporadic encroachments of Europe on then-feudal Japan including some Christian evangelizing; but after a number of military engagements at home as well as abroad, Ieyasu (founder of the Tokugawa shogunate) beat out his rivals and established unified rule from Edo (Tokyo) and, as a policy, self-isolation from the West. The weak emperor was sent off to retirement in Kyoto. Japanese contacts with Europeans were strictly limited over this period; but there was an orderly and creative economic, political, and cultural national development within Japan on the basis of, essentially, feudal technology.

The second phase was triggered by the enforced opening of Japan to external trade by Commodore Matthew Perry of the United States in 1854–1855. After much internal debate and even civil war, the Western clans, who advocated that Japan come out of its isolation, won. In the words of the Charter Oath written for the boy-emperor who was brought back to Tokyo, Japan was to seek science and technology throughout the world for the greater glory of the emperor. This spirit of reactive nationalism—that Japan had to catch up with or even outdo the Europeans and Americans—was climaxed by the Japanese campaign to establish an empire in East Asia in the 1930s and early 1940s. This effort was carried out in parallel to the German effort to establish hegemony in Europe, an aggression that had been initially neglected by nations distracted by post-1918 American isolationism and the Great Depression. This led ultimately to Japanese defeat and occupation by the Allied forces.

A third phase comprising the remarkable postwar period of economic recovery and growth occurred from the 1950s to the early 1990s. Central to this phase was the Japanese quick adoption of the technologies of the third and fourth industrial revolutions, symbolized by the automobile and the computer. Japan became technically a wholly modern economy, the second in the world, although the standard of living did not quite match Japanese technological virtuosity. Then the Japanese economy flattened out as it approached population decline and a period of stagnation in the course of the 1990s.

The fourth phase, which lies ahead, has not yet been fully formulated in Japan or elsewhere; it will require that Japan achieve a national consensus and then execute over coming decades a policy that will achieve the following:[2]

- *A time-buying program* that will expand the workforce during the period from the beginning of the fall of the Japanese population (say, 2007) to the reattainment of a total fertility rate of 2.1, the replacement rate. Japan's fertility rate is now about 1.4, and its population will begin to fall at the rate of some 650,000 persons per annum starting early in the twenty-first century—a major global economic and strategic event.[3]

- *A consensus achieved by the men and women of Japan* that will permit an expansion of the fertility rate to 2.1 from 1.4. This will require a kind of de facto treaty in which the women continue to expand their role in education and in the workforce while families are provided with well-run nurseries, pregnancy leave, substantial subsidies to early marriage and the bearing of children, and men share more than they do now the tasks of the family and household.[4] This will be, of course, the most difficult part of the task.

- *Acceptance, as a goal, of a constant population with continued R&D and innovation.* This would not only permit a continued regular growth in income per capita but an improvement in the quality of life in Japanese society.

These are the requirements of political economy of which Japan has urgent need, given its early population decline, as well as the opportunity to pioneer. Before indicating some of the substance of these three elements of

TABLE 12.1 TOTAL FERTILITY RATE BY LEVEL OF INCOME: 1965, 1987, 1997, 2000

	Total Fertility Rate			
	1965	*1987*	*1997*	*2000 (estimated in 1987)*
Low-Income Economies	6.3	4.0	3.2	3.3
Lower-Middle-Income Economies	6.2	4.1	2.5	3.2
Upper-Middle-Income Economies	4.7	3.5	2.4	2.8
High-Income Economies	2.8	1.8	1.7	1.8
World	5.4	3.6	2.8	3.1

Source: Reprinted by permission from *World Development Report 1989* (New York: Oxford University Press, 1989), pp. 216–217, Table 27, including estimate for 2000; 1997 figures from *Entering the 21st Century, World Development Report* (New York: Oxford University Press, 1999/2000), p. 247.

policy, it may be useful to lay out the major demographic situation the world now confronts.

THE DEMOGRAPHIC FACTS

The essential facts about the world's population at present can be briskly summarized.

- A gross fertility rate of 2.1 (children per family) defines the replacement rate. Above that number a population rises; in time, below, it falls. The interval between the fall in fertility and the fall in population depends on the size of the population of women of fertile age.
- There is a general tendency of fertility (and, later, population) rates to correlate inversely with urbanization, income per capita, education, and the proportion of the population using modern methods of birth control (see table 12.1).

These four determinants are obviously, to an important degree, related to one another.

- There are a number of transitional countries, including some with large populations, whose fertility rates are rapidly decreasing; and a few already have fertility rates below 2.1 (see table 12.2).
- Since the late eighteenth century, both birthrates and death rates have been falling; but the fall in death rates outpaced the fall in birthrates

TABLE 12.2 TOTAL FERTILITY RATE FOR SAMPLE TRANSITIONAL
COUNTRIES, 1970, 1992, 2000

	1970	1992	2000 (est.)
Thailand	5.5	2.2	2.0
Turkey	4.9	3.4	2.6
Brazil	4.9	2.8	2.0
Mexico	6.3	3.2	3.1
South Korea	4.3	1.8	1.5
Indonesia	5.9	2.9	2.7
India	5.8	3.7	3.4
China	5.8	2.0	1.8

Sources: The figures for 1970 and 1992 are from World Bank, *World Development Report, 1998–1999,* table 26. Those for 2000 are from Population Reference Bureau, *1998 World Population Data Sheet.*

Note: The PRB's *2001 World Population Data Sheet* gives the following *actual* fertility figures for 2000, as opposed to the estimates given in the table: Thailand 1.8, Turkey 2.5, Brazil 2.4, Mexico 2.8, India 3.2.

until the depression of the 1930s. After the Second World War, however, world population rose sharply, due to the spread of the new antibiotics and the control of malaria. Birthrates have subsequently declined and converged with death rates irrespective of stage of growth (see table 12.3).

While the length of life in most countries has crept up, circulatory diseases and cancers have thus far set a kind of limit to the fall of death rates.

- As already noted, Africa south of the Sahara is a regional exception to this pattern with a fertility rate of 5.6, not far below the maximum, yet shadowed by the AIDS epidemic.
- Against this background, the overall long-run estimates of peak global future population have been systematically falling. The medium figure now centers below 9 billion.

THE TWO DANGERS

Since overall world population will increase for some time, there is a real danger that we shall face regional crises in food, raw materials, and environmental conditions in the early part of the twenty-first century. In fact, there are such crises now in Africa. Instability in the Middle East may cause interruptions in the energy supply. And the possibility of environmental crises with global consequences cannot be dismissed. These crises, however, have been widely studied and debated.

The second type of danger has not been studied and debated. It arises from the noneconomic barriers to reachieving a 2.1 replacement rate and the length of time involved, if the fertility rate is permitted to fall below that level. This has already happened in the rich, industrial part of the world: in Europe, Canada, Japan, mainland China, Taiwan, Hong Kong, Singapore, and South Korea. There will also be a problem for transitional countries now above the 2.1 fertility rate but falling. In the United States the problem is masked by the high level of immigration. Population is more or less at the replacement rate of 2.1. The Anglo fertility rate, however, is 1.7, the Hispanic immigrants' rate, 2.3. All will also face the problem of maintaining full employment and a socially viable society with a stagnant population, if they opt for that objective. Fertility in Mexico is falling swiftly and its elderly population expanding. Its real per capita income is also rising. Immigration from Mexico to the United States is likely to hit its upper limit and decline.

THE FIRST REQUIREMENT: BUYING TIME

The first symptom of population dynamics finding its way into the political arena is the increased average age of the population in the rich industrialized countries and the more precocious developing countries. The proportion of the workforce to the dependent population is falling due to the attenuation of the population of fertile women and the lengthening of human life. A recent OECD paper concludes: "The current ratio in most developed countries is around four or five people of working age for every person over 65. But by

TABLE 12.3 DEATH RATE BY LEVEL OF INCOME, EXCLUDING INDIA AND CHINA, 1970 AND 1992 (per thousand)

	1970	1992
Low-income economies	19	12
Lower-middle-income economies	12	9
Upper-middle-income economies	10	7
High income economies	10	9

Sources: "Modern Japan's Fourth Challenge: The Political Economy of a Stagnant Population," *Japanese Economic Review* 51, no. 3 (September 2000). Also appeared in the American Philosophical Society's *Proceedings,* December 2000. World Bank, *World Development Report, 1989* (New York: Oxford University Press, 1989), p. 216, table 27.

2025 that ratio will be down to about three to one in America and around two and-a-half to one in most European countries. Add independent children and young people, and workers look seriously overstretched."[5] This is also a major issue in mainland China.

The situation of Japan was captured in a long, vivid article in the *New York Times,* international edition, of October 6, 1996.[6] Briefly summarized, here are the main points:

- The fertility rate is now 1.4. If that rate is sustained, the Japanese will have 55 million inhabitants in 2100 as opposed to 125 million now.
- Prizes up to $5,000 per child are being offered by local authorities to those who have children, but there are strong objections to a pronatalist policy.
- Objections include the following: The subsidies offered are insufficient; more children would take up women's "spare time"; men don't like "annoying things" around and would not help raise the children; women have "advanced" and do not wish to endanger their educations, prestige, and incomes.
- The government might take this issue more seriously, although the first effort of Prime Minister Ryutaso Hashimoto was to propose discouraging young women from higher education. This did not go over well, provoking a "furor."

The director general of the Institute of Population Problems in Tokyo is openly pessimistic about reversing the trend in fertility, which he attributes to the fact that "women have advanced."

The point is driven home by "Japan's Debt-Ridden Future," in the August 3, 1996, issue of the *Economist:*

> The problem starts and stops with the speed at which Japan is graying. Although still among the younger of the OECD countries with only fourteen percent of its population aged sixty-five or over, some twenty-six percent are likely to fit that description by 2025. Japan will then have a higher proportion of elderly people than any other country in the world, including even Germany and Sweden. And although today there are still 5.1 people who are working and contributing to a national pension scheme, for every person collecting an old-age pension, by 2025 there are likely to be only 2.4 workers per pensioner. The implications are clear. Either the pension contributions that working people make will have to rise from today's 16.5 percent of salary to around thirty-five percent by 2025, or pensioners will have to accept far lower benefits. As in most things, the outcome is bound to be a bit of both.

In China by the year 2030, 33 percent of the people will be over sixty, the retirement age, accounting for 21 percent of the population as opposed to 10 percent in 1992.[7] The total of elderly dependents will be 339 million, by official calculation.

In addition to raising the retirement age, which has been much talked about but not yet widely implemented, Hamish McRae lists the following measures that will increase the workforce in relation to the dependent population:

- Female participation in the workforce will climb.
- Part-time working (including working at home) will continue to increase.
- University students will be expected to work part-time while studying, a process already begun.
- Greater efforts will be made to reduce unemployment.
- Retraining for different jobs several times in a career will become more normal.
- Volunteer labor will be used to a greater extent.
- There will be more pressure on children to learn marketable skills.[8]

To this list should be added a solution to the problem of the "underclass," which is of a smaller relative size in Japan than in other affluent countries; that is, to educate and train for places in the workforce the disadvantaged men and women who are now on welfare. This will no longer be a matter of equity or budgets. The training of these men and women for the workforce will be a substantial contribution to buying time.

Immigration has already bought time in certain countries below 2.1 fertility. If there is a decline in the indigenous population, the shortfall can, in theory, easily be made up by men and women from another country with higher fertility rates, at least until the march of development dries up the pool of potential immigrants. There are two contrary forces that come into play, however: political resistance within the host country to a real or believed change in the demographic content of the society; and the initially unskilled character of many immigrants, resulting in long-term unemployment and a consequent rise in welfare expenditures. The balancing of these considerations against the additions to the workforce could limit the role of immigration in making up the labor shortfall.

Time-buying measures are, of course, important because it will take a considerable time to get the fertility rate back to the replacement rate. The conclusion of one social scientist and mathematician is to be taken seriously by all countries that have permitted their fertility rate to drop below 2.1 or where such a condition is imminent:

This evidence combined with the dynamic theory of population systems tell us that without promptly reversing the current trend of a declining birth rate in Japan, there seems little hope of preventing Japan's total population from declining, which will certainly emerge in the early decades of the next century. Actions for promoting reproduction in Japan have to be taken as soon as possible, because population development is a process with a great inertia. The probability of obtaining decisive results from population—and other social-economic policies—is extremely small for a short time period measured in terms of years. In the case of Japan, the great inertia of the population system will most likely drag the Japanese population down in the next several decades, due to the last fifty years of declining birth rates in that country. The policy of doing nothing and waiting for Japan's population to rise in the next century seems not right because it simply violates the natural rules governing the population system.[9]

THE SECOND PROBLEM: MEN AND WOMEN

The coming of an actual fall in population as opposed to the shadow cast by a decline in the fertility rate, is likely to raise acutely a problem that now exists: the relation between men and women. This is notably true in Japan, which lags behind the United States and perhaps Western Europe in the role of women in the workforce and especially in professional and executive jobs. Hence, the outcry of women when the Japanese premier stated, as reported in the *New York Times* of October 6, 1996, that the population problem was a function of a Japanese excess of education for women.

I doubt that women will give up their drive for education and for the highest place in the workforce that their God-given talents and ambition allow. I hold this view because the trend toward the full participation of women is a worldwide trend.

On the other hand, women are as good citizens as men and, when the implications of the population problem become clear, they are likely to accept their inescapable part in raising the fertility rate if two conditions are satisfied:

(a) that nurseries are set up near their places of work and, in general, their role as mothers as well as members of the workforce are respected (e.g., by subsidies for having additional children and maternity leave).

(b) that men share more fully than is traditional in the household and family tasks. This may well turn out to be the slowest and most profound task confronted, given the traditional role of men in Japanese society.

THE THIRD REQUIREMENT: THE POLITICAL ECONOMY
OF A STAGNANT POPULATION

If this analysis is correct, all nations will have to settle down to a stagnant population, at best, if they are to survive. We have all known instinctively that trees don't grow to the sky. In fact, with the passage of time, the population of the great empires before the industrial revolution rose and fell; and many of them disappeared. We have had a remarkable increase in the world's population since the eighteenth century and it is reaching its global limit. At this time, the recalcitrance of the circulatory diseases and cancer has caused the fall in the death rate to slow down. The birthrate, however, has continued to decline. Therefore, fertility has fallen below the replacement rate and, in a relatively short time, population—now still increasing—will begin to fall.

If we succeed in bringing population up in the more affluent countries and if its fall in other cases is checked at the 2.1 replacement rate, the third task (aside from the time-buying program and the pact between men and women) will begin.

First, the timing of the change in perception about the future of human population. This change runs inevitably into two of the most deeply rooted human impulses.

One has existed at least as long as human beings have lived in organized societies. Keynes once put it well: "We can not as responsible men do better than base our policy on the evidence we have and adapt it to the five or ten years over which we may suppose ourselves to have some measure of prevision."[10] Human beings are extremely conservative and, in the usual case, base their current decisions on the "evidence at hand." That evidence is that global population is still rising, which conforms to the extremely common view that it is overpopulation which is to be currently feared. Demography permits us to calculate roughly when a fertility rate below 2.1 will translate into a fall in population itself, given certain additional information that is generally ascertainable. But the fact is that an actual fall in population is only to be observed in the European parts of the former Soviet empire where perhaps temporary transitional problems obtain. Most of the world's citizens can go about their business operating on familiar assumptions. The average citizen does not study fertility statistics, and the shadows they may cast seem unreal or unlikely, or, as psychiatrists say, may be denied.

This tendency not to face this population problem is reinforced by the second force at work, from the late eighteenth century. The prevailing assumption in the Atlantic world has been that population increase was normal. And as the rest of the world moved gradually from the assumption of variations around a static norm to an environment of progress this assumption has spread, aided by the growing span of the media.

On the other hand, population stagnation got a bum rap. I suppose the bad repute of population stagnation versus progress takes its start from this passage from Adam Smith:

> It is in the progressive state, while the society is advancing to the further acquisition, rather than when it has acquired its full complement of riches, that the condition of the labouring poor, of the great body of the people, seems to be the happiest and the most comfortable. It is hard in the stationary, and miserable in the declining state. The progressive state is in reality the cheerful and the hearty state to all the different orders of the society. The stationary is dull; the declining melancholy.[11]

Smith's judgment was that the American colonies were in a progressive state; relatively rich but stationary China, stagnant; Bengal, declining. But Smith thought of innovation mainly as an incremental product as markets widened. He thought of major innovations as the relatively rare sporadic product of scientists. His thought was formed before the industrial revolution yielded innovation as a flow. He thought of international trade and specialization of function as the primary means to raise productivity.

Stanley Jevons cited this passage from Adam Smith when some ninety years later he published *The Coal Question* (1865). At the height of Victorian self-confidence, before the shadow of Bismarck and his less cautious successors fell across the Atlantic world, Jevons proclaimed in his peroration:

> If we lavishly and boldly push forward in the creation and distribution of our riches, it is hard to over-estimate the pitch of beneficial influence to which we may attain in the present. *But the maintenance of such a position is physically impossible. We have to make the momentous choice between brief greatness and longer continued mediocrity.*[12]

Jevons was thinking of the attenuation of the thick seams of coal on which the industrial revolution was carried forward from textiles to railroads, before the age of electricity, oil, and, in time, atomic energy. What is interesting, in retrospect, is not Jevons' application of diminishing returns to British coal mining but some of his reluctant reflections on British society losing its place at the head of the queue in the world economy.

And three quarters of a century forward there is a distinctly worried character to Alvin Hansen's presentation of what he believed in the 1930s was the end of the great innovations of the past and the coming of a stagnant population. After considering the uncertain impact of the enlarged role of government on the incentives for private investment, he concluded: "The great transition, incident to a rapid decline in population growth and its impact upon capital formation and the workability of a system of free enterprise, calls for high scientific adventure along all the fronts represented by the social science disciplines."[13]

My conclusion about timing is, then, quite simple: thought will turn, among economists, politicians, and all of us, to population stagnation or worse, when population decline actually begins among the most affluent societies, early in the twenty-first century. And, excepting Russia, it may begin first in Japan.

The macroeconomics of a stagnant population were briefly set out in 1937 by J. M. Keynes.[14] By rough calculation he estimated that for Britain "a stationary population with the same improvement in the standard of life with the same lengthening of the period of production would have required an increase in the stock of capital of only a little more than half the increase that actually occurred."[15] This population-related investment included housing, furnishing, and increasing consumer durables including automobiles. This rough figure was accepted as the gap that had to be filled in the contemporary discussion on the implication of a static population that was triggered by the rise in unemployment that occurred in the depression of 1937–1938 in the United States, when at the cyclical peak (1937) unemployment was as high as 14 percent.

There are, of course, specific contemporary investment possibilities to be considered that might go some distance in filling Keynes' gap: the repair of bridges, the modernization of air traffic control, the improvement of transport to and from airports, research and development expenditures designed to improve productivity and to reduce pollution, the improvement of education and educational facilities, preventive investment to expand the workforce and to reduce welfare expenditures, increased support for the arts, investment to produce a less polluting postpetroleum generation of automobiles, enlarged expenditures for the exploration of space, and so on.

It should be noted that the scenario considered in this chapter was first outlined by John Stuart Mill, a lifelong advocate of birth control and a constant population. But Mill was also a strong supporter of public investment in R&D and envisaged a continued rise in productivity and real wages under a regime of population stagnation.[16]

Such speculation as there is on the likelihood of an increase or decrease of R&D with a stagnant population is of two minds: on the one hand, it is argued that R&D might fall as part of the view that investment is population related; on the other hand, the incentive for productivity raising R&D might increase with a decline in the workforce. I suspect that the outcome will depend on the totality of the vision of the future that prevails. If it is

understood that continued future expansion in R&D and innovation is possible in this environment, and that increased productivity is the basis for full
employment and rising real wages, an increase in R&D might well occur.
The observation of J. R. Hicks is germane:

> If the population can once be controlled, there is no need for the econ-
> omy to go on expanding, in order that wages should be above the subsis-
> tence level. Instead of land being the main fixed factor, so that (as in the
> Ricardian stationary state) surplus production is swallowed up in rent,
> it is labour that becomes the main fixed factor, so that surplus produc-
> tion can be made to go, at least in large measure, to wages. This is an
> altogether different, and much more agreeable, picture. The Stationary
> State is no longer a horror. It becomes an objective at which to aim.[17]

The transition to a constant population would, indeed, have profound
social, psychological, cultural, military, as well as economic meaning, but
depending on the spirit in which the possibilities and challenges are pursued, the outcome could be salutary.

At this stage one can only conclude:

(a) That modern society offers many opportunities to expand investment
in highly productive ways and to maintain full employment under a
regime of stagnant population and rising real wages. The legitimacy of
increased public investment would, however, have to be accepted and
steps taken to assure that it would not descend into low-productivity
pork barrel expenditures.

(b) The success, however, of such a transformation of modern sophisticated societies would not simply consist of a correct series of measures
of political economy. A vision would have to be developed that the
world of stagnant populations can open many opportunities for creative work. In fact, at a difficult moment in interwar Britain Keynes
evoked that vision in charming if excessively optimistic terms.[18] In
short, there is no reason to accept passively Adam Smith's reflection
formulated before the Industrial Revolution, the diminished world of
Jevons as he contemplated the waning seams of British coal, or Alvin
Hansen's worries about the drying up of investment opportunities.

Now the third reflection about this transition. While it is going on, societies will be coming forward into technological maturity and demanding an
enlarged place in the world. It would not be difficult to envisage a world
of ugly struggle between those who came to affluence first and those who
came behind them.

This may happen, but it is an unrealistic nightmare. After all, the twentieth century was largely taken up with the consequences of such dreams by the rulers of Germany (twice), Japan, and the Soviet Union. If we count in the rather miserable interwar years, as we should, some three quarters of the past century were shadowed by war, hot or cold. The century was hard on those who thought that they could succeed to the hegemony of the colonial powers. And the twenty-first century, in that respect, will prove worse. But history has not stopped. The world of 2002 has demonstrated that minor as well as aspiring major powers can make ample trouble; and we do not know what the strategic instabilities caused by the population problem dealt with in this chapter may bring about.

On the other hand, the prospects for those who are coming along behind the present affluent powers could flourish in a world at peace. And they will not be far behind as China and India now show, with considerable industrial prowess and a fertility rate below 2.1 in China and on its way downward in India. It is not to be ruled out that an enlarging role in a world at peace is the best option for the people of China, India, the Middle East, Russia, as it has been for the Germans and Japanese. The past century should have taught us all that this is not a world that will be dominated by any one power. But that will depend not only on the arms commanded by the Atlantic, and European, and other Asian powers but also on their continued vitality and their positive vision of the future.

Thirteen

THE LONG AND SHORT PERIODS

A POSSIBLE BINDING THREAD

INTRODUCTION

What can I say in general about the eleven policy issues in which I was involved from the 1940s to the 1990s? They embrace problems of war and arms control, aspects of foreign and domestic policy; and they range in scale from global population prospects to the lives of disadvantaged citizens in the capital of Texas.

The first thing to be said about these cases is that they mirror the history of the last half century. A good many men and women of my generation found themselves engaged in a similar sequence of problems. We threw ourselves into each one as it came before us as part of the agenda of our time.

Looking back, however, I have come to the view that there is a binding thread that runs through the positions I have taken on these issues. It lies, I believe, in this proposition: what economists call the long period is, in fact, the sum of what we do or fail to do over short periods of time. Keynes commended to economists the dictum: "In the long run we are all dead." From undergraduate days I have held to the view that the long run is with us every day of our lives.[1] That goes for both history and the active world of policy when I got into it. It should be added immediately that Keynes practiced his craft mainly in interwar Europe where, unemployment rarely fell below 10 percent and reached, say, 25 percent in the Great Depression. It was natural for him to concentrate on the urgent problem of putting idled people to work, with a consequent focus on the short-run demand factors in play; although he was thoroughly capable of speculating a hundred years ahead.[2] In our time, however, I am inclined to hold that my dictum better fits the case than Keynes' *bon mot* of the interwar years.

In short, the binding thread in the eleven preceding chapters, sometimes only part of the story, often at the center, is that colleagues and I, for our own reasons, recognized the legitimacy of introducing long-run factors into the making of current policy. This holds, notably, for the three presidents for whom I was privileged to work.

Take the issues dealt with in this book.

THE USE OF AIR POWER IN EUROPE

The doctrines of the U.S. air forces in Europe (and of the EOU) were not to choose targets of obvious short-run interest, for example, cities and, later, marshaling yards. They were tempting as big physical targets against which much undifferentiated short-run damage could be done. EOU sought to find in the structure of production long-run targets of great concentration. If destroyed, they would have significant consequence for first-line enemy strength in a short period of time if attacked in a stubborn, thorough way — for example, oil, bridges and dumps in the context of the invasion of Europe. But there was an important exception. The attack on single-engine fighter factories was a necessary short-run compromise given the rapid approach of D-Day in 1943 and early 1944, and given the German plan for a four-fold, single-engine fighter expansion. That plan was half achieved by July 1944 when attacks by the U.S. air forces forced German dispersal of aircraft factories. Air supremacy over the Normandy beaches was a compelling Allied criterion, and thus an overriding, short-run objective. EOU accepted the legitimacy of that objective. But there was an irony in that story. It was not the limitation of production that was decisive. It was the disproportionate German loss of mature pilots in the course of these attacks — a long-run factor.

THE UNITED STATES AND THE SOVIET UNION, 1945-1989

Those who supported from the beginning of the Cold War the vision of a united, rather than a split Europe, had to wait some forty-five years before the Berlin Wall fell and the Cold War ended. But holding to that long-run vision became the American policy to which presidents subsequently adhered.

Vastly less important, I had formed from direct observation in 1947–1949 while working in Geneva for the Economic Commission for Europe the view that the Soviet Empire was historically transient. In 1958 I hazarded the guess that the Communist empire would break up in the third generation. (I had the grace not to attempt to persuade anyone to make that official U.S. policy): "[T]he Buddenbrooks' dynamics moves on, generation by generation. Those who seized power and used it to build an industrial machine of great resource may be succeeded by men who, if that machine cannot produce a decisive national or international result, decided that there are other and better objectives to be sought, both at home and abroad."[3] As noted in the present text, Lenin was born in 1871, Stalin in 1879—the first generation; Khrushchev, the second, was born in 1894; Gorbachev, the third, in 1931.

THE DEATH OF STALIN

Some would-be policymakers (as well as President Eisenhower and Prime Minister Churchill) thought that the death of Stalin was a good time to seek an end to the Cold War. Without fully understanding the view of Germany held by Beria and his uneasy colleagues, an early negotiation of long-run issues with the Soviet Union was, nevertheless, recommended on both sides of the Atlantic; but it failed. Others thought the effort would not only fail but it would obtrude upon urgent short-run Cold War business. In fact, the peace offensive of the USSR was primarily responsible for the successful popular demand for a negotiation. Although the delay in negotiation that resulted was unwise, the president's April 16, 1953, speech was a useful long-run reminder to the Soviet Union that the initial long-run American vision of a united democratic Europe was still alive; and it fairly defined Eisenhower early in his term as an active advocate of peace. This was a long-run policy that ultimately came to pass.

OPEN SKIES

Some sophisticated commentators thought President Eisenhower's July 1955 Open Skies proposal at Geneva was merely a short-run propaganda ploy; but he meant exactly what he said. Like most professional soldiers he believed nuclear weapons were only useful to deter others from using nuclear weapons. Moreover, his proposal, in fact, served two practical long-run purposes. First, it was a useful reply to the repeated official Soviet view that "the degree of inspection had to be proportional to the degree of disarmament." In the age of nuclear weapons and long-range delivery capabilities, it was a common interest that each side feel confident of the other side's military dispositions. This fact was understood by some Soviet officials under Khrushchev but denied in Soviet policy. Second, it may have helped prepare the way, through staffing out of the proposal in Moscow, for Khrushchev's subsequent acceptance of satellite photographic overflights in the otherwise disheveled Paris summit of 1960. A formal Open Skies treaty incorporating overflights was successfully negotiated in 1992—proving that not everything dies in the long run.

EISENHOWER AND KENNEDY ON FOREIGN AID

The clash of anti- and pro–foreign aid advocates of the 1950s is a textbook example of a difference in policy that had its origins in an intellectual debate concerning the long period versus the short period. At some risk of oversimplification, it can be argued that the anti–foreign aid forces applied a highly understandable short-term perspective to the underdeveloped areas. They argued that a successful American economic policy called for reliance on private entrepreneurship and investment that could be floated in private capital markets. Only aid in the form of technical assistance was, they argued, legitimate.

Foreign aid advocates took a dynamic, long-run, historical view that, in time, these short-run prescriptions might apply, but that most of the developing countries in the 1950s and 1960s were short of private entrepreneurs and were badly in need of large infrastructure investments, which they could not float successfully in private capital markets. Essentially those who argued against foreign aid applied the short-term standards of an advanced industrial society; those who took an opposing view applied a longer, historical perspective to the process of growth.

This struggle was carried on in the United States by two ardent phalanxes, both represented in the two major parties from 1953 to 1958. The former view prevailed in the House of Representatives. The Senate was inclined to the latter view. The executive branch was of two minds as was President Eisenhower, who was prepared to back an increase of development aid if someone else could produce a consensus in the split administration. Those who opposed foreign aid prevailed for five years. Between 1958 and 1961, however, the logjam broke under the reality of several factors: World Bank willingness to move on an international basis; pressure of the Democratic gains in a midterm election (1958); the withdrawal from Washington of a group of strongly opposed figures high in the Eisenhower administration; and above all, pressures from crises in the external world, including the essentially irrelevant launching of the first Soviet satellite. The Kennedy-Cooper initiative on India-Pakistan of 1958–1959 was one of the more important measures of this transitional period. Eisenhower's second term ended with a considerable unilateral increase of the U.S. budget for development aid, perhaps decided by the president after his trip to India. This eased Kennedy's problem when, as a Democratic president, he faced a somewhat more hostile Congress than the one elected in 1958. He nonetheless laid the long-run basis for a prodevelopment policy that embraced the whole industrial world and a technique of international consortia that was applied to at least sixteen developing countries. It was a nice bridge between an initiative in the Senate and long-run international policy.

KENNEDY-JOHNSON EFFORTS TO CONTROL INFLATION

Chapter 8 sets out its theme as follows: "The central intellectual issue was exceedingly simple. There were those who felt that it was legitimate and right to act on the short-term (demand) factors affecting the economy, notably fiscal and monetary policy. There were others who felt that it was legitimate and right to act in addition to make the average increase in wages equal to the average increase in productivity." Productivity is, of course, a long-run economic variable.

But this simple intellectual issue was by no means simple when it came on the agenda of the Kennedy and Johnson administrations.

After the 1960 election Samuelson and I (both Kennedy advisers) had set out the two themes clearly. The subsequent debate within the executive branch was, in fact, settled by a decision of the president. His long-run view was subsequently well articulated in *The Report of the President's Council of Economic Advisers' Report to the Congress* early in 1962. After a famous short-run battle with the steel industry over prices, the policy was adhered to until Dallas. It produced good results. As Table 8.1 indicates, the policy came under short-run inflationary pressure in the course of President Johnson's administration.

LBJ sought to check the price rise in the course of 1968 by a tax increase, and commended to his successor a price rollback; but President Nixon, as immediate business, explicitly reversed "jawboning" policy early in 1969 to assert the primacy of short-run monetary measures to control prices. Before long, the inflationary forces Nixon thus let loose required direct price and wage control to contain prices during the election period of 1972. Soon after, the extravagant wheat and oil price increases of 1973 engulfed the world in inflation.

The greatest weakness of the Kennedy-Johnson policy was the failure of the two presidents to institutionalize their correct long-run perception that the control of inflation required not merely a short term monetary and fiscal policy but also long-run annual negotiations (or effective consensus) that would equate the national average increase in money wages to the average increase in productivity.

CHINA

The issue of confrontation versus engagement with China has generated a considerable literature. The U.S.-China dialogue deals with a range of inescapable short-run issues: for example, Taiwan, Tibet, human rights, membership in the WTO. Here I supplement the argument for engagement by introducing six long-run forces that bear on that question: the Chinese experience both of Sun Yat-sen's failure to achieve political unity and the earlier long-term Confucianist experience of recurrent dynastic disintegration; the possible relevance to the Chinese future of the American and other experiences with federalism; the dynamics of generational change in China and the possibility that time might widen the possibility of democracy on the mainland; the danger to this progression that a world depression might represent; the importance to this progression of a steady and reliable American military posture. The current aging and future peaking of the Chinese population will take place before it occurs in India. This long-term force may strengthen the chances of engagement. The continued loyalty to the doctrines of Sun Yat-sen on both sides of the Taiwan Straits may also be a helpful force. If history decrees that the policy of engagement succeeds along the way, the agreed principles for a united China may well be Sun Yat-sen's triad: nationalism, democracy, and the people's livelihood.

VIETNAM AND SOUTHEAST ASIA

The central issue in the discussion of Vietnam can be regarded as a long- versus short-run issue. In the short run the issue was the war in Vietnam and its immediate outcome. In the long run, the issue was the control of Southeast Asia and the fate of the Southeast Asia Treaty, which enjoined the United States to hold that region as a whole on the side of the noncommunist world.

The clash of the president with the military centered, from beginning to end, on the terms of engagement—the issue of keeping U.S. forces within the borders of South Vietnam. This excluded using American ground troops to cut the Ho Chi Minh Trail through Laos. It also determined the attritional strategy pursued by the U.S. military within Vietnam, the length of the war, and the casualties suffered—by both sides—including civilian casualties. The military argued that no guerrilla war has been won with an open frontier for supplies, replacements, and sanctuary. The decisive view of President Johnson was that cutting off the trails in Laos on the ground risked a wider war involving the Chinese and/or the Soviets, both nuclear powers.

Lyndon Johnson's judgment was, in part, determined by painful memories of the Chinese entrance into the war in Korea as the United Nations forces approached the Manchurian frontier, although it could be argued that the two cases—Korea and Vietnam—were not geographically analogous.

All the presidents involved in the Vietnam War supported the economic development efforts of Southeast Asian nations, which made remarkable progress in the 1960s. But President Johnson in addition threw his weight behind the long-run movement for cooperation and regional organization of the Asian countries. This movement was begun, notably, with the Asian Development Bank and ASEAN. In a three-week trip through Asia in the fall of 1966 President Johnson devoted about 90 percent of his many speeches on Asia not to Vietnam but to the case for regionalism. Behind the American intervention in Vietnam was the Southeast Asia Treaty. The experience of the Korean War taught the American government that it had a vital interest in maintaining the balance of power in Asia as in Europe; and Southeast Asia as well as Northeast Asia had to be held against the Communists to satisfy that condition.

The third issue addressed was the possible disproportion between the casualties and pain suffered, Vietnamese and American, as compared to the interests at stake. This seems to depend on whether President Johnson's speech at San Antonio was correct: whether American withdrawal from Vietnam if it took place in the 1960s ran the risk, as he feared, of a larger and quite possibly a nuclear war.

THE URBAN PROBLEM IN THE UNITED STATES

My treatment of the urban problem involves, again, a conflict between short- and long-run considerations. In the short run, urban political authorities operate more reactively than proactively. A good case can be made for damage-control investment, but our current dispositions are grossly out of balance. In the long run, the pathology in disadvantaged neighborhoods will be substantially reduced only by investment in prevention—investment that will yield a long-run substantial positive return over cost in the form of reduced criminal activity and incarceration; reduced welfare and unemployment expenditures; and increased income and tax revenue. The fundamental problem with urban policy is that prevention is underfunded.

The cost of the disadvantaged neighborhoods to the city of Austin was conservatively estimated in 1992 at $390 million per annum; that is, the excess expenditures of the city as compared with the expenditures required if Travis County were uniform. The figure would now (2002) be at least $450 million.

The rules governing outlays in preventive investment are three:

Prevention: The maximum of outlays in an expanded urban program should be invested in long-run prevention rather than short-run damage control.

Continuity: The prevention program should extend without break from prenatal care to the workforce or professions.

Scale: Preventive investment should be built up to match the scale of the problem in most American cities.

The Austin Project is presented as an effort to mount a program loyal to these three principles. As of 2002, it has mounted successful experiments in prevention and now faces the formidable task of going to scale; that is, making Austin's combined effort in prevention match the scale of the problem.

THE WORLD POPULATION PROBLEM

Shifts in world population—and their policy implications—represent a long-run problem that is beginning to have immediate consequences. In the short run, the older industrial countries and the more advanced developing countries are rapidly aging. This process reduces the proportion the labor force bears to an expanding elderly population. This change in proportion is already moving toward a central position in short-run politics around the globe, and will cause profound economic and noneconomic changes as the falling proportion of workers to the elderly declines.

These forces are illustrated by the analysis of Japan's population problem in Chapter 12. Because Japan had a very short baby boom (1947–1949) and a very low rate of immigration, the workforce began its absolute decline as early as 2001, and its total population will begin its absolute decline in 2007. Only a policy that embraces the goal of a constant population with continued R&D and innovation, accompanied by a time-buying program to enlarge the workforce, and a social contract to raise (or hold) the fertility rate at 2.1 stands a chance to maintain an adequate quality of life. Such a policy is now urgent for Japan and Russia. It will soon be seen as urgent for the rest of the planet except Africa south of the Sahara, where neither industrialization nor the decline in fertility has yet begun.

Beyond lies the problem of creating full employment with a constant population. This problem is soluble by an increase in infrastructure investment plus, if necessary, a tax cut or a direct increase of consumption. In general the goals of a constant population and an increased standard of living can be reconciled by evoking both the policy recommended here and the high-tech revolution.

Fourteen

TWO FINAL REFLECTIONS

ONE ABOUT THE TWENTIETH AND TWENTY-FIRST CENTURIES, THE OTHER ABOUT THE INDIVIDUAL AND HISTORY

THE TWENTIETH AND TWENTY-FIRST CENTURIES

There are two further reflections on the episodes set out in this book. The twentieth century has been marked by tragedy, and suffused with global conflict. Consider the drumroll of events since Kitty Hawk: the First World War; the unsatisfactory interwar period climaxed by the Great Depression; World War II; forty-five years of Cold War followed by an anxious era when the world's longer-run problems, some military, asserted themselves, none yielding to a quick answer. From 1900 to the start of the new millennium, the years left their mark on the history of Russia and Japan, Western and Eastern Europe, the United States and Canada — indeed upon the world as a whole.

Yet the century was not simply a litany of disaster. It accelerated the process of decolonization in Asia, the Middle East, and Africa, eventually freeing many millions of people as newly independent nations, moved forward in length of life, education, technology, industrialization, and real wages. China and India were the largest countries to emerge and pursue these objectives, but they were not alone.

Just as the twentieth century saw the virtual ending of colonial or quasi-colonial relations among countries, the twenty-first century will see, as the diffusion of power continues, a world made up of many states whose independence is guaranteed in part by their often sturdy but difficult nationalism and by their increasingly industrialized and maturing economies. The twentieth century was not a nourishing environment for either imperialism or colonization. The twenty-first century will prove even less so. Attractive developing societies ripe for imperial control are virtually gone, and the proliferation of nuclear weapons will not make it easier for these days to return.

But also gone is the close linkage of industrial potential and the capacity to kill people. The diffusion of atomic weapons technology and of other means of mass destruction have broken that linkage and increased the powers of so-called rogue states to do damage. That, in turn, has revolutionized the problems of defense and intelligence for much of the rest of the world. And the diffusion of this capacity has posed the long-run problem for the international community of taming such weapons and the often-malignant nationalism that lies behind their threat.

The rendering of imperial control of other nations less easy and more improbable goes, of course, for the United States. In this hemisphere we have made great progress in the past century toward treating the Latin American nations as equals and friends, although we have some ways to go. On the world scene as a whole we are an island off the great continent of Eurasia. This means we are the natural enemy of powers that seek hegemony in Europe or Asia, the natural friend of smaller countries who want no external hegemony including that of America. It is for that reason that a strong United States is needed in the world not as "the last remaining superpower" but as "the critical margin" required to make any international collaborative effort succeed. That function requires an ability to listen as well as to lay down the law; the objective is to create a partnership of many nations, large and small, in a world where power is diffused. In time another major state may emerge as a critical margin. But now and for the foreseeable future, there is no one to take America's place.

The primary forces that will have great impact on the lives of men and women everywhere in the twenty-first century are two: changes in technology and in population.

As for technology, I claim no higher wisdom. The computer is approaching the limits of the speed of calculation as determined by the laws of physics. But men and women are at work in a good many places to combine biology and computation to transcend these limits and perhaps approximate in time the speed achieved by the human brain. If successful, no one knows what can be achieved with such "machines." There remain, however, major problems to surmount.

The mapping of the human genome opens up great new potential for biological engineering. Will this scientific field expand significantly the life of human beings in the workforce or simply extend gradually their average length of life? Will botanical research yield another Green Revolution?

More generally, from the time of the agricultural revolution men and women created great cities and empires (say, 5000 B.C.–A.D. 1750). Global population in the preindustrial age rose to something like 790 million. At 2000, it shot past 6 billion. Moreover, a much higher proportion of these 6 billion human beings had access to training in the sciences and the arts than in the agricultural and protoindustrial age, when innovation was sporadic and rare, not more or less continuous as it has been since the end of the eighteenth century. Nevertheless, the greatest achievements in philosophy, religion, and the arts, the most memorable reflections on the human condition, came in the earlier centuries.

We simply do not know what human ingenuity and wisdom will produce in the century ahead, but we know that we inherit the high standards from earlier preindustrial times, which will be difficult to surpass.

Nevertheless, it seems likely that the greatest challenge of the twenty-first century will prove to be: to make, if possible smoothly and peacefully, the adjustment from a world of expanding population to one, at best, of static population with continued increase in the quality of life and continued increase in real wages as they are conventionally measured. In short, to be successful, the two revolutions under way must be brought together in mutual support. The decline in population—illustrated in Chapter 12—is already under way in the European countries of the former Soviet Union and will shortly occur in Japan (2007), where the decline in the workforce has already begun. Some sixty countries in addition are already below 2.1 in fertility; that is, they will spiral into a decline of population unless the forces at work are changed to expand the fertility level. This includes all of the advanced industrial countries and more advanced developing countries, including mainland China. Moreover, fertility in the most populous developing countries outside sub-Saharan Africa is above 2.1 but has fallen roughly by half in the last thirty years. Clearly as I argued in Chapter 12, we confront a global problem: to bring fertility back to 2.1 in areas where it is currently below; and to halt the decline in fertility at 2.1 in those places where it is now above that figure but falling. There are a number of steps that can buy time—for example, immigration, an increase of the age of retirement, an increase of the educational level among the disadvantaged populations in our cities, and so on. But the consequences resulting from fertility below 2.1 will have to be reckoned with, plus the problem of full employment with a senior population.

Modern economies over the past two hundred years have depended for social policy on an expanding population. We do not yet know what will be the consequences of population decline. The economic changes required will go deep—but they appear possible; the social and cultural changes will be more profound, notably the change in the relationship between men and women. But they run with the grain of forces already evident around the world. Much too slowly but inevitably men and women are moving toward partnership in the affairs of the household and the world outside. This partnership will be needed to achieve and maintain peacefully an equilibrium between a more or less static population and a rising quality of life. This is a possible goal for the twenty-first century. But it is also an inescapable challenge that no country has yet surmounted.

THE INDIVIDUAL AND HISTORY

This book also raises, in the end, a problem that is universal and timeless. I was first aware of it in the story told in Chapter 1: a ten-year-old boy staring at the stars from his camp bed and wondering at the universe going its majestic way and giving no thought whatsoever to a kid filled with pride at an extremely modest award. The problem is, more seriously, the gap between the individual and the workings not of the solar system but of the society on Earth of which he is a part. Much of religion and philosophy and poetry is devoted to this question. At the level of philosophy it was said memorably by Adam Smith in the opening sentence of his *Theory of Moral Sentiments:* "How selfish soever man may be supposed, there are evidently some principles in his nature, which interest him in the fortune of others, and render their happiness necessary to him, though he derives nothing from it, except the pleasure of seeing it." The inevitable gap between the individual and the human community is partly closed, then, by the sense of linkage of one human being with another. This linkage has frequently been forged by the perceived imperatives of war toward objectives larger than oneself, often binding persons to the fate of those next to them, whether in a foxhole or in New York City on September 11, 2001. But it is not only in crisis that this principle operates, but also in the field of development. That is why I included the short chapter about South Korea (Chapter 7). The ties that grew up in Korea and elsewhere were an authentic expression of human fellowship as people from different societies and cultures came to share the challenge of assisting a poor country develop rapidly. That experience touched many men and women from many countries who joined forces with the disadvantaged to elevate the quality of life and to widen economic and social horizons. And it was true in the United States of the men and women who sought to achieve these objectives in the disadvantaged sections of our cities as illustrated in Chapter 11.

Some of the decisions dealt with in this book reached to the top of the American government. I was privileged to see something of the multiple considerations that an American president must confront day by day. The presidents I knew consulted with and listened to a great many people before establishing, if imperfectly, the facts and consequences bearing on a given decision. And the decision, more often than not, was a choice among unpleasant alternatives. In the end, as each fellow in the Oval Office finally stepped off into the dark or half-light, he had to make the final decision alone.

We are right to honor Washington both as an innovator and an administrator. Against many odds, including the Continental Congress, he helped
mightily to achieve independence and to set the country on its way. Lincoln
did not merely save the Union but also began the long, still incomplete task
of moving human beings into the mainstream of American life and liberty.
Franklin Roosevelt not only kept American society's faith in democracy in
the face of a debilitating Great Depression, but also mobilized for war its
great industrial potential, and set the framework for a second try at a world
system of global peace and comity. But even these rare figures, who moved
significantly toward a large objective, knew in their hearts that they had left
a full agenda for their successors. Similarly, Jean Monnet knew as he drew
toward the end of his life, that there was much to do in bringing the unity
of Europe to fruition. And he regretted that he would not be there to help
it happen.

The gap, of course, will remain between large historic objectives and
what any human beings can achieve in the time allotted to him or her. But
there is, still, a margin for human achievement. The large, implacable forces
of history do not wholly determine the outcome.[1]

Some fifty-four years since I expressed this thought, knowing something
of the frustrations and the failures that must be endured, and the patience
required, I still hold this view.

I am grateful that I have had the opportunity to express my full energies
and aspirations. And some days we made a nickel.

Appendix A

DRAFT OF PROPOSED U.S. PLAN
FOR A EUROPEAN SETTLEMENT:
FEBRUARY 1946

Note: This is the first version of the proposal for a unified Europe written in February 1946. It was not adopted by Secretary of State Byrnes, nor did he lay it before President Truman. But it won the support of Dean Acheson and Will Clayton and led to the creation of the Economic Commissions in Europe, the Far East, Latin America, and Africa. In August 1958 it was offered in the U.N. General Assembly by President Eisenhower to the Middle East but was not taken up.

I. *Aim*

The purpose of the following outline proposals is to check the tendency toward the formation of exclusive blocs in Europe, and to provide a framework of major power accord within which Europe might peacefully recover and develop an increasing measure of unity over the coming years. To execute these proposals requires that the United States bring the full weight of its diplomatic power and bargaining position to bear. The proposals are consistent with the principles of the UNO Charter. They require, however, some extension of the UNO structure.

II. *Present Position*

These proposals are based on an analysis which regards the following factors as basic to the present position:

A. The re-emergence of USSR after forty years of military defeat, revolution, and repression within its own borders, as a major power in East and South-East Europe;

B. Failure of Yalta, Potsdam, and UNO to provide adequate machinery in Europe capable of preventing the split of Europe into relatively exclusive East and West blocs;

C. Judgment by the governments of USSR, U.K., and France that the positive interest of the U.S. in the structure of Europe was likely to prove transitory;

D. A U.S. policy which has thus far prevented the split of Europe, but which has not halted the tendency in that direction.

III. *U.S. Plan: Summary*

In brief the proposed U.S. approach would consist of the simultaneous presentation of:

A. Plan, involving extension of UNO structure, to provide machinery for Continent-wide consultation on a specific range of issues, within a framework of major power accord;

B. Formulae, consistent with such a plan, for settling the range of major outstanding issues of diplomatic conflict in Europe.

This approach is based on a judgment that, until the question of whether Europe shall split in the near future is decided, the settlement of particular questions will prove virtually impossible. The presentation of A and B above, might well be accompanied by the public assertion of the following:

1. The continuing and direct U.S. security stake in the structure and stability of Europe, in the light of U.S. involvement in two European wars, and the development of new military weapons;

2. U.S. opposition to an exclusive bloc structure for Europe as unstable, dangerous, and corrosive to all the larger conceptions on which we have all agreed;

3. U.S. belief that tendency toward unilateral and regional actions incompatible with development of UNO must be halted, by extended exploration, of U.S. proposals A and B, above;

4. U.S. faith that if problems frankly faced and discussed — with strong assertion of U.S. interest — a framework of major power accord for Europe can be found.

IV. *Plan for European UNO Machinery*

The following outline plan would be related, structurally, to the appropriate branches of the UNO. It would constitute an extension of the central organization, but would be so organized as to avoid violating its basic unity. (Appendix required on structural details of organization, to be done by the United States experts on UNO.)

It is judged necessary that provision be made for treatment of European problems at two levels: an assembly level which would seek agreement on technical issues on a majority basis of some agreed kind; and a Security Council level where the security interests of the major powers might intervene. In general it would be hoped that the presence at the Assembly level of major-power non-voting, but active observers would serve to achieve solutions agreeable to the major powers, and thus minimize the issues which might be formally brought to the Security Council for settlement.

Assembly Level

The Assembly would consist simply of sub-committees, empowered to deal with a specified range of particular problems on a Continent-wide basis. Each member would have a single vote; and a majority (or perhaps ²/₃) vote would prevail. Voting membership would include all members of the United Nations in Europe, excluding U.K. and USSR. These latter powers and the U.S. would fully participate in the meetings on a non-voting basis. USSR might insist on the membership of the Ukraine and the Byelo-Russian Republics, which might well be accepted, so long as majority (or $^2/_3$) rule were maintained. The range of issues to be dealt with, and the terms of reference within which the Assembly organizations would be empowered to act would be set by the Security Council of the United Nations. A possible range of initial organizations within the Assembly would be the following:

1. Fuel and Power (Appendix required of LA/Stillwell, Jackson): This would involve an extension of the ECO, both with respect to membership, and to include issues connected with electric power distribution.

2. Trade: (Appendix required of CP) involving extension of EECE, acting as clearing house for trade agreements, and efforts to set up common trade policies for Europe in conformity with general ECOSOC principles.

3. Transport: (Appendix required of TRC) involving extension of scope of ECITO, with special role as guardian of common European policies on freedom of navigation for waterways.

4. Finance: (Appendix required of FN, in conjunction with Bretton Woods Fund officials) involving measures for stabilizing European currencies, common European measures to combat inflation, looking toward development of a common Continental currency, related to dollar.

5. Planning: (Appendix required of ED, in conjunction with Bretton Woods bank officials) involving coordination of capital development plans, including distribution of capacity removed from Germany as reparations; possibility of Danubian TVA, etc.

Other economic branches can easily be envisaged, as well as political branches dealing with such problems as Displaced Persons, uniformity of passport regulations, etc. The present list is illustrative, and is believed to be within the range of prompt negotiation and implementation.

Security Council Level

In addition to the ties that the organization within the Assembly would have with ECOSOC, Bretton Woods, and other worldwide organizations, direct screening of basic decisions, and definition of terms of reference would be reserved to the Security Council. Over a period of time it would be the hope that, as confidence grew, the range of issues and authority permitted the Assembly organizations would expand; and that the area of security intervention on the part of the Great Powers would contract. Voting procedures at this level would follow normal Security Council UNO procedures.

V. *Formulae for Settlement of Outstanding Issues*

It is evident that, while acceptance of machinery of this type would facilitate negotiation of many particular current issues, a European settlement must include specific provision for their solution. The following are possible formulae for some of the major current European problems, consistent with the assumption that major power accord in Europe will continue.

1. Rhineland-Ruhr: Political separation avoided with some limited concessions to French view (see EUR-ESP-OORI paper).

2. Danube: Riparian states only on permanent commission, with symmetrical arrangement for Rhine and other international European rivers; freedom of navigation guaranteed by European transport organization above.

3. Germany: Proceed promptly with Potsdam, reparations, central agencies, reactivation German economy.

4. Austria: Prompt settlement German assets issues, leaving some USSR ownership confined if possible to oil, and shipping on Danube; but no extra-territorial status for such ownership; proceed with Austrian treaty; entrance Austria to UNO and withdrawal of troops.

5. East Europe: Consolidation, and if possible, reduction USSR reparations out of current output; no extra-territorial status Russian ownership rights; U.S. recovery aid.

6. Mediterranean: The issues of Dardanelles, Turkey, and USSR relation to Middle East oil must be faced, probably, if this plan is to prove acceptable.

In general forcing of quadripartite forum extension represents weakening of most aggressive USSR elements, and threat to USSR of an independent Continent or growing independence; and short-run compensatory concessions might well be required.

VI. *Possible Objections*

There are a number of just and obvious queries to be made of the line of policy indicated above.

a) *International accord is not achieved by mechanisms, but from the outlook and spirit of the powers engaged in negotiation.* This judgment is clearly applicable. In the first instance, there can be little doubt that a European Organization would merely transfer to a new forum the present struggle for national power and influence. It would have initially only the advantage of promising that such struggle take place within a framework of international organization rather than as between virtually autonomous blocs. Over a longer period it holds the possibility that the measure of independence allowed the small European countries will expand, and that the intervention of the Great Powers will be confined to a narrowing range of problems affecting large questions of security.

b) *The UNO Assembly and Security Council already exist.* The machinery now in prospect within the UNO does not appear to offer a forum for the continuous issues of European housekeeping and national interplay. In any case, the fact that blocs are now rapidly in the process of emergence simultaneously with the development of UNO machinery, indicates *prima facie* the need for some additional structure.

c) *U.S. efforts to maintain major power accord have already indicated the impossibility of altering the unilateral basis on which the USSR is proceeding in Europe.* The weight attached to this judgment depends largely on whether it is believed that the USSR is acting on the assumption of future diminished U.S. concern in European affairs. USSR response to the alternatives of a

European Organization or vigorous U.S. support for a Western bloc cannot fairly be pre-judged. In addition it is to be noted that, despite firm insistence on certain minimum unilateral controls over the countries of Eastern Europe, USSR policy has varied widely, as between, say, Finland, Bulgaria, Czechoslovakia, and Hungary. The possibility that the USSR might ultimately permit, with certain security guarantees, the participation of Eastern European countries in a European organization can, on present evidence, by no means be excluded.

d) *USSR might make the European Organization a vehicle for attempted extension of Soviet influence.* It is undeniable that this will be the case. Similarly it is clear that the Western powers will attempt to extend their influence through such an organization. Conflict of political conception and of national or regional interest cannot, of course, be avoided by any organization, even if it were intrinsically desirable. The advantage of a European organization is that it offers the possibility of bringing the inevitable conflicts of East and West Europe within the orbit of rules of law; and of offering to the more than three hundred million people between the English Channel and the Curzon line an enlarging voice in their own affairs and a position somewhat more independent than at present of the security objectives of the major powers.

e) *The French might insist that such a scheme does not provide sufficient direct checks on the influence and power of a unified Germany.* It is known that the Socialist Party has only reluctantly accepted the French Government's Rhineland-Ruhr proposals, and that it has, in principle, opposed the dismemberment of Germany. The Communist Party [of France] had supported the Rhineland-Ruhr proposal with the reservation that the area not be subject to exclusively Western control. An effective re-assertion of Big Three accord, in the terms suggested above, might well remove much of the ground from the French Government's position. In addition, the following special limitations on Germany's relative power in Europe are contemplated under Potsdam, or might well be considered.

1. Sharp initial reduction in Germany's post-war economic strength;
2. relatively more rapid recovery and economic expansion in France and elsewhere on the Continent, due to reparations and U.S. loans;
3. permanent French acquisition of Saar;
4. ownership of Ruhr coal, iron and steel industries by European organization;
5. explicit guarantees against re-armament in German Treaty; with perhaps other limitations on German sovereignty;
6. opportunity for France to assume role of leadership, on Continent-wide basis, within European Organization.

f) *U.S. initiative in pressing for such a European solution may fail.* The nature of the alternative to a European Organization, which is discussed below, makes it desirable in the U.S. interest to press for the superior solution, however small the chances of success may initially appear to be. Only after exhaustion of the line of approach it represents does acceptance of a bloc alternative appear justified.

VII. *The Alternative*

The principal alternative to the re-establishment of major power accord in Europe is the formation of relatively exclusive blocs. The formation of such blocs, or the assumption that they will form, constitutes the basis of USSR, UK, and French policy in Europe. From the point of view of the West this is a policy frankly of despair, disruptive of every enunciated conception of U.S. political and economic foreign policy. It is doubtful, further, whether it will lead to a condition of even temporary stability in Europe.

In particular, crystallization of exclusive blocs would appear to involve the following:

    a) the association of German sentiment for unity with the more aggressive of the two blocs, almost certainly the East;

    b) intensification of efforts by each bloc to foster and maintain minority elements within the other bloc;

    c) development of the blocs toward military coalition engaged in active armaments competition.

In such a situation the Western Powers, due to the inhibitions within their political life, would be at a distinct disadvantage; and a progressive extension of the Eastern sphere would be anticipated.

From the outset the U.S. would be confronted with very strong pressures to support, economically and militarily, the Western bloc. Confronted with the choice of supporting such a bloc, or retiring to isolation, it is doubtful over a period of time whether popular sentiment in the U.S. would accept the former course, especially if the USSR were content to use means short of overt military action to secure its end. In short, it appears to be the main hope for the maintenance and extension of Western concepts and Western political power, that the structure of negotiation be elaborated to deal with an expanding range of issues, in Europe as elsewhere.

Appendix B

THE QUESTION OF EAST GERMANY
IMMEDIATELY AFTER STALIN'S DEATH

I shall present in this appendix two views of the "transient interval" between Stalin's death and the successful repression of the East German revolt. One of these views is based on the evidence known to the West up to 1992; the other reflects three articles by Mark Kramer published in the *Journal of Cold War Studies* 1, nos. 1–3 (1999), based on later evidence released by the Russian government. First the evidence up to 1992.

Those scholars who contended that Kremlin policy regarding the German question moderated significantly between March and June 1953 base their argument on two factors. Some cite the Soviet government's more conciliatory rhetoric and actions on a wide range of issues following Stalin's death. Others concentrate on the shadowy foreign policy activities of Lavrenti P. Beria, who supposedly favored a policy of détente with the West, including an all-German settlement. In both cases, the evidence is indecisive and the issue remains one for speculation rather than dogmatism.

Peter Lyon, *Eisenhower: Portrait of the Hero*, 2nd ed. (Boston: Little, Brown, 1974), pp. 531–534, and Leonard Mosley, *Dulles: A Biography of Eleanor, Allen, and John Foster Dulles and Their Family Network* (New York: Dial Press, 1978), pp. 337–338, argue that the new Soviet leadership was ready for serious discussions concerning disputes with the West. In their view, the United States missed an excellent opportunity to reduce East-West tensions by not responding to Russian peace initiatives sooner and with greater flexibility.

The primary evidence supporting the thesis of a Beria plan to accept a unified, noncommunist Germany is a subsequent accusation to that effect against Beria by Nikita Khrushchev published in the *New York Times*, March 11 and March 16, 1963. Khrushchev's 1963 speech is viewed by some as nothing more than a crude attempt by the Soviet leader to discredit a long-dead adversary. However, speculation concerning Beria's conciliatory goal existed even in 1953. Philip E. Mosely, in "The Kremlin's Foreign Policy since Stalin," *Foreign Affairs* 32, no. 1 (October 1953): 24–25, noted several signs that the Soviet government had relaxed its most onerous controls and was urging its German client state to adopt a less combative posture toward the West. Mosely speculated that Beria and his German protégé, Wilhelm Zaisser, hoped to make the East German regime more respectable in preparation for all-German negotiations.

Two of the most detailed and persuasive works advancing the thesis that Beria intended to abandon East Germany in favor of an all-German settlement are Boris I. Nicolaeveksy, "The Meaning of the Beria Affair" (December 1953), in *Power and the Soviet Elite: "The Letter of an Old Bolshevik," and Other Essays by Boris I. Nicolaevsky*, ed. Janet D. Zagoria (New York: Praeger, 1965), pp. 126, 135–137, 146; and Wolfgang Leonhard, *The Kremlin since Stalin* (New York: Praeger, 1962), pp. 70–73. Leonhard's arguments are the most intriguing since he relies, in part, on the testimony of two high-level East German defectors. Also relevant in the discussion of the "abandonment" issue are David J. Dallin, *Soviet Foreign Policy after Stalin* (Philadelphia: Lippincott, 1961), pp. 171–179; Walter Laqueur, *Russia and Germany: A Century of Conflict* (London: Weidenfeld and Nicolson, 1965), pp. 277–278; Arnold L. Horelick and Myron Rush, *Strategic Power and Soviet Foreign Policy* (Chicago: University of Chicago Press, 1966), pp. 26–30; Robert G. Wesson, *Soviet Foreign Policy in Perspective* (Homewood, Ill.: Dorsey Press, 1969), pp. 219–220; Thomas W. Wolfe, *Soviet Power and Europe, 1945–1970* (Baltimore: Johns Hopkins University Press, 1970), p. 77; and Adam B. Ulam, *Expansion and Coexistence: The History of Soviet Foreign Policy, 1917–67* (New York: Praeger, 1968), p. 543. Most of these authors, especially Dallin, Laqueur, Wesson, and Ulam, view with considerable skepticism the notion that Beria or any other Soviet leader would have advocated a policy of abandonment with regard to the East German regime.

Perhaps the most scholarly review of the evidence of the Beria initiative between Stalin's death and Beria's assassination, including the relations among Molotov, Beria, Khrushchev, and Malenkov, is James Richter's (Bates College) "Reexamining Soviet Policy towards Germany during the Beria Interregnum," Working Paper No. 3, History Project, Woodrow Wilson International Center for Scholars, June 1992.

There appears to be fairly solid evidence that Beria advocated the trading of East Germany for a united democratic but militarily neutralized Germany. At the other end of the spectrum, according to the conventional accounts, was Molotov, the redoubtable Communist, who would under no circumstances have surrendered East Germany. Malenkov and Khrushchev wavered but in the end supported Molotov's position.

Richter concludes:

> In sum, the new information suggests that no realistic opportunity to reunify Germany existed in the months after Stalin's death. The Soviets had decided in late May (before the East German revolt) not to abandon East Germany in return for a demilitarized, united Germany, and, though the instructions to East Berlin suggested the decision could have been reconsidered at a later date, no Western proposal could have changed their mind in the short time before Beria's arrest in late June. On the other hand, the new information also shows a fluidity in Soviet decision making after Stalin's death that most Western accounts have not appreciated, suggesting that even if the division of Germany could not have been avoided, U.S. actions may have had a significant impact on other aspects of Soviet foreign policy decision making.

Thus, we still do not have a clear-cut answer about the impact of U.S. actions on Soviet decision making after Stalin's death. But as the Soviet chapter of Russian history comes to a close, there may be some virtue in uncertainty. It spurs further research, reminding scholars with even greater clarity that Soviet development need not have taken the course it did, even after the Stalinist period, but that several moments existed in which different courses could have been chosen. It also illustrates the many factors contributing to the choices that were made; in particular, it shows how international pressures may have influenced fundamental internal debates about the Party's identity and its relations to the domestic and international environment. Finally, it offers the United States one good lesson from the cold war: look carefully at the domestic politics of the country the United States wishes to influence, and be aware that U.S. actions can affect other countries' foreign policies in unpredictable ways. (pp. 25–26)

Now the 1999 analysis of Mark Kramer, beginning with his summary of the three articles.

This is the final segment of a three-part article on Soviet policy in East-Central Europe during the first several months after the death of Josef Stalin in March 1953. Part 1 discussed the far-reaching changes in Soviet policy toward East-Central Europe in the spring of 1953, which would have been inconceivable before Stalin's death. Stalin's successors broadly agreed that they must halt the Stalinization of East-Central Europe and encourage political and economic liberalization. No sooner had these reforms begun, however, than they were shaken by upheavals in Czechoslovakia and the German Democratic Republic (GDR). Soviet troops had to intervene in East Germany on 17 June 1953 to crush a nationwide rebellion. Part of the article focused on the period right after the East German uprising, shifting back to the power struggle in Moscow. Well before the crisis in the GDR erupted, a few Soviet leaders had been plotting to remove one of their colleagues, Lavrenti Beria, the powerful minister of internal affairs. The East German crisis caused a slight delay in those plans, but once the crisis had been resolved, the conspiracy against Beria gathered pace. He was arrested during a meeting of the Presidium of the Soviet Communist Party (CPSU) on 26 June 1953. His downfall not only marked the end of the first phase of the post-Stalin succession struggle, but also proved to have lasting repercussions for Soviet policy in East-Central Europe.

Part 3 of the article, presented here, recounts the well-orchestrated denunciation of Beria at a CPSU Central Committee (CC) plenum in July 1953. It then considers the short-term and longer-term effects of the Beria affair on Soviet policy toward Germany and on Soviet–East European relations more generally. The final section ties together the three parts of the article by highlighting . . . the linkages between internal and external events in the Soviet Union and East-Central Europe in 1953. Drawing on recent theoretical literature about the connection between domestic politics and international relations, this final section explores the broader implications of the internal-external linkages in the Soviet bloc during the early post-Stalin period.

Mark Kramer's full and thoroughly documented account differs from earlier analyses of this interval in two related respects. First he asserts that all the major figures in the post-Stalin Politburo agreed that the situation in East Germany (and, indeed, in all the Eastern bloc) required amelioration in the wake of Stalin's death; and the negotiation of German unity was acceptable if Soviet troops were left in a neutralized, united, and presumably democratic Germany. Quite explicitly Kramer's account identifies Molotov not only as agreeing with this position but as its major expositor, which befitted his position as a foreign affairs expert. Two, the plot to remove Beria was contemplated by "a few Soviet leaders" before the East German revolt. The reason for this position had nothing to do with the agreed discussion about a new policy for Germany. It had a great deal to do with signs that Beria was contending for Stalin's place as the sole ruler of the Soviet Union and had been keeping files on his Politburo colleagues, which were removed and destroyed shortly after Beria's arrest.

In short Khrushchev's later public blaming the quarrel with Beria as due to his position on a German settlement was a lie.

The practical point developed by Kramer was that the arrest of Beria—a domestic political event—brought about a continued policy of holding on to East Germany. In a way Kramer's final position is much like James Richter's. They both emphasize that external circumstances may well influence and be determined by domestic policy.

Kramer's account does not deal with the possibility that the East German revolt and its highly professional suppression by the Soviet military might have itself led to an abandonment of their previous leaning toward an all-German settlement, nor does it deal with the possible role of the explosion of a thermonuclear device in August 1953 in affecting their thinking. But Kramer's account deserves great respect, although I am not inclined to feel this "transient interval" is fully explained.

Appendix C

TEXT OF W. W. ROSTOW'S
SEOUL NATIONAL UNIVERSITY SPEECH

Note: This talk was delivered on May 3, 1965, at the Seoul National University after discussion with President Park. It was among the least charismatic speeches ever delivered because it was translated into Korean, paragraph by paragraph. Spoken Korean takes approximately one and a half times English. The students, some of whom had literally climbed into the lecture hall's rafters, appeared to have listened carefully.

TEXT

U.S. Information Service, Seoul, Korea
Phone 2-711 Ext. 237

For publication or broadcast,
with or without credit to U.S.I.S.

65-83
May 3, 1965

I am more pleased than I can easily tell you to be here talking to a group of students in Korea. This is not a statement of courtesy or formality. I've been working in the government now since January 1961, when I came to work for President Kennedy, and I don't mind at all not adding to the list of books that the chairman was good enough to read to you. But I do mind greatly not spending time with students. It may be a kind of trade secret which we teachers don't tell our students often, but I tell you that we have the deepest kind of respect for those whom we teach. And there's a reason for this. Students can pick up very easily what may have taken us a generation to create. They climb up on our shoulders and they carry forward the life of ideas and the life of the nation from where we leave off, and it really is in that spirit in which a teacher looks at his students.

As for our being in Korea, perhaps you do not understand because time is passing, how deeply we in the United States feel towards Korea. We have been through a war together; many of my contemporaries died here alongside your people. Together we have been through this long difficult period of reconstruction. I know many Koreans, I have met them in Washington, but to be here among you at this stage is a source of great gratification.

It was in fact the Korean War which made me decide that I could not return, as I'd expected in 1950, to a pure academic life. I decided that we were in for a long crisis, and we set up at MIT the Center for International Studies, which in the 1950s engaged a part of my time in work on public policy. And so, in a sense I am here as a servant of my country because of that decision made in 1950 at the time of the Korean War. In preparing notes for my talk to you this afternoon I decided to exercise an old professor's prerogative and to change the subject.

I shall talk about Asian economic development a little at the beginning and end of my talk, but my subject is this: I'm going to tell you with great honesty what the problems and the prospects for the economic development of Korea look like to a State Department planner who only set foot in Korea yesterday.

I am conscious of my ignorance and how much more I have to learn about the Korean economy. Perhaps in the next day or so my friends here will have a chance to correct me, but nevertheless I thought it might interest you to know how a man sitting at a State Department desk far away looks at your prospects and your problems.

First, I should like to draw a quick map of the countries of Asia in terms of their stages of economic growth. In the stage of "preconditions" for takeoff, I think we can list Nepal, Laos, Cambodia, Burma, Indonesia, and Vietnam. I think that Indonesia technically could move into takeoff if it concentrated its energies and resources; and I believe South-Vietnam would move into takeoff if this war were not on its neck. But those are the "preconditions" countries.

Most of the other countries of Asia are in my view in takeoff position; that is, as you recall, the first sustained phase of industrialization. India, Pakistan, Thailand, Philippines, Malaysia, Taiwan. And for reasons that I will explain, I believe Korea is already in the early stages of takeoff.

Japan, whose first stage of industrialization came a long time ago, starting about 1885, is now I would say, in the early stage of high mass consumption.

Communist China is an interesting case of an interrupted takeoff. It moved forward in the 1950s from roughly 1952 to 1958 or so. It then went into a very deep crisis, mainly because of its bad agricultural policy. It has recovered slowly back towards the level of 1958, but it is still unclear whether Communist China has an agricultural policy consistent with a sustained takeoff.

You will note that there are no cases of the drive to technological maturity in this Asian list. This occurs simply because of the historical accident of the timing of modernization. You have the unique case of Japan starting late in the nineteenth century. Colonialism mainly prevented this kind of sustained modernization until after the Second World War—that's why the bulk of Asia is at a stage of completing the preconditions, or in takeoff.

When I spoke in Tokyo the other day on Asian economic development, I focused my generalizations around the problems of the countries in takeoff. I focused around three quite typical weaknesses in the takeoff: a systematic neglect of agriculture, a neglect of building a national market, and a neglect of nontraditional exports. Looked at in this way, Korea is a more hopeful case of a country in takeoff than many others in Asia, and I will tell you precisely why.

First, in agriculture, you have mounted here a serious agricultural program. If it is sustained, if there is a continuous effort to modernize your life, and especially to increase the application of chemical fertilizers, I believe that you will fully be able to feed your own population. If you use your agricultural base, not merely as a source of food but as a source of raw materials for industry and as a source of exports, then you can raise the level of standard of life in rural areas so that it becomes increasingly a market for Korean manufactured goods.

Secondly, you have launched your industrialization in part on the basis of import substitution, but you have not made the mistake, which many countries have done, of making your tariffs so high and your manufacturers so comfortable that they are inefficient. You have not stifled competition in manufacturing sectors behind high tariff barriers. Your manufacturers are beginning to face the winds of competition in international markets. You've avoided dangers which many other underdeveloped countries have faced because they have made their import substitution tariff protection so comfortable for their manufacturers that they never have learned to compete.

Finally, you've already begun a drive to increase your nontraditional exports and you are on the way to learning how to earn the foreign exchange you will need for full-scale industrialization.

This hopeful policy—that's moving forward in agriculture, in import substitution, in nontraditional exports—is underpinned by infrastructure investment in roads, in power, in institutions, and in hardworking and talented and educated human beings. This gives me confidence that you not only can launch takeoff but that you can see it through.

I conclude therefore that your takeoff is under way, that you're essentially, in terms of policy, pointed in the right direction and that your leading sectors are import substitution and nontraditional exports. But growth, human or national, always involves problems, and I'd like to talk about what I've seen from Washington as some of Korea's critical problems.

First, to make good this takeoff and to drive beyond to technological maturity you need a rapid buildup of the Korean industrial sector. In turn, this requires, first, that you produce in your own society many more entrepreneurs, modern businessmen, engineers, scientists, and industrial managers. This kind of industrial development must be based, in human terms, fundamentally on Koreans.

Second, you should be prepared to use for your own purposes of national development foreign capital and foreign technology. You should not be afraid of bringing in foreign enterprise which can contribute, as I say, not only capital but entrepreneurial skills and technology.

In the day I have been here, I have been asked quite often whether in my view, there is enough strength in the Korean economy so that it will not be overwhelmed if there is a normalization of economic relations with Japan. And I will tell you what my answer was. I have given a great deal of thought to this question, and I began by examining the practical experience that I could observe in the contemporary world with this kind of problem. One interesting case is the relationship between the United States and Mexico, because the gap in the stage of development between the United

States and Mexico is greater than that between Japan and Korea. There was a time in the 1930s when the Mexicans were very much afraid of foreign capital and indeed they nationalized the oil properties of an American oil company. What happened was that during the Second World War starting in 1940, Mexico began its takeoff with an import substitution boom which was imposed by the fact that it could not import from the United States and Europe many of the things it used to import. As they developed their own manufacturing industry, they began to bring in foreign private industry at the same time, and they discovered that the effect of bringing in foreign industry, when they had a movement forward of their own, was to accelerate the expansion of the Mexican industrial sector.

So, you end up now with the situation in 1965 where the Mexicans, who are a very proud people, with a firm strong government, plan to import 220 million dollars in private capital in the year 1965. And in the 25 years since their takeoff began in 1940, the purely Mexican private and public manufacturing sector has expanded very much more rapidly than the foreign ownership element.

Now the Mexicans have made very sure that all of this money that came in went into sectors that fitted Mexican national development. They've been extremely careful to make sure that this foreign private capital worked to the pattern of design of their development strategy, and they have proved it possible to use foreign private enterprise to fulfill a nation's development plan.

Other Latin American countries are now beginning to follow that pattern. The Philippines and Pakistan—especially Pakistan—is well worth your study because there has been very rapid growth in the Pakistani industrial sector with the bringing in of a lot of foreign capital. And India, after being suspicious and rather cautious of foreign private capital for a time, is moving over towards an acceptance of something closer I think, in spirit, to the kind of policy followed by Mexico, the Philippines, and other countries I've mentioned. I conclude, therefore, as nearly as I can perceive, that if you maintain the momentum you already have in your own industrial sector, if you have a national development plan in which it is clear what sectors you wish to see developed with the help of outside capital—not only Japan but also the United States and Germany and any other country you want to deal with—that private foreign capital will not overwhelm you. You can be confident that the net effect of the capital and managerial skill and technology you import will give you a higher rate of growth in the Korean industrial sector than you would otherwise have.

I conclude this section of my talk, then, by saying that if I am correct that your leading sectors are in the industrial area, that your job is to build up your own capacity to manage and push forward that industry as fast as possible and to learn how to use the advantages, how to exploit the advantages, of foreign private investment for your own development, while carrying forward the work on agriculture and infrastructure that will be necessary to underpin this rapid industrialization.

Now, I turn to a second technical problem, which is not in the last year a major problem in Korea, but I talk to you from the heart about avoiding it, and that is inflation.

Some of you may know, in addition to my job as planner in the State Department,

I am the United States member of the Inter-American Committee on the Alliance for Progress, called CIAP. It is kind of Board of Directors of the Alliance. There I have seen a great deal of inflation and its miseries. Inflation reduces the level of savings and forces down the total level of investment. It distorts the pattern of investment away from its most intelligent and productive uses by making people invest in order to hedge against inflation. It produces a kind of competition among the social classes as to who can best protect himself against inflation. It is, I assure you, something to be avoided if you are concerned with the serious development of your nation.

All of us on CIAP have designed a policy and a program to stop inflation, or prevent it, and I might just give you the headings briefly. First, insure tax collection; second, insure efficiency in government-owned corporations so that they do not require subsidies from the budget; third, attack the cost of living from the supply side through improved marketing of agricultural commodities, and the development of mass distribution methods and the marketing methods of the manufacturers to provide what the masses of the people need. To keep inflation out of a society, or to stop it, there needs to be a deep understanding among all the major elements in the society, a kind of social compact between government, industry, consumer, and labor. If any of you are interested in my views on this derived from the very hard experience in Latin America, I gave a talk to some students in Argentina not so long ago entitled "The Chapter Keynes Never Wrote" and I gather there are some copies that you can get from the U.S. Information Service if you are interested in greater detail.

I mentioned the concept of a social compact with respect to stopping inflation, but there is a deeper social compact that is needed to underpin a national development plan designed to modernize a society. Some of you may remember the French statesman Clemenceau during the First World War who said, "War is too serious a matter for Generals." I can say as an economist and a development planner that economic plans of a country are too serious a matter for economic planners alone. Technically, an economic plan is a set of statistical projections, but if it is to have meaning it must become a common vision of where a society wants to be in, say, five years. I would hope in the case of Korea, for example, that when your second five-year plan is prepared that the public would discuss it, analyze it, and come to understand what it is trying to achieve. A plan ought to be discussed in all the sectors of society, and then it ought to be taken out of the capital city and discussed in the regions of a country so that people feel what the plan means, the changes it will bring in their life. In short, looked at properly, a development plan is a nation's own vision of the future it wishes to make in a modern technological age in terms of its own history, its own traditions, its own ambitions for the future.

If I am right, if the takeoff of Korea has begun, if you have begun the process of sustained growth, what I have had to say is of quite profound significance for you in this room who are students.

You stand somewhat like the students in the early days, let's say of MIT, after the Civil War where a consciousness seized the country that it was on its way to industrialization and students turned to the question "Where will I fit, how can I play a part in the modernization of the United States?" Because once growth starts it is very powerful. I would estimate conservatively that if I am right and your takeoff has begun, within the span of the lifetime of most of you in this room, you will see a Korea at least where Japan now is, or Italy. You will see a Korea that has grown in the vocabulary of stages-of-growth to technological maturity, absorbed all the modern science and technology, and begun to turn its industrial machine to what I call the age of high mass consumption.

As you know, my view of the timing of economic development derives from my historical studies, but it might interest you to know the view of this problem that comes not from historical study but from the personal experience of President Johnson and Secretary of State Rusk.

President Johnson was born in a very poor part of central Texas. Secretary of State Rusk was born in a very poor part of Georgia. In both cases they grew up with a level of life that is not above that of the contemporary life of Korea.

In the span of their lives—they are both men in their fifties—they have seen a complete transformation in their regions, the regions of their boyhood in the United States. And this is one of the reasons that quite without the benefit of the stages of economic growth, they believe passionately in economic development and know how much can be done by purposeful men in the span of one lifetime.

And so the simplest message that I've got for you as a planner from Washington is that, as objectively as I can see it, you should approach the problems ahead of you not out of fear, and not merely out of hope, but out of confidence.

You've had your country split in a world war. You've had to try to begin your political and economic development, then came a second war. You had to reconstruct your country and found political institutions. Nevertheless, in 1965 you stand, on my quite objective assessment, already into the first sustained phase of your industrialization with intelligent and sound basic policies, and with a foundation in infrastructure, including a remarkably intelligent and energetic people that is capable of carrying forward the kind of modernization you want.

Now let me say in the final section of my talk something about the relations of Korea with the outside world in the next phase of its development.

First with the United States. We have been with you since the end of the war. We've gone through fighting together, through reconstruction and political difficulties, and my simple message is that now that the real adventure of development has begun, we do not intend to leave you. We intend to enjoy this adventure and participate in it with you.

Specifically we look forward to the formulation of your second five-year plan and as we look at the requirements of that plan, we intend to play our part in helping finance them, and inevitably as you move forward and move to a development phase, the forms of our aid will change from generalized support of the level of consumption, to development aid which enlarges the level of investment.

With respect to Japan, I've already discussed my view that Japanese and other external assistance in no way need overwhelm you if you maintain the momentum of your own private sector, and make sure that the investments fit your development plan. On the contrary, this kind of external assistance could be a force accelerating Korean industrial development.

It may interest you to know that in the days I spent in Japan very recently before coming here, in all my talks with Japanese who knew Korea, there were two convictions. One, a great respect for the skill and quality and intelligence of the Korean worker and his technical skills; and, secondly, an understanding that the takeoff phase of industrialization in Korea had already begun.

Third, in addition to whatever the help the United States and Japan can give in your development plan, I would hope that countries, aside from the United States and Japan, would come in, much as the Europeans are now coming increasingly into the Alliance for Progress.

There is another very interesting dimension to your development and all of Asia's. This is the emergence, I believe, which will come in the next years of more systematic regional work on the development within Asia.

There's been a lot of attention lately to Southeast Asian regional development; and there is indeed the Mekong Valley Authority working on the river development of that area.

There's a larger movement afoot, which is symbolized by the emergence of the concept of an Asian development bank.

President Johnson has just indicated that he is prepared for the United States to play its part and put up some money in that bank. The suggestion made by the Asian experts was that we put up 20%. I think Japan will put up 20%, Australia a little under 10%, and the rest of the countries of Asia, the remainder. We think that kind of regional development is sound.

In addition, our friends in Asia may wish to examine this instrument we call CIAP in the Alliance for Progress, in which under Latin American direction, country plans are reviewed, multinational projects are organized, trade problems are resolved. It may be that you want some kind of Asian leadership in the whole enterprise parallel to that which we have in the Alliance for Progress—but that only the people of Asia can decide and organize.

We have found that the development of a regional organization and a regional development effort in Latin America has not diminished the ties between us and the Latin Americans. They have never been so intimate. What it has done is to give the whole region a relationship of greater strength and dignity in dealing with the United States in the whole development process.

And now as I close, permit me to tell you if I may—and this is the first time I've ever told it in public—an incident that happened in the White House in 1961 when President Kennedy was there. We were talking about the future of Korea in the 1960s, and one man present said, "Korea has had a very hard history and a very hard time. I do not think we can count in the 1960s on any sustained upward movement in the Korean economy. That will have to wait until the 1970s."

Although I was a junior bureaucrat around the Cabinet table, I asked the President for permission to speak not as a bureaucrat but as an economist. I said that I thought this view was too pessimistic, that I know some of the young Korean economists and planners coming along, and that I had some feeling for the next generation that was emerging. I believed we would see Korea take hold and move forward in the course of the 1960s.

And so in coming here and seeing Korea at last, with many signs of vitality, and meeting face-to-face a good many members of this vigorous young generation that is emerging, I have had a special pleasure and I'm sure that it would have pleased President Kennedy as well.

I frankly told you this afternoon how a man at a great distance views your prospects and your problems, and I've tried to tell you with all the responsibility — not only of a bureaucrat but of a social scientist who must live with his judgments — of the confidence I deeply feel in you and the future of your country.

Appendix D

ANDREWS AND ORTEGA ELEMENTARY SCHOOLS: TEXAS ACADEMIC ACHIEVEMENT ANALYSIS, 1994-2001

ANDREWS TAAS ANALYSIS, 1994-2001 (percent passing)

	1994	1995	1996	1997	1998	1999	2000	2001
Grade								
Third	55.1	53.8	46.7	37.1	63.9	66.1	56.1	—
Fourth	46.6	34.5	47.8	53.5	74.6	51.8	58.1	—
Fifth	29.3	37.0	39.6	58.2	68.1	61.4	63.2	—
All Tests								
All students	43.0	40.5	44.7	49.5	69.0	49.8	56.4	—
African American	32.4	34.7	41.2	48.3	66.1	51.3	51.7	—
Hispanic	48.9	46.2	50.0	45.1	71.7	45.5	58.7	—
White	88.2	64.3	52.9	68.4	77.8	77.8	100.0	—
Economically								
Disadvantaged	41.6	39.0	41.7	45.8	69.7	43.3	53.6	—
Reading								
All students	65.2	63.0	62.2	58.8	78.7	62.6	73.3	76.3
African American	58.4	60.6	62.0	57.9	78.4	69.8	75.0	84.8
Hispanic	68.9	65.8	64.1	55.6	79.2	51.5	69.4	68.2
White	94.1	71.4	58.8	72.2	77.8	88.9	100.0	—
Economically								
Disadvantaged	64.6	62.1	57.5	53.8	78.1	56.6	69.9	73.5
Mathematics								
All students	49.4	45.5	53.2	65.4	75.5	63.0	68.2	79.7
African American	39.6	37.2	49.5	63.8	72.8	61.4	61.6	72.7
Hispanic	55.6	51.4	57.5	64.0	78.6	62.2	73.5	85.3
White	88.2	85.7	64.7	78.9	82.4	88.9	100.0	—
Economically								
Disadvantaged	49.1	45.1	51.9	62.6	75.7	58.2	65.3	78.3
Writing								
All students	79.3	72.7	84.8	79.1	94.2	76.9	77.8	72.7
African American	76.5	71.1	89.3	79.5	94.6	72.2	81.4	82.5
Hispanic	83.3	81.8	83.3	72.2	88.9	83.3	71.4	60.0
White	83.3	66.7	66.7	100.0	100.0	—	—	—
Economically								
Disadvantaged	75.7	75.7	81.8	74.0	95.1	69.7	74.6	66.7
Attendance	96.6	96.3	96.3	95.8	95.7	96.4	96.4	96.5

ORTEGA TAAS ANALYSIS, 1994–2001 (percent passing)

	1994	1995	1996	1997	1998	1999	2000	2001
Grade								
Third	52.0	48.8	65.2	46.2	48.4	53.3	47.4	—
Fourth	32.1	48.0	48.7	46.2	42.9	54.5	69.7	—
Fifth	53.6	45.5	63.0	40.0	58.6	71.8	67.6	—
All Tests								
All students	45.7	47.5	60.4	50.4	56.0	65.1	66.4	—
African American	28.6	47.6	60.0	29.4	42.1	48.3	44.8	—
Hispanic	46.8	48.7	60.2	53.2	58.3	69.7	71.3	—
White	—	—	—	—	—	—	—	—
Economically Disadvantaged	43.2	42.4	55.8	46.1	52.6	67.4	64.5	—
Reading								
All students	64.6	71.1	75.0	67.9	73.0	80.3	83.9	84.4
African American	42.9	61.9	60.0	52.9	68.4	68.0	66.7	88.5
Hispanic	66.7	73.0	77.9	69.9	73.7	83.3	87.9	83.3
White	—	—	—	—	—	—	—	—
Economically Disadvantaged	62.5	67.5	72.6	64.8	71.3	85.2	84.1	85.5
Mathematics								
All students	56.3	50.5	68.6	58.0	65.5	77.3	73.9	86.0
African American	50.0	52.4	73.3	41.2	52.6	65.4	53.8	76.9
Hispanic	55.7	51.4	67.8	60.2	67.7	80.4	78.1	88.1
White	—	—	—	—	—	—	—	—
Economically Disadvantaged	54.8	45.8	63.5	54.5	63.4	79.7	69.8	86.3
Writing								
All students	85.7	72.0	78.9	64.0	61.8	67.5	75.0	84.6
African American	100.0	—	85.7	—	—	50.0	71.4	—
Hispanic	81.8	75.0	76.7	68.2	66.7	73.3	73.9	88.9
White	—	—	—	—	—	—	—	—
Economically Disadvantaged	85.2	66.7	80.0	61.9	56.7	70.6	73.1	84.4
Attendance	—	96.5	96.4	96.2	96.6	97.4	96.7	97.5

NOTES

1. A BACKWARD GLANCE

1. The issue came to a head in 1903 when Martov (Yuly Tsederbaum) resisted Lenin's views and opposed Lenin's plan for a party restricted to professional revolutionaries. Martov called for a mass party modeled after western European social democratic parties. It was out of this cleavage that the Mensheviks emerged.

2. I later used the generational framework of Thomas Mann's first novel, *Buddenbrooks,* to predict the definitive change in the Soviet Union in my 1958 lectures at Cambridge. See *The Stages of Economic Growth* (Cambridge: Cambridge University Press, 1960, 1971, 1990), p. 162 (all editions).

3. Ferdinand Schevill, *A History of Europe* (New York: Harcourt Brace, 1925 ed.), p. 719.

4. The industry and resourcefulness of my colleague Patricia Schaub has verified the reports of this storm in the *New York Times,* which referred to it as a hurricane. The storm tore violently up the coast from North Carolina to New York on August 23–25, 1933, losing force as it went up the Hudson valley.

5. The editors in 1930–1931 were William Harlan Hale and Selden Rodman; in 1931–1932, Richard M. Bissell Jr. and Richard S. Childs; in 1932–1933, Eugene V. Rostow, William S. Harpham, and Herman W. Liebert; and in 1933–1934, Loren C. Berry, William J. Hull, Karl C. Parrish, and Andrews Wanning.

6. U.S. Department of Commerce, Bureau of Mines, *Minerals Yearbook 1932–1933,* p. 281, and *1939,* p. 671.

7. I fulfilled all requirements for the B.Litt. at Oxford writing a paper covering 1868–1886. At Yale in 1938–1939 I extended the text down to 1896, which was my Ph.D. thesis. All this was agreed to by Yale before I went to Oxford. The Ph.D. thesis was published in 1981: *British Trade Fluctuations, 1868–1896* (New York: Arno Press).

8. We dug up the *Times* accounts of the semifinals and finals of the elimination tournament. In the semifinals we first played a tie with Trinity (February 25, 1937, p. 6); Balliol then beat Trinity handsomely, 15-3 (March 3, 1937, p. 5). I had forgotten the tie and the two games. Having achieved the finals, Balliol lost in the second overtime period to University College, 6-3: the winning penalty kick "dropped on the cross-bar and fell on the far side" (March 6, 1937).

9. For another account of the Abdication crisis as seen by Alistair Cooke see his *Six Men* (London: Alfred A. Knopf, 1977), pp. 67–68 and 75. Cooke quotes the Laski argument, which was reprinted in the *New York Times* (p. 75): "The essential issue has never been more exactly put than by Harold Laski, in a dispatch printed in the *New York Times* three days before the abdication: 'This issue is independent of the personality of the King. It is independent of the personality of the Prime Minister. It does not touch the wisdom or unwisdom of the marriage the King has proposed. It is not concerned with the pressure, whether churches or the aristocracy, that is hostile to this marriage. It is the principle that out of this issue no precedent must be created that makes the Royal authority once more a source of independent political power in the State."

10. For another account of this organization focused on the 1938 tour, see Edward Heath's *Music: A Joy for Life* (London: Sidgwick and Jackson, 1976), pp. 50–51. Heath took over from me the writing of music for the 1938 tour, and the printed program for that tour records both our names.

11. Yale University, *Class of 1936: 50 Years Out* (ed. Oliver Jensen), published by Yale University Alumni Records Office, p. 28.

2. THE USE OF AIR POWER IN EUROPE, 1942–1945

1. Solly Zuckerman, *From Apes to Warlords* (London: Hamish Hamilton, 1978), pp. 197–198.

2. Solly Zuckerman, "Bombs and Illusions in World War II," *Encounter* 52, no. 6 (June 1979): 86. For a first-rate account of the oil vs. marshaling yards controversy, see Charles P. Cabell, *Man of Intelligence* (Colorado Springs, 1998), Ch. 13.

3. Zuckerman, *From Apes to Warlords,* p. 407 (Sicily Report, "General Conclusions," paragraphs 10, 12, 14). Zuckerman here makes clear the distinction between "tactical" and "strategical" targets he strongly denies making in his *Encounter* article (see note 2). For some reason Zuckerman does not include in this appendix the nine brief paragraphs of "Special Conclusions" that include his critically important negative assessment of bridges as "uneconomical and difficult targets."

4. Ibid., p. 239. There is an ambiguity here in the phrase "factual analysis." Within the considerable limits of time for research and availability of evidence, well specified in the text of the Sicily Report, the facts in the text are no doubt correct. The analysis and conclusions drawn from them were, however, contestable, as is often the case, for the same set of facts can lend themselves to diverse interpretations. For example, the data presented in the text of the Sicily Report on bridge attacks (pp. 56–60) lend themselves, as noted on pp. 39–40 and in note 41, to much more optimistic conclusions than were drawn from them by Tedder and Zuckerman.

5. Ibid., p. 217.

6. This is the date of the paper in the EOU files. Zuckerman dates the consideration of the AEAF/SHAEF plan as presented on February 15 ("Bombs and Illusions," p. 86). In *From Apes to Warlords,* p. 222, a process is suggested in which there may have been a succession of amended drafts. It should, perhaps, be noted that while

the plan promised to "paralyze movement in the whole region," the expected results in executing the plan as stated on March 25 by Tedder, Eisenhower, and Portal were more modest.

7. Sir Charles Webster and Noble Frankland, *The Strategic Air Offensive against Germany, 1939–1945* (London: Her Majesty's Stationery Office, 1961), 3:73. The British official history of the strategic bombing offensive heads the chapter "The Approach to Overlord and the Revival of United States Strategic Air Power, December 1943–February 1944."

8. Adolf Galland, *The First and the Last* (New York: Henry Holt, 1954; Bantam Edition, 1978), pp. 208–210.

9. Arthur William Tedder, *With Prejudice* (London: Cassell, 1966), p. 526.

10. Ibid., p. 513.

11. Ibid., p. 506.

12. Alfred P. Chandler et al., *The Papers of Dwight David Eisenhower, The War Years: III* (Baltimore: Johns Hopkins University Press, 1970), pp. 1784–1785.

13. Tedder, *With Prejudice*, p. 526.

14. Tedder (ibid., pp. 516–517) had assessed the oil plan in these terms:

I am frankly sceptical of the oil plan, partly because we have been led up that garden path before, partly because the targets are in difficult areas (six of them in the Ruhr, where we have been assured that the Americans could not do precision bombing on the railway targets because of flak and smoke, and the most important ones in the areas south and southwest of Berlin, where penetration is most difficult), and partly because I am not sure as to the real vulnerability of the new synthetic oil plants, where the enemy has presumably taken immense precautions against an air attack by means of dispersal, protection, etc. I am even less impressed by the arguments advanced for the tank targets as a help for "Overlord."

15. Wesley Frank Craven and James Lea Cate, eds., *The Army Air Forces in World War II* (Chicago: University of Chicago Press, 1951), 3:174. See also Webster and Frankland, *Strategic Air Offensive against Germany*, 3:46–47.

16. Ibid.

17. Craven and Cate, *Army Air Forces*, 3:174–176.

18. Quoted in an account of this affair, written by me in the late winter and spring of 1945, contained in an unpublished manuscript, "Economic Outpost with Economic Warfare Division," vol. 5, "War Diary of the OSS, London: The Enemy Objectives Unit (EOU) to April 30, 1945," p. 101; the manuscript is to be found in the National Archives in Washington.

19. Craven and Cate, *Army Air Forces*, 3:372–378. Some odd things went on in the Mediterranean toward the end of 1943. In the brief interval between Spaatz' departure for London and Eaker's arrival, a virtual embargo on bridge attacks was ordered by Tedder's headquarters on December 24, 1943, and seven northern Italian marshaling yards were accorded overriding priority among transport targets. On that day the Target Section of the MAAF recommended "complete, simultaneous, and continuous cutting of all German supply lines" across central Italy. It took several

months to resolve this confusion. Sir John Slessor, who left Coastal Command to become Eaker's deputy in the Mediterranean, played an important part in settling the conceptual battle over transport targets left in the wake of Tedder's and Zuckerman's departures for Britain. Here is Slessor's account of why he disengaged from Tedder's doctrine and helped lay the basis for Operation STRANGLE:

> . . . [T]here was at least one conclusion in the report [Zuckerman's Sicily Report] which had since been invalidated by experience, namely that bridges as targets were too uneconomical and difficult to be worth attacking except in special circumstances in the tactical area. . . .
>
> Moreover, looking at the map of Italy with its relatively few railways, it seemed from the lessons of the past at least possible that we had here a special opportunity for really decisive results. In a memorandum dated February 11 to the very able young Director of Operations, Brigadier-General Lauris Norstad, calling for a review of bombing policy, I wrote—
>
> > "There are now some seventeen German divisions in Italy south of Rome. I do not believe the Army—even with our support—will move them. But I think it more than possible that the Hun, by concentrating all this force so far south, has given us—the Air Forces—an opportunity. He has been able up to now just to support his smaller armies on the present line in spite of our air attacks on his communications. I find it hard to believe that, by increasing those forces, he has not put a load on to his communications which they will not be able to stand if we really sustain a scientifically planned offensive against the right places in his L. of C."
>
> Subsequent discussions led to the production of a new bombing directive, which was approved by Eaker and issued on February 18. (*The Central Blue* [London: Cassell, 1956], p. 568)

20. Craven and Cate, *Army Air Forces,* 3:157–162.

21. Gordon A. Harrison, *Cross-Channel Attack* (Washington, D.C.: GPO, 1951), p. 228. William F. Whitmore concludes as follows:

> World War II experience, both in Italy and in Normandy, indicated that fighter/bombers (dive and glide bombing) could cut bridges for 50 to 60 tons a cut, medium bombers (level bombing from, say, 10,000 feet) for 100 to 120 tons, and "heavies" (B-17 and RAF Bomber Command) for something over 200 tons. These were average figures for normal squadrons, and they were frequently improved on in particular cases. In the few instances where Air Force policy allowed squadrons to specialize in "bridge-busting" (that is, the use of AZON guided bombs in Burma), spectacular results were obtained—as low as 4 or 5 tons per cut. ("Logistics as a Target System," *Journal of Defense Research* 2B, no. 2 [summer 1970]: 188)

22. The official histories are not clear on how the bridge attacks of May 7 actually came about. What we have by way of formal documentary record is thin, indecisive, but not unilluminating. We have the minutes of target planning meetings on May 3

and May 6, 1944, held at Leigh-Mallory's headquarters. At both, bridges as pre-D-Day targets were considered. Here are the two relevant paragraphs summarizing the May 3 discussion:

8. As D Day approaches it is recognized that the enemy's lines of communication will become of increasing importance, and if a series of targets could be selected which would cut a number of lines for a period of two to three weeks from D-21 to D Day, this would contribute to the Tactical plan of railway cutting which will be put into force after D Day. It appeared that the Targets which fulfilled this need were Railway Bridges, provided that such attacks were technically practicable, and for this purpose it appeared that the 8th Air Force would be the best force to employ.

9. It was decided that the 8th Air Force should do a full scale attack on three SEINE Bridges and three MEUSE Bridges, any time after D-15. If this was not a success, the final policy would be adjusted. It was felt that the time spent on this attack would not substantially affect the attacks on Railway centres if it did not succeed.

On May 6 Spaatz initiated the discussion by urging that the heavy bombers not be diverted to bridges; but, apparently under pressure from Twenty-first Army Group and the British Second Tactical Air Force, Leigh-Mallory agreed, despite the difficulty of the targets and his fear of wasted effort, that some experimental attacks might be undertaken "between now and D-Day."

Evidently there is something missing here, for there is no suggestion that an experimental attack would be carried out the next day. In my memory and Kindleberger's, the central figure who forced the issue was Brigadier General Frederic H. Smith, Jr., the second-highest ranking U.S. officer (next to General Hoyt S. Vandenberg) assigned to Leigh-Mallory's headquarters. He was present at the meetings of both May 3 and May 6. His memory of the circumstances, as of November 9, 1979, is the following:

My plan was that we use P-47 fighter-bombers with delayed-action fuses to attack the bridges from the mouth of the Seine to Paris: 1,100-lb. bombs with 3-to 5-second delay fuses. Our thinking was that we could take out all the Seine bridges without tipping off the fact that Normandy was to be our main place of landing." [A systematic attack on the Loire bridges would have indicated, broadly, the landing site.]

Professor Zuckerman, who worked for Sir Trafford Leigh-Mallory, was present. Zuckerman said it would take something like 260 [sic] sorties of B-26's per bridge to carry out my plan. I said that's nonsense. [Presumably this occurred at the May 3 meeting.] However, Leigh-Mallory went along with Zuckerman and said no, we will not set those bridges as our objective. In the meantime, word of what I was proposing got to Fred Anderson. The next day he called me and said: "Freddie, stay a little later than usual today at your office. A Captain of the Horse Guards will call on you and get your plan for attacking bridges." So when the Captain of the Horse Guards duly arrived, I gave him my plan and went home. Two days later,

I believe, Leigh-Mallory said at the morning meeting, Smitty [Gen. Frederic H. Smith Jr.], I have reconsidered your plan and I authorize you to attack a bridge as you desire on the Seine River and we will see what happens. [Presumably this occurred after the May 6 meeting.] So I selected Vernon which was a double-tiered bridge which carried both rail and road traffic. And I called Brigadier General David Schlatter of Ninth Air Force — we lived together — and told him to go ahead. We had discussed this a number of times. Next morning a squadron of P-47's took off from somewhere in the Ninth Air Force with top cover of P-51's, as I remember, and attacked Vernon. The first plane ordered to attack later peeled off and sank his 1,100-lb. bomb in the abutment of the bridge. As he pulled over he saw sympathetic explosions. The Germans had mined it, and the whole thing fell flat in the river. Therefore, I got an okay to go ahead with the Seine bridge target plan as a whole.

I think the Captain of the Horse Guards took the plan to 10 Downing Street and that's where the pressure came from on Leigh-Mallory to reverse his decision. That's my theory. (F. M. Sallagar, *Operation "STRANGLE" (Italy, Spring 1944): A Case Study of Tactical Air Interdiction* [Santa Monica, Calif.: RAND, R-851-PR, February 1972])

23. Tedder, *With Prejudice,* p. 537. Tedder does not, however, provide an account of how the attacks on bridges were introduced. He dates the major attacks on bridges as beginning as late as May 21. Zuckerman continues to fight the bridges to the end of his book (*From Apes to Warlords,* pp. 282–283); but he shifts ground somewhat in his reply to Kindleberger ("Bombs and Illusions," pp. 86–89). He argues, in effect, that bridges were always part of the transport plan but that their attack was not as effective as the assault on marshaling yards.

24. W. W. Rostow, *Pre-Invasion Bombing Strategy* (University of Texas Press: Austin, 1981), pp. 66–71.

25. The attack on the German Air Force was conducted by the Jockey Committee, made up of high-ranking officers of the RAF and the U.S. Army Air Corps. I was secretary of that committee from 1943 to 1945 and sent to all commands the weekly target lists in the wake of its deliberations. It met on Tuesdays. On April 3, 1945, it decided that the German Air Force had no offensive or defensive capabilities. I sent out that day a message to all commands informing them of that decision and ended the telegram: "Sic transit Gloria Tuesday" (Craven and Cate, 3:753–754).

A note in Craven and Cate indicates that the original printed reference is in the official Fifteenth Air Force History, Appendix G. As a historian I should note that the Fifteenth Air Force quotes the final dispatch as saying: ". . . Jockey has unsaddled and weighed in. Sic transit Gloria Tuesday." The racetrack analogy is quite accurate. But I simply don't remember it. General Spaatz had promised to send me home promptly after the German Air Force was formally pronounced by the Jockey Committee to have no offensive or defensive capabilities. He was as good as his word: I was in New York City rowing Elspeth about the Central Park lagoon on V-E Day.

26. C. P. Kindleberger, *Encounter* 51, no. 5 (November 1978): 41.

27. Charles Curtis, *A Commonplace Book* (New York: Simon and Schuster, 1957), pp. 112–113.

28. Slessor, *Central Blue*, p. 521.

29. Webster and Frankland, *Strategic Air Offensive against Germany,* 3:242–243.

30. The Air War College was good enough to provide bomb tonnage and target figures for the Eighth Air Force. These provided a rough idea—but only a rough idea—of the weight of the attack on oil. Of the total tonnage dropped by the Eighth Air Force, 3 percent at the maximum was devoted to oil between April and December 1944.

31. Sir Arthur Harris, *Bomber Offensive* (London: Collins, 1947), p. 220.

32. Frederick M. Sallager, *Operation "Strangle" (Italy, Spring 1944): A Case Study of Tactical Air Interdiction* (Rand Corporation: Santa Monica, Calif., 1972).

3. THE UNITED STATES AND THE SOVIET UNION, 1945-1999

1. Appendix A contains the full text of the original memorandum I wrote in February 1946 entitled *Draft of Proposed U.S. Plan for a European Settlement: Spring 1946.* The plan went through several versions as it went through the bureaucracy and was approved by Messrs. Acheson and Clayton, then the undersecretary and the assistant secretary for economic affairs. Subsequent references are to the Acheson-Clayton Plan. An Economic Commission for Europe was, indeed, proposed in the original plan. It came to life as follows. Isador Lubin represented the United States at a London postwar meeting of UNRRA (United Nations Relief and Rehabilitation Administration). He came to Paris to tell Byrnes that the Poles and the British had gotten together to propose an Economic Commission for Europe. Byrnes said to Lubin: "Wait a minute. I have some such proposal in my briefcase." The long and short of it was that he told Lubin (who knew of the larger plan) he could support the British and Polish proposal in London which he proceeded to do. The commissions then had a quiet life of their own. In this order, UN Economic Commissions were set up in Asia and the Far East (Bangkok, 1947), Latin America, (Santiago, 1948), and Africa (Addis Ababa, 1958).

2. *Public Opinion Quarterly* 11 (winter 1946–1947): 582–592.

3. Public opinion polls over the period 1945–1946 show that a substantial American majority was prepared to keep troops in Europe, Japan, and even China; that the rate and terms of discharge from the armed services were judged fair; that a rapid shift occurred toward reliance on U.S. strength rather than on the United Nations for defense; that suspicion of Soviet intentions, never low, rapidly increased. On the other hand, most politicians took the view that the public clamor for demobilization was irresistible. For a discussion of the evidence for both views see Nancy Boardman, *Public Opinion and the United States Foreign Policy, 1937–1956* (Cambridge: Center for International Studies, MIT, n.d. [c. 1958]), pp. 49–62.

4. In 1930 the Republicans won both houses, but by an exceedingly narrow margin in the House of Representatives. The death of several members and subsequent by-elections shifted the balance to the Democrats—thus, the fifteen- rather than sixteen-year gap in the Republican control of both houses.

5. George F. Kennan, *American Diplomacy, 1900–1950* (Chicago: University of Chicago Press, 1951), p. 120. The theme appears also, in positive form, in Kennan's equally celebrated long telegram of February 22, 1946; see *The Truman Administration: A Documentary History,* ed. Barton J. Bernstein and Allen J. Matusow (New York: Harper and Row, 1966), pp. 211–212.

6. Winston Churchill, *Triumph and Tragedy,* vol. 5 of *The Second World War* (New York: Houghton and Mifflin, 1948–1953), p. 365. J. F. Byrnes, *Speaking Frankly* (New York: Harper and Brothers, 1947), p. 31, agrees that more time was spent at Yalta on Poland than any other subject. See also Charles E. Bohlen, *Witness to History, 1929–1969* (New York: W. W. Norton, 1973), pp. 187–192, on the central role of the Polish question at Yalta.

7. J. Stalin, letter to Lenin of June 12, 1920, quoted in V. I. Lenin, *Collected Works,* 3rd Russian ed. (Moscow, 1935), vol. 25, no. 141, p. 624.

8. Averell Harriman, *America and Russia in a Changing World* (Garden City, N.Y.: Doubleday, 1971), p. 44.

9. There is, literally, no reference of substance to U.S. policy toward Poland in Truman's *Memoirs,* vol. 1 (Garden City, N.Y.: Doubleday, 1955–1956), p. 411. Much the same is true of Byrnes' *Speaking Frankly,* where the last reference to the Polish government is in the context of the debate in London in September 1945 over the Romanian treaty (p. 101). The grim sequence from Yalta to the crudely fixed Polish election and the new constitution of February 1947 is traced out in detail by Edward J. Rozek, in *Allied Wartime Diplomacy: A Pattern in Poland* (New York: John Wiley, 1958), pp. 338–437.

10. Lucius D. Clay, *Decision in Germany* (Garden City, N.Y.: Doubleday, 1950), pp. 121–122.

11. For Clay's observations on the evolution of the U.S.-Soviet relationship and its limits, see ibid., pp. 107, 136–138, 159–162.

12. The passage that follows is based on conversations in Berlin with Clay, Robert Murphy, William Draper, and others in early June 1946. I was sent with J. K. Galbraith to negotiate with Clay a common American policy on Ruhr coal production to be urged on the British, within whose zone the Ruhr then lay. The protracted character of our negotiations with Clay provided ample time to exchange views on other issues.

13. Ellen Clayton Garwood, *Will Clayton: A Short Biography* (Austin: University of Texas Press, 1958), pp. 119–120.

14. Joseph M. Jones, *The Fifteen Weeks* (New York: Viking, 1955), p. 218.

15. George F. Kennan, *Memoirs, 1925–1950* (Boston: Little, Brown, 1967), pp. 325–326.

16. *Foreign Relations of the United States,* 1946, 5:518–519.

17. Ibid., 1945, 3:890; 3:916, n. 8; 1946, 5:505–507; 5:509.

18. Ibid., 1946, 5:506.

19. Robert Murphy, *Diplomat among Warriors* (Garden City, N.Y.: Doubleday, 1964), p. 303. Before I left London in late April 1945, a senior American colleague and I were invited to lunch at a Pall Mall club with an RAF friend and a representative of the Foreign Office whom we had never met. We were a bit surprised when it gradually

emerged that the purpose of the meeting was for the Foreign Office member to suggest gently but lucidly that we ought to begin thinking about an Anglo-American-led Western bloc to contain the Soviet Union in the postwar world.

20. Clifford informs me that the report was printed in ten copies. In the morning of the day after he sent it to Truman, he was called by the president on the telephone around 6:00 A.M. and asked how many copies existed and who had them. When informed that he alone had possession of the other copies, Truman ordered Clifford to bring them to the president's office early in the working day. Truman told Clifford that the document was explosive and must not be distributed. On being presented with the remaining copies, Truman counted them and locked them up. The document is now available at the Truman Library.

21. *Foreign Relations of the United States,* 1947, 3:241-247.

22. These conversations can be traced in ibid., 1945, 3:897-912.

23. This reaction to the French proposals is explicitly reflected in the following concurring opinion of March 15, 1946, filed by the ESP (the office containing GA), in an otherwise agreed-upon working-level State Department paper urging that the Ruhr-Rhineland not be detached from Germany:

ESP concurs with the recommendation that the French proposal for the separation of the Ruhr and Rhineland from Germany be rejected and with much of the underlying analysis of the supporting paper on which it has collaborated. It desires, however, to submit certain supplementary observations:
Analysis
. . . ESP regards the description of the status quo, in the subject paper, as incomplete in relation to the underlying French view. The French proposals arose in considerable part from the assumption that the United States interest and effective intervention in Europe would, as after 1918, prove to be transitory. From this assumption the French draw the conclusion that the long-run possibilities of a non-bloc structure for Europe, within the framework of Major Power accord, are remote.
It is appreciated that not only the French, by their proposal, but also the United Kingdom and the USSR by their action, are conducting foreign policy in Europe on a similar assumption and a similar conclusion. . . .
Recommendations
. . . ESP would . . . recommend for consideration . . . that the quadripartite negotiation of the French proposals for the separation of the Ruhr and the Rhineland from Germany be made the occasion for a major diplomatic offensive by the United States designed to halt and reverse the present movement towards an exclusive bloc structure in Europe. Out of its experience with a limited range of relevant issues, ESP has prepared a partial formulation for such an approach.

24. Eugene V. Rostow had served during the war as a State Department officer in North Africa in 1943 and subsequently as an assistant to Dean Acheson. After a long-delayed back operation, he returned as a professor to the Yale Law School. The cited conversation was by telephone. His views on Germany and Europe were published in "The Partition of Germany and the Unity of Europe," *Virginia Quarterly Review*

23, no. 1 (winter 1947): 18–33. He argues that European unity is the only method to prevent Germany from again disrupting the balance of power and that only an economically revived Germany partitioned into several component states could be safely absorbed in a unified Europe. The article also reflects anxiety that Byrnes' Stuttgart speech and concurrent Soviet verbal support for German unity signaled a competition for German nationalist sentiment of considerable danger.

25. Jean Monnet, *Memoirs* (Garden City, N.Y.: Doubleday, 1978), pp. 249–255.

26. W. W. Rostow, *The American Diplomatic Revolution* (Oxford: Clarendon Press, 1946), especially pp. 24–25. I left the State Department in September 1946 to accept the post of Harmsworth Professor of American History for the year 1946–1947. An inaugural lecture is delivered any time a new professor is ready to hold forth.

27. See Appendix A.

28. W. W. Rostow, *The United States in the World Arena* (New York: Simon and Schuster, 1969), p. 110 (1st pb ed.). First published in 1960 by Massachusetts Institute of Technology Press.

29. W. W. Rostow, *The Stages of Economic Growth* (Cambridge: Cambridge University Press, 1960, 1971, 1990), pp. 102–103 (all eds.).

30. For my discussion of the process of deceleration in the 1970s, see *The World Economy: History and Prospect* (Austin: University of Texas Press, 1978), pp. 436–437.

31. Rostow, *Stages of Economic Growth*, p. 162. In *Buddenbrooks*, Thomas Mann's first novel, the first generation of a German family made money selling supplies to the Prussian army during the Napoleonic Wars; the second generation held on to the money, but became burgomaster of the town; in the third generation the grandson played the piano and died young.

I was not, of course, alone in predicting an end to communism in Eastern Europe. John Lucacs, for example, reports in a note that Winston Churchill said to de Gaulle in November 1944 that "Russian rule [in Eastern Europe]" would not last ("After the meal comes the digestion period"). (*Five Days in London, May 1940* [New Haven: Yale University Press, 1999], p. 214, n. 44). Lucacs adds: "to Colville [Churchill's personal aide] on New Year's Day in 1953, he predicted that by the 1980s Communism would disappear from Eastern Europe." Colville's text is: "He [Churchill] said that if I lived my normal span I should assuredly see Eastern Europe free of Communism" (John Colville, *The Fringes of Power: 10 Downing Street Diaries, 1939–1955* [New York: W. W. Norton, 1985], p. 658).

4. THE DEATH OF STALIN, 1953

1. Prepared by the Steel Division Economic Commission for Europe (Geneva, 1949), this study of some 148 pages ended each section with a statement of "possible remedies." Although the study was highly technical, it was also suffused with a plea for European cooperation, for example:

> The measures that have been suggested . . . for putting the European steel industry on a sound competitive basis — the mutual adjustment of European steel plans, the

necessity for reducing the cost of European steel and the longer-range measures for increasing productivity and consumption — all involve a magnanimous attempt at international economic co-operation. With the immediate crisis of problems arising from the war now over, the choice lies before Europe, either to go forward in its co-operative endeavours to meet the new, difficult and often troublesome tasks, or relapse into the old modes of thought and action which have brought upon it its present troubles. (p. 76)

2. Jackson's account conforms to the lengthy report in *Foreign Relations of the United States, 1952–1954*, vol. 8, *Eastern Europe–Soviet Union: Eastern Mediterranean*, pp. 1107–1125.

3. A substantial number of secondary works have examined the president's speech before the American Society of Newspaper Editors on April 16, 1953, and its relationship to the Soviet "peace offensive" following Stalin's death. In *The United States in World Affairs, 1953* (New York: Harper and Brothers, 1955), pp. 105–108, 114–132, Richard P. Stebbins describes in considerable detail the crucial events of March and April 1953. Both Robert J. Donovan, in *Eisenhower: The Inside Story* (New York: Harper and Brothers, 1956), pp. 72–76, and presidential assistant Sherman Adams, in *First Hand Report* (New York: Harper and Brothers, 1961), pp. 95–98, also deal briefly with that period. Richard Goold-Adams, in *The Time of Power: A Reappraisal of John Foster Dulles* (London: Weidenfeld and Nicolson, 1962), pp. 85–86, 109–119, concentrates upon what he views as the essentially negative and obstructionist role played by Secretary Dulles.

President Eisenhower's version of the events leading to the speech is contained in his *Mandate for Change, 1953–1956* (Garden City, N.Y.: Doubleday, 1963), pp. 143–149. One of the most detailed accounts of the often agonizing drafting and redrafting of the speech can be found in Emmet John Hughes, *The Ordeal of Power* (New York: Atheneum, 1963), pp. 100–115. For some reason Hughes begins his account only in "mid March," although he was intimately involved from the March 6 draft forward; but his version contains much valuable information. Another useful participant's account of the administration's immediate response to Stalin's death is Robert Cutler, *No Time for Rest* (Boston: Little, Brown, 1965), pp. 320–323.

Louis L. Gerson, "John Foster Dulles," in *The American Secretaries of State and Their Diplomacy*, ed. Robert H. Ferrell (New York: Cooper Square Publishers, 1967), pp. 128–131, examines Dulles' role with greater sympathy than that found in Goold-Adams' work. However, both Townsend Hoopes, *The Devil and John Foster Dulles* (Boston: Little, Brown, 1973), pp. 170–175, 180, and Leonard Mosley, *Dulles: A Biography of Eleanor, Allen, and John Foster Dulles and Their Family Network* (New York: Dial Press, 1978), pp. 330–338, share Goold-Adams' view that the secretary of state harbored scant enthusiasm for an American peace overture to Stalin's successors.

Several general works on the Eisenhower period examine the administration's reaction to the Soviet dictator's death. A concise and generally accurate account is Herbert S. Parmet, *Eisenhower and the American Crusades* (New York: Macmillan, 1972), pp. 274–281. See also Peter Lyon, *Eisenhower: Portrait of the Hero*, 2nd ed. (Boston: Little, Brown, 1974), pp. 530–534; Charles C. Alexander, *Holding the Line: The Eisenhower Era, 1952–1961* (Bloomington: Indiana University Press, 1975), pp. 65–66; and Elmo Richardson, *The Presidency of Dwight Eisenhower* (Lawrence, Kans.: Regents Press, 1979), pp. 61–62.

4. Statement of March 15, in *Pravda,* March 16, 1953; *Current Digest of the Soviet Press* 5, no. 8 (April 4, 1953): 5.

5. Adams, *Firsthand Report,* p. 97.

6. Monnet's account of the evolution of the EDC, from the attack on South Korea to its failure in the French Assembly on August 30, 1954, is to be found in his *Memoirs* (Garden City, N.Y.: Doubleday, 1978), pp. 336–362, 368, 381–382, 394–399.

7. Ibid., p. 396.

8. Konrad Adenauer, *Memoirs, 1945–53,* trans. Beate Ruhm von Oppen (Chicago: Regnery, 1966), pp. 430–434.

9. Interview by Don North, December 17, 1970. John Foster Dulles Oral History Project, Seeley G. Mudd Library, Princeton University; transcripts available at the Dwight D. Eisenhower (DDE) Library. This image is also evoked by Charles Bohlen in his *Witness to History, 1929–1969* (New York: W. W. Norton, 1973), p. 311. Bohlen notes that he made the remark half jokingly to someone who repeated it to Dulles, who, presumably, was not amused.

10. John W. Hanes Jr., personal aide to Dulles, puts this point well in a letter to me of February 20, 1981:

> [Dulles] had been profoundly influenced by what he considered to be the failure of a number of his predecessors and specifically including Dean Acheson to be able to translate much of their foreign policy decisions into effective American govern-mental policy, because of a failure to gain congressional support (and, sometimes, because of having to endure active congressional hostility). He was determined to do his best not to let this happen to President Eisenhower and himself.
>
> Both he and President Eisenhower, from their separate experiences, were more aware than most men in Washington of the shortcomings, with respect to foreign policy, of what you describe as the 'Republican Right,' especially in the Senate— and, particularly, of the danger represented by a demagogue as personified by Joe McCarthy (who, I think, cannot properly be described in terms such as 'right' or 'left'). But, especially in 1953, these things existed; they were influential in the Senate (and beyond); and they could not be ignored as forces.

11. Bohlen, *Witness to History,* pp. 311–312.

12. See especially ibid., Chap. 18, pp. 309–336.

13. John W. Ford, member of the Foreign Service and an extraordinarily cou-rageous security officer at the time, records the climax of the Bohlen affair as fol-lows ("The McCarthy Years inside the State Department," *Foreign Service Journal,* November 1980, p. 12):

> Senator Joseph McCarthy and certain other members of Congress questioned the nomination by the Eisenhower administration of Chip Bohlen to be the next

ambassador to the Soviet Union. The so-called 'evidence' on which to question his appointment took several forms: innuendoes in his security file or in FBI reports — the 'raw' material which so frequently constitutes part of basic background investigations. The most highly advertised bit of 'evidence' was a tape recording, allegedly containing Ambassador Bohlen's voice. This tape purportedly implicated him in activities which made him a security risk. Secretary Dulles called me to his office, where the security office file and the FBI reports on Ambassador Bohlen were assembled on his conference table. I was instructed to bring a tape recorder.

As I entered Secretary Dulles's office, I was introduced to Senators Taft and Sparkman. The secretary, with a flourish, instructed me to review with the senators the files on Mr. Bohlen. The secretary noted, however, that allowing the senators to see these files was 'without prejudice to the concept of executive privilege.'

Neither senator found anything incriminating in the files and then we proceeded with the tape recording. Unfortunately the extension cord for the recorder was too short, the quality of the tape was poor and the volume potential of the recorder was low. This means that Senators Taft and Sparkman and I had to lie down on the floor of Secretary Dulles's office in front of his desk and listen to the recording. I certified in a document that it was not Ambassador Bohlen's voice. That was also evident to all present. Shortly thereafter Ambassador Bohlen was cleared and took off for his new assignment.

14. Donovan, *Eisenhower*, pp. 108–109.

15. W. W. Rostow, in collaboration with Alfred Levin and with the assistance of others, *The Dynamics of Soviet Society* (New York: W. W. Norton, 1953). See esp. pp. 244–245, 251–252.

16. Ibid., p. 252.

17. See George F. Kennan, *Memoirs, 1925–1950* (Boston: Little, Brown, 1967), esp. pp. 415–466, and *Memoirs, 1950–1963* (Boston: Little, Brown, 1972), esp. pp. 3, 39–54, 90–104, 131–144, 159–162.

18. Kennan, *Memoirs, 1925–1950*, pp. 462–464. On pp. 446–448 Kennan, with admirable candor, lays out, with hindsight, certain assumptions in his earlier argument that were proved false.

19. For an account of the development and fate of this paper, see ibid., pp. 415–448.

20. McGeorge Bundy was to be national security adviser from 1961 to 1966; Kingman Brewster was to be president of Yale (1963–1977).

21. Kennan's interview in the J. F. Dulles Oral History Project indicates that Bohlen, as well as Jackson, asked him to come to Washington to discuss "questions arising from Stalin's death."

22. Philip E. Mosely, "The Kremlin's Foreign Policy since Stalin," *Foreign Affairs* 32, no. 1 (October 1953): 20, 22.

23. Gerson, *Dulles*, pp. 129–130. Gerson evidently had access to diplomatic exchanges which have not yet been fully declassified.

24. Adenauer's full analysis is to be found in his *Memoirs*, pp. 434–435, and in

the account of his trip to the United States, pp. 438–455. The extracts in the text are from pp. 438, 442, 444, and 455.

25. Goold-Adams, *Time of Power,* p. 110.

26. Hughes, *Ordeal of Power,* pp. 102–104. Hughes' full account of the writing and development of the speech, as he saw it, is on pp. 100–115. There is every reason to believe from subsequent speech drafts and the transcript of the Hughes-Dulles conversation of the same day that Eisenhower spoke in the vein Hughes evokes.

27. Hughes, *Ordeal of Power,* pp. 117–118.

28. Harold Macmillan, *Tides of Fortune, 1945–1955* (New York: Harper and Row, 1969), p. 511.

29. The Berlin conference was the kind of occasion when Dulles, by all accounts, was most comfortable and, in human terms, at his best: completely focused on a single problem, surrounded by a small, supportive group of aides, in unambiguous command. In letters of February 1, 1954, to an unnamed recipient and February 9, 1954, to Robert Cutler, C. D. Jackson commented:

> Foster is also very good at working with his staff. He consults them constantly and listens and frequently takes suggestions contradicting his ideas without a quiver.
>
> I suspect that this is the kind of existence he loves and because he is enjoying it, his personality is blossoming. . . . Particularly interesting to me is the fact that his relations with his staff are very warm and human, with lots of humor and great understanding of the other fellow's problems. Furthermore, his background press conferences have been models of interesting lucidity.
>
> Are you beginning to think by now that I have gone soft?

Both letters are from the C. D. Jackson Papers, box 27, "Berlin Basics and Working Papers" folder, DDE Library.

30. The Bohlen interview is from the J. F. Dulles Oral History Project, Mudd Library, Princeton University. Bohlen's more measured statement of his retrospective view is in *Witness to History,* p. 371:

> Looking back, I believe I was remiss at the time of Stalin's death in not recommending that Eisenhower take up Churchill's call for a "meeting at the summit" — the first time this phrase was used — with Malenkov. Dulles batted down the idea. I was not asked for an opinion and doubt that I would have been listened to if I had expressed one at that time. Dulles had told the senators he did not want me as an adviser. But I think I made a mistake in not taking the initiative and recommending such a meeting.
>
> After the death of Stalin, there might have been opportunities for an adjustment of some of the outstanding questions, particularly regarding Germany. In addition to the extraordinary act of *Pravda*'s publishing the text of a speech by President Eisenhower calling for peace, the Soviet press let up on its hysterical Hate America campaign. May Day slogans — a clue to the Bolshevik line of thinking — showed a striking contrast to those published for the anniversary of the Bolshevik Revolution the preceding November, when Stalin was still living. Instead of "down with the warmongers" and references to "imperialist aggressors" and "foreign usurp-

ers," there were expressions of confidence in the ability to resolve all differences between nations. Soon after his assumption of power, Malenkov himself said in a statement that there were no issues that could not be negotiated. Khrushchev subsequently charged that Malenkov and Beria had been contemplating a change in Soviet policy on Germany, possibly relinquishing the hold on East Germany and permitting some form of unification in return for a demilitarized, neutralized Germany. Khrushchev, as he often did, was undoubtedly stretching the truth. I doubt if any Soviet leader ever seriously contemplated giving up the Sovietized area of Germany. But there might have been room for some other accommodation.

31. Goold-Adams, *Time of Power,* p. 119.

32. Appendix B discusses the evidence in the literature bearing on the question of whether there was or was not an interval between Stalin's death in March 1953, and the successful repression of the East German revolt in June 1953 in which a settlement might have been reached on Germany. The possibility that the post-Stalin leadership may have been willing, for a transient interval, to contemplate a good-faith negotiation leading to an all-German settlement remains an unresolved historical question.

33. *Wall Street Journal,* April 29, 1980. For the author's nonauthoritative reply to Arbatov, see the *Wall Street Journal,* May 8. Both pieces were published on the editorial page.

34. Eisenhower, *Mandate for Change,* pp. 503–505.

35. Richard H. Immerman cites a 1956 example of Eisenhower's instructing Dulles to avoid, in the context of the Suez crisis, "a long wearisome negotiation, especially with an anticipated probability of negative results in the end." See his "Eisenhower and Dulles: Who Made the Decisions?" *Political Psychology* 1, no. 2 (autumn 1979): 27.

36. Several close observers have noted in interviews in the J. F. Dulles Oral History Project that the Eisenhower-Dulles relationship changed with the passage of time. For example, James Hagerty, Rod O'Connor, and Emmet Hughes agree that the early months of the relationship were the most uncertain, as Dulles learned to accommodate to the style of his new client. They also agreed that, with the passage of time, Dulles' confidence in the relationship increased, although elements of uneasiness persisted down to 1955 at least (see Chap. 5). Stalin's death and the ensuing debates and activities within the administration occurred in the early shakedown months. The question raised is whether this fact significantly affected the policies pursued by the United States. Without dogmatism, I am inclined to believe that Eisenhower's 1953 reservations about summitry, as well as Dulles', were quite deeply rooted as were their instinctive differences with respect to the appropriate tone to be adopted at such a juncture. I would guess that transient uncertainties in their working relationship played no significant role in the outcome.

37. Three examples of this gap between presidential posture and subsequent governmental performance were Eisenhower's proposals at the 1955 Geneva summit; the passages on aid to developing nations in his second inaugural address; and his proposals for organizing development aid in the Middle East in his August 1958 Lebanon-Jordan speech before the United Nations General Assembly.

The idea was to fly balloons at a very high altitude (above known fighter capability), drifting them across the USSR, and recovering them over neutral or friendly territory. The use of polyethylene made it possible to fly the balloons at constant pressure-altitude (which means essentially at a pre-selected altitude). The Air Force had been experimenting with these balloons at Holloman Air Force Base, and, in the early 1950's, was using them to carry scientific equipment to high altitudes.

In the summer of 1951, while working at Air Force Headquarters, in the Pentagon, I wrote a directive to the Air Force Cambridge Research Center specifying a field program to study the very high altitude wind field. In 1940, the expression "high altitude" had meant above 10,000 feet; work with B-29's jumped the meaning to 25,000 feet. By 1950, 50,000 feet was a modern definition and it seemed to be a good idea to get some instruments at even higher altitudes: to get there, just for once, before the airplanes did. The directive required polyethylene balloons to be floated at staggered levels between 50,000 and 100,000 feet; the balloons would carry a transmitter which would enable one to locate them every two minutes. With launchings from three West Coast sites (Tillamook, Oregon; Vernalis, California; and Edwards Air Force Base, California), we believed we would get good coverage of the U.S. and that a typical crossing would take three days. The balloons used an automatic ballasting system whenever they needed to gain altitude. After about three days, they would descend to 28,000 feet, where a pressure-sensing cut-down device would take over. The balloon would float harmlessly to earth, the gondola would follow on a parachute, and the finder would receive a monetary reward for returning the gondola. We called this project MOBY DICK ("What a gleamy and dazzling thing, this splendid, great white whale!").

At the very time I was writing this directive, working in the Geophysics Branch, around the corner from my office another directive was being written by a friend in the Reconnaissance Branch. He was directing the Wright Air Development Center to produce an operational plastic balloon for overflying the USSR. The 1946 RAND study would guide Wright Field's thinking. My friend and I believed these programs would complement each other quite nicely, with MOBY DICK furnishing important developmental technology to its operational counterpart (named WS-119L); it would also furnish a practically perfect "cover" for at least the developmental phase of WS-119L.

I was transferred to the Air Force Cambridge Research Center, to a staff position, in the Fall of 1951. Over the next two years, I was pleased to note the success of MOBY DICK, as hundreds of balloons swept across the United States at altitudes which helped deliver unique data to the Air Weather Service and the (then) U.S. Weather Bureau. Occasionally, to the delight of everyone in the program, a MOBY DICK balloon would make a very fast trip across the U.S., and sail out over the Atlantic, beeping away. Not to worry.

WS-119L was another story. The Wright Field engineers were not acquainted with polyethylene balloons and delegated that part of the development program to Holloman Air Force Base, retaining gondola development, camera development, and recovery work. They concentrated on the recovery problem, which appeared to be the most difficult; they were unable to solve it. The WS-119L specifications called for a capability to pick up a 600-lb gondola on the ground, on the water, and in the air. By early 1953, Wright Field technicians considered the project a disaster: one aircrew had almost crashed in field tests and no one had much stomach for carrying the work any farther.

A series of unusual circumstances led to my transfer from the Cambridge staff to a new laboratory—the Atmospheric Devices Laboratory—in the Spring of 1953. This lab, among other responsibilities, was given the job of MOBY DICK *and* WS-119L.

WS-119L had these basic technical problems, all requiring "instant" solution:

a. How can one get polyethylene manufacturers to make a very high quality film for the balloon program (no thin spots, please!), when all the big money is in seat covers and carrot-wrap?

b. How can one develop a gondola that will stay warm enough to protect our electronics and camera, when they are flying in the stratosphere for more than the usual three days?

c. How does one design a parachute capable of floating a 600-lb load safely from altitudes of 75–90,000 feet?

d. How does one recover a gondola safely in mid-air, say at 12–14,000 feet? (Water recovery and land pickup looked solvable.)

Each of these problems was solved experimentally by August 1954. Production of equipment and crew-training were completed by August 1955. The flight program lasted from November 1955 to Spring 1956, producing, by the user's standards, excellent results. It was certainly the least expensive program that has ever been run on this specific problem. There was some Soviet rhetoric (not very tough) over failed flights which dropped gondolas to earth prematurely. The reason for termination was never explained to us, but I later associated it with the fine progress Kelly Johnson was making at Lockheed's Skunk Works [where the U-2 was developed]. The very high altitude wind field weakens and shifts radically in the late Spring, so we knew we would not be flying, whatever the political situation, during summer months. I did not see examples of the product until May 1961. Although Gary Powers' trial, in 1960, was a serious affair, I could not help but smile at that part of the prosecution testimony in which G. Istomin, D. Sc. Tech., said that "The film is of a special grade designed for aerial surveys from high altitudes. Compared with the film used in American spy balloons of the 1956 model, the given grade has been improved. . . ." In 1957, the WS-119L camera (a beauty!) became the basis for the DISCOVERER satellite camera. Also, in 1957, the WS-119L mid-air recovery system was used—exactly as was—for outfitting the C-130's which were to recover satellite capsules in mid-air. By that time, I was stationed on the West Coast, in the Air Force Ballistic Missile Division, and shared responsibility for developing the DISCOVERER program. We were all very grateful that there had once been a lighter-than Air Force.

Where We Stood in July 1955: U-2 Photo-Reconnaissance:

I did not participate in this program, but had a number of friends who did. The "Perry Dictum" was borne out when I asked one of the key persons when the first U-2 test flight was made and, after searching his memory, he missed it by a year. [The reference is to Robert Perry of RAND whose dictum is: "Don't give me your memories, give me your memoranda." I would modify the Perry Dictum only by saying a historian wants both, while maintaining, of course, a proper reserve about memories unsupported by documentary evidence.] The first test flight was made on August 6, 1955. The first overflight of the USSR was made in 1956. The USSR overflight program was curiously tentative; perhaps there was some feedback to President Eisenhower about which we do not know. The caution can be illustrated two ways, rather easily. If you plot all U-2 overflights of the USSR on a single map, the limitations of the effort are almost shocking. The second evidence is knowing that from early 1958 to April 1960, practically *no* overflights of the USSR were made (one uses the word "practically" because some of the overflights were so shallow as to scarcely qualify).

Where We Stood in July 1955: Satellite Photo-Reconnaissance:

In July 1955, we had no satellite photo-reconnaissance capability whatever. RAND had done a fine study of satellite reconnaissance in 1946; a second important set of studies was produced in 1952–3. There had been very limited development-testing of some sensor and read-out components. But the big problem — the unavailability of a booster — was simply insurmountable.

Recall that the first successful THOR did not fly until December 19, 1957, and the first ATLAS success did not occur until August 29, 1958.

Satellite photo-reconnaissance came into its own August 18, 1960. (Please to ignore the persons who will insist it was August 10; they are wrong.)

4. Paul Worthman commented as follows in a letter to me of May 15, 1981: "[V]ery little work was being done on the satellite system in 1955. From 1955 through 1957, 'space' was literally a dirty word, not to be used by anyone in our government except NASA, and sparingly there. As late as 1957, (then) Major General B. A. Schriever had tough sledding getting $10 million for a satellite reconnaissance system and was *ordered* (hardly necessary, with that funding) to limit his effort to component development."

5. Ibid. Worthman comments: "I'll wager no one in our community *really knows* if this flight [*Kosmos 1*] produced intelligence information, but it is certainly the first flight in the series which we identify with Soviet satellite reconnaissance."

6. This point is made by Stefan Possony in "Reconnaissance in Time Perspective," in *Open Space and Peace,* ed. Frederick J. Ossenbeck and Patricia C. Kroeck (Stanford: Hoover Institution, 1964), pp. 30–31.

7. Dwight D. Eisenhower, *Waging Peace, 1956–1961* (Garden City, N.Y.: Doubleday, 1965), p. 556.

8. On this point Worthman commented perceptively in his letter to me of May 15, 1981:

[O]ne of the fastest fading recollections for the American public—and even the intelligence community—is the fact that the closed society was an extraordinarily effective device for the purposes of the Soviets. I see the open skies proposal in that context; it was one of a series of acts of near-desperation by our frustrated, worried national leaders. No one seems to remember *how* frustrated and *how* worried.

When one tells today's citizens that our leaders were deeply concerned about a surprise attack or believed very sincerely that the probability of nuclear war was rather high, the listener shows nothing but disbelief. The listener has a great advantage: he knows how things turned out during that chapter—we were not attacked and we did not go to war.

9. *Khrushchev Remembers,* trans. and ed. Strobe Talbott (Boston: Little, Brown, 1970), pp. 392-393.

10. *Khrushchev Remembers: The Last Testament,* trans. and ed. Strobe Talbott (Boston: Little, Brown, 1974), pp. 374-375.

11. Marquis Childs adds another possible dimension to the reasons for Eisenhower's decision to go to Geneva, in *Eisenhower Captive Hero* (New York: Harcourt, Brace, 1958):

> There is some reason to believe that President Eisenhower's attitude toward the proposed summit meeting was different from that of his Secretary of State. By this time the Eisenhower reputation was sadly frayed. The image of the crusader had been blurred by the McCarthy madness and by the nagging, persistent futility of his efforts to bring his party together behind many important constructive measures. The Democrats had won control over both houses of Congress in 1954. With the dimming of the Eisenhower luster, his critics were becoming bolder, although he still had a powerful hold on the country as hero, a folk figure larger than life-size, and a large proportion of the press continued to treat him with veneration, if not with awe. With his intuitive sense of drama and popular response, and with the precedents of 1942 and 1950, the meaning of a return to Europe in the role of peacemaker can scarcely have escaped him. The symbol of the hero-leader was in need of refurbishing. His mandate, out of the great electoral victory of 1952, had been to bring peace to the United States and the world. And so this new opportunity glowed against the murky horizon of the recent past with both a challenge and a promise. (pp. 205-206)

12. Eisenhower details clearly the background to his decision to accept the summit meeting in his *Mandate for Change,* pp. 505-506.

13. Ibid., p. 508.

14. The individual supporting papers and their authors were:

Tab 1—"Soviet Estimate of the Situation" (George Pettee)

Tab 2—"The Requirements for U.S. NATO to Win in the Arms Race with the USSR" with two annexes (Ellis Johnson)

Tab 3—"Alliance and Coalition Problems"
   (a) "Does NATO Have a Position of Strength?" (Frederick S. Dunn)
   (b) "Asia Policy" (W. W. Rostow)

(c) "Japan" (Paul Linebarger)

(d) "Measures to Cope with Free-World Fears of the Bomb" (Stefan Possony)

(e) "Air Defense of the United States and Western Europe" (Elks Johnson)

(f) "Factors Influencing the Morale of Allies" (George Pettee)

Tab 4—"Straining the Sino-Soviet Alliance" with annex (Paul Linebarger)

Tab 5—"An Institute for the Study of Peace" (George Pettee)

15. From an interview conducted by Hugh Morrow, of Rockefeller's staff, on July 14, 1977.

16. Dwight D. Eisenhower Papers, Ann Whitman File, Whitman Diary Series, box 5, "Ann C. Whitman Diary, May 25, 1955" folder 2, Dwight D. Eisenhower (DDE) Library.

17. John Foster Dulles (JFD) Papers, Telephone Conversation Series, box 10, "White House Telephone Conversations, Mar.–Aug. 1955" folder 1, DDE Library.

18. "Ann C. Whitman Diary, May 25, 1955."

19. Sherman Adams, *Firsthand Report* (New York: Harper, 1961), pp. 90–91.

20. Memorandum of conversation with the president, August 5, 1955, JFD Papers, White House Memo Series, 196, box 3, "Meetings with the President-1955" folder 3, DDE Library.

21. "White House Telephone Conversations, Mar.–Aug. 1955."

22. Morrow interview (see note 15).

23. JFD Papers, Telephone Conversation Series, box 4, "Telephone Conversations, General, May–Aug. 1955" folder 6, DDE Library.

24. Memorandum of telephone conversation with the president, July 6, 1955, JFD Papers, Telephone Conversation Series, box 10, "White House Telephone Conversations, Mar.–Aug. 1955," folder 1, DDE Library.

25. Morrow interview.

26. Ibid.

27. Responding on May 4, 1981, to an earlier draft of this chapter, the late William Kintner recalled the meeting on July 18 as follows: "Nelson alone of our small group was sitting at the table. I was sitting directly behind him. After his initial presentation to Anderson, Radford, etc., the 'Open Skies' proposal fell like a lead balloon. He turned around and asked, 'What did I do?' And I said, 'Do it again.' It was at this time that Possony intervened and Radford finally got the idea—'I see what you fellows are doing—you are trying to open up the Soviet Union.' Radford's observation won general acceptance of the group for the 'Open Skies' proposal."

28. Reston's dispatch of July 20 undoubtedly reflected Dulles' background press conference of that day, given on a "not for attribution" basis, now available in the Dulles Papers at the Princeton University Library. The bulk of the briefing centered on whether progress could be made in reconciling Soviet proposals for an all-European security treaty with U.S., British, and French insistence that such a treaty must be accompanied by the emergence of a Germany unified on a democratic free-election basis. The disarmament discussion scheduled for the next day was mentioned briefly several times in the course of Dulles' briefing. He noted, for example, that "there is more room for imaginative thinking" on the German prob-

lem, "which has been quite thoroughly hacked over for a period now of approximately eight years." On the arrival of Gruenther and Radford, about which he was questioned, in connection with the European security–German issue, Dulles said: "There is no possibility of discussing and exploring these problems just in the few hours these gentlemen will be here. We will give them a general overall picture of the way things are going. There has been a talk with them but it is not for the purpose of giving any technical studies to any of these proposals." Dulles was asked bluntly: "Will the United States present any plan or proposal on disarmament?" He replied: "Well, we will follow the same practice with reference to disarmament that we have followed with reference to this matter [Germany]; namely, that we will indicate our broad philosophical approach. Indeed, that has already been done in the opening statement of the president, where he put special emphasis upon problems of inspection and viewing to prevent surprises. And there may be various illustrative things indicated by the various Ministers as to what might be done under that heading. But there again there will be nothing in the way of a concrete proposal of substance on a take-it-or-leave-it basis."

In a further question on disarmament Dulles went no further than the relevant passage in Eisenhower's opening statement at Geneva. When Dulles spoke to the press, Eisenhower had not yet indicated his firm decision to go ahead with Open Skies; and it would have been, in any case, inappropriate for Dulles to foreshadow it. But the background press conference makes quite clear why Reston and his colleagues were surprised on the next day when, indeed, "a concrete proposal of substance" was laid on the table by Eisenhower.

29. Log entry 1/16/54, C. D. Jackson (CDJ) Papers, box 56, "Log-1954" folder, DDE Library.

30. Charles E. Bohlen, *Witness to History, 1929–1969* (New York: W. W. Norton, 1973), pp. 384–385. Bohlen was Eisenhower's personal interpreter at Geneva.

31. James Desmond, *Nelson Rockefeller: A Political Biography* (New York: Macmillan, 1964), pp. 151–152. In the course of this study we sought and obtained declassification of the Quantico II report: "Psychological Aspects of United States Strategy," November 1955. It is to be found at the Eisenhower Library.

32. *International Security: The Military Aspect* (Garden City, N.Y.: Doubleday, 1958), pp. 62–64. The final text of the report of Panel II is to be found in *Prospect for America: The Rockefeller Panel Reports* (Garden City, N.Y.: Doubleday, 1958–1961), pp. 93–155.

33. Eisenhower, *Waging Peace*, p. 226.

34. Quoted in John Gittings, *Survey of the Sino-Soviet Dispute, 1963–1967* (London: Oxford University Press, 1968), p. 82.

35. I analyze this process in some detail in *The Diffusion of Power* (New York: Macmillan, 1972), pp. 28–35.

36. Arnold L. Horelick and Myron Rush, *Strategic Power and Soviet Foreign Policy* (Chicago: University of Chicago Press, 1966), p. 35.

37. "Department of Defense Statement on U.S. Military Strength," April 14, 1964.

38. Quoted in Horelick and Rush, *Strategic Power,* p. 64.

39. Ibid.

40. Eisenhower, *Waging Peace,* pp. 206–209.

41. Robert S. Rosholt et al., *An Administrative History of NASA, 1958–1963* (Washington, D.C.: NASA, 1966), Chap. 1, pp. 4–5, and relevant notes.

42. Letter from Nikolai A. Bulganin to President Eisenhower, September 19, 1955, Department of State *Bulletin* 33, no. 852 (October 24, 1955): 645; and letter from Premier Bulganin to President Eisenhower, February 1, 1956, Department of State *Bulletin* 34, no. 874 (March 26, 1956): 517.

43. Text supplied by Mr. Amrom Katz.

44. F. M. Cornford, *Microcosmographia Academica* (Cambridge, Eng.: Bowes and Bowes, 1933), preface to 3rd ed.

45. In a discussion of this matter while the text was being drafted, Robert Bowie suggested that satellite photography, reflecting the emergence of a new impersonal technology, was easier for the Soviet Union to accept than manned flight in aircraft, the latter carrying with it more of the flavor of conventional espionage. Ted Carpenter added the observation that U-2 flights, by violating airspace, violated existing international law, whereas no law existed with respect to outer space. And, as Khrushchev acknowledged to de Gaulle in April 1960, the Soviet decision to launch its first Sputnik, freely overflying other nations, made the acceptance of satellite photography inevitable.

46. Morrow interview. Clark Clifford, an authoritative source on this matter, recalled in a conversation of January 23, 1982, that the idea for Point Four did, indeed, derive from an official of modest status in the State Department. Clifford does not recall whether he served on Latin American affairs under Rockefeller. Acheson did not oppose the idea, as is generally believed, but fought and won a battle to have the Point Four program administered within the State Department rather than by the separate agency Clifford would have preferred.

47. Gerard C. Smith Oral History Interview, Philip A. Crowl, interviewer, October 13, 1965, J. F. Dulles Oral History Project, Mudd Library, Princeton University, transcript, p. 108.

6. EISENHOWER AND KENNEDY ON FOREIGN AID, 1953–1963

1. Kennedy's and Cooper's speeches on March 25, 1958, are to be found in the *Congressional Record,* 85th Cong., 2nd sess., 1958, 104, pt. 4:5246–5253 (JFK) and 5253–5555 (JSC).

2. Dillon's description and the illustrative quotation are included in a presentation to the Senate Committee on Foreign Relations of March 3, 1958, when he was deputy undersecretary of state for economic affairs. The text is to be found in the Department of State *Bulletin* 38, no. 978 (March 24, 1958): 469–475. The quotation was from an unnamed Soviet speaker at an Afro-Asian conference in December 1957.

3. For a contemporary skeptical view of the long-run viability of the initial Chinese Communist development strategy, see, for example, W. W. Rostow, in collaboration with Richard W. Hatch, Frank A. Kierman Jr., and Alexander Eckstein, *The Prospects*

for Communist China (New York: W. W. Norton, 1954), esp. pp. 271-274, 289-295, 299-314.

4. See, for example, Benjamin Schwartz, "China's Developmental Experience, 1949-72," in *China's Developmental Experience*, ed. Michel Oksenberg (New York: Academy of Political Science, vol. 31, no. 1, March 1973), pp. 18-21.

5. Alexander Eckstein, *China's Economic Development* (Ann Arbor: University of Michigan Press, 1975), p. 49. An excellent technical account of the sequence of events and policies in agriculture is the chapter by Alva Lewis Erisman ("China: Agricultural Development, 1949-71") in *People's Republic of China: An Economic Assessment, A Compendium of Papers*, submitted to the Joint Economic Committee, U.S. Congress (Washington, D.C.: GPO, May 18, 1972), pp. 112-146.

6. Bauer's book on India is *United States Aid and Indian Economic Development* (Washington, D.C.: American Enterprise Association, Nov. 1959). Some of Bauer's other writings during this period were: *West African Trade* (Cambridge: Cambridge University Press, 1954); with B. S. Yamey, *The Economics of Under-developed Countries* (Chicago: University of Chicago Press, 1957); *Economic Analysis and Policy in Under-developed Countries* (Durham, N.C.: Duke University Press, 1957). For further evaluation of Bauer's views, see my review of his *Equality, the Third World, and Economic Delusion* (Cambridge: Harvard University Press, 1981) in *Society* 20, no. 1 (Nov.-Dec. 1982): 88-89.

7. Russell Edgerton, *Sub-Cabinet Politics and Policy Commitment: The Birth of the Development Loan Fund* (Syracuse: Inter-University Case Program, 1970), pp. 77 and 80.

8. Ibid., pp. 128-129.

9. W. W. Rostow with Richard W. Hatch and others, *An American Policy in Asia* (New York: John Wiley with the Technology Press of MIT, 1955), pp. 50-51.

10. The complexity of the relationship between economic and political development was borne in on me since, starting in 1950, I taught regularly, as I still do, a course in the evolution of the world economy since the eighteenth century. Latin America figured substantially in that graduate seminar. Later reflections on the problem are incorporated in *Politics and the Stages of Growth* (Cambridge: Cambridge University Press, 1971). For a critical analysis of the views of CENIS and others on the allegedly automatic relation between economic development and democracy, see especially Robert A. Packenham, *Liberal America and the Third World: Political Development Ideas in Foreign Aid and Social Science* (Princeton: Princeton University Press, 1973). Packenham's judgments on CENIS' analysis of this complex relationship appear based more on paraphrase by others than on what members of CENIS actually wrote and said. We did, indeed, argue that societies that harnessed their strong nationalist aspirations to well-designed economic development programs, engaging the participation of all levels of the population concerned, would transit the inherently revolutionary process of modernization with less internal and external violence, less vulnerability to external intrusion, and a better chance of generating in time their own forms of democratic political life than those that turned their nationalist political energies in other directions. In *A Proposal*, we concluded: "We do not seek

societies abroad built in our own image. We do have a profound interest that societies abroad develop and strengthen those elements in their respective cultures that elevate and protect the dignity of the individual as against the claims of the state. Such elements of harmony with the Western democratic tradition exist in different forms everywhere" (p. 131). With the passage of almost five decades since those propositions were asserted, I see no reason to alter them.

11. In dealing with Kennedy's prepresidential years neither Arthur Schlesinger Jr. nor Theodore Sorensen has much to say about the formation of Kennedy's view of the world. James MacGregor Burns in his biography *John Kennedy: A Political Profile* (New York: Harcourt Brace and World, 1959) provides brief, but useful, insights at each stage from Kennedy's undergraduate thesis (published as *Why England Slept*) forward, but he does not address the questions Why the developing regions? Why India? Herbert S. Parmet's *Jack: The Struggles of John F. Kennedy* (New York: The Dial Press, 1980) is useful and quite detailed down to Kennedy's speech on Algeria in 1957, but does not deal with the Kennedy-Cooper resolution or, indeed, with any other aspect of Kennedy's foreign policy views in the period 1958–1960. James N. Giglio has produced a well-balanced book, *The Presidency of John F. Kennedy* (Lawrence: University Press of Kansas, 1991). He misses, however, the role of the 1951 trip to the East in shifting Kennedy's foreign policy from Western Europe to the underdeveloped areas (pp. 14–15).

12. *Congressional Record,* 82nd Cong., 2nd sess., 1952, 98, pt. 7:8492–8493.

13. Arthur Schlesinger Jr., *Robert Kennedy and His Times* (Boston: Houghton Mifflin, 1978), p. 93. Parmet, *Jack,* p. 228, quotes this observation of Robert Kennedy's. Parmet's account of the trip to the Middle East and Far East is quite full and sensitive to its meaning, notably the impact on Kennedy of the power of nationalism he observed; but Parmet does not pursue the lead he correctly identifies as it helped shape Kennedy's subsequent foreign policy positions, except for those taken in his well-known interventions on Indochina (1954) and Algeria (1957), to which Parmet does refer.

14. Quoted in the context of Kennedy's April 6, 1954, speech in the Senate on Indochina, in *The Strategy of Peace* (New York: Harper, 1960), p. 60.

15. Dutton's other observations are also germane: "He was definitely trying to establish a record as a knowledgeable, dynamic and wise leader in foreign affairs; at that time support for India seemed sensible and in U.S. interest."

B. K. Nehru, in a letter to me of August 5, 1982, added this *témoignage* from Kennedy himself in a conversation that probably took place in September 1959:

> I asked him point blank the question why he, as a Presidential candidate, was sticking his neck out for foreign aid, particularly for India, when both such aid and the country for which he wanted it were unpopular issues and would certainly lose him votes. He gave me two reasons, the first of which was certainly the most impressive. It was, as I remember his words, "I support foreign aid because I think it is right." He then went on to say that it could be that he did lose some votes because this was an unpopular issue but the fact was that the people who were against foreign aid were generally against most things. The image they projected

was a negative one; what the country was looking for in this view was a man with a positive outlook. By supporting foreign aid and by being positive in other matters he projected an image of a positive man which gained him votes.

16. Theodore Sorensen, *Kennedy* (New York: Harper and Row, 1965), p. 66.

17. A brief but authoritative account of the emergence of the Bank is to be found in Edward S. Mason and Robert E. Asher, *The World Bank since Bretton Woods* (Washington, D.C.: Brookings Institution, 1973), pp. 11-35. The authors supply full references to the primary sources.

18. The Commonwealth embraced both advanced industrial countries (e.g., Great Britain, Canada, and Australia) and developing nations. It was natural for the latter to press forward their development interests in the newly formed post-imperial club; and it was understandable that Britain, despite limitations on resources, would wish to make a positive response. The United States, South Korea, Japan, and some other Asian countries, not formally part of the British Empire, joined the Colombo Plan, which was an important pioneering venture in North-South collaboration, although, in itself, it did not generate large resources for development.

19. The title of the report of the Gordon Gray Commission was *Report to the President on Foreign Economic Policies* (Washington, D.C.: GPO, 1950); and of the Rockefeller Report, U.S. International Development Advisory Board: *Partners in Progress: A Report to President Truman* (New York: Simon and Schuster, 1951). Acheson's speeches dealing with foreign aid in Asia are summarized accessibly in *The Pattern of Responsibility*, ed. McGeorge Bundy (Boston: Houghton Mifflin, 1952), pp. 171-200.

20. Although it is clear that Communist policy had shifted prior to 1953 toward softer forms of aggression in Asia, the Middle East, and Africa, and although it is clear that the Soviet Union had every reason to maintain a soft policy until its missile delivery systems had matured, it is still possible, of course, that the ring of pacts helped confirm in Moscow the correctness and maintain the stability of that policy over the period 1953-1958.

21. *Europe after Stalin: Eisenhower's Three Decisions of March 11, 1953* (Austin: University of Texas Press, 1982).

22. Department of State *Bulletin* 28, June 15, 1953, p. 831.

23. *The United States in World Affairs, 1954* (New York: Harper and Brothers, 1955) p. 100. On Stassen's role in 1954 see also Burton I. Kaufman, *Trade and Aid: Eisenhower's Foreign Economic Policy, 1953-1961* (Baltimore: Johns Hopkins University Press, 1981), pp. 51-56.

24. Although Sherman Adams' account of the confrontation leaves a good deal to be desired, it is worth quoting as one of the few references in print to Jackson's World Economic Plan (*First Hand Report* [New York: Harper, 1961], pp. 115-116).

When Jackson gave up the struggle in Washington after the agreed term of his enlistment had more than come to an end, he left with Eisenhower and Dulles a recommendation for a bold foreign program. While the central point of view of Jackson's proposal was becoming more widely shared by the best-informed foreign observers, it suffered from the competition of other more pressing programs and the realities of the federal budget. Jackson pointed out that the Soviets were making significant headway in the cold war because they were concentrating on economic and trade offensives. Recalling the tremendously successful effect of the Marshall Plan in winning friends overseas, he said that the United States, to stay abreast in the race, needed to launch a down-to-earth world economic plan that could be made to work. With the hard lessons learned during his experience as the administration's cold war idea promoter vivid in his mind, Jackson went on to warn that such a plan could win support only in the hands of people who understood the nature of the Communist competition and would keep it from the watering-down process which the compromisers would put it through to make it politically acceptable to Congress. This, said Jackson, would so dilute it that it would be quite useless.

Jackson's plan never reached even that stage. The problems of applying such thinking to the policies already in operation, together with the necessity of keeping some control over the ceilings of public expense, staggered the imagination of those who nevertheless believed in Jackson's approach. In that spring of 1954 those ideas became submerged in the more immediate urgencies of the Indo-China crisis and the supreme effort of Eisenhower and Dulles to persuade France to accept the proposed European Defense Community program.

Echoes of the Princeton meeting and its aftermath are to be found in a column by Sylvia Porter in the *New York Post,* "Asian 'Marshall Plan'?" June 8, 1954; and in an article in the *Wall Street Journal,* August 27, 1954, on C. D. Jackson's "new world-wide economic aid offer." Burton I. Kaufman deals with some aspects of Jackson's proposal and its vicissitudes, *Trade and Aid,* pp. 49-51. Kaufman also discusses at some length the 1954 battle over the lending power of the Export-Import Bank, pp. 29-32. See also Robert E. Asher, "The World Bank, The Export-Import Bank of the United States, and the Developing Nations," in *International Review of the History of Banking,* no. 11 (1975): 19-36.

25. Both Dulles and Jackson were Princeton graduates. That fact, plus Princeton's location between Washington and New York, made it a natural place to gather, in a time when the railroads were still a conventional means of travel. Jackson's reference to a "new" Princeton conference is to a Princeton gathering in May 1952 of government and nongovernment men concerned with psychological warfare policy.

26. C. D. Jackson (CDJ) Papers, box 56, "Log-1954" folder, Dwight D. Eisenhower (DDE) Library.

27. Ibid., August 7, 1954.

28. Ibid.

29. Ibid.

30. CDJ papers, box 41, "Eisenhower Correspondence through 1956" folder 1, DDE Library.

31. CDJ Papers, box 40, "Dulles, John Foster" folder, DDE Library.

32. Ibid.

33. CDJ Papers, box 64, "Millikan, Max" folder, DDE Library.

34. CDJ Papers, box 49, "Hoover, Herbert, Jr." folder, DDE Library.

35. CDJ Papers, box 73, "Quantico Meetings" folder 5, DDE Library.

36. Rostow with Hatch, *American Policy in Asia,* pp. 50–51.

37. *Prospects for Communist China,* pp. 308–309.

38. *American Policy in Asia,* p. 49.

39. *The United States in World Affairs, 1955,* published for the Council on Foreign Relations (New York: Harper and Brothers, 1957), p. 122.

40. John Foster Dulles (JFD) Papers, Correspondence Series, box 1, Dwight D. Eisenhower folder, Seeley G. Mudd Manuscript Library, Princeton University. Since this letter was written by Eisenhower the day after his talk with Rockefeller in Gettysburg, it may reflect something of the latter's argument on behalf of the Quantico II report.

41. CDJ Papers, box 56, "Log-1956" folder, DDE Library.

42. Edgerton, *Sub-Cabinet Politics,* p. 148.

43. U.S. Council on Foreign Economic Policy, Office of the Chairman, Dodge Series, Subject File, box 2, "Economic Aid—Multilateral" folder, DDE Library.

44. Ibid.

45. CDJ Papers, "Log-1957" folder. I should, perhaps, add the following anecdote to supplement Jackson's account of the meeting on February 6, 1957. Eric Johnston, with whom I was closely in touch at this time, told me he had called Sherman Adams in the wake of Eisenhower's second inaugural address and asked what specifically the president had in mind in the key passage cited. Adams replied, according to Johnston: "Not a thing, Eric, not a goddamned thing. And don't you go about thinking he did."

46. Russell Edgerton's *Sub-cabinet Politics and Policy Commitment: The Birth of the Development Loan Fund* also contains a review of the evolution of foreign policy in the 1950s, with special attention to its congressional dimensions, that significantly supplements that presented here. His portrait of Dulles' views on development lending and of the Eisenhower-Dulles relationship on this matter differs from that presented here, mainly, I suspect, because documents are now available that were inaccessible to Edgerton when he assembled his data in the mid-1960s. The pilot project of 1957 proved to be the Development Loan Fund. The rather complex story of its creation is well told in Edgerton's monograph.

47. For a vivid account of these shenanigans, see ibid., pp. 90–96.

48. The text of Dulles' statement of April 8, 1957, is to be found in the *Congressional Record,* 85th Cong., 1st sess., 1957, 103, pt. 4:5409–5411. A later forthright statement by Dulles in support of the DLF is found in pt. 7:9123–9125.

49. At just about this time (in the spring of 1957) this theme was much on Eisenhower's mind. Quoting from one of Eisenhower's taped conversations, William Bragg Ewald Jr. in *Eisenhower the President: Crucial Days, 1951–1960* (Englewood Cliffs, N.J.: Prentice Hall), pp. 97–99, presents the following account of a confrontation on foreign aid between Eisenhower and Senator Styles Bridges that suggests, among other things, how effective Eisenhower could have been if he had chosen to crusade for a World Economic Plan including aid to India:

If transcribed verbatim, tapes have a conspicuous merit, they relay the exact words spoken, in jest, in reflection, or (as on one May morning in 1957) in wrath.

Through the spring of 1957 both Republicans and Democrats on the Hill had been making life hard for Ike, now a lame duck, by bellowing for cuts in his allegedly spendthrift budget and by denouncing foreign "giveaways." They would not see that the military defense of the free world depends upon the economic health of the free world. Senator Styles Bridges of New Hampshire, a crusty conservative, had made a speech calling foreign aid advocates "do-gooders." Jim Hagerty read the ticker and scribbled in ink on yellow pad a red-hot memo to Eisenhower recommending a woodshed hiding: a reminder to Bridges that "if anyone is getting sick of 'do-gooders' it's you—political do-gooders who can't or won't see the full picture and fulfill the obligations we have as a leader of the free world." The president, like Hagerty, also had had it up to here, and next morning, after the Legislative Leaders meeting, Ike called Bridges on the carpet, switched on the gadget, and left historians with the only extended verbatim record extant of an Ike chewing-out.

"I am convinced that the only way to avoid war," the president told the Senator, "the only way to save America in the long run from destruction, is through the development of a true collective system of defense.

"It is pretty hard when I have to bear the burdens not only of the Presidency, but of the titular head of the party, to have said by one of the principal people in the party that this is nothing but a do-gooder act. . . . I think nothing could be further from the truth. I realize that as of this moment it is a very popular thing to talk about saving a dollar. Frankly, I would rather see the Congress cut a billion off . . . defense [than off foreign aid]—as much as I think it would be a mistake. . . . If we depend exclusively on our own arms, we are headed for a war; there is going to be no other answer. . . .

"If I knew a cheap way out of this one, I certainly would take it. . . . If Mr. Truman (and, unfortunately, a Republican Congress in 1946 and 1948) had given us what the Chiefs of Staff authorized me to request—which was 15 billion dollars a year over and above stockpiling and pay increases—I believe there never would have been a Korean War.

"I begged them for 110 million dollars, but never could make them see the need for it. (I think you were among the group I went down to talk to.) I am not blaming anybody, but I want to say this is just another incident in a long lifetime of work on this.

"Finally, I think my party ought to trust me a little bit more when I put not only my life's work, but my reputation and everything else, on the line in favor of this. . . ."

Bridges, shaken, asked to see the ticker story. Then he started to explain: "What I meant by that statement was Yugoslavia, Indonesia, India and others—where I thought they in turn would contribute nothing to the mutual security, and therefore the money that you put into those countries was advocated particularly by do-gooders."

The President shot back: "Take some countries, like India for example. India has 350 million people. Suppose India said 'we take our stand with the West'— consider where we are, right up against an 1800 mile border against China.

"How much have we got to put into India to make it reasonably safe for them to even exist? Frankly, this is the one country I had in mind when I said that there are one or two countries in the world that I would want to be neutral. Now we have no obligation to defend them, and if the other fellow attacks them, they violate a world treaty because they are jumping on a neutral country. I had a long talk with Nehru about this, and he is up against the matter of 350 million people practically starving. You could put all the defenses in the world in there, and they will go Communistic. . . ."

Bridges backed and shuffled: "I don't blame you for being disturbed about that little statement given to you. That, in effect, is what I said, but it was only *part* of what I said."

Eisenhower's lecture did not, of course, keep Bridges from leading the fight in the Senate against the Kennedy-Cooper resolution on June 6, 1958.

50. Dwight D. Eisenhower Papers, Ann Whitman File, Dulles-Herter Series, box 7, "Dulles, John Foster—Nov. '57" folder, DDE Library.

51. Stevenson was initially asked to go to Paris as the third-ranking man on the U.S. delegation. As one of his biographers correctly reports (Kenneth S. Davis, *The Politics of Honor: A Biography of Adlai E. Stevenson* [New York: G. P. Putnam and Sons, 1967], p. 371), Stevenson was wary:

... Secretary of State Dulles, speaking, he said, for the President as well as himself, had approached Stevenson in early November to ask that the Democratic Party's titular head participate to the fullest extent in the formulation of the U.S. position for the forthcoming meeting. Indeed, the words Dulles used could be interpreted to mean that Stevenson, if he accepted, would be responsible for drafting the new American position, which would then be passed upon by the President and Secretary of State. Further, Stevenson was asked to come to Paris as a member of the U.S. delegation, wherein he would be outranked only by Eisenhower and Dulles. The appeal (for it had that quality) was couched in terms of patriotic duty: at this juncture, a 'bipartisan' approach was of the utmost importance.

Stevenson, nevertheless was wary. He was not unmindful of the disadvantages he would suffer and of the advantages his political opposition would gain if he were tagged with public responsibility for final policies with which he might or might not agree. He therefore suggested for himself a much more modest role, that of mere adviser or 'consultant.' Thus his publicly assigned responsibility for the event would be no greater than his actual authority to determine it, and his freedom to criticize, if criticism seemed needed, would be unimpaired.

52. Adlai Stevenson (AS) Papers, box 733, NATO: Black Notebook (2 of 2) folder, Mudd Library, Princeton University.

53. I had contributed some material to Stevenson's staff during the 1956 campaign, but our first meeting was at breakfast in the Commander Hotel in Cambridge

on the morning of the Princeton-Harvard football game, November 9, 1957. I worked with him quite closely, helping as best I could with drafts and other suggestions over the next month until his responsibility was fulfilled and Eisenhower was off to Paris. Stevenson's papers at the Mudd Library in Princeton indicate that Thomas Finletter and Hubert Humphrey filed memoranda with Stevenson on the NATO Summit on November 29 and December 2, respectively. I remained in touch with Stevenson, helping with speech drafts, and so on through the winter until he left on a world tour in 1955. We were next in touch as the Kennedy administration assembled for business in the last week of January 1961.

54. AS Papers, NATO: Black Notebook (2 of 2) folder.

55. The phrase is Robert Cutler's, in his *No Time for Rest* (Boston: Little, Brown, 1965), p. 375. Cutler was the first U.S. executive director of the IADB.

56. *Review of Foreign Policy,* Hearings before the Committee on Foreign Relations, Part 1 (Washington, D.C.: GPO, 1958), pp. 278-280.

57. The story of this enterprise is well, but briefly, told in James A. Robinson, *The Monroney Resolution: Congressional Initiative in Foreign Policy Making* (New York: Henry Holt, 1959). For a wider account of the origins of IDA and its evolution, see Mason and Asher, *World Bank since Bretton Woods,* Chap. 12, pp. 380-419.

58. I. G. Patel, *Foreign Aid* (Bombay: Allied Publishers, 1968), pp. 12-14.

59. Castro's deal with the orthodox Cuban Communist leadership and Moscow was probably struck in the summer of 1958. For a brief account see the author's *Diffusion of Power* (New York: Macmillan, 1972), pp. 49-52, 99-103, and relevant notes for sources.

60. Dwight D. Eisenhower, *Waging Peace, 1956–1961* (Garden City, N.Y.: Doubleday, 1965), p. 520.

61. Ibid., pp. 269-270.

62. Mason and Asher, *World Bank since Bretton Woods,* p. 514.

63. B. K. Nehru, "The Way We Looked for Money Abroad," in *Two Decades of Indo-U.S. Relations,* ed. Vadilal Dagli (Bombay: Vora and Company, 1969), pp. 20-21.

64. The full text of those presentations is to be found in the *Congressional Record,* 86th Cong., 1st sess., 1959, 102, pt. 2:2737-2740.

65. Escott Reid's name was ultimately dropped from the list of possible candidates because he was a Canadian ambassador. It was judged wise to include only private citizens in the mission to India. Reid later became a high official of the World Bank.

66. Patel, *Foreign Aid,* p. 17.

67. Letter to Millikan from author of December 10, 1958. From such records as I have, the period of most intense consultations in London was November–December 1958. The U.S. Embassy in London knew of and, to a degree, encouraged this enterprise in international crusading. Two officials at the British Treasury were particularly interested in the problem of mobilizing support for Indian development: Sir Denis Rickett and Chaim Raphael. The discussions were wide-ranging, including the British inflation–balance of payments problem, which inhibited the U.K.'s capacity to aid developing countries.

68. Box 718, Senate Legislation Files, Holborn, F. folder (1939), JFK Library. Writing to me in Europe on May 13, 1959, Millikan described his lobbying with the State Department on these residual issues:

> I have been politicking with the Department to try to get them to support the Kennedy resolution. This has been peculiarly frustrating because they have taken the line, first, that a resolution on India will get them into all kinds of trouble with all the other under-developed countries and, second, that the mission should be a U.S. Congressional one rather than an international wise men's mission. This is partly based on the view that a Congressional mission will have more influence on Congress (which I doubt) and partly on some doubts as to whether the European countries would really come through with contributions to a cooperative effort. Your evidence from both your British discussions and those with Monnet has been extremely helpful, and I hope we have brought them around but it is not quite clear yet.

69. Joseph Dodge was to have been the American member of the three-man team, backed by the Treasury, which wanted a banker who would avoid excessive U.S. commitments. Dodge's illness led to the appointment of Sproul, who proved to be appropriately cautious but in no way obstructive.

70. Patel, *Foreign Aid,* p. 14. In a letter to me of August 5, 1982, B. K. Nehru, described as follows how "the Wisemen" operated in India:

> The Wisemen operated at two levels. As far as I remember they used to have a meeting every day with one or the other section of the civil servants of the various Ministries concerned with economic development who explained their plans and programs to them and answered their questions. I do not recall who took these meetings on our side; it must, I should imagine, have been the Economic Secretary. They took place in the Finance Minister's room at his rather long conference table (I do not know what happened to the Minister!). The Wisemen did not have a formal leader but it was very clear that in fact Oliver Franks had been given the honour. He did most of the cross-questioning and was ably supplemented by Abs. As far as I can recall — and I was present at most, if not all, these meetings — Mr. Sproul was conspicuous by his total silence!
>
> The second level of operation was calls on the Ministers concerned. These were sometimes formal but sometimes, in the case of Ministers who knew their business, quite substantive. But I do remember Oliver Franks telling me at the very beginning that he would much rather spend time with civil servants who would know what they were talking about than spend it in discussing generalities with political leaders.

71. The reaction of Indian officials is well captured in a letter of March 21, 1960, from Harry G. Curran (the World Bank's resident representative in India) to Eugene Black:

> The Government of India awaited the arrival of the Wise Men with rather mixed feelings. They hoped and believed the Mission would prove helpful to them — and

were very appreciative of your friendly initiative in organizing it—but they were a little nervous about its composition. Franks, they believed, had an exceptional understanding of the problems confronting developing countries; but they were less sure of Abs and Sproul. They had fears of a hard German banker closely associated with private industry and the export trade, and a rigid old Federal Reserve conservative. In the event they were agreeably surprised.

Franks more than fulfilled their expectations. They sensed at once that he was fundamentally sympathetic to their aspirations, and were fascinated by his dynamic personality and quick mind and elegance of phrase. Abs also impressed them very favorably—a massive impression of power and quick grasp of fact. Although he didn't say very much, it was a genial silence with a twinkle in the eye, and when he spoke it was very much to the point. Sproul also they liked—they thought him a kindly older man, anxious to understand and less rigid than they had feared.

The Wise Men themselves were I believe favorably impressed by what they heard and saw, and by the Third Plan as it was exposed to them. You will know their general conclusions from their letter. . . . There remain no doubt question marks in their minds—e.g., whether the proclaimed drive for food production will be effective; whether the deficit financing in the Third Plan can be kept down to the intended relatively modest level; the need for a more positive effort to increase exports; the desirability of more positive Government action and declared intention to attract private foreign investment; whether even this large Third Plan can keep pace with the rising population. But on the whole I believe they were satisfied that the G.O.I. [Government of India] had achieved a good deal since independence, and that the Third Plan was a serious and not unrealistic attempt to continue what remains to be done. As regards the much discussed Public v. Private Sector argument, I believe the Wise Men were convinced that India was not moving towards a Socialist State in which private enterprise would be squeezed out of existence, but that on the contrary, the evidence suggested that the Government's approach to problems (although this was perhaps not openly admitted) was becoming more pragmatic, that private industry was undoubtedly expanding rapidly, and that in as far as its expansion was hampered, it was more by bureaucratic complexities (for which the Indians have a natural bent!) than by ideological intent.

The Mission's progress was therefore smooth, the relations with the Government very friendly and everyone parted on excellent terms.

There was however some disappointment that there was not an opportunity for more frank discussion on the conclusions reached by the Wise Men. Franks and Abs would, I believe, have welcomed this—and would also have liked to take advantage of the chance to make a number of points to the Government which they would not have wished to express publicly or even to have included in an official letter to you. Sproul however was strongly opposed to any discussion of their conclusions. As you will know from his cable to you, he was much concerned about what he would have to face on his return to the U.S., and, with visions no doubt of Congressional committees breathing over one shoulder and the press over the other, took the view that their conclusions must remain confidential until you had considered them and decided what should be made public. It proved impossible to move him from this position; and so although all three were very friendly in their last talks with the Prime Minister and Finance Minister, and Franks turned on all his eloquence and charm to say not much in as nice a way as possible, the G.O.I. await with great interest to hear from you what in fact the conclusions of the Mission are.

72. This increase in development aid in the foreign aid budget by an outgoing administration probably was connected with the impression made on Eisenhower by his trip to India in December 1959. Eisenhower was much impressed by the size and enthusiasm of the crowds that turned out for the American president and the evident poverty of the people.

73. Jean Monnet, *Memoirs* (Garden City, N.Y.: Doubleday, 1978), p. 109. Burton I. Kaufman, *Trade and Aid*, p. 198, notes an experience that might, at last, have converted Eisenhower to unambiguous support for enlarged development aid and that might account for the substantially enlarged final aid budget he submitted to the Congress, which was of considerable assistance to Kennedy: that is, the strong impact on Eisenhower of his visit to India and other parts of Asia in 1959.

74. For an account of Kennedy's view of this problem and the actions he undertook, see my *Diffusion of Power*, pp. 203–206. The fact is that Jawaharlal Nehru's visit to Washington in November 1961 was a grave disappointment to both U.S. and Indian officials. Nehru was passive and unresponsive, quite possibly because his health was already failing.

75. For elaboration of this theme, see my *Stages of Economic Growth*, pp. 26–30.

76. W. W. Rostow, *Why the Poor Get Richer and the Rich Slow Down* (Boulder, Colo.: Westview Press, 1987), pp. 266–267.

77. For a systematic effort to measure the improvement in "basic needs," see David Morawetz, *Twenty-five Years of Economic Development: 1950 to 1975* (World Bank, Baltimore: Johns Hopkins University Press, 1977), especially pp. 31–58.

78. The historians of the World Bank, E. S. Mason and R. E. Asher, share my view of the importance of this point but more wistfully: "The Bank can ally itself with the development-minded elements in the country and reinforce their efforts. But the Bank's biggest handicap is its inability to guarantee that development-minded officials will come into power or remain in power" (*World Bank since Bretton Woods*, p. 648). My point is, of course, that many more such officials rose to power and stayed in power than would have been the case if development aid had not been institutionalized.

7. THE REPUBLIC OF KOREA

1. See the extraordinary tribute to Bruce, the Marshall Plan Ambassador in Paris and Tomlinson, the Treasury representative, in Monnet's *Memoirs* (New York: Doubleday, 1978), pp. 269–270.

8. THE EISENHOWER, KENNEDY, JOHNSON EFFORTS TO CONTROL INFLATION, 1957-1972

1. One important extension of mathematical economics is not used in the cases that follow. A disaggregated sectoral approach to economic analysis and programming takes its approximate start with the article "On the Solution of Discrete Programming Problems" by Harry M. Markowitz and Alan S. Manne (*Econometrica* 25, no. 1 [January 1957]: 84-110). They argue: "For many years, he [the economist] has known that all theorems about the 'efficiency' of competitive equilibrium break down in the presence of indivisibilities or of increasing returns to scale. Market analogue solutions are of no avail here. Moreover, in optimization problems of this type, neither marginal analysis (i.e., calculus methods) nor linear programming is guaranteed to produce a correct solution" (p. 84). The development of this extension of mathematical techniques is discussed at some length in the section on "The Sectoral Planners" in my *Theorists of Economic Growth from David Hume to the Present,* pp. 359-362 and related notes. In the same family is Michael Kennedy's method for solving numerically the increasing returns problem, pp. 507-569.

2. Schumpeter lists "the carrying out of the new organization of an industry . . . as one of the five major forms of innovation" (quoted in Rostow, *Theorists of Economic Growth*), p. 235.

3. See, for example, W. W. Rostow "Monnet: Innovator as Diplomat," in *The Diplomats, 1939-1979,* ed. Gordon Craig and Francis L. Loewenheim (Princeton: Princeton University Press, 1994), pp. 280-281.

4. Richard Mayne, "Gray Eminence," Ch. 4 in *Jean Monnet: The Path to European Unity,* ed. Douglas Brinkley and Clifford Hackett (London: Macmillan, 1991), p. 124.

5. The phrase is from the title of Chap. 8, of *Waging Peace,* Eisenhower's memoir of the White House years (Garden City, N.Y.: Doubleday, 1965), p. 205.

6. H. Scott Gordon, "The Eisenhower Administration: The Doctrine of Shared Responsibility," in *Exhortation and Controls,* ed. Craufurd D. Goodwin (Washington, D.C.: The Brookings Institution, 1975), pp. 133-134.

7. Samuelson's report was entitled "Prospects and Policies for the 1961 American Economy: A Report to President-Elect Kennedy," January 6, 1961. Goodwin quotes Samuelson's more unbuttoned view: "Samuelson concluded with his proposed response to a hypothetical question that his grandchildren might raise about his contribution to the New Frontier: I shall sadly reply: I kept telling them down at the office, in December, January, and April that, WHAT THIS COUNTRY NEEDS IS AN ACROSS THE BOARD RISE IN DISPOSABLE INCOME TO LOWER THE LEVEL OF UNEMPLOYMENT, SPEED UP THE RECOVERY AND THE RETURN TO HEALTHY GROWTH, PROMOTE CAPITAL FORMATION AND THE GENERAL WELFARE, INSURE DOMESTIC TRANQUILITY AND THE TRIUMPH OF THE DEMOCRATIC PARTY AT THE POLLS" (*Exhortation and Controls,* pp. 144-145; uppercase in original).

8. William J. Barber, "The Kennedy Years: Purposeful Pedagogy," in *Exhortation and Controls,* p. 136.

9. Ibid., pp. 136-137, quoted from a letter of November 17, 1960, to the president-elect from me.

10. My role on this issue may seem odd given my task was foreign policy. But before the election I had as an economist expressed views to Kennedy on this issue, and we continued our dialogue on it after he took office. The Council of Economic Advisers gradually came to the conclusion that Kennedy took my view seriously on the use of the automobile and steel wage negotiations to link in general wage increases to productivity increases. I was primarily engaged in foreign policy in the Kennedy-Johnson years. My activities on the domestic front were strictly extracurricular, although initiated by the two presidents. For those interested, my earlier comments on the wage-price problem are contained in *The Process of Economic Growth*, 1st ed. (Oxford: Clarendon Press, 1953), pp. 220-237. The whole of Chap. 10, "Economic Theory and Public Policy," is relevant to the argument of the present book as a whole.

11. I talked with Blough in Boston on the occasion of the Brookings Conference on wage-price policy in November 1974 that resulted in the book by Craufurd Goodwin. Blough had helped my brother Eugene, who was then dean of the Yale Law School, raise money for the school. We got on well. When asked about the sudden rise in the steel price in 1962, Blough said the discussion in the Senate was a violation of the right of private enterprise to set prices freely; and he and his colleagues had to react.

12. John Sheahan, *The Wage-Price Guideposts* (Washington, D.C.: Brookings Institution, 1967), p. 37.

13. See, for example, Goodwin, *Exhortation and Controls*, pp. 186-191 (closing days of the Kennedy administration); pp. 265-293 (reflections within and after the Johnson administration); and Arnold C. Weber, "The Continuing Courtship: Wage-Price Policy through Administrations" (Chap. 6), pp. 353-398.

14. For a systematic treatment of these trend periods from 1790 to 1976, see pp. 109-304 in my *World Economy: History and Prospect* (Austin: University of Texas Press, 1978).

15. Goodwin, *Exhortation and Controls*, p. 178.

9. CHINA, 1949-

1. The whole literature of "engagement versus confrontation" is evidently too large to reference here. By way of illustration I am thinking of the compendium edited by Ezra Vogel, *Living With China*, (W. W. Norton, 1997). It was the outcome of a complex exercise which engaged authentic China experts, travel within the whole Pacific area, interviews with Chinese officials and experts at think tanks, and reflections from informed American officials and private citizens.

2. I would like to acknowledge the helpful comments on a draft of this chapter by Professor Dwight Perkins of Harvard. I alone, of course, am responsible for the final version.

3. See Chap. 4. On China see W. W. Rostow, in collaboration with Richard W. Hatch, Frank A. Kierman Jr., and Alexander Eckstein, *The Prospects for Commu-*

nist China (New York: W. W. Norton, 1954); and with Richard Hatch, *An American Policy in Asia* (New York: John Wiley and the Technology Press of MIT, 1955).

4. My conclusion about Chinese culture was somewhat unorthodox. Although it had a unique background and many special features, there was a basic harmony with cultures of the West. Chinese writings described a good father, a good son, a good soldier, a good ruler, and so on in terms of values familiar also in the West. On the other hand, I was struck by the fact that Aristotle never slept there. Truth was defined not in terms of long logical chains of thought but an arraying of the pros and cons of an issue followed by a net conclusion stated tersely and elegantly — often as a poem. I concluded this was not a bad way to search for the truth. As a tribute to this view I prefaced *The Prospects for Communist China* with sentences from a fourth-century-B.C. Legalist (hard-handed dictator); Mencius, a third-century-B.C. Confucianist (political moderate); and one third-century Confucianist, whose description of a failing dynasty sounds much like China caught up in Mao's Cultural Revolution.

The possible role of demographic factors in long Confucianist dynastic cycles was raised by the "Chinese Malthus," Hung Liang-chi (1746–1809) and discussed on pp. 49–50 of *Politics and the Stages of Growth*. The source for the quotation from Hung Liang-chi is Ping-ti Ho, *Studies on the Population of China, 1368–1953* (Cambridge: Harvard University Press, 1959).

The Chinese cyclical theory, in terms of human and institutional strength and frailty, but not demography, has been well paraphrased by Mary Clabaugh Wright in *The Last Stand of Chinese Conservatism* (Stanford: Stanford University Press, 1957), pp. 43–47:

> In brief, the theory was this: A new dynasty at first experiences a period of great energy, and vigorous and able new officials put in order the civil and military affairs of the Empire. In the course of generations the new period of vigor is followed by a golden age. Territories acquired earlier are held, but no new territories are conquered. Learning and the arts flourish in an atmosphere of elegance. Agricultural production and the people's welfare are supported by the maintenance of peace, attention to public works, and limitations of taxes. This golden age, however, carries within it the seeds of its own decay. The governing class loses first the will and then the ability to meet the high standards of Confucian government. Its increasing luxury places a strain on the exchequer. Funds intended for irrigation, flood control, maintenance of public grain reserves, communications, and payment of the army are diverted by graft to private pockets. As morale is undermined, corruption becomes flagrant.
>
> This process of decline may be retarded by the vigorous training of officials and people in the Confucian social philosophy, but the basic direction of events cannot be altered. Sooner or later, the governing class, blind to those reforms which alone can save it, taxes the peasants beyond endurance and fails to attend to the public welfare. Sporadic local rebellions result, necessitating additional taxes and the recruiting of troops from an increasingly disaffected population. Their stake in the existing order gone, the people express their disaffection in a great rebel-

lion. If the rebellion is successful, the "swarming bandits" become in the eyes of history the "righteous forces."

The great rebellion is usually successful. One of its leaders slowly consolidates his power by securing (1) military superiority; (2) support from the literati, to whom he offers a revived Confucian state that they will administer; and (3) support, at least tacit, from the peasantry, to whom he offers peace, land, reduced taxes, and a program of public works to protect the agricultural economy. The new dynasty thus begins where its predecessor began, and its destiny will follow the same pattern.

For a discussion of "China: Cycles with Continuity of Culture" including the quotation from Mary Wright, see W. W. Rostow, *Politics and the Stages of Growth* (Cambridge: Cambridge University Press, 1971), pp. 47–53.

5. *Prospects for Communist China,* p. v.

6. Ibid., pp. 305–309.

7. W. W. Rostow, *The Diffusion of Power* (New York: Macmillan, 1972), pp. 681, n. 9. This statement was made in the context of an interview of Mao by Edgar Snow.

8. *Diffusion of Power,* pp. 499–494

9. The Polish Palace of Culture was a quasi-public building. As someone in Warsaw said, the U.S.-Chinese dialogue could be heard by any taxicab in the area with a transistor radio. Although we regularly sent a thoroughly qualified Foreign Service officer to Warsaw for these talks, they were empty of content until the move was made to the Chinese and American embassies in Warsaw.

10. Richard M. Nixon, "Asia after Vietnam," in *Foreign Affairs* 46, no. 1, October 1967, pp. 111–125.

11. This characteristic of Chinese communism as a mixture of traditional Chinese and Communist ideas and texts is illustrated by Lucian Pye in *Mao Tse-tung: The Man in the Leader* (New York: Basic Books, 1976), p. 240, by reference to Vsevolod Holubnychy, "Mao Tse-tung's Materialistic Dialectics," *China Quarterly,* no. 19 (July–September 1964), p. 16. Holubnychy includes the following percentage table of reference from Mao's *Selected Works* (see table 9.2).

TABLE 9.2 SOURCES QUOTED BY MAO

Confucian and Neo-Confucian writings	22%
Taoist and Mohist writings	12%
Folklore legends, pure belles lettres	13%
Other Chinese and foreign writers, unclassified	7%
Marx and Engels	4%
Lenin	18%
Stalin	24%
Total	100%

Sources: Lucian Pye, *Mao Tse-tung: The Man in the Leader* (New York: Basic Books, 1976), p. 240; Vsevolod Holubnychy, "Mao Tse-tung's Materialistic Dialectics," *China Quarterly,* no. 19 (July–September, 1964), p. 16.

12. Isaac Kramnick, ed., *The Federalist Papers,* (Middlesex, Eng.: Penguin Books, 1987).

13. See, notably, Chap. 5, by Frank A. Kierman Jr., in *The Prospects for Communist China,* pp. 105-123.

14. *China Economic Review* 9, no. 1 (Stamford, Conn.: JAI Press, Inc., spring 1998). The editor of this issue points out that the lead article by Bruce Reynolds, Jiang Wang, and Chun Chang ("Economic Transition under a Semi-Federalist Government: The Experience of China," pp. 1-23) already makes the link between federalism and movement toward democracy: "They hypothesize that the political federalism that has developed in China since 1978 may be a stepping stone toward democratization. This halfway house, they argue, has enabled China's economic reform to be gradual, rather than the 'big bang' reform that is melting down in Russia as the issue goes to press."

15. *China 2020: Development Challenges in the New Century* (Washington, D.C.: World Bank, 1997). The study consists of some 161 large pages written by a team led by Vikram Nehru, Aart Kraay, and Xiaoqing Yu. A distinguished set of peer reviewers, commentators, and discussants involving some 179 scholars, Chinese and Western, were consulted. The book is more coherent than its provenance would suggest.

16. Ibid., p. 9.

17. Quoted in the *International Herald Tribune,* from the *New York Times,* August 13, 2001, the *New York Times* editorial goes on:

> The challenge of governing and feeding so large and poor a country should not be underestimated. But, despite the protestations of President Jiang and other authoritarian leaders of developing nations, there is no inherent conflict between food and freedom or between democracy and social order.
>
> China can be proud of moving beyond the starvation years of civil war and early Communist rule into a period of greater national well-being. The market reforms that were begun two decades ago by Deng Xiaoping and continued under Mr. Jiang helped bring this about. But China's people need not be condemned to another generation of authoritarianism in the name of avoiding future famines and unrest. Quite the contrary. Greater government accountability can enhance prosperity and the construction of an adequate social safety net.
>
> China's 5,000-year-old culture sustains an orderly democracy in Taiwan. It can do so on the mainland, too. The threat of social disorder is very much on the mind of Mr. Jiang and other Chinese leaders today. In recent years spontaneous and sometimes violent strikes, along with rural protests over corruption and excessive taxation, have shaken numerous areas of the country. Fear of further unrest as the Communist Party prepares to select a new generation of leaders is a dominant concern in Beijing. These anxieties help explain Mr. Jiang's crackdown on the Falun Gong religious cult and his repression of democratic dissent.
>
> China's next leaders are likely to be more accustomed to economic freedom and less traumatized by the chaos of the middle decades of the 20th century than Mr. Jiang, who came of age during those years. Perhaps they will better be able

to recognize that political freedom can be the natural partner of economic growth and social stability.

18. In dealing with China's rate of growth the World Bank (*China 20 20,* p. 3) produced for 1978–1985 both "official" GDP figures of 8.6 and a lower calculation with "alternative deflators" of 6.8.

Several further alternatives are also given. These are presented as honest errors of calculation for such a large economy or due to alternative assumptions or weights.

Starting in 1997–1998, however, a different and far more serious shadow has fallen over Chinese statistics. The overall estimates of aggregate growth have not been consistent with the sectoral official data. This new phase of skepticism is reflected in this brief summary quotation from Thomas G. Rawski, "What Is Happening to China's GDP Statistics," in *China Economic Review* 12, no. 4 (2001): 348.

> China's recent official growth story is an obvious misfit: in every other instance, including China's own experience 10 years earlier, substantial GDP growth co-incided with increased energy use, higher employment, and rising consumer prices.
>
> . . . [T]he clash between output and energy trends is only one of many unlikely elements. The figures for 1997/1998 bristle with inconsistencies. Could farm output increase in all but one province despite floods that rank among China's top 10 natural disasters of the 20th century? Could industrial production rise 10.75% even though only 14 of 94 major products achieved double-digit growth and 53 suffered declining physical output? Could investment spending jump 13.9% even though steel consumption and cement output rose by less than 5%? Skeptical Chinese analysts point to many such puzzles.

The *China Economic Review* is a much-respected journal to which reputable Chinese scholars—a few from the mainland, the bulk from outside—contribute. It has devoted an entire issue to this matter, from which Rawski's quotation is drawn. One cannot help concluding, looking at the evidence as a whole, that real growth of 7–8 percent has not been achieved in China in recent years and, for whatever reasons, high-level Chinese officials have decided to maintain the impression of continuity in overall growth. Economists have not firmly established what the figures should be, but they may have reached as little as 2 percent per annum at its nadir.

This setback may have resulted from the industrial boom in agricultural areas reaching its natural limits plus the effect of acute natural disasters. We evidently have much to learn; but whatever the short-term setback, there is reason to believe that China will resume a high rate of progress like the rest of Asia—although not, perhaps, the extraordinary growth figures of the 1980s and most of the 1990s. For a somewhat disabused view of the Chinese economy as a whole, see "Survey of China," *Economist,* June 15, 2002, Special Section.

19. Ibid., p. 15. When Elspeth and I spent several weeks lecturing in China in early autumn 1984, the picture of a robust, smiling peasant woman appeared in newspapers throughout China. She stood beside a shiny Toyota with an account of how

she made enough money to buy the car from selling eggs in the open market produced on the family farm. She was presented as an example of Deng's advice: "It is
glorious to be rich."

20. Pye, *Mao Tse-tung,* pp. 314–315.

21. Ezra Vogel, ed., *Living with China,* esp. the introduction and Chaps. 4, 7,
and 8.

22. Nancy Boardman Eddy, *Public Opinion and American Foreign Policy, 1937–
1956,* Working Paper of American Project, MIT, CENIS, p. 23.

23. Ibid., pp. 26–27.

24. This lecture ("The American Diplomatic Revolution") was reprinted in W. W.
Rostow, *Essays on a Half-Century* (Boulder, Colo.: Westview Press, 1988), p. 13. It
was originally published by the Clarendon Press in Oxford (1948).

25. These, among other comparative figures for China and India, have been com-
piled down to 2050 by George Purcell Jr., who speculates imaginatively about their
possible operational meaning in "Demographic Shifts and Asian Security," soon to
be published.

26. "New Challenges to Social Safeguard System," *People's Daily,* April 10, 1997,
p. 17, translated and published in English by Li Jianxing in *Inside China Mainland*
19 (July 1997): 72–74.

10. VIETNAM AND SOUTHEAST ASIA

1. A full bibliography on Vietnam would, of course, be out of place here. For those
interested in my views, passages on Vietnam appear in *The Diffusion of Power: An
Essay in Recent History* (New York: Macmillan, 1972), pp. 7–58, 108–110 (Eisenhower
administration); pp. 260–295 (Kennedy administration); pp. 435–533 (Johnson administration); pp. 550–563 (Nixon administration to March 1972). See also my review
of Robert McNamara's *In Retrospect: The Tragedy and Lessons of Vietnam, Times
Literary Supplement,* June 1994, pp. 4–6, reprinted in *Parameters* 26, no. 4 (winter 1996–1997): 39–50; and *Society* 35, no. 6 (September–October 1998): 78–84. A
useful recent book on ASEAN is M. Dutral's *Economic Regionalism in Asia-Pacific:
Challenges to Economic Cooperation* (Cheltenham, U.K.: Edward Elgar Press, 1999).

2. On the Geneva Accords, see *Diffusion of Power,* pp. 267–268 and 284–288.

3. Lyndon B. Johnson, *The Vantage Point* (New York: Holt, Rinehart and Winston, 1971), pp. 122–123.

4. James E. Cross, *Conflict in the Shadows* (Garden City, N.Y.: Garden City Press,
1963), p. 10. Looking further back Cross pointed out that Wellington was in the position to supply the guerrillas in the Iberian peninsula who won over Napoleon at great
cost. De Gaulle could not win in Algeria due to supply from neighboring countries.
On the other hand, the Communists had no sanctuary in Malaya or the Philippines
or Indonesia.

I had the occasion to express this view of aggression in the Kennedy and Johnson
periods. For example, in a speech at Fort Bragg on June 28, 1961 ("Guerrilla Warfare
in the Underdeveloped Areas"), which Kennedy had personally cleared, I said:

[I]t is important that the whole international community begin to accept its responsibility for dealing with this form of aggression. It is important that the world become clear in mind, for example, that the operation run from Hanoi against South Viet-Nam is as clear a form of aggression as the violation of the 38th parallel by the North Korean armies in June 1950. In my conversations with representatives of foreign governments, I am sometimes lectured that this or that government within the Free World is not popular; they tell me that guerrilla warfare cannot be won unless the peoples are dissatisfied. These are, at best, half truths. The truth is that guerrilla warfare, mounted from external bases — with rights of sanctuary — is a terrible burden to carry for any government in a society making its way towards modernization. As you know, it takes somewhere between ten and twenty soldiers to control one guerrilla in an organized operation. Moreover, the guerrilla force has this advantage: its task is merely to destroy; while the government must build and protect what it is building. A guerrilla war mounted from outside a transitional nation is a crude act of international vandalism. There will be no peace in the world if the international community accepts the outcome of guerrilla war, mounted from outside a nation, as tantamount to a free election.

The sending of men and arms across international boundaries and the direction of guerrilla war from outside a sovereign nation is aggression; and this is a fact which the whole international community must confront and whose consequent responsibilities it must accept. Without such international action those against whom aggression is mounted will be driven inevitably to seek out and engage the ultimate source of the aggression they confront.

I suspect that, in the end, the real meaning of the conference on Laos at Geneva will hinge on this question: it will depend on whether or not the international community is prepared to mount an International Control Commission which has the will and capacity to control the borders it was designed to control.

In the negotiation in Geneva we were given some reason to hope that Hanoi's infiltration of South Vietnam might be stopped by the creation of an International Control Commission that was formally agreed to by Ambassador Georgy Pushkin and Ambassador Averill Harriman. The treaty went into effect at the end of the first week of October 1961. Hanoi did not cease infiltration for one day, nor did the Soviets or the International Control Commission interfere with them.

From the planning staff in the State Department I addressed on November 28, 1962, the following to Kennedy (and Rusk) on the occasion of Mikoyan's visit to Washington after the Cuban missile crisis:

You will recall that in the course of the Geneva conference Pushkin agreed with Governor Harriman that the Soviet Union would take responsibility for ending infiltration into Viet Nam and Laos. There is no question but that such infiltration continues. The order of magnitude is debatable; but the most responsible estimate runs at something like the rate of 500 per month. . . .

The essence of the matter appears to me to be this:

The Soviets are not assuming their responsibilities under the Geneva agreement, after the passage of enough time for us to be clear that this is either a willful act or a lack of capacity to impose their position on Ho Chi Minh.

We are continuing to accept on our side of the truce lines of the cold war a serious illegal act at a place where U.S. prestige and interests are heavily committed. . . .

The whole lesson of the cold war, including the recent Cuban crisis, is that the Communists do not escalate in response to our actions taken to preserve our side of the truce lines of the cold war.

It is much better to put pressure on now, against the background of recent Vietnamese progress, than in a waning situation.

I informed President Johnson of my view when I moved back to the White House as national security adviser on April 1, 1966. He later asked me to set that view down, and he sent it to the members of the Joint Chiefs of Staff.

5. The Greek-Yugoslav case is particularly vivid. On March 12, 1947, President Truman in his Truman Doctrine speech announced American support for a Greek government hard-pressed by supplies and men that flowed across the Greek border with Yugoslavia. At that time Tito appeared a well-behaved member of the Comintern and other Communist clubs set up in Eastern Europe under Soviet aegis. But by March 18, 1948, the Soviet Union recalled from Belgrade its military and technical advisers. Tito then closed down his border supply operations against the Greek government. The Greek Communist movement was then rolled up. By the end of 1951 military aid had been negotiated by Tito from the United States, and in subsequent years Tito moved to establish a Balkan defense pact with France, Turkey, and Italy, finalized on May 26, 1955. Khrushchev arrived in Belgrade to apologize for his earlier treatment of Tito, but the belated courtship did not go very well. After various conferences Khrushchev adjourned the talks on February 19, 1957. The Yugoslavs could expect no economic favors from the USSR.

6. W. W. Rostow, "The Case for the Vietnam War," *Parameters* 26, no. 4 (winter 1996–1997): 47.

7. Richard H. Shultz Jr., *The Secret War against Hanoi* (New York: Harper-Collins, 1999), pp. 205–206.

8. Ted Gittinger, ed., *A Vietnam Round Table* (Austin: Lyndon B. Johnson School of Public Affairs, 1993), p. 76.

9. Charles J. V. Murphy, "New Building Blocs for Asia," *Fortune,* December 1966, p. 136. In London, the *Economist* carried a strongly supportive lead article in the October 29, 1966, issue entitled "The Pacific Consensus." It began: "The Johnson doctrine for Asia is starting to pay off." The *Economist* article was the most detailed current analysis of the potential meaning of Asian regionalism.

10. Lee Kuan Yew's statement was made at the close of a speech at the University of Singapore Democratic Socialist Club.

11. A special place in history ought to be reserved for those political leaders who settle old quarrels as President Park normalized relations with Japan (Chap. 7). The leaders of Malaysia and Indonesia in 1967 belong in the select club of those who made the choice Park did in 1965.

12. Keynote address by (H. E.) Tan Sri M. Ghazali Shafie, "ASEAN—Today and

Tomorrow," at the Fletcher School of Law and Diplomacy, Boston, November 11, 1981, pp. 14–15.

13. John Wong, *ASEAN Economies in Perspective* (Philadelphia: Institute for the Study of Human Issues, 1979), p. 194.

14. In an op-ed piece in the *New York Times* of May 28, 1990, General Westmoreland ended an elaborate and formal analysis as follows:

> All this makes evident a significant and, until now unappreciated, situation. The U.S., by its military efforts, blocked the expansion of communism for ten years, removing the pressure on ASEAN. Three ASEAN nations provided troops or other support to America's efforts in Indochina. In the process, America encouraged and provided for those insecure countries fourteen years to mature and develop confidence in self-government.
>
> Ironically, Vietnam, albeit now a communist state, is serving our strategic interest by confronting the Chinese along China's southern border with strong military forces. In contrast to Korea, where there are 41,000 U.S. troops, we have no troops tied down in or near Indochina, and the strategically important ASEAN alliance is an entrenched part of the non-communist world.
>
> The wisdom of President Johnson's strategy of avoiding a larger and possibly uncontrollable war and at the same time protecting our strategic interest has been sustained by history. (Gittinger, *Vietnam Round Table*, pp. 191–192)

On July 28, 1995, Vietnam, evidently concerned with the economic and military rise of China, and concerned with the Chinese incursion into Vietnam, joined ASEAN.

11. THE URBAN PROBLEM, 1991–

1. City of Austin and Travis County, Strategic Partnerships for Urban Revitalization proposal, June 8, 1994, IV-4.

2. The Austin Project, *An Investment Plan for the Young: The Austin Project, First Phase,* September 8, 1992, pp. 35–36.

3. W. W. Rostow and Elspeth Rostow, *The Austin Project.* This early version included the letter of transmittal to Mayor Bruce Todd (August 19, 1991). The paper was published in the *Proceedings of the American Philosophical Society* 136, no. 3 (September 1992): 353–409.

4. Center for Demographic and Socioeconomic Research and Education Department of Rural Sociology, *Texas Challenged: The Implication of Population Change for Public Service Demand in Texas,* summary report prepared and published for the Texas Legislative Council (Texas A&M University, 1996). This is an analytic summary of a three-volume research report prepared by the state demographer and staff at Texas A&M.

5. For the United States as a whole, the nearest equivalent of the figures in the text are for total population, and they stop at 2020 rather than 2030. They nevertheless indicate roughly the degree to which Texas is exceptional, notably with respect to the

TABLE 11.3 U.S. POPULATION BY RACE/ANCESTRY, 2000–2020

Anglos		Black		Hispanic		Other	
2000	2020	2000	2020	2000	2020	2000	2020
70.6%	62.5%	12.8%	13.9%	11.3%	15.7%	4.4% (0.9)[a]	7.0% (0.9)[a]

Source: W. W. Rostow, *The Great Population Spike and After: Reflections on the 21st Century* (New York: Oxford University Press, 1998), p. 217.
[a] The figures in parentheses indicate the proportion of American Indians. The figure for "Other" therefore indicates the proportion of Asians in the population.

future proportion of Hispanics. Frank D. Bean, Robert G. Cushing, and Charles W. Hayes, "The Changing Demography of U.S. Immigration Flows: Patterns, Projections, and Contexts," in *Migration Past, Migration Future: Germany and the United States*, ed. Klaus J. Bade and Myron Weiner (Oxford, Eng.: Berghahn Books, 1997), table 3. (See table 11.3.)

6. Ibid., pp. 59–60.

7. The anonymous White House briefing on May 10, 1994, was even more explicit: "No applicant will be eligible for a single dollar of federal enterprise support unless it submits a comprehensive strategic plan that brings together the community, the private sector and local government and demonstrates how the community will reform the delivery of government services. The challenge-grant process is designed to empower local communities to be as innovative as possible."

12. POPULATION, MODERN JAPAN'S FOURTH CHALLENGE

1. W. W. Rostow, *Theorists of Economic Growth with a Perspective on the Next Century* (New York: Oxford University Press, 1990), pp. 490–495. I should note that Lincoln Day has presented a quite different argument in *The Future of Low Birth-Rate Populations* (London: Routledge, 1992). In an elegant and ingenious analysis Day depicts a static population with a higher proportion of older people, a substitution for pensions financed by higher lifetime private savings, and many other social adjustments including a taming of the automobile. Perhaps the decisive assumption in this argument is that the decline in fertility may reverse producing a static population (pp. 18–23). Richard A. Easterlin has produced a book, *Growth Triumphant* (Ann Arbor: University of Michigan Press, 1996), that uses much the same method as *The Great Population Spike and After: Reflections on the 21st Century* (New York: Oxford University Press, 1998). It differs from *The Great Population Spike* in its view of what lies ahead in the twenty-first century.

It, too, traces in its own way the manner in which the focus of modern growth has systematically decreased both human fertility and human mortality. But he ends with a look at the twenty-first century as the triumph of science and real income, whereas I am more impressed with the sixty-plus countries that have fallen below the replacement rate of 2.1 and their struggle ahead to get back to 2.1. Along the way

Easterlin probes at length (pp. 131-144) an issue dealt with in the present book only briefly—namely, "Does satisfying material needs increase human happiness?"

2. For a full exposition of the world population situation, see Rostow, *Great Population Spike.*

3. Nicholas D. Kristof, "Empty Isles Are Signs Japan's Sun Might Dim," *New York Times,* August 1, 1999, p. 1. The workforce in Japan was due to begin its decline in 2001.

4. Rostow, *Great Population Spike,* p. 4.

5. See Chap. 2, note 17, in ibid., pp. 206-208.

6. An authoritative paper on the present Japanese population situation by Shinachi Ichimura and Naghiro Ogawa, "Policies to Meet the Challenge with Declining Fertility: Japan and Other East Asian Countries," was presented at the Annual Meeting of the Population Association of America, Los Angeles, March 23-25, 2000.

7. Ibid., pp. 201-202.

8. Hamish McRae, *The World in 2020: Power, Culture, and Prosperity: A Vision of the Future* (London: HarperCollins, 1994), p. 97.

9. Piyu Yue, "A Brief on Dynamics of the Population System and the Future of Japan's Population," unpublished note (Austin: IC² Institute, 1999), pp. 5-6.

10. J. M. Keynes, *Economic Consequences of the Peace* (New York: Harcourt Brace, 1920), p. 204.

11. Adam Smith, *Wealth of Nations* (New York: The Modern Library, Random House, 1937), Chap. 8 ("Of the Wages of Labour"), pp. 69 and 81.

12. Stanley Jevons, *The Coal Question* (London: Macmillan, 1865), p. 349.

13. Rostow, *Great Population Spike,* p. 131.

14. J. M. Keynes, "Some Economic Consequences of a Declining Population," *Eugenics Review* 29, no. 1 (April 1937).

15. Ibid., p. 18.

16. J. S. Mill, *Principles of Political Economy,* ed. V. W. Bladen and J. M. Robson (Toronto: University of Toronto Press, 1960), pp. 706-754.

17. J. R. Hicks, *Classics and Moderns: Collected Essays on Economic Theory,* vol. 3 (Cambridge: Harvard University Press, 1983), p. 68. Hicks' reflections on the stationary state (pp. 68-72) including the views of J. S. Mill, are relevant to the present discussion.

18. Rostow, *Great Population Spike,* pp. 7-8 and p. 204, n. 3.

13. THE LONG AND SHORT PERIODS

1. In plain English, my commitment to the Marshallian long period means a commitment to take account of the short-run supply as well as the short-run demand factors in the life of economies—above all, changes in population and the workforce as well as technological change, which lies at the heart of economic growth. But it means also taking account of noneconomic factors as they affect the economy—for example, wars, the play of politics—which often can weaken or strengthen the will of peoples to absorb new technologies. Thus my work at Yale and Oxford, requiring